# Consumer Behavior I

SAGE LIBRARY IN BUSINESS & MANAGEMENT

# Consumer Behavior I: Research and Influences

## VOLUME 1

*Consumer Behavior as a Field of Study*

Edited by

**Margaret K Hogg**

SAGE Publications

London • Thousand Oaks • New Delhi

First published 2005



SAGE Publications Ltd
1 Oliver's Yard
55 City Road
London EC1Y 1SP

SAGE Publications Inc
2455 Teller Road
Thousand Oaks, California 91320

SAGE Publications India Pvt Ltd
B-42, Panchsheel Enclave
Post Box 4109
New Delhi 110 017

**British Library Cataloguing in Publication data**

A catalogue record for this book is available from the British Library

ISBN 1-4129-0841-8 (set of three volumes)

**Library of Congress Control Number: 2005900845**

Typeset by Pantek Arts Ltd, Maidstone, Kent
Printed on paper from sustainable resources
Printed and bound in Great Britain by TJ International Ltd, Padstow, Cornwall

# Contents



# VOLUME 1

## CONSUMER BEHAVIOR AS A FIELD OF STUDY

# VOLUME 2
# CONSUMER DECISION-MAKING

# VOLUME 3

## CONSUMER SOCIALIZATION: CHILDHOOD, CHILDREN AND FAMILIES

# Appendix of Sources

1. "Comparing *Journal of Consumer Psychology* and *Journal of Consumer Research*", *Anat Alon, Maureen Morrin and Nada Nasar Bechwati*
   *Journal of Consumer Psychology* 12 (1) (2002): 5–21. Mahwah, New Jersey and London: Lawrence Erlbaum Associates. Reproduced by kind permission of the publisher and authors.
2. "On Method in Consumer Research: A Critical Relativist Perspective", *Paul F. Anderson*
   *Journal of Consumer Research* 13 (September) (1986): 155–173. Chicago: University of Chicago Press. Reproduced by kind permission of the publisher.
3. "Hermeneutics and Consumer Research", *Stephen J. Arnold and Eileen Fischer*
   *Journal of Consumer Research* 21 (June) (1994): 55–70. Chicago: University of Chicago Press. Reproduced by kind permission of the authors and publisher.
4. "Feminist Thought: Implications for Consumer Research", *Julia M. Bristor and Eileen Fischer*
   *Journal of Consumer Research* 19 (3) (March) (1993): 518–536.
   Chicago: University of Chicago Press. Reproduced by kind permission of Eileen Fischer and the publisher.
5. "Consumption: The New Wave of Research in the Humanities and Social Sciences", *Colin Campbell*
   *Journal of Social Behavior and Personality* 6 (6) (1991): 57–74. Society for Personality Research. Reproduced by kind permission of Select Press.
6. "Hedonic Consumption: Emerging Concepts, Methods and Propositions", *Elizabeth C. Hirschman and Morris B. Holbrook*
   *Journal of Marketing* 46 (3) Summer (1982): 92–101. Chicago: American Marketing Association. Reprinted with permission from *Journal of Marketing*.
7. "Alternative Ways of Seeking Knowledge in Consumer Research", *Laurel Anderson Hudson and Julie L. Ozanne*
   *Journal of Consumer Research* 14 (March) (1988): 508–521. Chicago: University of Chicago Press. Reproduced by kind permission of the authors and publisher.
8. "Positivism and Paradigm Dominance in Consumer Research: Toward Critical Pluralism and Rapprochement", *Shelby D. Hunt*
   *Journal of Consumer Research* 18 (June) (1991): 32–43. Chicago: University of Chicago Press. Reproduced by kind permission of the author and publisher.
9. "Interpreting Consumer Mythology: A Structural Approach to Consumer Behavior", *Sidney J. Levy*
   *Journal of Marketing* 45 (3) (1981): 49–61. Chicago: American Marketing Association. Reprinted with permission from *Journal of Marketing*.
10. "Roots of Marketing and Consumer Research at the University of Chicago", *Sidney J. Levy*
    *Consumption, Markets and Culture* 6 (2) June (2003): 99–110. London: Taylor and Francis, Routledge. Reproduced by kind permission of the author and publisher.

11. "Consumer Research and Semiotics: Exploring the Morphology of Signs, Symbols and Significance", *David Glen Mick*
*Journal of Consumer Research* 13 (September) (1986): 196–213. Chicago: University of Chicago Press. Reproduced by kind permission of the author and publisher.
12. "Philosophical Tensions in Consumer Inquiry", *J. Paul Peter*
*Handbook of Consumer Research*, ed. T.S. Robertson & H.H. Kassarjian. Englewood Cliffs, NJ: Prentice-Hall, (1991): 533–547. Reprinted by permission of Pearson Education, Inc., Upper Saddle River, NJ.
13. "Consumer Research: In Search of Identity", *Itamar Simonson, Ziv Carmon, Ravi Dhar, Aimee Drolet and Stephen M. Nowlis*
*Annual Review of Psychology* 52 (2001): 249–275. Palo Alto, CA: Annual Reviews. Reprinted with permission, from the *Annual Review of Psychology*, Volume 52 © 2001 by Annual Reviews, www.annualreviews.org.
14. "Putting Consumer Experience Back into Consumer Research: The Philosophy and Method of Existential-Phenomenology", *Craig J. Thompson, William B. Locander and Howard R. Pollio*
*Journal of Consumer Research* 16 (September) (1989): 133–146. Chicago: University of Chicago Press. Reproduced by kind permission of the authors and publisher.
15. "Beyond Consumerism: New Historical Perspectives on Consumption", *Frank Trentmann*
*Journal of Contemporary History* 39 (3) (2004): 373–401. London: Sage. Reprinted with permission.
16. "Discovery-Orientated Consumer Research", *William D. Wells*
*Journal of Consumer Research* 19 (March) (1993): 489–504. Chicago: University of Chicago Press. Reproduced by kind permission of the author and publisher.
17. "Consumers and Consumption", *Sharon Zukin and Jennifer Smith Maguire*
*Annual Review of Sociology* 30 (2004): 173–197. Palo Alto, CA: Annual Reviews. Reprinted, with permission, from the *Annual Review of Sociology*, Volume 30 © 2004 by Annual Reviews, www.annualreviews.org.
18. "Constructive Consumer Choice Processes", *James R. Bettman, Mary Frances Luce and John W. Payne*
*Journal of Consumer Research* 25 (3) Dec (1998): 187–217. Chicago: University of Chicago Press. Reproduced by kind permission of the authors and publisher.
19. "Self Generated Validity and Other Effects of Measurement on Belief, Attitude, Intention and Behavior", *Jack M. Feldman and John G. Lynch, Jr.*
*Journal of Applied Psychology* 73 (3) (1988): 421–35. © 1988 by the American Psychological Association. Reprinted with permission.
20. "Rediscovering Satisfaction", *Susan Fournier and David Glen Mick*
*Journal of Marketing* 63 (4) (1999): 5–23. Chicago: American Marketing Association. Reprinted with permission from *Journal of Marketing*.
21. "Product Experience is Seductive", *Stephen J. Hoch*
*Journal of Consumer Research* 29 (December) (2002): 448–454. Chicago: University of Chicago Press. Reproduced by kind permission of the author and publisher.

22. "Managing What Consumers Learn From Experience", *Stephen J. Hoch and John Deighton*
*Journal of Marketing* 53 (2) (1989): 1–20. Chicago: American Marketing Association. Reprinted with permission from *Journal of Marketing*.
23. "Preconscious Processing Effects: The Independence of Attitude Formation and Conscious Thought", *Chris Janiszewski*
*Journal of Consumer Research* 15 (September) (1988): 199–209. Chicago: University of Chicago Press. Reproduced by kind permission of the author and publisher.
24. "Order-of-Entry Effects on Consumer Memory and Judgment: An Information Integration Perspective", *Frank R. Kardes and Gurumurthy Kalyanaram*
*Journal of Marketing Research* 29 (3) (1992): 343–357. Chicago: American Marketing Association. Reprinted with permission from *Journal of Marketing Research*.
25. "Choosing to Avoid: Coping with Negatively Emotion-Laden Consumer Decisions", *Mary Frances Luce*
*Journal of Consumer Research* 24 (March) (1998): 409–433. Chicago: University of Chicago Press. Reproduced by kind permission of the author and publisher.
26. "Memory and Attentional Factors in Consumer Choice: Concepts and Research Methods," *John G. Lynch Jr. and Thomas K. Srull*
*Journal of Consumer Research* 9 (June) (1982): 18–37. Chicago: University of Chicago Press. Reproduced by kind permission of John G. Lynch and the publisher.
27. "Contrast Effects in Consumer Judgments: Changes in Mental Representations or in the Anchoring of Rating Scales?" *John G. Lynch Jr., Dipankar Chakravarti and Anusree Mitra*
*Journal of Consumer Research* 18 (December) (1991): 284–297. Chicago: University of Chicago Press. Reproduced by kind permission of the authors and publisher.
28. "How Does Motivation Moderate the Impact of Central and Peripheral Processing on Brand Attitudes and Intentions?", *Scott B. MacKenzie and Richard A. Spreng*
*Journal of Consumer Research* 18 (March) (1992): 519–529. Chicago: University of Chicago Press. Reproduced by kind permission of Scott B. MacKenzie and the publisher.
29. "The Effect of New Product Features on Brand Choice", *Stephen M. Nowlis and Itamar Simonson*
*Journal of Marketing Research* 33 (1) (1996): 36–46. Chicago: American Marketing Association. Reproduced with permission from *Journal of Marketing Research*.
30. "Whence Consumer Loyalty?", *Richard L. Oliver*
*Journal of Marketing* 63 (4) (1999): 33–44. Chicago: American Marketing Association. Reproduced with permission from *Journal of Marketing*.
31. "Consumer Learning and Brand Equity", *Stijn M.J. van Osselaer and Joseph W. Alba*
*Journal of Consumer Research* 27 June (2000): 1–16. Chicago: University of Chicago Press. Reproduced by kind permission of Stijn van Osselaer and the publisher.

32. "Consumer Knowledge: Effects on Evaluation Strategies Mediating Consumer Judgments", *Mita Sujan*
*Journal of Consumer Research* 12 (June) (1985): 31–46. Chicago: University of Chicago Press. Reproduced by kind permission of the author and publisher.
33. "Dealing with Children's Advertising: Public Policy Issues and Alternatives", *Gary M. Armstrong and Merrie Brucks*
*Journal of Public Policy and Marketing* 7 (1) (1998): 98–113. Chicago: American Marketing Association. Reproduced from *Journal of Public Policy and Marketing*.
34. "The Role of Parental Socialization Types on Differential Family Communication Patterns Regarding Consumption", *Les Carlson, Sanford Grossbart and J. Kathleen Stuenkel*
*Journal of Consumer Psychology* 1 (1) (1992): 31–52. Mahwah, New Jersey and London: Lawrence Erlbaum Associates. Reproduced by kind permission of Les Carlson and the publisher.
35. "Socializing Children About Television: An Intergenerational Study", *Les Carlson, Russell N. Laczniak and Ann Walsh*
*Journal of Academy of Marketing Science* 29 (3) (2001): 277–288. London: Sage. Reprinted with permission.
36. "The Influence of Familial and Peer-based Reference Groups on Consumer Decisions", *Terry L. Childers and Akshay R. Rao*
*Journal of Consumer Research* 19 (Sept) (1992): 198–211. Chicago: University of Chicago Press. Reproduced by kind permission of Akshay R. Rao and the publisher.
37. "Spatial Biographies of Children's Consumption: Market places and spaces of childhood in the 1930s and beyond", *Daniel Thomas Cook*
*Journal of Consumer Culture* 3 (2) (2003): 147–169. London: Sage. Reprinted with permission.
38. "Family Members' Perceptions of Adolescents' Influence in Family Decision Making", *Ellen R. Foxman, Patriya S. Tansuhaj and Karin M. Ekstrom*
*Journal of Consumer Research* 15 (March) (1989): 482–491. Chicago: University of Chicago Press. Reproduced by kind permission of the authors and publisher.
39. "The Emergence of Adaptive Decision Making in Children", *Jennifer Gregan-Paxton and Deborah Roedder John*
*Journal of Consumer Research* 24 (1997): 43–56. Chicago: University of Chicago Press. Reproduced by kind permission of the authors and publisher.
40. "Age Differences in Product Categorization", *Deborah Roedder John and Mita Sujan*
*Journal of Consumer Research* 16 (March) (1990): 452–460. Chicago: University of Chicago Press. Reproduced by kind permission of the authors and publisher.
41. "Age Differences in Children's Choice Behavior: The Impact of Available Alternatives", *Deborah Roedder John and Ramnath Lakshmi-Ratan*
*Journal of Marketing Research* 29 (May) (1992): 216–226. Chicago: American Marketing Association. Reproduced by kind permission of the authors and publisher.
42. "Consumer Socialization of Children: A Retrospective Look at Twenty-Five Years of Research", *Deborah Roedder John*
*Journal of Consumer Research* 26 (December) (1999): 183–213. Chicago: University of Chicago Press. Reproduced by kind permission of the author and publisher.

43. "Preschoolers' Learning of Brand Names from Visual Cues", *M. Carole Macklin*
*Journal of Consumer Research* 23 (December) (1996): 251–261. Chicago: University of Chicago Press. Reproduced by kind permission of the author and publisher.

44. "Children's Understanding of the Intent of Advertising: A Meta-Analysis", *Mary C. Martin*
*Journal of Public Policy and Marketing* 16 (2) (1997): 205–217. Chicago: American Marketing Association. Reproduced with permission from *Journal of Public Policy and Marketing*.

45. "Passing the Torch: Intergenerational Influences as a Source of Brand Equity", *Elizabeth S. Moore, William L. Wilkie and Richard J. Lutz*
*Journal of Marketing* 66 (2) (2002): 17–37. Chicago: American Marketing Association. Reproduced with permission from *Journal of Marketing*.

46. "The Role of Family Communication in Consumer Socialization of Children and Adolescents", *George P. Moschis*
*Journal of Consumer Research* 11 (March) (1985): 898–913. Chicago: University of Chicago Press. Reproduced by kind permission of the author and publisher.

47. "Consumer Socialization: A Theoretical and Empirical Analysis", *George P. Moschis and Gilbert A. Churchill Jr.*
*Journal of Marketing Research* 15 (1978): 599–609. Chicago: American Marketing Association. Reproduced with permission from *Journal of Marketing Research*.

48. "Relationships Between Family Communication and Consumer Activities of Adolescents: An Exploratory Study", *Kay M. Palan*
*Journal of the Academy of Marketing Science* 26 (4) (1998): 338–349. London: Sage. Reprinted with permission.

49. "How Do Young Children Learn to Be Consumers? A Script-processing Approach", *Laura A. Peracchio*
*Journal of Consumer Research* 18 (March) (1992): 425–440. Chicago: University of Chicago Press. Reproduced by kind permission of the author and publisher.

# Acknowledgements

I would like to thank all the academic colleagues and friends who have generously shared their ideas with me in many conversations (e.g. at Association of Consumer Research (ACR)[1] conferences in the U.S.A. and Europe; and at Manchester School of Management and at Lancaster University Management School in England) about the structure and content of these volumes. It is impossible to name everyone here. However, I promised to formally acknowledge those who responded to my written requests for suggestions about what to include, and also about what would be appropriate criteria to use, when making a very difficult selection, and they include *inter alia*: Eric Arnould, Carlos Ballesteros, Emma Banister, Stephen Brown, Lan Nguyen Chaplin, Carolyn Costley, June Cotte, Karin Ekstrom, Bob Fennis, Charles Hofacker, David Glen Mick, Barbara Phillips, Gad Saad, Mary-Anne Twist and Rajiv Vaidyanathan (2004).

There will be academic colleagues not acknowledged by the inclusions, and also some potentially offended by exclusion; to them, and to those whose nominations I have not included, my apologies. The opportunity to make this selection obviously came with constraints. Most importantly, ninety articles represented the boundary for this project, and this number cannot comprehensively represent the variety of topics (theoretical and empirical) encompassed by research into consumer behavior and consumption. Ultimately, these are my selections, and reflect my interpretation of how the field of consumer research and consumption studies has evolved, and is evolving.

Margaret K. Hogg
Lancaster
March 15 2005

## Editor's Overview and Introduction: Research and Influences in Consumer Behavior

**Margaret K. Hogg**

After an overview, I begin my introduction with a preamble (deliberately so called). This establishes the context within which I approached the question: what constitutes consumer behaviour research? And the associated challenge of identifying just some of the major works in consumer behaviour for this set of edited volumes. From the preamble I move to issues which relate to the sociology of knowledge and the philosophy of science; after that I discuss the papers within Volumes 1–3; and then look briefly ahead to Volumes 4–6.

Overview

Any selection of papers involves choices. In the light of Simonson *et al.*'s (2001:249 Vol. 1) point that there remain considerable disagreements about what constitutes consumer research, it could be regarded as a problematic (if not foolhardy) task to try and select key articles to represent the field of consumer behaviour research within these volumes. It has not been my ambition to produce an all-defining collection of major papers for consumer behaviour research which would meet everyone's criteria. Rather, what I have tried to do in these volumes is to demonstrate the richness and complexity represented by research into consumer behaviour. The field is so varied in terms of theoretical and empirical coverage. My selection represents one mapping of the field. For some readers, the volumes will provide an overview of the key debates in the field; whereas for other readers they will provide the starting point for further reading in the different topic areas. My choices are informed by a historical and European view [see below] of the debates across the continents about what constitutes consumer behaviour research; and about the situated practice of consumer research undertaken in order to generate knowledge (whether theory testing or theory building; whether deductive or inductive; whether informed by positivist or non positivist approaches to research). I hope that the articles I have selected will provide the starting point for many individual journeys [see below] through the field of consumer research.

Some very difficult choices had to be made. I recognize that there will be *lacunae* – which will be more significant in some researchers' eyes than in others. This applies not just to articles, but also to topic areas, some of which have had to be, regretfully, neglected (e.g. sex and gender; gift-giving; rituals) not because they lacked importance or status, but because I did not have the space to deal with every topic area. Even now, I recognize that enthusiasts for family research will feel that I have only skimmed the surface (Volume 3), and similarly those interested in behavioural decision theory and social cognition (Volume 2) will feel I could usefully have devoted all six volumes to these important areas (as identified extensively by Simonson *et al.*'s (2001) paper (Volume 1)). But to concentrate on just one area to the total exclusion of others would not have allowed me to capture the flow of research within the field.

Most of the papers in these two sets (Volumes 1–6) are drawn from the US debates about consumer behaviour. However, to concentrate exclusively on the US reputational field would have been to ignore the important work done in consumption studies in other areas, for instance, the sociology of consumption tradition within northern Europe. Miller (1995) provides a valuable overview which moves beyond the US perspective and demonstrates how different disciplines have contributed to our understanding of consumers and consumption. In these volumes papers from the sociology of consumption (Bennett 1999; Jagger 1998; Komter 2001; Lucas 2002; Warde 1994 [Vols. 4–6]) provide a small counterbalance to the predominance of US voices in the research on consumer behaviour reported here. However, I recognize firstly that I cannot do justice to all the themes within sociology of consumption in this set (for instance, the discussion about ordinary consumption which arose out a series of conferences run by the European and British Sociological Associations in the mid 1990s, and is reported in Gronow and Warde's 2001 set of edited papers, and which would link with the interest in mundane consumption (Kleine, Kleine and Kernan (1993) see Volume 6); and secondly, that many of the debates are beyond the immediate scope of this project, though they are important in informing our understanding of consumers and consumption (particularly individuals' relationships with consumer and material culture (see for instance the *Journal of Consumer Culture* and the *Journal of Material Culture*)). European sociologists of consumption will feel that their field is under-represented here. However, I wanted to capture the range of voices that talk about consumers and consumption – whilst recognizing that it was beyond the scope of these volumes to capture everything. I hope I have succeeded in demonstrating the richness and variety of research on consumer behaviour drawn from a range of disciplinary foundations, academic sites and geographical locations – to show that consumer research as a field of academic practice is growing and evolving rapidly – and that these volumes will therefore provide some glimpses into the pools of activity around which consumer research is swirling.

# Introduction

## Preamble

The Road Not Taken

Robert Frost

Two roads diverged in a yellow wood,
And sorry I could not travel both
And be one traveller, long I stood
And looked down one as far as I could
To where it bent in the undergrowth;

Then took the other, as just as fair,
And having perhaps the better claim,
Because it was grassy and wanted wear;
Though as for that, the passing there
Had worn them really about the same,

And both that morning equally lay
In leaves no step had trodden black.
Oh, I kept the first for another day!
Yet knowing how way leads to way,
I doubted if I should ever come back.

I shall be telling this with a sigh
Somewhere ages and ages hence:
Two roads diverged in a wood, and I –
I took the one less travelled by
And that has made all the difference.

My choice of path through the field – and thus the context for my journey along the roads (Peck 1997), highways and buyways (Belk 1991) – of consumer research is characterized by a number of features. First of all, I am a historian by training. Historians nowadays acknowledge that they bring to their work their own research background, training and experience (along with their situational context e.g. culture, gender, political viewpoint) so that their interpretation cannot be completely free of their own contextual understanding – but as far as possible they try to maintain a reflexive distance from their own personal viewpoints when analyzing their data set.

It is important to begin by recognizing that historians offer just one interpretation of a dataset from amongst many. The main criterion for their interpretation is "plausibility", i.e. how well does the analysis they offer "fit" in terms of existing world views and interpretations, *and* in the light of the data that is available in that time and place. It could be argued that I am faced here with a complete data set of consumer research publications. There are no hidden data sets (i.e. journal articles) to be (re)discovered, whereas undiscovered (or distorted) data (whether diaries, government records, lost films, pottery shards) is a possibility which always faces historians. This is true; my data set is complete – but rather less clear were the criteria by which to assess the data that I had.

An important challenge for me, in this selection, was not only to try and include papers which had already had a significant impact on the field (as evidenced by extensive citations, e.g. many of the papers in Volumes 1–3); but also to try and capture some sense of the direction in which consumer research was moving (new emerging foci of activity) by including more recent papers (e.g. Volumes 4–6). What evidence could I call on here? How could I begin to argue for the plausibility of my selection? Mapping the field (Hart 1998: 142ff) – where it has been; where it is at; where it might go – and thereby capturing some of the key articles in the major debates over the past thirty years would represent a rather different task from trying to also capture some sense of where the flow of debate might go, how discussions might evolve – and thus identify some of the articles which will be influencing debates over the next thirty years. It is not so easy to use citation counts and best paper awards for evidence for that part of the exercise. In response to a classic question posed in many research seminars, and just as regularly confronted by historians: how can we be sure that this explanation takes fullest account of the information available – or to spin this within the context of this task – how I can be sure that this selection takes fullest account of all the published materials within the field? I cannot.

At this point it might be useful to consider that, although a historian by training, my "lived experience" for the past fifteen years has been as a consumer behaviour researcher (informed by the disciplinary training of a historian). Within the context of this project then, I am also a participant observer, maybe a "quasi ethnographer" of my field; and this is the second feature which characterizes my journey through the field. Here it might be helpful to recall Golden-Biddle and Locke's (1993)[2] discussion about how ethnographic texts "convince" as some clear parallels can be drawn with the way that historians seek to convince.

Golden-Biddle and Locke (1993:595) identified three dimensions that are central to the arguments which ethnographers use to convince: plausibility, authenticity and criticality. Translated into historical terms, plausibility is about accounting for as much of the information as possible, so that there is some degree of well argued "fit" between the information (or data), whether textual or visual records (e.g. diaries; government and parish records; news and film archives; artefacts), and the explanation offered to account for the interpretation offered of the data. In these volumes, bounded by ninety papers, I cannot account for every publication, but I can endeavour to capture some sense of the debates in the field. Authenticity is about convincing the readers that the interpretation is drawn from the data; about convincing readers that the researcher has "been present in the field and grasped how members understood their world" (Golden-Biddle and Locke 1993:595) rather than, in the case of historians, colouring the interpretation with a *post hoc* view of events: that the researchers have searched systematically and conscientiously through existing archives of material, and also hunted for new material. Strategies that historians adopt to achieve authenticity echo Golden-Biddle and Locke (1993) in the importance placed on "depicting the disciplined pursuit and analysis of data, and qualifying personal biases" [hence this preamble] and also demonstrating clearly how all the points link back to some type of historical record or artefact [hence the quotations and footnotes]. Criticality and reflexivity are the two other key features of historians" approach to their task. Criticality, for Golden-Biddle and Locke (1993:595), incorporates reflexivity, searching for "carving out room to reflect, provoking the recognition and examination of differences, and enabling readers to imagine new possibilities". These all inform the choice of papers in this set. At the same time, historians also seek to achieve criticality by examining the underlying assumptions which researchers bring to their field of study notably via "scepticism towards rhetoric, tradition, authority and objectivity" (Mingers 2000:219).[3]

Objectivity brings me directly to one of the crucial areas of debate for consumer behavior researchers as well as for historians; and links to the issues which I touch on below about the sociology of knowledge, philosophy of science and the paradigm debate within consumer research (see particularly Volume 1). On objectivity I find myself, on this particular path of my journey through the field, in company (and agreement) with an eminent historian, Paul Thompson. His work, using oral methods to collect historical data, placed him at the forefront of an important emergent area of historical study in the mid 1970s. He describes his own journey through the objectivity/subjectivity debates as he moved from history into sociology. This resonates with my experience as I moved from history into consumer research.

Paul Thompson (1996/2004) observed that for a long time the field of history did not debate subjectivity and objectivity. This informed the "world view" which he brought with him from history into sociology (and parallels the world view which I brought with me from history into consumer research at the beginning of my journey in the early 1970s and when I re-joined the path in the mid 1980s):

> "I came out of history where there's no subjectivist tradition. I then moved into sociology where, again, at that time [mid/late 1970s], there was no post-modern interest in subjectivity. It was a tremendously strong tradition of doing social research to establish facts ... I don't think for the time, it was particularly positivistic, there just wasn't very much of an alternative vision ... ten years later, all the people in oral history had been very strongly influenced both by Luisa Passerini on her ideas about subjectivity and silence, and memory, and I think even more by Sandra Portelli and his ideas about

> the way in which people changed memory ... but I haven't moved as far as the postmodern position ... I would argue that it is always very difficult to know what's happened in the past, and in a way, it's a delusion to imagine that you can get at what really happened, but if you work in a genuine social scientific way, you can get nearer to understanding what it was like in the past. And I think we should [aim for] that, and at the same time, understand the difficulties of doing it; and also the way in which the distortions of memory, in themselves, do help us to understand the past... to my mind, everything is somewhere on a line between being objective and being subjective, and you never get to the pure objective... [nor to the pure subjective] because people's subjectivity is made up of their real experiences... you don't invent dreams from nothing" (Paul Thompson 1996/2004).

So, I make my way as a historian, informed by both modernist and postmodernist arguments, along the highways and buyways of consumer behaviour. My lived experience as a participant observer in and of the field provides me also with an ethnographic viewpoint. I therefore pick up Lievrouw's argument here that: "both the bibliographic map and its ethnographic interpretation are necessary to move through the territory of scholarly communication" (1990:69, cited in Hoffman and Holbrook 1993:06). I recognize that even describing consumer behavior research as a field to be explored and mapped could be challenged as a "positivist" reading of the task. It suggests a reality that exists independently of the constructionist understanding of the world. An alternative argument would be to take a Foucauldian perspective to uncover the different discourses and power in the field. As Foucault (1977:27–28) argues:

> "power produces knowledge ... power and knowledge directly imply one another ... there is no power relation without the creative constitution of a field of knowledge, nor any knowledge that does not presuppose and constitute at the same time power relations" (cited in Clegg 2001)

However, having flagged up that issue, I will leave that argument to one side at the moment, and instead recognize a third characteristic that distinguishes my particular journey along the roads of consumer research. My cultural context is Europe. As a European making the journey through consumer behaviour research, certainly in the early days, I could assume the guise of a stranger, in line with Schutz's (1943, 1944) view of the role of a stranger as:[4]

> "...someone who is passing through, but who needs to establish an adequate grasp of existing social relationships in order to get back. The stranger is neither unreflective like the person on the street nor trapped within the narrow vantage point of an academic specialism ... Strangers have a unique vantage point, able to participate in everyday life yet still maintain a degree of detachment ... the stranger sees beyond the lived experience of everyday life, but is not so detached as to lose contact with the people being studied" (Schutz 1943 and 1944 cited in Smith 1998:16).

A stranger combines participation with a degree of detachment informed by reflexivity (again reminiscent of the role of a historian). Clegg (2002) argued that "history, power and imagination constitute the three dimensional space within which reflexivity is constituted". This echoes earlier arguments about reflexivity and criticality (Golden-Biddle and Locke 1993; Mingers 2000). Mingers (2000) stresses the importance, firstly, of examining claims to authority, and the associated assumptions about legitimacy and whose views should be privileged: "recognizing that there is a multiplicity of perspectives, questioning the dominant view or privileged position, and trying to 'see the world through another's eyes' (Checkland and Scholes, 1990, Churchman, 1968)" (cited in Mingers 2000: 226). Secondly, Mingers (2000) calls for claims to objectivity to be examined, as well as the assumptions about "the validity of knowledge and information ... . Recognizing that it [knowledge and information] is *never* value-free and objective" (Mingers 2000:226). Thirdly, Mingers (2000) proposes scepticism towards tradition, most notably questioning taken-for-granted assumptions about factual matters or acceptable social practices or values (Mingers 2000: 226). Finally, Mingers (2000) calls for scepticism towards rhetoric by questioning the logical soundness of arguments and of how they are expressed; evaluating "whether people's arguments and propositions are sound in a logical sense (Hughes 1996)" (Mingers 2000:226). However, the longer I am in the field, the less of a stranger I become. My world view is increasingly informed by the world views which I encounter in the academic field of practice (Reckwitz 2002; Whitley 1995) of consumer behavior research. The pressure to maintain an independent and reflexive viewpoint becomes increasingly difficult as my initiation into the field continues apace; and my understanding of the tensions, conflicts and arguments within the different consumer behavior intellectual networks (Collins 1998; Harrington 2001) becomes more informed; and my reading of them becomes more refined.

## Truth, world views, paradigms and disciplinary matrices

Which brings me to the debates about "world views", schools of thought and positivist and non positivist paradigms within consumer research that I encountered inter alia via the presidential and ACR Fellows" luncheon speeches (e.g. Bettman 1993; Lutz 1989a; Richins 2001; Tybout 1995); the debates in ACR conference proceedings (e.g. Levy 1992; Sheth 1985; Sternthal and Zaltman 1974; Zinkhan, Saxton, Roth and Zaltman 1990); the editorials (Lutz 1989b; 1989b; 1989d; Monroe 1991) and articles in *Journal of Consumer Research* (including Calder and Tybout 1987; Holbrook 1987); and during the paper sessions and luncheon discussions. Truth, power and discourse are the three poles around which many of these discussions revolved and where many of the arguments were (and are still being) played out: sometimes explicitly; sometimes less explicitly. Let's stop to look briefly at truth, before moving on to paradigms and disciplinary matrices.

> "To argue that truth is a subjective construction is not, however, to suggest that knowledge is an idiosyncratic product. Knowledge is generated ... through a rigorous examination of ideas in public communication ... the discipline is... highly systematic in its formulation of knowledge. Ideas usually survive an exacting process of intellectual scrutiny by advocates of diverse theoretical positions before they graduate to the status of truth statements ... . knowledge ... is, in fact, intersubjectively generated." (Astley 1985: 499)

Astley's view (1985) is rather different from the usual conception of science as being "a cumulative discovery of objective truth" (Astley 1985: 497). Yet I would like to suggest that these volumes might follow Astley's (1985) approach and be seen as a contribution to a "reflective conversation" (Morgan 1983:406; Astley 1985: 510–511) about the stories told by different schools of thought within consumer behavior research. Deighton and Narayandas (2004: 19) argue that

> "Stories can be read as illustrations of theory ... . Stories can also be read as challenges to theory ... telling stories is a tradition in anthropology, history, and some of the other interpretive social sciences, and if V & L [Vargo and Lusch 2004] are correct that marketing scholarship must increasingly contend with value not frozen in objects but flowing in events, then, as anthropologists and historians do, marketing scholars may find that offering stories to one another to support or repudiate claims about the meaning of a sequence of events is a useful way to perform scholarship ... ."

This exhortation sits neatly with this attempt to "map the flows in the field" of what constitutes consumer behavior research where conversations are often described in terms of positivist and non-positivist camps, although members of both groups recognize the heterogeneity (rather than homogeneity) of the alignment of approaches within their own part of the knowledge production system.

The poles of meaning around which consumer research activities flow are represented by two theoretical perspectives, which can be very broadly classified as positivism and non positivism (Crotty 1998: 5). Positivism and non positivism have both encompassed various schools of thought which have adopted inductive and deductive approaches to knowledge generation at different times. Positivist incorporates as many as twelve varieties of positivism (Crotty 1998, p. 21) which are all identified with objectivism, that is "the epistemological view that things exist as meaningful entities independently of consciousness and experience, that they have truth and meaning residing in them as objects ('objective' truth and meaning, therefore) and that careful (scientific?) research can attain that objective truth and meaning" (Crotty 1998: 5–6). Non positivist perspectives incorporate interpretivism (e.g. symbolic interactionism (Solomon 1983: Volume 5), hermeneutics (Arnold and Fischer 1994: Volume 1), and phenomenology (Thompson, Locander and Pollio 1989: Volume 1)) as well as feminism (Bristor and Fischer 1993: Volume 1), critical inquiry, poststructuralism (Holt 1997, Volume 6) and postmodernism. These use a variety of methodological approaches and hold two different epistemological views. Firstly, there is constructionism which rejects the view that there is objective truth waiting for us to discover, rather "truth, or meaning, comes into existence in and out of our engagement with the realities of our world ... meaning is not discovered but constructed ... in this view of things, subject and object emerge as partners in the generation of meaning" (Crotty 1998: 8–9). Secondly, there is subjectivism (relevant to structuralist, post-structuralist and postmodernist forms of thoughts) where "meaning does not come out of an interplay between subject and object but is imposed on the object by the subject. Here the object as such makes no contribution to the generation of meaning" (Crotty 1998: 9). An important feature which distinguishes positivist from non positivist approaches, in their approach to knowledge generation and construction, is their different view of the relationship between facts and values. This has implications for their research designs, choice of methods and views of the purpose of research. Research is seen as either generating nomothetic knowledge about consumer behavior and thereby identifying rule-governed behavior from which generalizations can be offered (e.g. Calder and Tybout 1987; Tybout 1995); or as eliciting idiographic understanding of situated consumer behavior, linked to its social and cultural contexts (Belk 1995).

## Consumer behavior as an academic field of practice

By recognizing the situated nature of knowledge production, Olsen (2000) linked the debates in the sociology of knowledge with the philosophy of science.[5] The situated nature of knowledge construction and production in the social sciences (Smith 1998; Olsen 2000) is underscored by the "socio-political context in conventional consumer research" (Sherry 1990:548). Like other fields of academic practice (Whitley 1988; 1989; 1995) consumer behavior is characterised by key social networks and groups of scholars; and associated places/spaces for public performance e.g. conferences; proceedings; journals. Schutz (1943, 1944) pointed to the paramount importance of understanding the social networks within a field.

What then characterizes consumer behavior research as an academic field of practice (Whitley 1995:81)? It is difficult to achieve complete agreement on the characteristics which define consumer behavior as a field of academic practice. There are a number of contested sites for understanding consumers and consumption: geography (e.g. U.S., Northern Europe); discipline (social sciences or humanities); organizations (academic and managerial); journals; and conferences (with their associated proceedings). There are arguments (see Volume 1; and the presidential addresses reported in the conference proceedings of the Association for Consumer Research) about different types of knowledge; and struggles to establish the status and authority of particular types of knowledge. To capture the contested nature of knowledge (its generation and credentialization) in this field of academic practice (Whitley 1984; 1995) is also to recognize the situated nature of knowledge generation (Smith 1998, Olsen 2000) represented by the different paradigms in the field, or what Kuhn (1996: 182) subsequently described as the "disciplinary matrices" around a body of knowledge. Kuhn (1996: 11) argued that "it remains an open question what parts of social science have yet acquired...paradigms at all" where paradigms are derived from achievements agreed by particular scientific communities and are defined as having two characteristics.[6] Following substantial critiques of his original usage of the term "paradigm", in his third edition Kuhn's (1996: 182) text introduced the term "disciplinary matrix" to cover the shared understanding of a body of theory by a community of scholars, where *disciplinary* referred to "the common possession of the practitioners of a particular discipline" and *matrix* because it was "composed of ordered elements of various sorts, each requiring further specification".

The field of academic practice represented by research into consumers and consumption is distinguished by a number of different disciplinary matrices (Kuhn 1996:182) – sometimes competing (e.g. Tybout 1995), sometimes overlapping (Lutz 1989), and in some cases largely oblivious to each other (Gronow and Warde 2001). A range of different disciplines touch on consumers and consumption in their fields of endeavour; and bring a variety of lenses to their studies of consumers and consumption. The field draws on a variety of disciplines which are represented to a greater or lesser extent in mainstream marketing journals, but some issues around consumption are found further afield e.g. in sociology of consumption, as the focus moves from the individual (psychology and cognitive information processing) to encompass the broader cultural and structural contexts in which individuals operate as consumers.

In order to understand the structure of consumer behavior as a field of academic practice (Whitley 1995) it is important to have a sense of the wider field of marketing from which consumer research emerged nearly sixty years ago. Wilkie and Moore (2003) provide an excellent overview of the credentializing of the field of marketing (Whitley 1995), particularly the changing emphasis in journal editorial membership; and the disappearance of practitioners as authors from the academic journals, as members of the journal editorial boards; and as conference participants. These changes are also mirrored in consumer behavior research, notably in the history of the Association for Consumer Research (see for instance Cohen 1995; Engel 1995; Kardes and Sujan 1995 Kassarjian 1995; Kernan 1995a; Wells 1995 and also Wilkie and Moore 2003:127ff) and of the *Journal of Consumer Research*. One example of the increasing credentialization of consumer research as a field of academic study can be seen in the introduction of double blind manuscript review process in 1982 by *JCR* co-editors Kassarjian and Bettman (1982 cited in Kernan 1995b:491).

The situated nature of knowledge production in this field is indicated by the struggle to establish the status of particular types of knowledge – as generated via positivist and non positivist research – and their respective claims to define what constitutes research in consumer behavior. This represents a key thematic in all these volumes. The challenge is to map (Hart 1996) the topology (Folkes 2002) of consumer research as an academic field of practice (Whitley 1995); and to capture the areas of contestation represented by the different disciplinary matrices, most notably the debates amongst and between positivist and non positivist researchers about their respective approaches to consumer behavior research. The interdisciplinary richness of the field of consumer behavior is reflected in the impact of the social sciences (e.g. sociology, anthropology and psychology) on the key publications. These volumes capture the inter-change and application of social science theories, concepts, conceptual frameworks and empirical results within the field of consumer behavior research. The topological shape of the academic field has changed considerably since the publication of a series of key citation articles in the late 1980s and early 1990s; most notably because of the growing influx of influences from sociology and anthropology; and the arts and humanities – although applied psychology remains the foundational discipline for much of the published work in the field (e.g. Volume 2).

## Volume 1: Consumer Behavior as a Field of Study

The first volume in this set focuses on consumer behavior as a field of study. The papers explore the debates about what constitutes research into consumer behavior; and revolve around four questions: how might we map consumer behavior as a field of academic practice? how do we study consumer behavior and/or research consumers? i.e. – the paradigm debate; how are debates on consumer behavior framed within specific philosophy of science approaches? and what are the wider (and widening) debates about consumption?

How might we map consumer research? Five papers in this volume (Alon, Morrin and Bechwati 2002; Campbell 1991; Simonson, Carmon, Dhar, Drolet and Nowlis 2001; Trentmann 2004; Zhukin and Maguire 2004) offer important – and very different – answers to the question: what constitutes consumer behavior research? First of all, Alon, Morrin and Bechwati (2002) provide an analysis of the bibliographical structure of consumer research, most notably of the US voices in the field, represented largely by the *Journal of Consumer Research*; and more recently by the *Journal of Consumer Psychology*. This first volume explicitly (Alon, Morrin and Bechwati 2002) and implicitly (e.g. Anderson 1986; Arnold and Fischer 1994; Bristor and Fischer 1993; Hudson and Ozanne 1988; Hunt 1991; Mick 1986; Thompson, Locander and Pollio 1989; Wells 1993) is testament to the influence that the *Journal of Consumer Research* has had on consumer behavior. A number of significant reviews of the influence of *JCR* are available (including Cote, Leong and Cote 1991; Zinkhan, Martin, Roth and Saxton (1992), Hoffman and Holbrook (1993); Frank 1995; Kernan 1995b). These reflect the important role played by key academic journals in marking the academic boundaries of a subject area (cf. Whitley 1984) (Baumgartner and Pieters 2003).

Secondly, Simonson *et al* (201) and Zhukin and MacGuire (2004) provide classic reviews of consumer research, and consumers and consumption respectively, drawing on different disciplinary foundations: psychology and sociology. Simonson *et al.* (2001: 252–254) offer a valuable overview of published work in consumer research for the previous thirty years. They draw parallels between trends in psychology and consumer research, with particular reference firstly to social versus cognitive research (notably behavioral decision theory compared with social cognition consumer research); and secondly between "hot" ("affect and mood, arousal, regret, low involvement peripheral persuasion, hedonic aspects of consumption, conflict and self-expressive motives for brand preference", Simonson *et al.* 2001:254) and "cold" topics ("role of beliefs in attitude formation, attention, perception, information acquisition, learning, expertise, attribution, and decision rules", Simonson *et al.* 2201: 254). Zhukin and MacGuire (2004:173) see consumption as an "institutional field" where social groups shape the institutional framework for consumption spaces created by "new technologies, ideologies and delivery systems"; and where individuals use consumption to form and express identities (a view critiqued by Warde 1994, Volume 5). Finally, Campbell (1991) and Trentmann (2004) provide overviews of the insights offered by the arts and the humanities, as well as the social sciences, into consumption. Campbell (1991) draws briefly on historical trends to provide a context for his discussion. This is in contrast to Trentmann who, as a historian, asks "what should be the unit of enquiry for historical research? … a history of 'consumerism' or 'consumer society', of 'consumption regimes' or 'consumer culture'", and then proceeds to examine the different theoretical and empirical approaches taken by historians.

The next question addressed by papers in Volume 1 is: How do we study consumer behavior and/or research consumers? Here we move on to try and give some sense of the ontological and epistemological debates which surround research into consumer behavior. The selection of articles (Anderson 1986; Hudson and Ozanne 1988; Hunt 1991; Peter 1991) shows the changing emphasis in research approaches to understanding consumers and indicates how the theoretical context for the study of consumer behavior has changed over time. The paradigm debate within marketing can be traced back at least as far as Converse (1945) and Bartels (1951). Their early papers posed questions about the relationship between science and marketing. Peter and Olson (1983) reopened these issues in their paper "Is Science Marketing?" and thus initiated the next phase of the discussion between positivists and non positivists about what counts as research within consumer behavior. These paradigm debates took particular hold in consumer behavior research (Wilkie and Moore (2003:132): Anderson 1983; Arndt 1985; Deshpande 1983; Hunt 1983, 1990, 1992; Peter 1992; Peter and Olsen 1983; Zinkhan and Hirschheim 1992) – and have continued to the present day (Levy 2003).

The third set of papers revolve around specific examples of consumer behavior research framed within different philosophy of science approaches ranging from the structuralist (Levy 1981) to hermeneutics (Arnold and Fischer 1994); phenomenology (Thompson, Locander and Pollio 1989); semiotics (Mick 1986) through to feminism (Bristor and Fischer 1993). These represent just a small selection of papers which range widely through the objectivist – constructionist – subjectivist issues (Crotty 1998) and include *inter alia* Arnould and Thompson 2005; Calder and Tybout 1987; Firat and Venkatesh 1995; Hirschman 1991;

Holbrook 1987; Holbrook and O'Shaughnessy 1988; Levy 2005; Sherry 1990; and Tybout 1995.

The two remaining papers raised important issues about the direction of consumer behavior research in their respective periods. Hirschman and Holbrook (1982) (see also Holbrook and Hirschman 1982) pointed to the need to consider hedonic, i.e. non rational and emotional, aspects of consumer decision-making, which had been largely excluded from the classic comprehensive models of buyer behavior then extant (e.g. Engel *et al* 1968; Howard and Sheth 1969; Nicosia 1966). Wells (1993:489) called for re-visioning of consumer behavior research for "wider horizons, a larger audience, a different talent mix, more emphasis on discovery, more attention to consumers, and more single-minded dedication to meaningful results".

## Volume 2: Consumer Decision-making

> "That all our knowledge begins with experience, there is indeed no doubt ... but although our knowledge originates with experience, it does not all arise out of experience" (Immanuel Kant 1998, p. 41 cited in Hoch 2002:448).

The second volume in this series continues the theme of exploring the production of knowledge within the academic field of practice represented by consumer behavior research. These papers focus on aspects of consumer decision-making, drawing on the extensive and prolific work done within applied psychology on consumer behavior (e.g. attitude; memory; learning; knowledge; motivation; perception; personality; satisfaction and dissatisfaction) with a selection of the major key papers framed mainly within the information-processing approach of cognitive psychology, notably behavioral decision theory and social cognition consumer research.

Simonson, Carmon, Dhar, Drolet and Nowlis (2001, see Volume 1) provide a detailed review of the range and depth of research under "hot" and "cold" topics. Under the theme of decision-making and choice, Lynch and Srull's (1982) study of "Memory and Attentional Factors in Consumer Choice" represents one of most cited papers in this field; along with Feldman and Lynch's (1988) classic paper on measuring belief, attitude, intention and behavior; and Lynch, Chakravarti and Mitra's (1991) examination of consumer judgments. Bettman has produced a stream of research on consumer decision-making which is represented here by the important Bettman, Luce and Payne (1998) paper which examines the *constructive* aspects of consumer choice. Choice is the theme also in Luce's (1998) prize winning paper on negative emotions and choice (which shows how difficult it can be always to categorize papers neatly into "hot" or "cold" topics). Nowlis and Simonson (1996) extend the examination of consumer choice into the context of brand choice within the marketing managerial context of new product development; which links with MacKenzie and Spreng's (1992) classic study of the impact of motivation on information-processing (central and peripheral) on brand attitudes and intentions. Processing effects are picked up again in Janiszewski's (1988:199) paper on preconscious processing effects which suggests that "consumers use differential hemispheric strategies for task performance to form preconsciously based attitudes". The importance of knowledge and learning as topics is reflected by Sujan's early paper (1985) on knowledge effects; by van Osselaer and Alba's (2000) work on consumer learning and brand equity; and by Kardes and Gurumurthy's (1992) examination of order of entry effects in consumer memory and judgment. The implications of consumer learning not just for the pre-purchase search stage, and the purchase and choice stage, but also for the post-purchase and evaluation stage of consumer decision-making is captured by Hoch's (2002) paper on "Product Experience is Seductive"; and also Hoch and Deighton's (1989) earlier discussion of what consumers learn from experience.

The managerial issues around consumer decision-making are reflected in Oliver's (1999) paper on consumer loyalty. The final paper by Fournier and Mick (1999)[7] "Rediscovering satisfaction" provides a neat coda to the volume as it combines the use of deductive and inductive approaches to research in consumer behavior and marketing on a classic topic, where it was possibly felt that there was not much more work to be done (the authors themselves describe it as "a mature research area"). Yet their paper showed how other feelings and emotions linked to Consumer Satisfaction/Dissatisfaction could be elicited by using a different phenomenological and longitudinal approach, compared with the more usual cognitive information processing studies.

## Volume 3: Consumer Socialization: Childhood, Children and Families

Consumer socialization is the focus of the third volume which primarily addresses the question: "how do we learn to become consumers?". The contribution of Ward's seminal article (1974) to consumer socialization can be seen in the stream of publications which has flowed from it; and in the variety of directions which research on families and children have taken over the past thirty years. Only a few papers from this very rich stream of research can be included here; and they provide some indication of the scope and scale of our changing understanding of consumer behavior and of the processes involved in pre-purchase, purchase and post-purchase consumption at different life stages. Roedder John's (1999) superlative review of a quarter century of work on consumer socialization of children provides a nicely detailed context for the papers in this volume which can be loosely grouped as follows: consumer socialization; social and family influences in consumer socialization; children and adolescents as consumers; children and advertising (with links to papers in Volume 4); and ending with a brief glance at the historical context.

Moschis and Churchill's large scale study of adolescents (1978) was an important early contribution to understanding "consumption-related skills in the context of sociological and developmental theories of socialization". The influence of the family was explored in a number of studies including Moschis'

(1985) examination of the role of family communication in consumer socialization; a theme that was also taken up by Carlson, Grossbart and Stuenkel (1992) in their discussion of the inter-relationship between general socialization types and specific communication dimensions as shown in mothers' parenting styles; and by Palan (1998) in her study of the relationship between family communication and adolescent consumer activity. Foxman, Tansuhaj and Ekstrom (1989: 481) used family triads to "document structural relationships between parents and children in family decision-making"; while Childers and Rao (1992) extended Bearden and Etzel's (1982) study of peer influence on product and brand choice to examine intergenerational influences across cultures. Carlson, Laczniak and Walsh (2001:276) use an intergenerational study with mothers and adolescents to investigate the relation between family communication patterns and mothers' marketplace motivations, attitudes and behaviors. Moore, Wilkie and Lutz (2002) also examined intergenerational influences, this time within the context of brand equity, as well as the interaction between advertising and product experience in children's experience of the market place (Moore and Lutz 2000. Unfortunately there was not space to include this paper here).

Armstrong and Brucks (1988) examine some of the recurring themes in the controversy which surrounds advertising to children; and in a similar vein, Martin (1997) provides a meta-analysis of the extent to which children understand the intent of advertising. These link to studies which concentrate on how children learn to become consumers (Peracchio 1992); many of which focus on trying to identify significant ages at which different skills develop such as adaptive decision-making (Gregan-Paxton and John 1997; see also Gregan-Paxton and John 1995 [not included here]); product categorization (John and Sujan 1990); choice behavior (John and Lakshmi-Ratan 1992); and learning of brand names as visual cues (Macklin 1996).

The historical theme identified in the first volume in Trentmann's paper is revisited again in Cook's paper in Volume 3 which examines how two intersecting spatial dimensions: aspirational and proprietary, shaped children's experience of consumption in the marketplace from the 1930s onwards; and also how these dimensions affected our views of children as consumers.

## Volumes 4–6: Looking ahead

The thematic elements traced at the beginning of this introduction, which linked papers to positivist and non-positivist approaches to knowledge and their associated (if implicit) intellectual networks (Collins 1998; Harrington 2001), are reflected in the next three volumes which cover: Advertising and Consumption (Vol 4); Possessions, brands and the self (Vol 5); and (Sub)cultures of consumption (Vol 6).

The topics dealt with in Vol 4 (Advertising and Consumption) include consumer memory and processing of information; the impact of advertisements; interpretation of advertisements; and adolescents and advertising. The papers in Volume 4 reflect the division between positivist and non positivist researchers' examination of the consumption of advertising, thus paralleling the substantive themes from Volumes 1–3. Some papers in Volume 4 fit neatly with the mainstream information processing research found in applied psychology research and discussed at some length in Volume 2 including Petty, Cacioppo and Schumann's classic paper (1983) on "Central and Peripheral Routes to Advertising Effectiveness"; Keller's much cited paper (1987) on "Memory Factors in Advertising"; MacInnis, Moorman and Jaworski's (1991) key paper on "Enhancing and Measuring Consumers" Motivation, Opportunity and Ability to Process Brand Information from Ads"; and Braun-LaTour's prize winning paper (1999) "Post-experience Advertising Effects on Consumer Memory", to mention just a few. Scott's important paper (1994) on the need for a theory of visual rhetoric and Ritson and Elliott's (1999) prize-winning paper, which reported an ethnographic study of adolescents' social uses of advertising, both illustrate the growing impact of non positivist approaches on how we study the consumption of advertising; while McQuarrie and Mick's (1999) innovative paper combined multiple research traditions (text-interpretive, experimental and reader-response) to examine visual rhetoric in advertising.

Possessions, brands and the self are the central themes in Volume 5; and here the non positivist approach predominates, but not to the exclusion of positivist papers. Levy's classic paper "Symbols for Sale" sets the scene for this volume. Some of the key papers on brands include Aaker and Keller's (1990) work on brand extensions; Aaker's (1997) study of brand personality; Holt's (2002) post-structuralist approach to brands; and Fournier's (1998) prize-winning paper about consumers' relationships to their brands. Belk's much cited (1988) paper on "Possessions and the Extended Self" played an important role in propelling non positivist papers into the mainstream of consumer behavior research; and is central to the set of papers on possessions, which also includes Price, Arnould and Curasi (2000) on disposition; and two papers from the sociology of consumption: Lucas (2002) on "Disposability and Dispossession in The Twentieth Century"); and Komter (2001) on "Heirlooms, Nikes and Bribes: Towards a Sociology of Things". Papers on the self draw on symbolic interactionism (Solomon 1983); and Warde's (1994) paper from the sociology of consumption tradition problematizes the notion of consumer choice in relation to identity creation via consumption.

A number of current and topical themes under the umbrella title of (Sub)cultures are the focus of the sixth and last volume in the series. McCracken's (1986) much cited paper "Culture and Consumption" and Belk, Wallendorf and Sherry's (1989) prize-winning paper "The Sacred and Profane in Consumer Behavior: Theodicy on the Odyssey" are central to this volume; along with papers on subcultures of consumption (Schouten and McAlexander 1995 and Bennett 1999); and newly emergent debates about brand communities (Muniz and O'Guinn 2001; and McAlexander, Schouten and Koenig 2002); the social patterning of consumption (Holt 1997); and distastes (Wilk 1997; and Turner and Edmunds 2002).

## Choosing the road ...

At this point I leave readers to make their own personal journeys through the literature – hoping that everyone will find here something to his/her taste; and also something that provokes further thought and discussion in that all-important reflective conversation (Morgan 1983:406; Astley 1985:510–511) which should be the defining characteristic of our field of consumer behavior research.

## Notes

1. The Association for Consumer Research (ACR) which emerged from The American Marketing Association Consumer Behavior Workshop in Ohio 1969 held its first conference in 1970 (Engel 1995:548–9). It represents the main international academic forum for researchers into consumer behavior, holding an annual conference in North America; and, since the 1990s, biennial conferences in Europe and Asia-Pacific.

2. I am grateful to Dr. Ellen Pruyne and Professor Ian Clarke, Department of Marketing, Lancaster University Management School, for drawing my attention to this article.

3. With thanks to Dr. Maria Piacentini (Department of Marketing) and Dr. Patrick O'Shea (Centre for the Enhancement of Learning and Teaching) at Lancaster University for drawing my attention to Mingers' paper.

4. At my first ACR conference in Vancouver 1992 I clearly was a "stranger" (and described by one participant, in as many words, as "exotic other" i.e. foreign and different). My status as stranger was brought home to me not so much via my experience of the papers at the academic sessions but at the social events where one could hover, almost invisibly, on the edge of groups in the evening receptions; and very nervously, and clearly alone, at the intimidating luncheons. No European academic training at that stage had prepared me for the social challenge of the US academic circuit, and the initiation rituals which I was witnessing. I had a sense of "being on the outside, looking in", rather like Alice in Wonderland. Of particular relevance here is Harrington's (2001) discussion of Collins's (1998) argument about the centrality of the "intellectual network": "I am arguing that if one can understand the principles that determine intellectual networks, one has a casual [sic] explanation of ideas and their changes. In a very strong sense, networks are the actors on the intellectual stage… The network dynamics of intellectual communities provides an internal sociology of ideas" (p.xviii). Intellectual networks arise when individuals enter into Goffmanian "interaction rituals": primarily in the face-to-face situations of gatherings, conferences and disputations, but also along the "vertical" dimension of master-pupil relations and intergenerational discipleship and polemic… participation in "interaction ritual chains" for Collins yields a quantum of intellectual creativity or "emotional energy", which increases or decreases according to the thinker's place at the centre or periphery. Prolonged exposure to the network generates a degree of Bourdieurian "cultural capital", defined by Collins as "a personal repertoire of symbols loaded with membership significance… a symbolic repertoire of varying degrees of abstraction and reification, of different generalized and particularized contents" that varies "depending on the degree of cosmopolitanism and social density of the group situations" (Collins 1998: 29). "Intellectual communities feed on conflict and attention-seeking" (Harrington 2001: 127). At Vancouver ACR 1992 I was launched into this n(N)ew w(W)orld.

5. There is not space here to pursue at length the important debates about the relationship between sociology of knowledge and philosophy of science, see for instance Vratusa-Zunjic's (2001) review of Meja and Stehr (1999) eds. Weseley (1997) identifies two important strands in the debate: the first strand with an "interest in the socio-historical conditioning of the knowledge claims"; and the second strand with "its attempt to grasp the social nature of the forms of gaining and organizing knowledge"; and she quotes Ludwik Fleck who "joined the traditions and critically confronted them with the ideas of the Vienna Circle… and generalized his findings in a sociological theory of knowledge….. 'In science, just as in art and in life, only that which is true to culture is true to nature' (Fleck 1979:35). Truth is both historically contingent and socially necessary" (Weseley 1997: 7ff); so that for Fleck (1979, p.21) "The form of scientific theories – their socially embedded plausibility, closed structure and stylistic

consonance with other accepted theories – is the social precondition to their advancement" (Wesely 1979 p. 8).

6. "Their achievement was sufficiently unprecedented to attract an enduring group of adherents away from competing modes of scientific activity. Simultaneously, it was sufficiently open-ended to leave all sorts of problems for the redefined group of practitioners to solve" (Kuhn 1996:10).

7. I am very grateful to Dr Gillian Hopkinson (Lancaster University Management School) for drawing my attention to this paper; and generously sharing with me her creative use of this article as the foundation for a postgraduate research methodology seminar at Manchester School of Management, UMIST, UK.

## References


Anderson, Paul F. (1983) "Marketing, Scientific Progress and Scientific Method" *Journal of Marketing* 47 (Fall) 18–31

Arndt, Johan (1985) "On Making Marketing Science More Scientific: Role of Orientations, Paradigms, Metaphors, and Puzzle Solving" *Journal of Marketing* (Summer) 11–23

Arnould, Eric J. and Craig J. Thompson (2005) "Consumer Culture Theory (CCT): Twenty Years of Research" *Journal of Consumer Research* 31 March

Astley, W. Graham (1985) "Administrative Science as Socially-Constructed Truth" *Administrative Science Quarterly* 30 497–513

Bartels, R. (1951) "Can Marketing Be A Science?", *Journal of Marketing* 15 (3) 319–329.

Baumgartner, Hans and Rik Pieters (2003) "The Structural Influence of Marketing Journals: A Citation Analysis of the Discipline and Its Subareas over Time" *Journal of Marketing* 67 (April) 123–39

Bearden, William O. and Michael J. Etzel (1982) "Reference Group Influence on Product and Brand Purchase Decisions" *Journal of Consumer Research* 9 (September) 183–194

Belk, Russell (1991) ed. *Highways and buyways* Provo, Utah: Association for Consumer Research.

Belk, Russell (1995) "Studies in the New Consumer Behavior" in *Acknowledging Consumption* ed. Daniel Miller, London: Routledge, 58–95

Belk, Russell W., Melanie Wallendorf and John F. Sherry (1989) "The Sacred and the Profane in Consumer Behavior: Theodicy on the Odyssey" *Journal of Consumer Research* 16 (June) 1–38

Bettman, J.R. 1993 "The decision maker who came in from the cold" *Advances in Consumer Research* 20:7–11 Provo, Utah: Association of Consumer Research

Calder, B.J. and Tybout, A.M. 1987 "What consumer research is" *Journal of Consumer Research* 14 (1) 136–140

Checkland, P. and J. Scholes (1990) *Soft Systems Methodology in Action* Chichester: Wiley

Churchman, C.W. (1968) *The Systems Approach* New York: Dell Publishing

Clegg, Stewart (2001) ed. "Editor's Introduction: Frameworks and Applications" Central Currents in Organization Studies I, London: Sage, vii–xxiii

Clegg, Stewart (2002) ed. "Editor's Introduction: Contemporary Trends" Central Currents in Organization Studies II, London: Sage, ix–xxxi

Cohen, Joel B. 1995 "Abbott and Costello Meet Frankenstein: An ACR Retrospective" *Advances in Consumer Research* 22 Provo UT: Association for Consumer Research, 545–547

Collins, Randall (1998) *The Sociology of Philosophies: A Global Theory of Intellectual Change* Cambridge, MA: Harvard University Press, reviewed in Harrington (2001)

Converse, Paul (1945) "The Development of the Science of Marketing: An Exploratory Survey" *Journal of Marketing* 10 (July) 14–34

Cote, Joseph A., Siew Meng Leong and Jane Cote (1991) "Assessing the influence of *Journal of Consumer Research*: A Citation Analysis" *Journal of Consumer Research* 18 (December) 402–410

Crotty, Michael (1998) *The Foundations of Social Research: Meaning and Perspective in the Research Process* London: Sage.

Deighton John and Das Narayandas (2004) "Stories and Theories" an invited commentary on "Evolving to a New Dominant Logic for Marketing" *Journal of Marketing* 68 (1) January 19–20

Deshpande, Rohit (1983) "Paradigms Lost: On Theory and Method in Research in Marketing" *Journal of Marketing* 47 (Fall) 101–110

Engel, James F 1995 "ACR's 25th Anniversary: How It All Began" *Advances in Consumer Research* 22 Provo UT: Association for Consumer Research, 548–549

Engel, J., D. Kollat, R. Blackwell 1968 *Consumer Behavior* New York: Holt, Rinehart & Winston

Firat, A. Fuat and Alladi Venkatesh (1995) "Liberatory postmodernism and the re-enchantment of consumption" *Journal of Consumer Research* 22 (December): 239–267

Fleck, L. (19798) *Genesis and Development of a Scientific Fact* Chicago: University of Chicago Press (cited in Wesely 1997)

Folkes, Valerie (2002), "Presidential Address: Is Consumer Behavior Different?" *Advances in Consumer Research*, Volume XXIX, Valdosta, GA: Association of Consumer Research p. 1–4

Fournier, Susan (1998), "Consumers and Their Brands: Developing Relationship Theory in Consumer Research" *Journal of Consumer Research*, 24 (March), p. 343–373.

Frank, Ronald E. (1974) "The *Journal of Consumer Research*: An Introduction" *Journal of Consumer Research* 1 (June) i–ii

Frank, Ronald E. (1995) "Notes on *The Journal of Consumer Research:* The Unprecedented Challenges of a Start-up" *Advances in Consumer Research* 22 Provo UT: Association for Consumer Research, 486–487

Frost, Robert (1920) *The Road Not Taken* Henry Holt and Company

Golden-Biddle, Karen and Karen Locke (1993) "Appealing work: an investigation of how ethnographic texts convince" *Organization Science* 4 (4) November 595–616

Gregan-Paxton, J. and D.R. John (1995) "Are Young Children Adaptive Decision Makers? A Study of Age Differences in Information Search Behavior" *Journal of Consumer Research* (21) 4 March: 567–580

Gronow, J. and A. Warde (2001) "*Ordinary consumption*" London: Routledge

Hart, Chris (1998) *Doing a Literature Review* London: Sage

Harrington, Austin (2001) "From Hegel to the Sociology of Knowledge: Contested Narratives" Review essay of Randall Collins (1998) *The Sociology of Philosophies* Cambridge, MA: Harvard University Press, in *Theory, Culture and Society* 18 (6) 125–133

Hirschman, Elizabeth C. (1991) "Secular Mortality and the Dark Side of Consumer Behavior: Or How Semiotics Saved My Life" *Advances in Consumer Research* 18 pp. 1–4 Provo, Utah: Association for Consumer Research

Holbrook, Morris B. and Elizabeth C. Hirschman (1982) "The Experiential Aspects of Consumption: Consumer Fantasies, Feelings and Fun" *Journal of Consumer Research* 9 (September) 132–140

Hoffman, Donna L. and Morris B. Holbrook (1993) "The Intellectual Structure of Consumer Research: A Bibliometric Study of Author Cocitations in the First 15 Years of the *Journal of Consumer Research*" 19 (March) 505–517

Holbrook, M.B. (1987) "What is consumer research?" *Journal of Consumer Research* 14 (June): 128–132

Holbrook, M.B. and J. O'Shaughnessy (1988) "On the scientific status of consumer research and the need for an interpretive approach to studying consumption behavior" *Journal of Consumer Research* 15 (December) (1988): 398–402

Howard, J.A. and J. N. Sheth (1969) *The Theory of Buyer Behavior* New York: Wiley

Hughes, W. (1996) *Critical Thinking* Ontario: Broadview Press

Hunt, Shelby D. (1983) "General Theories and the Fundamental Explananda of Marketing" *Journal of Marketing*, 47 (Fall) 9–17

Hunt, Shelby D. (1990) "Truth in Marketing Theory and Research" *Journal of Marketing* 54 (July) 1–15

Hunt, Shelby D. (1991) "Positivism and Paradigm Dominance in Consumer Research: Toward Critical Pluralism and Rapprochement" *Journal of Consumer Research* 18 (June) 32–44

Hunt, Shelby D. (1992) "For Reasons and Realism in Marketing" *Journal of Marketing* 56 (April) 89–102

Hunt, Shelby D. (1993) "Objectivity in Marketing Theory and Research" *Journal of Marketing* 57 (2) 76–92

Hunt, Shelby D. and Terry Clark (2001) "The Influence of Philosophy, Philosophies, and Philosophers on a Marketer's Scholarship" *Journal of Marketing* 65 (4) October 117–123

Kuhn, Thomas (1996) *The Structure of Scientific Revolutions* 3rd ed. Chicago and London: University of Chicago Press

Kardes, Frank R. and Mita Sujan 1995 eds. *Advances in Consumer Research* 22 Provo UT: Association for Consumer Research

Kassarjian, Harold H. and James R. Bettman (1982) "Editorial" *Journal of Consumer Research* 9 (June) 1–3

Kassarjian, Harold H. (1995) "Some Recollections from a Quarter Century Ago" *Advances in Consumer Research* 22 Provo UT: Association for Consumer Research, 550–552

Kernan, Jerome B. (1995a) "Declaring a Discipline: Reflections on ACR's Silver Anniversary" *Advances in Consumer Research* 22 Provo UT: Association for Consumer Research, 553–560

Kernan, Jerome B. (1995b) "Framing a Rainbow, Focusing the Light: JCR's First Twenty Years" *Advances in Consumer Research* 22 Provo UT: Association for Consumer Research, 488–496

Kleine, R.E. Kleine, S.S. and Kernan, J.B. 1993: 209: "Mundane Consumption and the Self: A Social-Identity Perspective", *Journal of Consumer Psychology* 2 (3) (1993) 209–235

Levy, Sidney J. (1992) "Presidential Address: Constructing Consumer Behavior: A Grand Template" *Advances in Consumer Research* 19 pp. 1–6

Levy, Sidney J. (2005) "The evolution of qualitative research in consumer behavior" *Journal of Business Research* 58 341–347

Lievrouw, Leah A. (1990) "Reconciling structure and process in the study of scholarly communication" in *Scholarly Communication and Bibliometrics* ed. Christine L. Borgman, Newbury Park, CA : Sage 59–72

Lutz, Richard J. (1989a) "Positivism, Naturalism and Pluralism in Consumer Research: Paradigms in Paradise" *Advances in Consumer Research* 16 Provo, Utah: Association of Consumer Research, 1–7

Lutz, Richard J (1989b) "Editorial" *Journal of Consumer Research* 16 (1) June

Lutz, Richard J. (1989c) "Editorial" *Journal of Consumer Research* 17 (4) March

Lutz, Richard J. (1989d) "Editorial" *Journal of Consumer Research* 18 (2) September

McQuarrie, Edward F. and Mick, David Glen (1999), "Visual Rhetoric in Advertising: Text-Interpretive, Experimental, and Reader-Response Analyses" *Journal of Consumer Research* 26 (1) (June): 37–65.

Meja, Volker and Nico Stehr (1999) eds. *The Sociology of Knowledge* Edward Elgar, Cheltenham UK/Northampton MA.

Miller, Daniel (1995) ed. *Acknowledging Consumption: a review of new studies* London: Routledge

Mingers, John (2000) "What is it to be Critical?" *Management Learning* 31 (2) 219–237

Monroe, Kent (1991) "Editorial" *Journal of Consumer Research* 18 (1) June

Moore, E.S. and R.J. Lutz (2000) "Children, Advertising and Product Experiences: A Multimethod Inquiry" *Journal of Consumer* Research 27 (June): 1–48

Morgan, Gareth (1983) (ed) "In research, as in conversation, we meet ourselves" in *Beyond Method: Strategies for Social Research*, Newbury Park, California: Sage, 405–407

Nicosia, F. (1966) *Consumer Decision Processes* Englewood Cliffs, NJ: Prentice-Hall

Nicosia, Francesco M. and Robert N. Mayer (1976) "Toward a Sociology of Consumption" *Journal of Consumer Research* 3 (September) 65–75

Olsen, Wendy K. (2000) "Originality or collective progress in the social sciences" *Feminist Economics* available at http://www.raggedclaws.com/criticalrealism/archive/wkolsen_ocpss.html accessed 5/11/2004

Peck, M. Scott (1997) *The Road Less Travelled* London: Random House

Peter, J.P. (1992) "Realism or Relativism for Marketing Theory and Research: A Comment on Hunt's "Scientific Realism" *Journal of Marketing* 56 (April) 72–79

Peter, J.P. and Olson J.C (1983) "Is Science Marketing?" *Journal of Marketing* 47 (Fall) 111–125
Pratt, Robert W. (1974) "ACR: A Perspective" *Advances in Consumer Research* 1 Chicago: Association for Consumer Research 1–8
Randles, S., Andrew McMeekin and Alan Warde (2002) "The Making of a "KIS": the professionalisation and industrialisation of market research" RESER Conference on Innovation and Services, Manchester September *unpublished paper*
Reckwitz, A. (2002) "Toward a Theory of Social Practices" *European Journal of Social Theory* 5 (2) 243–263, cited in Randles *et al.* (2002)
Richins, Marsha L. (2001) "Consumer Behavior as Social Science" Presidential Address *Advances in Consumer Research* 28 Provo, Utah: Association for Consumer Research, 1–5
Schutz, Alfred (1943) "The Problem of Rationality in the Social World" *Economica* Vol X, May 130–149 [cited in Smith 1998]
Schutz, Alfred (1944) "The Stranger: An Essay in Social Psychology" *American Journal of Sociology* 49, 6 May 499–507 [cited in Smith 1998]
Scott, Linda M. (1994a), "Images in advertising: the need for a theory of visual rhetoric" *Journal of Consumer Research* 21 (2) (September): 252–274
Scott, Linda M. (1994b), "The Bridge from Text to Mind: Adapting Reader-Response Theory to Consumer Research" *Journal of Consumer Research* 21 (December): 461–480.
Sherry, John F. (1990) "Postmodern Alternatives: The Interpretive Turn", Consumer Research *Handbook of Consumer Research* eds. H.H. Kassarjian and T.S.Robertson, Englewood Cliffs, NJ: Prentice-Hall, Chapter 16 549–591.
Smith, Mark J. (1998) *Social Science in Question* London: Sage
Sprott, David E. and Anthony D. Miyazaki (2002) "Two Decades of Contributions to Marketing and Public Policy: An Analysis of Research Published in *Journal of Public Policy and Marketing*", *Journal of Public Policy and Marketing* 21 (Spring) 105-125
Sternthal, Brian and Gerald Zaltman (1974) "Broadening the Concept of Consumer Behavior" *Advances in Consumer Research* 1 Chicago: Association for Consumer Research, 488-496
Thompson, Paul (1996) Life Story Interview www.esds.ac.uk/qualidata/online/data/edwardians/biography/PaulThompsonLifeStoryInterview1996.doc accessed 3 November 2004
Tybout, Alice (1995) "The Value of Theory in Consumer Research" Presidential address *Advances in Consumer Research* 22 Provo, Utah: Association for Consumer Research, 1–8
Vaidyanathan Rajiv (2004) "Field of Dreams: An Informal Examination of the Discipline of Consumer Behavior as Defined by Doctoral Seminar Reading Lists" *ACR* Newsletter
Vargo, Stephen L. and Robert F. Lusch (2004) "Evolving to a New Dominant Logic for Marketing" *Journal of Marketing* 68 (1) Jan 1–18
Venkatesan, M. (1972) ed *Proceedings of the Third Annual Conference of the Association for Consumer Research*, Chicago: Association of Consumer Research
Ward, S. (1974) "Consumer Socialization", *Journal of Consumer Research* 1 (September) :1–14.
Vratusa-Zunjic, Vera (2001) Review of Meja, Volker and Nico Stehr (1999) eds. *The Sociology of Knowledge* Cheltenham UK/Northampton MA: Edward Elgar in *Journal of the History of the Behavioral Sciences* 37 (3) Summer 290–292
Wells, William D. Wells (1993) "Discovery-oriented Consumer Research" *Journal of Consumer Research* 19 (March) 489–504
Wells, William D. (1995) "What Do We Want To Be When We Grow Up?" *Advances in Consumer Research* 22 Provo UT: Association for Consumer Research, 561–563
Wesely, Anna (1997) "Philosophy of science and sociology of knowledge" *Innovation: The European Journal of Social Sciences* 10 (1) March 7–16
Whitley, Richard (1984) "The Fragmented State of Management Studies: Reasons and Consequences" *Journal of Management Studies* 21 (3) 331–348
Whitley, Richard (1988) "The Management Sciences and Managerial Skills" *Organization Studies* 9 (1) 47–68
Whitley, Richard (1989) "On the Nature of Managerial Tasks and Skills: their Distinguishing Characteristics" *Journal of Management Studies* 26 (3) 209–224
Whitley, Richard (1995) "Academic Knowledge and Work Jurisdiction in Management" *Organization Studies* 16 (1) 81–105

Wilkie, William and Elizabeth S. Moore (1999) "Marketing's Contributions to Society" *Journal of Marketing* 63 (Special Issue) 198–218
Wilkie, William L. and Elizabeth S. Moore (2003) "Scholarly Research in Marketing: Exploring the '4 Eras' of Thought Development" *Journal of Public Policy and Marketing* 22 (2) Fall 116–146
Zinkhan, George M. and Rudy Hirschheim (1992) "Truth in Marketing Theory and Research: An Alternative Perspective" *Journal of Marketing* 56 (April) 80–88
Zinkhan, George M., Martin S. Roth and Mary Jane Saxton (1992) "Knowledge Development and Scientific Status in Consumer-Behavior Research: A Social Exchange Perspective" *Journal of Consumer Research* 19 (September) 282–291
Zinkhan, George M., Mary Jane Saxton, Martin S. Roth and Gerald Zaltman (1990) "Citation Analysis of the ACR Proceedings: A Knowledge Development and Social Exchange Perspective" *Advances in Consumer Research* 17 Provo, Utah: Association for Consumer Research, 627–635

# 1

# Comparing *Journal of Consumer Psychology* and *Journal of Consumer Research*

**Anat Alon, Maureen Morrin and Nada Nasr Bechwati**

**Source:** *Journal of Consumer Psychology* 12 (1) (2002): 5–21.

The *Journal of Consumer Psychology (JCP)*, which published its first issue in 1992, came into being at a time when the number of researchers in the field of consumer research was growing (Lutz, 1991). From the outset, *JCP's* stated goal has been to publish research that will "contribute to our understanding of consumer psychology in all of its domains and all of its forms" by encouraging scholars "of widely divergent backgrounds and orientations" to submit "both experimental and nonexperimental studies that report original data, as well as theoretical, methodological, and review articles" (*JCP*, Vol. 1, No. 1, back cover). Interestingly, *JCP's* statement of purpose is similar in many respects to that of the *Journal of Consumer Research* (*JCR*; Frank, 1974; Monroe, 1991), which was launched over two decades ago and is considered by many researchers in the field as the premier journal of consumer research.

Although *JCP's* stated goal seems quite similar to that of *JCR*, *JCP's* raison d'être has been perceived by some as not simply being an alternative outlet for publication of consumer research. That is, *JCP* is not generally viewed as simply a "me too" journal. Instead, the journal has been perceived by many as having a research focus somewhat different from that of *JCR*. Specifically, *JCP* has been perceived by some as having been created partly in response to what was interpreted as a shift in the methodological focus of *JCR* in the last decade or so. During that time, *JCR* began to increase its accommodation of postmodern approaches, compared to more positivistic approaches (Hunt, 1991), perhaps in response to growing calls for such an accommodation by leading members of its professional organization, the Association of Consumer Research (see, e.g., Hirschman, 1991). In comparison to *JCR*, *JCP's* mission was thus perceived by many to be more methodologically homogeneous, with a greater focus on traditional experimentalism, as opposed to other approaches such as postmodernism. To our knowledge, this assumption has not been empirically tested. Neither have other issues of comparison between the two journals, such as the extent to which they publish articles on the same or different topics, or the extent to which its authors come from diverse disciplines of interest. Thus, at present, we do not know whether *JCP* acts as a supplement or a complement to *JCR*. *JCP* recently reached a significant milestone by having published a total of over 100 articles since its inception. This, combined with the start of a new millennium, suggested it was an appropriate time for pausing to assess the degree to which the *JCP's* editorial objectives are being met and to examine its mission and positioning, especially in relation to *JCR*. How does *JCP* compare to *JCR*, the leading journal in consumer research? Is *JCR* just a "me too" journal, essentially a clone of *JCR*, or does it have a unique mission and focus? Is *JCR* really less diverse, interms of methodology, than *JCR*? Are there ways in which *JCP* is more diverse than *JCR*? In what other ways are the two journals similar or different? This review seeks to address these questions.

This article consists of an in-depth review of the articles published in *JCP* and *JCR* from 1992 to 1998. The review is intended to provide perspective on key differences and similarities between the journals, as well as on trends that may indicate where these journals are headed – in terms of research focus and overall stature within the discipline. We focus on issues such as output, authorship, content, research design, and data analysis. To our knowledge, this article constitutes the first major attempt to review *JCP*. However, researchers have previously assessed JCR's impact (e.g., Zinkhan, Roth, & Saxton, 1992) – for example, in terms of its level of diversity (Leong, 1989; Tellis, Chandy, & Ackerman, 1999). Tellis *et al.* (1999) conducted a citation analysis from which they concluded that "*JCR*, which strives to be diverse, appears not to achieve its goal" (p. 120). In their review, Tellis *et al.* (1999) chose to compare *JCR* with other journals that are considerably broader in nature (*Journal of Marketing, Journal of Marketing Research, and Marketing Science)* as they cover marketing topics other than consumer behavior (e.g., distribution and logistics, quantitative models, sales force management issues, etc.). In this article, by choosing to focus the comparison on *JCP* and *JCR*, we are able to conduct a more in-depth analysis of the published research. In addition, we adopt a more multidimensional view of diversity than that applied in previous comparisons, several of which have been based on citation analyses. In this research, we investigate how diverse a journal is within its own subdiscipline – namely, within the field of consumer research (vs. marketing, more broadly). We assess diversity on a number of measures such as methodological approach and author affiliation. Each of these issues is discussed later, followed by a concluding section on implications.

## Output and Authorship

During its initial 7-year life span, *JCP* published a total of 117 articles, written by over 198 different authors. In that time, the journal published four issues annually (with the exception of 1994, when two issues were published). The typical issue of *JCP* contained four to five 22-page articles written by two co-authors. During the same period, *JCR* published nearly a third more articles ($n$ = 269). However, the average number of articles contained in a typical issue of *JCR* fell rather dramatically during that time period ($M$ = 12.25 from 1992 to 1994; $M$ = 7.625 from 1995 to 1998). This may have been the result of the creation of *JCP* as an alternative outlet for consumer behavior research, or other factors such as changing editorial policies and directions at *JCR*. Not only were there more articles published in *JCR* in the 1992 to 1998 time span, the average article length was somewhat longer.

The average number of pages in a typical *JCR* article was 14, compared to an average page length of 11 for *JCP*. (Note that the different format of the two journals was taken into account by calculation of a conversion ratio whereby two *JCP* pages equaled about one *JCR* page.)[1]

As one of *JCP's* stated goals is to attract researchers from across several disciplines, author affiliation was examined.[2] The vast majority of authors publishing in *JCP* in its first 7 years were academic researchers (97.5%). The majority of these academics held positions in marketing or business departments (76.7%), with psychology the next most prevalent departmental affiliation (15.0%). Other areas, such as communications (1.7%) and advertising (1.7%) were represented to a significantly lesser degree. Hence, it would appear that the journal has not attracted a significant number of researchers from outside of academic disciplines, however, it has managed to attract a significant proportion of academics from outside the field of marketing. Nonmarketing disciplines were less well represented in *JCR* during the same time period. Almost all the researchers published in *JCR* held positions in marketing or business departments (91.0%). Other departments, such as psychology (2.6%), were represented to a much lesser degree than in *JCP*.

## Content

Each article published in the two journals during the past 7 years was classified by content area based on a typology from a recent review of the consumer psychology literature (Jacoby, Johar, & Morrin, 1998). This system classifies articles according to whether they are concerned with the following: (a) Contributions of Broad Relevance, such as philosophy of science and methodological advances; (b) Domain-Specific Research, such as information processing, attitudes, affect, choice, and intrinsic and extrinsic factors affecting these processes; or (c) Public Policy Issues. Each of these three major content areas is further broken down into several subcategories, resulting in a total of 33 different categories into which an article could be classified (Table 1). Each article was independently coded by two of the three authors for an agreement rate of 80.6%.[3] Disagreements were resolved with discussion. Most of the disagreements resulted from decisions regarding whether to categorize an article based on the focus of independent (e.g., gender) versus dependent variables (e.g., satisfaction).

Most of the articles in *JCP* focused on domain-specific research (84.8% of all articles), such as information processing or attitude formation, rather than on contributions of broad relevance such as philosophy of science (0.9%) and methodological advances (7.7%), or on public policy issues (6.8%). The results further indicate that, of the topical domains, information processing received the greatest amount of attention from *JCP* authors (22.2% of all articles), followed by a focus on extrinsic factors (19.7%; e.g., context effects), intrinsic factors (16.3%; e.g., personality), attitudes (14.6%; e.g., formation), and choice (7.7%; e.g., heuristics). Within the area of information processing, most attention was focused on the topics of memory and categorization, which together accounted for nearly two thirds of the information processing articles.

An interesting aspect of *JCP* was the significant amount of space devoted to comments and rebuttals on controversial issues, such as the issue of cognitive versus affective routes to attitude formation see *JCP*, Vol. 6, No. 1), the conduct of social marketing (see *JCP* Vol. 6, No. 2), and the robustness of the mere ownership effect (see *JCP*, Vol. 6, No. 3).

To what extent do these results regarding content indicate a desirable degree of coverage of the various topics within consumer research? Although nearly all of the major topical domains were addressed to some extent in *JCP*, some topics received considerably less attention than others. The topic of affect, for example, received relatively little attention from *JCP* authors (4.3% of all articles), whereas cognitively-based approaches attracted a rather large share of attention. Also, remarkably little attention was devoted to philosophy of science issues such as the positivism and postmodernism debate.

A comparison of content coverage between *JCP* and *JCR* reveals that *JCR* exhibits a somewhat less narrowly focused approach, with 74% of its articles devoted to domain-specific research (vs. 84.8% for *JCP*). Contributions of broad relevance such as philosophy of science (7.8%), methodological advances (16.3%), and public policy issues (2.3%) received considerably more attention from *JCR* authors than from *JCP* authors. Of the domain-specific areas, extrinsic factors received the greatest amount of attention from *JCR* authors (23.5%), followed by a focus on information processing (16.4%), intrinsic factors (14.8%), and choice (9.7%). The greatest disparity between *JCR* and *JCP* in domain-specific interests occurred in the relative degree of focus on attitude theory. *JCP* devoted more than twice the amount of attention to attitudes than did *JCR* (14.6% of total articles vs. 5.9%, respectively). Overall, it appears that although the authorship of *JCR* is more highly concentrated in the business disciplines (especially marketing), compared to *JCP*, the topics addressed by the *JCR* authors are broader.

## Research Design

Most of the articles published in *JCP* (85.5%) were of an empirical nature, with the rest consisting primarily of commentary and perspective articles. On average, the empirical articles reported a combined sample size of 284.[4] Interestingly, the average number of participants reported in *JCP's* empirical articles appears to be rising over time ($M\ n = 229$ from 1992 to 1994; $M\ n = 328$ from 1995 to 1998). This finding mirrors a similar trend in the increasing number of studies reported in each article from an average of 1.7 from 1992 to 1994, to 2.5 from 1995 to 1998. The situation in *JCR* was a bit different. Most of the articles published in *JCR* (86.9%) were of an empirical nature, similar to *JCP*. The average number of participants reported in *JCR* articles was larger than that of *JCP* overall and quite stable over time ($M\ n = 328$). If sample size can be considered one measure of a journal's level of rigor, this set of results seems to indicate that *JCP* is, over time, approaching the level of rigor historically associated with *JCR*.

**Table 1** Content Area in *JCP* and *JCR* from 1992 to 1998

| *Content* | *JCP Total* | *JCP %* | *JCP Subtotal* | *JCR Total* | *JCR %* | *JCR* |
|---|---|---|---|---|---|---|
| *Subtotal* | | | | | | |
| Contributions of broad relevance | | | | | | |
| Philosophy of science | | | 0.9% | | | 7.8% |
| General | 0 | 0.0% | | 5 | 1.9% | |
| Postmodernism | 1 | 0.9% | | 16 | 5.9% | |
| Methodological advances | | | 7.7% | | | 16.3% |
| General | 2 | 1.7% | | 24 | 8.9% | |
| Survey and questionnaire design | 1 | 0.9% | | 6 | 2.2% | |
| Construct development | 6 | 5.1% | | 14 | 5.2% | |
| Domain-specific research | | | | | | |
| Information processing | | | 22.2% | | | 16.4% |
| Sensation and perception | 7 | 6.0% | | 8 | 3.0% | |
| Attention | 0 | 0.0% | | 2 | 0.7% | |
| Categorization | 8 | 6.8% | | 8 | 3.0% | |
| Inference making | 3 | 2.6% | | 9 | 3.3% | |
| Information search | 0 | 0.0% | | 5 | 1.9% | |
| Memory | 8 | 6.8% | | 12 | 4.5% | |
| Attitudes | | | 14.6% | | | 5.9% |
| Formation and persuasion | 14 | 12.0% | | 13 | 4.8% | |
| Conditioning | 0 | 0.0% | | 1 | 0.4% | |
| Attitudes and behavior | 3 | 2.6% | | 2 | 0.7% | |
| Affect | | | 4.3% | | | 3.7% |
| As independent variable | 5 | 4.3% | | 8 | 3.0% | |
| As dependent variable | 0 | 0.0% | | 2 | 0.7% | |
| Choice | | | 7.7% | | | 9.7% |
| Heuristics and biases | 9 | 7.7% | | 19 | 7.1% | |
| Variety seeking and decision timing | 0 | 0.0% | | 3 | 1.1% | |
| Satisfaction | 0 | 0.0% | | 4 | 1.5% | |
| Factors affecting information processing, attitudes, and choice | | | | | | |
| Intrinsic factors | | | 16.3% | 1 | | 14.8% |
| Age | 1 | 0.9% | | 10 | 3.7% | |
| Gender, ethnicity | 4 | 3.4% | | 4 | 1.5% | |
| Personality | 12 | 10.3% | | 9 | 3.3% | |
| Perceptions | 2 | 1.7% | | 17 | 6.3% | |
| Extrinsic factors | | | 19.7% | | | 23.5% |
| Family, group, and so forth | 4 | 3.4% | | 11 | 4.1% | |
| Social roles and identity | 2 | 1.7% | | 3 | 1. 1 % | |
| Culture | 1 | 0.9% | | 14 | 5.2% | |
| Source credibility | 0 | 0.0% | | 1 | 0.4% | |
| Type of claim | 5 | 4.3% | | 8 | 3.0% | |
| Ad repetition | 0 | 0.0% | | 1 | 0.4% | |
| Context | 11 | 9.4% | | 25 | 9.3% | |
| Public policy and issues | | | 6.8% | | | 2.3% |
| Labeling effects | 0 | 0.0% | | 0 | 0.0% | |
| Health care | 6 | 5.1% | | 5 | 1.9% | |
| Advertising | 2 | 1.7% | | 1 | 0.4% | |
| | 117 | 100.0% | | 268 | 100.0% | |

*Note. JCP = Journal of Consumer Psychology; JCR = Journal of Consumer Research.*

The two major types of empirical studies conducted in *JCP* were laboratory experiments and field surveys. Researchers who published in *JCP* relied very heavily on laboratory experimentation (80.0% of the empirical articles) and the use of student participants (88.0% of the empirical articles). Surveys, typically consisting of field surveys, were the next most common empirical approach, accounting for most of the remaining empirical articles (21.0%; note that some articles reported using both experiments and surveys). Alternative techniques, such as content analysis and projective techniques, were also reported, but relatively rarely.

Although the two major types of empirical studies conducted in *JCR* were also laboratory experiments and field surveys, the situation there is less "one-sided". Researchers who published in *JCR* used laboratory experimentation to a lesser extent (60.2% of the empirical articles vs. 80.0% for *JCP)*. Also, the use of student participants was less prominent (61.5% of the empirical articles vs. 88.0% for *JCP)*. Alternative techniques such as depth interviews (8.1%) and content analysis (4.3%) were used to a greater extent in *JCR*. These results suggest that, methodologically, *JCR* does indeed exhibit a broader orientation than does *JCP*.

## Data Analysis

The techniques *JCP* and *JCR* researchers used to analyze their data sets are summarized in Table 2. The articles were categorized based on a typology developed by Wind, Rao, and Green (1991). Their framework classifies articles according to whether the data analysis involves the following: (a) Simple Methods, such as cross tabulations, *t* tests, and correlation; (b) Interdependent Structures, such as factor analysis, cluster analysis, and multidimensional scaling; or (c) Dependent Structures, such as regression, analysis of variance, and causal modeling. (Note that the percentages reported in this section of the article and in Table 2 total more than 100%, as several researchers reported more than one analytical technique.)

By far, the most popular technique employed by *JCP* authors, used in 73.0% of the empirical articles, was analysis of variance (ANOVA) and its offshoots, such as multivariate analysis of variance, analysis of covariance (ANCOVA), and so forth. This result is not surprising given the heavy emphasis on the experimental approach noted previously. Interestingly, the emphasis on ANOVA techniques in *JCP* (73.0% of empirical articles) is much greater than that of *JCR* (53.0%). This is likely due to the fact that *JCP* exhibits a heavier focus on experimental research than does *JCR*. Regression analysis (15.0%) and simple methods (13.0%) were the next most popular techniques utilized by *JCP* authors, followed by causal modeling (10.0%). Analysis of interdependence structures was considerably less prevalent (5%).

Postmodern discussions were very popular (15.8%) in *JCR*, especially compared to the small proportion of *JCP* articles devoted to this topic (1%). ANOVA type analyses were used to lesser extent in *JCR* compared to *JCP* (53.0% vs. 73.0%, respectively). Regression analysis (23.5%) was the second most popular technique in *JCR*, followed by causal modeling (9.4%), simple methods (8.6%), and analysis of interdependence structures (7.2%). *JCR* thus exhibits a broader range of data analytic approaches than *JCP*, likely reflecting its more diversified content, method, and research design approaches.

**Table 2** Primary Data Analysis Techniques in *JCP* and *JCR* Empirical Articles from 1992 to 1998

| *Content* | *JCP Total* | *JCP %* | *JCP Subtotal* | *JCR Total* | *JCR %* | *JCR Subtotal* |
|---|---|---|---|---|---|---|
| Simple methods | | | 13.0% | | | 8.6% |
| Cross tabs, frequencies | 5 | 5.0% | | 10 | 4.3% | |
| *T* test | 3 | 3.0% | | 4 | 1.7% | |
| Correlation | 5 | 5.0% | | 6 | 2.6% | |
| Interdependence structures | | | 5.0% | | | 7.2% |
| Factor analysis | 3 | 3.0% | | 11 | 4.7% | |
| Cluster analysis | 2 | 2.0% | | 1 | 0.4% | |
| Multidimensional scaling | 0 | 0.0% | | 5 | 2.1% | |
| Dependence structures | | | 98.0% | | | 85.9% |
| Regression | 15 | 15.0% | | 55 | 23.5% | |
| ANOVA, ANCOVA, MANOVA, and so forth | 73 | 73.0% | | 124 | 53.0% | |
| Causal modeling, path analysis, and so forth | 10 | 10.0% | | 22 | 9.40% | |
| Postmodern discussion | 1 | 1.0% | 1.0% | 37 | 15.8% | 15.8% |

Note. *JCP* = *Journal of Consumer Psychology*; *JCR Journal of Consumer Research*; ANOVA = analysis of variance; ANCOVA = analysis of covariance; MANOVA = multivariate analysis of variance. Columns total to more than 100% as many articles reported the use of more than one data analytic technique.

## Conclusions

The number of academic journals devoted to marketing has proliferated in the past several decades. The *Journal of Marketing*, which used to be the main outlet for publication, has been supplemented by the *Journal of Marketing Research*, the *Journal of Consumer Research*, and *Marketing Science*, to name just a few. This review suggests that a relatively recent addition to this group, *JCP*, is emerging as a respected journal, as is evidenced by its stabilized publication schedule, its ability to attract researchers from academic disciplines outside of business, and its willingness to encourage lively intellectual debate. The journal also appears to exhibit increasing methodological rigor in terms of the mean number of studies and mean sample sizes reported in its empirical articles overtime.

Has *JCP* maintained a unique place in the universe of marketing journals? The results of this review suggest that it has. To avoid a head-to-head attack on the market leader in the area of consumer research (i.e., *JCR)*, *JCP* appears to have pursued a niche or focused strategy. It has not become just a "me too" journal. The results of the current review of *JCP's* first 7 years of publication in comparison to that of *JCR* suggest that its positioning to date lies toward the positivist, empirical, and experimental camp (vs. the relativist, interpretivist, and postmodern camp) – witness the focus on laboratory-based experimental studies using student participants, and the relatively small numbers of postmodern articles and discussions.

Based on a citation analysis, Tellis *et al.* (1999) concluded that *JCR* was not very diverse, relative to other major marketing journals. In this analysis, we measured diversity in a number of different ways and compared the level of diversity between two more similar journals: *JCR* and *JCP.* The current analysis suggests that, of the two major journals devoted to publishing research related to consumer behavior, *JCR* is more diverse in several respects such as content coverage and data analytic approaches. *JCP,* however, is more diverse in terms of the range of authors it attracts from the academic disciplines, with a significantly greater proportion of nonbusiness researchers, particularly those in the basic discipline of psychology.

Is *JCP* less diverse than desired? Journal diversity can be measured in many ways. It could be argued that interdisciplinary diversity is as important or more important than is diversity of content coverage or analytic approach, in assessing journal quality. It is also open to argument whether diversity, in all its forms, should be a primary goal of every major journal in the field. Discovering here that most of *JCP's* articles are focused on positivistic and experimental type research approaches should not necessarily be interpreted in a negative light. Perhaps, rather than all journals striving for all types of diversity, they should attempt to carve out a niche strategy, deciding in what ways they should be focused (i.e., not diverse) and in what ways they should be diverse. We would suggest that it is advantageous for *JCP* to not simply be a "me too" journal; that is, that it should not necessarily aim for the same types of diversity as other journals such as *JCR.*

The issue of journal positioning is critical. Given that where we publish plays an essential role in defining who we are in an academic field, the way a journal positions itself will likely impact the body of researchers it draws. Hence, whether the decision is to be more diverse or more focused on one or more of the attributes discussed herein, active measures should be taken to support this decision. Although the question of whether the mission of a journal is defined by what it strives (or aspires) to be or by what it ends up being, that is, *de facto*, remains to be answered, having a factual review of what it has been is definitely a prerequisite to review this mission. This article constitutes an attempt to tell the *JCP* story the way it is, that is, to provide a factual review.

## Notes

1. We randomly selected five pages with different formats (i.e., a first page in an article, a page full of words with no subtitles or tables, a page with subtitles, a page with one table, a reference page), counted the words, added them up for the five pages for each journal, and then divided the sum for one journal by that of the other. The conversion rate in article length is approximately 1.97.

2. Affiliations for 97.5% of the authors were obtained. In those instances where department affiliation was not identified on the title page of an article, attempts were made to establish the author's affiliation using membership directories for Association for Consumer Research and Society for Consumer Psychology, the 1995 *Wiley Guide to Marketing Faculty* (Hasselback, 1995), as well as university Web sites. The analysis was based on counting each authorship as "1" (e.g., if an author, who was a marketing academic, published twice in *JCP*, that counted as two academic marketing affiliations). In multiple-authored articles, each author was allocated a value of 1.

3. No double counting was allowed.

4. Sample sizes reflect summations across the studies reported in a single article. Included were the number of participants who successfully completed all requirements in the studies reported in the article. Pretest participants were excluded.

## References

Frank, Ronald E. (1974). Editorial. *Journal of Consumer Research, 1.*

Hasselback, James R. (1995). *Wiley Guide to Marketing Faculty 1995*. New York: Wiley.

Hirschman, Elizabeth C. (1991). Secular mortality and the dark side of consumer behavior: Or how semiotics saved my life. In R.H. Holman & M.R. Solomon (Eds.), *Advances in consumer research* (pp. 4–9). Provo, UT: Association for Consumer Research.

Hunt, Shelby D. (1991). Positivism and paradigm dominance in consumer research: Toward critical pluralism and rapprochement. *Journal of Consumer Research, 18*, 32–44.

Jacoby, Jacob, Johar, Gita, & Morrin, Maureen. (1998). Consumer behavior: A quadrennium. *Annual Review of Psychology, 49*, 319–344.

Leong, Siew Meng. (1989). A citation analysis of the *Journal of Consumer Research*. *Journal of Consumer Research, 15*, 492–497.

Lutz, Richard. (1991). Editorial. *Journal of Consumer Research, 17.*

Monroe, Kent. (1991). Editorial. *Journal of Consumer Research, 18.*

Tellis, Gerald J, Chandy, Rajesh K., & Ackerman, David S. (1999). In search of diversity: The record of major marketing journals. *Journal of Marketing Research, 36*, 120–131.

Wind, Jerry, Rao, Vithala R., & Green, Paul E. (1991). "Behavioral Methods." In Thomas S. Robertson & Harold H. Kassarjian (Eds.), *Handbook of consumer behavior* (pp. 506–532). Englewood Cliffs, NJ: Prentice Hall.

Zinklian, George M., Roth, Martin S., & Saxton, Mary Jane. (1992). Knowledge development and scientific status in consumer–behavior research: A social exchange perspective. *Journal of Consumer Research, 19*, 282–291.

# 2

# On Method in Consumer Research: A Critical Relativist Perspective

**Paul F. Anderson**

**Source:** *Journal of Consumer Research* 13 (1986): 155–173.

> Relativism is often attacked not because one has found a fault, but because one is afraid of it. – Paul Feyerabend.

## Prolegomenon

In recent years many of the academic areas that have an interest in consumer research have begun to display a certain self-consciousness concerning matters epistemological. Indeed, the topic has recently generated a lively debate within the discipline of marketing between those who wish to defend the traditional views of logical empiricism (Brodbeck 1982; Hunt 1983a, 1984) against the challenge of various forms of relativism (Anderson 1983; Peter 1982, 1983; Peter and Olson 1983). The origins of this particular debate, however, can be traced to consumer research; for it was before an audience of consumer researchers that Jerry Olson (1981) first confirmed that the rumors of positivism's death were not greatly exaggerated. At about this same time, privately circulated working papers by Peter (1981) on consumer behavior and Anderson (1981) on marketing also questioned the hegemony of positivism in disciplines. Since this time, discussions of philosophy and sociology of science have been a regular feature at ACR meetings and at theory conferences and workshops sponsored by the American Marketing Association. In addition, the entire Fall 1983 issue of the *Journal of Marketing* was given over to articles on marketing theory and philosophy of science. It should be noted, however, that this is not a new phenomenon; methodological and epistemological debates within many of consumer behavior's cognate disciplines can be traced at least to the 19th and early years of the 20th centuries (see, for example, Comte 1830–42; Durkheim 1895; Mill 1843; Weber 1922).

While this renewed interest in epistemological considerations is of fundamental significance for consumer research, it is important to recognize that it appears to be just one manifestation of a more general reordering within western intellectual thought. For example, a recent special issue of the *Partisan Review* on "New Directions in Modern Thought" notes that the epistemic orthodoxy is currently under attack in such diverse fields as philosophy, economics, ethics, law, and philosophy of science. Moreover, as Daniel Bell (1984, p. 216) suggests, the current

> upheavals in philosophy and social thought are not "simply" one more turn in intellectual fashion, but epitomize the new efforts of the disciplined imagination to find some ways of making consistent, meaningful, and persuasive statements about fundamental issues, when the established ways have been found wanting or have become exhausted.

While Bell's rhetoric may be somewhat overstated, it is clear that the collapse of the positivistic consensus that dominated methodological discussions in the sciences for much of this century has left a void that is yet to be filled. Where positivism seemed to offer a firm foundation or "Archimedian point" (Bernstein 1983, p. 8) from which to judge competing knowledge claims, proffered alternatives have been made to appear as relativistic flights of fancy that lead to epistemological anarchy and the abandonment of rationality and objectivity.

It is indeed unfortunate that opponents of relativism have seen fit to couch the debate in these terms, for it appears to reflect the (wholly unwarranted) "fear" that Feyerabend refers to in the opening quote. As Bernstein (1983) points out, since the time of the Enlightenment western thought has been afflicted with what he calls the "Cartesian Anxiety." (Because in the *Meditations* Descartes established one of the enduring metaphors of western philosophy – the idea of the secure foundation on which scientific knowledge can be built.) In this view, epistemology faces a Kierkegaardian either/or decision. Either there exists a solid, ahistorical foundation on which we can ground our knowledge claims, or we are led to an inescapable relativism in which "anything goes" and there is no basis for preferring "the knowledge-claims of medical science over palmistry" (Hunt 1984, p. 30).

Happily for consumer research, however, the choice is not this stark, for the type of relativism attacked by Hunt (1984) has never been advocated by any of the participants in the current debate. The object of Hunt's critique is a straw man known as judgmental (Knorr-Cetina and Mulkay 1983) or "nihilistic" relativism. In this view, all knowledge claims are equally valid and there is no basis on which to make judgments among the various contenders. (Indeed, a careful reading of even the most radical of contemporary relativists will reveal that this does not even approximate their views, e.g., Collins 1975, 1981; Feyerabend 1975, 1978a).

In contrast, the version of relativism I will be arguing for here may be referred to as "critical epistemic relativism" or simply critical relativism. While clearly influenced by the work of Kuhn (1970, 1977), Laudan (1984b), and the cognitive sociologists of science (Anderson 1983), all of the views espoused here would not necessarily be championed by any particular school of thought within the philosophy or sociology of science. Critical relativism is a multifaceted philosophy of science, but one of its major assertions is that there exists no single "scientific method." Instead, disciplinary knowledge claims are viewed as contingent upon the particular beliefs, values, standards, methods, and cognitive aims of its practitioners. Moreover, critical relativism recognizes that knowledge production in the social sciences is impacted by the broader cultural milieu in which it is embedded. In short, science is a social and historical enterprise, and its knowledge-products can be affected as much by sociological factors as by purely "cognitive" or empirical considerations. However, it is vital to recognize that cognitive and social factors do not necessarily pull science in opposite directions (Bloor 1982). That is to say, sociological influences do not lead science down the path of prejudice and error while adherence to the canons of "logic" and empiricism lead ever upward toward ultimate truth. Social and cognitive factors are inextricably linked in all in science simply because it is a human and cultural activity. Thus, what is judged (ex post) to have been "good" or "bad" science will reflect the influence of both types of factors.

Indeed, it is the very recognition of science's dependence upon contingent disciplinary commitments, unique historical factors, and complex sociological processes that makes this view a *critical* relativism. Traditional positivistic philosophies of science assume that the social sciences adhere to a single scientific method for the justification of their knowledge claims. However, this acceptance of scientific monism has the untoward consequence of committing its adherents to the verisimilitude of the currently accepted body of social scientific knowledge. This follows from the fact that such claims have presumably been verified by the positivist's own standards of scientific adequacy. In contrast, critical relativism is skeptical of all claims to scientific knowledge because it recognizes that there are multiple scientific objectives and alternative methods for attaining these objectives (Anderson 1983; Laudan 1984b; Peter and Olson 1983). Moreover, critical relativism recognizes that the value of such claims must be assessed in light of their unique modes of production and their methods of justification. To suggest that the hallmark of scientific knowledge is its empirical testability (Hunt 1983a, pp. 368–372) is to settle for far less than we should demand of such an important enterprise as science. As will be demonstrated below, the requirement of empirical testability is notoriously ambiguous within the recognized sciences, and as demonstrated elsewhere (Laudan 1983), it is a criterion that is allegedly met by patently "nonscientific" disciplines. (Understood in the sense of Anderson's (1983) science$_2$.)

Thus, empirical testability and intersubjective certification are far weaker criteria (see Anderson 1983) than we have been led to believe by contemporary positivists and "modern empiricists." However, critical relativists do not eschew empirical testing as suggested by Hunt (1984); nor do they necessarily retreat to hermeneutical or interpretive approaches as suggested by Deshpande (1983). Indeed, critical relativists are actually more "hard-headed" than positivists in their analysis of "scientific" knowledge claims. (In the remainder of the paper "positivism" will be employed as a rubric to encompass the older varieties of logical positivism, logical empiricism, and all forms of falsificationism (see Anderson 1983 for a review), as well as the recently constructed fallibilistic version that Hunt (1984) calls "modern empiricism.") The critical relativist demands to know a theory's mode of production, the criteria by which it is judged, the ideological and value commitments that inform its construction, and the metaphysical beliefs that underwrite its research program. Most importantly, the critical relativist wishes to know the realizable cognitive and practical aims of a theory so that its range of applicability can be assessed.

One of the most serious mistakes of the positivist tradition is its assumption that the objective of all science is the attainment of a description of the "reality" of the natural and social world. Given this commitment, positivists are hard pressed to explain the radically different descriptions of human behavior offered by contemporary social science (e.g., cognitive psychology, radical behaviorism, Freudian psychology, cultural anthropology, the new home economics (e.g., Becker 1981), structural-functionalism, symbolic interactionism, phenomenological sociology, etc.).

Faced with this degree of disparity, positivists generally retreat to one or more of the following positions. Some will argue that a number of these research programs will be discovered to be false and will be abandoned by a more "mature" social science. This would appear to be the claim of naive falsificationists. Others suggest that the various social sciences and the various "schools" within these sciences are like the proverbial blind men touching different parts of the elephant. Thus, they are accurately describing different "aspects" or "levels" of social and psychological reality. Finally, and closely related to this last view, is the belief that at some point in time a grand synthesis of these positions will be achieved and we will find that they can all be subsumed under some overarching framework. This, I take it, is the hope of those who talk of "general theories" (Bartels 1968; Hunt 1983a, 1983b) or the "systems" approach to knowledge construction (Reidenbach and Oliva 1981; von Bertalanffy 1968).

In contrast, critical relativism rejects each of these options because it rejects their basic premise: that there is a single knowable reality waiting "out there" to be discovered via *the* scientific method (Olson 1981). The critical relativist has no quarrel with the metaphysical notion that there may well be a single social and natural reality, but he or she will resist the assertion that science is capable of revealing or even converging upon this "reality" (Laudan 1981). Instead, the relativist accepts competing research programs for what they are – different ways of exploring and analyzing natural phenomena, each with its own advantages and liabilities. As argued elsewhere, there are good reasons for believing that "realism" (the notion that science discovers or at least converges on "reality") is an untenable position (Laudan 1981; Leplin 1984).

Thus, critical relativism is first and foremost a descriptive enterprise. In the following section it will be argued that the best way to make sense of how social science is actually practiced is to construe it relativistically. Moreover, it will be suggested that positivism (in all its varying forms) is neither a practical nor a desirable ideal toward which we should strive. Once these positions are established, we can then move on in the second major section of the article to develop some of the implications of critical relativism for research in consumer and buyer behavior. Initially, however, it will be necessary to deal with two crucial issues. The first is the alleged self-refuting nature of relativism, and the second is the relevance of abstract philosophical debate for "workbench"-level research in consumer behavior. (That is, research issues that affect the day-to-day activity of researchers in our field.)

### Is Relativism Self-Refuting?

Since the time of Plato's attack on the Greek sophist Protagoras, it has been argued that relativism is incoherent because it offers evidence in support of the "truth" of its own positions (Bernstein 1983; Flew 1979; Rosenberg 1984). Thus, it is said that on pain of logical inconsistency relativists cannot claim that their own doctrines are true while at the same time arguing that truth itself is "relative" (Laudan 1982, 1984b). Unfortunately, this argument goes astray at the very beginning by assuming that "truth" plays a role in the ontology of critical relativism. Relativists do not claim that their positions are true in some absolute sense. They simply argue for their positions by employing the intellectual resources that are sanctioned by the "scientific culture" of the present age and/or by attempting to change the evaluative criteria, aims, or methods of contemporary intellectual discourse (McCullagh 1984). For example, in this article I will not argue that relativism should be adopted because its principles are in accord with the will of a Supreme Being. While such a claim was viewed as perfectly rational and "scientific" when made by Newton in support of his mechanics in the 17th century, it would be considered ludicrous by contemporary scientific standards. Relativism simply reminds us that appraisal criteria are relative to a specific research community and a particular epoch. There is no guarantee that our current evaluative criteria will not appear to be similarly quaint some 300 years hence.

Of course, at this point, some will object that the relativist's position implies that (for any given time period) there must exist some transprogrammatic standards for theory selection. However, this view ignores the fact that criteria are applied by human beings and, as Wittgenstein (1953) might put it, what a person believes is ultimately shown by how he or she behaves. Thus, what might count as decisive refutation of a theory for one scientist could be considered completely irrelevant by another (Leibenstein 1981). Therefore, nothing in critical relativism requires transcendent standards of scientific adequacy. Indeed, it will be shown below that an important implication of the relativistic construal is that appraisal criteria in the social sciences are highly parochial!

Moreover, relativists readily admit that their own knowledge claims are as much a function of social, cultural, and cognitive factors as are any beliefs held by members of a scientific community (Pinch 1982). Indeed, in his seminal program statement on the nature of a cognitive sociology of science, Bloor explicitly states that the discipline must be "reflexive" (1976, p. 5). That is, it must be able to explain the construction of its own knowledge base by appeal to social, cultural, historical, and cognitive factors. Thus, any claim made by a relativist can be criticized on the basis of social and/or empirical factors. Indeed, some of the strongest criticisms of relativistic sociology of science have been leveled by other sociologists on both empirical and nonempirical grounds (Gieryn 1982; Woolgar 1981; Yearly 1982). Thus, there is nothing inherently self-refuting in the relativists' program. The charge is simply a red herring made by those who misunderstand the claims of contemporary relativists.

### Is Philosophy of Science Relevant to Day-to-Day Research Practice in Consumer Behavior?

It will be argued here that not only is philosophy of science relevant at the workbench level, but the entire field of science and technology studies (STS) contains important insights for our discipline. Unfortunately, however, debates in this area are often carried on at such an abstract level that, once the dust settles, research in the natural and social sciences generally goes on much the way it did before. This seems to imply that practicing researchers view philosophy, sociology, and history of science issues as secondary to the main job of designing studies, generating data, and analyzing results. For most researchers the connection between abstract philosophical issues and concrete research practice has not been made explicit. For example, the great majority of methodological articles appearing in our journals concern themselves with technical rather than philosophical matters. The latter are viewed as interesting, but largely irrelevant for the day-to-day practice of research. This state of affairs is indeed regrettable, since it can be argued that epistemic considerations are actually primary for any discipline with scientific pretensions.

Like Molière's M. Jourdain who spoke prose all his life without knowing it, we all invoke implicit philosophies of science when we conduct studies, interpret results, criticize others' work, or decide between competing theories. Epistemological issues can be viewed as primary because they underwrite all of the knowledge claims of a discipline. Consumer research's right to speak with authority on matters within its domain is a function of the "well-foundedness" of its knowledge base. While technical criticisms of statistical or design procedures affect only those studies using the suspect techniques, philosophical critique can call into question a field's entire corpus.

Philosophy of science considerations are particularly important for an area like consumer research that seeks to be interdisciplinary (Ferber 1977). The fact that the topic is studied by so many disciplines with widely varying research traditions immediately raises the question of how one evaluates the (often conflicting) knowledge claims of its various practitioners. Closely related to this is the issue of whether it is even possible to study the topic in a truly interdisciplinary fashion or whether a multidisciplinary approach is the most that can be hoped for (Ferber 1977). It will be shown here that these questions can only be answered after a meta-theoretical analysis of the nature of social scientific knowledge.

Thus, a major objective of the present article is to develop a descriptive model of how social scientific knowledge is constructed and validated. As noted earlier, this will be a relativistic model that will have significant normative implications for the practice of consumer behavior research. Of necessity, such an ambitious enterprise will be far reaching in the issues engaged and topics discussed. Of course, the claim that normative prescriptions can be derived from this model does not seek to deny the validity of Hume's (1740) "naturalistic fallacy," which notes that statements of "ought" cannot be logically deduced from statements concerning what "is." The far weaker position is taken here that descriptive statements "underdetermine" ought statements. That is, reasonable observers may disagree on the normative implications of descriptive accounts.

At this point it might be valuable to lay out some of the central claims of a relativistic model of social science before each is explicated and defended in detail. Among other things, a critical relativist position asserts that:

1. Research programs in the social sciences are high encapsulated.
2. Scientific methods underdetermine theory choice and scientific goals underdetermine methods. That is to say, methods do not uniquely pick out particular theories, and scientific goals may be achieved via alternative methods.
3. Social scientific research programs exhibit a "weak form" incommensurability. In other words, scientists can understand each other perfectly well, yet disagree violently on the appropriate program for researching a particular topic.
4. Falsificationism is not a workable methodology for the social sciences.
5. Empirical tests are not intersubjectively certifiable in any strong sense.
6. Social scientific constructs may be more profitably characterized as researchers' artifacts than as reified "unobservables."
7. The content of social scientific knowledge is impacted by social, historical, cultural, and economic factors.
8. There are many alternative ways of constructing and justifying knowledge in the social sciences.
9. While there exists no privileged epistemological platform from which to assess competing knowledge claims, *relative judgments can be made among competing programs on the basis of social and cognitive aims, metaphysical beliefs, and preferred methodologies.*

While each of these points will be discussed below, their interrelationships will not always make it possible to discuss them in the exact order presented above.

## Encapsulated Research Programs

Perhaps the most significant breakthrough in the field of science studies in this century is the recognition that the crucial unit of analysis is not at the level of the proposition, hypothesis, or theory, but at the level of the macrostructures in which these concepts are embedded. Referred to by various authors as paradigms (Kulm 1962), research programmes (Lakatos 1974), research traditions (Laudan 1977), and research areas (Feyerabend 1978a, 1978b), these macrostructures are best thought of as a series of empirical, metaphysical, methodological, axiological, and ideological commitments made by individuals who choose to study social and natural phenomena from a particular perspective. Perhaps the easiest way to explicate the concept through the examples shown in the Exhibit. This Exhibit displays four positivistic research programs that have been employed in consumer research – positivistic in the sense that each attempts to employ the alleged methods of natural science to the study of social phenomena. As shown in row 4, each aims to "explain," predict, and control human behavior by subsuming it under deterministic or statistical laws that are assumed to be universal in nature. An example of a well-known statistical "law" employed in consumer behavior research is the extended Fishbein model

(Fishbein 1967; Fishbein and Ajzen 1975). Of course, Ajzen and Fisbein do not claim that their model is truly universal in nature. They admit that some behaviors like "emotional outbursts" and the "performance of well-learned skills" may not be explained by their theory (1980, p. 245). However, they do suggest that "the theory is useful for most individuals and with respect to most social behaviours," and that "many behaviors which appear unplanned turn out, on closer examination, to be quite intentional" (1980, p. 245).

Positivists assert that the performance of a particular action by an agent is "explained" if one can point to a general "law" of which the action is a specific exemplar. All four of the programs shown in the Exhibit "explain" behavior in this fashion. However, despite their common cognitive aims, positivistic research programs can be quite heterogeneous in their other commitments. As a result, a particular research program often functions as a a rubic for a wide variety of theoretical claims and methodological procedures. Thus, for the sake of coherence and intelligibility, a specific exemplar has been chosen to represent each program. As shown in the first row of the Exhibit, the cognitive program will be represented by the theory of Fishbein and Ajzen (1975), the behaviorist program by B. F. Skinner's (1953, 1969) theory of operant conditioning, the economic program by the approach of Becker (1965, 1976) and the structuralist or sociological program by the work of Blau (1977). The second row gives examples of work in consumer behavior that either derives directly from the specific exemplar (e.g., Lutz and Bettman 1977; Nord and Peter 1980) or is highly consonant with the methods, procedures, and approach of the program's exemplar (e.g., Martineau 1958). Finally, the third row gives an indication of the historical, intellectual, and disciplinary foundations of each program.

The remaining rows of the Exhibit display the various commitments of researchers that constitute the very nature and scope of the program. As noted earlier, these will include commitments to a series of "facts," theories, metaphysical beliefs, ontological entities, ideological positions, and cognitive aims. Taken together, these features define the program and the Weltanschauung of its practitioners.

Despite the plethora of commitments in each of the columns, Laudan (1984a, 1984b) has recently argued that three of these elements are central to an understanding of scientific progress and rationality. Since Laudan's approach appears to be particularly useful for the analysis of social scientific research programs, it will be used (with some modifications) as a foundation for our relativistic model of social scientific knowledge construction.

### A Reticulated Model of Scientific Rationality

Figure A is an adapted version of Laudan's (1984b, p. 63) reticulated or network model of scientific research programs. According to Laudan, the three key elements in any research program are its cognitive aims, its empirical beliefs or theories, and its methodological prescriptions. This reticulated model seeks to replace the traditional hierarchical models of positivistic philosophy of science that assume a one-way justificatory flow from aims, to methods, to theories.

**Exhibit** Some Positivist Research Programs in Consumer Behavior

| Exemplars and commitments | Cognitive program | Behaviorist program | Economic program | Structuralist program |
|---|---|---|---|---|
| **A. Exemplars and intellectual foundations:** | | | | |
| 1. Specific exemplar | Fishbein and Ajzen (1975) | Skinner (1953, 1969) | Becker (1965,1976, 1981) | Blau (1977) |
| 2. Consumer behavior exemplars | Wilkie and Pessemier (1973); Lutz and Bettman (1977) | Nord and Peter (1980); Peter and Nord (1982) | Becker (1976); Ferber and Birnbaum (1977a, 1977b) | Martineau (1958); Warner and Lunt (1941); Coleman (1983) |
| 3. Intellectual foundations | Cognitive Psychology, Social Psychology/ Thurstone, Likert, Guttman, Allport, Dulany | American Behaviorism/ Watson, Thorndike | Microeconomics/Jevons, Walras, Marshall, Mincer | Structural-Functionalism/ Durkheim, Weber, Parsons, Merton |
| **B. Programmatic commitments:** | | | | |
| 4. Overriding cognitive aim | "Explanation" via subsumption of behavior under universal laws; Prediction and control | "Explanation" via subsumption of behavior under universal laws; Prediction and control | "Explanation" via subsumption of behavior under universal laws; Prediction and control | "Explanation" via subsumption of behavior under universal laws; Prediction and control |
| 5. Predominant mode of inference | Hypothetico-Deductive | Inductive | Hypothetico-Deductive | Hypothetico-Deductive |
| 6. Interpretation of ontology | Realist | Realist | Instrumentalist | Realist |
| 7. Sample ontology | Behavioral intention, Attitude, Beliefs, Motivation to comply | Operants, Stimulus, Reinforcement, Extinction | Utility, Production function, Full income, Marginal utility | Social structure, Social strata, Cosmopolitanism, Social mobility, Status |
| 8. Primary research methods/appraisal criteria | Production of predicted effects in experimentation; Correlation in ex post facto studies at the micro level; Consistency with ontology of cognitivism | Production of predicted effects in experimentation; Consistency with ontology of behaviorism | Correlation in ex post facto studies at the macro level; Internal consistency: Mathematical elegance; Simplicity; Consistency with ontology of economics | Correlation in ex post facto studies at the macro level; Consistency with ontology of structuralism |

**Exhibit** *(Continued)*

| Exemplars and commitments | Cognitive program | Behaviorist program | Economic program | Structuralist program |
|---|---|---|---|---|
| 9. Concept of mind | Accessible to others via survey research; Actors have privileged access to their cognitive states | Not accessible to others: Actors have privileged access to some mental states; Access to mental events not necessary for scientific explanation | Not accessible to others; Actors do not have privileged access; Access to mental events not necessary for scientific explanation | May or may not be accessible to others; Actors may or may not have privileged access; While human behavior is influenced by cognitive events, it is also influenced by social-structural variables that cannot be reduced to psychological constructs |
| 10. Concept of human nature | Cognitive man: A rational information processor who forms beliefs, attitudes, and intentions that are causally determinant of his behavior | Behavioral man: Operates on the environment and experiences consequences that determine his future behavioral response probabilities | Economic man: Behaves in a manner that maximizes a utility function subject to the constraints of time, money income, information, and technology | Social man: Exhibits psychological predispositions but behavior at the group level is largely determined and/or constrained by social-structural factors |
| 11. Sample proposition: specific exemplar | Behavioral intention is a function of the sum of the weighted attitude toward the behavior and the social norm regarding the behavior (Fishbein and Ajzen 1975, p. 301) | Ratio schedules of reinforcement produce highly stable levels of behavioral occurrence and are reasonably resistant to extinction (Skinner 1953, p. 99) | The purchase of "luxury" or time-saving products and services by wealthy households does not reflect diminishing marginal utility of income but is an efficient substitution of a plentiful resource (money) for a scarce resource (time) (Becker 1976, p. 141) | The higher the rates of vertical mobility between two social strata, the more prevalent the associations between their members (Blau 1977, p. 74) |

**Exhibit** *(Continued)*

| Exemplars and commitments | Cognitive program | Behaviorist program | Economic program | Structuralist program |
|---|---|---|---|---|
| 12. Sample proposition: consumer behavior exemplar | Belief modification rather than evaluation modification is the more promising strategy for attitude change (Lutz and Bettman 1977, p. 146) | Product purchase, store visits, etc., can be encouraged via intermittent reinforcement in the form of lotteries, door prizes, etc. (Nord and Peter 1980, p. 39) | Input "factors" used in producing the same household "commodity" will have greater cross-price elasticities than factors used in producing different "commodities" (Becker 1976, p. 140) | The buying behavior of the overprivileged blue-collar workers is much closer to the behavior of the over privileged professional and white-collar workers than it is to the behavior of the (lower-income) blue-collar workers (Zaltman and Wallendorf 1983, p. 123) |
| 13. Ideological/Value commitments/ Policy implications: specific exemplar | Individuals are free to seek and evaluate information that may lead to changes in their beliefs, attitudes, intentions and behavior. Policies can be designed to affect both cognitive structure and behavior through various forms of information dissemination | Human freedom and autonomy are illusory. Contingencies of reinforcement in the environment can be designed to assure that individuals achieve personal well-being and that societies solve their problems | Individuals have identical preference functions and differ only in their access to information. Thus, if higher levels of education allow households to achieve higher levels of productive output, policies can be developed to encourage higher educational attainment | Integration and heterogeneity in large and complex societies should be encouraged; however, strong ingroup bonds are detrimental to the integration of the various strata in society. Policies can, therefore, be developed to discourage strong ingroup bonds |

In the traditional view, science is a goal-directed activity that seeks to attain a variety of objectives (also referred to as scientific values). Some of the cognitive aims that have figured prominently in the history of natural and social science include: truth, falsifiability, parsimony, consistency, extensibility, explanatory power, predictive accuracy, fruitfulness, mathematical elegance, verisimilitude, practicality, metaphysical consistency, and uniqueness. The hierarchical model assumes that scientific methods are the procedural rules designed to achieve the goals of science. In the social sciences such rules usually take the form of prescriptive generalizations. Some examples would include: assign subjects randomly to treatment and control groups, validate theoretical constructs, use multiple item measures of constructs, test for homogeneity of treatment difference variances when using within-subjects designs, and so on. The conventional account of scientific progress asserts that conflicts concerning competing theories are settled by moving "one step up the hierarchy to the level of shared methodological rules" (Laudan 1984b, p. 24). Indeed, Laudan suggests that most theoretical controversies in the natural sciences are dealt with in this fashion. If scientists disagree on the appropriate theory, experiments are conducted and common methdological rules are consulted in order to settle the matter.

**Figure A** A Reticulated Model of Scientific Rationality

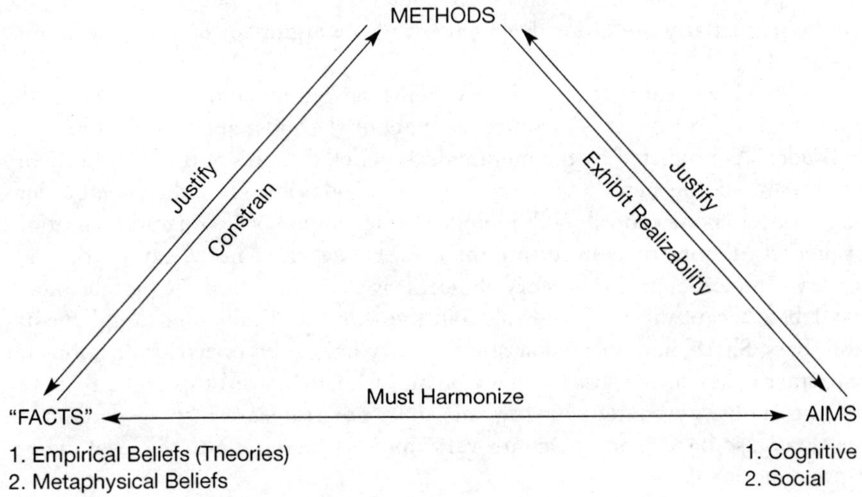


Source: Larry Laudan (1984b), *Science and Values*, Berkeley, CA: University of California Press.

Unfortunately, not all theoretical disputes in the natural and social sciences can be resolved in this manner. The reason is that methods "underdetermine" theory choice. That is to say, methodological rules do not always allow us to discriminate among alternative theories. Consider, for example, the rule: validate theoretical constructs. Put very simply, this means that we should make sure that we are measuring what we think we are measuring. As straightforward as this prescription appears, it has proven to be a notoriously slippery concept in actual practice.

As an illustration we might return to a well-known controversy within the cognitive paradigm that took place during the early 1970s: the famous "Fishbein-Rosenberg" debates (Bass 1972; Bass and Talarzyk 1972; Cohen, Fishbein, and Ahtola 1972; Sheth 1972; Sheth and Talarzyk 1972; Talarzyk 1972). To make a rather long story unconscionably short, Sheth and Talarzyk (1972) and Bass and Talarzyk (1972) tested what they claimed to be the early Rosenberg (1956) and Fishbein (1963) "expectancy-value" models of attitude using the same measurement scales. However, in response, Cohen, Fishbein, and Ahtola (1972) charged that these studies had not properly operationalized the constructs in either model and had in fact constructed a new "adequacy-importance" model of attitude. In reply, Bass (1972), Sheth (1972), and Talarzyk (1972) argued that it is necessary to modify the constructs in the Fishbein and Rosenberg models and the methods of testing these theories because of the different purposes of marketing and social psychological research.

This old controversy has not been dredged up in order to settle any of the substantive issues at stake in the debate; the multiattribute model research program in consumer behavior has moved far beyond the specific points raised by the disputants. Rather, the Fishbein-Rosenberg debate provides us with a concrete case study that illustrates the limitations of both the hierarchical and reticulated models of scientific rationality. Indeed, this controversy has been chosen precisely because we know the "outcome" of the debate – a factor that will be particularly useful for development of the argument in a later section of this article.

It should be clear that the debate is being carried on at all three levels of the hierarchy. At bottom, it is a controversy about the most appropriate theory of "attitude." As predicted by the hierarchical model, disputes at the level of theory will be shifted one step up to the realm of methodology. Here the debate essentially concerns one central methodological rule: employ valid operationalizations of theoretical constructs in testing theories. However, as noted earlier, this rule tends to "underdetermine" theory choice. It is clear that all of the participants in the debate accept this as a valid rule, but they differ radically on its implementation. Bass, Sheth, and Talarzyk argue that they have valid operationalizations for consumer behavior purposes, while Cohen, Fishbein, and Ahtola argue that they do not. Thus, agreement on the rule does not translate into agreement on the theory; so once again the controversy moves one step up to the level of cognitive aims or values.

But agreement at this level is also thwarted by underdetermination. All of the disputants agree that predictive capability is an important objective of scientific theories, and each presents empirical data demonstrating the "predictive" success of their model. Unfortunately, though, they disagree on what is to be predicted and the appropriate setting for a test of predictive accuracy. Cohen, Fishbein, and Ahtola point to average correlations between the Fishbein model and independently measured affect of 0.70. Sheth dismisses the importance of these correlations because of the different settings, purposes, and procedures used in consumer behavior studies, but he also presents data from another consumer behavior study showing average correlations of 0.76 between affect and "belief scales comparable to Rosenberg's perceived instrumentality component" (1972, p. 464). Similarly, Bass points out that their purpose in testing the modified Fishbein model was to determine if "brand preference is related to product and brand-specific measures as opposed to more general measures such as demographic and personality variables" (1972, p. 46 1). Talarzyk reiterates this point and shows data that illustrate that the Bass-Talarzyk "Fishbein" model has high predictive success for brand preference.

It would appear that once again we have consensus on a cognitive value but disagreement on its "meaning" or "operationalization." However, the conflict is more complex than this because the participants are actually working with more than one cognitive objective. A careful reading of the comment and replies will reveal that the concept of purposes is mentioned quite frequently. Bass, Sheth, and Talarzyk go to great lengths to point out that their purposes are very different from those of social psychology. Thus, they feel justified in altering the nature of the models and the analytical testing procedures. In contrast, Cohen, Fishbein, and Ahtola stress fidelity to the original Rosenberg and Fishbein models as an overriding objective. In other words, we see that a second cognitive value has been smuggled into the debate: consistency with established theoretical frameworks.

In the traditional hierarchical view (Figure B), this is where the debate must end, because the participants differ on the application of one key value (prediction), and they disagree on the weight or importance of the second value (consistency). Thus, the disputants find themselves in a classic case of Kuhnian incommensurability. In his later writings, Kuhn (1977) argues that value conflicts in science can be inherently open-ended when (1) scientists disagree on the application of shared values to concrete cases, or when (2) scientists place differential weights on shared values. As Kuhn puts it, two scientists "fully committed to the same list of criteria [values] for choice may nevertheless reach different conclusions" on the most appropriate theory (1977, p. 324). When this occurs Kuhn argues that we must turn to psychological, social, and historical factors to explain the initial value commitments and any subsequent resolution of the conflict.

Laudan (1984a, 1984b) disagrees with this relativistic construal of value choice and conflict resolution. He argues, using historical case studies from the natural sciences as evidence, that mechanisms exist by which value conflicts can be resolved. In Laudan's view, there are two broad categories of procedures that can be employed to criticize scientific aims. The first may be referred to as the utopian critique. A cognitive aim can be said to be utopian when, in the light of our current background knowledge, we know of no means by which it can be achieved.

*The Utopian Critique.* There are three specific subcategories of the utopian critique: (1) demonstrable, (2) semantic, and (3) epistemic. A cognitive goal can be said to be *demonstrably* utopian when we can show, "given our understanding of logic or the laws of nature" (Laudan 1984b, p. 52), that the objective cannot be achieved. An example would be the desire to generate scientific laws that can be shown to be universally applicable. Given that our evidence for any putative law will always be finite, how can we logically conclude that the law applies universally? This is simply a restatement of the age-old problem of induction – a problem that is generally conceded to have no adequate solution (Black 1967).

*Semantic* utopianism, on the other hand, arises when the "meaning" of a cognitive value cannot be explicated or "cashed out" in concrete terms. For example, the objectives of simplicity and elegance are notoriously vague and ambiguous in application (Laudan 1984b). That is to say, it is difficult to provide the specific criteria by which one theory can be judged to be simpler or more elegant than a rival. As an illustration we might consider the famous argument for the greater "simplicity" of Copernican cosmology over the rival Ptolemaic system. While it is true that Copernicus's heliocentric theory required only seven circular orbits to account for the aberrant behavior of the known planets (as compared to Ptolemy's 12), Copernicus was forced to include additional epicycles and eccentrics in order to predict the actual position of the planets (Kuhn 1957). Thus, both systems employed over 30 circular orbits, and when the actual computational labor required to predict planetary positions is compared, they prove to be "substantially equivalent" (Kuhn 1977, p. 324).

**Figure B** The Traditional Hierarchial Model of Research Programs

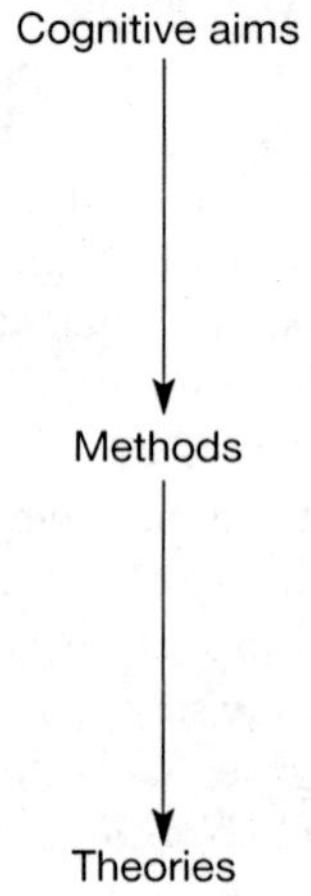


Closely related to the concept of semantic utopianism is the argument of *epistemic* utopianism. In Laudan's view, a scientist may be able to provide a perfectly coherent definition of a cognitive aim, but be unable to specify "a criterion for determining when the value is present or satisfied and when it is not" (1984b, p. 53). Consider, as an example, the goal of falsifiability (Calder, Phillips, and Tybout 1981, 1982, 1983; Leong 1985; Popper 1962). A theory or hypothesis can be said to be falsifiable when its (deductively derived) predictions can be confronted with empirical data. If the predictions from the theory do not manifest themselves, we may say that the theory has been falsified. To see the difficulties here, we need to look more closely at the "logic" of hypothesis testing. Any test of an hypothesis or theory can be shown to be an inductive argument of the following form (Giere 1979, 1984):

> If [Not *H*, but *IC* and *AA* hold], then very probably not *P*.
> *P* occurs.
> *IC* and *AA* (by assumption).
> Thus (inductively) *H*,
> where *H* = the hypothesis under test,
> *IC* & *AA* = the initial conditions and auxiliary assumptions implied by the test and,
> *P* = the empirically testable prediction deduced from the hypothesis *and* the initial conditions and auxiliary assumptions.

The first premise of the argument is a conditional statement that indicates that if the hypothesis is false, but the initial conditions and auxiliary assumptions are true, it will be very unlikely that we will observe the predicted datum *P*. The second premise gives the results of the test (*P* was in fact observed). The third premise is simply the assumption that *IC* and *AA* hold, and the final statement in the argument is the (inductive) conclusion that the hypothesis is, in fact, the case.

Presented in this fashion we can see that any test of an hypothesis depends on much more than the theory or hypothesis putatively under investigation. A real world study will implicate a myriad of initial conditions and auxiliary assumptions concerning measuring instruments, sample selection, subject abilities, statistical tests, potential confounds, and so on. The key point here is that a researcher can never know with certainty that the *IC* and *AA* are as specified. In fact, it is not even possible to know all of the initial conditions and auxiliary assumptions that are implicated in a particular study. (Indeed, this is the upshot of Lynch's (1982, 1983) critique of Calder *et al.*'s (1981, 1982, 1983) position on external validity.)

So in a posttest only with control group experimental design, it is not possible to know for certain if the experimental and control groups are "equivalent" on the dependent measure because we can make no pretest comparisons. Thus, one of the initial conditions in studies using this design is that random assignment has equalized the groups. (At least with respect to the dependent variable.) Of course, this will not be the case for some (presumably small) subset of experiments (especially those with small sample sizes). The problem is that we may never know which studies are confounded by selection bias.

A similar problem arises when falsifications result from the auxiliary assumptions implicated in a study. To use one of Calder *et al.*'s (1982) own illustrations, consider Hertz's search for the electromagnetic radiation predicted by Maxwell's equations. Maxwell's theory predicted that radio waves move at the speed of light, but Hertz consistently found that their speed differed significantly from that of light (Chalmers 1976). Thus, in a naive sense, Hertz had falsified Maxwell's model. It was subsequently found that the difficulty was caused by the fact that the radio waves were being reflected back off the walls of the laboratory and were interfering with the experimental apparatus. Thus, Hertz's implicit auxiliary assumption that the size of the laboratory was an irrelevant "background" factor proved to be the cause of the apparent "falsification." While Calder *et al.* (1982) recognize this fact, they fail to draw the appropriate lesson because of their patently "whiggish" reading of the historical record. (In this context, a whig history is one in which we use our knowledge of how historical events actually worked out to interpret or draw lessons from said events.) Our knowledge of the interference effects in late 19th century electromagnetic experiments will not help us one whit in identifying the sources of "falsifications" in the as yet unsettled cases of gravity waves (Collins 1975, 1981), solar neutrinos (Pinch 1980), or free quarks (Pickering 1981). (In fairness, it must be noted that Tybout and Calder (see Tybout, Sternthal, and Calder 1985) are in no sense naive falsificationists. They recognize that other values (like parsimony) play a role in scientific theory choice and that realism is an untenable philosophical position.) The key point here is that, while it is possible to specify the meaning of falsification, it is very difficult to determine in concrete cases the cause of any particular falsifying result.

*The Inconsistency Critique.* The argument of inconsistency is Laudan's (1984b) second major mode for criticizing scientific values. This becomes relevant when a discipline or subdiscipline espouses one set of goals or aims while actively pursuing very different objectives. A classic illustration of this type of criticism in the social sciences can be found in Mark Blaug's attack on contemporary economics. Blaug, a committed falsificationist, states that (1980, pp. 259–260):

> Mainstream neoclassical economists ... preach the importance of submitting theories to empirical tests, but they rarely live up to their declared methodological canons. Analytical elegance, economy of theoretical means, and the widest possible scope obtained by ever more heroic simplification have been too often prized above predictability and significance for policy questions ... the battle for falsificationism has been won in modern economics. The problem now is to persuade economists to take falsificationism seriously.

While it is highly unlikely that falsificationism could ever be successfully implemented in economics (Caldwell 1984), Blaug's attack demonstrates how subtle the process of goal displacement can be within a research program. It is clear that economics sees itself as an empirical discipline, but as many economists and philosophers of economics have pointed out, significant portions of the corpus of economic theory are devoid of empirical content (Hands 1984; Hausman 1981, 1984; Rosenberg 1983). Thus, in Laudan's model, economists should be facing a philosophical crisis. Either they must admit the rather weak empirical support for their doctrines and openly substitute such values as mathematical elegance, simplicity, and theoretical consistency as overriding objectives, or (on pain of inconsistency) they must continue to assert that theirs is a fully empirical discipline despite rather persuasive evidence to the contrary. On the other hand, the fact that no such crisis appears to exist within mainstream economics (in spite of claims to the contrary, e.g., Bell and Kristol 1981; Eichner 1983) should raise the question of whether Laudan's methods of resolving value disputes are commonly employed within the social sciences. It is to this issue that we now turn.

## Incommensurability in the Social Sciences

As noted earlier, the research programs shown in the Exhibit share a common overriding cognitive aim – the subsumption of human behavior under general laws with the ultimate objective of prediction and "control." Thus all four programs are anchored in the same axiology, yet they differ significantly in their empirical, metaphysical, ontological, and ideological commitments. In other words, each program employs very different means to attain what are ostensibly the same cognitive ends. It will be the burden of this section to show that in cashing out their putative objectives in different terms, these programs actually change the very nature of what counts as explanation, prediction, and control within them and, in turn, redefine the objects of their inquiry. Thus, as suggested by Figure A, empirical beliefs, metaphysical beliefs, and methodological rules feed back on and help determine the aims of a research program. The major consequence of this fact is that it leads to what I shall call a "weak form" incommensurability across programs designed to "explain" what is putatively the same category of human behavior.

To see this we need only look down any set of columns and across any set of rows numbered 5 through 13 in the Exhibit. Here we observe that, taken as a whole, the various commitments made by adherents of each research program do not mesh very well. For example, consider the predominant mode of inference (row 5) and interpretation of ontology (row 6). We immediately notice that while the cognitive and behaviorist programs share a realist orientation toward their ontologies,[1] they differ significantly in their preferred modes of inference. (Very roughly, a realist asserts that the constructs mentioned in successful theories genuinely refer to things that actually exist in the world.) Similarly, while the cognitive and economic programs have the hypothetico-deductive method in common, the former is realist in its orientation and the latter is clearly instrumentalist. (In general, an instrumentalist asserts that the constructs in a theory need not refer so long as the theory generates successful predictions. For an overview of economic instrumentalism, see Hausman 1984.) The only programs that match on these two dimensions are the cognitive and the structuralist. This would tentatively suggest that (as long as the disjunction on the other commitments of the two programs is not too great) we should expect to find attempts to integrate these programs into a more general model of consumer behavior. Of course, this is exactly what we observe in the Engel and Blackwell (1982) and Howard and Sheth (1969) theories. However, it should be noted that the propriety of combining cognitive and social "facts" in explanations of human conduct and the common practice of reducing social constructs to psychological states remain hotly debated issues in the philosophy of social science (Blau 1977; Garfinkel 1981; Rubinstein 1981).

*Ontological Barriers.* Whatever the merits of combining cognitive and structural schemata, it should be clear from the sample ontologies in row 7 that a fusion between or among the cognitive, behavioral, or economic programs would be difficult indeed. The problem, of course, is that variables that perform an explanatory role in one program do not necessarily fulfill this role in the others. Thus, while attitudes, intentions, and beliefs are causally determinant of behavior in the cognitive program, they are, at best, "verbal responses" under the control of reinforcements generated by the linguistic community in Skinner's (1984) program, and make no appearance whatsoever in Becker's.

A second ontological barrier to programmatic integration is the fact that the "meaning" of terms can differ radically across programs. Consider, for example, the construct "reward," which can appear in all four theories in the Exhibit. In the Fishbein model a reward could be one of the cognitively anticipated outcomes of a behavior, whereas in the Skinnerian program a reward is any stimulus presented to an individual that increases the probability of a behavioral response when the stimulus is presented to the individual in the future. In contrast, in Becker's model a reward will be viewed as anything that increases the utility of an economic agent and in Blau's theory (if the term appears at all) it is only implied by psychological axioms like "people prefer [obtain rewards from?] associates with whom they share social attributes" (1977, p. 245). Thus we see that while the term "reward" can occur in all four programs, its meaning and function differ significantly across programs. In other words, the meaning of a construct is relative to the program in which it appears, and we should not be misled into thinking that because the same word is used in different programs, its meaning is invariant across programs. Moreover, it should be noted that this is not an unusual occurrence in science. It is notorious that the term "Mass" does not mean the same thing in classical and relativistic physics (Bernstein 1973; Hoffmann 1972; Kuhn 1977), and that the term "gene" had no less than 16 different referents over the period 1903–1966 (Carlson 1966). The lesson to be learned from all this is that it is not always possible to take a single concept or construct from one theory and employ it unproblematically in another theory. In many cases, a scientific term loses its original meaning when removed from the research program in which it is embedded.

*Programmatic Dominance.* Of course, it might be objected at this point that there have been successful syntheses of the programs listed in the Exhibit. For example, the work of Bandura (1971, 1977) and the early work of Bern (1964) could be viewed as filling the "seams" between the cognitive and behaviorist columns. However, on closer examination, it is clear that the theories developed by both of these scholars exhibit what I shall call "programmatic dominance." That is to say, their respective programs of research are dominated by either the cognitive or behaviorist orientations. In the case of Bandura's social learning theory, the fact that reinforcements are cognitively mediated places this approach on the cognitive end of the spectrum. On the other hand, Bern's early attempts to define beliefs and attitudes as sets of operants clearly places this theory on the behaviorist end. Moreover, it is important to note that by combining cognitive and behaviorist ontologies, these theories do not fall neatly into either camp. By granting a causal or mediating role to "mental" constructs, both programs ensure rejection by mainstream radical behaviorists. Moreover, while Bandura's theory is acceptable to many cognitivists, it is clear that Bern's early work falls well outside of the cognitive program.

Thus, we see that the columns in the Exhibit are simply discrete points along a continuum of research programs that represent, more or less, "pure form" alternatives for the investigation of consumer behavior. The existence of other approaches in the "seams" of the Exhibit does not vitiate the incommensurability argument. It simply demonstrates that incommensurability is itself a continuum and that some theory pairs are more incommensurable than others.

In addition, it is quite possible for programs to "migrate" along this continuum. For example, Bem's (1964, 1965, 1967) original formulation of the self-perception hypothesis (which has been used by some consumer researchers to explain the foot-in-door phenomenon) was constructed by employing the theoretical perspective and ontology of radical behaviorism (see Tybout, Sternthal, and Calder 1983 for a review). However, when Bem's *Beliefs, Attitudes and Human Affairs* appeared in 1970, self-perception theory remained intact, but its behavioristic origins were not mentioned, and its behavioristic ontology had been dropped. (A factor that, no doubt, made the theory more palatable to both consumer researchers and social psychologists.)

Moreover, it is also possible for new programs to evolve from, or in reaction to, established research traditions. Thus, Fishbein (1967) considers his extended model to be a "liberal interpretation" of Dulany's (1961, 1964, 1968) theory of propositional control. In turn, Dulany's theory was developed in response to what he viewed as experimental anomalies in Skinner's theory of verbal operant conditioning. What is interesting about this case is that Dulany's (1968) model is couched in a quasi-behavioristic ontology, while Fishbein (1967) makes a clean break with behaviorism by employing a fully cognitive ontology.

Thus, while it is possible for theories to migrate away from one program toward another and for new theories to evolve from earlier programs, it should also be clear that these movements are not always gradual shifts brought about by compelling empirical evidence. Rather, they may well be discrete "jumps" that can be a function of both empirical and nonempirical factors. Of course, only detailed historical research can shed light on the question of which mode of theory change predominates in the social sciences. But whatever the outcome of such research, it should be obvious that once a certain critical distance is reached, research programs tend to become incommensurable. In this context, incommensurability means that it will not be possible to construct empirical tests (that would be acceptable to adherents of both programs) that would ultimately adjudicate between the competing theories. This can be seen in row 8 of the Exhibit, which shows the methodological commitments and appraisal criteria (referred to as cognitive aims and methods in Figure A) of each of the four programs. If we look across this row we see both congruence and incongruence between and among programs. For example, while mathematical elegance and simplicity figure prominently in the economic program, they are not of overriding importance in the other three research areas. On the other hand, we do find that some programs share a common methodology. For example, both cognitivists and radical behaviorists employ the experimental method. But before we take this as evidence that an empirical adjudication between these programs is possible, we must remember that methods and appraisal criteria function as a whole in theory testing. Thus, while Fishbeinians and Skinnerians might agree on the experimental method, their adherence to very different ontologies would cause them to design and interpret their experiments in radically different ways. As such, an experimental test of the extended Fishbein model would involve the elicitation of subject self-reports concerning mental states, while a test of Skinner's theory of operant conditioning would eschew all self-reports and focus solely on "observables" such as operants, reinforcements, and stimuli. An identical argument could be made for the incommensurability of Becker and Blau's programs, despite their common methodological commitments.

It can thus be seen that there is little hope of constructing "crucial experiments," Platt style (1964) "strong inference" procedures, or "falsifying" experiments (Calder *et al.* 1981, 1982, 1983) that would ultimately adjudicate between cognitive and behaviorist world views. Given the disparate commitments of the two camps, there are no purely empirical procedures that both sides could accept as valid tests of their veridicality. Similarly, the fact that the economic and structuralist programs share the method of correlation at the macro level does little to enhance the comparability of the two programs because of their disjunction at the ontological level.

*Metaphysical Beliefs.* Rows 9 through 13 further illustrate the incommensurability of the four programs. In particular, row 9 (the concept of mind) and row 10 (the concept of human nature) are the key metaphysical beliefs from Figure A that undergird each program. Indeed, it can be argued that the so-called "problem of mind" is the most significant and fundamental problem of the social sciences. The problem of mind is actually a set of interrelated problems that arise from the fact that mental events appear to be "private" phenomena for the actor. Moreover, differences across programs at the methodological, ontological, metaphysical, empirical, and axiological level can be traced, in large part, to the way in which each program goes about "solving" the various problems of mind. (A complete explication of this claim must be left to another paper because of the complexities involved.) In the present case it can be seen that the key issues are: (1) the accessibility of the subject's mind to others, (2) the question of whether subjects have "privileged access" to their own mental states, (3) the necessity of access (by either party) for scientific explanation, and (4) the issue of whether social-structural variables can be reduced to psychological states. As can be seen in the Exhibit, the four programs offer disparate answers to these questions. The most important differences concern the issue of access. The Fishbeinian program deals with the problem of access via subject self-reports, while the radical behaviorist eschews self-reports entirely. In contrast, Becker and Blau deal with access by simply assuming certain "psychological" dispositions among actors and deducing the consequences that follow logically from these axioms.

Furthermore, it can be seen that each program's "philosophy of mind" directly informs its concept of human nature (row 10), and that jointly these two metaphysical commitments help to determine a program's mode of inference (row 5), the nature and interpretation of its ontology (rows 6 and 7), its research methodologies and realizable cognitive aims (row 8), and its empirical claims (rows 11 and 12).

Thus, to a large extent, research programs in the social sciences may be viewed as "self-justifying" networks of commitments. This can be seen in Figure A, where aims, methods, and facts jointly support one another. Moreover, it is important to note that what count as facts within a program are under different degrees of empirical constraint. The "output" of a program – its empirical beliefs, theories, propositions, and hypotheses – must be justified by whatever methodologies are sanctioned within the research program. Metaphysical beliefs, however, are under a far weaker empirical constraint. As such, a program's concept of mind and human nature constitutes the taken-for-granted bedrock on which its knowledge claims are based. Such beliefs are only rarely questioned or subjected to empirical investigation.

For example, if one should question the lack of "realism" in the assumptions that underwrite the Beckerian program, one would be politely referred to Friedman's (1953) famous essay in which he argues that unrealistic assumptions are irrelevant as long as the program generates empirically accurate "predictions" (Becker 1976, p. 7). (Note that it is the adherents of the program themselves who determine the acceptable degree of accuracy in its predictions!) Thus, we see that the program is able to "immunize" itself from an outsider's criticism of its metaphysical beliefs by appeal to yet another of its commitments – the philosophical position of instrumentalism.

Similarly, even within programs committed to realism, there is very little questioning of basic assumptions concerning the concept of mind and human nature. Moreover, when such considerations are raised (e.g., Nisbett and Wilson 1977; Wilson and Nisbett 1978), they are usually subjected to severe criticism (e.g., Adair and Spinner 1981; Ericsson and Simon 1980; White 1980), which tends to leave the basic issue (in this case the veridicality of self-reports) unresolved. This results because of the fundamental fact that we have no means for gaining "privileged access" to the mental life of our subjects. Thus, research in these programs is, in many respects, immune from criticisms of its basic assumptions. This immunity (which need not be total or even permanent) arises because of the inherent open-endedness of metaphysical debates, and because it is clearly not in the interests of program adherents to question their most fundamental assumptions (Barnes 1977; Bloor 1976; Earl 1983).

Thus, it can be seen that by accepting as given a particular concept of mind and of human nature, the research programs in the Exhibit actually redefine the objects of their inquiry. This has profound implications for consumer research because it means that, in many cases, proponents of the different programs are not even talking about the same subject matter! It is a linguistic (or as Wittgenstein (1953) might put it) a "grammatical" mistake to assume that because theories of "consumer behavior" can be derived from these programs, they must all be trying to explain the same thing. As has been illustrated, the incommensurability of these approaches cuts right across almost all of a program's commitments. Of course, there is nothing in principle that rules out programmatic synthesis. But, at the same time, there are few social factors driving consumer research toward Ferber's (1977) interdisciplinary ideal. As long as there are professional rewards to be gained by remaining within one program (as well as disincentives and "entry barriers" discouraging synthesis) we can expect to see the field characterized by encapsulation.

## Summary and conclusions

One of the major implications of the foregoing is that, when viewed as the sole arbiter of theory choice, the empirical testability requirement of logical empiricism, modern empiricism, and naive falsificationism is a relatively weak criterion of scientific adequacy. As the Exhibit demonstrates, each of the four programs we have discussed produces empirically justified claims concerning consumer behavior, yet there is often radical divergence in the content of these claims. We have shown that when there is conflict between theories or research programs at the level of factual assertions or methodological preferences, the debate tends to shift up to the next level in the justificatory hierarchy (Figure B). However, we have also seen that this schema is less of a hierarchy and more of a "self-justifying" network characterized by underdetermination at each of its nodes (Figure A). Moreover, it does not appear that Laudan's (1984b) methods of resolving value disputes have functioned effectively for either intra- or interprogram disputes in the social sciences. (In part, this may reflect the previously mentioned social, professional, and institutional factors inhibiting programmatic integration or adjudication.)

It can thus be seen that the way in which social and consumer behavior research is actually practiced is best construed from a critical relativist perspective. Moreover, suggestions that positivistic alternatives should be adopted as normative ideals tend to miss the point that the history of great scientific advance is rarely in accord with positivistic algorithms (Anderson 1983). What must be taken as given is the fact that science is a social, historical, cultural, and economic enterprise. As such, both cognitive and sociological factors will be implicated in any adequate philosophy of science.

### Hardheaded Relativism

It has also been shown that critical relativism is more "hard-headed" than positivism in its requirements for scientific adequacy. Unlike positivists, who are committed to the thesis of scientific monism, critical relativists do not take programmatic knowledge claims a face value. A critical relativist demands to know a program's methodological, ontological, metaphysical, and axiological commitments before he or she is willing to grant epistemic authority to its knowledge products: Most importantly, critical relativists want to know a program's realizable cognitive (and social) aims before they are willing to give it serious consideration. Different aims may require very different programs of research.

For example, if one is interested in understanding the complex process by which husbands and wives negotiate their consumption decisions at the individual household level, I would submit that Becker's program does not have the resources to deliver the requisite goods. This can be seen if one is willing to roll up one's sleeves and dig into the intricate web of commitments that constitute the Beckerian program. From this vantage point it can be shown that the most that Becker can provide are some mathematically elegant theorems that can be interpreted as being consistent (in a correlational sense) with data gathered at the macro level.

The lesson to be learned from all this is that every research program has its limitations when it comes to achieving its putative aims. Each of the theories in the Exhibit has explanation via subsumption as its cognitive aim, but each cashes out this cognitive aim in very different terms. For the critical relativist, there is no question of accepting the prima facie theories of a research program until its methods of construction, its underlying metaphysical and ideological beliefs, its ontological commitments, and its capacity to achieve its cognitive and social aims have been assessed. This, of course, involves a great deal of work, but an important enterprise like science demands a commitment of this magnitude.

In the final analysis, critical relativists would prefer to make their theory choices on the basis of realizable cognitive and social aims. Unfortunately, this is not always possible. For example, radical behaviorists have been quite ingenious in constructing explanations for human actions that cognitivists view as anomalies for behaviorism. In this and many other cases, I suspect that actual choices among programs are often made on the basis of preferred ontologies, metaphysical beliefs, ideologies, and methodologies. These are, in turn, sustained by academic training, professional and/or social interests, and introspective or social experience. Thus, perhaps the ascendance of cognitivism in the last few decades may have more to do with its implications for human freedom and autonomy than with decisive empirical refutation of behaviorism.

### Policy and Ideology

This may be seen in row 13 of the Exhibit where some very specific ideological/value commitments and "policy" implications have been derived directly from the specific exemplar theories. What is immediately noticeable about these commitments is that (1) they are, at least in part, metaphysical in nature, (2) they are highly value laden, and (3) each contains factual assertions that are "justified" by methods acceptable within each research program. What is most disturbing about this state of affairs is that public or other policy officials rarely have the expertise, time, or staff to critically evaluate the epistemic, metaphysical, and ideological underpinnings of policy recommendations. Each of the programs in the Exhibit can claim to speak with scientific authority on matters of consumer policy, yet there is little that policy officials can do to assess the epistemic merits of such claims (except to call in other "scientific" experts). Thus, the "users" of consumer research findings are faced with a classic "agency" problem (Barnea, Haugen, and Senbet 1985; Pratt and Zeckhauser 1985) that can actually serve the interests of those officials who are less than honest brokers for their constituencies.

Critical relativism's response to problems of this sort is to be, at one and the same time, more tolerant and more critical of alternative models of knowledge production. It is more tolerant because it recognizes that there is no single scientific method and that different research programs are able to achieve very different cognitive and social ends. However, critical relativism is also highly skeptical of a program's claims to have achieved those ends, and it recognizes that only through a detailed analysis of a program's commitments, its modes of theory construction, and its validation procedures can a judgment be made concerning the adequacy of its knowledge-products. Moreover, a critical relativist perspective makes it clear that scientific aims and values are not "rigid designators" that uniquely pick out the correct theory or research program – and it is fully cognizant of the fact that incommensurability and underdetermination can operate within, as well as across, established research programs.

### The Multiattribute Model Redux

In closing, these claims can be made more concrete by returning to our earlier example of the multiattribute model debate. It will be recalled that one of the major points of contention in that controversy was the question of whether the adequacy-importance version of that model was more appropriate than the other alternatives – especially the Fishbein attitude-toward-an-object model (Cohen, Fishbein, and Ahtola 1972). It would appear that the adequacy-importance model was eventually "deconstructed" by influential studies conducted by Bettman, Capon, and Lutz (1975a, 1975b) and an important review article by Lutz and Bettman (1977). (Here "deconstructed" is used as a technical term borrowed from the sociology of science to indicate that the adequacy-importance model ceased to be a major option for research in consumer behavior. Of course, this does not mean that the model and its residuum have been completely expunged from our literature.)

Drawing on work by Bass and Wilkie (1973) and Birnbaum (1973), Bettman *et al.* argued that cross-sectional regression analysis was an inappropriate method for "validating" multiattribute models. Moving to an individual level analysis, Bettman *et al.* showed that the Fishbein (1963) model was more appropriate because of its greater "homogeneity of response patterns across subjects and ... [its] ultimate usefulness ... to the policy-maker" (1975b, p. 162).

What is especially interesting about this example is the fact that the extended Fishbein (1967) model was simultaneously being "constructed" (made a live option) for consumer researchers through the exclusive use of cross-sectional regression analysis (e.g., Harrell and Bennett 1974; Lutz 1973a, 1973b; Ryan 1973, 1974; Ryan and Bonfield 1975; etc.). (And subsequently, via multiple validation procedures.) Thus, we have a classic case study in which the research cornmunity seems to have initially rejected a particular methodology for the justification of one model, while at the same time it accepted another model by using the very same methodological procedure.

As might be expected, however, lurking behind this apparent paradox at the methodological level there appears to have been something of a consensus forming around the scientific aim of maintaining consistency with established theoretical frameworks. (The same issue that was at stake in the earlier

"Fishbein-Rosenberg" debates.) This can be seen quite clearly in the Lutz and Bettman review article in which they attack the adequacy-importance model for, among other things, its lack of a "theoretical foundation" (1977, p. 140).

If we leave aside for the moment the fact that a theory is just an artifact created by the human imagination, and that (on this score at least) the adequacy-importance and Fishbein models fall in the same category, we can begin to see exactly what the "consistency" value meant to the research community at that time. It appears that consistency meant that the model was derived from an established research program in social psychology. This interpretation is supported by the fact that it would have been difficult during this time period to make a purely empirical case for the superiority of the original Fishbein (1963) model (Mazis, Ahtola, and Klippel 1975; Sheth 1972; Talarzyk 1972). Indeed, in another study employing single attribute versions of the models, Bettman *et al.* (1975a) found that the Fishbein approach was superior to the adequacy-importance and a newer "adequacy-evaluation" model on only one of three different methodological procedures. However, when the Bettman *et al.* (1975b) article appeared, the Fishbein model was declared the superior theory because of its lower heterogeneity of response across subjects at the individual level.

The upshot of all this is to suggest that, even within programs, theory choice need not necessarily be a straightforward, empirically-driven phenomenon. As we have seen, while much of the argumentation surrounding the early development of multiattribute models in consumer research appeared to concern empirical issues, the consistency value was an ever-present background factor that played an important (and perhaps decisive) role in the outcome of the debate.

This conclusion is consistent with a substantial body of literature in the cognitive tradition in contemporary sociology of science. This literature suggests that aims and methods are best conceived of as "flexible resources" employed to confirm some theoretical claims and to disconfirm others (see, for example, Collins 1975; Gilbert and Mulkay 1984; MacKenzie 1981; Pickering 1981, 1984; Pinch 1980, 1985; Potter 1984). What this means is that values, aims, and methods do not function as formal rules that are unambiguously applied by the scientific community to choose the best theory. Rather, the community selectively employs and interprets such criteria in response to empirical, social, cultural, and economic factors. Thus, it should not be surprising to find (as Potter (1984) demonstrated in his analysis of psychologists' scientific discourse) that research communities and individual scientists may appear to be inconsistent in their application of choice criteria. Nor, in light of Laudan's (1984b) model and the empirical work in sociology of science, should it be surprising to find, at any specific point in time, a significant degree of unanimity on scientific values underlying this apparent inconsistency (if approximately the same factors are impinging on the discipline as a whole). For example, consumer research's interest in maintaining consistency with established psychological paradigms in the mid-1970s might be explained, in part, by the discipline's legitimate desire to improve its standing as a bona fide scientific area. However, only a detailed historical and sociological analysis of this and similar cases can shed light on the role of such factors in the outcome of scientific progress in consumer research.

Toward the Workbench

It should be clear that a relativistic construal of social science will have profound implications for "workbench"-level issues in consumer research. For example, a relativistic model can help to explicate the important distinctions that must be made in the social sciences among the concepts of explanation, prediction, and understanding. Closely linked to this issue is the significance of the concept "meaning" as it relates both to the cognitive goal of "understanding" and to the ontological status of social scientific concepts. The latter consideration is at the heart of the crucial realism-instrumentalism controversy (Chalmers 1982) and is closely connected to the problem of mind and human agency (Bagozzi 1980). Other issues that can be illuminated by relativism would include: the inability of the social sciences to match the predictive and manipulative success of the natural sciences, the relationship between psychological/social-psychological explanations at the individual level and sociological/anthropological explanations at the group or cultural level, the role of "folk" psychology and sociology in scientific explanations of human behavior, and the important challenge to positivistic social science posed by the "interpretive" tradition. At a more concrete level, a relativistic perspective can have important implications for such day-to-day considerations as the nature and meaning of construct validity (Peter and Churchill 1984), the relationship between internal and external validity, the function and importance of replication, the value of programmatic research and meta-analysis, the role and definition of empirical testing in scientific progress, and many others. Unfortunately, a full development of these issues will require another paper. As Dostoevsky put it at the end of *Crime and Punishment*, that must be "the subject of a new story, but our present story is ended."

## Notes

1. Of course, this does not mean that every individual cognitivist or behaviorist is also a realist. These labels are used to capture the general tenor of discourse within each program.

## References

Adair, John G. and Barry Spinner (1981), "Subjects' Access to Cognitive Processes: Demand Characteristics and Verbal Report," *Journal for the Theory of Social Behavior*, (March), 31–52.

Ajzen, Icek and Martin Fishbein (1980), *Understanding Attitudes and Predicting Social Behavior*, Englewood Cliffs, NJ: Prentice-Hall.

Anderson, Paul F. (1981), "A Review of Some Recent Philosophy and Sociology of Science Literature," working paper, Virginia Polytechnic Institute and State University.

– (1983), "Marketing, Scientific Progress and Scientific Method," *Journal of Marketing*, 47 (Fall), 18–31.

Bagozzi, Richard P. (1980), *Causal Models in Marketing*, New York: John Wiley.

Bandura, Albert (1971), *Psychological Modeling*, Chicago: Aldine-Atherton.

– (1977), *Social Learning Theory*, Englewood Cliffs, NJ: Prentice-Hall.

Barnea, Amir, Robert A. Haugen, and Lemma W. Senbet (1985), *Agency Problems and Financial Contracting*, Englewood Cliffs, NJ: Prentice-Hall.

Barnes, Barry (1977), *Interests and the Growth of Knowledge*, London: Routledge & Kegan Paul.

Bartels, Robert (1968), "The General Theory of Marketing," *Journal of Marketing*, 32 (January), 29–33.

Bass, Frank M. (1972), "Fishbein and Brand Preference: A Reply," *Journal of Marketing Research*, 9 (November), 461.

– and W. Wayne Talarzyk (1972), "An Attitude Model for the Study of Brand Preference," *Journal of Marketing Research*, 9 (February), 93–96.

– and William L. Wilkie (1973), "A Comparative Analysis of Attitudinal Predictions of Brand Preference," *Journal of Marketing Research*, 10 (August), 262–269.

Becker, Gary S. (1965) "A Theory of the Allocation of Time," *The Economic Journal*, 75, 493–517.

– (1976), *The Economic Approach to Human Behavior*, Chicago: University of Chicago Press.

– (1981), *A Treatise on the Family*, Cambridge, MA: Harvard University Press.

Bell, Daniel and Irving Kristol (1981), *The Crisis in Economic Theory*, New York: Basic Books.

– (1984), "The Turn to Interpretation," *Partisan Review*, 51, 215–219.

Bem, Daryl J. (1964), "An Experimental Analysis of Beliefs and Attitudes," unpublished dissertation, University of Michigan, Ann Arbor, MI.

– (1965), "An Experimental Analysis of Self-Persuasion," *Journal of Experimental Social Psychology*, 1, 199–218.

– (1967), "Self-Perception: An Alternative Interpretation of Cognitive Dissonance," *Psychological Review*, 74, 183–200.

– (1970), *Beliefs, Attitudes and Human Affairs*, Belmont, CA: Brooks/Cole.

Bernstein, Jeremy (1973), *Einstein*, New York: Penguin Books.

Bernstein, Richard J. (1983), *Beyond Objectivism and Relativism*, Philadelphia, PA: University of Pennsylvania Press.

Bettman, James R., Noel Capon, and Richard J. Lutz (1975a), "A Multimethod Approach to Validating Multi-Attribute Attitude Models," in *Advances in Consumer Research*, Vol. 2, ed. Mary Jane Schlinger, Chicago: Association for Consumer Research, 357–374.

– Noel Capon, and Richard J. Lutz (1975b), "Cognitive Algebra in Multi-Attribute Attitude Models," *Journal of Marketing Research*, 12 (May), 151–164.

Birnbaum, Michael H. (197 3), "The Devil Rides Again: Correlation as an Index of Fit," *Psychological Bulletin*, 79 (April), 239–242.

Black, Max (1967), "Induction," *Encyclopedia of Philosophy*, 4, ed. Paul Edwards, New York: Macmillan.

Blau, Peter M. (1977), *Inequality and Heterogeneity*, New York: The Free Press.

Blaug, Mark (1980), *The Methodology of Economics*, Cambridge, U.K.: Cambridge University Press.

Bloor, David (1976), *Knowledge and Social Imagery*, London: Routledge & Kegan Paul.

– (1982), "A Reply to Gerd Buchdahl," *Studies in History and Philosophy of Science*, 13, 305–311.

Brodbeck, May (1982), "Recent Developments in the Philosophy of Science," in *Marketing Theory: Philosophy of Science Perspectives*, eds. Ronald F. Bush and Shelby D. Hunt, Chicago: American Marketing Association.

Calder, Bobby J, Lynn W. Phillips, and Alice M. Tybout (1981), "Designing Research for Applications," *Journal of Consumer Research*, 8 (September), 197–207.

–, Lynn W. Phillips, and Alice M. Tybout (1982), "The Concept of External Validity," *Journal of Consumer Research*, 9 (December), 240–244.

–, Lynn W. Phillips, and Alice M. Tybout (1983), "Beyond External Validity," *Journal of Consumer Research*, 10 (June), 112–114.

Caldwell, Bruce J. (1984), "Some Problems with Falsificationism in Economics," *Philosophy of the Social Sciences*, 14 (December), 489–495.

Carlson, Elof Axel (1966), *The Gene: A Critical History*, Philadelphia, PA: W.B. Saunders.

Chalmers, Alan F. (1976), *What Is This Thing Called Science?* St. Lucia, Australia: University of Queensland Press.

– (1982), *What Is This Thing Called Science?* 2nd ed., St. Lucia, Australia: University of Queensland Press.

Cohen, Joel B., Martin Fishbein, and Olli T. Ahtola (1972), "The Nature and Uses of Expectancy-Value Models in Consumer Attitude Research," *Journal of Marketing Research*, 9 (November), 456–460.

Coleman, Richard P. (1983), "The Continuing Significance of Social Class to Marketing," *Journal of Consumer Research*, 10 (December), 265–280.

Collins, H.M. (1975), "The Seven Sexes: A Study in the Sociology of a Phenomenon, or the Replication of Experiments in Physics," *Sociology*, 9, 205–224.

– (1981), "Son of Seven Sexes: The Social Destruction of a Physical Phenomenon," *Social Studies of Science*, 11, 33–62.

Comte, Auguste (1830–1842), *Cours de Philosophie Positive*, Paris: Herman.

Deshpande, Rohit (1983), "Paradigms Lost: On Theory and Method in Research in Marketing," *Journal of Marketing*, 47 (Fall), 101–110.

Dulany, Don E., Jr. (1961), "Hypotheses and Habits in Verbal 'Operant Conditioning'," *Journal of Abnormal and Social Psychology*, 63, 251–263.

– (1964), "The Separable Effects of the Information and Affect Conveyed by a Reinforcer," paper presented at the Psychonomic Society Meetings.

– (1968), "Awareness, Rules, and Prepositional Control: A Confrontation with S-R Behavior Theory," in *Verbal Behavior and General Behavior Theory*, eds. Theodore R. Dixon and David L. Horton, Englewood Cliffs, NJ: Prentice-Hall, 340–387.

Durkheim, Emile (1895), *Les Regles de la Methode Sociologique*, Paris: Felix Alcan.

Earl, Peter E. (1983), "A Behavioral Theory of Economists' Behavior," in *Why Economics is Not Yet a Science*, ed. Alfred S. Eichner, Armonk, NY: M.E. Sharpe, 90–125.

Eichner, Alfred S., ed. (1983), *Why Economics Is Not Yet a Science*, Armonk, NY: M.E. Sharpe.

Engel, LF. and R.D. Blackwell (1982), *Consumer Behavior*, New York: Holt, Rinehart, and Winston.

Ericsson, K. Anders and Herbert A. Simon (1980), 'Verbal Reports as Data," *Psychological Review*, 87 (May), 215–251.

Ferber, Robert (1977), "Can Consumer Research Be Interdisciplinary?" *Journal of Consumer Research*, 4, 189–192.

Ferber, Marianne A. and Bonnie G. Birnbaum (1977a), "The 'New Home Economics': Retrospects and Prospects," *Journal of Consumer Research*, 4 (June), 19–28.

– and Bonnie G. Birnbaum (1977b), "Rejoinder," *Journal of Consumer Research*, 4, 183–184.

Feyerabend, Paul (1975), *Against Method*, Thetford, England: Lowe and Brydone.

– (1978a), "From Incompetent Professionalism to Professionalized Incompetence – The Rise of a New Breed of Intellectuals," *Philosophy of the Social Sciences*, 8 (March), 37–53.

– (1978b), *Science in a Free Society*, London: Verso.

Fishbein, Martin (1963), "An Investigation of the Relationships Between Beliefs About an Object and the Attitude Toward that Object," *Human Relations*, 16, 233–239.

– (1967), "Attitude and the Prediction of Behavior," in *Attitude Theory and Measurement*, New York: John Wiley, 477–492.

– and Icek Ajzen (1975), *Beliefs, Attitude, Intention and Behavior*, Reading, MA: Addison-Wesley.

Flew, Anthony, ed. (1979), *A Dictionary of Philosophy*, 2nd ed., New York: St. Martin's.

Friedman, Milton (1953), "The Methodology of Positive Economics," in *Essays in Positive Economics*, Chicago: University of Chicago Press.

Garfinkel, Alan (1981), *Forms of Explanation*, New Haven, CT: Yale University Press.

Giere, Ronald N. (1979), *Understanding Scientific Reasoning*, New York: Holt, Rinehart, and Winston.

– (1984), *Understanding Scientific Reasoning*, 2nd ed., New York: Holt, Rinehart, and Winston.

Gieryn, Thomas F. (1982), "Relativist/Constructivist Programmes in the Sociology of Science: Redundance and Retreat," *Social Studies of Science*, 12, 279–297.

Gilbert, Nigel and Michael Mulkay (1984), *Opening Pandora's Box*, Cambridge, U.K.: Cambridge University Press.

Hands, Douglas W. (1984), "What Economics Is Not: An Economist's Response to Rosenberg," *Philosophy of Science*, 51 (September), 495–503.

Harrell, Gilbert D. and Peter D. Bennett (1974), "An Evaluation of the Expectancy Value Model of Attitude Measurement for Physician Prescribing Behavior," *Journal of Marketing Research*, 11 (June), 269–278.
Hausman, Daniel N. (1981), *Capital, Profits and Prices: An Essay in the Philosophy of Economics*, New York: Columbia University Press.
– (1984), *The Philosophy of Economics*, Cambridge, U.K.: Cambridge University Press.
Hoffman, Banesh (1972), *Albert Einstein, Creator and Rebel*, New York: New American Library.
Howard, John A. and Jagdish N. Sheth (1969), *The Theory of Buyer Behavior*, New York: John Wiley.
Hume, David (1740), *A Treatise of Human Nature*, Oxford, U.K.: Clarendon Press.
Hunt, Shelby D. (1983a), *Marketing Theory*, Homewood, IL: Irwin.
– (1983b), "General Theories and the Fundamental Explananda of Marketing," *Journal of Marketing*, 47 (Fall), 9–17.
– (1984), "Should Marketing Adopt Relativism?" in *Scientific Method in Marketing*, eds. Paul F. Anderson and Michael J. Ryan, Chicago: American Marketing Association, 30–34.
Knorr-Cetina, Karin D. and Michael Mulkay (1983), "Introduction: Emerging Principles in Social Studies of Science," in *Science Observed*, London: Sage.
Kuhn, Thomas S. (1957), *The Copernican Revolution: Planetary Astronomy in the Development of Western Thought*, Cambridge, MA: Harvard University Press.
– (1962), *The Structure of Scientific Revolutions*, Chicago: University of Chicago Press.
– (1970), *The Structure of Scientific Revolutions*, 2nd ed., Chicago: University of Chicago Press.
– (1977), *The Essential Tension*, Chicago: The University of Chicago Press.
Lakatos, Imre (1974), "Falsification and the Methodology of Scientific Research Programs," in *Criticism and the Growth of Knowledge*, eds. Imre Lakatos and Alan Musgrave, Cambridge, U.K.: Cambridge University Press, 91–195.
Laudan, Larry (1977), *Progress and Its Problems*, Berkeley, CA: University of California Press.
– (1981), "A Confutation of Convergent Realism," *Philosophy of Science*, 48 (March), 19–49.
– (1982), "A Note on Collins's Blend of Relativism and Empiricism," *Social Studies of Science*, 12, 131–132.
– (1983), "The Demise of the Demarcation Problem," in *The Demarcation between Science and Pseudo-Science*, Vol. 2, ed. Rachael Laudan, Blacksburg, VA: Center for the Study of Science in Society, Virginia Polytechnic Institute.
– (1984a), "Reconstructing Methodology," in *Scientific Method in Marketing*, eds. Paul F. Anderson and Michael J. Ryan, Chicago: American Marketing Association 1–4.
- (1984b), *Science and Values*, Berkeley, CA: University of California Press.
Leong, Siew Meng (1985), "Metatheory and Metamethodology in Marketing: A Lakatosian Reconstruction," *Journal of Marketing*, 49 (Fall), 23–40.
Leplin, Jarrett, ed. (1984), *Scientific Realism*, Berkeley, CA: University of California Press.
Liebenstein, Harvey (1981), "Microeconomics and X-Efficiency Theory: If There Is No Crisis, There Ought To Be," in *The Crisis in Economic Theory*, eds. Daniel Bell and Irving Kristol, New York: Basic Books, 97–110.
Lutz, Richard J. (1973a), "A Comparison of Two Alternative Models of the Attitude-Behavior Relationship," paper presented at the Eighty-First Annual Convention of the American Psychological Association, Montreal, Canada.
– (1973b), "Cognitive Change and Attitude Change: A Validation Study," unpublished dissertation, University of Illinois, Urbana-Champaign.
– and James R. Bettman (1977), "Multiattribute Models in Marketing: A Bicentennial Review," in *Consumer and Industrial Buying Behavior*, eds. Arch G. Woodside, Jagdish N. Sheth, and Peter D. Bennett, New York: North-Holland, 137–149.
Lynch, John G., Jr. (1982), "On the External Validity of Experiments in Consumer Research," *Journal of Consumer Research*, 9 (December), 225–239.
– (1983), "The Role of External Validity in Theoretical Research," *Journal of Consumer Research*, 10 (June), 109–111.
MacKenzie, Donald (1981), *Statistics in Britain 1865–1930*, Edinburgh, U.K.: Edinburgh University Press.

Martineau, Pierre (1958), "Social Classes and Spending Behavior," *Journal of Marketing*, 23 (October), 121–130.
Mazis, Michael B., Olli T. Ahtola, and R. Eugene Klippel (1975), "A Comparison of Four Multi-Attribute Models in the Prediction of Consumer Attitudes," *Journal of Consumer Research*, 2 (June), 38–52.
McCullagh, C. Behan (1984), "The Intelligibility of Cognitive Relativism," *The Monist*, 67 (July), 327–340.
Mill, John Stuart (1843), *A System of Logic*, London: Longman, Green, & Company, 1959.
Nisbett, Richard E. and Timothy D. Wilson (1977), "Telling More Than We Can Know: Verbal Reports on Mental Processes," *Psychological Review*, 84 (May), 231–259.
Nord, Walter R. and J. Paul Peter (1980), "A Behavior Modification Perspective on Marketing," *Journal of Marketing*, 44 (Spring), 36–47.
Olson, Jerry C. (1981), "Towards a Science of Consumer Behavior," in *Advances in Consumer Research*, Vol. 9, ed. Andrew A. Mitchell, Ann Arbor, MI: Association for Consumer Research, v–x.
Peter, J. Paul (1981), "Some Methodological Issues in Consumer Research," paper presented at the Association for Consumer Research Annual Conference.
– (1982), "Current Issues in the Philosophy of Science: Implications for Marketing Theory: A Panel Discussion," in *Marketing Theory: Philosophy of Science Perspectives*, eds. Ronald F. Bush and Shelby D. Hunt, Chicago: American Marketing Association, 11–16.
– (1983), "Some Philosophical and Methodological Issues in Consumer Research," in *Marketing Theory*, Shelby D. Hunt, Homewood, IL: Irwin, 382–394.
– and Walter R. Nord (1982), "A Clarification and Extension of Operant Conditioning Principles in Marketing," *Journal of Marketing*, 46 (Summer), 102–107.
– and Jerry C. Olson (1983), "Is Science Marketing?" *Journal of Marketing*, 47 (Fall), 111–125.
– and Gilbert A. Churchill, Jr. (1984), "The Relationships Among Research Design Choices and Psychometric Properties of Rating Scales: A Meta-Analysis," working paper, Graduate School of Management, University of Wisconsin-Madison (August).
Pickering, Andrew (1981), "The Hunting of the Quark," *Isis*, 72 (June), 216–236.
– (1984), *Constructing Quarks*, Chicago: University of Chicago Press.
Pinch, T.J. (1980), "Theoreticians and the Production of Experimental Anomaly: The Case of Solar Neutrinos," in *The Social Process of Scientific Investigation*, eds. Karin D. Knorr, Roger Krohn, and Richard Whitley, Dordrecht: D. Reidel, 77–106.
– (1982), "The Three-Sigma Enigma: On the Negotiation of Error in Physics," paper presented at the Society for Social Studies of Science Meetings, Philadelphia, PA, 28–31, October.
– (1985), "Towards an Analysis of Scientific Observation," *Social Studies of Science*, 15 (February), 3–36.
Platt, John R. (1964), "Strong Inference," *Science*, 46 (October), 347–353.
Popper, Karl R. (1962), *Conjectures and Refutations*, New York: Harper & Row.
Potter, Jonathan (1984), "Testability, Flexibility: Kuhnian Values in Scientists' Discourse Concerning Theory Choice," *Philosophy of Social Science*, 14, 303–330.
Pratt, John W. and Richard J. Zeckhauser (1985), *Principals and Agents: The Structure of Business*, Boston: Harvard Business School Press.
Reidenbach, R. Eric and Terence Oliva (1981), "General Living Systems Theory and Marketing: A Framework for Analysis," *Journal of Marketing*, 45 (Fall), 30–37.
Rosenberg, Alexander (1983), "If Economics Isn't Science, What Is It?" *The Philosophical Forum*, 14, 296–314.
– (1984), "Methodology, Theory and Philosophy," paper presented at the Workshop on Scientific Methodology, Virginia Polytechnic Institute, Blacksburg, VA, 57, April.
Rosenberg, Milton J. (1956), "Cognitive Structure and Attitudinal Affect," *Journal of Abnormal and Social Psychology*, 53 (November), 367–372.
Rubinstein, David (1981), *Marx and Wittgenstein*, London: Routledge & Kegan Paul.
Ryan, Michael J. (1973), "Purchase Behavior: An Exploratory Theory, A Predictive Model," in *Proceedings* of the Southern Marketing Association, ed. Robert L. King, Blacksburg, VA.

– (1974), "An Empirical Test of a Causal Chain Derived from Fishbein's Behavioral Intentions Model and Applied to a Purchase Intention Situation," unpublished dissertation, University of Kentucky, Lexington, KY.

– and Bonfield, E.H. (1975), "The Fishbein Extended Model and Consumer Behavior,', *Journal of Consumer Research*, 2, 118–136.

Sheth, Jagdish N. (1972), "Reply to Comments on the Nature and Uses of Expectancy-Value Models in Consumer Attitude Research", *Journal of Marketing Research*, 9 (November), 462–465.

– and W. Wayne Talarzyk (1972), "Perceived Instrumentality and Value Importance as Determinants of Attitude," *Journal of Marketing Research*, 9 (February), 6–9.

Skinner, B.F. (1953), *Science and Human Behavior*, New York: The Free Press.

– (1969), *Contingencies of Reinforcement*, New York: Appleton-Century-Crofts.

– (1984), "The Operational Analysis of Psychological Terms," *The Behavioral and Brain Sciences*, 7 (December), 547–581.

Talarzyk, W. Wayne (1972), "A Reply to the Response to Bass, Talarzyk and Fishbein," *Journal of Marketing Research*, 9 (November), 465–467.

Tybout, Alice M., Brian Sternthal, and Bobby J. Calder (1983), "Information Availability as a Determinant of Multiple Request Effectiveness," *Journal of Marketing Research*, 20 (August), 280–290.

–, Brian Sternthal, and Bobby J. Calder (1985), "Theory Testing Procedures: A Falsificationist's View," paper presented at the AMA Workshop on Marketing Theory, Virginia Polytechnic Institute, Blacksburg, VA, 12–14, May.

von Bertalanffy, Ludwig (1968), *General Systems Theory*, New York: George Braziller.

Wallis, Roy (1979), *On the Margins of Science*, Keele, U.K.: University of Keele.

Warner, W. Lloyd and Paul S. Lunt (1941), *The Social Life of a Modern Community*, New Haven, CT: Yale University Press.

Weber, Max (1922), *The Methodology of the Social Sciences*, Glencoe, II: Free Press.

White, Peter (1980), "Limitations on Verbal Reports of Internal Events: A Refutation of Nisbett and Wilson and of Bem," *Psychological Review*, 87 (January), 105–112.

Wilkie, William L. and Edgar A. Pessemier (1973), "Issues in Marketing's Use of Multi-Attribute Attitude Models," *Journal of Marketing Research*, 10 (November), 428–441.

Wilson, Timothy D. and Richard E. Nisbett (1978), "The Accuracy of Verbal Reports About the Effects of Stimuli on Evaluations of Behavior," *Social Psychology*, 41 (June), 118–131.

Wittgenstein, Ludwig (1953), *Philosophical Investigations*, Oxford, U.K.: Basil Blackwell.

Woolgar, Steve (1981), "Interests and Explanation in the Social Study of Science," *Social Studies of Science*, 11, 365–394.

Yearly, Steven (1982), "The Relationship Between Epistemological and Sociological Cognitivist Interests: Some Ambiguities Underlying the Use of Interest Theory in the Study of Scientific Knowledge," *Studies in History and Philosophy of Science*, 13, 353–388.

Zaltman, Gerald and Melanie Wallendorf (1983), *Consumer Behavior*, New York: John Wiley.

# 3

# Hermeneutics and Consumer Research

**Stephen J. Arnold and Eileen Fischer**

**Source:** *Journal of Consumer Research* 21 (1994): 55–70.

The term "hermeneutics" and related derivations have appeared with increasing frequency in consumer research (App. A). Although these terms have most often appeared in studies taking an "interpretive approach" (Hudson and Ozanne 1988), the relationship of hermeneutics to this approach remains obscure. Moreover, the questions, What is hermeneutics? and Does hermeneutics have a unique contribution to make to consumer research? remain unanswered. This article attempts to answer these questions and, in the process, follows Hudson and Ozanne by identifying differences among interpretive approaches.

Hermeneutic philosophy is concerned with the interpretation of understanding (Bernstein 1983; Bleicher 1980; Gadamer 1989). This philosophy holds that understanding has an ontological status. It emphasizes that all understanding is linguistic. Furthermore, hermeneutic philosophy explores how the subject-object dichotomy may be bridged by an interpreter engaging the "other" through a reading that is grounded in, but not determined solely by, the interpreter's [pre-]understanding.

The relevance of hermeneutics to consumer research is threefold. First, in purporting to understand understanding itself, philosophical hermeneutics is basic to any scientific or scholarly endeavor. The concept of [pre-]understanding accounts not only for existing theory and research findings but also for the knowledge that researchers as subjects share with the human objects of their inquiry.

Second, hermeneutic philosophy refines our understanding of the interpretive approaches used in consumer research. Hermeneutic philosophy partially informs Mick's (1986) semiotics, Levy's (1981) structuralism, Stern's (1989) literary criticism, Thompson, Locander, and Pollio's (1989) existential-phenomenology, Hirschman's (1986) humanistic inquiry, and Belk, Sherry, and Wallendorf's (1988) naturalistic inquiry. Several of these interpretive approaches incorporate procedures directly related to hermeneutic philosophy.

Finally, hermeneutic philosophy can be shown to have distinct implications for approaches to consumer research, although hermeneutic philosophy is not strictly associated with one particular method. Of particular relevance are the concepts of [pre-] understanding, the hermeneutic circle, the fusion of horizons, self-understanding, and the ideal of the dialogic community.

In support of the preceding claims, we provide an account of major themes in hermeneutic philosophy. We include a brief historical sketch and a summary of the tenets characterizing hermeneutics. We discuss the similarities between hermeneutic philosophy on the one hand and certain interpretive approaches and critical theory on the other. Finally, we outline a research approach consistent with hermeneutic philosophy, compare it to other emergent approaches, and illustrate it with two interpretations.

## Historical Overview of Hermeneutics

The meaning of hermeneutics has evolved over time as understandings of understanding have grown and changed. This section briefly highlights this evolution, although the meaning of some of the developments may not be apparent until the discussion is expanded in later sections. Furthermore, while the various meanings are presented sequentially, it is emphasized that no version ceases to exist. Proponents of each might be found today, and later views incorporate elements of their predecessors. "There does not exist a general hermeneutics, that is, a general theory of interpretation, ... there are only various separate and contrasting hermeneutic theories" (Thompson 1981, p. 46).

The term "hermeneutics" derives from Hermes, messenger of the Greek gods, who announced messages verbatim to mortals and made them understandable. The implication is that hermeneutics has two tasks: to determine what a text has to say and to provide instruction about what to do (Bleicher 1980, p. 12).

An important impetus in the development of hermeneutics was the practice of exegesis, the determination of divine meaning in sacred texts through close reading. As a consequence, a "hermeneutical method" developed in the context of religious studies. This method is summarized in a Reformation account of biblical hermeneutics in which the interpreter is instructed to analyze a passage's grammar and to consider the passage in the broader contexts of the complete text and the felt experience of Christian life (Bleicher 1980, p. 12). The significant development here is the recognition that individual textual components have to be dealt with as part of a larger whole.

Hermeneutics was, in time, generalized to a theory of textual interpretation not restricted to religious works. The nearly unanimous opinion of pre- and early twentieth-century hermeneutic thinking was that, if an interpreter followed prescribed procedures, it was possible in principle to determine an "objective," immutable meaning either as intended by the author or as contained in the text. This form of hermeneutics is known as "hermeneutical theory."

A contemporary proponent of hermeneutical theory is Emilio Betti. Influenced by, among others, the theologian Friedrich Schleiermacher, the philosopher Wilhelm Dilthey, and the linguist Wilhelm von Humboldt, Betti (1980) identified "meaning-full forms" (p. 53) in which the mind of the other has objectivated itself. The task of the reader or listener is to re-experience, re-cognize, and re-think *(Verstehen)* what the other originally felt or thought (Bleicher 1980, pp. 110–112). Betti formulated a set of "hermeneutical canons" to facilitate this process of interpretation and argued that, when the meaning-complex or "objective" knowledge is acquired through interpretation, understanding occurs at intellectual, emotional, and moral levels. Misunderstanding occurs, he suggested, with increases in space and time between the author and reader.

"Philosophical hermeneutics" developed through the middle to late twentieth century and was very much a consequence of Martin Heidegger's *Sein und Zeit* (published in English as *Being and Time*) and Hans-Georg Gadamer's *Wahrheit und Methode* (published in English as *Truth and Method).* In contrast to hermeneutical theory, philosophical hermeneutics took the position that interpretations are not decidable (Connolly and Keutner 1988). In other words, understanding is not the objective re-cognition of an author's intended meaning. Instead, understanding is a practical task in which the interpreter is changed by becoming aware of new possibilities of what it is to be a human being.

Another aspect of philosophical hermeneutics that is different from hermeneutical theory is a movement away from an epistemology of subject-interpreting-object – a legacy of Cartesian subject-object dualism. Instead, attention shifts to an ontology of the interpreter in the continuous act of coming-into-understanding.

"Critical hermeneutics" emerged in response to philosophical hermeneutics. It is closely related to critical theory (see Murray and Ozanne 1991) and diverges from philosophical hermeneutics most notably in its recognition of systemic distortion of [pre-] understanding (i.e., false consciousness) and in its use of analytic procedures (e.g., psychoanalysis, neo-Marxian analysis) to remove this distortion. Jürgen Habermas (1980) and Karl-Otto Apel (1984) argued that uncritical acceptance of [pre] understanding could perpetuate the exclusion of past suppressed interests. Furthermore, the recognition of the linguisticality of understanding by philosophical hermeneutics does not acknowledge that language is also a medium of domination. Thus, the critical thinkers developed theory and techniques that address power interests and systemic distortions of understanding.

The most recent version of hermeneutics to emerge is "phenomenological hermeneutics." It is claimed by its proponents to bridge hermeneutical theory, philosophical hermeneutics, and critical hermeneutics (Bleicher 1980; Valdés 1987). Based primarily on the work of Paul Ricoeur, phenomenological hermeneutics mediates between a recapture of an objective sense of the text and an existential appropriation of its meaning into understanding. Semiotic-structural analysis acts to show how the text works and what it says before this sense of it is used to give insights into the interpreter's own situation.

In our account of hermeneutic philosophy, we emphasize philosophical hermeneutics informed by certain insights from critical and phenomenological hermeneutics. We describe the tenets of hermeneutic philosophy and show how these relate to implicit or explicit assumptions of critical theory and various interpretive approaches.

## Tenets of Hermeneutic Philosophy

### [Pre-] understanding and Prejudice

A concept emphasized in hermeneutic philosophy is [pre-]understanding. It has also been described as prejudice or pre-judgment. [Pre-]understanding follows from the recognition that, prior to any interpretation, we and the object of our interpretation exist. In advance of any reflection, we belong to a cultural world. Heidegger designated this relationship "being-in-the-world" (Bleicher [1980, p. 118], citing Heidegger [1949]).

The implication of being-in-the-world is that the interpreter and that which is interpreted are linked by a context of tradition – the accumulation of the beliefs, theories, codes, metaphors, myths, events, practices, institutions, and ideologies (as apprehended through language) that precede the interpretation. While taken for granted, ordinarily unnoticed, and never made fully explicit, tradition nonetheless weaves together the interpreter and that which is interpreted. Even prior to interpretation, the boundary between the two is incomplete because of the tradition that they mutually know and constitute.

Philosophical hermeneutics stresses that [pre-] understanding enables rather than constrains the interpreter. In anyone's experience, things are either familiar or strange only because there is a starting or reference point, or what Gadamer (1989) termed "prejudice." Prejudice is not necessarily unjustified or erroneous. In fact, prejudice is our window on the world, our base for recognition and comparison. Without prejudice, it would not be possible to make sense of the events and objects we observe or to find meaning in the words and actions of others.

[Pre-]understanding or prejudice is continually being realized and worked out. In the trial-and-error, dialectic nature of inquiry, [pre-]understanding's adequacy to encompass the subject matter is continually tested. When things, events, objects, words, or actions seem alien, puzzling, or contradictory, [pre-]understanding is challenged to change.

The [pre-]understanding of consumer researchers is found in two interrelated traditions – experience as a consumer and experience as a researcher. If we, for instance, knew nothing of shopping in modern stores with complex arrays of merchandise, of the artistry and imagination that inform advertising, or of the complex emotions associated with gift giving, we could not begin to make sense of the many phenomena we study. Philosophical hermeneutics counsels us to capitalize more fully on [pre-]understanding rather than trying to put it aside when we take up our research.

[Pre-]understanding also results from knowledge of accumulated theories and research findings concerning consumer behavior. Our theoretical knowledge of attitudes, learning, socialization, and other consumer behavior concepts gives us an additional basis for making sense of consumer behavior. We acknowledge that the enterprise of seeking such insight is shaped by our particular temporally, socially, and culturally conditioned [pre-]understanding of our subject and of science in general. We do not put this prejudice aside but instead use it to construct a coherent account.

Hermeneutics' emphasis on [pre-]understanding is paralleled in the doctrine that informs Mick's (1986) semiotics, some forms of structuralism (see, e.g., Hirschman 1988),[1] and the more integrative forms of literary criticism (see Stern 1989). Semiotics "insists on an ongoing reflexivity where the researcher's presuppositions – prior beliefs, theories, models, metaphors, etc. – are regarded as integral to the inquiry's outcome" (Mick 1986, p. 208). Mick's tutorial on semiotics stresses the importance of tacit knowledge, both as what shapes the researcher and as what the researcher seeks to learn about.

McCracken's (1988) second step in the "qualitative research circle" (p. 29) of the long interview is the "review of cultural categories" (p. 32). This step involves a review of the researcher's personal experience as it relates to the topic of investigation. Associations, incidents, and assumptions are identified and considered as the self is made an instrument of inquiry.

Other research approaches seem to regard [pre-]understanding largely as an obstacle to be overcome. In critical theory, [pre-]understanding is regarded with suspicion and is overcome if dogma is discerned. While naturalistic inquiry acknowledges that the research team is an instrument and that inquiry is not value free, some accounts advocate the use of external auditors and member checking. Prejudice is regarded as distorting the researchers' apprehension of the informants' reality; the researcher-as-instrument in this view is to function as a conduit for the meaning of the informants rather than as a co-constituter of that meaning. Similarly, in existential phenomenology, while it is acknowledged that multiple interpretations are possible, effort is made to bracket (hold in abeyance) the researchers' prejudices.

Hermeneutic philosophers acknowledge the limitations in each person's [pre-]understanding but place the emphasis on its enabling role and advocate drawing as consciously as possible on [pre-]understanding as a starting point for interpretation. Moreover, they do not believe it is possible to penetrate the subjectivity of the other and seek instead to move beyond the subject-object distinction in acknowledging that all understanding is a product, in part, of the interpreter's [pre-]understanding.

### Ideal of the Dialogic Community

An ideal to be striven for in hermeneutic philosophy is the dialogic community. A dialogic community shares [pre-]understanding mediated through language. The community is characterized by a sense of collective identity and by voluntary participation in purposive social action. This action is grounded in dialogue – conversation where participants listen as well as speak and accept other points of view as worthy of consideration (Bernstein 1983; Gadamer 1989, p.385). They have the "good will" to try to understand one another.

The community plays both a constitutive and a regulative role. Through dialogue, the community collectively creates new understanding. As a part of this process, the community responds to emergent interpretations without subscribing to a correspondence view of truth. New interpretations are evaluated with the goal of better taking up another's perspective as opposed to deciding whether the statements are moving closer to or further from "Truth" (Valdés 1987, p. 55). The imperative in the term "regulative" is on being open to the other as opposed to performing a gatekeeper role.

Consumer research comes closest to the ideal of dialogic community in the "invisible college," the give-and-take of an academic seminar, the exchanges in a conference special session, and the double-blind review process of a peerrefereed journal. In the case of a journal, the dialogic community is composed of the editor, members of the editorial board, occasional reviewers, and readers of the journal. Dialogue is represented in the submission of a manuscript and successive iterations of reviewer and author responses until consensus is achieved. Members of this community author new manuscripts and play a regulative role.

This tenet may be related to the assumptions underlying critical theory. In some versions of critical theory the notions of "general symmetry" and the "ideal speech situation," where all participants have an equal chance to engage in unrestrained discourse (see Murray and Ozanne 1991, pp. 132, 141–142), are directly related to the tenet of a dialogic community. These ideas are rooted in a common intellectual heritage – they share an emphasis on the linguistic nature of understanding and on the need for iteration in interpretation.

The difference between the two traditions concerns the respective views of the dialogic community. Whereas hermeneutic philosophers focus on the constitutive creative potential of the dialogic community, the emphasis in critical theory is on the hazards of power differences in constraining dialogic interchange. Critical theorists regard general symmetry and the ideal speech situation as guides or standards that should be striven for but that cannot be sustainedly achieved. It is only when power differences are removed that critical theory acknowledges the reconstructive potential of the dialogic community. The idealism of hermeneutics is like that of liberal democracy; in the practice of both, the constitutive creative potential is not always realized, but this potential is realized with sufficient frequency to lend credibility to pursuit of the ideal.

The tenet of the dialogic community also bears some relationship to a methodological feature of existential phenomenology identified by Thompson *et al.* (1989): the "interpretive group." They suggest that, among other benefits, a group effort at interpretation may be useful since a group may collectively see patterns not recognized by any single researcher. Although this is a methodological edict, it appears to point to an assumption of existential phenomenology ("people who share a common interest [may serve] ... a recognition function" [Thompson *et al.* 1989, p. 141]) similar to an implication of hermeneutics (people who share [pre-]understanding are more likely to make similar interpretations of the same text. Conversely, people with different [pre-]understanding are more likely to create dissimilar interpretations).

The use of external auditors in naturalistic inquiry (Belk *et al.* 1988) or humanistic inquiry (Hirschman 1986),[2] while apparently similar at the operational level to the idea of the dialogic community in philosophical hermeneutics, differs in a crucial way. External auditors are advocated in these approaches as a means of ensuring that "findings [flow] from the data rather than being imposed by the biases of the inquirers" (Belk *et al.* 1988, p. 456) or that an "interpretation is drawn in a logical and unprejudiced manner" (Hirschman 1986, p. 246). Philosophical hermeneutics does *not* regard [pre-]understanding as a constraint to be overcome; moreover, it would argue that "findings" should and must "flow from the interpreter" in the sense that the interpreter's [pre-]understanding is a crucial element of interpretation.

### Linguisticality of Understanding

Hermeneutic philosophy stresses that "language is the universal medium in which understanding occurs" (Gadamer 1989, p. 389). Through language, experience is filtered, encoded, and communicated in dialogue. It bridges past and present, interpreter and text; it conveys and propels tradition.

There is no perspective outside language from which to view language as an object (Bernstein 1983; Gadamer 1989, p. 452; Rorty 1989). Gadamer's (1989) statement "Being that can be understood is language" (p. 474) implies that language always shapes and constrains our experience of the world. There is no world outside of language to be discovered with language as a tool; language is the world we know. This universality of understanding is always partial, and our language determines that partiality or horizon of prejudice.

Taking into account this linguisticality of understanding, Heidegger (1949) stresses that it is not possible to appropriate a text's meaning by an attempt at neutrality. In advance of any interpretation, the interpreter belongs to the world and, as a consequence, has inherited [pre-] understanding mediated by language.

The assumption that understanding is linguistic is largely shared by the various language- or sign-based approaches to studying consumer behavior that include structuralism (Levy 1981), semiotics (Mick 1986), and some of the integrative approaches to literary criticism (Stern 1989). The linguisticality of understanding is not discussed in consumer research representations of existential phenomenology (Thompson *et al.* 1989), naturalistic-humanistic inquiry (Belk *et al.* 1989; Hirschman 1986), or critical theory (Murray and Ozanne 1991).

### Nonobjectivist

We share tradition, but we do not all share all elements of tradition. The world we know is the language we use. As a consequence, our [pre-]understanding sensitizes us to certain issues and not to others. The lens through which we view texts both highlights and obscures particular components. There is never any one, or objective, understanding of a text. Rather, there are many; no one understanding can embody all the elements of tradition.

This does not, however, mean that all interpretations are equally persuasive. The emergent consensus of the dialogic community confers greater authority on some interpretations than on others. The impossibility of an objective interpretation implies that, while some interpretations will be judged superior to others, multiple interpretations are possible, and no interpretation can ever claim to be final or correct (Madison 1989). Note that this means hermeneutic philosophy is not consistent with extreme relativism; rather, as Madison argues, it is consistent with our everyday understanding that "there is more than one side to every story" and that all understanding is perspectival.

To a greater or lesser extent, most of the research approaches being compared here to hermeneutics share this underlying tenet. In existential phenomenology, for instance, Thompson, Locander, and Pollio (1990) argue that "texts are always open to multiple interpretations" (p. 347); however, they stress that not all interpretations are equally adequate in describing respondent perspectives (the goal of existential phenomenology). Likewise, humanistic and naturalistic inquiry are based on non-objectivist assumptions. Hirschman (1986) observes that "research inquiry is inherently value-laden because researcher values inevitably influence the choice of *phenomenon*, choice of *method*, choice of *data*, and choice of *findings*" (p. 238). She states that "the humanist approach denies the possibility of discovering objective truth" (1986, p. 242). Similarly, Mick, in explicating semiotics, states that "objectivity is impossible: theories precede facts and interpretation precedes perception," and that "the cybernetic matrix of the symbol-human environment will not permit us to arrive at the truth" (1986, pp. 207, 209). And, while the literary criticism approaches outlined by Stern (1989) vary considerably, in few of them is there "one right reading" of a text. According to critical theorists, "facts cannot be separated from values" (Murray and Ozanne 1991, p. 131). Although reality is thereby socially constructed, it can then be objectified in constraining social structures.

### Understanding

According to hermeneutic philosophy, understanding is not what we believe we learn about the other from the text. As we derive a sense of the text, our own self-knowledge is changed. As Ricoeur says: "To understand *is to understand oneself in front of the text*" (Ricoeur 1981, p. 143; emphasis in the original). Hermeneutic understanding is in part self-understanding, self-reflection, and self-development.

Interpretation of a text involves the explication, the clarification, and the working out of the possibilities of our existence as humans. We appropriate for ourselves new alternatives and project into our own lives their potential. "Thus it is true in every case that a person who understands, understands himself [or herself] *(sich versteht)*, projecting himself [or herself] upon his [or her] possibilities" (Gadamer 1989, p. 260).

Hermeneutical understanding has an ontological status (Gadamer 1989, p. 293). The ontological status of understanding in hermeneutic philosophy refers to the nature of human beings, which is one of always trying to understand. We are in a continuous state of coming into understanding; "understanding is always in the process of being concretized" (Gadamer 1989, p. 476). Understanding is reflected in interpretation(s). This insight is opposed to the position of hermeneutical theory that interpretation leads to understanding. Instead, "interpretation is the explicit form of understanding" (Gadamer 1989, p. 307).

In the continuous process of understanding, the boundary between subject and object is transcended. As researchers who are humans (and consumers), we are simultaneously trying to understand the other as well as be an other who is being understood. The stranger becomes familiar and is constituted into our comprehension of humanity (and consumption). Thus, hermeneutical philosophy moves beyond the dichotomies that surfaced in Enlightenment thinking between objectivism and relativism, mind and body, and subject and object (see Bernstein 1983).

This transcendence of the subject-object dichotomy has an important implication for what is meant by "self" in "self-understanding." The self is neither the object, for example, the informant, nor the subject, for example, the researcher. Following Apel (1984, p. 239), the self is the "ideal communication community." We can equate this meaning narrowly to the dialogic community and broadly to the human community to which we all belong.

Hermeneutic self-understanding is not a detached, pregiven theory, principle, or universal to be applied without change again and again to various issues (Gadamer 1989, p. 341). Instead, hermeneutic understanding is an action-oriented, practical-moral knowledge brought to, and derived from, a specific situation or problem. An example adopted from Gadamer (1989, pp. 310, 325) illustrates this aspect of hermeneutic understanding: a judge is required to render a judgment regarding an alleged violation of the law. The judge approaches the text of the law with [pre-]understanding in the form of accumulated precedent, related judgements, and past experience. In deciding the outcome of the case, the law is interpreted, [pre-]understanding is modified, and understanding of the law is advanced. The meaning of the law and the meaning of the specific case are codetermined. This understanding provides the basis for [pre-]understanding for the next case. "We consider application to be just as integral a part of the hermeneutical process as are understanding and interpretation" (Gadamer 1989, p. 308).

Hermeneutic understanding is different from explanation (Apel 1984). Explanation abstracts from experience. Theoretical constructs are distilled from lived experience and linked together in a reductionist, Hempelian nomological net. Underlying causal laws and principles are assumed in the search for "Nature's Own Vocabulary" (Rorty 1982, p. 192). A hermeneutic perspective on understanding, by contrast, assumes many vocabularies, which include the vocabulary of explanation. Vocabularies are revised as new words and metaphors are formed and old ones die away. Explanation's vocabulary is seen to be just one more vocabulary for creating narratives by which humans tell stories about themselves.

This relationship between explanation and understanding is similar to the relationship between a map of a city and an inhabitant's description of the city (Packer 1985). A map abstracts city elements at a point in time and presents them as a related system of objects. An account of city life by an inhabitant is a reflection on the accumulations of discovery and experience. It is "a system of possibilities and resources, frustrations and obstacles, and two people will find both commonalities and differences in their accounts of it" (Packer 1985, p. 1092). Understanding brings to consciousness those possibilities of being that explanation, by reason of its abstraction, conceals and closes off.

Hermeneutic understanding is not the same as *Verstehen*. *Verstehen* is seeing "the world from an insider's perspective" (Hudson and Ozanne 1988, p. 511). It assumes the ability to appropriate the life experience of the other: to relive it, reproduce it, coincide with it, and empathize with it. It has an "objective-idealist form" (Bleicher 1980, p. 271).

In contrast to *Verstehen*, hermeneutical understanding does not assume that a "true" meaning exists or, even if it did, that it could be apprehended. It is inappropriate to think of "somebody's own account of his [or her] behavior or culture as epistemically privileged" (Rorty 1982, p. 202). This account is just as much an interpretation as will be our account of his or her account.

Other "fallacious views" of hermeneutical understanding described by Ricoeur (1981, pp. 191-193) include trying to describe the original audience's understanding of the text such as would be done if we tried to describe how consumers of another era responded to an advertisement of that time. Another nonhermeneutic view is that the meaning of the text is subsumed into the [pre-]understanding of the reader without changing that understanding. In hermeneutic understanding, there must be observed some shift, change, or expansion of the horizon or frame of reference of the interpreter.

Hermeneutic understanding is partially consistent with that implicit in semiotics and structuralism, some of the integrative forms of literary criticism (see Stern 1989), and naturalistic-humanistic inquiry. For instance, in Levy's (1981) use of structuralism, "a protocol in which a consumer tells the story of how the product is consumed can be examined for how the consumer interprets the consumption experience, what it tells about people related to consumption ... and what the instance explains about the general nature of consuming" (p. 50).

In this description, hermeneutic understanding could occur in either the experience of the consumer in a specific consumption-related instance ("how the consumer interprets the consumption experience") or when the researcher realizes an insight in working with the protocol ("what the instance explains about the possible nature of consuming"). The difficulty in being able to explicate the first kind of understanding, consumer self-understanding, is that we are removed from it by levels of interpretation. There is a first level of interpretation that occurs in the consumer's original experience. There is a second level of interpretation when the consumer recalls the experience for the researcher and creates the protocol. There is a third level of interpretation when the researcher interprets the protocol. Rather than claiming to have penetrated these dense layers of interpretations to describe consumer self-understanding, it seems easier to describe what I (the researcher) or we (the research team) believe *we* (the dialogic or human community) have learned about the nature of consumer behavior. The researcher could say either "I think what we have learned here is that..." or "As compared to what our literature said about this phenomenon, our understanding has been revised as follows."

Naturalistic-humanistic inquiry likewise appears to be underpinned by different views of understanding, some of which are consistent with that of hermeneutics. For instance, Belk *et al.* (1988) note that the research team seeks to understand an activity from the perspective of the participants, and eventually moves from this to "themes that organize the way in which analysts and informants perceive" the activity (p. 458). Analytically organized themes would appear to be understanding of ourselves as consumers through the realization of other modes of consuming.

Hermeneutic philosophy's view of understanding is more at odds with that implicit in existential phenomenology. In this approach, the understanding that is sought is simply that of the "lived experience" of the individual (Thompson *et al.* 1989, p. 139) or *Verstehen.* Self-understanding seems neither explicitly nor implicitly a part of the understanding that is to be achieved.

Similarly, in critical theory, it is regarded as possible to understand the perspective of the multiple "others" who are stakeholders in a concrete problem. Critical researchers "are successful to the extent that they come to see and talk about the world as the social actors do... . By grasping the social actors' view of the world ... the researcher hopes to understand social action" (Murray and Ozanne 1991, p. 137).

## Implications of Hermeneutic Philosophy for Consumer Research

Some researchers have referred to hermeneutics as a method that might be compared to phenomenology (see, e.g., Murray and Ozanne 199 1, Fig. 1, p. 130). An important difference, however, is that, in comparison to those for phenomenology (see, e.g., Thompson *et al.* 1989), there exist no detailed and explicit guidelines for *the* hermeneutic method. Gadamer (1989, p. xxviii) emphasizes that his intent was not to elaborate a methodical procedure for the human sciences. Hermeneutic philosophy might be consistent with many alternative methodological approaches. For instance, Schouten's (1991) investigation of "selves in transition" and Belk's (1988) study of the "extended self" differ dramatically in methodological details. Yet both are highly consistent with hermeneutic philosophy. Both draw on [pre-]understanding to interpret a range of materials and both end up with new [self-]understanding. For instance, Belk suggests, "*Our* accumulation of possessions provides a sense of past and tells us who we are, where we have come from, and perhaps where we are going" (1988, p. 160; emphasis added).

Although there is no specific hermeneutic methodology, it is possible to identify and illustrate features of an approach to consumer research that are consistent with hermeneutic philosophy. These features concern the nature and autonomy of the text, semiotic-structural analysis, hermeneutic circle, fusion of horizons, and critical response. In the remainder of this section, we will describe each of these features and compare them, where possible, to the assumptions and features of interpretive and critical research. Table 1 adapts Murray and Ozanne's (1991) comparative framework to summarize and contrast these features.

Reference to McCracken's (1991) interpretation of the original version of Michael Jackson's *Black and While* music video (App. B) provides a convenient way of illustrating our exposition.'[3]

### Nature of the "Text"

The existential orientation of hermeneutic philosophy suggests that the texts to be studied will represent the contextualized personal expressions of an individual consumer. While early versions of hermeneutics would suggest that these texts be written, philosophical hermeneutics' emphasis on ontological understanding may lead to the study of a broader variety of textual forms. Forms originating with the consumer include interview transcripts, verbal protocols, and audiovisual recordings. Photographs and artifacts may also form the basis for an interpretation. McCracken's text is a music video. The common characteristic of these "texts" is the opportunity to be able to return to them again and again. Texts are "enduringly fixed expressions of life" (Gadamer [1989, p. 3871, citing Droysen [1937, p. 63]).

In published consumer research, the texts most readily recognizable as candidates for hermeneutic assessment are those studied by linguistically based research approaches, such as semiotics, structuralism, and most types of literary criticism. A hermeneutic approach, however, could also be applied to the texts of interviews used as data in naturalistic-humanistic inquiry, existential phenomenology, and critical theory. The field notes collected in naturalistic-humanistic inquiry are, in effect, the first iteration of interpretation.

### Autonomy of the Text

It is consistent with hermeneutic philosophy to believe that, once authored or recorded, a text assumes a life of its own. That is, it can lead to understanding that does not coincide with what the author or actor meant. It can generate insight that the author did not realize. This potential makes the interpretation much different than some "objective" re-cognition of the author's intended meaning. McCracken (App. B) acknowledges he cannot recover Michael Jackson's intended meaning in the violent smashing of car and shop windows, saying: "The significance of this? We can't know."

Methodological emphasis on the autonomy of the text is common to semiotic and structural approaches, and to text and reader-focused and integrative forms of literary criticism (but not author-focused literary criticism). In naturalistic inquiry, texts are regarded as autonomous in that "there is no attempt to corroborate a respondent's description" (Thompson *et al.* 1989, p. 140); however, the text is not autonomous from its "author" in that it is precisely the author's unique perspective (their lived experience) that the analysis attempts to uncover. Similarly, in humanistic-naturalistic inquiry, the "texts" created are treated as representative of, not autonomous from, informants.

In critical methodology, texts may be regarded as partially autonomous. That is, as the critical researcher searches for "contradictions between intersubjective understanding and objective social conditions" (Murray and Ozanne 1991, p. 136), the text (of an interview, for instance) may be regarded as a reflection of something more or different from that which the informant intended.

### Semiotic-Structural Analysis

To account for the linguisticality of understanding, it is necessary to give close reading to the language (or other signifiers, such as pictures or gestures) of the text. Nonobjectivist semiotic and structural analyses serve this end (see n. 1). Semiotic analysis focuses on meaning-producing events (Eco 1976; Innes 1985; Sebeok 1976). A fundamental concept in semiotics is the *sign* – a symbol, icon,

**Table 1** Alternative Approaches to Consumer Research

| Research process | Interpretivism | Critical theory | Hermeneutics |
|---|---|---|---|
| Initial stage | Identification of a general phenomenon of interest | Identification of a concrete practical problem | Concern with a specific situation or problem |
| | Phenomenon's boundaries are left open and undelineated | Identification of all groups involved with this problem | |
| Data collection stage: General structure | "Bracketing" of prior conceptions | The interpretive step: construction of an inter-subjective understanding of each group | Reflexivity re [pre-]understanding: recognition of own horizon and the enabling role of prejudice |
| | Immersion in a natural setting for an extended time period | The historical-empirical step: examination of the historical development of any relevant social structures or processes | Review of tradition in human activities and research literature |
| | Design, questions, and sampling strategies evolve as phenomenon is studied | The dialectical step: search for contradictions between the intersubjective understanding and the objective social conditions | Semiotic-structural analysis: determination of the horizon of the text what it says and how it works<br>Hermeneutical circle: Resolution of contradictions among and between elements and the larger whole of the text |
| | Reliance on the human instrument for generating "thick description" | The awareness step: discuss alternative ways of seeing their situation with the repressed group(s) | Fusion of horizons: recast [pre-]understanding to encompass sense of the text |
| | Content or textual analysis to yield an interpretation | The praxis step: participate in a theoretically grounded program of action to change social conditions | Understanding: insight into self and recognition of new practical-moral way in which to act |
| Standard data – gathering techniques | Participant observation<br>In-depth interviews | In-depth interviews<br>Historical analysis | Autonomous text |
| Sample evaluative criteria | Length of immersion and creation of thick description | Improvement of quality of life | Persuasiveness of rhetoric<br>Consensus of dialogic community |

*Source*. – This table was adapted from Murray and Ozanne (1991, p. 136).

or index. The text is regarded as a system of signs and the analysis focuses on the relationships between the signs (syntactics), as well as the relationships between the signs and the objects to which they refer (semantics).

Structural analysis (Kurzweil 1980) is closely related to semiotics, especially in its identification of relationships between signs. Of particular interest are oppositional relationships, such as masculinity versus femininity, which rely for their meaning on their opposition to one another and which represent ways in which thinking is organized. Structuralists recognize that signs have many meanings; they limit the range of possibilities by seeking an inner logic on the basis of the distinctions drawn and relationships recognized between symbols used in human expressions.

In McCracken's (1991) interpretation of *Black and White*, he analyzes both lyrics ("I don't care if you're black or white") and visual images ("We see a mesmerizing succession of men and women, perhaps 10 in all. By a trick of the camera, one face literally becomes another. A white woman becomes a black man, who becomes a white man, who becomes an Asian woman").

He parses the symbolism of these words and images in context of one another, stating "This is Ovid made contemporary. This is the new Metamorphosis… . In a few seconds of video, all the distinctions of culture, race and gender disappear. Every difference is negotiable. We are all merely versions of one another."

McCracken also pays keen attention to opposites. He plays with the notion that, in this video, Jackson represents himself as having moved beyond the oppositional categories by which we traditionally define ourselves and others: "He is no longer black. He is not really white. He is no longer male. He is not quite female."

The semiotic-structural aspect of the hermeneutic approach has, obviously, much in common with semiotics as described by Mick (1986), structuralism as outlined by Levy (1981), as well as by Hirschman (1988), and the structuralist form of literary criticism as summarized by Stern (1989). It is probably fair to say that a more detailed and technical semiotic-structural analysis would often be found in applications of these latter methodologies than would a hermeneutic analysis, since an explanation of the way specific sets of signs make certain meanings may be their endpoint. Semiotic-structural analyses as such are not a core element of existential phenomenology or naturalistic-humanistic inquiry.

### Hermeneutic Circle

The idea of a hermeneutic circle, or iterative spiral of understanding, is central to hermeneutic philosophy. This idea has been widely seized upon by various interpretive researchers seeking to describe the back and forth, specific-general-specific movement of interpretation. The term "hermeneutic circle" represents the idea that the meaning of a whole text is determined from the individual elements of a text, while, at the same time, an individual element is understood by referring to the whole of which it is a part (Bernstein 1983). Specific elements are examined again and again, each time with a slightly different conception of the global whole. Gradually, an ever more integrated and comprehensive account of the specific elements, as well as of the text as a whole, emerges.

An individual element in the whole is not unlike a word in a sentence. By itself, the word may communicate little, especially since words have multiple meanings. In the context of a sentence, however, the sense of the word becomes apparent. In addition, the word contributes to the meaning of the sentence.

The objective of hermeneutic circling is to achieve an understanding free of contradictions. This is an important goal to achieve because contradictions are often overlooked as being minor errors or aberrations. The interpreter must persist until, eventually, an account is derived in which all passages in the text are woven into a coherent interpretation. At this point, it is often found that certain portions of the text, originally thought to be understood, have changed their meaning (Bernstein 1983).

In McCracken's interpretation (see App. B), his first pass at interpreting the lyrics "I don't care if you're black or white" and the images of Jackson surrounded by Africans, Thais, North Americans, South Asians, and Russians is as follows: "At first glance, this looks like another cliché: rock musician calls for international understanding (yawn), Michael Jackson doing his version of 'I'd like to buy the world a Coke.'" The notion that the video's multiracial theme is a cliché reflects how McCracken's [pre-]understanding shapes the way he approaches the text.

In the process of hermeneutic circling, however, McCracken comes to interpret the passage in a different way. In his revised interpretation, he realizes that Jackson "isn't using these cultures as exotica. No, he skips from culture to culture because he now belongs in all of them." He also appears to draw on this reinterpretation of the specific lyrics and images noted above when he summarizes his interpretation of the boundary breaking message of the entire video by saying that Jackson "is experimenting in cultural definitions we may some day embrace."

The dialectical tacking of the hermeneutic circle does not necessarily have to appear in the written interpretation. It appears in McCracken's account as a useful rhetorical device. It is usually not so transparent.

The hermeneutic circle is also explicitly claimed to be a tool of existential phenomenology (Thompson *et al.* 1989, 1990). Semiotic-structural, literary criticism, and naturalistic-humanistic approaches may also incorporate iterative movements back and forth between elements of data and the entire body of data in creating an interpretation that is ever more complete. Critical researchers would be less likely to draw on circling techniques to resolve apparent inconsistencies or contradictions in data; they would tend more to regard these as evidence of the tensions between subjective understanding and objective social conditions (Murray and Ozanne 1991).

### Fusion of Horizons

Both literally and figuratively, everything that is "visible" from a particular vantage point is the horizon (Gadamer 1989, p. 302). Both the interpreter and the text (representative of the other) have a horizon. It is in the fusion of horizons that the subject-object dichotomy is transcended.

The horizon of the interpreter is his or her [pre-]understanding. The horizon of the text is its sense discerned through semiotic-structural analysis and progressive iterations of the hermeneutical circle. The interpreter's horizon is finite but neither limiting nor closed. When the interpreter moves or changes position through developing understanding, his or her horizon moves as well. Fusion of horizons implies that the horizon of the interpreter comes to encompass or integrate the discerned horizon of the text. In the process, [pre-]understanding is changed until it is able to account for the sense of the text. [Pre-]understanding becomes understanding.

This fusion of horizons is evident in McCracken's response to his interpretation of the video. He states (App. B): "Plainly this [loosening conventional definitions of culture] is a personal project for Michael Jackson. Something in his own biography made him wish to evade traditional gender and racial categories. But, just as plainly, something in us responds to this. The cultural categories of race and gender are constantly being written and rewritten in our society, and we marvel at his definitional versatility. In a changing society, he is a metamorph and, to this extent, an exemplar."

The implications of hermeneutics' emphasis on fusion of horizons and the breakdown of the subject-object dichotomy is that a hermeneutic interpretation makes statements about the collective "self." Geertz (1988) suggests research of this nature can "open (a bit) the consciousness of one group of people to (something of) the life-form of another, and in that way to (something of) their own" (p. 143). As Bernstein (1983) stresses, it is only through efforts to sharpen our understanding of the other that we gain deeper understanding of ourselves. The process of hermeneutic interpretation, then, does lead to generalizations *of a sort.* These generalizations will not be factlike statements or causal explanations of human behavior; rather, they will be reflective insights not so much about the other as about a collective human community.

McCracken's conclusions (see App. B), on the basis of his interpretation, are that "We are all beginning to see that transformation will be the theme of the 21st century, which will force us out of the old pattern of stasis-change into continual change. The future will be a place of relentless transformation.... Michael Jackson is, in his way, an astonishing creator of culture. His *Black and White* gives us a glimpse of some of the remarkable things that await us in the next century."

### Critical Response

The nonobjectivity of hermeneutics and the linguisticality of understanding mean there is no one single or correct interpretation (Gadamer 1989, p. 397). A hermeneutic interpretation, however, is similar to other products of human talent and will be subject to a range of accomplishment. How does the reviewer differentiate better from worse interpretations?

The reviewer's response to a hermeneutic interpretation is not unlike the critical review of an artistic performance (Bernstein 1983, pp. 124–125; Gadamer 1989, p. 191) and suggests several features. An artistic performance has both technical and artistic elements. Reviewing the conduct of the semiotic-structural analysis or the adequacy of the literature review would seem like judging technical ability. Responding to claims of understanding would be akin to judging artistic rendition.

This analogy suggests several points the critical reviewer might consider when responding to a hermeneutic interpretation:

- The interpretation must be coherent and free of contradiction. Themes must be documented. Observations should be supported with relevant examples.
- A command of the relevant literature will be evident. Tradition must be acknowledged.
- The interpretation should be comprehensible to the reading audience, given their [pre-]understanding. It should show "good will" by adapting to them and taking into account their world view.
- The interpretation should "enlighten." It is "fruitful" in revealing new dimensions of the problem at hand. "[W]hat is evident is always something surprising as well, like a new light being turned on," says Gadamer (1989, p. 486). It yields insight that leads to revision of [pre-]understanding. This revision should be made quite explicit.
- The prose should be persuasive, engaging, interesting, stimulating, and appealing (McCloskey 1983). Allusions, metaphors, similes, and analogies serve hermeneutics well. The cultural literacy of the authors will be apparent.

The last points emphasize the rhetorical nature of a hermeneutic interpretation, and that the selection among alternative interpretations is a matter of argumentation and debate (Thompson 1981, p. 53). "And so we see that the rhetorical and hermeneutical aspects of human linguisticality completely interpenetrate each other" (Gadamer 1976, p. 25). Rhetoric is argumentation aimed at the dialogic community. It covers all modes of discourse that aim at persuasion and conviction (Madison 1989; Perelman 1989).

McCracken's (1991) interpretation of Michael Jackson's *Black and White* video is a good one on all these counts. He draws explicitly on the words and images of the "text" to document specific themes. He creates an overall interpretation that is consistent and coherent. His prose is compelling as he leads the reader from an initial tendency toward jaded indifference through a grudging recognition of the nuances of the video's import to an enthusiastic appreciation. He addresses his intended general readership audience with both a terminology and a set of ideas to which they should easily relate, and builds on these ideas so as to draw his audience along with him to new insights. Whether, of course, these insights are "enlightening" to all members depends on their own [pre-]understanding.

Anyone attempting to evaluate a hermeneutic interpretation must accept that there may be a multiplicity of equally good or better readings. Different artists (or even the same artist at different times) perform distinct, but equally compelling, renditions of the same score or script. In an analogous way, the same text can continue to lead to new sources of understanding (Gadamer 1989, p. 298). It is possible, for instance, that someone else's reading of the *Black and White* video might attempt to make sense of those images that McCracken regards as "mystifying details of personal biography," those where Jackson smashes the windows of cars and shops.

As a way of illustrating the possibility of multiple readings, we provide a second interpretation of Michael Jackson's video (App. C). In contrast to McCracken's idea of transformation, this interpretation reads the video as a vilification of the persistence of racism.

We believe the second interpretation provides a complementary illustration of the features of a hermeneutic interpretation. Following from the notion of the autonomy of the text, we do not claim Michael Jackson's intention is to expose the threats of racism. In fact, with his wealth and power, it would be surprising if it were his aim. However, our structural analysis of the black-white opposition and our semiotic analysis of the black panther image and the physical actions in the latter part of the video lead us to see in the text a cry of outrage.

McCracken's interpretation expresses more satisfaction with the status quo; our interpretation urges change. The understandings yielded by the two readings thus differ starkly, yet each is grounded in the same text and uses demonstrably similar interpretive techniques.

## Challenges to Hermeneutic Philosophy

Any account of hermeneutics based on Gadamer's philosophical hermeneutics faces opposition from critical theorists and others (see, e.g., Apel 1984, pp. xviii–xix). We provide an admittedly simplified account of these views and the responses of hermeneuticians.

One concern of critical theorists is that the hermeneutic interpreter is "subject to the false consciousness of pseudonormal understanding" (Habermas 1980, p. 191). Critical theorists believe false consciousness occurs because there exists a causal system of empirical contingencies (i.e., social structures) that lie outside of consciousness. Both text and [pre-]understanding may be imbued with classism, sexism, racism, ethnocentrism, and speciesism – that is, domination. This potential is recognized in "systematically generated misunderstanding recognized as such – without, at first, being able to 'grasp' it" (Habermas 1980, p. 191). On this view, the idealism of hermeneutics renders it "blind to the perception of material factors that assert themselves 'behind the backs' of social actors" (Bleicher 1980, p. 175). Instead of self-understanding, it generates self-misunderstanding.

The response of hermeneuticians to the criticism of vulnerability to systemic [mis-]understanding is based on the tenet of the linguisticality of understanding. Gadamer's reply to Habermas would be that "in the mirror of language everything that exists is reflected" (Habermas [1980, p. 1987], citing Gadamer [1967, p. 1181]. The idea that there is a truth outside the mirror of language is inconsistent with hermeneutic understanding. Truth is a property of sentences, and sentences are parts of a human language. Since human languages are human creations, so is truth (Rorty 1989).

"Who denies that our specific human possibilities do not subsist solely in language?" adds Gadamer. "One would want to admit, instead, that every linguistic experience of the world is experience of the world, not experience of language" (Gadamer 1989, p. 546). Even domination is experienced in language. Once encountered, it presents itself to ourselves to be appropriated into hermeneutic understanding and, in turn, to become the [pre-]understanding of a subsequent interpretation. An illustration of this point comes in the second interpretation of the Michael Jackson video (App. C). This hermeneutic interpretation is partially informed by insights that a critical perspective, such as that introduced to consumer research by Rogers (1987) and Murray and Ozanne (1991), might generate. As critical perspectives are introduced, they become part of our [pre-]understanding and are likely to influence subsequent interpretations. Critiques of ideology are now part of our tradition and may well inform subsequent research. "We can no longer oppose hermeneutics and the critique of ideology. The critique of ideology is the necessary detour which self-understanding must take" (Ricoeur 198 1, p. 144).

A final response of hermeneuticians to the criticism of vulnerability to systemic [mis-]understanding relates to the consequences of the semiotic-structural analysis. This analysis acts to distance the interpreter from the text by focusing attention on how it works and what it says. It is another "detour" (Ricoeur 1981, p. 158) prior to engagement with [pre-]understanding and a subsequent fusion of horizons. The semiotic-structural analysis creates a kind of maneuvering space in which the interpreter is challenged to find a revision to his/her [pre-]understanding, such that it encompasses the sense of the text. In this way, prejudice, preconceptions, and illusions are critically reviewed (Bleicher 1980, p. 234).

A second concern of critical theorists is the dialogically constituted nature of hermeneutic interpretations. They regard as unacceptably context-dependent an argument that merely convinces a given dialogic community at a given time. They hold to the ideal that there exists independently a best argument or way – the ideal that has constantly propelled Enlightenment science and liberal social thought (Rorty 1985). Habermas rejected the claim that the Enlightenment project was dead and elaborated a universalistic philosophy of rationality he called communicative action or competence – "action oriented to mutual understanding" (Bernstein 1985, p. 3).

Michel Foucault (see Dreyfus and Rabinow 1982) and Jean-François Lyotard (see Lyotard 1984) argue against any form of global theorizing and reject Habermas's project. They see it as just another narrative, a "metanarrative," because of its claim to generalize in a more comprehensive theory what was accomplished by Marx, and Freud. They doubt that Habermas's theory can provide universalistic criteria and succeed where transcendental philosophy and all other similar attempts failed.

No metanarrative is needed, says Rorty (1985). "What is needed is a sort of intellectual analogue of civic virtue – tolerance, irony, and a willingness to let spheres of culture flourish without worrying too much about their 'common ground,' their unification, the 'intrinsic ideals' they suggest, or what picture of [humankind] they 'presuppose'" (p. 172).

This democracy of approaches has been adopted by some of those who have challenged hermeneutics. Apel (1984), for instance, legitimated the deductive-nomological and the critical-reconstructive, as well as the historical-hermeneutic, approaches. This "transcendental pragmatic" perspective converges remarkably with that of Bernstein (1983), who advocated movement beyond the objectivism-relativism dilemma with a merger of science (as it is practiced), hermeneutics, and praxis (moral practice). It is also consistent with Ricoeur (1981), who mediates between an objective sense of the text and hermeneutic understanding. Note that, in each of these schemas, dialogically constituted hermeneutic interpretations remain an essential element.

The implication of this convergence is the basis of an argument for pluralism in consumer research whether labeled "epistemic pluralism" (Madison 1989: p. 277) or "paradigmatic pluralism" (Sherry 1991, p. 572). In consumer research, positivist, interpretive, critical, and hermeneutic narratives can be sustained simultaneously.

## Conclusions

This exposition of hermeneutic philosophy has attempted to clarify what is both a ubiquitous and an illusive term. It has also permitted a comparison of the assumptions and features of hermeneutics, critical theory, and various interpretive research approaches. Finally, it has allowed us to emphasize the relatively unique features of hermeneutic interpretation: [pre-]understanding, the linguisticality of understanding, the autonomy of the text, the hermeneutic circle, the fusion of horizons, and self-understanding. Research that is not hermeneutic does not reflect these features or the tenets of nonobjectivism and the ideal of the dialogic community.

The incorporation of these ideas in consumer research would enable researchers to draw more consciously, critically, and powerfully on their own [pre-]understanding of the everyday phenomena that we study. We often treat commonplace behaviors, like bargain hunting, brand choice, and coupon usage as though we were not ourselves consumers. To be more explicit, drawing on and challenging our [pre-]understanding with regard to these phenomena, and regarding what we learn as insights into not only consumer behavior but our own lives as consumers, should serve to sharpen our instincts, heighten our humility, and increase our sense of moral ownership of the research that we do.

These insights can also extend into our lives as humans. Although our texts are about consumption, the self-understanding that is realized may involve family, community, and even the world to which we all belong. The reflexive nature of hermeneutics encourages us to consider our situation and to engage the dialogic community, no matter how broadly defined, with our insights. Hermeneutics makes us actors in the broader stage of social democracy.

Hermeneutic philosophy underdetermines the choice of methodological technique, the context of application, and the form of expression. Hermeneutic philosophy seeks to understand understanding as an ontological state, not to prescribe a method for interpreting texts in a set fashion. As such, it leaves the way open for methodological innovation in pursuit of the fusion of horizons and for paradigmatic pluralism as to what constitutes a legitimate form of expression. The method of hermeneutics is deeply democratic.

## Appendix A

Hermeneutics Terms in Consumer Research and Sources

| | |
|---|---|
| Hermeneutics | Mick 1986, p. 207; Murray and Ozanne 199 1, p. 130; O'Shaughnessy and Holbrook 1988, p. 197; Ryan and Bristor 1987, p. 191 |
| Hermeneutic circle | Hudson and Ozanne 1988, p. 5 10 |
| Hermeneutical circle | Thompson *et al.* 1989, p. 141 |
| Hermeneutical approach | Hirschman 1990, p. 31 |
| Hermeneutic logic | Holbrook and Grayson 1986, p. 374 |
| Hermeneutic analysis | Holbrook 1988, p. 55 |
| Hermeneutical tradition | O'Shaughnessy 1985, p. 305 |
| Hermeneutic fashion | Hirschman 1988, p. 352 |
| Hermeneutic endeavor | Thompson *et al.* 1990, p. 346. |

## Appendix B

Seeing the Future in Black and White

Last Thursday, all the world (well, about 500 million of us) tuned in to watch the new Michael Jackson video. We had to. After all, Michael Jackson's a wonder. He has sold more than 100 million records. A man with these numbers is important even when he's wrong. Even bad Michael Jackson is prime viewing.

The video *Black and White* is a funny mixture of elements. It begins with the silliest notion of rock 'n' roll: rock as scourge of the parent. This is the dumbest cliché and cheapest hook in an industry that excels in dumb and cheap. With beginnings as inauspicious as this, things look pretty grim. You knew the video couldn't get any worse. What, you wondered, if it didn't get any better?

The video's second theme was more promising. As Mr. Jackson sings and dances, he is magically transported from one culture to another. He is shown surrounded by Africans, Thais, North American aboriginals, South Asians and Russians. The lyric is "I don't care if you're black or white," and the theme is something like "cultural differences mean nothing in the face of human sameness."

At first glance, this looks like another cliché: rock musician calls for international understanding (yawn), Michael Jackson doing his version of "I'd like to buy the world a Coke." But then you get it. He isn't using these cultures as exotica. No, he skips from culture to culture because he now belongs in all of them. He is a fully international presence; all cultures are his province. One hundred and ten million records in the global village have seen to that.

The third theme is quite breathtaking. This part of the video is reputed to have cost $10,000 a second. It's worth every penny. We see a mesmerizing succession of men and women, perhaps 10 in all. By a trick of the camera, one face literally becomes another. A white woman becomes a black man, who becomes a white man, who becomes an Asian woman. Faces form and reform before your eyes. This is Ovid made contemporary. This is the new Metamorphosis.

No longer is Mr. Jackson flitting between cultures. He is dissolving them. And not just cultures. Now race and gender are dissolved as well. In a few seconds of video, all the distinctions of culture, race and gender disappear. Every difference is negotiable. We are all merely versions of one another. In the perfect mix of the Jackson video and the computer-controlled image, all men and women, all races, all cultures, are one.

This is not the first time Michael Jackson has warmed to the theme of metamorphosis. Indeed, you might say he has devoted his life to it. Growing up in the public eye, he was called upon to change continually as music, clothing and a fickle public changed.

But then he left the Jackson Five, and the real changes began. As a result of plastic surgery and bleaching, he has undergone further, more extraordinary metamorphoses. The object of this seems clear enough. He has deliberately transcended traditional notions of race and gender. He is no longer black. He is not really white. He is no longer male. He is not quite female. He loosened the conventional definitions of culture and escaped.

Plainly this is a personal project for Michael Jackson. Something in his own biography made him wish to evade traditional gender and racial categories. But, just as plainly, something in us responds to this. The cultural categories of race and gender are constantly being written and rewritten in our society, and we marvel at his definitional versatility. In a changing society, he is a metamorph and, to this extent, an exemplar. Michael Jackson has made himself a laboratory. He is experimenting in cultural definitions we may some day embrace.

More than that, we are all beginning to see that transformation will be the theme of the 21st century, which will force us out of the old pattern of stasis-change into continual change. The future will be a place of relentless transformation. There is a creature in *Terminator II* that becomes whatever it touches, illustrating one effortless, metamorphic shape of things to come. Michael Jackson illustrates another.

The "metamorphic" part of the video takes his own preoccupation and turns it into something more public, into something like art. It's the only time the video addresses anything with larger proportions. But this brush with art is short-lived. No sooner have we glimpsed it than we are again driven into the mystifying details of personal biography.

Michael Jackson, transformed into and then out of the shape of a panther, enters a ghetto street. He begins to dance. The dance is, as it always is with him, a demonstration of virtuoso control of the body. He is marionette under its own flawless control. But then comes violence. Suddenly he begins to smash the widows of cars and shops. Perfect control of the body turned into an inability to control the social self. Suddenly, he becomes an agent of anarchy and destruction.

The significance of this? We can't know. The video has once again descended from the public into the private. Perhaps this virtuoso of control secretly hates control. Perhaps this master of order is an anarchist. In any case, the video contains private and cryptic sentiments, ones that have so offended the public that Mr. Jackson has promised to take them out.

All in all, *Black and While is* a puzzle. The parts that work are powerful. The parts that don't are dreadful. What we know is that Mr. Jackson is a key fabricator of the global village, that his music and personas will help construct the international culture of the 21 st century.

Naturally, many of us are appalled at this. The idea that the new world order will be shaped by a man who has spent his life on the stage, lives as a recluse and regards Elizabeth Taylor as a formative intellectual influence is not a happy one. But this is too harsh. Michael Jackson is, in his way, an astonishing creator of culture. His *Black and White* gives us a glimpse of some of the remarkable things that await us in the next century.

Source: Grant MeCracken, "Seeing the Future in Black and White," *The Globe and Mail*, November 21, 1991.

## Appendix C

Black or White, Not Black and White

"It's not about races, it's about faces," sings Michael Jackson in his video *Black and White*. "I'm not going to spend my life being one color."

We watch with amazement as faces, male and female, black and white, Caucasian and Asian, blend into one another. These metamorphosing faces are a piece of cunning technological wizardry, which is typical of Jackson's sophisticated showmanship.

"It doesn't matter if you're black or white," he continues. We are persuaded that historical oppositions, such as those between races, are breaking down. Racial, gender, and ethnic boundaries can be transcended, not just between groups, but by individuals.

"Cut. That was perfect." says a voice on the video signaling a conclusion to the music but not to the visual images.

The gender- and race-blending face sequence ends. Our gaze wanders, and we are startled to discover a black panther brooding in the corner of the studio. It appears taut with silent rage. Discovered, the panther darts out the back door and down a flight of stairs. We follow it into a dark alley.

This new setting is definitely "off-stage." There is no music playing now. We are suddenly far from a clean and well-lit world of cheerful singing and dancing that celebrates the unimportance of racial boundaries. The only sound now is an occasional scream – or is that the panther's growl? – and the sound of the wind as it stirs up stray bits of newspaper. Steam rises from the sewer grates.

The panther metamorphoses into Michael Jackson. He begins to dance. At first the body movements are tightly controlled, almost as though Jackson were a puppet and some unseen hand controlled him. Jackson, despite his wealth and power, remains a black man. We see in his rigidity the shackles of social institutions constraining society's underprivileged groups. His "remote-controlled" dancing symbolizes the plight of those controlled by the strings of poverty, inadequate access to quality education and health care, and constrained job opportunities. Their fates are jerked about beyond their own control.

Jackson's movements are emblematic of one whose freedom is curtailed. He splashes up dirty water from a puddle–disturbing the smooth surface that belies a rank reality. He grabs his crotch, an aggressive taunt threatening physical harm. It says to us: "Hey! Fuck you!"

Jackson tap dances under a streetlight in a manner not unlike the famous "Singin' in the Rain" dance sequence. But there is an eerie difference. Instead of gentle music, we hear howling wind. And instead of hurdling dexterously over and around objects, Jackson deliberately kicks things in his path.

Jackson smashes the windows of a car with his hands. He jumps on its hood and smashes the wind-shield. He hurls the steering wheel of the ravaged car through the window of a nearby building. We feel directly threatened by his actions.

The scene makes us think of what it is to be marginalized. Like malevolent marionettes, the oppressed respond to their constraints in ways that hurt others – and themselves. These behaviors are unacceptable, but what are the alternatives? How else is it possible to obtain a vestige of power and control in a consumer society where one can never fully partake?

The final sequence of images reinforces the pervasive feeling of anger and despair. The camera on Jackson's face shows him grimace, seemingly with pain. He rips his clothes, rubbing his hands over his body with eyes closed, an expression of anguish on his face. He falls to his knees in a puddle, his clothes in tatters, his face contorted. As the filthy water threatens to drown him, Jackson becomes the panther again. The lyrics "It doesn't matter if you're black or white" are repeated for the last time.

We attempt to make sense of the seeming inconsistency of this final portion of the video. Are we to conclude that the violation of social norms is a futile gesture? Hostile behaviors may express one's sense of oppression, but they offer no chance of moving beyond the indignities associated with the categories into which one is born. No matter what society wishes us to believe, it matters a great deal whether you are black or white. The choices are still more constrained, the access to the "good life" still restricted.

In this light, the initial portion of the video can be seen to be a wishful fantasy or a poignant satire. We are not moving toward an egalitarian utopia where the American dream is equally accessible to all. For those who are members of marginalized groups, equity is a laughable myth.

The video as a whole is threatening. We understand that, despite the optimistic rhetoric and images, oppression, particularly racial oppression, is pervasive; moreover, this oppression is breeding a violent backlash that threatens social order. It suggests to us that, unless racial and other forms of oppression are addressed, disruptive violence (like that which occurred in Los Angeles after the first Rodney King trial) will persist and grow. The image of the black panther, symbol of the militant black rights group, has connotations quite different from the pleasant message in the lyrics of the song.

This may not be a message we all want to hear. The last segment of the video, which occurs after the music has ended and shows Jackson smashing cars and grabbing his crotch, was regarded as puzzling, inconsistent, and, above all, offensive by many of the millions who watched the video the evening it was first aired. In response to public outcry, Michael Jackson dropped the final portion of the video. All subsequent screenings have contained only the portion of the video that appears to support the message suggested by the lyrics.

Given the unpalatable nature of this message, it is not surprising so many of us rejected the warning by rejecting the portion of the video that delivered the disturbing news. Why do we find it so hard to face up to the truth?

## Notes

1. Semiotic and structural approaches will generally be grouped together for the purposes of this article. Many scholars hold that structural and semiotic analyses are inseparable, since the study of signs necessarily involves investigation of the system of relations through which meaning is produced and vice versa (Hirschman 1988).

2. Humanistic and naturalistic inquiry will be grouped together and treated as essentially the same methodological approach throughout this article. The expositions of both approaches draw heavily on the methods outlined by Lincoln and Guba (1985) and largely conform to standard descriptions of participant observation.

## References

Apel, Karl-Otto (1984), *Understanding and Explanation: A Transcendental-Pragmatic Perspective*, Cambridge, MA: MIT Press.

Belk, Russell W. (1988), "Possessions and the Extended Self," *Journal of Consumer Research*, 15 (September), 139–168.

—, John F. Sherry, Jr., and Melanie Wallendorf (1988), "A Naturalistic Inquiry into Buyer and Seller Behavior at a Swap Meet," *Journal of Consumer Research*, 14 (March), 449–470.

Bernstein, Richard J. (1983), *Beyond Objectivism and Relativism: Science, Hermeneutics, and Praxis*, Philadelphia: University of Pennsylvania Press.

— (1985), *Habermas and Modernity*, Cambridge, MA: MIT Press.

Betti, Emilio (1980), "Hermeneutics as the General Methodology of the *Geisteswissenschaften*," in *Contemporary Hermeneutics: Hermeneutics as Method, Philosophy and Critique*, ed. Josef Bleicher, London and New York: Routledge & Kegan Paul, 51–4. Originally published in *Die Hermeneutik als allgemeine Methode der Geisteswissenschaften* (Tobingen: J. C. B. Mohr, 1962).

Bleicher, Josef (1980), *Contemporary Hermeneutics: Hermeneutics as Method, Philosophy and Critique*, London and New York: Routledge & Kegan Paul.

Connolly, John M. and Thomas Keutner, eds. (1988), *Hermeneutics versus Science? Three German Views*, Notre Dame, IN: University of Notre Dame Press.

Dreyfus, Hubert and Paul Rabinow (1982), *Michel Foucault: Beyond Structuralism and Hermeneutics*, Chicago: University of Chicago Press.

Droysen, Johann Gustav (1937), *Historik*, ed. Hübner, Munich.

Eco, Umberto (1976), *A Theory of Semiotics*, Bloomington: Indiana University Press.

Gadamer, Hans-Georg (1967), "Rhetorik, Hermenutik und Ideologiekritik," in *Kleine Schieften*, Vol. 1, Tübingen: J. C. B. Mohr, 113–130.

– (1976), *Philosophical Hermeneutics*, trans. and ed. David E. Linge, Berkeley: University of California Press.

– (1989), *Truth and Method*, New York: Crossroad. Originally published as *Wahrheit und Methode* (Tübingen: J. C. B. Mohr, 1960).

Geertz, Clifford (1988), *Works and Lives: The Anthropologist as Author*, Stanford, CA: Stanford University Press.

Habermas, Jürgen (1980), "The Hermeneutic Claim to Universality," in *Contemporary Hermeneutics: Hermeneutics as Method, Philosophy and Critique*, ed. Josef Bleicher, London and New York: Routledge & Kegan Paul, 181–211. Originally published as "Der Universalitätsanspruch der Hermeneutik" in *Kultur und Kritik* (Frankfurt: Suhrkamp, 1973).

Heidegger, Martin (1949), *Sein und Zeit*, Tübingen: Neomarius. Published in English as *Being and Time* (New York: Harper & Row, 1962).

Hirschman, Elizabeth C. (1986), "Humanistic Inquiry in Marketing Research: Philosophy, Method, and Criteria," *Journal of Marketing Research*, 23 (August), 237–249.

– (1988), "The Ideology of Consumption: A Structural Syntactical Analysis of 'Dallas' and 'Dynasty,' " *Journal of Consumer Research*, 15 (December), 344–359.

– (1990), "Secular Immortality and the American Ideology of Affluence," *Journal of Consumer Research*, 17 (June), 31–42.

Holbrook, Morris B. (1988), "An Interpretation: *Gremlins* as Metaphors for Materialism," *Journal of Macromarketing*, 8 (Spring), 54–58.

– and Mark W. Grayson (1986), "The Semiology of Cinematic Consumption: Symbolic Consumer Behavior in *Out of Africa*," *Journal of Consumer Research*, 13 (December), 374–381.

Hudson, Laurel Anderson and Julie L. Ozanne (1988), "Alternative Ways of Seeking Knowledge in Consumer Research," *Journal of Consumer Research*, 14 (March), 508–521.

Innis, Robert E., ed. (1985), *Semiotics: An Introductory Anthology*, Bloomington: Indiana University Press.

Kurzweil, Edith (1980), *The Age of Structuralism: Lévi Strauss to Foucault*, New York: Columbia University Press.

Levy, Sidney J. (1981), "Interpreting Consumer Mythology: A Structural Approach to Consumer Behavior," *Journal of Marketing*, 45 (Summer), 49–62.

Lincoln, Yvonna S. and Egon G. Guba (1985), *Naturalistic Inquiry*, Beverly Hills, CA: Sage.

Lyotard, Jean-François (1984), *The Postmodern Condition: A Report on Knowledge*. Manchester: Manchester University Press.

Madison, Gary B. (1989), "The New Philosophy of Rhetoric," *Texte*, Vol. 8/9, pp. 247–277.

MeCloskey, Donald N. (1983), "The Rhetoric of Economics," *Journal of Economic Literature*, 21 (June), 481–517.

McCracken, Grant (1988), *The Long Interview*, Beverly Hills, CA: Sage.

— (1991), "Seeing the Future in Black and White," *The Globe and Mail*, November 21.

Mick, David Glen (1986), "Consumer Research and Serniotics: Exploring the Morphology of Signs, Symbols, and Significance," *Journal of Consumer Research*, 13 (September), 196–213.

Murray, Jeff B. and Julie L. Ozanne (1991), "The Critical Imagination: Emancipatory Interests in Consumer Research," *Journal of Consumer Research*, 18 (September), 129–144.

O'Shaughnessy, John (1985), "A Return to Reason in Consumer Research: An Hermeneutical Approach," in *Advances in Consumer Research*, Vol. 12, ed. Elizabeth C. Hirschman and Morris B. Holbrook, Provo, UT: Association for Consumer Research, 305–311.

– and Morris B. Holbrook (1988), "Understanding Consumer Behaviour: The Linguistic Turn in Marketing Research," *Journal of the Market Research Society*, 30 (April), 197–223.

Packer, Martin J. (1985), "Hermeneutic Inquiry in the Study of Human Conduct," *American Psychologist*, 40 (October), 1081–1093.

Perelman, Chaïm (1982), *The Realm of Rhetoric*, Notre Dame, IN: University of Notre Dame Press.

Ricoeur, Paul (1981), *Hermeneutics and the Human Sciences: Essays on Language, Action and Interpretation*, Cambridge: Cambridge University Press.

Rogers, Everett M. (1987), "The Critical School and Consumer Research," in *Advances in Consumer Research*, Vol. 14, ed. Melanie Wallendorf and Paul F. Anderson, Provo, UT: Association for Consumer Research, 7–11.

Rorty, Richard (1982), *Consequences of Pragmatism (Essays: 1972–1980)*, Minneapolis: University of Minnesota Press.

– (1985), "Habermas and Lyotard on Postmodernity," in *Habermas and Modernity*, ed. Richard J. Bernstein, Cambridge: Polity.

– (1989), *Contingency, Irony, and Solidarity*, Cambridge: Cambridge University Press.

Ryan, Michael J. and Julia M. Bristor (1987), "The Symbiotic Nature of Hermeneutical vs. Classically Generated Knowledge," in *1987 AMA Winter Educators' Conference: Marketing Theory*, ed. Russell W. Belk *et al.*, Chicago: American Marketing Association, 191–194.

Schouten, John W. (1991), "Selves in Transition: Symbolic Consumption in Personal Rites of Passage and Identity Reconstruction," *Journal of Consumer Research*, 17 (March), 412–425.

Sebeok, Thomas A. (1976), *Contributions to the Doctrine of Signs*, Bloomington: Indiana University Press.

Sherry, John F., Jr. (1991), "Postmodern Alternatives: The Interpretive Turn in Consumer Research," in *Handbook of Consumer Behavior*, ed. Thomas S. Robertson and Harold H. Kassarjian, Englewood Cliffs, NJ: Prentice Hall, 548–591.

Stern, Barbara B. (1989), "Literary Criticism and Consumer Research: Overview and Illustrative Analysis," *Journal of Consumer Research*, 16 (December), 322–334.

Thompson, Craig J., William B. Locander, and Howard R. Pollio (1989), "Putting Consumer Experience Back into Consumer Research: The Philosophy and Method of Existential-Phenomenology," *Journal of Consumer Research*, 16 (September), 133–146.

–, William B. Locander, and Howard R. Pollio (1990), "The Lived Meaning of Free Choice: An Existential Phenomenological Description of Everyday Consumer Experiences of Contemporary Married Women," *Journal of Consumer Research*, 17 (December), 346–361.

Thompson, John B. (1981), *Critical Hermeneutics: A Study in the Thought of Paul Ricoeur and Jürgen Habermas*, Cambridge: Cambridge University Press.

Valda, Mario J. (1987), *Phenomenological Hermeneutics and the Study of Literature*, Toronto: University of Toronto Press.

# 4

# Feminist Thought: Implications for Consumer Research

**Julia M. Bristor and Eileen Fischer**

**Source:** *Journal of Consumer Research* 19 (3) (1993): 518–536.

The premise of this article is that consumer research, like other bodies of knowledge, has sometimes misrepresented women. More fundamentally, we will argue that a portion of consumer research's theory and knowledge are gendered in unrecognized ways, and that feminist critique is required to clarify the implicit assumptions. Such critiques have been directed at many other disciplines and exposed pervasive, systemic assumptions about women and about gender that reflect ungrounded stereotypes and beliefs (Calás and Smircich 1992; Langland and Gove 1981). Feminist reappraisals typically strive to raise the consciousness of members of the academy – female and male – to the pervasively gendered nature of their disciplines. They also seek to offer insights on how scientific practice and thought can be enhanced, not merely by "adding women' to existing theory and research, but also by identifying alternatives to current practice and thought based on feminist perspectives. This article strives to lay the groundwork for a parallel reappraisal, revision, and enrichment of consumer research by examining it in the light of feminist thought.

In suggesting that consumer research will benefit from feminist reappraisal and revision, we are neither implying nor presuming conscious sexist motivations on the part of specific individuals. To the contrary, we contend that, precisely because gender biases and gendered assumptions are long-standing, pervasive, and subtle aspects of our worldviews and research traditions, they are widely and unconsciously taken for granted. Thus, they are also very difficult to identify and revise. We wish to state clearly that we are not suggesting that the corrective is to dismiss science and our existing knowledge base. We propose that this knowledge base can be revised once researchers acquire a heightened sensitivity to the gendered nature of our discipline.

While some initial efforts have been made to bring certain feminist perspectives to bear on some aspects of consumer research,[1] no integrated effort that draws on the range of feminist thought has yet appeared. This article attempts to provide a more comprehensive basis for heightening sensitivity to gender biases and gendered assumptions in consumer research by first summarizing some major strands of feminist thought. It then draws on these feminist perspectives to illustrate the types of biases and assumptions rooted in dominant conceptions of science, as well as in the problematics – decisions about what aspects of the world need explaining (Harding 1986) – theory, and methods of data collection and analysis common in consumer research. Our goal is to be both critical and constructive: we seek to develop practical approaches to broadening and enriching consumer research.

**Table 1** An Overview and Comparison of Major Feminist Perspectives

| Features | Liberal feminism | Women's voice/experience feminism | Poststructuralist feminism |
|---|---|---|---|
| Intellectual underpinnings | Liberal political philosophy | Marxism, psychoanalysis | Deconstructionism, postmodemism |
| Assumptions about human experience | Experience gives direct access to (the same) objective knowledge for women and men | The experiences, and therefore the knowledge, of women and men differ systematically | All experiences are mediated by dominant discourses; all knowledge Is therefore constituted by language and potentially open to revision |
| Assumptions about sex and gender | Men and women are not different in their rationality; any observed differences are due to differences in socialization or access to opportunities and are open to change if men and women gain equal opportunities | Fundamental differences in nature and perspective are linked to sex and/or gender; these differences stem from either biology or socialization or both; while sex differences are influential, psychological gender is not fully determined by biological sex | A bipolar opposition between the terms related to men/masculinity vs. women/femininity is pervasive in dominant discourses; this filters the experiences of both men and women such that they take for granted assumptions about sex and gender differences; these assumptions can be challenged by deconstructions of dominant discourses |
| Strategies and goals for change | Enact and enforce legislation to ensure women have equal access to opportunities; strive to eliminate all sex-related differences in day-to-day behaviors, i.e., pursue androgyny | Demonstrate that female and/or feminine nature and perspectives are not inferior; pursue a state in which different sexes/genders are equally valued and empowered | Challenge the hegemony of dominant discourses that systematically disenfranchise women and other marginalized groups; seek to develop a heightened openness in society to multiple equally valued perspectives |

## An Overview of Major Feminist Perspectives

While feminist writings can be traced back to at least the seventeenth century, most feminist thinking has developed fairly recently. No single feminist perspective now dominates; rather, many viewpoints, some quite incommensurable, have been developed and exist simultaneously (Black 1989; Hirsch and Keller 1990; Jagger 1983; Tong 1989). We do not wish to obscure the differences that exist among perspectives. Thus, we have chosen to summarize a range representative of the breadth of feminist thought. Recognizing that no review can be exhaustive of all feminist viewpoints, we have selected only three of the major ones. Like all categorical schemes, however, ours may be challenged for grouping distinct ideas, for failing to group logically linked ideas, or for failing to include important elements. We provide below an overview of three perspectives (see Table 1), liberal feminism, women's voice/experience feminism (Calás and Smircich 1992), and poststructural feminism, which offer a complementary range of critiques on consumer research.

Before discussing these perspectives, distinctions among three key terms need to be drawn. First, *sex* is a biological concept that allows us to distinguish between males and females purely on the basis of physiological characteristics. While biological sex per se does not predetermine behavior, it has a profound influence on a person's socialization experience (Fischer and Arnold 1990). Second, *gender is* a social concept referring to psychologically, sociologically, or culturally rooted traits, attitudes, beliefs, and behavioral tendencies. Because gender is a pervasive filter through which individuals experience their social world, consumption activities are fundamentally gendered. Although the concepts of sex and gender are related, gender is not fully determined by sex. For instance, not all women are feminine and not all men are masculine (Bern 1974). Considerable gender variation has been detected between *and* among women and men. Third, although (as discussed below) feminist perspectives differ widely, it is commonly agreed that a feminist is one who believes there are inequities in contemporary society that disadvantage women relative to men and who supports the goal of eradicating these inequities. Feminism, like gender, is not isomorphic with sex. Being a woman is neither a necessary nor a sufficient condition for being a feminist: many men adopt a feminist perspective; many women do not.

### Liberal Feminism

Liberal feminism is rooted in liberal political philosophy, which encompasses basic beliefs in the equality of all beings and views human beings as essentially rational, self-interest-seeking agents (Jagger 1983; Tong 1989). Rationality is assumed to be a purely mental capacity and is regarded as what is especially valuable about human beings (Jagger 1983). Individual psychological differences resulting from differences in social opportunities are acknowledged, but rationality, the human essence, is viewed as a capacity for which every human being has the same potential.

Liberalism stresses the ultimate value of individuals and holds that individual rights have priority over general community welfare; it views the just society as one that allows individuals to exercise their autonomy and to fulfill themselves (Tong 1989). Because the resources that allow self-fulfillment are believed to be limited in every society, the fundamental problem for liberalism is to devise social institutions that protect individuals' rights to a fair share of those resources while guaranteeing maximum freedom from state intervention for each (Jagger 1983). While classical liberals believed that allowing a free market to operate while guarding civil liberties would provide everyone with an equal opportunity to determine her or his own fate within the market, contemporary liberals tend to believe that individuals come to the market with such differences in initial advantage, talent, and luck that some of them cannot take their fair share of market opportunities without adjustments via government intervention (Tong 1989).

At present, liberal feminists feel that liberal principles are not applied equally to men and women. Men have tended to be treated as the "self" whose "self-interests" are to be protected. Women have tended to be treated as the "other"; as such, their interests were largely ignored or violated. The goal of liberal feminism is the application of liberal principles to women *and* men and a resultant sexual equality (Eisenstein 1986). Liberal feminists tend to hold the contemporary view that state intervention is required to achieve this goal since women have less frequently realized their full rational capabilities because they were deprived of essential opportunities such as education (Jagger 1983; Wendell 1987). They advocate eliminating laws that establish different rights for men and women, promoting legislation that prohibits various kinds of discrimination against women, undertaking major economic reorganization, and redistributing wealth (Jagger 1983; Tong 1989; Wendell 1987). Liberal feminists stress that opportunities for paid employment for women are particularly important in order to overcome the more insidious factors that keep women from full rational development (Tong 1989). The allocation of most domestic work and child care to women diminishes their opportunities for well-paying and/or prestigious jobs that would enhance their autonomy and self-fulfillment.

Liberal feminists argue that any detected psychological male/female differences are not innate but develop out of women's socially allocated roles, which discourage women from developing their full capacities for reason. They deny that the physical differences between men and women are relevant since they view rationality as having no physical basis. They argue that, as women gain access to equal opportunities through the necessary state interventions, women and men will actualize their potential rationality more equally and observed psychological differences will diminish or disappear, resulting in widespread psychological androgyny (Jagger 1983). Some contemporary liberal feminists specify that the ideal would be for individuals to possess a combination of masculine *and* feminine traits that would result if men took on some traditional female roles at the same time women gained access to traditional male roles (Tong 1989).

Liberal feminists are probably the most numerous today. Through the effort of contemporary and historical liberal feminists, improvements in legislation to protect women from many forms of discrimination have occurred. Liberal feminism is, however, most protective of the interests of white, middle-class, heterosexual feminists for whom preservation of many elements of the current sociopolitical status quo is acceptable (Jagger 1983; Tong 1989).[2] Other forms of feminism that represent more diverse perspectives and needs, and promote more radical agendas for sociopolitical change, flourish as well.

### Women's Voice/Experience Feminism

This grouping includes a wide array of feminist perspectives grounded in diverse philosophical bases. These include, for instance, radical feminism and some versions of social and psychoanalytic feminism. What women's voice/experience perspectives have in common is a belief that there are differences between male and female experiences and that female experiences are at least an equally valid basis for developing knowledge and organizing society (Calás and Smircich 1991).[3] In contrast to liberal feminist thought, women's voice/ women's experience feminism does not consider men and women to be essentially the same; among men and among women, shared experiences are assumed to help define a group-based rationality or mode of knowing. Further, feminists in this category tend to subscribe to the view that "distinctions of gender, based on sex, structure virtually every aspect of our lives and indeed are so all-pervasive that ordinarily they go quite unrecognized" (Jagger 1983, p. 85).

Some feminists in this category believe that differences between men and women are primarily or largely innate and linked to biology (e.g., Brownmiller 1976; Daly 1978). They recognize that antifeminists have often used biological arguments to justify the oppression of women but feel that this interpretation of the implications of biological determinism is unwarranted. They focus on how innate differences in the physical strength of women and men have enabled men to unjustly oppress women. They also stress the unique biologically based (pro)creative capacities of women and suggest that this forms the basis of a distinctive female perspective. Such theories imply a direct link between biological sex and psychological gender.

Other feminists in this category reject biological determinism (e.g., Oakley 1981; Smith 1987). They believe in a "distinctive standpoint for women, not necessarily as a general attribute of women as a class of persons, but as a mode of experience that is distinctive to women and in important ways an experience that has marked [women] off from men and still continues to do so. This is an experience of work around particular individuals, particularly children" (Smith 1989, p. 34). Feminists in this group view gender as a socially constructed category but believe that the deep embeddedness of the construct leads to real differences in the life-worlds of most women versus those of most men.

A central concern of feminists in this category is to eradicate the subordination of women by validating that which is associated with femaleness. Androgyny is generally not considered an ideal that will help to achieve this goal. Many suggest that blending masculinity and femininity is as absurd as putting "master and slave language or imagery together to define a free person" (Raymond 1979,

p. 161). Some feminists in this group would argue that the ideal to strive for is some form of matriarchy ranging from a society based on matriarchal values to one ruled by women, which privileges women's voices and ways of knowing (Jagger 1983). Others believe a preferable state can be achieved by developing alternate social arrangements (such as organizations run by and for women) that create an environment where women's voices and experiences are fully valued. Most would argue that, at a minimum, it is essential to recognize the ways in which knowledge is gendered and to gain legitimacy for that feminine knowledge that has been suppressed or marginalized. Feminist theorists in this group have begun to identify numerous theories and practices that have been male gendered and to articulate female alternatives (Belenky *et al.* 1986; Chodorow 1978; Gilligan 1982). For instance, definitions of moral development and of what constitutes moral behavior have been argued to be male biased (Gilligan 1982). Gilligan argues that traditional notions of morality are based on the masculine tendency to assume a sharp distinction between the self and the other; feminine notions of morality differ because they are informed by women's tendencies to regard the boundaries between self and other as fluid and undefined.

### Poststructuralist Feminism

Also known as postmodernist feminism or postfeminism, poststructuralist feminism is most recent in vintage.[4] It is rooted in the multifaceted postmodernist movement developed in and from the works of Derrida (1973), Foucault (1979, 1981, 1986), and others. While these works vary considerably, they share certain assumptions about language, subjectivity, and discourse. Language is viewed as the forum where actual and possible forms of social organization and their likely consequences are defined and contested. It is through language that meaning is constituted: for instance, the meanings of "femininity" and "masculinity" and of "self" and "other" vary from language to language, as well as among discourses within a language.

Given that language works in this way, it is regarded as the medium in which our subjectivity (our sense of ourselves and of situations) is constructed. Thus, an individual's subjectivity is not viewed as fixed or coherent, and the idea that knowledge can be validated by experience is seriously questioned. (Such a view contrasts with liberal feminism, which assumes that every human being possesses a unified rational consciousness, and with women's voice/experience feminism, which assumes women share a common experience base.) Poststructuralism views subjectivity as contradictory and open to constitution or reconstitution, through discourse, each time we think or speak.

The term "discourse" refers to the historical, social, and political aspect of language and hence of subjectivity. The meanings of social reality that shape the way individuals interpret their lived world, including the meanings they have for "femininity" and "masculinity," vary among discourses within a language. For instance, the term "politically correct" is now being pejoratively associated, by certain powerful voices, with refusals to condone speech or action that is discriminatory; social activists might label such refusals in a positive way as ethically appropriate. Variations among discourses are socially and historically situated, and political; particular discourses support particular social structures and processes embodied in institutions such as the law, the educational system and the family. Each institution has a discursive field, or set of competing discourses, that are a site of struggle for meaning and power. The power structures that prevail depend on which discourses are dominant. Thus, if the pejorative term "politically correct" continues to be applied prevalently to nondiscriminatory practices, groups who benefit from such discrimination are likely to maintain or gain power and institutions are unlikely to be challenged to eliminate discriminatory practices.

Poststructural feminism draws on the notions of language, subjectivity, and discourse to understand existing power relations that disadvantage women and to identify opportunities and strategies for a change. For instance, poststructural feminists could note the current condemnation of "political correctness" and argue that this rhetoric supports patriarchy since it undermines attempts to discourage sexist language and behaviors. The method for identifying opportunities and strategies for change relies on historical analysis of discourses that structure institutions and modes of thought, deconstructing binary oppositions (such as "feminine" vs. "masculine." or "self" vs. "other") in language, and seeking to recognize the power hierarchies supported by particular discourses. Poststructuralist feminist analyses, which are challenging certain institutional discourses and practices, are only beginning to emerge (see Calfás and Smircich 1991; Firat 1991; Mumby and Putnam 1990; Scott 1990).

It should be noted that, while poststructural feminists view other feminists as ineffective to the extent that they fail to deconstruct dominant discourses, some feminists of other perspectives would argue that poststructuralism is not well suited to feminist critique since it is antifoundational and hence apolitical. Any poststructuralist critique could in turn be deconstructed; for instance, a poststructuralist feminist analysis of criticisms of political correctness could in turn be deconstructed. Feminists from other perspectives have rejected poststructuralism both because it has this potential to undermine its own critique (and thus its own political agenda) and because many thinkers associated with poststructuralism have been unconcerned with, or even opposed to the aims of, feminism and have perpetuated the privileging of nonfeminist interests. Hekman (1991) insists these concerns are serious but argues that poststructuralism can usefully be conjoined with feminism. She notes that engaging poststructuralism reveals to feminists the futility of any attempt they might make to define an essentialist feminine nature or to replace masculine epistemology with feminine epistemology. She argues that poststructuralism shows feminists both the necessity and the political power inherent in rejecting masculine/feminine dualisms and the worldview that hierarchically orders these categories. Poststructural feminism thus advances the goal of challenging the patriarchal status quo by pointing up the arbitrary nature of the assumptions on which it is based.

## Feminist Critiques of Consumer Research

Each of the feminist perspectives discussed above provides distinct grounds for critically assessing various aspects of consumer research. While elements of some of these critiques could be raised equally well from other perspectives (such as Anderson's [1986] critical relativism), it is unlikely that critics speaking from nonfeminist perspectives will fully develop those aspects of their thought relevant to feminists. Just as it can be argued that no research is value neutral, so it must be recognized that no critique is value neutral; those who do not consciously reflect feminist values will be unlikely to devote attention to the feminist implications of their work. It is, therefore, necessary to review some criticisms that have been raised previously in the consumer behavior literature in order to address those facets of the criticisms with particular relevance to a feminist agenda.

### Objectivity

The ideal of scientific objectivity has been insightfully critiqued by other consumer research scholars (e.g., Anderson 1983, 1986; Peter and Olson 1983). Contributing to the philosophy of science debates during the last decade, they argue that no science is objective and what counts as valid knowledge is relative to programmatic standards and commitments. These views are no longer considered heretical. Even among conservative scholars, the possibility that scientific objectivity cannot be absolute has been conceded (Hunt 1990). Feminist critiques of objectivity are nonetheless worth discussing since they help us to see commonly overlooked androcentric research assumptions.

*Liberal Feminism.* The mildest critique comes from liberal feminism, which accepts contemporary notions of objectivity (such as sophisticated falsificationism [Calder and Tybout 1987]). Liberal feminism suggests that lapses in objectivity reflect a correctable failure to rigorously adhere to proper scientific procedure (Harding 1987). For instance, liberal feminists would argue that early consumer research that assessed the relative influence of female versus male spouses in purchase decisions was nonobjective simply because improper research techniques were used. Specifically, only one partner, usually the wife, was questioned about both her influence and that of her spouse, and no account was taken of the fact that self-versus spouse-reported levels of influence often vary greatly. This measurement problem forestalled understanding of variations in family decision-making patterns (Davis 1971). Stronger concerns about objectivity in science are raised by both women's voice/experience feminism and poststructural feminism.

*Women's Voice/Experience Feminism.* Women's voice/experience versions of feminism assume that the differences between men and women result in incommensurable experiences and points of view. These views offer critiques of objectivity that fall into two categories. The first critique is raised by those feminists who believe that female/male differences are biologically based and unbridgeable. They tend to reject "objectivity" altogether as a male value (e.g., Daly 1978). In the extreme, such feminists would accept that in the following pairs of bipolar terms, the former truly more aptly characterizes men and the latter more aptly characterizes women: cultured versus natural, public versus private, scientific versus artistic, rational versus emotional, thinking versus feeling, hard versus soft, quantitative versus qualitative, and objective versus subjective. If these dualistic cultural gender stereotypes are regarded as true, it follows that the standard of objectivity is a male standard and that women are alienated from any science – including consumer research – that embraces this standard.

The second critique is raised by those who believe male/female differences are socially based. The historical association of objectivity with men and subjectivity with women (Fee 1983; Jordanova 1980) leads to concerns about the assumption that women can be objects but not subjects of knowledge, known but not knowers (Keller 1978; Oakley 1981; Smith 1974; Westkott 1979). Further, this association equates scientific activity with masculine characteristics, thus implying that a woman scientist can only be a subject, and a knower, by adopting a male perspective. However, many women have found themselves enmeshed in conflict over the relation of their respective disciplines to their personal experiences because they feel that to practice research from a male perspective compels them to discard or repress their experienced world as a valid source of information (Simeone 1987; Smith 1974).

However, the implication here is not that women are ill suited to research or defective because they cannot maintain the subject/object separation. The ability of anyone to maintain subject/object separation has already been severely questioned by postpositivists (e.g., Belk, Sherry, and Wallendorf 1988; Hirschman 1986). Rather, the implication is that, since historically men have largely been the sole proprietors of knowledge (in that they alone were likely to receive higher education and enter into the "knowledge creating" professions) and since objectivity is socially perceived as a valued masculine trait, it is easy to see how the perception of an objective, unbiased, and ungendered perspective could be created and perpetuated (Keller 1978, 1982). But, as these critiques suggest, scientific objectivity is not achieved at times because male (or white or socially privileged) scientists do not study some matters as female (or nonwhite or socially disadvantaged) scientists might pursue them. Since male experiences and resultant viewpoints are fundamentally different, men have difficulty asking objective questions or developing objective theories about subjects related to *others'* experiences. This difficulty is not due to disinterest in others' experiences. Harding (1986) argues that socialized differences in men's and women's roles not only structure understanding, they set limits on understanding. The perspective of someone in a given role (male vs. female, white vs. Black vs. Hispanic vs. Asian, upper vs. lower class) is thus inherently partial in both senses of the word.

The concerns of women's voice/experience feminism can be applied to objectivity in consumer research. For instance, it is consistent with this feminist perspective to argue that the predominantly middle-class white male scholarly community has persistently studied the consumption of labor-saving durables in a way that reveals a severe breach of understanding of female consumers and of families who do not conform to the North American prototype (i.e., a married woman and man with one or more children). As women entered the full-time paid work force outside the home in greater numbers, consumer researchers searched for a connection between family expenditure on time-saving durables and whether the wife had paid employment outside the home (Reilly 1982; Schaninger and Allen 1981; Strober and Weinberg 1977, 1980; Weinberg and Winer 1983) based on an economic metaphor likening the household to a factory. The rationale offered for investigating this connection is either that the family will need to save time on domestic duties if the wife is working fewer hours in the home (see Weinberg and Winer 1983) or that wives' earnings are regarded as transitory and therefore durables are purchased as a form of savings (Mincer 1960). The consistent finding has been, contrary to these economic arguments, that families in which the wife works outside the home do not differ in their expenditure on time-saving durables from those families in which the wife does not have outside paid employment (holding constant the total family income). Several concerns about this research stream's objectivity are highlighted by feminist critiques.

The very posing of the question reflects traditional assumptions about the relative valuation of women's work, the sex of the "main bread winner" in mixed-sex couples, and the structure of contemporary families. Specifically, it is assumed that women's paid employment is a "consumer behavior construct" (Schaninger and Allen 1981) whereas men's paid employment is to be taken for granted. Moreover, families are assumed to be headed by one employed male who is the main breadwinner and one woman who is not. In order to carry out these studies, researchers are forced to discard from public data sets the large portion of families in which this norm does not apply. Such studies would probably not be very meaningful in cultures and sub-cultures in which women's roles, family structures, and consumption patterns differ from the North American prototype. Thus, the objectivity of the manner in which questions concerning wife's role status and labor-saving durables consumption are posed must be questioned if only because the research question is relevant to such a select group (i.e., those who conform to the [decreasingly representative] prototypical family) but does not represent the growing numbers of "non-traditional" households (see Roberts and Wortzel 1984). Further, the persistence with which a relationship between women's employment status and consumption of time-saving durables is sought, despite the "null results" findings of initial studies, suggests that researchers are less than objective in their beliefs regarding whether such a relationship should exist.

The objectivity with which findings are interpreted must also be called into question. For instance, one explanation of the finding that time-saving durables are not consumed more by families in which wives work outside the home is that families "do not treat wives' and husbands' earnings differently" (Weinberg and Winer 1983, p. 259). This explanation may not in itself be wrong (though Zelizer [1989] provides evidence that wives' and husbands' monies have been regarded as separate and unequal), but it appears to be partial (i.e., biased and incomplete). The perspective of the women in the families studied seems to be inaccessible to the researchers; the female subjects remain the "other." An equally plausible explanation for the "no difference" findings is that women employed outside the home feel compelled to serve their families in much the same manner they would if they were not employed; that is, they use no more – and no fewer – labor-saving devices than their counterparts who do not work outside the home since they are trying to fulfill their social role expectations by conforming to whatever the standards are for good wives and mothers despite having the role of breadwinner. If having labor-saving durables is considered consistent with the role, then we might expect a family who could afford such durables to purchase them, regardless of the wife's paid employment status. In fact, Firat and Lewis argue that "the advent of 'timesaving durables,' while presented in the public domain of ideas as emancipation of women from housework, in effect has expanded the social expectation of efficiency and has increased the physical and psychological pressures upon women" (1985, p. 228). The tendency toward the "social reproduction" (Chodorow 1978) of traditional gender roles is a factor deeply ingrained in the minds of contemporary consumers, but its impact is ignored in studies in this research stream.

Women's voice/experience critiques do not imply that the notion of objectivity should be dismissed as futile, but that it needs to be revised because of the "partiality" of individual knowledge. Keller (1982), for example, suggests reconceptualizing objectivity as a dialectical process involving critical self-reflection. In practice, the use of mixed-sex research teams sensitive to gender issues may help mitigate this partiality (e.g., Costa 1991; Easterday *et al.* 1977; Warren 1988; Young 1991), although no single man or woman can be expected to fully represent the masculine or feminine point of view. This implies that an extended interaction between "knowers" from various groups (e.g., men and women) is required to obtain more complete, more objective, less distorted knowledge. Without such interaction, female consumers will continue to be represented as the "other," that is, as someone different in kind from the researcher.

*Poststructuralist Feminism.* Poststructuralist feminist criticisms of objectivity are the most pervasive and least readily addressed. These critiques cast doubt on the possibility of objectivity since they deny that objective knowledge can be obtained through experience (Flax 1990; Weedon 1987). They argue that all knowledge derived through experience is socially constructed by historically, socially, and politically shaped discourses. Poststructuralists in general focus on the manner in which language serves to structure knowledge as it is perceived. Feminist poststructuralists pay particular attention to the way gender-related language pervasive in our culture shapes what is viewed as objective knowledge; they problematize "knowing" as an already (male) gendered sphere of action (Flax 1990). For instance, the language of consumer research includes several terms for female consumers, such as "house-wives," "work-wives," just-a-job wives," "career women," and "super-women" (see, e.g., Bartos 1978, 1989; McCall 1977) but has no corresponding set of terms (e.g., career men) for male consumers. This terminology reflects vivid differences in our knowledge about female and male consumers. As objects of study in consumer research, women are frequently defined in terms of their marital roles. On the other hand, men's status is taken for granted, and their consumption behaviors are rarely singled out as interesting consumer phenomena.

Such examples from poststructural feminism reinforce the premise that all knowledge is open to revision since it is only apprehended through the categories that shape perceptions. This does not imply that knowledge can be corrected via intersubjective verification or critical reflection since everyone is socialized through some set of discourses and her or his knowledge is thus filtered. Rather, it implies that objective knowledge of reality is impossible and that knowledge claims tend to empower some and disadvantage others because they are shaped by dominant discourses.[5] Knowledge claims about women in consumer research largely have been generated within the dominant patriarchal discourse and reflect the taken-for-granted status of women as objects of investigation. These knowledge claims thus appear to convey "knowledge about" rather "knowledge of" female consumers (see Langer 1963) that entrenches the status of women as the "other" about whom knowledge must be sought (vs. the "self" who creates knowledge). Rather than seek truth via objectivity, poststructural feminism enjoins scholars to challenge seeming objectivity in extant thought in order to reveal patterns of domination (of women or other less powerful groups) and clarify patriarchal interests that are sustained by specific scientific discourses.

### Problematics

A discipline's cognitive aims and values both shape and limit its problematics (Laudan 1983). Problematics are decisions about what aspects of the world need explaining and what is puzzling about these aspects (Harding 1986). Consumer research problematics have been criticized for their alignment with marketer interests (see Holbrook 1987); alternative problematics might reflect consumer interests, political interests or nonapplied interests (i.e., interest for interest's sake; Belk 1986; Bristor 1985; Holbrook 1987). Similarly, the different feminist perspectives can suggest problematics that reflect concerns especially relevant to women consumers.

*Liberal Feminism.* Liberal feminism, which views individuals as rational agents in pursuit of self-interests, suggests that, so long as women are less likely to become scientists (e.g., as a result of inequities in the social and educational opportunities afforded to women), then their interests are less likely to be reflected in the questions that are pursued. An implicit assumption is that questions of interest to women tend not to be asked by male scientists simply because they are, rationally and inevitably, pursuing self-interests. For example, much research on family consumption arguably reflects the self-interests of married men who may wish to devote minimal time and effort to household production activities, regardless of whether their wives also work outside the home. Taking for granted that men will not take responsibility for major household production activities such as child care and food preparation, even when their wives work outside the home, Soberon-Ferrer and Dardis (1991) assume that household responsibilities that cannot be met by wives will be supplemented by purchases, not husbands' labor. The interests of women might be better served by research that both challenges this assumption about primary responsibility and seeks to identify ways in which husbands might be motivated to assume more equal responsibility. As another example, Choe, Yoon, and Johnson (1991) explored sex differences in durable-goods payment methods. Their data suggest that women heads of household (who were, by definition, all unmarried) in comparison to the men household heads (who were almost all married) were significantly worse off economically. The knowledge generated by the Choe *et al.* study might assist in the development of a durable-goods marketing strategy. An alternative problematic more relevant to the interests of many women is whether women heads of one-adult households, compared to their male counterparts, are economically disadvantaged or have fewer, more restrictive, payment options (and if so, why).

Liberal feminism stresses, however, that increases in the numbers of women in academe, or in the numbers of consumer researchers interested in "women's issues," do not ensure that feminist research will necessarily be undertaken or published. Researchers wishing to study consumer issues using feminist perspectives may face problems similar to those encountered by feminists in other fields. Feminist perspectives often do not fit accepted traditional paradigms, theories, and research methods (Smith 1974). Further, pursuing topics of interest to women is often viewed as lacking generality or academic value, and researchers who choose such topics are systematically less likely to obtain access to critical resources and, thus, less likely to receive tenure or promotions (see Simeone 1987; Spender 1981). The difficulties of obtaining outside funding faced generally by researchers affiliated with business schools (AMA Task Force 1988) may be more acute for feminist consumer researchers. As a main, albeit limited, source of outside funds for business school researchers, the Marketing Science Institute is explicitly dedicated to the study of management issues; women's issues were not listed in a recent statement of research priorities (Marketing Science Institute 1992). The kinds of alternative problematics suggested above to be reflective of the interests of many women consumers may not be viewed as relevant for advancing managerial marketing knowledge.

In fact, some research of interest to women could be antithetical to the interests of marketers. For instance, the interests of marketers and women may be at odds with regard to product proliferation in the household cleaning-product category. Whereas marketers are interested in growing sales within the category by developing increasingly specialized products and suggesting ever-higher standards of cleanliness, women might be better served by studies of how to minimize housework by using fewer, generalized all-purpose cleaning products and how to resist any tendency to escalate standards of cleanliness (Friedan 1963). While exceptions certainly occur, it seems likely that obtaining funding to study a consumer topic of particular interest to women would be more difficult if the topic did not coincide with the interests of marketers.

*Women's Voice/Experience Feminism.* Feminism based on women's voice/experience can suggest additional consumer problematics that, because they arise from women's experiences, have been largely ignored. No exhaustive list of such topics is possible. However, the types of problematics indicated by women's voice/experience feminism can be illustrated by discussing one major example of distinctively female experience and tracing out some of its implications. A notable theorist who explored certain unique female experiences is Nancy Chodorow (1978). She argues that the early childhood of girls differs fundamentally from that of boys because women have been the primary early childhood caregivers. The fact that boys and girls experience the caregiving element of their environment differently, she suggests, accounts for the development of basic sex differences in personality. Girls identify more with their mothers and develop more flexible ego boundaries. Boys are encouraged to differentiate themselves from their mothers and identify with their fathers, who are more remote during the child's early years, which Chodorow posits leads boys to identify with the "position" of the father rather than the actual person. Further, she suggests that differences between the positional identification boys experience and the personal identification girls experience is the definitive factor in the differential constitution of masculinity and femininity. Specifically, it makes women open to forming numerous deep, primary relationships while leaving men without an ability to form extended networks of deep personal relationships. Women develop the propensity to form and nurture relationships not only on their own behalf but also as part of their role in the domestic sphere.

Chodorow's argument that women are more "relationship focused" than men opens up some distinctive problematics for consumer research. Research questions to date have lacked much consideration of the relational aspects of consumption. When the role of the "other" in consumption is questioned, the stress has been either on how self-image is derived through others' view of our consumer behaviors (e.g., Solomon 1983) or on types of reference group influence on individual tastes and preferences and on susceptibility to influence (e.g., Bearden, Nettemeyer, and Teel 1989; Burnkrant and Cousineau 1975). Both approaches are characterized by inherently atomistic views of consumption that accord more closely with the masculine tendency toward individuation than with the feminine tendency toward relationship building (Gainer 1992). An alternative view of consumption is based on the notion that individuals' activities are a function of the social networks in which they are embedded (Granovetter 1985). Sensitivity to the importance of social relationships in consumption is evident in studies that focus on consumer's social networks (e.g., Brown and Reingen 1987; Frenzen and Davis 1990; Reingen *et al.* 1984), some of the work on gift giving (e.g., Belk and Coon 1991; Fischer and Arnold 1990), on holiday rituals (e.g., Wallendorf and Arnould 1991), and on the meaning of possessions (e.g., Belk 1988). As yet, however, little research in our discipline has directly explored the implications for consumer behavior of the importance (to women) of relationship building and maintenance. Research that acknowledges a "moral economy" (i.e., a system of transactions that are defined as socially desirable or "moral" because through them social ties are recognized and balanced social relationships are maintained) as opposed to the traditional exchange paradigm is needed to correct this imbalance. For instance, Cheal's (1988) study of gift exchanges among a community of Winnipeg residents explicitly explored how respondents created and maintained their social worlds partially through the yearly cycle of gift giving; his analysis reveals that his respondents did not participate in gift exchanges in order to receive valued goods but rather to affirm their kin and friend networks.

Such a relationship-based focus could be used to conceptualize new problems, such as how the relationship between consumers and organizations figures in the construction of consumers' social worlds. Agentic (masculine) perspectives on consumer-organization relationships have focused on how the marketing organization can use them to achieve business goals (Hirschman 1991). For instance, brand loyalty, the term used to describe a consumer's commitment to a brand or company, tends to be defined simply in terms of the repeat-buying patterns of individual consumers and studied strictly so as to enable marketers to maintain market share in the face of competition (Kotler and Turner 1989). In contrast, a communal perspective on consumer-organization relationships might focus on relationships that were not strictly a means to an end. For instance, loyal donors' relationships to one another and to a particular not-for-profit organization could usefully be studied so as to increase understanding of how shared goals bind consumers to one another and the organization and how the organizations are shaped by their relationships to their donor base (Gainer 1992). It is likely that a better understanding of the manner in which interpersonal relationships are created and sustained through consumer behaviors could be developed if our typical narrow focus on market-based exchanges were broadened and non-market-based transactions (e.g., "handing down" goods) were also studied. Though this discussion deals with the implications of but one idea about the differences between men and women, it illustrates the impact on consumer research problematics that the feminism of women's voice/experience might have.

*Poststructuralist Feminism.* While liberal and women's voice/experience feminisms contribute additional problems to study, or additional ways of studying existing problems, poststructural feminism can both deconstruct existing problematics and suggest new ones. Deconstructionism draws heavily on Derrida's (1973) antiessentialist analyses of language, which shows that no signifiers have a fixed signification and that the meaning of signifiers is always in flux. A feminist deconstruction of consumer research focuses on the gendered language in existing problematics and asks how gendered signifiers shape our view of existing problematics. For example, Hirschman's (1991) content analysis of current research published in the *Journal of Marketing* shows that marketers' relationships to consumers are almost always described in terms that portray marketers as agentic beings who seek to wield power over consumers rather than as communally oriented beings who seek to coexist in harmony with consumers. The most common agentic themes include gaining power and control over others; instrumentalism; competition; and conflict, war, and aggression. This analysis can help us to challenge some of the patriarchal assumptions that inform our current problematics.

New problematics associated with a poststructuralist feminist approach, which recognizes the way gendered signifiers are associated with seemingly neutral things or ideas, are exemplified by the works of Forty (1986) and Heisley (1991). Forty (1986) shows that, in the nineteenth century, differential product designs (e.g., wristwatches) began to communicate socially constituted ideals of femininity and masculinity that were held to correspond to biological sex differences; his work illustrates how the interplay of gendered signifiers and that which they signify is an integral part of the dynamic between social norms, gender, and consumption styles. Heisley's (1991) work on the gender symbolism in food found the signifier "feminine" to be highly associated with unprocessed foods such as milk and eggs, and the signifier "masculine" to be highly associated with meat.

To summarize, although extant consumer research problematics represent a variety of different interests, especially those of managers, they are often informed by unacknowledged gendered assumptions. Feminist perspectives can be used to demonstrate that many seemingly gender-neutral or gender-inclusive problematics actually incorporate gender biases, such as formulating problems that serve male self-interests, overlooking problems that reflect women's unique experiences, and shaping problematics on the basis of masculine language and signifiers. Additionally, feminist perspectives can suggest new problematics that seek to remedy this imbalance by explicitly focusing on the female and the feminine.

### Theories

While we have suggested many ways in which consumer research problematics might be broadened or challenged by feminist perspectives, it must be recognized that gendered problematics are difficult to recognize and correct because of the mutually reinforcing relationship between problems on one hand and theories and methods of data collection and analysis on the other (Bernard 1973). In other words, problems chosen for investigation are greatly limited by available theories and methods; theories and methods are used because they facilitate investigations of certain problems. This discussion will focus in particular on the theoretical perspectives on sex and gender that characterize or are absent from our literature.

*Liberal Feminism.* Although liberal feminism acknowledges biological differences, it does not theorize that they determine differences in rational abilities and processes. Thus, liberal feminism would call into question implicit assumptions that biological differences determine observed differences in cognitive style or capacity. For example, recent studies of the impact of various stimuli on men versus women are premised on the theory that males and females differ innately in their tendency to be agentic or communal and in their hemispheric information-processing styles (Meyers-Levy 1988, 1989; Meyers-Levy and Sternthal 1991). Using biological sex as an independent variable, the research design suggests an implicit belief that the cause of detected male/female differences is biologically "hard wired." A liberal feminist perspective would caution that different results might be found using subjects who had been raised under different social or cultural conditions that were more nearly equal for men and women. It suggests, at a minimum, that the interpretation of results in such studies should consider that detected sex-related differences in cognitive processing might not be stable across all social and cultural settings.

At the same time, liberal feminism would also question whether results from studies using single-sex samples lack validity for generalized consumer behavior knowledge. For instance, Reingen and his colleagues (Reingen *et al.* 1984; Ward and Reingen 1990) have sampled college sororities to investigate the role of interpersonal relationships in consumer decision making; Richins (1991) examined the effects of physically attractive ad models on young women's satisfaction with their own attractiveness; and MacInnis and Park (1991) studied the effects of music indexicality (the extent to which it arouses emotion-laden reactions) on young women's high- and low-involvement and processing. While single-sex sample designs have certain advantages, they forgo the opportunity to empirically investigate whether phenomena are sex specific. Thus, generalizing knowledge claims about "consumers" from single-sex samples is theoretically indefensible without additional research involving the other sex.

To summarize, while liberal feminists reject the notion that cognitive abilities are biologically determined, they accept the premise that sex differences currently exist because of social inequities. So long as inequities exist, and particularly since so much of consumer behavior (who shops, who chooses, who pays, who consumes what) is demonstrably linked in some way to sex, liberal feminism would argue that sex differences should be investigated empirically. However, it should not be assumed that the cause of these differences is biological.

*Women's Voice/Experience Feminism.* Women's voice/experience feminism stresses that theories should take into account experientially based differences in the viewpoints of men and women. The use of gender-related constructs provides one means of doing so. For instance, two psychological constructs commonly used in consumer research acknowledge that individuals are variably socialized into gendered perspectives. One is gender identity, that is, the extent to which women and men identify with both masculine and feminine traits (e.g., Allison *et al.* 1980; Gentry and Doering 1977; Gentry, Doering, and O'Brien 1978; Gentry and Haley 1984; Golden, Allison, and Clee 1979; Stern 1988). The other construct is gender role attitudes, that is, the extent to which individuals have traditional views about the rights and responsibilities of women and men (e.g., Fischer and Arnold 1990; Green and Cunningham 1975; Qualls 1987; Schaninger and Buss 1985).

Women's voice/experience feminism helps us see two types of problems that may characterize some consumer theory that does not incorporate gender explicitly. The first concerns theories and concepts that disregard gender but contain gender-based asymmetries. For example, some constructs contain asymmetric gender referents based on men's experiences as the norm. The construct "working wives" (cf. Soberon-Ferrer and Dardis 1991) makes sense only if one regards childcare and household management as nonwork or leisure and defines work only as paid employment outside the home. From a male perspective, it may be easy to differentiate housework from "real" work because housework is paid for with emotional, not economic, currency. However, from a female perspective housework compares badly to most paid employment – it is boring, physically demanding, never ending (Forty 1986) and is not recognized as a legitimate occupation. Gender bias in the perception of meaningful work may help explain why Bartos (1989) concluded that the search for behavioral differences among women based solely on their occupational status has proved unsatisfactory. This is not to say that all constructs must be gender symmetric or inclusive. Recognizing asymmetries would help us appreciate the scope and/or limitations of our concepts and might suggest the need for new ones. For example, Belk (1988) very appropriately acknowledges his concept of the extended self to be inherently masculine and Western, thereby raising the possibility that feminine or Eastern constructs might be sought.

The second problem concerns research that ignores gender as a theoretical variable on the assumption that it is irrelevant to the matter of interest. This assumption pervades much of the theory in which consumer research is rooted yet is undermined by recent findings that the differential socialization of boys and girls relates to many adult behaviors (e.g., Chodorow 1978; Dinnerstein 1976; Gilligan 1982). One implication of this point applies to studies in which gender is ignored at a theoretical level, yet significant male/female differences are empirically detected. For instance, Feick and Price (1987) find sex differences in consumers' propensity to provide shopping and marketplace information. Since shopping is socially stereotyped as "women's work," theoretical attention to the role of gender-related socialization differences might help explain observed sex differences in the market maven construct.

A second implication is that a consideration of gender at the theoretical level might shed light on empirical problems seemingly unrelated to gender. For example, emotion has been the topic of several recent articles (e.g., Hui and Bateson 1991; MacInnis and Park 1991; Olney, Holbrook, and Batra 1991; Westbrook and Oliver 1991). This is encouraging since consumer researchers have historically preferred to study rational, logical consumer processes associated with the masculine, such as information processing, over processes associated with the feminine, such as emotion (Holbrook 1990). However, the emerging body of knowledge about emotion may be distorted by overlooking gender as an explicit theoretical issue. For instance, in linking emotion to satisfaction with a recent car purchase, Westbrook and Oliver (1991) clustered their largely male (74 percent) sample into groups representing different emotional patterns. They were puzzled because the "unemotional" group (which contained the largest number of respondents) was related to "moderately high" satisfaction levels. Although the number of men and women in each group was not reported, gender may shed some theoretical light: since men tend to be socialized to hide their emotions, gender may moderate the relationship between expressed emotion and satisfaction. Incorporating gender theories into future research on emotion and/or customer satisfaction might yield a better understanding of such phenomena.

Awareness of the different ways feminists theorize gender may help consumer researchers to articulate their own theoretical positions more clearly. It may also help them to choose which theories to apply more knowledgeably; there is a tendency to assume certain constructs are relevant to certain consumer behaviors without exploring or explaining the rationale for such suppositions. For instance, in their research into gender differences in durable-goods payment methods, Choe *et al.* (1991) assign gender merely on the basis of biological sex. They base their analysis on a comparison of the payment methods of female- versus male-headed households, where a household is defined as female headed only if she is not married. Although, not surprisingly, numerous differences between male- and female-headed households are reported, alleged gender differences are confounded by marital status. Researchers interested in gender differences may wish to read more widely in the feminist literature on women's experience to help select more applicable theories.

*Poststructuralist Feminism.* Poststructural feminist perspectives regarding gender are the most radical. They stress that signifiers (e.g., words like "masculine" and "feminine") associated with sex and gender are coupled with many phenomena not necessarily linked to sex or gender (e.g., activities like managing and shopping) and that cultural notions regarding sex and gender thus tend to inform our understanding of these phenomena. Theories centrally related to our view of consumers, such as the marketing concept, can be argued to be partially reliant on gendered signifiers for their meaning because the taken-for-granted linguistic opposition between marketer and consumer is related to our culture's binary oppositions of male versus female and masculine versus feminine. "Marketer" is associated with masculinity and "consumer" with femininity since this dichotomy corresponds directly to practices in place when modern marketing arose: men were more likely to be managers or those who controlled the public world of commerce and woman were likely to be consumers or those who controlled the private world of consumption (Firat 1991; Firat and Venkatesh, forthcoming). This historical interplay between the development of the definition of "feminine" and the development of consumer culture would be hard to overestimate. Numerous scholars have noted that consumption-related duties became "women's chores" in the latter part of the last century and that, at the same time, these duties became one of the major activities occupying the time of middle-class women (Benson 1986; Ewen 1977; Firat and Venkatesh, forthcoming; Gordon and McArthur 1984; Leach 1981). Today, the image of many consumption activities as "women's work" and the tendency for women to define themselves in part through their consumer behaviors persists (Fischer and Arnold 1990; Fischer and Gainer 1991; Jansen-Verbeke 1987). Noting these associations raises questions concerning what kinds of gendered assumptions might underlie the way the marketer/consumer relationship is construed in our theories.

Links between gender imagery and marketer/consumer relationships can be traced to some of the earliest marketing texts (such as Naether's [1928] *Advertising to Women* and Frederick's [1929] *Selling Mrs. Consumer),* which explicitly cast the consumer as female and pit the marketing manager (referred to with masculine pronouns) against the consumer, advising him on how to get her to buy something she might not otherwise have purchased. The contemporary marketing concept (i.e., that "the key to achieving organizational goals consists in determining the needs and wants of target markets and delivering the desired satisfactions more effectively and efficiently than competitors" [Kotler and Turner 1989, p. 171]) belies a lingering connection between masculine/feminine relationships and marketer/consumer relationships: a poststructural feminist reading of the language in which the concept is couched points up the sexual connotations of the statement that marketers are seeking to "determine consumers' wants and needs" (which can be read either as "discovering" or, more perniciously, as "dictating" needs, that is, deciding for consumers what those consumers *really* want) and "delivering desired satisfactions" (giving them what they are asking for) to achieve their own goals (get what the marketer wants). This reading has striking parallels to stereotypes of exploitive male/female relationships in which a man decides what a woman really wants and "delivers satisfaction," thereby achieving his own sexual gratification.

Clearly, there are many female marketing managers and even more male consumers; equally clearly, marketers cannot universally be characterized as exploitively seeking to violate consumers' interests. Nonetheless, there are persistent tendencies to characterize consumers (male and female) in terms consistent with stereotypes of women (as passive entities, easily duped by a superficial show of interest, and essentially powerless) and to construe marketers in relation to consumers in terms consistent with stereotypes of men (as self-serving agents, less concerned with permanent relationships than with immediate gratification, and as aggressors). Such a gendered marketer/consumer dichotomy is evident, for example, in the portrayal of consumers as struggling to maintain self-control over their desires for immediate gratification in the face of numerous actions taken by marketers to exploit consumer impatience (Hoch and Loewenstein 1991). In another example, as described in consumer research (e.g., Frenzen and Davis 1990), direct sellers appear to be clever exploiters of consumers' needs for social relationships to achieve their own ends. That consumers might resist excessive pressure or even "use" marketing venues to their own purposes (without buying products) is never intimated even though there is evidence that women are not as susceptible to marketing pressures as is sometimes hypothesized (Frenzen and Davis 1990).

The point here is that the discourse of consumer research constrains our perception of marketer/consumer relationships. It is not accurate to characterize consumers as largely passive dupes, and marketers are not necessarily scheming aggressors. Envisioning other constructions of reality that place more emphasis on the trust and respect that can characterize relationships may help develop more mutually beneficial consumer/marketer relationships. A starting point for consumer researchers would be to devote greater attention to exchange relationships in which the power is more balanced between consumer and marketer (such as garage sales; see Soiffer and Herrmann [1987]). It is worth noting that more nearly balanced power differentials between buyer and seller are a feature of business-to-business marketing, and that industrial marketers have introduced the concept of "relationship marketing," which speaks to the need for trust, mutual respect, and a long-term orientation in buyer-seller relationships (see Jackson 1985).

### Methods of Data Collection

A key component in scholarly training is learning the data collection methods that are consistent with the discipline's aims and theories (Laudan 1983). Proper and standard procedures are emphasized. However, rigorous adherence to such standards may both fail to ensure objectivity and introduce systematic gender bias in the name of proper method (Harding 1986). Since liberal feminism accepts traditional scientific method as fundamentally sound, it merely exhorts scientists to follow established research norms more closely. Both women's voice/experience feminism and poststructuralist feminism hold important insights into gendered aspects of data collection.

*Women's Voice/Experience Feminism.* Women's voice/experience feminism points to several opportunities to sensitize us to gender issues in the data collection process. One opportunity involves a heightened awareness of the various ways in which sex and gender may affect data collection. For example, Rao and Steckel (1991) asked respondents to rate marketing faculty candidates individually and then to reach a group consensus. The sex of respondents and candidates was not taken into consideration. Since research employing scenarios that systematically vary the sex of the main character find that respondent judgments are affected both by the sex of the respondent and by that of the main character (see Simeone 1987), including sex might have led to insights about potential two- and three-way interactions involving respondent sex, candidate sex, and judgments on other reported characteristics such as personality and collegiality. As a second example, since an all-male research team was used to interview married women (Thompson, Locander, and Pollio 1990), it might have been useful for them to speculate how their posing of questions about experiences unique to women affected their data collection (Harding 1987; Oakley 1981) and/or to consider using mixed-sex research teams sensitized to gender issues in the future (Costa 1991; Young 1991). As a final example, Pechmann and Ratneshwar (1991, p. 149) asked respondents to view an ad for a powdered cleanser as they "normally" would and to rate attributes. Since many view cleansers as a "woman's product," men's viewing habits, knowledge, and experience may be quite limited. These examples show not a violation of some ideal design but rather that sex and gender may have unavoidable effects. To better understand these effects, reporting sample sex composition and testing for response homogeneity across sex should be routine. Further, including gender-related measures such as gender identity and gender-role attitudes might lead to important new insights about consumption processes.

A second opportunity for sensitivity relates to gaining a better understanding of the nature of the researcher/ respondent relationship. Women's voice/experience feminism challenges the assumption that the researcher/respondent relationship can ever be nonreflexive, that is, independent and separate (Belk 1991; Oakley 1981), or that the relationship is either gender neutral or gender inclusive (Eichler 1988; Sherif 1979). For example, the goal of nonreflexivity is thought to be achieved by maintaining the hierarchy and distance between the interviewee and interviewer by shrugging or laughing off interviewee questions, and not revealing information lest it affect responses (see Selltiz *et al.* 1965). When Oakley (1981) interviewed women about their childbearing experiences, her initial attempt to follow such textbook interviewing prescriptions created a dilemma for her. If she refused to answer such questions as "Which hole does the baby come out of?" hierarchy and distance would have been maintained. However, it also would have negatively affected respondents' willingness to provide data. By using her research as a vehicle to offer information and advice to her respondents (she had recently had a child herself and so was able to give them information they were uncomfortable requesting from their male doctors) she was able to use her gendered and reflexive relationship with her respondents to mutual advantage. She obtained insights into their experience; they benefited from advice based on hers. Acknowledging the gendered, reflexive nature of the researcher/respondent relationship has several research implications. First, it validates emergent subjective experiences as a basis of knowledge (Oakley 1981; Smith 1974; Westkott 1979) and thus can lead to new insights into women's unique experiences (e.g., Thompson *et al.* 1990). Second, it rejects the traditional hierarchical assumption that the scholar speaks as the voice of authority, suggesting instead a more collaborative relationship between the "narrator" and "interpreter" (Personal Narratives Group 1989b) in which, for example, the respondents participate in the interpretation process (e.g., Thompson et al. 1990). Third, it suggests that scholars must acknowledge how their own class, gender, culture, and race affect interpretation (Harding 1987; Personal Narratives Group 1989b). For example, since Thompson *et al.*'s (1990) interpretations of married women's experiences were unavoidably influenced by the researchers' respective backgrounds, acknowledging them and their likely influence would provide an interpretive context for interested readers.

The recent trend toward more qualitative consumer research suggests that gender issues may receive more attention since qualitative researchers are more likely to seek a fully contextualized understanding of phenomena (Belk 1991) and to report respondents' sex, gender, race, and age (see, e.g., Meha and Belk 1991; Wallendorf and Arnould 1991). Although such methods are well suited to the exploration of women's perspectives, they have no inherent immunity to gender problems and require continued sensitivity to gender (see Warren 1988). Scholars may wish to consult feminist sources such as *Interpreting Women's Lives*, edited by the Personal Narratives Group (1989a, 1989b), for research that is exemplary in this regard.

*Poststruclturalist Feminism.* Poststructuralist feminism, with its attention to discourse, suggests somewhat different sources of bias in our methods of data collection. One source arises because wording may invoke certain unintended implicit meanings and elicit reactions that do not accord with intended meanings. Eichler (1988), for instance, points out that just as the pronoun "you" can be interpreted either as singular (i.e., you, yourself) or plural (i.e., you, everyone else in some category), the pronoun "he" can be interpreted in either the gender inclusive or the gender exclusive sense. She also notes that responses to gendered language may vary depending on the respondent's sex, as well as the respondent's interpretation of whether the question was gender inclusive or particular to men. Numerous analyses of gendered terminology in language (e.g., Moulton 1977) have shown that the use of terms such as he, his, man, and so forth, are never neutral, regardless of intention. Even when the term is unambiguously inclusive, the result may be odd, amusing or insulting (e.g., "Some men are female"; Moulton 1977).

Despite widespread adoption of gender inclusive language in consumer research articles and textbooks, insensitivities to the effects of gendered language persist in data collection. Although question wording is of paramount importance and books on research methods usually contain detailed discussions on the subject in general, gender issues are overlooked. For example, Sudman and Bradburn's (1982, p. 1) highly regarded book on questionnaire design opens with a discussion of the critical importance of question wording in maximizing validity and a warning that "seemingly small changes can cause large differences in responses." The fact that they ignore the issue of gendered language is an indication of the extent to which unquestioned assumptions about gender neutral language pervade our discourse.

In practice, the ambiguous use of "he" is not uncommon in consumer research instruments. For instance, Wilson and Peterson (1989, p. 24) presented respondents with the following scenario in a word-of-mouth study: "Suppose you found out your neighbor had purchased Brand [A or B] (of a digital tape recorder) and that he had to take it back." It is unclear as to whether "he" was intended to mean male or any human. Yet responses are likely to have varied depending on how this was interpreted, as well as on respondents' sex and gender. We suggest that, because of the product involved, it is more likely that respondents would have interpreted the neighbor as male. This is theoretically problematic given that nowhere in the article is it suggested that the research question is about the evaluation of positive versus negative word-of-mouth information from *male* sources.

As another example, the Wallach and Kogan (1964) scale of risk-taking behavior has been used a number of times in consumer research. In the 12 scenarios used to create an index of risk-taking behavior, there is only one female mentioned, a "girl," Miss X whom Mr. Y is considering marrying. Not only are all the actors male; the contexts and decision situations are all traditionally associated with men (e.g., electrical engineering, war, and football). Given its age, it is to be expected that some biases would appear in the scale; the issue is how it has been applied and/or tailored to contemporary research contexts. For example, when Zinkhan and Kirande (1991) used the Wallach and Kogan scale in a cross-cultural study, they eliminated the football scenario as inappropriate for Spanish subjects, but the asymmetrical gender content of the scale was overlooked. Undoubtedly, women and traditional female activities were not consciously excluded from the scale; gender simply remains an unmarked category in our discourses. Interestingly, in their analyses, these authors discovered significant differences between male and female responses. Their results lend credence to the critiques raised by women's voice/experience and poststructuralist feminism and suggest that greater efforts to be sensitive to gender in language are imperative.

### Methods of Data Analysis

One of the final steps in the knowledge-generation process is the analysis and interpretation of data. Since data analysis decisions are largely influenced by decisions about problematics, theory, and data collection methods, the possibilities for gender biases before this step are numerous. Those who would argue that analyses, at least quantitative ones, are fairly mechanical might regard this phase as the least susceptible to introducing gendered assumptions. Two of the feminist perspectives give insight, however, as to how gender biases can be incorporated into analyses.

*Women's Voice/Experience Feminism.* The feminism of women's voice/experience would suggest it is necessary to at least consider the possibility of sex- and gender-based differences in the phenomenon of interest. If, as argued in the previous section, too few consumer researchers report sample sex and gender characteristics, fewer yet report analyses involving these characteristics, thus ensuring that nothing will be learned about the influence of these characteristics on consumption. This omission is especially true for quantitative analyses, but, even in qualitative analyses that tend to report respondent sex, the opportunity to incorporate it into analysis is not always taken. For instance, Schouten's (1991) analysis overlooked systematic differences in men's and women's self-concepts and motivations for self-alteration through plastic surgery. There are profound implications that could be drawn from an interpretation of the fact that the two men had pragmatic reasons for self-alteration (e.g., sinus problems), while the seven women (or their relatives) were dissatisfied with their bodies (e.g., breasts too big, too small). As Wolf (1990) points out, pressures to achieve ideal beauty lead women to experience intense dissatisfaction with their natural appearance and to exert heroic efforts to conform to socially defined standards of beauty.

Even if the relatively easy step of comparing the sexes becomes routine, problems may persist since this approach is underwritten by the view that all differences are biologically based. Those who view gender as socially constructed and variable within as well as between the sexes would argue that this is insufficient, if not misleading. They would suggest that, if a quantitative approach to data analysis is to be used, then quantitative measures of gender-related constructs must also be developed and their impact analyzed in order to fully understand any phenomenon of interest. Similarly, qualitative approaches must also be more sensitive to the influence of gender on consumption. Simply put, sex or gender differences cannot be presumed not to exist if no attempt is made to analyze data to detect their presence. As argued at the beginning of this article, gender is a pervasive filter through which individuals experience their social world. Since consumption is a ubiquitous cultural phenomenon, much remains to be analyzed about gendered aspects of consumption.

*Poststructuralist Feminism.* Poststructuralist feminism offers a somewhat different critique of data analysis, leveled at the dominant discourses and practices within science and scholarly journals. The practice of hypothesis testing, and the dominant discourse in which it is embedded, may introduce a tendency in studies of sex or gender to find differences where few or none exist. The standard hypothesis-testing format is for $H_O$ to hypothesize no sex/gender difference, and for $H_A$ to hypothesize a sex/gender difference. Despite extensive criticisms of the ingrained prejudice against publishing findings supporting the null hypothesis (Greenwald 1975), journals still display a bias toward publishing significant results (Eichler 1988; Hyde 1981). This practice must lead to careful reading of studies reporting significant results because they can support unfounded gender assumptions in several ways. First, they can create the impression that differences are more numerous than nondifferences, when in fact many "no difference" studies may be stored in file cabinets or omitted from the research report. Further, when differences are reported, the discussion is often framed so that the male results are described as the norm while the female results are described as deviations from the norm, thereby implying not only that females are different but also that they are inferior (Spender 1981). Second, through lack of a priori conceptual development and/or post hoc discussion about gender, reported gender differences (e.g., Meyers-Levy 1988, 1989; Meyers-Levy and Sternthal 1991) can appear to be biologically "hardwired" and thus reinforce cultural stereotypes about men's and women's inherent abilities. Third, even if statistically significant, the differences may be too small to be substantively significant (Hyde 1981). Hyde meta-analyzed the data from which Maccoby and Jacklin (1974) concluded that four cognitive gender differences (in verbal, quantitative, visual-spatial, and visual-analytic spatial abilities) were "well established." She found effect sizes to be small, accounting for only 1–5 percent of the population variance and thus not meaningful in a practical setting. Yet publishing results reporting significant differences confers a legitimacy and credibility that can form the basis of self-fulfilling prophecies. For example, telling people that scientists have found sex differences in some domains may promote the enactment of these differences.

Only by critical examination of our data analysis techniques and publication strategies can practices biased in these ways be eliminated. In papers that argue that empirical gender-based differences exist (e.g., Meyers-Levy and Sternthal 1991), journal reviewers might press authors to articulate fully the nature and implications of the theoretical bases (as well as empirical precedents) in which they have grounded their investigations. This would help to ensure that discussions distinguish carefully whether biologically based sex differences or sociologically based gender differences are being posited and to delimit the applicability of the study in terms of the contexts in which it is thought to be relevant.

## Summary and Conclusions

This critical discussion of consumer research in light of feminist theories has identified many ways in which unwarranted assumptions are embedded in and perpetuated by our practices. First, feminist perspectives were shown to reveal androcentrism in traditional definitions of objectivity and to add to the debate on the feasibility and the desirability for consumer research of pursuing objectivity as it is traditionally defined. Second, problematics reflective of the interests and experiences of women were argued to have been largely ignored in mainstream consumer research. The dominance of patriarchal interests and perspectives in existing problematics was also addressed. Third, feminist challenges to certain theories used in consumer research were raised. Undefended assumptions of biologically determined sex differences, unacknowledged assumptions of asymmetry in the socialization of men and women, failures to take gender into account when relevant, and lack of awareness of the way gendered signifiers inform theoretical discourses were all discussed. Fourth, feminist insights about the need to take sex of respondents and researchers into account in both qualitative and quantitative data collection, and to be sensitive to the effects of gendered language during data collection, were reviewed. Finally, feminist critiques both of failures to take into account the sex and/or gender socialization of respondents and of tendencies to reify sex differences in data analysis were discussed.

There are several reasons for optimism concerning the discipline's ability to reduce sex/gender biases and thereby develop more accurate and useful knowledge. For example, the 1991 ACR-sponsored conference on sex and gender and consumer research in Salt Lake City, and the increasing number of ACR papers and special sessions exploring sex- and gender-related topics, suggests that such issues are increasingly salient and important to consumer researchers. Also, the openness to qualitative and interpretive research methods that are consistent with some feminist theory has been demonstrated in the increasing amount of such work published in *JCR*.

In the long term, consumer research has the potential to become a discipline with a heightened sensitivity not only to sex and gender but also to issues such as race, class, culture, and sexual orientation. To develop in this way, the field must support a plurality of theoretical and methodological approaches capable of capturing rich and complex consumption phenomena, as well as engage in ongoing and critical self-reflectiion.

Research that incorporates the following can help achieve these goals:

- Problematics that reflect the perspectives and concerns of those groups that have been systematically marginalized
- Theories and concepts that are inclusive of marginalized groups, or that explicitly delimit the domain of their applicability
- Data collection methods that recognize emergent subjective experiences of women and minority groups as epistemologically valid, and instruments that are sensitive to the effects of gendered, or otherwise biased, language
- Data analysis methods that do not assume a priori that there are, or that there are not, differences related to sex, gender, or other biological, social, or cultural categories, but that facilitate examining their presence and their nature

Whether our goals are merely to improve on our current practices or, more ambitiously, to broaden and enrich our discipline, the ideas expressed here should prove invaluable. That such an effort is worthwhile seems incontrovertible.

## Notes

1. Although the field of consumer research is clearly broader, in this article the term refers primarily to research appearing in outlets such as the *Journal of Consumer Research*, marketing journals, and conferences sponsored by the Association for Consumer Research.

2. In fact, minority women's viewpoints (from women of color, lesbian women, non-middle-class women, etc.) have often been completely ignored or distortionally represented by liberals and other relatively empowered feminists who view the interests of women too generally as monolithic and unified. Extensive discussions of minority issues in feminism can be found, e.g., in Barrett and McIntosh (1986), Childers and Books (1990), Books (1984), and King (1990).

3. The profound differences in tenets and foci between the forms of feminism included in this category must not be misrepresented. For instance, radical feminists tend to focus on innate female/male differences (such as reproductive anatomy and roles) and to trace women's oppression to exploitation of these differences; they seek to alter the hierarchical ordering of male/female relationships based on these differences while preserving that which is uniquely, and innately, female. In contrast, many psychoanalytic feminists are concerned with differences in preconscious psychic development that stem from girls' and boys' identification with, versus differentiation from, their mothers; these psychoanalytic feminists believe that the development of psychologically healthy and empowered women and men requires alterations in the standard parenting arrangements. Most social feminists focus on neither physical nor psychic differences but on the social structures, particularly of patriarchy and capitalism, which constrain the roles into which men and women are socialized. They call for revisions in these social structures in order to open a wider range of roles for women and men, and to end the subordination of women to men on the basis of their traditional roles.

4. This section draws extensively on Weedon (1987).

5. Critics of general poststructuralism argue that it goes too far in rejecting the possibility of some shared knowledge and of some progress toward less biased understanding. In its extreme versions, poststructuralism is regarded as bordering on both nihilism and solipsism.

## References


Allison, Neil, Linda Golden, G. Millet, and Donna Coogan (1980), "Sex-typed Product Images: The Effects of Sex, Sex Role Self Concept, and Measurement Implications," in *Advances in Consumer Research*, Vol. 7, ed. Jerry C. Olson, Ann Arbor, MI: Association for Consumer Research, 604-609.

AMA Task Force on the Development of Marketing Thought (1988), "Developing, Disseminating, and Utilizing Marketing Knowledge," *Journal of Marketing*, 52 (October), 1–25.

Anderson, Paul (1983), "Marketing, Scientific Progress, and Scientific Method," *Journal of Marketing*, 47 (October), 18–31.

– (1986), "On Method in Consumer Research: A Critical Relativist Perspective," *Journal of Consumer Research*, 13 (September), 155–173.

Barrett, Michele and Mary McIntosh (1985), "Ethnocentrism and Socialist-Feminist Theory," *Feminist Review*, 20 (Summer), 23–47.

Bartos, Rena (1978), "What Every Marketer Should Know about Women," *Harvard Business Review*, 56 (May–June), 73-85.

– (1989), *Marketing to Women around the World*, Boston: Harvard Business School Press.

Bearden, William, Richard Nettemeyer, and Jesse Teel (1989), "Measurement of Consumer Susceptibility to Interpersonal Influence," *Journal of Consumer Research*, 16 (September), 183–194.

Belenky, Mary, Blythe Clinchy, Nancy Goldberger, and Jill Tarule (1986), *Women's Ways of Knowing*, New York: Basic.

Belk, Russell (1986), "What Should ACR Want to Be When It Grows Up?' in *Advances in Consumer Research*, Vol. 13, ed. Richard J. Lutz, Provo, UT: Association for Consumer Research, 423–424.

– (1988), "Possessions and the Extended Self," *Journal of Consumer Research*, 2 (September), 139–168.

– (1991), "Real Men DO Collect Soft Data," in *Gender and Consumer Behavior*, ed. Janeen Costa, Salt Lake City: University of Utah Printing Service, 387–393.

– and Gregory Coon (1991), "Men and Women on Dating and Gift-Giving: Same Planet, Different Worlds," in *Gender and Consumer Behavior*, ed. Janeen Costa, Salt Lake City: University of Utah Printing Service, 941–103.

–, John Sherry, and Melanie Wallendorf (1988), "A Naturalistic Inquiry into Buyer and Seller Behavior at a Swap Meet," *Journal of Consumer Research*, 14 (March), 449–470.

Bem, Sandra (1974), "The Measurement of Psychological Androgyny," *Journal of Consulting Clinical Psychology*, 42 (2), 155–162.

Benson, Susan Porter (1986), *Counter Cultures: Saleswomen, Managers and Customers in American Department Stores*, Urbana: University of Illinois Press.

Bernard, Jesse (1973), "My Four Revolutions: An Autobiographical History of the ASA," *American Journal of Sociology*, 78 (January), 773–791.

Black, Naomi (1989), *Social Feminism*, Ithaca, NY: Cornell University Press.

Bristor, Julia (1985), "Consumer Behavior from a Contemporary Philosophy of Science Perspective: An Organizational Framework," in *Advances in Consumer Research*, Vol. 12, ed. Elizabeth C. Hirschman and Morris B. Holbrook, Provo, UT: Association for Consumer Research, 300–304.

Brown, Jacqueline Johnson and Peter H. Reingen (1987), "Social Ties and Word-of-Mouth Referral Behavior," *Journal of Consumer Research*, 14 (December), 350–362.

Brownmiller, Susan (1976), *Against Our Will: Women, Men and Rape*, New York: Bantam.

Burnkrant, Robert and Alain Cousineau (1975), "Informational and Normative Social Influence in Buyer Behavior," *Journal of Consumer Research*, 2 (December), 205–215.

Calás, Marta and Linda Smircich (1992), "Using the 'F' Word: Feminist Theories and the Social Consequences of Organizational Research," in *Gendering Organizational Analysis*, ed. Albert J. Mills and Peta Tancred, Newbury Park, CA: Sage, 222–234.

– and Linda Smircich (1991), "Voicing Seduction to Silence Leadership," *Organization Studies*, 12 (4), 567–601.

Calder, Bobby and Alice Tybout (1987), "What Consumer Research Is ..." *Journal of Consumer Research*, 14 (June), 136–140.

Cheal, David (1988), *The Gift Economy*, London: Routledge.

Childers, Mary and Bell Hooks (1990), "A Conversation about Race and Class," in *Conflicts in Feminism*, ed. Marianne Hirsch and Evelyn Fox Keller, New York: Routledge, 44–59.

Chodorow, Nancy (1978), *The Reproduction of Mothering*, Berkeley and Los Angeles: University of California Press.

Choe, Hyuncha, S. J. Yoon, and Dixie P. Johnson (1991), "Gender Differences in the Choice of Payment Method for Purchasing Goods," in *Gender and Consumer Behavior*, ed. Janeen Costa, Salt Lake City: University of Utah Printing Service, 32–42.

Costa, Janeen Arnold (1991), "The Bi-Gender Research Team," paper presented at the Gender and Consumer Behavior Conference, Salt Lake City.

Daly, Mary (1978), *Gyn/Ecology: The Metaethics of Radical Feminism*, Boston: Beacon.

Davis, Harry (1971), "Measurement of Husband-Wife Influence in Consumer Purchase Decisions," *Journal of Marketing Research*, 8 (August), 305–312.

Derrida, Jacques (1973), *Speech and Phenomenon*, Evanston, IL: Northwestern University Press.

Dinnerstein, Dorothy (1976), *The Mermaid and the Minotaur*, New York: Harper & Row.

Easterday, Lois, Diana Papademas, Laura Schorr, and Catherine Valentine (1977), "The Making of the Female Researcher," *Urban Life*, 6 (3), 333–348.

Eichler, Margrit (1988), *Non-sexist Research Methods: A Practical Guide*, Boston: Allen & Unwin.

Eisenstein, Zillah (1986), *The Radical Future of Liberal Feminism*, Boston: Northeastern University Press.

Ewen, Stewart (1977), *Captains of Consciousness: Advertising and the Social Roots of the Consumer Culture*, New York: McGraw-Hill.

Fee, Elizabeth (1983), "Women's Nature and Scientific Objectivity," in *Woman's Nature*, ed. Marian Lowe and Ruth Hubbard, New York: Pergamon, 9–28.

Feick, Larry F. and Linda L. Price (1987), "The Market Maven: A Diffuser of Marketplace Information," *Journal of Marketing*, 51 (January), 83–97.

Firal, A. Fuat (1991), "Consumption and Gender: A Common History," in *Gender and Consumer Behavior*, ed. Janeen Costa, Salt Lake City: University of Utah Printing Service, 378–386.

– and Alladi Venkatesh (forthcoming), "The Making of Postmodern Consumption," in *Consumption and Marketing: Macro Dimensions*, ed. Russell Belk and Nikhilesh Dholakia, Boston: PWS-Kent.

Fischer, Eileen and Stephen Arnold (1990), "More than a Labor of Love: Gender Roles and Christmas Gift Shopping," *Journal of Consumer Research*, 17 (December), 333-345.

– and Brenda Gainer (1991), "I Shop Therefore I Am: The Role of Shopping in the Social Construction of Women's Identities," in *Gender and Consumer Behavior*, ed. Janeen Costa, Salt Lake City: University of Utah Printing Service, 350–357.

Flax, Jane (1990), *Thinking Fragments: Psychoanalysis, Feminism, and Postmodernism in the Contemporary West*, Berkeley and Los Angeles: University of California Press.

Forty, Adrian (1986), *Objects of Desire*, New York: Pantheon.

Foucault, Michel (1979), *Discipline and Punish*, Harmondsworth: Penguin.

– (1981), *The History of Sexuality, Vol. 1, An Introduction*, Harmondsworth: Pelican.

– (1986), *The History of Sexuality, Vol. 2, The Use of Pleasure*, Harmondsworth: Viking.

Frederick, Christine (1929), *Selling Mrs. Consumer*, New York: The Business Bourse.

Frenzen, Jonathan and Harry Davis (1990), "Purchasing Behavior in Embedded Markets," *Journal of Consumer Research*, 17 (June), 1–12.

Friedan, Betty (1963), *The Feminine Mystique*, New York: Dell.

Gainer, Brenda (1992), "The Impact of Between Buyer Relationships on Consumer Behavior," unpublished dissertation, Faculty of Administrative Studies, York University, North York, ON, Canada.

Gentry, James and Mildred Doering (1977), "Masculinity-Femininity Related to Consumer Choice," in *Contemporary Marketing Thought*, ed. Barnett A. Greenberg and Danny N. Bellenger, Chicago: American Marketing Association, 423–427.

–, Mildred Doering, and Terence O'Brien (1978), "Masculinity and Femininity Factors in Product Perception and Self Image," in *Advances in Consumer Research*, Vol. 5, ed. H. Keith Hunt, Ann Arbor, MI: Association for Consumer Research, 326–332.

– and D. Haley (1984), "Gender Schema Theory as a Predictor of Ad Recall," in *Advances in Consumer Research*, Vol. 11, ed. Thomas C. Kinnear, Provo, UT: Association for Consumer Research, 259–264.

Gilligan, Carol (1982), *In a Different Voice*, Cambridge, MA: Harvard University Press.

Golden, Linda, Neil Allison, and Mona Clee (1979), "The Role of Sex Role Self Concept in Masculine and Feminine Product Perceptions," in *Advances in Consumer Research*, Vol. 6, ed. William L. Wilkie, Ann Arbor, MI: Association for Consumer Research, 599–605.

Gordon, Jean and Jan McArthur (1984), "American Women and Domestic Consumption, 1800–1920: Four Interpretive Themes," *Journal ofAmerican Culture*, 8, 35–46.

Granovetter, Mark (1985), "Economic Action and Social Structure: The Problem of Embeddedness," *American Journal of Sociology*, 3 (November), 481–510.

Green, Robert and Isabella Cunningham (1975), "Feminine Role Perception and Family Purchasing Decisions," *Journal of Marketing Research*, 12 (August), 325–332.

Greenwald, Anthony G. (1975), "Consequences of Prejudice against the Null Hypothesis," *Psychological Bulletin*, 82 (January), 1–20.

Harding, Sandra (1986), *The Science Question in Feminism*, Ithaca, NY: Cornell University Press.

– (1987), "Introduction: Is There a Feminist Method?" in *Feminism and Methodology*, ed. Sandra Harding, Bloomington: Indiana University Press, 1–14.

Heisley, Deborah (1991), "Gender Symbolism and Usage Expectations in Food," paper presented at the Gender and Consumer Behavior Conference, Salt Lake City.

Hekman, Susan (1991), *Gender and Knowledge: Elements of Postmodern Feminism*, Oxford: Polity.

Hirsch, Marianne and Evelyn Fox Keller (1990), *Conflicts in Feminism*, New York: Routledge.

– (1991), "A Feminist Critique of Marketing Theory: Toward Agentic-Communal Balance," in *Gender and Consumer Behavior*, ed. Janeen Costa, Salt Lake City: University of Utah Printing Service, 324–340.

Hoch, Stephen J. and George F. Loewenstein (1991), "Time-inconsistent Preferences and Consumer Self-Control," *Journal of Consumer Research*, 17 (March), 492–507.

Holbrook, Morris B. (1987), "What Is Consumer Research?' *Journal of Consumer Research*, 14 (June), 128–132.

– (1990), "The Role of Lyricism in Research on Consumer Emotions: Skylark, Have You Anything to Say to Me?" in *Advances in Consumer Research*, Vol. 17, ed. Marvin E. Goldberg *et al.*, Provo, UT: Association for Consumer Research, 1–8.

hooks, bell (1984), *Feminist Theory: From Margin to Center*, Boston: South End.

Hui, Michael K. and John E. G. Bateson (1991), "Perceived Control and the Effects of Crowding and Consumer Choice on the Service Experience," *Journal of Consumer Research*, 18 (September), 174–184.

Hunt, Shelby D. (1990), *Modern Marketing Theory*, Cincinnati: South-Western.

Hyde, Janct Shibley (1981), "How Large Are Cognitive Gender Differences?" *American Psychologist*, 36 (8), 892–901.

Jackson, Barbara Bund (1985), *Winning and Keeping Industrial Customers*, Lexington, MA: Lexington.

Jagger, Alison (1983), *Feminist Politics and Human Nature*, Totowa, NJ: Rowman & Allenheld.

Jansen-Verbeke, Myriam (1987), "Women, Shopping and Leisure," *Leisure Studies*, 6, 71–86.

Jordanova, L. J. (1980), "Natural Facts: A Historical Perspective on Science and Sexuality," in *Nature, Culture and Gender*, ed. Carol P. MacCormack and Marilyn Strathern, Cambridge: Cambridge University Press, 42–69.

Keller, Evelyn Fox (1978), "Gender and Science," *Psychoanalysis and Contemporary Thought*, 1 (3), 409–433.

– (1982), "Feminism and Science," *Signs: Journal of Women in Culture and Society*, 7 (3), 589–602.

King, Katie (1990), "Producing Sex, Theory and Culture: Gay/Straight Remappings in Contemporary Ferninism," in *Conflicts in Feminism*, ed. Marianne Hirsch and Evelyn Fox Keller, New York: Routledge, 60–81.

Kotler, Philip and Ronald E. Turner (1989), *Marketing Management*, Canadian 6th ed., Scarborough, ON: PrenticeHall Canada.

Langer, Susan (1963), *Philosophy in a New Key: A Study of Symbolism, Reason, Rite and Art*, Cambridge, MA: MIT Press.

Langland, Elizabeth and Walter Gove, eds. (1981), *A Feminist Perspective in the Academy: The Difference It Makes*, Chicago: University of Chicago Press.

Laudan, Larry (1983), *Science and Values*, Berkeley and Los Angeles: University of California Press.

Leach, William (1981), *True Love and Perfect Union: The Feminist Reform of Sex and Society*, London: Routledge & Kegan Paul.

Maccoby, Eleanor E. and Carol N. Jacklin (1974), *The Psychology of Sex Differences*, Stanford, CA: Stanford University Press.

MacInnis, Deborah J. and C. Whan Park (1991), "The Differential Role of Characteristics of Music on High- and Low-Involvement Consumers' Processing of Ads," *Journal of Consumer Research*, 18 (September), 161–173.

Marketing Science Institute, (1992), *Research Priorities 1990–992*, Cambridge, MA: Marketing Science Institute.

McCall, Suzanne (1977), "Meet the 'Workwife'," *Journal of Marketing*, 41 (July), 55–65.

Mehta, Raj and Russell W. Belk (1991), "Artifacts, Identity, and Transition: Favorite Possessions of Indians and Indian Immigrants to the United States," *Journal of Consumer Research*, 17 (March), 398–411.

Meyers-Levy, Joan (1988), "The Influence of Sex Roles on Judgement," *Journal of Consumer Research*, 14 (March), 522–530.

– (1989), "Priming Effects on Product Judgments: A Hemispheric Interpretation," *Journal of Consumer Research*, 16 (June), 76–86.

– and Brian Sternthal (1991), "Gender Differences in the Use of Message Cues," *Journal of Marketing Research*, 28 (February), 84–96.

Mincer, Jacob (1960), "Labor Supply, Family Income and Consumption," *American Economic Review*, 50 (May), 574–583.

Moulton, Janice (1977), "The Myth of the Neutral 'Man,"' in *Feminism and Philosophy*, ed. Mary Vetterling-Braggin *et al.* Totowa, NJ: Littlefield, Adams, 124–137.

Mumby, Dennis and Linda Putnam (1990), "Bounded Rationality as an Organizational Construct," paper presented at the Academy of Management, San Francisco.

Naether, Carl (1928), *Advertising to Women*, New York: Prentice-Hall.

Oakley, Ann (1981), "Interviewing Women: A Contradiction in Terms," in *Doing Feminist Research*, ed. Helen Roberts, London: Routledge & Kegan Paul, 30–61.

Olney, Thomas J., Morris B. Holbrook, and Rajiv Batra (1991), "Consumer Responses to Advertising: The Effects of Ad Content, Emotions, and Attitude toward the Ad on Viewing Time," *Journal of Consumer Research*, 17 (March), 440–453.

Pechmann, Cornelia and S. Ratneshwar (1991), "The Use of Comparative Advertising for Brand Positioning: Association versus Differentiation," *Journal of Consumer Research*, 18 (September), 145–160.

Personal Narratives Group (1989a), "Truths," in *Interpreting Women's Lives*, ed. Personal Narratives Group, Bloomington: Indiana University Press, 261–264.

– (1989b), "Origins," in *Interpreting Women's Lives*, ed. Personal Narratives Group, Bloomington: Indiana University Press, 3–15.

Peter, J. Paul and Jerry C. Olson (1983), "Is Science Marketing." *Journal of Marketing*, 47 (Fall), 111–125.

Quails, William (1987), "Household Decision Behavior: The Impact of Husbands' and Wives' Sex Role Orientation," *Journal of Consumer Research*, 14 (September), 264–279.

Rao, Vithala R. and Joel H. Steckel (1991), "A Polarization Model for Describing Group Preferences," *Journal of Consumer Research*, 18 (June), 108–118.

Raymond, Janice (1979), *The Transsexual Empire*, Boston: Beacon.

Reilly, Michael (1982), "Working Wives and Convenience Consumption," *Journal of Consumer Research*, 8 (March), 407–418.

Reingen, Peter H., Brian L. Foster, Jacqueline Johnson Brown, and Stephen B. Seidman (1984), "Brand Congruence in Interpersonal Relations: A Social Network Analysis," *Journal of Consumer Research*, 11 (December), 771–783.

Richins, Marcia L. (1991), "Social Comparison and the Idealized Images of Advertising," *Journal of Consumer Research*, 18 (June), 71–83.

Roberts, Mary Lou and Lawrence H. Wortzel, eds. (1984), *Marketing to the Changing Household*, Cambridge, MA: Ballinger.

Schaninger, Charles and Chris Allen (1981), "Wife's Occupational Status as a Consumer Behavior Construct," *Journal of Consumer Research, 8 (September)*, 189–196.

– and Christian Buss (1985), "The Relationship of Sex Role Norms to Household Task Allocation," *Psychology and Marketing*, 2 (2), 93–104,

Schouten, John (1991), "Selves in Transition: Symbolic Consumption in Personal Rites of Passage and Identity Reconstruction," *Journal of Consumer Research*, 17 (March), 412–425.

Scott, Joan (1990), "Deconstructing Equality-versus-Difference: or, the Uses of Poststructuralist Theory for Feminism," *Conflicts in Feminism*, ed. Marianne Hirsch and Evelyn Fox Keller, New York: Routledge, 134–148.

Selltiz, C., M. Jahoda, M. Deutsch, and S.W. Cook (1965), *Research Methods in Social Relations*, London: Methuen.

Sherif, Carolyn Wood (1979), "Bias in Psychology," in *The Prism of Sex: Essays in the Sociology of Knowledge*, ed. Julia A. Sherman and Evelyn Torton Beck, Madison: University of Wisconsin Press, 93–133.

Simeone, Angela (1987), *Academic Women*, South Hadley, MA: Bergin & Garvey.

Smith, Dorothy (1974), "Women's Perspective as a Radical Critique of Sociology," *Sociological Inquiry*, 44 (1), 713.
– (1987), *The Everyday World as Problematic*, Boston: Northeastern University Press.
– (1989), "Sociological Theory: Methods of Writing Patriarchy," in *Feminism and Sociological Theory*, ed. Ruth Wallace, Newbury Park, CA: Sage, 34–64.
Soberon-Ferrer, Horacio and Rachel Dardis (1991), "A Multistage Model of Customers' Assessments of Service Quality and Value," *Journal of Consumer Research*, 17 (March), 375–384.
Soiffer, Stephen and Gretchen Herrmann (1987), "Visions of Power: Ideology and Practice in the American Garage Sale," *Sociological Review*, 35 (1), 48–83.
Solomon, Michael (1983), "The Role of Products as Social Stimuli: A Symbolic Interactionism Perspective," *Journal of Consumer Research*, 10 (December), 319–329.
Spender, Dale (1981), "The Gatekeepers: A Feminist Critique of Academic Publishing," in *Doing Feminist Research*, ed. Helen Roberts, London: Routledge & Kegan Paul, 186–202.
Stern, Barbara (1988), "Sex-Role Self Concept Measures and Marketing: A Research Note," *Psychology and Marketing*, 5 (Spring), 85–99.
Strober, Myra and Charles Weinberg (1977), "Working Wives and Major Family Expenditures," *Journal of Consumer Research*, 4 (December), 141–147.
– and Charles Weinberg (1980), "Strategies Used by Working and Nonworking Wives to Reduce Time Pressures," *Journal of Consumer Research*, 6 (March), 338–348.
Sudman, Seymour and Norman M. Bradburn (1982), *Asking Questions: A Practical Guide to Questionnaires*, San Francisco: Jossey-Bass.
Thompson, Craig, William Locander, and Howard Pollio (1990), "The Lived Meaning of Free Choice: An Existential-Phenomenological Description of Everyday Consumer Experiences of Contemporary Married Women," *Journal of Consumer Research*, 17 (December), 346–361.
Tong, Rosemarie (1980), *Feminist Thought: A Comprehensive Introduction*, Boulder, CO: Westview.
Wallach, Michael A. and Nathan Kogan (1964), *Risk Taking: A Study in Cognition and Personality*, New York: Holt, Rinehart & Winston.
Wallendorf, Melanie and Erie Arnould (1991), "'We Gather Together': Consumption Rituals of Thanksgiving Day," *Journal of Consumer Research*, 18 (June), 13–31.
Ward, James C. and Peter H. Reingen (1990), "Sociocognitive Analysis of Group Decision Making among Consumers," *Journal of Consumer Research*, 17 (December), 245–262.
Warren, Carol, A. B. (1988), *Gender Issues in Field Research*, Newbury Park, CA: Sage.
Weedon, Chris (1987), *Feminist Practice & Poststructuralist Theory*, New York: Blackwell.
Weinberg, Charles and Russell Winer (1983), "Working Wives and Major Family Expenditures: Replication and Extension," *Journal of Consumer Research*, 10 (September), 259–263.
Wendell, Susan (1987), "A (Qualified) Defense of Liberal Feminism," *Hypatia*, 2 (Summer), 65–94.
Westbrook, Robert A. and Richard L. Oliver (1991), "The Dimensionality of Consumption Emotion Patterns and Consumer Satisfaction," *Journal of Consumer Research*, 18 (June), 84–91.
Westkott, Marcia (1979), "Feminist Criticism of the Social Sciences," *Harvard Educational Review*, 49 (4),422–430.
Wilson, William R. and Robert A. Peterson (1989), "Some Limits on the Potency of Word-of-Mouth Information, *Advances in Consumer Research*, Vol. 16, ed. Thomas K. Srull, Provo, UT: Association for Consumer Research, 23–29.
Wolf, Naomi (1990), *The Beauty Myth*, Toronto: Vintage.
Young, Melissa Martin (1991), "The New View: W1727, Ethnographer, Seeks Homeless Male Informant to Live with in Platonic Relationship for Purposes of Data Collection and Research," in *Gender and Consumer Behavior*, ed. Janeen Costa, Salt Lake City: University of Utah Printing Service, 317–323.
Zelizer, Viviana (1989), "The Social Meaning of Money: 'Special Monies'," *American Journal of Sociology*. 95 (2), 342–377.
Zinkhan, George and Kiran Kirande (1991), "Cultural and Gender Differences in Risk-taking Behavior among American and Spanish Decision Makers," *Journal of Social Psychology*, 131 (5), 741–742.

# 5

# Consumption: The New Wave of Research in the Humanities and Social Sciences

**Colin Campbell**

**Source:** *Journal of Social Behavior and Personality* 6 (6) (1991): 57–74.

Occasionally a special combination of events causes a topic or field of study to spring to prominence in several disciplines at approximately the same time. This is indeed what has happened over the past decade with respect to 'consumption.' Previously deemed unworthy of much serious interest by academics within the social sciences or the humanities and hence largely the preserve of those in such applied fields as marketing or consumer affairs, it has quite suddenly become a major topic of academic study. Not surprisingly, this has been accompanied by a considerable inter-disciplinary exchange of ideas with scholars often feeling that they have more in common with researchers in other disciplines who are studying the same topic than with their erstwhile colleagues. Thus, in recent years anthropologists, sociologists, historians, psychologists and economists have all been eagerly reading each others' work and attending each others' conferences. This unusual state of affairs constitutes the background for this article, which does not pretend to be a normal review of a field of work so much as an attempt at a general trans-disciplinary overview of the background to the current state of research into consumption.

This term is used in a wide sense to cover not just the selection and purchase of goods and services offered for sale but also the broader social and cultural context which gives these activities their meaning. Consequently, it covers such associated topics as advertising, fashion and the organization of domestic life. Naturally there is also a close association with the institution of private property as most items of consumption are also valued as possessions. There are, however, also important differences between research on these two topics. In the first place, consumption is typically viewed as a process in which items are selected, acquired, used and then disposed of, whilst possession relates to one aspect of certain phases of this cycle. In that sense, consumption is to do with activities (including dispossession) in contrast to the concern with relationships which tends to mark the study of possession. But, secondly, in so far as the study of consumption does involve a concern with an individual's relationship with objects these tend to focus on rights of use rather than on rights of ownership.

Several factors have combined over the past decade to bring about a remarkable outburst of research and scholarship which can be described as dealing with the subject of consumption. These are (1) the growing recognition in historical studies that the characteristics of a consumer society are not limited to the modem era. (2) A new awareness on the part of Marxist and neo-Marxist thinkers of the need to incorporate a more adequate and sophisticated theory of consumption into this tradition of thought. (3) The increasing recognition within cultural sociology and cultural studies generally of the centrality of consumerism to the understanding of the culture of postmodern societies. (4) Finally, these three major factors have been supplemented by other lesser influences, including (a) trends in urban sociology, (b) the rise of feminism, and (c) the influence of a few highly influential French theorists.

*Historical Trends*. For several decades the belief that the consumer society was the latest and most recent stage in the evolution of industrial societies constituted the prevailing assumption underlying most historical studies of the modern and pre-modern period, with the consequence that consumption related activities were not subject to the same degree of historical investigation in transitional societies. This presumption has recently been overthrown and more and more attention paid to the study of consumption in the early modern period. The crucial changes here occurred first in economic history (McKendrick *et al.*, 1981), but have spread rapidly throughout all branches of the discipline. One could say that a vast endeavour to rewrite the history of the early period of industrialization is under way, an endeavour which is changing our understanding of the great transformation and hence of modernity itself.

*Marxist Thinking*. Marx, although very concerned with the institution of property, paid little attention to consumption, tending to dismiss it as no more than the natural corollary of production. Thus it is that Marxism (together with that other essentially productionist body of thought, neo-classical economics) faces a major challenge from the growing interest in consumptionist issues. As a consequence, Marxist thinkers have embarked on a determined effort to adapt Marxist ideas to deal successfully with the accepted reality of a modem consumer society and these efforts constitute one of the principal themes within the new wave writing. At the same time, an old-style Marxist productionism is widely used by those without Marxist sympathies as an epitome of an outmoded and inapplicable theory of society in contradistinction to which they can present their own relevant consumerist theories.

*Consumer Culture*. Finally, within cultural analysis, there has been a growing recognition of the centrality of consumption to an understanding of the systems of meaning which characterize modem post-industrial society. Whilst analysts have been using the term "consurner society" for some years (see Riesman, Glazer, and Denny, 1966; Bell, 1978; Martin, 1981), it is only during the past decade that the precise nature of the culture of consumption has itself become the focus of study; a development which is linked both to the rise in popularity of semiotic-style analyses (Barthes, 1968; Mick, 1986) and the debate over postmodemism in the arts.

A number of other, more specific factors can also be seen to have played some part in the emergence of the new wave of research. These would include (a) developments in urban sociology which have made collective consumption its predominant subject matter (b) the rise of feminism and women's studies which have given greater prominence to such topics as fashion, the body, diet, advertising, shopping and housework (c) the influence of a few seminal thinkers, especially the French writers Braudel, Baudrillard and Bourdieu. The work of these writers, together with the points listed under (a) through (b), will be considered later in the paper.

As suggested above, these developments have had repercussions outside the particular discipline or field of study in which they first occurred, thereby multiplying their impact on academic research as a whole. Thus innovations in some disciplines have, in their turn, prompted the adoption of new perspectives in others, or, in some cases helped to set a new research agenda. The emergence of semiotic and post-structuralist approaches within anthropology, for example, stimulated parallel developments within sociology and history. Similarly, work in history can be said to have had a profound effect upon the way in which some sociologists have come to regard the origin and character of the consumer society (see Campbell, 1987) as well as causing a reassessment of theories of consumption by those working in a Marxist tradition (see, for example, Miller, 1987). At the same time, there have been specific attempts at interdisciplinary collaboration (see Appadurai, 1986) together with a growing openness on the part of those professionals who work in departments of marketing and commerce to the influence of research in the more traditional academic disciplines (see McCracken, 1988 for evidence of this development).

## Social sciences

There is a traditional literature on consumption within the social sciences. Once economics has been set aside, this can be said to have concentrated upon how the consumption practices of individuals and groups are affected by their membership of society or social classes, whilst tending to view consumption itself as a form of meaningful interaction. The major contributions here would be those of Veblen on conspicuous consumption (1925), Simmel on fashion and money (1957, 1978), Malinowski on the kula (1922), Boas on the potlatch (1944), Mauss on the gift (1976), Marx on commodity fetishism, use and exchange value (1971, 1973), Sombart on luxury (1967), and Weber on status groups and the Protestant ethic (1958, 1978). But this classic body of literature, much of which has been largely neglected for decades, has been supplemented over the past ten to fifteen years by a new one. Whilst drawing on the classics to some extent, it also promises to constitute new perspectives on old problems. The disciplines which have been in the forefront of this renaissance in the study of consumption have been anthropology and sociology.

### Anthropology

It could be said that, alone among the social sciences, anthropology has never consistently relegated the study of consumption to second place behind the primacy accorded the examination of the world of production. This stems from the fact that anthropologists are not inclined to see societies as merely "economies writ large" but rather as complex social systems or structures of interaction. At the same time, the discipline's sharp focus on kinship has carried with it a natural concern with such matters as property rights and inheritance. Thus the influence of such figures as Durkheim, Malinowski, Benedict and Mauss has worked to favour the examination of consumption practices as they relate to a larger svstem of social relations. Consequently, in the nineteen-seventies when the study of consumption was still in the doldrums, Douglas and Isherwood's book *The World of Goods* (1978) stood out as a virtually isolated attempt to remind social scientists that as yet there was no satisfactory answer to the question, "why do people buy goods?" They stressed that the use and exchange of objects should be seen as cultural, meaningful experiences located in a shared system of communication. In so doing they were not only usefully reemphasising one of the central messages contained in the works of the founders of social and cultural anthropology mentioned above, but they were also laying the basis for the subsequent growth of structuralist and semiotic approaches to consumption. In this respect they played a significant part in accomplishing that shift from a dominantly social to a dominantly cultural perspective which has been such a feature of the new wave of research as a whole.

Whilst the work of Douglas and Isherwood clearly played an important part in prompting the revival of interest in consumption in the social sciences and is cited by most new wave researchers there have been other influences at work. One of these is a strong Marxist tradition of analysis which has grown up within the framework of anthropology (see Sahlins 1972, 1976). Its overall aim, as Appadurai puts it, is to do for consumption what Marx did for production, that is "to demystify the demand side of economic life." (1986, p. 58) Understandably, perhaps, this perspective tends to view the study of consumption as concerned with 'material culture' with a consequent focus on 'exchange' and 'commodities.' In this respect it has points of contact with archaeology which perhaps has the best claim of any discipline to be described as the study of material culture. It is thus pertinent to observe that the collection of essays edited by Appadurai includes a contribution by an archaeologist, and that when it comes to the study of consumption the social sciences needs to be recognised as including archaeology within its orbit (see, for example, Gould and Schiffer, 1981).

### Sociology

Within sociology, Baudrillard (1975, 1981, 1983) has emerged as the key figure in the movement to fully incorporate 'consumption' into a neo-Marxist theory of society. This he attempts by drawing upon semiotics and focusing on the "commodity-sign" rather than the commodity. He argues that, in capitalist societies, consumption should be understood as a process in which only the signs attached to goods are actually consumed. Baudrillard's work involves a meeting of Marxist thought with semiotic analysis such that Marx's distinction between use and exchange value is linked to the analysis of commodities as signs. Hence his theory of the commodity sign and the claim that, in modern capitalist society, commodities are not valued for their use but understood as possessing a meaning which is determined by their position in a self-referential system of signifiers.

Another aspect of this movement of accommodation is illustrated by Daniel Miller's book *Material Culture and Mass Consumption* (1987). Although drawing on Simmel and Hegel as much as Marx, it can still be seen as an attempt to build a theory of consumption out of a basically Marxist tradition of thought. Thus the central thesis presupposes that modem industrial societies produce alienation among their members, a familiar enough Marxist theme. Miller's twist, and this is where he draws on both Simmel and Hegel, is to represent these same socio-economic and cultural structures as also offering the possibility of an escape from alienation; something which can be achieved by means of consumption. This then becomes the crucial, de-alienating, activity, one through which the product of labour can, in turn, be "de-commodified."

What is particularly significant about Miller's thesis is less that it serves to accommodate a basically Marxist style of thought to deal with the fact of modern consumerist society, than that it achieves this end in such a way as to present consumption itself as a central "liberating" experience. This particular theme is echoed by other new wave writers on consumption (see Otnes, 1988), even by those who reject the Marxist tradition. What these liberationists all have in common is the tendency to view consumption as the significant area of autonomy for individuals in what is, in all other respects, presented as an increasingly bureaucratic and alienating society. But there is another strand within the emerging area of consumption studies which has its origins, if only indirectly, in a Marxist tradition. This is in the field of urban sociology. Deemed to be in a state of crisis in the nineteen seventies it was given a fresh impetus by Manuel Castells' suggestion (1983) that its distinctive subject-matter should be collective consumption, that is the way in which the state provides the facilities for the reproduction of labour power in advanced capitalist societies. Dunleavy (1980; with Husbands, 1985) was one of the first to follow up Castells' suggestion. Peter Saunders (1986) has been prominent in developing theories of collective consumption in direct opposition to a Marxist or neo-Marxist framework.

Saunders, who in his own way is also a liberationist, sees the putative sociology of consumption as emerging out of three areas of work within the discipline–urban sociology, feminist writing and the sociology of work and leisure (1988, p. 142). What all three have in common is that "they have challenged the preoccupation of so much of sociology with the formal workplace and workplace relations, and have shown how social relations beyond the factory and the office may be crucial in determining life chances, shaping power relations, influencing social identities, stimulating social movements, and so on." (1988, p. 142). For Saunders the emerging sociology of consumption is a riposte to the long dominant influence of Marxist sociology and the assumption that production was the crucial process in advanced industrial societies. A concern with the "relationship to the means of consumption" is substituted for the more traditional concentration on the "means of production." The fundamental social and political cleavages are related to divisions between consumers not producers. From this perspective, the study of consumption and consumers becomes embroiled in claims about the virtues of self-help versus dependence and the operation of the market versus the collective provision of services. In place of the old Marxist analysis of a conflict between classes differentially related to the means of production, Saunders suggests a fundamental conflict between producers and consumers. Predictably enough Saunders has come under fierce attack (Warde, 1988; Burrows and Butler, 1989), principally on the grounds of his apparently unqualified endorsement of consumption and uncritical championing of consumer rights. But it is also noted that he does not so much explore the nature of consumption as study the contrasting social and political contexts in which it occurs, substituting categories of consumer for the traditional concepts of social class. Hence it has been suggested that he is not so much correcting the production bias of Marxist analyses as proposing his own equally general theory of industrial societies (Warde, 1988).

By far the most important single work to influence the new wave of research in consumption is Bourdieu's *Distinction: A Social Critique of the Judgement of Taste*, first published in France in 1979 and only available in English since 1984. Although this book can be seen as related both to a semiotic strand of cultural analysis and as a contribution to neo-Marxist thought, when considered as a study of consumption it is perhaps best understood as a development and extension of Veblen's work.

It is based on a wealth of research data gathered through questionnaires and interviews in the nineteen sixties and seventies. This complex and densely argued book has a main thesis which, like Veblen's, stresses the hierarchical character of modem societies and the centrality of consumption practices (especially the manifestation of taste) in the creation and maintenance of the relationships of domination and submission upon which such a hierarchy is built. However, whereas Veblen emphasised the extent to which consumption served to maintain and enhance status through its function in displaying pecuniary strength or wealth, Bourdieu plays down material possessions, stressing instead the importance of the individual's possession of symbolic or cultural capital and the way in which this can be put to use to display taste. There is, none the less, the same emphasis upon competition between individuals for the scarce resource of status as one finds in Veblen, with the addition of a subtle analysis of the character and historical development of the various *champs* or markets in which this takes place.

Unlike Veblen, however, Bourdieu recognises that there are inherent limitations on an individual's chances of succeeding in moving up through such a system as a consequence of their "habitus" or personal cultural inheritance, and that not even newly acquired wealth will necessarily enable individuals to advance their status. An impressive study which deserves to rank with Veblen's *Theory of the Leisure Class*, it has generated a great deal of discussion and comment. Much of this is favourable but certain problematic aspects of Bourdieu's analysis are frequently noted. Like Veblen, Bourdieu treats consumption as an essentially other-regarding activity and hence has little to say about invisible or "inconspicuous" forms of consumption activity. Similarly, he tends to extrapolate from the consequences of conduct (in maintaining distinctions and relationships of domination, for example) to the intentions of consumers, when evidence might suggest that these outcomes were largely unintended (see Elster,

1983, pp. 70–71). In this respect, Bourdieu can be said to exemplify the failure to deal adequately with the real subjective motives of consumers which has been a marked feature of most social theories of consumption.

## Economics

Economics has long been identifiable as the discipline in which major attention is given to the production process whilst consumption is regarded, in the words of Adam Smith, as "the sole end and purpose of all production" (1937, p. 625). Naturally such a view tends to accord consumption the status of a taken for granted activity about which little or nothing can be said, With some small exceptions this is still true today and economics remains the one social science discipline in which least progress has occurred with respect to the study of consumption. The observations of writers of the stature of Keynes (1936) and Galbraith (1984) on this topic warrant note but it is true to say that Thorstein Veblen (1899) is still the only significant social scientist whose writings on consumption have had any real impact on the discipline. In recent decades some of Veblen's insights have become revived as a few economists have strived to break free of what they see as the restrictive framework of productionist assumptions. Important works here would include Nurkse (1957) on the intemational demonstration effect, and Hirsch (1976) and Scitovsky (1976) on the inadequacies of conventional theories of consumer demand, together with Mason's (1981) important attempt to develop and test Veblen's ideas. However, despite these promising developments, it is still the case that economics lacks an adequate theory of consumer behaviour in the full sense and has yet to be affected significantly by the new interest in the topic which is so apparent in the other social sciences.

## Psychology[1]

The turning away from an overly-rationalistic perspective as represented by economics has also, somewhat unfortunately, involved a turning away from psychology. Social psychology, or at least, more properly, a micro-sociological interactional perspective, can be said to be influential in the wider research context in so far as Goffman's work is still cited (see Gould and Schiffer, 1981; Weatherill, 1988). But psychology proper now plays a less prominent part in research on consumption than was the case a decade ago. Within the discipline itself, and especially within the applied area of consumer research, there is evidence that the formerly popular "information processing models" (Bettman, 1979) are in the process of being displaced by an "experiential approach" (Holbrook and Hirschman, 1982) and by a greater focus on the symbolic aspects of consumption. In this respect it could be said that psychologists have actually taken heed of Kassarjian's (1982) admonition concerning the neglect of the role of cultural values in the study of consumption. There is, however, clearly room for greater inter-disciplinary collaboration here. The cognitive revolution in psychology and the concomitant comparative decline of behaviourism has removed what many sociologists and anthropologists have long regarded as one of the major obstacles to such cross disciplinary cooperation. The work of Csikszentmihalyi and Rochberg-Halton (1981) can be seen as an illustration of the way forward in this respect. Their emphasis upon meaning and the symbolic significance of material objects is clearly compatible both with the cultural orientation so marked in history and the social sciences and the cognitive concerns of contemporary psychologists. On the other hand, Kassarjian's observation on the neglect of consumer motivation as a topic of study (1982) is still true (as noted above) and has a significance outside of psychology itself.

## Humanities

### History

One of the major developments in recent years has been a recognition of the important role played by consumption in the historical processes which have moulded modern Western societies. Long considered to be a crucial characteristic of modem society, its role in the great transformation which was The Industrial Revolution has only recently become a focus of study. The assumption that consumption was an insignificant or trivial feature of "early" or "pre-modern" societies has also been increasingly challenged. The path-breaking works here are those of Fernand Braudel (1973, 1981) especially *Capitalism and Material Life 1400-1800* in which a forceful case is made for the claim that an understanding of the development of modernity in the West requires an appreciation of changes in consumer behaviour. As Braudel expresses it, the "right string to pull to start the engine of capitalism was demand." (1973, p. 12) Taking this position as the starting point for their researches, and building on the previous work of Appleby (1978) and Thirsk (1978), McKendrick, Brewer and Plumb (1982) set about demonstrating that a consumer revolution was the necessary historical concomitant of the eighteenth century English revolution in production. They stress how England at that time possessed exactly the right conditions for such a revolution, with an aspiring bourgeoisie flush with wealth from trade, a fluid social structure and ambitious and innovative market-manipulating entrepreneurs like Josiah Wedgwood.

At almost the same time other historians and historically-minded sociologists were also turning their attention to the question of the origins of modern consumer society. Mukerji (1983) finds the basis of what she calls "modern materialism" in fifteenth and sixteenth-century Europe, identifying the growing international trade in prints, maps and calicoes as both forming and diffusing a new orientation to objects. By contrast Campbell (1987), building on the evidence of McKendrick *et al.* and employing a Weberian model, has proposed that "the spirit of modem consumerism" arose in the eighteenth century as an ironic by-product of The Romantic Movement. The link between the two is modern autonomous hedonism or "day-dreaming," a practice effectively given the highest possible legitimation by Romantic teachings and yet vital to the dynamic cycle of desire, purchase, use and disillusionment characteristic of modern consumption.

Other historians have examined the same issue but with an emphasis on developments on the continent of Europe. These include Miller (1981) and Williams (1982) on the emergence of a consumer society in France and especially the nineteenth century department store, or Schama's (1987) dazzling and impressive examination of the Dutch attitude toward commodities and possessions during the sixteenth and seventeenth centuries. These works are perhaps most significant for their collective pathbreaking contribution to our historical understanding of modernity and its origins in a negative rather than a positive sense. That is to say, despite the diversity of views which they contain, all agree in emphasising the vital contribution which consumption made to the emergence of modern society and hence in rejecting the old productionist paradigm (see Fox and Lears, 1983). They therefore seem destined to provide the basis for a new wave of research endeavour predicated on a consumerist paradigm. Having said this, these studies are remarkable for their diversity of methods and theoretical perspectives and cannot be said to offer anything approaching a coherent or unitary framework for such research.

### Philosophy

The debate in philosophy which is probably most relevant to issues in the study of consumption is that which focuses on the concept of "need" ("real" and otherwise) and the associated ideas of "necessity" and "luxury". This was a matter of some concern to the nineteenth and early twentieth century social theorists, and exercised the minds of thinkers as diverse in outlook as Adam Smith, Karl Marx, Thorstein Veblen and Werner Sombart. The question at the heart of this debate, which concerns whether or not human beings can be said to have any basic or real needs, and if they do, what these might be, has not gone away. It figured prominently for example in the otherwise very different analyses of modem society offered by Kenneth Galbraith (1958) and Herbert Marcuse (1964), and more recently in the neo-Marxist formulation of Preteceille and Terrail (1985). It is a subject of debate which also takes in the question of the difference between "need" and "want", together with the definition of "interest" (for an up to date discussion of these issues see Garrett Thomson, 1987).

Generally speaking it seems reasonable to conclude, as Agnes Heller suggests (1982), that nearly all the distinctions made between "true" and "false" needs are untenable for "all needs humans recognise as real should also be considered as real" (1982, p. 9. Cited by Otnes, 1988, p. 174). This position makes it quite clear that those who insist on such a distinction are making what is basically an ideological claim. This does not mean that there are no important issues which remain to be resolved in this respect. There are still significant questions relating to the distinction between "needs," "wants," "desires," and "interests" which require clarification (see Ilmonen, 1988). However, these issues no longer occupy their earlier prominence in social theory as the focus of concern has increasingly moved away from systems of action to systems of meaning.

### Linguistics and Literature

To a considerable extent this change has been due to the impact of developments in linguistics, which, at least in the form of semiotics, has proved a powerful influence in recent years. The major figure here has been Saussure especially through the development and popularization of his ideas by Barthes (1968, 1983) and Eco (1976, 1984). The stress placed by these writers on culture as a complex system of communication and meaning has had an important influence on the study of consumption as is evident, for example, in the work of Levy (1978, 1982) and Belk (1982a, 1982b, 1984). However, Mick (1986) has argued that, to date, the full potential of semiotics has yet to be realised.

In addition to the study of language, the study of literature may be said to have played some small part in the revival of interest in consumption. For, in the absence of detailed case studies of consumption practices in the eighteenth and nineteenth centuries, theorists have turned to the novel for insights. Miller's (1981) work on the department store draws on fiction, as does Schudson in his exploration of the historical roots of consumer culture (1984, chap. 5). Finally, both Rosalind Williams (1982) and Campbell (1987) employ literary material as evidence in support of their arguments.

## Conclusion

It would seem that one can safely observe that the early pre-paradigmatic phase of the new wave of research on consumption is coming to an end. The clear characteristics of this phase were, firstly, the repeated laments over the neglect of consumption as a topic of research; secondly, the prominence given to a critique of the conventional utility theory prevailing in economics, and thirdly, the repeated calls for the tendency to evaluate and condemn consumption practices and the associated consumer society to be replaced by detailed and objective research.

Laments over the lack of research have, understandably, gradually given way to assessment and comment as the sum total of studies gradually mounts. At the same time, critiques of the inadequacy of the conventional utilitarian perspective employed by economics have been replaced by the simple observation that such a rationalistic perspective has now been eclipsed. There has also been a steady decline in the number of works which primarily constitute an evaluation of some aspect of modern consumer society (nearly always a condemnation). This can be seen clearly in an area like advertising where up to the beginning of this decade most books still tended to moralize if not sensationalize the topic. Now, although evaluation may not be eschewed, works are much more likely to contain serious discussions of the nature of the phenomenon. Schudson's observation in the course of his appeal for a "new sociology of consumption" that "it is time for a study that will not be a reflex-like intellectual revulsion at the world of goods but an effort to understand what place material culture might hold in a good world" (1981, p. 243) has, in general, been heeded. However, there are also signs of an evaluative reaction, with some writers making an overt and deliberate connection between the academic study of consumption and a popular movement both to "liberate" the consumer and redress some of the perceived evils of modern industrial society. To the extent that this trend persists then there must still be doubt as to whether the field has indeed entirely emerged from its pre-paradigmatic stage.

One can also anticipate the decline in importance of some of the present trends in the study of consumption. For example, that tradition of inquiry which treats consumption as a semiological system, whilst a major influence in both the social sciences and humanities over the past decade, could be said to have passed the peak of its influence. Whilst some commentators feel that its full potential in the context has yet to be realised (Mick, 1986), others have increasingly criticised the focus on a societal meta-language and especially the value of treating products and their uses as if they were no more than a system of signs (see McCracken, 1988, pp. 66 ff). Although an approach of proven value, commodities are material objects and as such possess characteristics which are not consistent with their treatment as mere signs. What is more, whilst a semiotic approach successfully focuses attention on the meaning of consumer goods, services and practices, it tends both to concentrate on meaning in the context of communication and to analyze this at a collective or system level. Consequently there is a tendency to overlook the subjective meanings actually held by consumers themselves. This topic is, however, precisely the predominant concern of the more recent phenomenological and interpretive analyses which seek to emphasize the extent to which individual consumers appropriate consumer goods to their own purposes and one can anticipate that this will be a growing focus of research. This process, whether understood as one of "individuation," "customization," "personalization" or "decommodification," is clearly destined to be a topic of further study having successfully displaced the previous preoccupation with the way in which producers, advertisers and marketers of goods were involved in the "creation of meaning."

If the field is emerging from its pre-paradigmatic or "neo-natal" stage and no longer has "no history, no community of scholars, no tradition of scholarship" (McCracken, 1988, p. 139) it still cannot be judged to be fully paradigmatic. As yet no clear consensus exists as to what consumption might be taken to include, let alone agreement on the paradigm to be adopted for its study. The two problems are, of course, closely related, the question of the scope of the phenomena to be included under the heading being intimately connected with assumptions concerning how it should be studied. Generally the first problem has been dealt with so far in a common sense fashion, with the simple working premise being that the field of consumption studies includes whatever people think it reasonable to include. Thus one can note that Otnes's (1989) collection includes articles on the cultural significance of food, on shopping and the provision of housing, whilst Appadurai's edited collection (1989) includes articles on medieval relics and the production, distribution and use of carpets and cloth. Other examples of topics which writers have treated the term as covering include advertising (Schudson, 1984), fashion (Barber *et al.*, 1953; Blumer, 1969; Bell, 1976; Barthes, 1983) taste (Lynes, 1954; Bourdieu, 1984), gift-giving (Belk, 1982; Caplow, 1982; Cheal, 1986), possessions (Rudmin, 1986), the body (Featherstone, 1982), the department store (Miller, 1981; Williams, 1982; Benson, 1986) and such leisure-time activities as customizing cars (Moorhouse, 1983). Although this is a reasonable enough ad hoc list, it will obviously have to be replaced before too long by a more theoretically justifiable and thoughtful delineation of the field. In any case, the consensus of opinion which exists concerning the inclusion of such topics under the general heading of "consumption" is more apparent than real, as these are frequently defined in different ways. This, in turn, naturally leads into the second problem where it is abundantly clear that no consensus exists, even in sub-fields within individual disciplines like sociology and anthropology.

It is possible to distinguish four very broad (and overlapping) lines of cleavage which effectively divide new wave researchers. Firstly, there is a distinction between those who espouse a form of methodological individualism which involves viewing consumption primarily as a set of micro-processes (even if studied in aggregate forms) concerning the attitudes, decisions and actions of individual consumers. By contrast, others focus on those structural or institutional forms which can be said to comprise the consumption "order" or "system." Secondly, there is a distinction between those who adopt an interpretive or phenomenological approach to the subject-matter, focusing on the meanings and motives of those who consume, and those who adopt a more positivist approach, analyzing consumption behaviour without making presuppositions about internal or mental states. Thirdly, there is a distinction between those who view consumption as if it were an essentially cultural phenomenon comprising either a system of beliefs and attitudes or one of symbols and signs, as opposed to those who see it primarily as a socio-economic network of institutions and relationships. Finally, one may note the distinction between those whose real interest is indeed in consumption *per se* and those whose primary concern lies in what an examination of this area might reveal about the nature and dynamics of modern "post-industrial" or "post-modern" society in general.

These are, of course, some of the same major lines of cleavage which can be found to divide social scientists on many issues so it should not be surprising to find that they also characterize the study of consumption. What this suggests is that it would be a brave person who attempted to predict which perspective will, in time, come to predominate. Some observations may be hazarded, however, on the basis of current trends. In the first place one can assume that the tendency, prevalent in economics, to see consumption as an end of human activity has most definitely given way to a presumption that it is indeed better understood as a means to some further end; whatever that may be taken to be. At the same time, consumption is by no means automatically viewed as an individual matter, the examination of collective consumption being a major topic within new wave research. Secondly, the assumption that consumption refers specifically to the selection, purchase and use of material objects has increasingly been questioned, as has its association with acquisitiveness, property rights and materialism itself. This is not merely because of an increasing recognition of the importance of the consumption of services and other invisible products, but rather because of a growing awareness that it is not so much objects as their meanings which are indeed consumed. It is this trend, of course, which has led to the nature and function of consumption being regarded as a central issue in contemporary debates over modernity and the culture of capitalism. But this move, whilst promising to free the study of consumption once and for all from the restrictive stranglehold of utilitarianism does pose new problems. For meaning is too easily "discovered in" or more accurately "imputed to" objects and activities where it does not, in fact, exist. That complex of significance analyzed by the researcher may not correspond to the motives and intentions which actually informed the conduct of the consumer. Thirdly and finally, one might predict that the study of consumption will slowly free itself from its present close involvement with cultural theory in general and the larger theoretical and ideological debates over postmodernism and the culture of capitalism. Although this connection is one of the principal reasons why the new wave has occurred it is not only likely to become an increasing embarrassment to further serious study in this field but it seems very possible that those whose primary interest lies in meta-theory and ideological debate will soon move on to greener pastures.

## Notes

1. As the psychology of property, ownership, and consumption is dealt with at length in other articles in this issue, this brief discussion is limited to an outsider's expression of developments in the disclipline.

## References


Appadurai, A. (Ed.). (1986). *The social life of things: Commodities in cultural perspective*. Cambridge: Cambridge University Press.

Appleby, J. (1978). *Economic thought and ideology in seventeenth-century England*. Princeton, NJ: Princeton University Press.

Bargyer, B., and Lobel, L. (1953). 'Fashion' in women's clothes and the American social system. In R. Bendix and S. Lipset (Eds.), *Class, status and power*. Glencoe. IL: Free Press.

Barthes, R. (1968). *The fashion system* (M. Ward and R. Howard, Trans.). New York: Hill and Wang.

Baudrillard, J. (1975). *The mirror of production*. St. Louis, MO: Telos Press.

Baudrillard, J. (1981). *Towards a critique of the political economy of the sign*. St. Louis, MO: Telos Press.

Baudrillard, J. (1983). *Simulations*. New York: Semiotext.

Belk, R.W. (1975). Situational variables in consumer behavior. *Journal of Consumer Research*, *2*, 157–164.

Belk, R.W. (1982). Effects of gift-giving involvement on gift-giving strategies. In A. Mitchell (Ed.), *Advances in consumer research* (Vol. 9). Ann Arbor, MI: Association for Consumer Research.

Bell, D. (1978). *The cultural contradictions of capitalism*. New York: Harper and Row.

Bell, Q. (1976). *On human finery*. New York: Schocken Books.

Benson, S.P. (1986). *Counter cultures: Saleswomen, managers and customers in American department stores, 1890–1940.* Urbana: University of Illinois Press.
Bettman, J.R. (1979). *An information processing theory of consumer choice.* Reading, MA: Addison-Wesley.
Blumer, H. (1969). Fashion: From class differentiation to collective selection. *Sociological Quarterly, 10*(3), 275–291.
Boas, F. (1944). *The mind of primitive man.* New York: Columbia University Press.
Bourdieu, P. (1984). *Distinction: A sociological critique of the judgement of taste* (R. Nice, Trans.). London: Routledge and Kegan Paul.
Braudel, F. (1973). *Capitalism and material life: 1400–1800.* London: Weidenfeld and Nicolson.
Braudel, F. (1981). *Civilization and capitalism. 15th–18th century* (Vols. 1–2). London: Collins.
Burrows, R., and Butler, T. (1989). Review article: Middle mass and the pitt: A critical review of Peter Saunders's sociology of consumption. *Sociological Review, 32*, 338–364.
Campbell, C. (1987). *The Romantic ethic and the spirit of modern consumerism.* Oxford: Basil Blackwell.
Caplow, T. (1982). Christmas gifts and kin networks. *American Sociological Review, 47*, 383–392.
Castells, M. (1983). Crisis, planning and the quality of life. *Society and Space, I*, 3–21.
Cheal, D. (1986). The social dimensions of gift behavior. *Journal of Social and Personal Relationships*, 3, 423–439.
Csikszentmihalyi, M., and Rochberg-Halton, E. (1981). *The meaning of things: Domestic symbols and the self.* Cambridge: Cambridge University Press.
Douglas, M., and Isherwood, B. (1978). *The world of goods: Towards an anthropology of consumption.* New York: Norton.
Dunleavy, P., and Husbands, C. (1985). *British democracy at the crossroads.* London: Allen & Unwin.
Eco, U. (1976). *A theory of semiotics.* Bloomington, IN: Indiana University Press.
Eco, U. (1984). *Semiotics and the philosophy of language.* Bloomington, IN: Indiana University Press.
Elster, J. (1983). *Sour grapes: Studies in the subversion of rationality.* Cambridge: Cambridge University Press.
Featherstone, M. (1982). The body in consumer culture. *Theory, Culture and Society, 1*(2), 18–33.
Fox, R.W., and Lears, T.J.J. (Eds.). (1983). *The culture of consumption: Critical essays in American history 1880–1980.* New York: Pantheon.
Galbraith, J.K. (1984). *The affluent society.* New York: New American Library.
Goffman, E. (1971). *The presentation of self in everyday life.* Harmondsworth, Middlesex: Penguin Books.
Gould, R.A., and Schiffer, M.B. (Eds.). (1981). *Modern material culture: The archaeology of us.* New York: Academic Press.
Hirsch, F. (1977). *Social limits to growth.* London: Routledge & Kegan Paul.
Holbrook, M.B., and Hirschman, E.C. (Eds.). (1982). The experiential aspects of consumption: Consumer fantasies, feelings and fun. *Journal of Consumer Research, 9*, 132–140.
Ilmonen, K. (1988). How to limit the quantitative growth in needs. In P. Otnes (Ed.), *The sociology of consumption.* Oslo: Solurn Forlag A/S.
Kassarjian, H.H. (1982). Consumer psychology. *American Review of Psychology, 33*, 619–649.
Keynes, L.M. (1936). *The general theory of employment, interest and money.* Cambridge: Cambridge University Press.
Levy, S.J. (1982). *Marketplace behavior: Its meaning for management.* New York: AMACOM.
Levy, S.J. (1982). Symbols, selves and others. In A. Mitchell (Ed.), *Advances in consumer research* (Vol. 9). Ann Arbor, MI: Association for Consumer Research.
Lynes, R. (1954). *The tastemakers.* New York: Harper.
Malinowski, B. (1922). *Argonauts of the western Pacific.* London: Routledge & Kegan Paul.
Marcuse, H. (1964). *One-dimensional man.* Boston: Beacon Press.
Martin, B. (1981). *A sociology of contemporary cultural change.* Oxford: Blackwell.
Marx, K. (1971). *Capital: Vol. 1. A critical analysis of capitalist production.* Moscow: Progress Publishers. (Original work published 1887)
Marx, K. (1973). *Grundisse: Foundations of the critique of political economy.* New York: Vintage Books.

Mason, R.S. (1981). *Conspicuous consumption: A study of exceptional consumer behaviour*. Farnborough, Hants: Gower Press.

Mauss, M. (1976). *The gift*. New York: Norton.

MeCracken, G. (1987). The history of consumption: A literature review and consumer guide. *Journal of Consumer Policy, 10*, 139–166.

MeCracken, G. (1988). *Culture and consumption: New approaches to the symbolic character of consumer goods and activities*. Bloomington, IN: Indiana University Press.

McKendrick, N., Brewer, L, and Plumb, J.H. (1982). *The birth of a consumer society: The commercialization of eighteenth-century England*. London: Europa Publications.

Mick, D.G. (1986). Consumer research and semiotics: Exploring the morphology of signs, symbols and significance. *Journal of Consumer Research, 13*, 196–213.

Miller, D. (1987). *Material culture and mass consumption*. New York: Basil Blackwell.

Miller, M. (1981). *The Bon Marche: Bourgeois culture and the department store, 1869–1920*. Princeton, NJ: Princeton University Press.

Moorhouse, H. (1983). American automobiles and workers' dreams. *Sociological Review, 31*, 403–426.

Mukerji, C. (1983). *From graven images: Patterns of modern materialism*. York: Columbia University Press.

Nurkse, R. (1957). *Problems of capital formation in underdeveloped countries*. New York: Basil Blackwell.

Otnes, P. (1988). The sociology of consumption: "Liberate our daily lives." In P. Otnes (Ed.). *The sociology of consumption: An anthology*. Oslo: Solum Forlag A/S.

Preteceille, E., and Terrail, J. (1985). *Capitalism, consumption and needs*. London: Basil Blackwell.

Riesman, D., Glazer, N., and Denny, R. (1966). *The lonely crowd: A study in the changing American character*. New York: Doubleday.

Rudmin, F. (1986). Psychology of ownership, possession and property: A selected bibliography since 1890. *Psychological Reports, 58*, 859–869.

Sahlins, M. (1972). *Stone age economics*. New York: Aldine.

Sahlins, M. (1976). *Culture and practical reason*. Chicago: University of Chicago Press.

Saunders, P. (1988). The sociology of consumption: A new research agenda. In P. Otnes (Ed.), *The sociology of consumption: An anthology*. Oslo: Solum Forlag AIS.

Schama, S. (1987). *The embarrassment of riches: An interpretation of Dutch culture in the golden age*. New York: Knopf.

Schudson, M. (1981). *Advertising, the uneasy persuasion: Its dubious impact on American society*. New York: Basic Books.

Scitoysky, T. (1976). *The joyless economy*. New York: Oxford University Press.

Simmel, G. (1957). Fashion. *American Journal of Sociology, 62*, 541–558.

Smith, A. (1937). *The wealth of nations*. New York: Modern Library.

Sombart, W. (1967). *Luxury and capitalism*. Ann Arbor, MI: University of Michigan Press.

Thirsk, J. (1978). *Economic policy and projects: The development of a consumer society in early modern England*. Oxford: Clarendon Press.

Thompson, M. (1979). *Rubbish theory*. Oxford: Oxford University Press.

Thomson, G. (1987). *Needs*. London: Routledge & Kegan Paul.

Veblen, T. (1925). *The theory of the leisure class: An economic study of institutions*. London: George Allen & Unwin.

Warde, A. (1988). *Production, consumption and social change: Reservations concerning Peter Saunders' sociology of consumption*. Unpublished manuscript.

Weatherill, L. (1988). *Consumer behavior and material culture in Britain*. London: Routledge.

Weber, M. (1958). *The Protestant ethic and the spirit of capitalism*. New York: Scribner's.

Weber, M. (1978). Classes, status groups and parties. In W.G. Runciman (Ed.), *Max Weber: Selections in translation*. Cambridge: Cambridge University Press.

Williams, R. (1982). *Dream worlds: Mass consumption in late nineteenth-century France*. Berkeley, CA: University of California Press.

# 6

# Hedonic Consumption: Emerging Concepts, Methods and Propositions

**Elizabeth C. Hirschman and Morris B. Holbrook**

**Source:** *Journal of Marketing* 46 (3) (1982): 92–101.

## Introduction

During the 1950s there was substantial discussion concerning the symbolic aspects of products (Gardner and Levy 1955, Levy 1959). As Levy noted, "People buy products not only for what they can *do*, but also for what they *mean*" (p. 118). This line of thought went forward during the 1960s to incorporate the notion of congruence between the lifestyle a consumer chose and the symbolic meaning of the products he/she purchased (Levy 1963).

However, during the 1970s there was a hiatus of research and discussion regarding product symbolism. This dearth of interest possibly was due to the excesses of the motivation research era, yet there is much to be gained – both pragmatically and conceptually – from inquiries into the esthetic, intangible and subjective aspects of consumption (Hirschman 1980a, Holbrook 1980, Levy 1980). These factors pertain to phenomena that we shall refer to as "hedonic consumption." *Hedonic consumption designates those facets of consumer behavior that relate to the multi-sensory, fantasy, and emotive aspects of one's experience with products.* Because the terms *multisensory*, *fantasy*, and *emotive* evoke a variety of meanings, we shall define them formally at the outset to forestall confusion in their subsequent interpretation.

By multisensory we mean the receipt of experience in multiple sensory modalities including tastes, sounds, scents, tactile impressions and visual images. While consumer researchers typically assume these experiences to be *afferent* (e.g., a product taste test), the hedonic perspective also posits *efferent* experiencing of multisensory impulses as an important form of consumer response (Berlyne 1971). Individuals not only respond to multisensory impressions from external stimuli (a perfume) by encoding these sensory inputs but also react by generating multisensory images within themselves, For example, smelling a perfume may cause the consumer not only to perceive and encode its scent but also to generate internal imagery containing sights. sounds and tactile sensations, all of which are also "experienced."

These internal, multisensory images can be of two types, First, *historic imagery* involves recalling an event that actually did occur. The scent of a perfume, for example, can cause the consumer to evoke a past episode involving a romance with one who wore the perfume. Second, *fantasy imagery* occurs when the consumer responds by producing a multisensory image not drawn directly from prior experience (Singer 1966). Instead of replaying a historic sequence the consumer constructs an imaginary one. The colors and shapes that are seen, the sounds that are heard, and the touches that are felt have never actually occurred, but are brought together in this particular configuration for the first time and experienced as mental phenomena.

Of course, even those sensations that originate in the consumer's mind draw upon real events for their construction (Singer 1966). It is unlikely that a consumer could generate a detailed, multisensory imaginative sequence without having some access to relevant real experiences. Thus, one should view multisensory imagery as a continuum from purely historic recollections to complete fantasy. Although both may play roles in hedonic consumption, we shall focus here on the latter, less explored area of fantasy.

In addition to the development of multisensory imagery, another type of response related to hedonic consumption involves *emotional arousal.* Emotions represent motivational phenomena with characteristic neurophysiological, expressive and experiential components (Izard and Beuchler 1980). They include feelings such as joy, jealousy, fear, rage and rapture (Freud 1955). Emotive response is both psychological and physiological in nature, generating altered states in both the mind and body (Ornstein 1977, Schacter and Singer 1962), It includes but extends beyond the affect or preference variables often studied by marketing researchers.

Rarely in marketing research has the full scope of emotional response to products been investigated. In research on hedonic consumption, however, this range of feelings plays a major role. The seeking of emotional arousal is posited to be a major motivation for the consumption of certain product classes, e.g., novels, plays and sporting events (Holbrook 1980), Further, emotional involvement is tied to the consumption of even simple products such as cigarettes, food and clothing (Levy 1959),

In sum, hedonic consumption refers to consumers' multisensory images, fantasies and emotional arousal in using products. This configuration of effects may be termed *hedonic response.* The characteristics and causes of hedonic response are further developed in the sections that follow.

## Theoretical background

The systematic, empirical investigation of hedonic response in consumption is quite new, with most relevant research dating from the late 1970s (e.g., Hirschman and Holbrook 1981. Holbrook 1980, 1981; Holbrook and Huber 1979, Levy and Czepiel 1974). However, the theoretical origins of the field may be traced to several specialized subfields in a variety of behavioral sciences: culture production systems within sociology (Becker 1973, Crane 1976, Hirsch 1972), esthetics within philosophy (Jaeger 1945), affective response within psycholinguistics (Osgood, Suci and Tannenbaum 1957), and fantasy imagery/daydreaming studies within psychology (Singer 1966, Swanson 1978).

In marketing an important precursor of research on hedonic consumption involved the stream of investigations termed *Motivation Research*. This research began in the 1950s (Dichter 1960) and continued into the 1970s; it focused on the emotional aspects of products and the fantasies that products could arouse and/or fulfill. However, many of the clinically oriented studies conducted by motivation researchers were subject to well-known criticisms concerning their rigor and validity (Kassarjian 1973), Wells and Beard 1973). Hence their long-term contribution has been limited.

A thematically related but more conceptually robust body of literature relevant to hedonic consumption dealt with product symbolism (Grubb and Grathwohl 1967, Levy 1959, 1964). The intellectual debt owed to these earlier efforts is quite apparent in several recent studies of symbolic consumption and its relation to hedonic experiences (Hirschman and Holbrook 1981).

The literature from these varied areas provides insights that can usefully extend and supplement the traditional orientation toward consumer research in marketing. These insights are evolutionary progressions of current paradigms and perspectives; however, in some ways they represent a fundamentally different orientation toward the examination of the interaction between consumers and products. Using a hedonic consumption perspective, products are viewed not as objective entities but rather as subjective symbols. The researcher is concerned not so much with what the product is as with what it represents. Product image, not strict reality, is a central focus; consumer emotive response, rather than just semantic learning, is a key criterion. Thus, the hedonic perspective seeks not to replace traditional theories of consumption but rather to extend and enhance their applicability.

Hedonic perspectives can be applied to several areas of current concern to marketers. In this paper we examine four: Mental Constructs, Product Classes, Product Usage and Individual Differences. In each area contrasts between the traditional and hedonic approaches are delineated. The incremental contributions that the study of hedonic consumption can make toward increasing knowledge of consumer behavior are explored by developing a series of propositions. These propositions highlight some discoveries that have been made using a hedonic focus. Most of these could not have been anticipated from the vantage point of traditional theory. Also, we shall cite some key deficiencies of current hedonic consumer research in each area. These limitations lie primarily in the domain of conceptualization and measurement and represent challenging obstacles to be overcome by researchers in this area.

## Mental Contructs

### Comparison of Traditional and Hedonic Approaches

Plato theorized that the human mind possessed three distinct faculties: *cognition* or knowing, *emotion* or feeling, and *conation* or willing (Scott, Osgood and Peterson 1979). Remarkably enough, these three constructs have remained largely intact over the years and are doubtless recognizable to most marketing researchers as the *belief, affect* and intention components of the familiar multiattribute attitude paradigm (Holbrook 1978). In much present consumer research there is an emphasis on the belief component of mental activities. Further, current investigations of consumer information processing focus almost exclusively on verbal information. Information occurring in other modalities – gustatory, olfactory, tactile, pictorial, aural – remains largely unexamined (Holbrook and Moore 1981). Additionally, within the multiattribute framework emotion is represented almost entirely by the subconstruct of affect. Emotive response, however, as it is usually measured, represents little more than a consumer's evaluation of tangible product attributes. The broader dimensions of emotion, such as strong feelings of anguish or rapture in response to products, are little explored or accounted for (Holbrook 1980).

This neglect probably results from the traditional economic view of products as objects for which the consumer desires to maximize utility, where utility typically is measured as some function of the product's tangible attributes. While this approach is quite valid and useful for goods whose tangible qualities and utilitarian performance serve as primary determinants of their value to the consumer, it would seem inappropriate for products whose selection and use are based upon satisfying emotional wants, rather than fulfilling utilitarian functions.

Traditional consumer research has largely ignored multisensory afferent and efferent consumer response, while measuring semantic rather than emotive and imaginal reactions to products. While not denying the utility of the traditional view, hedonic consumer research seeks to augment its focus by acknowledging the several sensory channels used by consumers to perceive and experience products. Pictorial stimuli appear to be particularly important in this light (Holbrook and Moore 1981). Thus, this approach supplements verbal data with that supplied by other sensory modalities and the internal generation of sensory impressions.

### Propositions

Several propositions can be derived from a consideration of hedonic mental constructs. First, in some instances, *emotional desires dominate utilitarian motives in the choice of products* (Maslow 1968). For example, as was clearly recognized by the motivation researchers, there are contexts in which emotions such as love, hate or jealousy will override consumers' economic decision rules based on deductive reasoning (Dichter 1960). Although they are depicted with great frequency in classical and popular literature *(Candide, The Godfather)*, plays *(Othello, Romeo and Juliet)*, movies *(Kramer vs. Kramer)* and television shows *(Dallas)*, and firmly supported by psychoanalytic work (Freud 1955), situations such as this have remained largely unexplored in much recent consumer research.

Second, *consumers imbue a product with a subjective meaning that supplements the concrete attributes it possesses* (Hirschman 1980a, 1981b). This process may be reinforced by exposure to evaluative (as opposed to factual) advertising content (Holbrook 1978). For some products such as esthetic objects, these intangible, symbolic attributes can be key determinants of brand selection. Indeed, perceptions of the product as a subjective symbol rather than a concrete object can account for the selection of brands that are clearly inferior in terms of their tangible features but are viewed as subjectively superior symbols (Levy 1959).

Third, *hedonic consumption is tied to imaginative constructions of reality* (Singer 1966), Thus, hedonic consumption acts are based not on what consumers know to be real but rather on what they desire reality to be. This, of course, echoes a proposition raised 20 years ago by motivation researchers (Dichter 1960). Indeed, the consumer's internal construction of reality may not be congruent with the external, objectively verifiable world. It follows that researchers probing the mental imagery that the consumer constructs around a product require measures of how the product is seen in the consumer's subjective reality, beyond its objective context. One way of accomplishing this is to ask consumers if they ever pretend that something other than reality is occurring when they are consuming a product (Swanson 1978).

For example, recent research indicates that members of an audience may imagine themselves as one of the actors while viewing a movie, play or other performance; there is evidence that some of those who engage in this type of projective fantasy may purposely attend a performance because they have foreknowledge that it contains a role in which they would like to imagine themselves (Hirschman 1982a). Similarly, the great popularity of pornography suggests that many who consume pornographic books, movies and paraphernalia are doing so to act out or enhance their sexual fantasies (Green 1981). Thus, fantasies on various themes are important determinants and consequents of hedonic consumption. Swanson (1978) terms these *absorbing experiences* because the consumer is absorbed into the reality created by the product.

Another example of self-constructed reality is that of cigarette smokers who enjoy imagining themselves as "Marlboro Men." The traditional assumption has been that the effectiveness of the cowboy theme depended on lending the cigarette and, hence its user, a masculine image. It is likely, however, that the image adopted by some Marlboro consumers is a much more literal one – these consumers actually want to generate self-images as the idealized cowboy. Thus, one important set of motives for consumption is the desire to enter or create an altered state of reality.

Fourth, a growing body of *evidence suggests that sensory-emotive stimulation seeking and cognitive information seeking are two independent dimensions.* Extensive investigations by Zuckerman (1979) on the construct of sensation seeking (the desire for sensory-emotional arousal) followed by recent studies on hedonic consumption (Hirschman 1982) indicate that consumers seek sensory-emotional and/or cognitive stimulation – that is, some consumers are above average on both dimensions, others above average on one dimension only, and others below average on both.

This orthogonality of sensory-emotive and cognitive stimulation seeking could lead to a major reformulation of notions concerning optimal stimulation level and innovativeness (Hirschman 1980b). Apparently, two (or more) distinct optimums exist for any given consumer.

### Limitations

The hedonic approach to consumer behavior raises important issues concerning the role of mental constructs such as multisensory imagery and emotional arousal. However, to examine these areas requires the further development of research methodologies, the operationalization of several new variables and an extended conceptual framework.

First, techniques for better manipulating and measuring consumer acquisition and processing of multisensory images are needed. The present emphasis on the use of verbal descriptions in consumer research needs to be supplemented with data on consumers' use of other sensory impressions in experiencing products. Some researchers already make use of pictorial (Holbrook and Moore 1981), aural (Huber and Holbrook 1980) and gustatory stimuli and employ nonverbal response measures such as the information display board or eye-movement camera (Jacoby *et al.* 1976). However, the underlying nonverbal stimulus-response connections require more systematic, empirical investigation.

Another need concerns the nature of emotional response. Reliable and valid operationalization of emotions is essential in two areas. The first involves *the role emotion plays in the selection of products*. The choice contexts in which emotion may operate have not yet been fully identified but represent great potential for better comprehending consumer decision making. This could be especially appropriate in situations when the product is being purchased primarily as an expressive symbol, for example, as a gift or to commemorate an important life event.

Second, measures of *emotional arousal during acts of product consumption* are needed. Consumers may purchase certain products with the intent of generating an emotional reaction within themselves. This intervening hedonic response must be monitored during consumption so as to determine its linkage to consumer satisfaction and product enjoyment. One potential source of such process measures is chemical changes in blood serum and cortical areas of the brain (Kroeber-Riel 1979). Another involves overt, observable behaviors that evince the consumer's emotional response (Izard and Beuchler 1980). A third deals with alterations of vital signs indicating arousal and excitement (Schachter and Singer 1962).

## Product Classes

### Comparison of Traditional and Hedonic Approaches

A second difference between hedonic consumption and traditional consumer research concerns the product classes selected for investigation. Traditional consumer research has tended to focus on package goods (toothpaste, cigarettes, cereal, detergent, beer) and major durables (appliances, automobiles) as objects of study (Holbrook 1980). In contrast, hedonic consumer research investigates the performing arts (opera, ballet, modern dance, legitimate theater), the plastic arts (painting, photography, sculpture, crafts) and the corollaries of these high culture products within popular culture (movies, rock concerts, fashion apparel).

Numerous examples of these latter substantive concerns may be found in the conference sessions edited by Hirschman and Holbrook (1981), Hirschman and King (1980) and Holbrook (1980).

The divergence of product focus between hedonic and traditional consumer research mirrors the divergence in theoretical philosophies underlying each discipline. Each has chosen products where a priori one might anticipate that the assumptions and propositions it advanced would most likely be found valid. For example, one might logically expect that selection decisions concerning utilitarian products such as washing machines would be best predicted and explained using the expectancy-value formulation of the traditional multiattribute attitude model. Similarly, hedonic consumption researchers have typically played their strong suit by selecting emotion laden, subjectively-experienced products such as ballet, music and theater.

This emphasis on esthetic products is constructive for several reasons. First, it provides an impetus for exploring several classes of products that have been largely ignored in traditional consumer research: audio records and tapes, novels, plays, movies, opera, sporting events and so forth. Such products play an important role in the consumer's life – providing him/her with entertainment and an outlet for emotion and fantasy. Second, despite the fact that all products can be hedonically experienced by consumers, those upon which research has been focused deserve special attention because of their capacity to generate unusually strong emotional involvement (Holbrook 1980). In contrast to the low involvement experienced in using toothpaste or detergent, the response to observing a sporting event, watching a film or hearing a rock concert is more intense, more involving and potentially more important in the life of the consumer (Maslow 1968).

Third, an intriguing characteristic of esthetic products is that, while they may be consumed in anticipation of the pleasure they provide, the consumer may also choose to consume them even with foreknowledge that they will cause emotional pain (Suomi and Harlow 1976). Such consumption situations may help consumers deal with unpleasant or unhappy events that they feel the need to confront, via fantasy and emotional arousal (Freud 1955). Two instructive examples are the recently televised docu-dramas, *Roots* and *Holocaust*. Paradoxically, viewing of these series was especially strong, respectively, among blacks and Jews whose consumption of the product was certain to evoke violent and fearful images drawn from their own history (*Time* 1980). Other recent examples of painful hedonic consumption would include the viewing of *Kramer vs. Kramer* by parents involved in child custody fights, *Unmarried Woman* and *Starting Over* by people deserted by their spouses, or *And Then You Cry*, by persons afflicted with cancer.

Such consumption behavior seems irrational if one assumes that consumers pursue maximization of the "sum-of-pleasures-minus-pains" according to Bentham's felicific calculus. Using the traditional utility-maximizing multiattribute paradigm, such behavior would represent selection of a product in which several strong, negative attributes were known to be present. However, the hedonic perspective acknowledges that consumers can utilize painful knowledge to expend emotions and construct fantasies that enable them to deal with unhappy realities better. In this light such consumption behavior is constructive and rational (Freud 1955, Suomi and Harlow 1976). Indeed, recent exploratory research reveals that consumption of movies, plays and books is often consciously undertaken to help consumers deal with "unhappy events they had experienced" (Hirschman 1982a).

Two psychological theories provide further rationales for such acts of painful hedonic consumption. Psychoanalytic theory (Freud 1955) suggests that purposeful exposure to frightening experiences enables the consumer to purge anxieties. If left unattended, these anxieties might eventually emerge as neurotic symptoms. For example, Jews who are unable consciously to deal with knowledge of their historic persecution may later manifest their anxieties in the form of paranoia. An alternative but noncompeting rationale for the consumption of anxiety-arousing products stems from work on behavior modification (Suomi and Harlow 1976). By exposing oneself to such experiences on a self-controlled basis, the consumer can build up a gradual tolerance (desensitization) concerning the frightening knowledge and thereby reduce its ability to arouse fear and anxiety.

### Propositions

Some important propositions are suggested by the hedonic perspective regarding product classes. First, *the product classes discussed tend to be more emotionally involving than those traditionally examined in consumer research.* Products such as movies, concerts, plays and novels can evoke complex fantasies and fulfill deep-seated and salient emotional needs. Their consumption often represents an act of profound importance to the consumer.

Second, *the consumption of such products generates and requires substantial mental activity on the part of the consumer.* This is true because of the multisensory imagery inspired by (say) a ballet and the expenditure of emotional resources used to experience and interpret the product. Further, it is likely that the mental activity engendered by consuming hedonic products is predominantly right brain-oriented (Ornstein 1977), since the capacity for responding to visual-spatial stimuli and emotion laden events is believed centered in this hemisphere. If later research supports this contention, then it is likely that such products may also be experienced as gestalts, since the right brain seems to respond to stimuli in a holistic rather than analytical fashion.

Third, *patronage decisions regarding hedonically consumed products are based primarily on the symbolic elements of the products rather than their tangible features.* A novel or play is selected primarily because of its ability to transport the consumer to a more desirable reality and/or to help in coping with an unpleasant emotional dilemma. Recent research indicates that even physical activities such as bicycle riding and skiing can be undertaken because of their symbolic qualities (Hirschman 1982a).

### *Limitations*

The primary limitation encountered with respect to hedonically-consumed product classes involves the special challenges they pose in developing adequate measurement methodologies. First, as a threat to *reliability*, many of the products discussed (a concert, ballet or play) are live performances and subject to variability across time. The composition of performing units may change, as in the substitution of an understudy for the leading lady. Further, even if the cast of performers is constant, the quality of their performance is susceptible to variation. In either case, the content of the product changes. thereby reducing the reliability of measures taken. Moreover, even for products not created via live performance (movies, records), such external factors as instrumentation (poor quality TV reception, speaker distortion) and consumption conditions (hot and crowded theaters, street noises) may threaten reliability.

A second measurement problem concerns the question of *validity*. Achieving valid measurement is difficult enough in most behavioral research. Yet these difficulties are compounded when the stimulus of interest is composed of both real and imagined aspects and when the consumer's hedonic response may be manifested both physically and mentally. Here, a combination of traditional scaling techniques (semantic differential scales, forced-choice tasks) and physiological indices of arousal (galvanic skin response, brain waves) will doubtless be required to reflect the complexity of hedonic consumer responses (Krober-Riel 1979).

## Product Usage

### Comparison of Traditional and Hedonic Approaches

Within traditional consumer research the most studied consumption activity is the decision making process (Bettman 1979). This focus originates in the strategically oriented concern of marketers with the prediction and explanation of brand choice. While the hedonic perspective in no sense advocates a reduction of research on consumer decision making, it does argue for increased attention to phenomena involved in product usage. The hedonic perspective includes the psychological experiences that accompany product usage. Thus, hedonic responses may be viewed as the essence of the usage experience.

Within this general framework the dynamic interaction between product and consumer is especially important. For example, the reaction of an audience has complex reciprocal effects on both performers and viewers during a play or sporting event *(Rolling Stone* 1980). Many hedonic products are consumed over time. An opera may last several hours; a painting may be contemplated in a museum for a few minutes or in the home for years. The emotions and fantasy images experienced by the consumer are in continuous flux throughout this usage period. One objective of hedonic consumption research is to monitor and, if possible, to predict emotional reactions and fantasy imagery during product usage.

During product usage the consumer's mental energies expended in emotional and imaginal responses pose a problem of resource allocation (Ornstein 1977, Schacter and Singer 1962, Singer 1966). Thus, if consumers know in advance that hedonic consumption will require a certain level of imaginal participation and emotional expenditure, they may choose to use (or to avoid) a certain product because they wish (or refuse) to make such an investment of their imaginal-emotional resources (Singer 1966, Zuckerman 1979). This notion of imaginal-emotional effort allocation during product usage extends the traditional marketing focus on money expenditures, while also moving beyond the emphasis of information theorists on cognitive processing effort during decision making (Bettman 1979).

Consider a consumer who is contemplating entertainment choices on Friday night and has narrowed the options to two movies both costing $4 per person, thereby controlling for demands on money resources across alternatives. One movie is a noninvolving situation comedy *(Nine to Five)* while the second is an intense saga of love, hate, violence and sexuality *(Raging Bull)*. We believe that consumers desiring a minimal expenditure of their imaginal-emotional energy would likely choose the former, while those desiring a more cathartic experience would probably opt for the latter.

### Propositions

Some interesting propositions emerge from regarding hedonic consumption as a dynamic usage experience. First, *there appears to be a preferred or most desirable pattern of emotional arousal for products experienced over a specific time frame* (Osborne and Farley 1970). For example, a novel, a movie, a rock concert or a football game are products that are experienced over time, during which varied emotions and fantasies are aroused in the consumer. Often the most preferred pattern of arousal is one that begins at a low level, increases in intensity, reaches a climax and then gradually subsides. This pattern appears in the structure of most operas, ballets, movies, novels, plays, jazz solos, and orchestral pieces and is more formally represented by the prologue, chorus, climax, epilogue sequence of classical Greek literature and drama (Jaeger 1945). In a clear parallel to sexual intercourse, the sequence represents a classic instance of art imitating life, perhaps with characteristic rhythm drawn largely from the survival value of procreation (Berlyne 1971, Maslow 1968).

According to Zuckerman (1979), sexual arousal is one of the primary concomitants of many types of hedonic consumption. For example, a popular hedonic experience for high school and college students is the rock concert. A vivid account of the role the rock concert can play in fulfilling the sexual fantasies of both audience and performers was recently provided by David Lee Roth, lead singer in a popular rock group: "As for me personally, I feel sexy a whole lot of the time. That's one of the reasons I'm in this job: to exercise my sexual fantasies. When I'm onstage, it's like doing it with 20,000 of my closest friends. And you don't have to ask them if they 'came.' They'll let you know"*(Rolling Stone 1980*, p. 21).

A second proposition stems from recent findings that *the capacity and desire for expending imaginal-emotional resources varies within one consumer over time* (Zuckerman 1979). Such temporal shifts in hedonic energy raise important questions concerning the dynamic patterns of product usage. However, their investigation raises serious methodological problems, to which we now turn.

### Limitations

Exploration of hedonic consumption as a dynamic process requires the development of appropriate measures of imaginal-emotive effort, capacity and desire. Yet, in contrast to the progress that has been made in measuring cognitive effort and capacity (Jensen 1980, Sternberg 1977), the measurement of imaginal-emotive effort and capacity remains largely unexplored.

In seeking measures of imaginal-emotive expenditures, there are two primary sources from which to draw: Zuckerman's (1979) sensation seeking scale and the scales Hilgard (1970) and Swanson (1978) developed to assess tendencies toward absorbing experiences. Sensation seeking encompasses four interrelated dimensions: thrill and adventure seeking, experience seeking, disinhibition and boredom susceptibility (Zuckerman 1979). The construct is measured using a 72-item, forced-choice instrument. Despite the pencil-and-paper nature of this operationalization the scale has been found to correlate quite strongly with several indicative behaviors, such as risky physical activities (hang gliding), drug and liquor consumption, frequency and variety of sexual intercourse, preference by women for infant breastfeeding and enjoyment of complex visual and auditory stimuli.

The measures developed by Hilgard (1970) for assessing tendencies toward absorbing experiences have been shown to correlate with susceptibility to hypnosis and altered states of consciousness. Moreover, the absorbing experiences scales applied in clinical settings have recently been revised by Swanson (1978) for application to normal, consuming populations. Exploratory research has shown that tendencies toward absorbing experiences are related to the seeking of sensory-emotional arousal and to the escape from reality by engaging in fantasy (Hirschman 1982a).

Both the sensation seeking and absorbing experiences scales are readily administered in survey research designs and are, therefore, potentially usable in the large sample studies favored by marketing researchers. Need for their use is suggested by the fact that sensation seeking has been found to be independent of cognitive information processing characteristics such as divergent processing ability, short-term memory capacity and information transfer, but strongly related to other hedonic consumption measures such as imagery and projective consumption (Zuckerman 1979).

An accompanying disadvantage stems from their essentially static nature, which renders them poorly suited to trace the dynamic changes in the consumer's general degree of hedonic effort and capacity. Moreover, it is likely that they tap chronic levels of hedonic energy associated with basic personality structure rather than acute levels of momentary sensory-emotive expenditures. In this sense, they are less appropriate to the study of usage experience than to the investigation of individual differences, a subject to which we now turn.

## Individual Differences

### Comparison of Traditional and Hedonic Approaches

A final area of demarcation between the hedonic and traditional approaches to consumer research concerns the issue of individual differences. In accord with its strategic orientation, much traditional marketing research has taken a post hoe approach to sources of interpersonal variance, in which consumers evincing certain behaviors (brand loyalty, high usage rate, low satisfaction) are profiled according to their discriminating characteristics. This descriptive profile approach is one common method of market segmentation and also appears in the many audience profile studies conducted by hedonic consumption researchers (Andreasen and Belk 1980), However, a complementary orientation more typical of hedonic research employs an approach in which subcultural groups are defined a priori – before being compared on the basis of hedonic responses (Hirschman 1982a, Singer 1966). Here, the central proposition is that individual differences in ethnic background, social class and gender cause products to vary greatly in the emotions and fantasies they inspire in a consumer.

Given this premise, recent research has begun to investigate differences between various subcultures in their emotions toward and fantasies about products. For example, six ethnic groups (Chinese, English, Greek, Irish, Italian, Jewish) were found to differ greatly in their emotional motives for pursuing consumption activities, their tendencies toward fantasy and altered states of consciousness, and their projection into consumption experiences (Hirschman 1982a). This subcultural approach to individual differences helps enrich research results by focusing attention on the social origins of variation in hedonic response. Further, it helps efforts to identify and understand the cultural sources of images – both of a real and fantasy nature – that guide consumers in their adoption and usage of products.

### Propositions

Given this perspective, some important propositions follow. First, *differences in consumer emotional and imaginal response to products appear closely tied to a variety of subcultural differences.* Ethnic groups, whether defined along racial, religious or nationality dimensions, represent complex systems of socialization, educating their members into a certain world view and enforcing adherence to a set of customs (Hirschman 1981a, 1982b). Hence, an individual tends to treat a product according to the perspective learned from his/her ethnic group. Similarly, the values shared by members of a given social class or gender affect desires for and responses to products.

Second, *subcultures vary in the amount of fantasy and emotionality encouraged/permitted in their members* (Hirschman 1982b, Singer 1966). Differences of this type can greatly influence the potential for and exhibition of hedonic response by consumers. For instance, Jews and Italian Catholics are generally permitted by their ethnic norms to be emotionally expressive, whereas such displays are discouraged among Protestants (Patai 1977). It has also been found that fantasizing and complexity of imagery are distributed in similar fashion across these three religious groups (Singer 1966). Jews and Catholic Italians not only report more and richer fantasies than do Protestants but also report significantly more erotic and sensual content in their fantasies (Singer 1966).

Third, *subcultural groups vary in their perception of what products are appropriate for hedonic consumption*. For example, consumers of many hedonically-experienced products are characterized by very distinctive social class profiles (Lapso 1981, Wachtel 1981). Operagoers are typically older, wealthier and higher in social status than theatergoers. Similarly, large socioeconomic differences exist between those who patronize basketball games and those attending museum exhibits (though cost differentials between these two products are minimal or even countervailing). These differences suggest that social class acts as a subcultural socialization agent, channeling consumers into those hedonic activities appropriate to their social positions. Marketers attempting to broaden the performing arts audience confront the problem that, if middle-class consumers begin attending in large numbers, upper-class patrons may leave in favor of something more exclusive. Notions of social appropriateness appear to extend to gender and ethnic group influences on hedonic consumption. Ethnic groups share norms that encourage and discourage certain kinds of hedonic consumption. For example, recent research on weekend evening entertainment choices by Catholics, Jews and Protestants shows several significant differences (Hirschman 1982b). There are also various social norms concerning masculine entertainment forms (e.g., sporting events) and feminine entertainment forms (e.g., shopping).

#### Limitations

Research on subcultural differences in hedonic consumption has thus far neglected the effects of cultural pluralism associated with the heterogeneous ethnic composition of American society. For example, because religious affiliation transverses the social class hierarchy, mutually facilitative or suppressive moderating effects may occur. Thus, if Protestants (say) are predisposed to the consumption of literature, one might find upper-, middle- and lower-class members of this religious denomination reading philosophy, best-sellers and romance paperbacks, respectively. Such potential interaction effects have not yet been explored systematically in hedonic research.

## Conclusions

We have defined hedonic consumption as those facets of consumer behavior that relate to the multisensory, fantasy and emotive aspects of product use. We have argued that this hedonic viewpoint represents an important extension of traditional consumer research and offers a complementary perspective for conceptualizing many otherwise neglected consumption phenomena. Accordingly, constructs of multisensory experience, fantasy imagery and emotive response have been introduced, defined and linked to various consumption processes.

Hedonic consumption is tied theoretically to work in several of the behavioral sciences – including sociology, esthetics, linguistics, psychology and psycholinguistics – as well as to motivation research and product symbolism in marketing theory. Given its comparative neglect in marketing research, we have sought to put forward a framework for its conceptualization and study. Four areas have been examined in terms of comparisons with the traditional approach. These four areas include Mental Constructs, Product Classes, Product Usage and Individual Differences.

The framework offered is admittedly both tentative and ambitious. We expect that it will provoke controversy but hope that it will also stimulate reflection on the nature of consumer behavior. The behavior of consumers, we believe, is far more sensorily complex, imaginative and emotion laden than has been reflected in the traditional approach to marketing research. The hedonic approach, while certainly no complete solution, may take us further toward comprehending the multiple facets of the consumption experience.

## References

Andreasen, Alan R. and Russell W. Belk (1980), "Predictors of Attendance at the Performing Arts," *Journal of Consumer Research*, 7 (September), 112–120.

Becker, Howard S. (1973), "Art as Collective Action," *American Sociological Review*, 39 (Spring), 767–776.

Berlyne, D. F, (1971), *Aesthetics and Psychobiology*. New York: Meredith.

Bettman, James R. (1979), *An Information Processing Theory of Consumer Choice*, Reading, MA: Addison-Wesley Publishing Company.

Crane, Diane (1976), "Reward Systems in Art, Science and Religion," in *The Production of Culture*, R.A. Peterson, ed., Beverly Hills: Sage.

Dichter, Ernest (1960), *The Strategy of Desire*, New York: Doubleday.

Freud, S. (1955), "Beyond the Pleasure Principle," in *The Standard Edition of the Complete Psychological Works of Sigmund Freud*. Vol. 18. J. Strackey, ed., London: Hogarth Press.

Gardner, Burleigh and Sidney J. Levy (1955), "The Product and the Brand," *Harvard Business Review*, 33 (March–April), 33–39.

Green, Bob (1981), "An Unmentionable Occasion," *Esquire*, 98 (March), 15–18.

Grubb, Edward L. and Harrison L. Grathwohl (1967), "Consumer Self-Concept, Symbolism and Market Behavior: A Theoretical Approach," *Journal of Marketing*, 31 (October), 22–27.

Hilgard, Josephine R. (1970), *Personality and Hypnosis: A Study of Imaginative Involvement*, Chicago: University of Chicago Press.

Hirsch, Paul M. (1972), "Processing Fads and Fashions: An Organization Set Analysis of Cultural Industry Systems," *American Journal of Sociology*, 77 (Winter), 639–659.

Hirschman, Elizabeth C. (1980a), "Attributes of Attributes and Layers of Meaning," in *Advances in Consumer Research*, Vol. 7. J.C. Olson, ed., Ann Arbor: Association for Consumer Research.

– (1980b), "Innovativeness, Novelty Seeking and Consumer Creativity," *Journal of Consumer Research*, 7 (December), 283–295.

– (1981a), "American Jewish Ethnicity: Its Relationship to Some Selected Aspects of Consumer Behavior," *Journal of Marketing*, 45 (Summer), 102–110.
– (1981b), "Commonality and Idiosyncracy in Popular Culture: An Empirical Examination of the 'Layers of Meaning' Concept," in *Symbolic Consumer Behavior*, E. C. Hirschman and M. B, Holbrook, eds., Ann Arbor: Association for Consumer Research.
– (1982a), "Ethnic Variation in Hedonic Consumption," *Journal of Social Psychology*, in press.
– (1982b), "Religious Affiliation and Consumption Processes: An Initial Paradigm," in Jagdish N. Sheth, ed., *Research in Marketing*, Vol. 6, JAI Press, forthcoming.
– and Morris B. Holbrook, eds. (1981), *Symbolic Consumer Behavior*, Ann Arbor, MI: Association for Consumer Research.
– and Charles King (1980), "Understanding Style and Taste," Special Topic Session. *Advances in Consumer Research*, Vol. VII. J.C, Olson, ed., Ann Arbor, MI: Association for Consumer Research.
Holbrook, Morris B. (1978), "Beyond Attitude Structure: Toward the Informational Determinants of Attitude," *Journal of Marketing Research*, 15 (November). 545–556.
– (1980), "Some Preliminary Notes on Research in Consumer Esthetics," in *Advances in Consumer Research*, Vol, VII, J.C. Olson, ed., Ann Arbor: Association for Consumer Research.
– (1981), "Integrating Compositional and Decompositional Analyses to Represent the Intervening Role of Perceptions in Evaluative Judgments," *Journal of Marketing Research*, 18 (February), 13–28.
– and Joel Huber (1979), "Separating Perceptual Dimensions from Affective Overtones: An Application to Consumer Esthetics," *Journal of Consumer Research*, 5 (March), 272–283.
– and William L. Moore (1981), "Feature Interactions in Consumer Judgments of Verbal Versus Pictorial Presentations," *Journal of Consumer Research*, 8 (June), 103–113.
Huber, Joel and Morris B. Holbrook (1980), "The Determinants of Esthetic Value and Growth," in *Advances in Consumer Research*, Vol. VII, J.C. Olson, ed., Ann Arbor: Association for Consumer Research.
Izard, C.E. and S. Buchler (1980), "Aspects of Consciousness and Personality in Terms of Differential Emotions Theory," in *Emotion: Theory, Research and Experience*, Robert Plutchik and Henry Kellerman, eds., New York: Academic Press,
Jacoby, Jacob, Robert W. Chestnut, Karl C. Weigl and William Fisher (1976), "Pre-Purchase Information Acquisition: Description of a Process Methodology, Research Paradigm and Pilot Investigation," in *Advances in Consumer Research*. Vol. III. B.B. Anderson. eds., Ann Arbor: Association for Consumer Research.
Jaeger, Werner (1945), *Paideia: The Ideals of Greek Culture*, Vol. I, translated by Gilbert Highet, New York: Oxford University Press.
Jensen, Arthur A. (1980), *Bias in Mental Testing*, New York: Free Press.
Kassarjian, Harold H. (1971), "Personality and Consumer Behavior: A Review," *Journal of Marketing Research*, 8 (November), 409–418.
Kroeber-Riel, Werner (1979), "Activation Research: Psychobiological Approaches in Consumer Research," *Journal of Consumer Research*, 5 (March), 240–250.
Lapso, Russell (1981), "Direct Marketing of Modern Dance," in *Symbolic Consumer Behavior*, E.C. Hirschman and M.B. Holbrook, eds., Ann Arbor: Association for Consumer Research.
Levy, Sidney J. (1959), "Symbols for Sale," *Harvard Business Review*, 37 (July-August), 117–119.
– (1963), "Symbolism and Life Style," in *Toward Scientific Marketing*, Stephen A. Greyser, ed., Chicago: American Marketing Association.
– (1980), "Symbolic Analysis of Companies, Brands, and Customers," University of Pittsburgh, (April), Twelfth Annual Albert Wesley Frey Lecture.
– and John A. Czepiel (1974), "Marketing and Acsthetics," *Proceedings*, Chicago: American Marketing Association, 386–391.
Maslow, A.H, (1968), *Toward a Psychology of Being*, 2nd ed., Prinecton, N.J.: Van Nostrand.
Ornstein, R.E. ( 1977), *The Psychology of Consciousness*, 2nd ed., New York: Penguin Books, Inc.
Osborne, J.W. and F.H. Farley (1970), "The Relationship Between Aesthetic Preference and Visual Complexity in Abstract Art," *Psychonomic Science*, 19 (February), 69–70.

Osgood, Charles E., George J. Suci and Percy H. Tannenbaum (1957), *The Measurement of Meaning*, Urbana: University of Illinois Press.
Patai, Raphael (1977), *The Jewish Mind*, New York: Charles Scribner's Sons.
*Rolling Stone* (1980), "Touring with Van Halen," (September 4), 21.
Schacter, S. and J.E. Singer (1962), "Cognitive, Social and Physiological Determinants of Emotional States," *Psychological Review*, 69 (July), 379–399.
Scott, William A., D. Wayne Osgood and Christopher Peterson (1979), *Cognitive Structure: Theory and Measurement of Individual Differences*. New York: John Wiley and Sons.
Singer, J.L. (1966), *Daydreaming: An Introduction to the Experimental Study of Inner Experience*, New York: Random House.
Sternberg, R.J. (1977), *Intelligence, Information Processing and Analogical Reasoning*, Hillsdale, NJ, Erlbaum.
Suomi, S.J. and H.F. Harlow (1976), "The Facts and Function of Fear," in *Emotions and Anxiety*, M. Zuckerman and C.D. Spielberger, Hillsdale, NJ: Lawrence Erlbaum Associates.
Swanson, Guy E. (1978), "Travels Through Inner Space: Family Structure and Openness to Absorbing Experiences," *American Journal of Sociology*, 83 (January), 890–919.
*Time* (1980), "Perspectives on 'Holocaust,"' (February 17), 67.
Wachtel, George A. (1981), "Marketing Broadway: A Case Study in Audience Research," in *Symbolic Consumer Behavior*, E, C. Hirschman and M. B. Holbrook, eds., Ann Arbor, MI: Association for Consumer Research.
Wells, William D. and Arthur D. Beard (1973), "Personality and Consumer Behavior," in *Consumer Behavior: Theoretical Sources*, Scott Ward and T.S. Robertson. eds., Englewood Cliffs, NJ: Prentice-Hall.
Zuckerman, M. (1979), *Sensation Seeking*, Hillsdale, NJ: Lawrence Erlbaum Associates.

# 7

# Alternative Ways of Seeking Knowledge in Consumer Research

**Laurel Anderson Hudson and Julie L. Ozanne**

**Source:** *Journal of Consumer Research* 14 (1988): 508–521.

Many ways of seeking knowledge about consumers exist. Knowledge may be gained from such diverse approaches as reading a novel to conducting a laboratory experiment. Each form of knowledge is valuable. However, as individual researchers, we must choose the processes through which we gain knowledge. Our field is dominated by various versions of positivism (Anderson 1986), even though the problems of positivism are well articulated in the literature (Anderson 1983; Olson 1981; Peter and Olson 1983). However, the interpretive approach is beginning to receive some attention as an alternative way of seeking knowledge (Belk, Sherry, and Wallendorf 1988; Hirschman 1985, 1986; Holbrook 1986; Hudson and Murray 1986; Solomon 1986; Wallendorf 1987).

The purpose of this article is to explore the assumptions and goals that underlie the two predominant approaches to gaining knowledge in the social sciences. By comparing positivism to interpretivism, we seek to highlight the existence of a number of diverse ways of seeking knowledge. Both of these research approaches include theories and methods based on different goals and underlying assumptions (Anderson 1986; Geertz 1973; Laudan 1984; Shulman 1986). These underlying philosophical assumptions include beliefs about the nature of reality, of social beings, and of what constitutes knowledge. By juxtaposing ways of seeking knowledge, we can learn and reflect on the strengths and weaknesses of both research approaches. This reflection is critical if we are to improve the ways in which we study consumers (Morgan 1983a).

This article (1) presents the major philosophical assumptions that underlie the general positivist and interpretive approaches, (2) demonstrates how these assumptions translate into different research processes, (3) explores the interdependency of assumptions, theoretical structures, and methodology, (4) compares the evaluative criteria used in each approach, (5) discusses problems within each approach, (6) highlights the range of positions within the interpretive approach, and (7) draws out implications of diverse ways of seeking knowledge for consumer research. Just as Anderson (1986) concluded that a weak form of incommensurability exists among research programs within the positivist approach, we conclude that the positivist and interpretive approaches (as used in this article and as practiced by many researchers) are incommensurable because they are based on different goals and philosophical assumptions (Kuhn 1962). Nevertheless, we hope this article makes it clear that incommensurability does not mean that the two approaches cannot peacefully coexist or that other alternative middle-ground approaches cannot or should not be developed.

**Table 1** A Summary of the Positivist and Interpretive Approaches

| Assumptions | Positivist | Interpretive |
|---|---|---|
| **Ontological** | | |
| Nature of reality | Objective, tangible<br>Single<br>Fragmentable<br>Divisible | Socially constructed<br>Multiple<br>Holistic<br>Contextual |
| Nature of social beings | Deterministic<br>Reactive | Voluntaristic<br>Proactive |
| **Axiological** | | |
| Overriding goal | "Explanation" via subsumption under general laws, prediction | "Understanding" based on Verstehen |
| **Epistemological** | | |
| Knowledge generated | Nomothetic<br>Time-free<br>Context-independent | Idiographic<br>Time-bound<br>Context-dependent |
| View of causality | Real causes exist | Multiple, simultaneous shaping |
| Research relationship | Dualism, separation<br>Privileged point of observation | Interactive, cooperative<br>No privileged point of observation |

Certain caveats apply to the study of these two approaches. First, philosophical assumptions are statements accepted without direct empirical support and are based on different views of reality, social beings, and knowledge. (However, these assumptions are sometimes based on strong philosophical arguments.) Second, we use the term "methodology" to refer to how one answers research questions. Methodology includes not only the data-gathering techniques, but also the research design, setting, subjects, analysis, reporting, and so on. Third, we chose the label of "interpretive" to describe the interpretive paradigm, although other labels abound, e.g., subjective (Rubinstein 1981), naturalistic (Lincoln and Guba 1985), qualitative (Van Maanen, Dabbs, and Faulkner 1982), and humanistic (ACR Special Session 1985). "Positivist" and "interpretive" are summary labels that refer to general research approaches that differ in their philosophical assumptions and goals. A number of positions can be loosely grouped under positivism: logical positivism, the received view, logical empiricism, modern empiricism, neopositivism, foundationalism, and objectivism. Likewise, the interpretive approach loosely captures a number of positions: subjectivism, phenomenology, symbolic interactionism, hermeneutics, and so on. Within positivism and interpretivism, a range of stances exists for each of the assumptions. In the first section of the article, the philosophical underpinnings of the two research approaches are discussed (see the Table). We emphasize how these philosophical assumptions translate into different ways of doing research within the two approaches. Then, the range of positions within the interpretive approach is further discussed by comparing three specific interpretive approaches.

## Positivist and Interpretive Approaches

### Ontological assumptions

*Nature of Reality.* All research approaches in the social sciences make ontological assumptions about the nature of reality and social beings. The positivists tend to take a realist position and assume that a single, objective reality exists independently of what individuals perceive. The social world, like the physical world, also exists independently of individuals' perceptions as a real, concrete, and unchanging structure. Reality exists as a structure composed of relationships among its parts. This reality is divisible and fragmentable; therefore, precise, accurate measurements and observations of this world are possible (Bagozzi 1980; Burrell and Morgan 1979; Morgan and Smircich 1980). The greatest understanding of this reality may come in a laboratory setting, where confounding variables can be controlled (Calder, Phillips, and Tybout 1981). Although individual inquiries may only approximate this reality, eventually all inquiries will converge on the same objective reality. Ford (1975) and others refer to this reality as "truth."

The laboratory experiment exemplifies these beliefs about the nature of reality. Parts of reality are separated from their usual context and placed in controlled settings for observation. For example, a problem under investigation might be the influence of different types of information on consumers' brand evaluations and their subsequent purchasing behaviors. Different types of information might be presented to an individual in a laboratory, and the researcher might measure behavioral or attitudinal responses. One assumption inherent in the laboratory experiment is that these relationships can be taken out of their natural and complex context, and the behavior that is displayed in the laboratory may correspond to the subject's behavior in the natural context. Thus, it is assumed that the responses to the information in the laboratory will reflect how subjects behave in a natural setting. This assumption enables the researcher to identify and unravel complex relationships while controlling for unstudied variables.

In contrast, the interpretivists deny that one real world exists; that is, reality is essentially mental and perceived. Individuals create devices, such as theories and categories, to help them make sense of their worlds (Burrell and Morgan 1979). Reality is also socially constructed in that "all human knowledge is developed, transmitted, and maintained in social situations" (Berger and Luckman 1967, p. 3). Thus, multiple realities exist because of different individual and group perspectives. The interpretivists believe that no amount of inquiry will converge on one single reality because multiple realities exist and these realities are changing. This approach also views these individual realities holistically – as more than the sum of their parts. That is, reality is made up of systems that are dependent on other systems for their meaning (Lincoln and Guba 1985). It is crucial for the researcher to know the context of a behavior or event because social beings construct reality and give it meaning based on context. Therefore, consumers would view information differently if they are in a retail store or laboratory setting. Furthermore, these interdependent systems must be viewed holistically. If the systems are separated and fragmented, their meanings change. For example, a researcher cannot grasp the meaning of an exchange ritual without also knowing about the norm of reciprocity.

Taylor and Bogdan's (1984) approach to the participant-observer technique is consistent with the interpretivists' assumptions about reality. For example, they suggest that when using the participant-observer technique the researcher should study people in their natural context and view people holistically; people should not be studied out of context or reduced to variables. Furthermore, people should be studied according to their own perspectives or frames of reference rather than from that of the researcher. Although it is impossible to see the world through the eyes of another, the researcher consciously tries to bracket personal beliefs and views. All perspectives are of interest in such an enterprise because the researcher is interested in describing multiple realities and does not believe a single reality exists.

*Nature of Social Beings.* These two approaches also make different assumptions about the nature of social beings. On one hand, the positivist approach holds a deterministic view: human behavior is determined. Some positivists modify this view and take a more stochastic approach. This model is exemplified, in the extreme, by certain forms of behaviorism that employ operant conditioning, where individuals behave *reactively*, in a response-reinforcement fashion, to the external world (Morgan and Smircich 1980; Rubinstein 1981). For example, the idea that individuals behave reactively is demonstrated by the belief that rewarding a purchase behavior with trading stamps may lead to a change in the probability of a purchase behavior. While cognitivists do not explain behavior generally in terms of external factors, they do reify internal subjective states and explain behavior as being determined by these states. Anderson describes the cognitivists' concept of human nature as "a rational information processor who forms beliefs, attitudes, and intentions that are causally determinant of his behavior" (1986, p. 160). On the other hand, the interpretive approach views people as more voluntaristic: people *actively* create and interact in order to shape their environment. They are not merely acted upon by outside influences. For example, Blumer's symbolic interactionism assumes that people create meaning through their interaction in the world: "It means that the human individual confronts a world that he must interpret in order to act instead of an environment to which he responds because of his organization" (1969, p. 15). For instance, consumers might engage in activities such as collecting cents-off coupons and trading stamps because they want to communicate to others that they are good, cost-efficient shoppers.

### Axiological assumptions

Underlying each of these world views are different fundamental goals or axiologies. World views differ, however, not so much in the presence or absence of a specific goal, but in the relative weighting of a goal and in what counts as fulfilling the goal.

The positivists' overriding goal is "explanation" via subsumption of the behavior under universal laws (Anderson 1986; Bredo and Feinberg 1982; Hunt 1983; Kerlinger 1973); the goal of explanation entails prediction. An explanation is achieved when one demonstrates the systematic association of variables underlying a phenomenon. Moreover, if one successfully demonstrates this systematic association, one "understands" the phenomenon (Kerlinger 1973). For instance, if a researcher wants to explain how consumers' involvement influences the processing of subsequent advertisements, the researcher must identify the antecedent variables (e.g., social or financial risk) and show how these variables are related to information processing. An explanation of a phenomenon – the demonstration of a systematic association of variables – should also enable the researcher to achieve some level of prediction.

For the interpretivists, the primary goal of research is understanding behavior, not predicting it (Rubinstein 1981). The interpretivists' view of understanding, however, is radically different from the positivists' view. First, interpretive researchers view understanding as more of a process than an end product. At points in time, researchers may state interpretations – their present understanding. However, the process of understanding is a never-ending process – a hermeneutic circle (this is one usage of the term). In other words, what was interpreted enters into current interpretations, just as the current interpretations will influence future interpretations. Therefore, interpretations are always incomplete. One never achieves *the* understanding; one achieves *an* understanding (Denzin 1984).

A prerequisite for doing research and seeking understanding is *Verstehen*. Wax (1967) focuses on *Verstehen* as the goal that separates the social sciences from the physical sciences by allowing access to the essential human aspects of individuals. We will use one of the more common definitions of *Verstehen:* grasping the shared meanings within a culture of language, contexts, roles, rituals, gestures, arts, and so on (Wax 1967). For example, Wallendorf (1987) discusses an informant who has rooms full of "junk" that he has collected. The *Verstehen*, or shared meaning, necessary to grasp the significance of this type of collecting is that people in American culture normally do not accumulate this many broken and discarded products. Knowing this shared meaning was a prerequisite to further understanding. Through active participation in the culture, the researcher strives for an insider's view, a knowledge of the shared meanings. Seeking *Verstehen* is an active process because language, customs, meanings, and culture are continuously being created by the joint activities of people. Meaning is dynamically created in the act of living (Wax 1967).

Although *Verstehen* is a necessary prerequisite to understanding, it is not sufficient for understanding. In addition to knowing the culturally shared meanings, it is necessary to obtain more comprehensive understanding by identifying, for example, the motives, dynamic uses of shared meanings, individual meanings, and interactions between shared meanings and individual meanings.

For instance, an interpretation of the collecting just discussed is that the man collected products so he would have available parts; collecting this "junk" often saves him from having to go to the hardware store. Another interpretation is that other people started expecting him to have parts that they needed, so he collects because people depend on him. As the individual and shared meanings are identified, the understanding becomes more comprehensive.

It should be noted that most research is conducted in the researcher's culture where a high degree of *Verstehen* already exists. Few researchers consider the number of shared meanings required to create and implement a positivistic survey. The shared meanings are taken for granted and the research questions are often framed, for instance, from the perspective of the researcher's social class, subculture, culture, training, and so on. To gain *Verstehen*, however, the interpretive researcher tries to drop the assumption of shared meanings and tries to see the world from an insider's perspective, as in Liebow's 1967 participant-observer study of lower-class black life. By actively seeking out the perspective of the members of this subculture, Liebow observed that these individuals operate within a value system that has little in common with middle-class values.

### Epistemological Assumptions

*Knowledge Generated.* The difference between what counts as knowledge within the two research approaches is striking. Based on their goals and their assumptions of reality, positivists take a generalizing approach to research; that is, they seek out general, abstract laws that ideally can be applied to an infinitely large number of phenomena, people, settings, and times. In other words, the positivists endeavor to identify time- and context-free generalizations, or nomothetic statements (Keat and Urry 1975). Conversely, interpretivists take a more historical, particularistic approach to research; that is, they study a specific phenomenon in a particular place and time. Rather than seeking to determine lawlike regularities, the interpretivists seek to determine motives, meanings, reasons, and other subjective experiences that are time- and context-bound. Geertz (1973) labeled this context-dependent form of explanation a "thick description." This difference in focus – generalistic vs. particularistic – is the primary difference between the two research approaches.

The difference in focus is fundamental: it changes what each approach views as important problems, facts, and evaluative criteria. For example, positivists, using a generalizing approach and investigating the influence of source credibility on consumers' attitudes, would attempt to derive an abstract, general formulation of this phenomenon. Positivists might seek out initial conditions, the process, causes, and effects. Because they are trying to derive a generalizable law, any number of different observations of this phenomenon would be appropriate. Nevertheless, the particular details of a single instance of the phenomenon have no intrinsic significance. Investigation of the particulars plays only an instrumental role in achieving the real purpose: general laws.

For the interpretivists, it is the particulars of a phenomenon that are of primary importance. In fact, some interpretivists create only idiographic knowledge. If an interpretivist studied people's perceptions of Bloomingdale's retail atmosphere, the researcher would focus on as many details as possible. Bloomingdale's retail environment is not chosen for instrumental reasons; it is chosen because an understanding of people's perceptions of this store is itself intrinsically appealing. A description of this store and people's perceptions of it will only be successful to the extent that the researcher accounts for contextual details. By adding variance, or details, the process will become more complex, and the researcher will achieve a thicker description. But complex processes are not easily generalizable. Therefore, these two approaches are at cross purposes because they produce different knowledge outputs. The particularistic approach creates thick descriptions from which it is difficult to create generalized knowledge statements (Berger, Zelditch, and Anderson 1982). Geertz uses the metaphor of a clinician making a diagnosis and says that "conceptualization is directed toward the task of generating interpretations of matters already in hand, not toward projecting outcomes of experimental manipulations or deducing future states of a determined system" (1973, p. 26). Although the interpretivist approach to research does not readily facilitate the statement of generalizations outside the context of the study, the approach does facilitate generalization within the context or case. For example, a researcher studying Bloomingdale's retail atmosphere would be able to discuss patterns and shared meanings within Bloomingdale's retail atmosphere, but these patterns and meanings would not necessarily transfer to the retail atmosphere of Saks. (It should be noted that some interpretivists do make generalizations between contexts.)

*View of Causality.* The assumptions regarding causality are closely connected with the assumptions regarding generalization and are also reflective of the differing goals of the two perspectives. The positivists, with their goal of explanation and prediction, place a high priority on identifying causal linkages. They believe that human action can be explained as the result of a real cause that temporally precedes the behavior (Hunt 1983). The deterministic assumption regarding the nature of man further supports their effort to identify the causes of individuals' behaviors.

The interpretivists view the world as being so complex and changing that it is impossible to distinguish a cause from an effect. Viewing the world holistically, the interpretivists' stance is that mutual, simultaneous shaping occurs between entities (Lincoln and Guba 1985; Rubinstein 1981). The voluntarist assumption regarding the nature of social beings also supports this position against causality. The interpretivists do not believe that reality is composed of parts or facts. If one attempts to fragment reality, then reality is changed (Rist 1977).

For instance, in studying family decision-making in dining-out decisions, the interpretivists would focus on the dynamic shaping that occurs. They would take into account not only the children's influence on the parents' choices, but the parents' influence on children's preferences. They would also recognize many other shaping factors, including contextual aspects. However, these factors cannot be separated into a temporally ordered causal sequence.

Data-collection techniques that tend to be used by the two approaches reflect these differing views of causality. The positivists often use experimentation in which there is an attempt to control the variables, the context, and the temporal order of events so that causal relationships can be inferred. The interpretivists often use the descriptive analysis of participant observations and historical documents in their attempt to view the entities holistically, in the context of political, social, economic, cultural, and other systems.

*Research Relationship.* The positivists' position regarding the relationship of the researcher to the subject is to assume a pronounced separation in which the researcher does not influence and is independent from the subject. Positivist researchers rely on their expertise to develop the research questions, designs, settings, and so forth. A detached stance is necessary to maintain objectivity, a prerequisite for legitimate knowledge (Bredo and Feinberg 1982). Because the positivists believe that it is possible for researchers to stand outside their object of inquiry and minimize or control for their own influence on it, they assume that a privileged vantage point exists from which researchers can view their subjects.

In contrast, the interpretivists hold that the researcher and the people under investigation interact with each other, creating a cooperative inquiry (Reason and Rowan 1981; Wallendorf 1987). If the social reality is based on individuals' or groups' perceptions, then, in order to be able to understand those perceptions, these individuals must be involved in creating the research process. Thus, the individual who is studied becomes a participant in the experiment, guiding the research as well as supplying information. The interpretivists believe that in the social sciences the scientist is a member of the social reality; no privileged, Archimedian vantage point exists (Giddens 1976; Lincoln and Guba 1985). This view results in emerging research designs that require ongoing adaptability on the part of the researcher. From the interpretivists' point of view, the emerging designs are better able to take into account the subject's knowledge.

Labels used by each approach to describe people under investigation exemplify differing assumptions about the research relationship. In the laboratory experiment, a person under investigation is called the subject, and an effort is made to maintain a separation between the researcher and the subject so that the manipulation of the independent variables, not the researcher, influences the subject's behavior. In the closed-ended survey, the individual is called the respondent, a term presupposing that the researcher knows the best questions to ask in order to discover a phenomenon. In more interpretive data-gathering techniques, such as participant-observation, the person is usually called the informant. These techniques tend to be unstructured, taking their leads from the informant, who informs and guides the research.

## General Research Process

These two research approaches, then, differ in their assumptions about the world and their goals. In this section, we discuss some of the general differences in research process arising from each approach and give specific examples.

Although general differences exist, it should be noted that neither approach translates into a single, unique research process. For example, the two approaches often use the same data-gathering technique, yet the technique changes as it is adapted from one approach to the other. Furthermore, the nature of the phenomenon studied changes as it is embedded in a different research process; this is highlighted in the section on data-gathering techniques.

### Positivist Research Approach

The positivists' approach to research includes the adherence to scientific protocol. The protocol for the proper research process is well established; we refer to this step-by-step organization as the principles of research design (Campbell and Stanley 1963). The research design is the fixed structure of the research, and adherence to this structure allows for "accurate answers" to research questions. This is not to ignore the use of pretests and pilot tests that allow the structure of the study to evolve, but at some point the questions to be addressed, the design and the hypotheses become fixed, at least until the next study. Although different research designs exist, "the ideal of science is the controlled experiment" (Kerlinger 1973, p. 315). The experiment, as used in a positivist research process, allows the researcher to select and assign subjects randomly to experimental groups, control extraneous variables, manipulate the relevant independent variables, and observe the dependent variables. Positivists argue that the controlled experiment allows the researcher the most confidence in discovering causal relationships among variables (Kerlinger 1973). This control provides the ability to isolate and examine only those behaviors that are specified by the hypotheses.

This use of protocol is exemplified in research by Bierley, McSweeney, and Vannieuwkerk (1985). They conducted an experiment to test whether preferences for stimuli, colored geometric figures, could be classically conditioned using music – knowledge that might be useful in advertising. Subjects were randomly assigned to experimental or control groups, separated by partitions, and given prerecorded instructions through headphones. The presentation of conditioned and unconditioned stimuli was carefully controlled and extraneous sources of variance were minimized: each session had 84 trials, conditioned stimuli were presented for five seconds and unconditioned stimuli for 10 seconds, music was played through headphones at 60 db., and experimenter-subject contact was minimized. Preference, the dependent variable, was then measured.

This stance regarding protocol reflects the connection between positivist assumptions and values and their concomitant research process. Through adherence to protocol, the positivists strive toward certitude that the researcher's descriptions correspond to true reality. The use of protocol is based on the researcher's assumptions about reality as well as on assumptions about social beings, the need for the separation of the researcher from the subject, the possibility of causal relations, and the desire to reveal the true reality and predict the outcome of events in reality.

## Interpretivist Research Approach

The interpretivists' approach to research, on the other hand, is typified by a continually evolving research design. The interpretivists seek to describe many perceived realities that cannot be known a priori because they are time- and context-specific. Thus, research is actually an emergent process. As perceived realities change, the research design adapts. In contrast to the experimentalists, to whom the control of all experimental conditions is paramount, the interpretivists conduct research in a natural, changing environment. The interpretivists consider that each researcher comes into the research environment with some knowledge or preunderstanding. However, this a priori knowledge is deemed inadequate for choosing a research design because of the complex and changing patterns of perceived realities. Although the interpretivists enter a research setting with some preunderstanding and a general plan, attempts are made to be open to new information. The study is allowed to unfold with the assistance of informants. Ideas, meanings, questions, and data-collection techniques are cooperatively developed.

Eugenia Shanklin (1979) discusses the evolving research design she used in a village in Ireland. The datacollection technique of visual documentation through photography was used. She found that perceptions of the role of the researcher changed throughout the research process: she felt that she passed through phases of being perceived as a tourist, a guest, a participant, and a neighbor. In each phase, her informant and photographical approach varied. For example, in the tourist phase, she faced the problem that the individuals who first acknowledged her presence (the town drunk and the village "nuisance") were at the margins of society. Shanklin explained that individuals at the margins of society often approach outsiders in an effort to gain the approval being withheld by their neighbors. To establish her role and status in the community, a distancing from these individuals was necessary. To get beyond the limited welcome she received for the photography, she examined the ways photographs were used and displayed in Irish homes. She noted that cameras recorded special occasions, but not commonplace ones. Also, few pictures were taken of children. She responded to this discovery by photographing children and giving the snapshots to parents. As informants became more comfortable with the researcher's photography, she continued to take the research photographs back to the informants and discuss them, often eliciting information or directions Shanklin would "never have known enough to ask about" (1979, p. 144).

The use of an evolving design is consistent with the interpretivists' belief that, due to the human's ability to adapt, the best approach to understanding is through the use of the human instrument. It is also consistent with their belief that one cannot have a priori knowledge of the many socially-constructed realities.

We have highlighted some general differences in research design and linked these differences to the positivists' and interpretivists' values and assumptions. Many other differences in the research process exist (see Hirschman 1986 for an example of one interpretive research process). Nevertheless, as demonstrated in the next section, a difference does not necessarily exist between the data-gathering techniques used by each approach.

### Data-gathering Techniques

Although it is tempting to assign quantitative data-gathering techniques to the positivist world view and qualitative techniques to the interpretivist world view, it is apparent that many techniques can be and are used by both approaches. But in embedding the same technique within different research processes, researchers change the technique and the data produced by the technique. The participant-observer technique is one that changes between the two approaches (Reason and Rowan 1981).

Whiting *et al.* (1966) provide an example of the participant-observer data-gathering technique in positivist research. In examining parental responses to emotions – in particular, to anger – Whiting *et al.* spent approximately one year in field work developing an ethnography of socialization and enculturation. The research design was set up to "test the degree to which field work can be preplanned according to fairly explicit theory" (1966, p. 3). Thus, the procedures were structured a priori, dependent and independent variables were identified, hypotheses suggested by psychoanalytic and learning theory were tested, statistical analyses were performed, and concern for reliability was expressed and identified as a priority.

Compare this use of technique to an interpretive study of emotion using the same technique. In Denzin's (1984) Emotions Project, an ongoing study of emotion in everyday life, he argues that one should use the language and meanings of the people. No hypotheses were proposed because it was felt that an a priori conceptual framework could not capture the flow of human experience. The goal of Denzin's inquiry was not to test theories but to describe and interpret emotions. Furthermore, each situation was seen as unique. "Nor will these streams of experience submit to experimental, statistical, comparative, or causal control and manipulation" (Denzin 1983, p. 132).

These studies exemplify what Geertz notes with regard to ethnography (1973, p. 6):

> From one point of view, that of the textbook, doing ethnography is establishing rapport, selecting information, transcribing texts, taking genealogies, mapping fields, keeping a diary, and so on. But it is not these things, techniques, and received procedures that define the enterprise. What defines it is the kind of intellectual effort it is.

Even if a researcher is creating an ethnography, we do not know the researcher's orientation. In other words, we cannot merely look at the data-gathering techniques to know what methodological orientation is held; we must examine the assumptions, the aims, and the research process.

Furthermore, even though different research approaches may study the same phenomenon, the phenomenon of inquiry is changed as it is approached from the different perspectives. For example, Whiting *et al.* approached anger from a learning theory perspective and operationalized anger as "gritting teeth, growing red in the face, clinching fists, taking an aggressive stance, losing oneself in temper tantrum and crying out with rage" (1966, p. 18). Here, consistent with learning theory, the external manifestations of anger are stressed. Compare this view of anger to a description of anger from Denzin's Emotion Project (1984, p. 100):

> When I get mad and angry, especially at my wife, I feel humiliated. I remember my father, when my mother used to get mad at him. She would yell and scream at him when he would come home drunk. He would sit at the kitchen table and hang his head and cry, and then go off to bed ... I hate myself when I get mad. Afterwards I am always embarrassed. Then I get resentful toward my wife, especially. If I keep this inside of me, we have a fight all over again.

Denzin's theory of emotions stresses that emotions are self-feelings that must be studied as lived phenomena from the point of view of the emotional person. The same philosophical assumptions that underlie Denzin's methodology underlie his theory. The methodology is consistent with the theory, and the theory supports the methodology. The same parallel holds for the relationship between Whiting *et al.'s* assumptions, theory, and methodology: consistent with learning theory, they define anger by a set of external behaviors that can be assessed by the methodology that they are using. Within each researcher's approach, these three components combine to form an interdependent system that is both self-justifying and self-perpetuating (Anderson 1986). Thus, the phenomenon of anger changes when studied within the two approaches.

## Criteria

The extent to which the two world views are encapsulated is highlighted by a comparison of their evaluative criteria. The positivists have a more definitive list of criteria, which is consistent with their desire for a standardized research process. Although the interpretivists have several general criteria, many specific criteria arise because of the differences among individual studies and theorists. In this section, we will discuss (1) Whiting *et al.*'s research and how it exemplifies positivistic criteria for evaluation, (2) the criteria that are consistently applied to interpretive research, (3) Denzin's specific criteria for judging interpretive research, and (4) the comparison of positivistic and interpretivistic criteria.

As noted previously, the positivists have a standardized and definitive protocol that allows for a more consistent application of fixed evaluative criteria. Whiting *et al.'s* (1966) work reflects these more definitive criteria. Whiting *et al.* discuss and evaluate their research on such criteria as the following:

1. The establishment of a theoretical basis: discussion of previous research, definition of independent and dependent variables a priori, and specification of hypotheses a priori.
2. The adherence to the proper protocol: rules for sample selection to avoid biases, standard questionnaire format across research settings, and antecedent and dependent variables.

3. Demonstration of reliability and generalizability: adherence to a priori definitions and procedures, and sampling within and across cultures.
4. The establishment of the statistical significance of the data.

To interpretivists, these criteria may seem rigid, but they are consistent with the positivists' goal of identifying general laws.

Perhaps the most consistently applied criterion for interpretive research is that the phenomenon be examined in the natural setting (Blumer 1969; Knorr-Cetina 1983; Patton 1980). Because meaning is derived from the context, studies must use natural settings. Also, the researchers must get to the point where they feel at home within the setting, or, as Sanday (1979) states, where they can communicate the patterns and expectations for conduct within the context. This comfort level allows researchers to see things similarly to the way the people being studied see them and to know the questions, problems, and data that are meaningful (Blumer 1969). Another criterion, which refers to Geertz's (1973) "thick description," is that the description of the phenomenon be detailed and inclusive of contextual and historical aspects. A related criterion is that the language and terminology of people being investigated be used (Fielding and Fielding 1986; Knorr-Cetina 1983). Interpretive research holds that language taxonomies and classification systems, subcultural vernaculars, and professional argots all reflect linguistic-cultural differences that the subtle processes of translation may miss: interactions should be recorded verbatim when possible. But while a researcher attempts to capture interactions verbatim – the emic perspective, the researcher does not retain this vocabulary when writing the results – the etic perspective.

Denzin's research incorporates these predominant interpretive criteria and specifies in the following summary additional evaluative criteria that are not as consistently applied (1984, p. 9):

1. Does the interpretation illuminate, disclose, and reveal the lived experience?
2. Does the interpretation rest on thickly contextualized, thickly described materials and on concepts near to experience?
3. Is the interpretation historically embedded and temporally grounded?
4. Does the interpretation reflect the phenomenon as a process that is relational and interactive?
5. Does the interpretation engulf what is known about the phenomenon?
6. Does the interpretation incorporate prior understandings and interpretations (the investigator's and others', including emergent ones) as part of the final interpreted, understood structural totality?
7. Does the interpretation cohere?
8. Does the interpretation produce understanding; that is, do the elements that are interpreted coalesce into a meaningful whole?
9. Is the interpretation unfinished? All interpretation is necessarily provisional and incomplete, to begin anew when the investigator returns to the phenomenon.

To positivists, these criteria may seem vague, but they are consistent with the flexible, adaptive nature of the interpretivists' research process.

If we used the criteria put forth by one of these researchers to assess the results obtained by the other, both approaches would be found lacking. For instance, Bonoma (1985) and Deshpande (1983) view qualitative data techniques as exploratory, not confirmatory, because they use positivist criteria to evaluate these techniques. In fact, many of the criticisms of both approaches arise from judging one approach by the criteria of another approach. For example, if we apply Denzin's and the interpretivists' criteria of (1) the researcher being a competent practitioner in the group, and (2) a thick description to Whiting *et al.'s* results, the results would fall short of the criteria. Whiting *et al.* would be criticized for believing that they maintained objectivity, fragmenting realities, and forcing their own conceptual framework on the people studied. Likewise, Denzin would not meet the positivists' criteria of a designated research protocol, a priori hypotheses that identify independent and dependent variables, standardized instruction and communication on the part of the researcher, and statistical significance. Denzin would be criticized for his sloppy research process, post hoc theorizing, unreplicable studies, and the exploratory status of his findings.

## General Criticisms

Although problems arise from judging one approach by another's evaluative criteria, some general criticisms from the philosophy and history of science exist for both approaches. Because the problems of positivism are discussed at length in the literature (Anderson 1983; Peter and Olson 1983; Rubinstein 1981; Suppe 1977), we will just list some of the major attacks. (These attacks also hold for Hunt's (1984) more moderate position of modern empiricism.) Positivists face the problem of induction: a universal statement cannot be verified by a finite number of observations, thus, universal laws are unachievable (probabilistic statements also face the problem of induction). Positivists assume a secure observational base from which objective observations can be made, but observations are value-laden, theory-laden, and interpreted (Anderson 1983; Peter and Olson 1983). Positivists reify subjective states and treat them like objects. Positivists try to conceive of the objective features of society apart from their social context and the perceptions of people (Rubinstein 1981). Positivists focus on truth content when no defensible method for establishing that truth exists (Peter 1983; Suppe 1977).

Because the interpretive view is not as familiar to consumer researchers, we will spend more time examining some of the prominent criticisms of this world view. One criticism of some interpretivist researchers is that they rely on empathetic identification as a basis for understanding (Hirschman 1986; Rubinstein 1981). Wilhelm Dilthey (Hodges 1969, p. 15) defines empathetic understanding as an observer's reliving of another's mental experiences. Many symbolic interactionists (Denzin 1970, p. 80) suggest that the researcher engage in role taking, whereby the researcher imagines how the receiver of a communication understands that communication. The criticism holds that, to begin with, empathetic identification is nonsensical because one cannot experience the thoughts of another – one can only experience one's own thoughts. Second, empathetic identification cannot be validated. Third, having a mental experience does not mean that one understands it; for example, in the area of mental health, it is the psychiatrist who understands manic depression, not the patient experiencing it (Rubinstein 1981).

Another criticism derives from the interpretivists' tendency to focus on individuals' intentional actions and individuals' consciousness, making it difficult to gain an understanding of macroscopic features of society. For example, one cannot understand the concept of family by just focusing on the knowledge of the individual members; part of the meaning of family is its role in the larger social system (Rubinstein 1981). The criticism holds that a theoretical grasp of the larger social context and social structures is crucial for understanding individual behaviors (Smart 1976).

A third area of criticism is reactivity (Thorns 1976): methods such as participant-observation are intrusive and may disrupt the normal activities of the people being studied. A related criticism concerns the biases of both the researcher and the informant: it is questionable whether researchers can really bracket their biases and social/cultural backgrounds. Furthermore, bias may arise because of the informant's expectations of the researcher, or, as has occurred in a number of studies, the informant may intentionally mislead the researcher. A final criticism concerns the establishment of the boundaries of the culture or group being studied: unless one studies an isolated group, the boundaries may be amorphous and changing, and clear divisions may not exist.

## Three Variations of Interpretivism

The world views presented for positivism and interpretivism are generalizations (Bogdan and Taylor 1975; Bredo and Feinberg 1982; Bruyn 1966; Burrell and Morgan 1979; Keat and Urry 1975; Lincoln and Guba 1985; Morgan and Smircich 1980; Rubinstein 1981). However, as Anderson (1986) points out, encapsulated research programs exist even within a world view. Anderson explicates various positivist programs; each has the cognitive goal of "explanation" but varies in the degree of adherence to various assumptions. Also, within the interpretive world view, research programs' common cognitive aim may be "understanding," but their other commitments may be different. Thus, within each world view there is variation in the degree to which different assumptions are emphasized. Furthermore, the meaning of understanding and what counts as fulfilling the goal may also vary. In order to illustrate some of the range within the interpretive world view, the research programs of Clifford Geertz, Yvonne Lincoln and Egon Guba, and Herbert Blumer are examined. Each of these programs is examined to highlight their different interpretations of the cognitive aim of understanding, the assumptions they emphasize or on which they vary, and the issues and problems that may arise from these different emphases.

### Geertz

Clifford Geertz is a leading exponent of what he calls the interpretive approach to anthropological understanding (Geertz 1973, 1983). Geertz claims that understanding involves interpreting others' modes of expression or symbol systems. Understanding "is more like grasping a proverb, catching an allusion, seeing a joke – or, as I have suggested, reading a poem – than it is like achieving communion" (1983, p. 70). Geertz identifies concrete cases and illustrative concepts that can be felt personally by those reading the research and that are also important to the people or group studied. He describes how he personally comes to understand the meaning of a concept. These meanings are often expressed through the use of metaphors, analogies, parables, and so on. For example, in the following illustration Geertz beautifully sensitizes the reader to the Javanese term "alus," which refers to an individual being refined, smooth, and civilized in both inward feelings and outward actions (1979, p. 231):

> Only when you have seen, as I have, a young man whose wife – a woman he had in fact raised from childhood and who had been the center of his life – has suddenly and inexplicably died, greeting everyone with a set smile and formal apologies for his wife's absence and trying, by mystical techniques, to flatten out, as he himself put it, the hills and valleys of his emotion into an even, level plain ("That is what you have to do," he said to me, "be smooth inside and out.") can you come ... (to) appreciate, however inaccessible it is to you, its own sort of force.

One appreciates the Javenese concept of "alus" by relating the sensitizing example to our own experiences and definitions of self.

As opposed to some interpretivists who base their understanding on empathetic identification, Geertz's interpretation of understanding highlights that the researcher cannot live the subject's perceptions, feelings, or meanings, but that the researcher can interpret them. Thus, the understanding is an interpretation of "thick description" (Geertz 1973). In fact, Crapanzano (1986) criticizes Geertz for conveying his interpretation in such vivid terms and images that he attributes experiences, meanings, and dispositions to people without adequate evidence or perhaps by projecting too much of his own culture on the interpretation. Crapanzano claims that there is little understanding from the native's point of view, but rather a "constructed understanding of the constructed native's constructed point of view" (1986, p. 74).

Geertz focuses on culture or collective meaning, as opposed to particular individual's meanings, and stresses the importance of the epistemological assumption regarding the particularist, nongeneralizing approach to research of a culture. Utilizing his "thick description" of a culture, he emphasizes a context-dependent form of explanation. However, Geertz does compare the concept of self in society across cultures. And he does say that the interpretations should fit not only past realities, but also survive future ones. Thus, the task is "not to codify abstract regularities but to make thick description possible, not to generalize across cases but to generalize within them" (Geertz 1973, p. 26). So in the previous example, Geertz would suggest patterns within Javanese life, but these patterns would not be expected to apply to another culture. Geertz's particularistic unit of analysis is a culture.

This assumption gives rise to one of the most prominent issues regarding Geertz's philosophy: the boundaries of the context. Especially in studying less isolated cultures, it is difficult to define both the breadth and the depth of the culture or context. For example, Geertz, while focusing on the individuals and their interaction with culture, does not include the examination of social/political structures in his view of context. In fact, a short time after Geertz left Bali, a revolt in Djakarta left between 40,000 and 80,000 Balinese dead (Geertz 1973), yet we have no hint of this tension between the social structure and the culture in his writing.

### Lincoln and Guba

Lincoln and Guba's (1985) approach to research from the field of education provides the basis for Hirschman's (1986) recent work on humanistic inquiry. Lincoln and Guba do not spend a lot of time in their recent book discussing the aims of their methodology; instead, they emphasize their ontological and epistemological assumptions and provide a step-like approach for doing research. What can be gleaned from their book is that contrary to what they see as the aim of scientific research – prediction – they seek understanding. Understanding in this context involves (1) gaining "an appreciation of the myriad mutual shapings that are synchronously ongoing and abstracting from that complexity a subsystem that serves the investigator's needs" (1985, p. 152), and (2) developing "an idiographic body of knowledge in the form of 'working hypotheses' that describe the individual case" (1985, p. 38).

An issue that arises from this definition is the distinction between understanding and prediction. Lincoln and Guba talk about the scientific goals of prediction and control as opposed to the naturalistic goals of understanding and management. Understanding and management imply that although you cannot predict case by case, you can look for patterns and develop working hypotheses that can be examined in pertinent situations to see whether they can be upheld. Management implies that although there cannot be control in the causal sense, there can be attempts to shape based on the tentative patterns a researcher develops.

Given a range of different emphases, Lincoln and Guba fall closer to many positivist programs in their axiological assumption than do interpretivists such as Geertz. However, their explication of ontological and epistemological assumptions are consistent with the general interpretivist world view presented in this article. In fact, Lincoln and Guba are attacked for the inconsistency between their assumptions and evaluative criteria. Lincoln and Guba's (1985) criteria of credibility, transferability, dependability, and confirmability closely parallel the positivist criteria of internal validity, external validity, reliability, and objectivity (Smith and Heshusius 1986).

Although Lincoln and Guba (1985) claim to use these interpretive assumptions, they ignore them in their discussion of criteria. The authors define confirmability as nonbiased, factual, confirmable findings. However, Lincoln and Guba assume that reality is determined by individuals' and groups' perceptions. If this assumption is held, then there is not one reality that can be captured in an unbiased/neutral way. Furthermore, the researcher's expectations may influence the construction and interpretation of these realities. Even if one evaluated the "raw," uninterpreted data to see if "objective" interpretations were made, the researcher still selects the data that are recorded and the vantage point that is taken. Thus, to interpretivists, there can be no such thing as objective data or confirmable results. Similar arguments can be made for the other criteria.

### Blumer

Herbert Blumer, a sociologist who worked closely with George Herbert Mead, is a leading proponent of one of the symbolic interactionist schools of thought (Solomon 1983). The two major schools of symbolic interactionism orient themselves to the two different world views discussed in this article: Blumer's Chicago school subscribes to a more interpretive world view, and M.H. Kuhn's Iowa school follows a more positivist philosophy (Meltzer, Petras, and Reynolds 1975).

For Blumer, understanding is "feeling one's way inside the experience of the actor." This is necessary because an individual's behavior is based on his/her own particular meanings. Thus, Blumer subscribes to empathetic identification. While Geertz stresses culture, Blumer emphasizes the individual as an actor. He views the individual's actions toward others as being based on the meanings of the others for the individual (Meltzer *et al.* 1975). These meanings are developed through individuals' interpretations of social interaction with each other. Thus, reality is composed of individuals' perceptions of it. Yet, in his view of reality, Blumer believes that "the empirical world can 'talk back' to our pictures of it or assertions about it – talk back in the sense of challenging and resisting, or not bending to, our images or conceptions of it" (1969, p. 22). Therefore, as opposed to the general interpretivist position, his stance on reality contains an objective and a subjective aspect. Blumer outlines the following tenets of his stance (1980, p. 410):

1. There is a world of reality 'out there' that stands over against human beings and that is capable of resisting actions toward it;
2. This world of reality becomes known to human beings *only* in the form in which it is perceived by human beings;
3. Thus, this reality changes as human beings develop new perceptions of it; and
4. The resistance of the world to perceptions of it is the test of the validity of these perceptions.

This combination of objectivity and subjectivity is carried over into his stance on generalization, and is perhaps most difficult to reconcile there. On one hand, Blumer is very particularistic in his emphasis on the individual and the individual's meanings; on the other hand, he states that researchers should try to formulate problems in a theoretical form and "unearth generic relations" (1969, p. 43).

These three interpretive programs illustrate a range of emphases and adherences to the different philosophical assumptions, demonstrating a "weak form of incommensurability" within the world view as well as between world views (just as Anderson (1986) points out exists within the positivist world). Geertz emphasizes understanding culture – the symbolic construction the group places on the world, while Blumer and Lincoln and Guba place more emphasis on the individual. For Geertz, the unit of analysis is culture and his focus of understanding is on the collective consciousness; for Blumer, the unit of analysis is the individual (actor) and his focus of understanding is on that individual's meanings and perceptions; and for Lincoln and Guba, the unit of analysis is individuals and the focus of understanding is on their meanings. The other ontological and epistemological assumptions discussed were highlighted to demonstrate the variation in assumptions within a world view. Thus, every researcher develops his/her own unique set of assumptions that fall within the parameters of a general world view.

## Implications

We examined the philosophical assumptions that underlie the positivists' and the interpretivists' research approaches. Each approach's assumptions justify and are consistent with their research methodology. In our discussion of Whiting *et al.*'s positivist and Denzin's interpretivist approach to anger, we demonstrated that the same assumptions also underlie their concepts and theories.

Assumptions and goals underlie all theories and methods. These components combine to form an interdependent, self-justifying system that is inextricably linked to the knowledge that this system produces. In other words, we cannot sever our knowledge products from the approaches that produced them. In our choice of methodologies for studying any phenomenon, we must consider the assumptions to which we adhere because the phenomenon is different when studied within different approaches (Anderson 1986); the end results and their applicability are different as well. For example, Whiting *et al.*'s results are aimed at generating laws and making predictions, but Denzin strives for comprehensive understanding.

What we recommend is that researchers recognize that philosophical assumptions underlie their theories and that they should identify their own philosophical assumptions (Gouldner 1970; Murray 1986). We suggest that researchers generally pursue methodologies that are consistent with the assumptions to which they adhere. For example, if a researcher holds a theory that is based on one set of assumptions, s/he should use a methodology that is based on the same set of assumptions. A researcher's assumptions, of course, will constrain the range of goals that can be attained; for instance, the assumption of mutual, simultaneously shaped systems and the context dependency of phenomena prohibits prediction as a goal.

Nevertheless, the violation of assumptions may at times lead to valuable insights. For example, a violation of assumptions may lead to a better understanding of one's own assumptions. But dangers exist. If one ignores guiding assumptions, problems may arise in the process of research and in the achievement of goals. We are a discipline that borrows. A major hazard of borrowing can be the lack of awareness of the assumptions to which these borrowed theories and methodologies adhere (Anderson and Thatcher 1986). For example, in the 1940s and 1950s, Freudian psychoanalytic theory was borrowed to explain consumers' motives for buying. However, this motivation research did not progress far. Murray suggests that this was due in part to the era of logical empiricism and to attempts to force an interpretive theory into positivist methodologies. In other words, the theory was based on interpretive assumptions and the methodology was based on positivist assumptions. Imagine the difficulty of operationalizing the concept of the unconscious or the superego (Murray 1986).

## Future Directions

Although we only highlighted some of the positivist and interpretive approaches to research, it is clear that a range of positions exists within both approaches. As a discipline, what should consumer research do with this diversity? The following alternatives adapted from the work of Anderson (1986), Churchman (1971), Feyerabend (1975), Mason and Mitroff (1981), and Morgan (1983b) illustrate some of the ways of dealing with this diversity that can be and/or are used within consumer research. Some of these alternatives overlap but differ in their focus and goals.

### Supremacy Alternative

The first alternative involves advocates of each research approach continuing to debate and persuade others that their approach is better. The supremacy response to the existence of different world views is to call for an evaluation to determine which of the opposing approaches – for example, positivist vs. interpretive – is best. The supremacy alternative requires supraordinate goals; however, agreement over supraordinate goals probably will not exist because goals acceptable to each world view will depend on each view's assumptions. Examples of supraordinate goals that have been advanced include problem-solving ability or the emancipation of humans (from the critical theory school). However, even if supraordinate goals are agreed upon, the interpretation of these goals may differ (Anderson 1986). For example, if all researchers accepted the goal of problem-solving ability, problems would still exist because each world view would acknowledge different problem sets. Nevertheless, supremacy is a commonly employed alternative.

### Synthesis Alternative

The second alternative is to combine elements of different world views through an additive process. For example, one specific response might be to advocate the synthesis of two approaches, combining the strengths and minimizing the weaknesses of each. This response is evident in attempts to find an all-embracing paradigm or to translate the different strategies of one paradigm into the language of another; these are often attempts to fill the seams between positivism and interpretivism. Elements of this alternative are seen in Lincoln and Guba's 1985 (and consequently Hirschman's 1986) explication of criteria for evaluating research. Here, positivist-like criteria are added to interpretive assumptions and methodology. In the synthesis alternative, it should be clear that if the knowledge products and guiding assumptions are different, they cannot be merged to create a single, unified approach. In this case, the blending of two approaches either ignores differing, underlying assumptions or changes the approaches and creates a world view that becomes a third approach.

### Dialectic Alternative

In contrast to the alternatives that seek to eliminate diversity by looking for the best world view, the dialectic alternative seeks diversity by counterposing aspects of the different world views in the hope of resolving conflict and developing a completely new mode of understanding through the debate generated by this juxtaposing. Belk (1987) advocates a similar stance in his Presidential Address to the Association for Consumer Research. Morgan (1980) promotes the use of multiple research strategies – accepting that each has something to offer – but attempts to utilize their competing insights within a single analysis. (The challenge here is how to accomplish this single analysis.) Thus, it is hoped that the end result will extend beyond the original formulation of either world view. If synthesis occurs, it happens only at the final stage, following the debate of conflicts, and is in a form of understanding that goes beyond the original formulations.

### Relativistic Alternative

Another alternative, receiving much attention in consumer research, is relativism. One version of relativism is critical relativism. This alternative leaves open the option that any research strategy may have something to offer, but the process and output must be evaluated based on the research program's own specified criteria. Thus, anything does not go. Anderson states that (1986, p. 156)

> critical relativists are actually more 'hard-headed' than positivists in their analysis of 'scientific' knowledge claims ... The critical relativist demands to know a theory's mode of production, criteria by which it is judged, the ideological and value commitment that inform its construction, and the metaphysical beliefs that underwrite its research program. Most importantly, the critical relativist wishes to know the realizable cognitive and practical aims of a theory so that its range of applicability can be assessed.

Thus, although a program is evaluated by its own standards, this does not mean that an individual evaluating the research must accept these standards as his/her own. Instead, positivist research is evaluated by positivist standards, and interpretive research is evaluated by interpretivist standards. There is no single set of standards that can be used across research programs.

Another variety of relativism is the position advocated by Feyerabend (1975) that "anything goes": epistemological anarchy. Here, every and any research strategy has something to offer; it is not necessary to synthesize, evaluate, be pragmatic, or utilize dialectic analysis.

In conclusion, a variety of options exist for the individual researcher regarding how to handle the diversity of research approaches. The last two alternatives are based on the premise that every approach to consumer research may have something to offer. This article was written in the spirit of encouraging an appreciation of the merits of diversity. We hope that exposure to alternative ways of seeking knowledge will inspire researchers to "explore and enrich research rather than constrain it through a search for an optimum way of doing things" (Morgan 1983b, p. 381). Consumer research, as a multidisciplinary field, is well suited to fostering diversity. Assumptions should be questioned and alternative ways of seeking knowledge should be sought. Our methods and theories are at an embryonic stage, and we can ill afford to stunt their development. Perhaps diversity will provide the challenge needed to stimulate new growth.

## References

ACR Special Session (1985), "Applying Humanistic Methods to Consumer Research: Four Practical Examples," in *Advances in Consumer Research*, Vol. 13, ed. Richard J. Lutz, Provo, UT: Association for Consumer Research, xiv– xv.

Anderson, Paul F. (1983), "Marketing, Scientific Progress, and Scientific Method," *Journal of Marketing*, 47 (Fall), 18–31.

– (1986), "On Method in Consumer Research: A Critical Relativist Perspective," *Journal of Consumer Research*, 13 (September), 155–173.

– and John G. Thatcher (1986), "On Borrowing, Epistemology, and Category Mistakes in Business Research," Working Paper No. 1-786-035, Harvard Business School, Boston, MA 02163.

Bagozzi, Richard P. (19 80), *Causal Models in Marketing*, New York: John Wiley.

Belk, Russell W. (1987), "ACR Presidential Address: Happy Thought," in *Advances in Consumer Research*, Vol. 14. eds. Melanie Wallendorf and Paul Anderson, Provo, UT: Association for Consumer Research, 1–4.

–, John Sherry, and Melanie Wallendorf (1988), "A Naturalistic Inquiry into Buyer and Seller Behavior at a Swap Meet," *Journal of Consumer Research*, 14 (March), 449–470.

Berger, Joseph, Morris Zelditch, and Bo Anderson (1982), "Historical and Generalizing Approaches to Sociology," in *Knowledge and Values in Social and Educational Research*, eds. Eric Bredo and Walter Feinberg, Philadelphia, PA: Temple University Press.

Berger, Peter L. and Thomas Luckman (1967), *The Social Construction of Reality: A Treatise in the Sociology of Knowledge*, New York: Irvington Publishers.

Bierley, Calvin, Frances K. McSweeney, and Renee Vannieuwkerk (1985), "Classical Conditioning of Preferences for Stimuli," *Journal of Consumer Research*, 12 (December), 316–323.

Blumer, Herbert (1969), *Symbolic Interactionism: Perspective and Method*, Englewood Cliffs, NJ: Prentice-Hall.

– (1980), "Mead and Blumer: The Convergent Methodological Perspectives of Social Behaviorism and Symbolic Interactionism," *American Sociological Review*, 45 (June), 409–419.

Bogdan, Robert and Steve Taylor (1975), *Introduction to Qualitative Research Methods: A Phenomenological Approach to the Social Sciences*, New York: John Wiley.

Bonoma, Thomas V. (1985), "Case Research in Marketing: Opportunities, Problems, and a Process," *Journal of Marketing Research*, 12 (May), 199–208.

Bredo, Eric and Walter Feinberg (1982), *Knowledge and Values in Social and Educational Research*, Philadelphia, PA: Temple University Press.

Bruner, Edward M. (1986), "Experience and Its Expressions," in *The Anthropology of Experience*, eds. Victor W. Turner and Edward M. Bruner, Urbana, IL: University of Illinois Press, 3–30.

Bruyn, Severyn T. (1966), *The Human Perspective in Sociology: The Methodology of Participant Observation*, Englewood Cliffs, NJ: Prentice-Hall.

Burrell, Gibson and Gareth Morgan (1979), *Sociological Paradigms and Organizational Analysis*, London: Heinemann.

Calder, Bobby J., Lynn W. Phillips, and Alice M. Tybout (1981), "Designing Research for Application," *Journal of Consumer Research*, 8 (September), 197–207.

Campbell, Donald T. and Julian C. Stanley (1963), *Experimental and Quasi-Experimental Designs for Research*, Chicago, IL: Rand McNally.

Churchman, C. West (1971), *The Design of Inquiring Systems*, New York: Basic Books.

Crapanzano, Vincent (1986), "Hermes Dilemma: The Masking of Subversion in Ethnographic Description," in *Writing Culture: The Poetics and Politics of Ethnography*, eds. James Clifford and George E. Marcus, Berkeley, CA: University of California Press, 51–76.

Denzin, Norman K. (1970), *The Research Act: A Theoretical Introduction to Sociological Methods*, Chicago, IL: Aldine.

– (1983), "Interpretive Interactionism," in *Beyond Method: Strategies for Social Research*, ed. Gareth Morgan, Beverly Hills, CA: Sage, 129–146.

– (1984), *On Understanding Emotion*, San Francisco, CA: Jossey-Bass Publishers.

Deshpande, Rohit (1983), "Paradigms Lost": On Theory and Method in Research in Marketing," *Journal of Marketing*, 47 (Fall), 101–110.

Feyerabend, Paul (1975), *Against Method*, London: New Left Books.

Fielding, Nigel G. and June L. Fielding (1986), *Linking Data*, Beverly Hills, CA: Sage.

Ford, Julienne (1975), *Paradigms and Fairy Tales, Volume 1*, Boston, MA: Routledge & Kegan Paul.

Geertz, Clifford (1973), "Thick Description," in *The Interpretation of Cultures*, New York: Basic Books, 3–30.

– (1979), "From the Native's Point of View: On the Nature of Anthropological Understanding," in *Interpretive Social Science*, eds. Paul Rabinow and William Sullivan, Berkeley, CA: University of California Press.

– (1983), *Local Knowledge: Further Essays in Interpretive Anthropology*, New York: Basic Books.

Giddens, Anthony (1976), *New Rules of Sociological Method: A Positive Critique of Interpretative Sociologies*, London: Hutchinson.

Gouldner, Alvin (1970), *The Coming Crisis of Western Sociology*, New York: Basic Books.

Hirschman, Elizabeth C. (1985), "Primitive Aspects of Consumption in Modern American Society," *Journal of Consumer Research*, 12 (September), 142–154.

– (1986), "Humanistic Inquiry in Marketing Research: Philosophy, Method, and Criteria," *Journal of Marketing Research*, 23 (August), 237–249.

Hodges, H. A. (1969), *Wilhelm Dilthey*, New York: Howard Fertig.

Holbrook, Morris B. (1986), "I'm Hip: An Autobiographical Account of Some Musical Consumption Experiences," in *Advances in Consumer Research*, Vol. 13, ed. Richard J. Lutz, Provo, UT: Association for Consumer Research, 614–618.

Hudson, Laurel Anderson and Jeff B. Murray (1986), "Methodological Limitations of the Hedonic Consumption Paradigm and a Possible Alternative: A Subjectivist Approach," in *Advances in Consumer Research*, Vol. 13, ed. Richard J. Lutz, Provo, UT: Association for Consumer Research, 343–348.

Hunt, Shelby D. (1983), *Marketing Theory*, Homewood, IL: Richard D. Irwin.

– (1984), "Should Marketing Adopt Relativism?" *1984 Winter Educators' Conference*, eds. Paul F. Anderson and Michael J. Ryan, Chicago, IL: American Marketing Association, 30–34.

Keat, Russell and John Urry (1975), *Social Theory as Science*, London: Routledge & Kegan Paul.

Kerlinger, Fred N. (1973), *The Foundation of Behavioral Research*, New York: Holt, Rinehart & Winston.

Knorr-Cetina, Karin D. (1983), "The Naturalistic/Ethnographic Analysis of Social Life," working paper, Sociology Department, Virginia Polytechnic Institute and State University, Blacksburg, VA 24060.

Kuhn, Thomas S. (1962), *The Structure of Scientific Revolutions*, Chicago, IL: University of Chicago Press.

Laudan, Larry (1984), *Science and Values*, Berkeley, CA: University of California Press.

Leibow, Elliot (1967), *Tally's Corner*, Boston, MA: Little, Brown & Co.

Lincoln, Yvonna S. and Egon G. Guba (1985), *Naturalistic Inquiry*, Beverly Hills, CA: Sage.

Mason, Richard O. and Ian I. Mitroff (1981), *Challenging Strategic Planning Assumptions*, New York: John Wiley.

Meltzer, Bernard N., John W. Petras, and Larry T. Reynolds (1975), *Symbolic Interactionism: Genesis, Varieties and Criticism*, Boston, MA: Routledge & Kegan Paul.

Morgan, Gareth (1980), "Paradigms, Metaphors and Puzzle Solving in Organization Theory," *Administrative Science Quarterly*, 25 (October), 605–622.

– (1983a), "Exploring Choice: Reframing the Process of Evaluation," in *Beyond Method: Strategies for Social Research*, ed. Gareth Morgan, Beverly Hills, CA: Sage, 392–404.

– (1983b), "The Significance of Assumptions," in *Beyond Method: Strategies for Social Research*, ed. Gareth Morgan, Beverly Hills, CA: Sage, 377–382.

– and Linda Smircich (1980),"The Case of Qualitative Research," *Academy of Management Review*, 5 (4), 491–500.

Murray, Jeff B. (1986), "Theory Appraisal and Theory Choice in Interdisciplinary Fields," working paper, Marketing Department, Virginia Polytechnic Institute and State University, Blacksburg, VA 24060.

Olson, Jerry C. (1981), 'Towards a Science of Consumer Behavior," in *Advances in Consumer Research*, Vol. 9, ed. Andrew A. Mitchell, Ann Arbor, MI: Association for Consumer Research, v–x.

Patton, Michael Q. (1980), *Qualitative Evaluation Methods*, Beverly Hills, CA: Sage.

Peter, J. Paul (1983),"Some Philosophical and Methodological Issues in Consumer Research," in *Marketing Theory: The Philosophy of Marketing Science*, ed. Shelby D. Hunt, Homewood, IL: Richard D. Irwin, 382–394.

– and Jerry C. Olson (1983), "Is Science Marketing?", *Journal of Marketing*, 47 (Fall), 111–125.

Reason, Peter and John Rowan (1981), *Human Inquiry: A Sourcebook of New Paradigm Research*, New York: John Wiley.

Rist, Ray (1977), "On the Relations Among Education Research Paradigms: From Disdain to Detente," *Anthropology and Education*, 8 (2), 42–50.

Rubinstein, David (1981), *Marx and Wittgenstein*, London: Routledge & Kegan Paul.

Sanday, Peggy Reeves (1979), "The Ethnographic Paradigms," *Administrative Science Quarterly*, 24 (December), 527–538.

Shanklin, Eugenia (1979), "When a Good Social Role is Worth a Thousand Pictures," in *Images of Information*, ed. Jon Wagner, Beverly Hills, CA: Sage, 139–145.

Shulman, Lee S. (1991), "Disciplines of Inquiry in Education: An Overview," *Educational Researcher*, 10 (June/July), 5–23.

Smart, Barry (1976), *Sociology, Phenomenology and Marxian Analysis*, London: Routledge & Kegan Paul.

Smith, John K. and Louis Heshusius (1986), "Closing Down the Conversation: The End of the Quantitative-Qualitative Debate," *Educational Researcher*, 15 (January), 4–12.

Solomon, Michael R. (1983), "The Role of Products as Social Stimuli: A Symbolic Interactionism Perspective," *Journal of Consumer Research*, 10 (December), 319–329.

– (1986), "Deep-Seated Materialism: The Case of Levi's 501 Jeans," in *Advances in Consumer Research*, Vol. 13, ed. Richard J. Lutz, Provo, UT: Association for Consumer Research, 619–622.

Taylor, Steven and Robert Bogdan (1984), *Introduction to Qualitative Research Methods: The Search for Meanings*, New York: John Wiley.

Thorns, David C. (1976), "Whither Sociology," in *New Directions in Sociology*, ed. David C. Thorns, Totowa, NJ: Rowman and Littlefield, 161–177.

Van Maanen, John, James M. Dabbs, Jr., and Robert R. Faulkner (1982), *Varieties of Qualitative Research*, Beverly Hills, CA: Sage.

Wallendorf, Melanie (1987), "On Intimacy," paper presented at the American Marketing Association Winter Educators' Conference, San Antonio, TX.

Wax, Murray L. (1967), "On Misunderstanding Verstehen: A Reply to Abel," *Sociology and Social Research*, 51 (April), 323–333.

Whiting, John W.M., Irvin L. Child, William W. Lambert, Ann M. Fischer, John L. Fischer, Corrine Nydegger, William Nydegger, Hatsumi Maretski, Thomas Maretski, Leigh Minturn, A. Kimball Romney, and Romaine Romney (1966), *Field Guide for a Study of Socialization, Six Cultures Series*, Vol. 1, New York: John Wiley.

# 8

# Positivism and Paradigm Dominance in Consumer Research: Toward Critical Pluralism and Rapprochement

**Shelby D. Hunt**

**Source:** *Journal of Consumer Research* 18 (1991): 32–43.

> For the philosopher, clarity is a matter of good faith.
> [Marquis de Vauvenargues, *Oeuvres Complétes*]

> I ask for greater acceptance of poetic insights in consumer research … .
> [Morris Holbrook, "Farewell Address"]

> Something there is that doesn't love a wall.
> [Robert Frost, "Mending Wall"]

The 1980s witnessed a spirited debate on the appropriate philosophical and methodological foundations for consumer research. Many writers attacked the philosophical and methodological foundations of contemporary social science and offered alternative "ways of knowing," including that of naturalistic inquiry (Belk, Wallendorf, and Sherry 1989), humanistic inquiry (Hirschman 1986), ethnographic methods (Sherry 1983), historical methods (Fullerton 1987), "enchanted inquiry" (Monieson 1988), critical theory (Dholakia 1988), semiotics (Holbrook and Grayson 1986; Mick 1986), literary explication (Stern 1989a, 1989b), existential-phenomenological methods (Thompson, Locander, and Pollio 1989), relativism/constructionism (Peter and Olson 1983, 1989), and critical relativism (Anderson 1986, 1989). Although these views differ in numerous respects, they all share a common characteristic: Each is offered as an alternative to contemporary social science, which is characterized as being dominated by "positivism" as a philosophy and "positivistic social science" as a methodology.[1]

"Spirited" is certainly not too strong an adjective to describe the ongoing debate. Not only do some participants contend that their opponents' "criticisms largely reflect misrepresentations and misunderstandings" (Calder and Tybout 1989, p. 205), "misconceptions" (Peter and Olson 1989, p. 25), and "honest misunderstandings" (Anderson 1989, p. 11), but others contend more strongly that the debate is full of "mischaracterizations and caricaturizations" (Hunt 1989a, p. 185) or, even worse, "nastiness and purposeful distortions" (Hirschman 1989, p. 209) and "ridicule" (Pechmann 1990, p. 7). This article's underlying thesis is that these "misses" (*mis*conceptions, *mis*understandings, *mis*representations, and *mis*characterizations), which constitute a divisive wall separating consumer researchers, stem, at least in part, from the fact that much of the debate has been historically ill informed. In particular, the debate has been poorly informed about the origins and fundamental beliefs of a group of philosophers called logical positivists. Thus, in accordance with those advocating historical method, this article uses historical sources to illuminate and clarify certain aspects of the ongoing debate. I first discuss the historical development of logical positivism and then use this historical material to clarify some of the "misses" in the debate. The purpose here is to move the debate to a more productive, historically informed level, not to end it; to clarify issues, not to conquer opponents. In short, the goal is to move toward rapprochement by punching a hole in the present wall that separates consumer researchers.[2]

## Misconceptions about Positivism

In the 1920s and 1930s, a group of German philosophers in Vienna (hence, Vienna Circle) developed a philosophy – later given the label "logical positivism" – that relied heavily on Machian neopositivism, Humean skepticism, Wittgenstein's *Tractatus Logico-Philosophicus*, and Russell's *Principia Mathematica.*[3] From Mach, the positivists drew their conviction that science should avoid metaphysical concepts and rely exclusively on observables. From Hume, they derived their belief that inductive reasoning is impermissible. (For Hume, only the conclusions of deductive logic and the beliefs derived from direct observational experience could be known with certainty. Since, according to "foundationalism" science should restrict itself to knowledge with certainty, inductive reasoning is therefore impermissible.) From Wittgenstein, the positivists developed both their famous "verifiability principle" (only statements that can be shown *conclusively* to be true or false are "cognitively meaningful") and the belief that the objective of philosophical inquiry should be the "critique of language" or "meaning analysis." From Russell, they adopted formal (symbolic) logic as an analytical tool for their meaning analyses.

The objectives of the logical positivists were to (1) help science make sense of the indeterministic nature of quantum mechanics, (2) help science avoid another Newtonian debacle, (3) help draw together or "unify" the various scientific disciplines, and (4) effect a rapprochement between science and the discipline of philosophy. (Under Hegelian idealism in the preceding half- century, philosophy had been, at best, irrelevant to modern science and, at worst, openly hostile to it.) The positivists were successful in effecting a rapprochement between large portions of the philosophical and scientific communities, and they did explicate and emphasize the commonalities of apparently diverse scientific disciplines. They did, indeed, develop a philosophy that could accommodate a major interpretation of the indeterminism of quantum mechanics, (the "Copenhagen view"), and, at least to the present, there has been nothing in science comparable to the Newtonian debacle (Stove 1982, p. 51). However, misconceptions about the logical positivists and their philosophy abound in the current consumer research literature. Here, I focus on three major ones: causality, the machine metaphor, and the nature of reality.

### Causality

The consumer research literature claims that the search for causal relations or causal explanations figures prominently in "positivistic social science." For example, in delineating "alternative ways of seeking knowledge in consumer research," Hudson and Ozanne (1988, p. 512) state: "The positivists, with their goal of explanation and prediction, place a high priority on identifying causal linkages." Hirschman (1986, pp. 239, 241) contrasts the "positivistic metaphysic" with the "humanistic metaphysic" and claims that the former implies that "elements of reality can be segregated into causes and effects," "first stage causes," "second stage causes," and "third stage causes." Thompson *et al.* (1989, p. 134) believe that a broad "set of assumptions underlies the use of positivist methods" and that "these assumptions are manifested in many normative methodological prescriptions," including the prescription that "science should uncover causal laws that explain the functioning of phenomena." Ryan and Bristor (1987, p. 193) claim that the "positivistic approach" emphasizes "causal explanation," and Lutz (1989, pp. 4, 7) asserts that "whereas, the Positivist aspires to causal explanation, the Naturalist eschews notions of linear causality." He further notes that "positivist consumer research" will seek "causal explanation" because the assumption of "real causes" is an "axiom" of the "Positivist paradigm."

Ozanne and Hudson (1989, p. 3) claim that a "basic assumption" of positivism is that "real causes exist." Anderson (1989, p. 17), in discussing the "implications for positivism and interpretivism" of Wittgenstein's philosophy, asserts that "perhaps the most damaging implication for positivistic psychology is Wittgenstein's acausalism." Positivistic research is discredited because, "on a Wittgensteinian construal, there can be no question of invoking a memory as a *cause* of behavior" (p. 18). Finally, Wallendorf and Belk (1989, p. 74), in developing criteria for assessing trustworthiness in naturalistic consumer research, point out that "triangulation does not always mean that only one interpretation will emerge," noting that, "given the post-Positivist rejection of the assumption of a single causal reality, this is entirely appropriate."

Statements in the consumer research literature notwithstanding, it is historically false that research guided by a positivistic philosophy would seek causal explanations or linkages or assume that real causes or a single causal reality exists. Any research guided by positivism would necessarily *avoid* both the assumption of causality and the search for "real causes." For example, Brodbeck (1962, p. 250) defended Hempel's "thesis of structural symmetry in explanation" (which states that explanation equals prediction and nothing "more") by derisively noting that Hempel's critics had adopted the "causal idiom" and that the truth content of "statements like" 'C is the cause of E' is problematic." Kyburg (1968, p. 236) claimed that causality is in the "realm of metaphysics" and stated that "it is questionable to what extent causality is of scientific interest." Braithwaite (1968, p. 308) asserted that attempting to identify causal laws would be a "thankless task." Finally, in discussing the concept of causal explanations, Hempel (1965, pp. 353–354) concluded, "It is not clear what precise construal could be given to the notion of factors 'bringing about' a given event, and what reason there would be for denying the status of explanation to all accounts invoking occurrences that temporally succeed the event to be explained."

The positivists rejected causality because they viewed "cause" as an unobservable, metaphysical concept that violated their Humean skepticism. As noted by Ayer (1959, p. 4), "it is indeed remarkable how much of the doctrine that is now thought to be especially characteristic of logical positivism was already stated, or at least foreshadowed, by Hume." For the positivists, following Hume, if a scientist observes that phenomena A and B occur with uniform regularity, there is no way to show *deductively* anything other than a regularity relationship. In particular, one cannot (and should not) conclude that A *causes* B.

### Determinism and the Machine Metaphor

A second major misconception about "positivistic social science" is that such a science would necessarily be deterministic, machine-like, or mechanistic. Thus, Ozanne and Hudson (1989, pp. 3, 7) contend that a "basic assumption" of the "positivist approach" is that the "nature of social beings" is "deterministic" or, even more strongly, "entirely deterministic." Similarly, Thompson *et al.* (1989, pp. 134, 137) believe that one of the assumptions that "underlies the use of positivist methods" is the "machine metaphor": "Cartesianism's world view is a *mechanistic* view in which reality is perceived as a machine-like event determined by forces and constraints." Like the view that positivism implies causality, these views also are ahistorical.

"Determinism" is "the view that every event has a cause... . All things in the universe are 'governed' by, or operate in accordance with, causal laws" (Angeles 198 1, p. 60). Because of the success of Newtonian mechanics, the philosophy of mechanistic materialism, with its Laplacian, deterministic "machine metaphor," was a prominent one at the close of the 19th century. In tracing the historical origins of logical positivism, Suppe (1977, p. 10) notes that "by the turn of the century, the three main philosophic positions held in the German scientific community were mechanistic materialism, neo-Kantianism, and Machian neo-Positivism... . [However,] relativity theory and quantum theory were thought to be incompatible with all three of these philosophies of science." Since the logical positivists were all German-speaking scientists, primarily mathematicians and physicists, they were well aware that quantum mechanics was incompatible with mechanistic materialism, the machine metaphor, and Laplacian determinism. Indeed, a primary objective of the Vienna Circle was to develop an alternative to such a view. They did so by creating one that replaced the Newtonian machine metaphor with the view that indeterministic, probabilistic prediction was appropriate for science (Carnap 1966). In short, since the best that could be accomplished with quantum mechanics is probabilistic prediction (the positivist "Copenhagen view"), such an accomplishment must be an acceptable goal for all science. Again, it should be emphasized that only prediction is sought, not "deeper" or causal explanations. Theories and laws, therefore, must be treated solely as calculation instruments for making predictions. Any research motivated by the "positivistic metaphysic" would view as naively misguided the belief that ultimate reality, either physical or social, follows the Newtonian/Laplacian "machine metaphor." Steven Hawking, originator of the big bang theory and probably the most prominent theoretical physicist living today, specifically acknowledges the debt his (non–"machine metaphor") position owes to the positivists. "You can say that the use of imaginary time [to explain the origins of the universe] is just a mathematical trick that doesn't tell us anything about reality… . But if you take a *positivist* position, as I do, questions about reality don't have any *meaning*. All one can ask is whether imaginary time is useful in formulating mathematical models that describe what we *observe*" (Strong 1990, p. 71; italics added).

### Reality

How the positivists viewed the nature of reality (their "ontology") is a third confused area in the debate. Hirschman (1986, p. 239) contends that the "humanistic metaphysic" proposes that "human beings construct multiple realities," while the "positivistic metaphysic" believes that "there is a single reality composed of discrete elements." Similarly, Hudson and Ozanne (1988, p. 509) claim, "The positivists tend to take a *realist* [italics added] position and assume that a single, objective reality exists independently of what individuals perceive. … In contrast, the interpretivists deny that one real world exists; that is, reality is essentially mental and perceived."

The concept "reification" also figures prominently in the debate on reality: "Positivists reify subjective states and treat them like objects," according to Hudson and Ozanne (1988, p. 515). In much stronger terms, Monieson (1988, p. 7) claims that "positivistic social science" is pernicious because it "reifies social relations so that they … are forged into marketable traits, into commodities." Again, these claims are ahistorical.

In philosophy, the study of ontology asks, "What does 'to be,' 'to exist' mean?" (Angeles 1981, p. 198). Although ontology has been perhaps the most prominent area of philosophical inquiry for millennia, space limitations dictate that the analysis here be restricted to certain fundamental issues regarding idealism, realism, and reification.

Although many different philosophies are "idealistic," all share the fundamental belief that the material world of tangible objects, such as trees and rocks, does not exist unperceived: "All reality is mental (spiritual, psychical). Matter, the physical, does not exist" (Angeles 1981, p. 120). In direct contrast, "realism" holds that the world of tangible objects exists unperceived: "Philosophical idealism is … opposed to realism and is thus the denial of the common-sense realist view that material things exist independently of being perceived" (Acton 1967, p. 110). "Reification" is inextricably associated with the concept "reality." (Both words have the common Latin root *res*, meaning "thing.") Reification implies treating an abstract concept as having a real existence in the same sense that a "thing" exists: It is "the fallacy of taking abstractions and regarding them as actual existing entities that are causally efficacious and ontologically prior and superior to their referents" (Angeles 1981, p. 243). Given that it is a fallacy by definition, "reification" is customarily used pejoratively in philosophy to indicate that one has somehow *improperly* treated an abstraction as having a "thinglike" reality. With the preceding distinctions in mind, we can now investigate the ontology of logical positivism.

Were the positivists realists? If, by "realist," we mean only the minimal position that tangible objects, such as what we call "trees" and "rocks," exist independently of our perception and labeling (i.e., they exist "out there"), then the logical positivists were definitely realists. Recognizing that idealism always degenerates into nihilism, sophistry, and/or solipsism,[4] the positivists embraced a minimal realism called "empirical realism" (Manicas 1987, p. 247). But, when philosophers today refer to their own positions or to science as "realist," they customarily mean something much stronger than the minimal belief that the existence of trees and rocks is independent of human thought.

Although operating under the common rubric of "scientific realism," there are almost as many versions of realism today as there are realist philosophers.[5] Nevertheless, all realists, either explicitly or implicitly, reject Humean skepticism with respect to the ontology of scientific theories: "The basic claim made by scientific realism ... is that the long-term success of a scientific theory gives reason to believe that something like the entities and structure postulated by the theory actually exists" (McMullin 1984, p. 26). Thus, scientific realism contends that the explanatory, predictive, and pragmatic success of a theory provides evidence for the existence of its associated entities, be they observable or unobservable, tangible or intangible, "thinglike" or "non-thinglike." The evidence is not presumed *conclusive*, in that "success" does not enable us to know with certainty that the entities and structure exist. For example, the long-term success of viral theory in explaining, predicting, and solving pragmatic problems with respect to diseases provides evidence warranting our belief in the existence of the entity labeled "virus" (a tangible unobservable). Similarly, to the extent that theories in consumer research incorporating latent constructs, such as "attitude," "intentions," and "beliefs" (*in*tangible unobservables), have been successful in explaining, predicting, and solving pragmatic problems, such evidence provides warrant for believing that these psychological states of consumers exist independently of researchers' labeling of them, that is, they are *real.*

Did the positivists adopt a realist ontological view? According to how "realism" is most commonly used today in the philosophy of science (i.e., unobservables can exist and are appropriate for theory construction), the positivists were, most definitely, not realists. The positivists, guided by the views of Mach and Hume, viewed unobservables as metaphysical concepts to be strictly avoided. In fact, many philosophers of science actually use positivism's opposition to realism as its major *defining characteristic:* "A philosophy (of science) [is] positivist if it holds that a scientific explanation must thoroughly eschew appeal to what is in principle beyond experience... . By contrast, a realist holds that a valid scientific explanation can appeal to the in principle nonobservable" (Manicas 1987, pp. 9–10).

Did the positivists engage in reification? That is, did the positivists improperly treat abstract concepts as having a real existence in the sense that a "thing" has existence? Most assuredly, they did not. Their Humean skepticism and revulsion toward metaphysics led them to insist that theories must contain only observables, that is, labels for "things."[6] In contrast, those scientists and philosophers of science guided by scientific realism, because they contend (on the basis of "success") that some unobservables may actually exist, could potentially be faulted for reification. Therefore, the claim that positivist researchers engage in reification is historically false. Exactly the opposite is true; researchers adhering strictly to positivism *cannot* engage in reification.

In fairness, there is an alternative perspective that draws on Marxist social philosophy and that can potentially lend credence to the claim that positivistic social science engages in reification.[7] Marxist philosophers (e.g., Berger and Pullberg 1966; Lukacs 1971) castigate contemporary social science on the basis of charges of "reification" and "commoditization."

Marxist philosophers see "a general 'drive to commoditization' in capitalist society" (Belk *et al.* 1989, p. 24). This "commodity fetishism" is uniquely associated with capitalism, Marxists contend, because only in capitalism does the production of commodities dominate society. Such societies necessarily, then, reify social relations. For example, the relationship between two people called "love" becomes nothing more than a commodity, a "thing" to be bought and sold. This reification extends to Western science, particularly sociology, which reifies societal institutions so that they are taken to have the causal power to determine how humans behave. Thus, Western science and society assume that societal institutions (e.g., corporations, the Roman Catholic church, and "bourgeois science") have an existence separate from the people that produce them and that, important for Marxist theory, individual human beings are thus powerless to change these "immutable" institutions. From the Marxist view, then, "positivistic social science" just means Western science or bourgeois science in toto and, therefore, it must engage in reification because this is an underlying characteristic of all aspects of Western societies. Since the objective of Marxist social philosophy is to "liberate the proletariat" from the "false consciousness" that a market economy serves their interests, Marxist philosophers offer the following argument: (1) social science is dominated by positivism, a "dead" philosophy; (2) positivism implies reification; (3) reification is pernicious; therefore, (4) contemporary (bourgeois) social science is not only fundamentally misguided (in adopting a "dead" philosophy), but pernicious as well (by reifying social relations).[8] Among the many things wrong with this argument is that it is historically false. The positivists, insisting as they did that science restrict itself to observables, could not engage in reification; neither, therefore, could any social science guided by positivism. If social science is pernicious, it is not because its adoption of positivism has led to reification. If social science is misguided, it is not because it is dominated by positivism (as will be shown later in this article).

### Rampant Antipositivism

In a section entitled "Rampant Antipositivism" Phillips (1987, p. 94) reviews the social science literature and concludes that "there have been many exaggerated claims about the evils of positivism ... [and] many factual errors are made when researchers refer to [it]." As we have seen, there have been similar errors in the consumer research literature. Antipositivist claims to the contrary, the positivists did not search for causal explanations or causal linkages; they did not adopt, nor hold that science should adopt, the machine metaphor; they did not have a realist view with respect to scientific theories; and they could not possibly have been guilty of reification. Phillips (p. 44) also compares the views of social science antipositivists with the actual positions of the positivists and concludes that "some of the most boisterous celebrants at positivism's wake are actually more positivistic than they realize, or have more in common with the positivists than they would care to admit." As we shall see, a similar situation prevails in the consumer research literature.

## Positivism versus Contemporary Antipositivism

Although often reaching their positions by different routes, those who advocate alternatives to "positivistic social science" actually share many views with their supposed antagonists. It is important to note that we have seen that both the positivists and contemporary antipositivists[9] reject the search for causal explanations and causal linkages. Second, the positivists explicitly embraced Humean skepticism, and, similarly, many antipositivists are strongly influenced by it (see, e.g., Anderson 1983, p. 19; Anderson 1989, p. 11; Hudson and Ozanne 1988, p. 515). Even those who (correctly) believe that "the term positivist is used much too loosely to be descriptive of any approach" (Calder and Tybout 1989, p. 200) embrace Humean skepticism. For example, in explaining why the "comparative" approach is superior to the "confirmatory" approach in testing theories, Sternthal, Tybout, and Calder (1987, p. 124) put forth the standard Humean position that it is impermissible to reason inductively from the successful predictions of a theory to its truth content: "The goal of the confirmatory approach cannot be realized because theories cannot be proven." Similarly, Calder and Tybout ( 1987, p. 137) argue in favor of "sophisticated falsificationist methodology" by contrasting their view with the "common view of science ... that empirical data are used to accumulate evidence for a theory until it is proven. This view of science is, of course, unacceptable ... [because, in part] inductive proof is logically impossible."[10]

As a third similarity, many antipositivists specifically reject the realist view with respect to unobservables, as did the positivists. Thus, Anderson (1989, p. 14) believes realism is "bankrupt": "As such, a position of 'ontological agnosticism' is strongly recommended."

Fourth, and finally, antipositivist methodology shares a striking similarity to that of the positivists in the use of meaning analysis. The positivists adopted the tool of formal logic and the goal of meaning analysis to clarify the language employed in the scientific community. Contemporary antipositivists, often under the rubric of "interpretivism," explore how the language of consumers consists of "shared meanings" (Ozanne and Hudson 1989, p. 2). As Hirschman

(1989, p. ix) puts it, "The best definition I have encountered of interpretive consumer research is that presented recently by Holbrook and O'Shaughnessey (1988). They view interpretation as 'the critical analysis of a text for the purpose of determining its single or multiple meaning(s).'"

### Differences

Numerous similarities not withstanding, contemporary antipositivists diverge from positivism on several issues. Not only did the positivists, in contrast to contemporary antipositivists, use formal logic, but they also held mathematics and statistics in high regard. Given the Positivists' view that quantum mechanics is "just mathematics,"[11] they were sympathetic to quantification in science. In contrast, contemporary antipositivists not only avoid the use of mathematics and statistics, but (consistent with Hegelian idealism) at times seem hostile to these tools. Some commentators even characterize the very essence of the debate as being between advocates of quantitative and qualitative methods: "Very simply, the logical positivist view of the world is synonymous with the quantitative paradigm" (Deshpande 1983, p. 102). In like manner, others claim the "opposing research camps" to be the "relevant researchers" versus the "rigorous researchers" and contend that the latter value the "quantifiable results" of "positive empiricism" (Dholakia 1985, p. 3). Similarly, Beck, Wallendorf, and Sherry (1989, p. 13) state that "we have not called for the development of quantitative measures because the nature and experience of the sacred may be antithetical to such measurement. The ontological and epistemological assumptions of positivist methods are not sympathetic to the mystical and experiential nature of sacredness."

However, equating positivism with quantitative methods is ahistorical: "A positivist, *qua* positivist, is not committed to any particular research design. There is nothing in the doctrines of positivism that necessitates a love of statistics or a distaste for case studies" (Phillips 1987, p. 96). Indeed, contemporary antipositivists could draw upon positivist writings to buttress their case for qualitative methods.[12] According to Brodbeck (1968, pp. 573–574), "The qualitative-quantitative dichotomy is spurious... . Although quantification has considerable merit, it is neither a necessary nor a sufficient condition for science."

Because the positivists were sympathetic toward both philosophy and science as institutions, a major part of their program was to effect a rapprochement between them. In contrast, some contemporary antipositivists are openly hostile to the institution of science, relying on the views of such bitterly antiscience authors as Feyerabend (1987, p. 297), who contends that "Western science has now infected the whole world like a contagious disease." Discussing the history of science, Firat (1989, pp. 95–96) asks, "Is science an institution we want to preserve?"[13] He concludes that it may be desirable to "erase the accumulation of scientific knowledge" because "science is a political institution ... [that] has lost its relevance for the solution of present human problems. Thus, the scientific establishment has become anti-change and reactionary." Not only would Firat's assessment of science differ from that of the positivists, the "book burning" implicit in "erasing the accumulation of scientific knowledge" would have been repugnant to them (as well as to most scholars).

A final difference between positivism and contemporary antipositivism centers on two different meanings of "meaning analysis." The English word "meaning" (and, therefore, "meaning analysis") suffers from systematic ambiguity. It can refer to the *communicative* characteristics of a word, phrase, or "text" and "meaning analysis" can then explore how such expressions serve this communicative role. However, "meaning" is also used in an *evaluational* sense, referring to something's importance, value, or significance. The positivists recognized this systematic ambiguity (Rudner 1966, pp. 75–83) and restricted their meaning analyses to communicative meaning. Similarly, as previously mentioned, those referring to their research as "interpretivist" often define their area of inquiry as exploring communicative meaning, as do those using the label "semiotics": "[Semioticians] investigate the sign systems or codes essential to all types of communication for the latent rules that facilitate sign production and interpretive responses" (Mick 1986, p. 197). However, contemporary antipositivists, in contrast to the positivists, have not restricted their meaning analyses to communicative meaning only. In fact, most of their published works have actually focused on evaluational meaning. The most obvious example is the extensive work of Belk *et al.* (1989), which explores how things become either "sacred" or "profane" and thereby acquire "personal meaningfulness" (p. 31), "transcendent meaning in their lives" (p. 32), or "significance" (p. 32) through a "process of meaning investment and divestment" (p. 2).

### Paradigm Dominance in Consumer Research

The preceding enables us to reexamine a premise underlying the entire debate, namely, that positivism dominates contemporary social science and consumer research. To this point, our analysis reveals not only that "positivism" does not imply "quantitative," but also: (1) Mesmerized as they were by Humean skepticism, the positivists considered the concept "cause" to be metaphysical and (at best) superfluous to science. (2) Absorbed as they were with quantum mechanics, they did not contend that science should adopt the machine metaphor. (3) Obsessed as they were with restricting scientific theories to nonmetaphysical observables, the positivists did not adopt a "realist view" with respect to scientific theories and could not possibly have been guilty of reification. Therefore, if antipositivist writers are correct on these issues (i.e., that *consumer research* is dominated by the search for causality, by the machine metaphor, by reification, and by the realist view with respect to unobservables), then consumer research is "antipositivist" or, more accurately, "nonpositivist."[14] Thus, the entire debate has had a demonstrably false underlying premise. Contemporary social science and consumer research are neither motivated by the "positivistic metaphysic" nor, most assuredly, "dominated by logical positivism."

### The Dominance of Positivism: An Alternative View

Fairness dictates that an alternative perspective of "positivism" be acknowledged.[15] Firat (1999, p. 94) discusses the major themes of "postmodern culture" and, drawing on the Marxist social philosophy of Baudrillard, advocates adopting "hyperreality":

> A second major reason for the attacks on science is clarified in the postmodernist critique and analysis of culture... . Currently, the most powerful articulator of this recognition [that social reality is produced or constructed] in the postmodernist literature seems to be Baudrillard... . His theory articulates the creation of the culture of "hyperreality," a reality that is constructed based on signifiers that become separated from their original referents and "free floating," [to] which, then, are attached new meanings. Thus, new symbols are created as well as a new reality independent of the original referents or foundations. Hyperreality is produced when these new symbols are accepted as real and so acted upon by the social actors.

On the basis of postmodernism, then, one might attempt to sanction the use of the term "positivism" stripped from its "original referents" (what the positivists actually believed in and advocated) and use it to refer to any set of beliefs or methods one chooses. The only restraint is rhetorical success, that is, whether this new "constructed reality" is "accepted as real and so acted upon by the social actors." Thus construed, "positivism" becomes a pejorative term of rhetorical abuse that can effectively stifle discussion and critique. If one's work is subjected to critical evaluation, rather than defending the research on its merits, one can shut down all discussion by retorting, "You're just using outmoded positivistic criteria to evaluate my post-positivistic, postmodern study." Phillips (1987, p. 94) reviews the debate in the social sciences and concludes that many writers do appear to be socially constructing a hyperreality: "Without suggesting that those who make the errors are deliberately dishonest, it seems as if the word 'positivism' arouses such negative feelings that it is often used in a blanket way to condemn any position at all that the writer disagrees with, irrespective of how positivistic that position really is."

A major problem with the current use of "positivism" as a socially constructed hyperreality dominating consumer research is that it violates the integrity of history. Lavin and Archdeacon (1989, p. 62) review the advantages of historical method and discuss its two "central imperatives": "Respect the integrity of the past and ... call attention to what was unique about it." No one disputes that the positivists were real people in an identifiable historical period and that they shared some common views. One may argue that some of their views were correct and others incorrect, or some well reasoned and others poorly thought out. One may further argue that some of the consequences of positivism were good for science and society and others were bad for both. Nevertheless, historical integrity and respect for those who can no longer speak for themselves obligate us (at the very least) to criticize the positivists for the beliefs they actually held and the views they actually espoused. As Hirschman (1989, p. 209) movingly reminds us, "Researchers, whether empiricist or interpretivist, are people, too." So also, we might add, were the positivists.

### On the Dominant Paradigm in Consumer Research

If logical positivism is not the dominant paradigm in consumer research, what is? Some might be tempted to conclude that, if not logical positivism, then surely logical empiricism must dominate consumer research. History, however, shows that this position is also untenable.

Logical empiricism was (in Lakatosian terms) a "research program" that emerged directly from the logical positivist movement. Indeed, prominant logical empiricists, such as Carnap and Feigl, had themselves been logical positivists. The major characteristic distinguishing logical empiricism from logical positivism was the substitution of the "testability principle" for the "verifiability principle." Because they accepted Humean skepticism with respect to induction, the positivists came to realize that the generalized nature of scientific laws rendered them "unverifiable," that is, incapable of being proved conclusively true. Therefore, Carnap (1936) replaced the verifiability principle with the "testability principle," which requires that all statements must be observationally "testable" to be "cognitively meaningful" (for them to have done otherwise would have implied the absurd claim that scientific laws were "meaningless"). However, what is most important for our purposes here is that the logical empiricists continued to embrace Humean skepticism, continued to reject "realism" with regard to theories, laws, and explanations, and continued to consider "causality" to be a metaphysical concept that (at best) was superfluous to science. Therefore, on the very same grounds as for logical positivism, we may conclude with great assurance that logical empiricism does not dominate consumer research.

The issue of the dominant paradigm in consumer research can be best addressed by first returning to the work of Kulin, whose *Structure of Scientific Revolutions* (1962) originated the view that each "mature" science has a dominant paradigm, consisting of (1) a knowledge content (i.e., theories, laws, concepts, symbolic generalizations, and "exemplars"), (2) a methodology (i.e., procedures by which knowledge is to be generated), and (3) an epistemology (i.e., criteria for evaluating knowledge claims). The construct "dominant paradigm" assisted Kuhn in his efforts to explain, among other things, why "mature" sciences progressed and others (e.g., the social sciences) did not. For Kuhn, each "mature" science has a dominant paradigm and, rather than engage in endless, unproductive disputation on methodological and epistemological issues, researchers spend their time making progress by "fleshing the dominant paradigm out" through "puzzle-solving." Like almost all the major views in *Structure*, that of the "dominant paradigm" or Weltanschauung has been totally discredited. For example, Laudan (1977, pp. 74 and 151) reviews the history of science and concludes, "Virtually every major period in the history of science is characterized both by the co-existence of numerous competing paradigms, with none exerting hegemony over the field, and by the persistent and continuous manner in which the foundational assumptions of every paradigm are debated within the scientific community... . Kuhn can point to no major science in which paradigm monopoly has been the rule, nor in which foundational debate has been absent."

If paradigm dominance has been found to be absent in the historical development of even mature sciences, one would hardly expect to find a dominant paradigm in consumer research, an area of inquiry whose systematic study is only several decades old. Indeed, as pointed out by numerous observers (e.g., Jacoby 1978), consumer research's history is best characterized by the open, often indiscriminate, borrowing of disparate methods and theories from everywhere. Most recently, Kassarjian (1989, pp. 124, 126) reviews the history of consumer research and points out: "In actuality, change and resistance to change, revolutionaries and counter-revolutionaries, have always been present – the media and survey researchers of the 1940s, the motivation researchers of the 1950s, the marketing science and cognitive types of the 1960s, consumer protection and public policy people of the 1970s and in the 1980s the proponents of the consumer behavior odyssey, relativism, and the approaches promulgated in this volume... . *The appropriate question is whether or not it is good science, rather than what kind of science it is. Is it making a contribution to knowledge?*" (italics added).

In conclusion, neither logical positivism nor logical empiricism dominates consumer research. *Yes*, the history of consumer research, like that of other disciplines (Hunt 199 1, p. 3), reveals periods when a particular method or theory becomes so popular as to be almost faddish. *Yes*, the proposers of new methods and theories, Kassarjian's "revolutionaries," must defend the trustworthiness of their methods and the veracity of their theories and other knowledge claims. And *yes*, other consumer researchers, Kassarjian's "counter-revolutionaries," will critically evaluate every new method and theory proposed. But *no*, the problems of the revolutionaries of the 1980s have not stemmed from their being victims of consumer research's "dominant paradigm." In truth, consumer research has no such paradigm: no paradigm or philosophical "ism" dominates consumer research. Given the prominent roles that "dominant paradigm" and "positivism" have played in the ongoing debate, it is no wonder that participants on both sides have complained about "misses" (i.e., mischaracterizations, etc.).

The preceding should not be interpreted to mean that there are no genuine differences between antipositivists and their colleagues in contemporary social science, for there are. For example, many consumer researchers do indeed believe that it is important to try to separate genuine, "causal" relationships from those that are purely accidental or "spurious." In contrast, many antipositivists disclaim any interest in this activity. Furthermore, much contemporary social science makes extensive use of mathematics and statistics, whereas many antipositivists see these tools as inappropriate or unnecessary for their scholarship. These differences notwithstanding, there is nothing on either side of the current debate resembling a monolithic, dominant paradigm. Indeed, much work needs to be done to fully explicate and clarify the actual differences between the two sides, as an extension of our previous discussion of the "realism" issue will demonstrate.

Consider the pluralistic manner by which contemporary social science addresses the ontology of concepts like "intelligence." Many consumer researchers accept the realist view that the long-run success of the intelligence-testing research program gives us reason to believe that what we label "intelligence" is a real, cognitive aptitude that manifests itself in a variety of problem-solving tasks and that such measures as IQ tests are (either good or bad) "indicants" of this real, underlying, "latent construct." In contrast, other consumer researchers agree with measurement theorist Nunnally's (1978, p. 108) positivist view: "The words that scientists use to denote constructs, e.g., anxiety and intelligence, have no real counterparts in the world of observables; they are only heuristic devices for exploring observables... . Although words relating to constructs are undeniably helpful to the scientist, they also can be real trouble. *Such words are only symbols for collections of observables*" (italics added).

Now consider the intended ontological status of concepts like "extended self," "sacred," and "profane," which have been prominent in antipositivist scholarship. Do researchers intend these concepts to be considered as *real?* If yes, on the basis of what criteria, and do these criteria differ from those of contemporary social science? If no, what is the ontology of such concepts, and how does it differ from contemporary social science? Surely, concepts such as "extended self," "sacred," and "profane" are not meant to be interpreted as positivist "collections of observables." However, many antipositivists have positioned their work (perhaps unnecessarily?) as being opposed to realism and, by implication, the realist view that the success of theories in which "unobservable" concepts are imbedded gives us reason to believe in the reality of the concepts.

Three points need to be emphasized with respect to my brief exposition on ontology and realism. First, since the intended ontological status of many concepts in antipositivist writings is unclear, much work needs to be done to clarify the status of such concepts before anyone could confidently claim that the ontology implicit in antipositivist scholarship significantly differs (or does not differ) from that in contemporary social science. Second, the rhetoric of the "dominance of logical positivism" has, if anything, delayed and obscured real progress in identifying and clarifying the substantive differences between antipositivist views and contemporary social science. And third, rapprochement in consumer research need not await the complete articulation of supposed differences, for, indeed, significant steps toward rapprochement have already been taken.

## Toward Rapprochement

Holbrook (1989, p. 4) analogizes that the current situation in consumer research is similar to the "rapprochement between science and poetics." With respect to this insight, I ask, is rapprochement possible in consumer research? Is the disciplinary wall separating researchers already so tall, so thick, that it is unbreachable? Moving the discussion away from "dominant paradigms" and "positivism" and toward historically informed debate will undoubtedly augment other recent moves toward rapprochement, as we shall see.

A major concern has been that those advocating alternative methodologies seemed to be adopting relativism (Calder and Tybout 1987). Since most philosophers of science associate relativism with nihilism, sophistry, and solipsism, any methodology grounded on it is highly suspect.[16] However, even avowedly relativist writers concede that "interpretive" research need not be relativistic (Anderson 1989, p. 13). Moreover, there is an emerging consensus among the debate's participants for pluralism, not relativism: "There can be little doubt that. at this stage in the development of consumer research, methodological pluralism is desirable" (Calder and Tybout 1989, p. 199). In like manner, Hirschman (1986, p. 428) calls out for "conscious pluralism in research practice" and Lutz (1989) adopts the position of "critical pluralism." Lutz's clarion call for *critical* pluralism provides the key for developing our prognosis on rapprochement.

"Critical pluralism" is a label originally suggested by Siegel (1988) to characterize how scholars should view their own and others' theories and methods.[17] The "pluralism" part reminds us that dogmatism is antithetical to science; we should adopt a tolerant, open posture toward new theories and methods. The "critical" half stresses that nonevaluational, nonjudgmental, noncritical, or mindless pluralism (viewing the supposed encapsulation of rival theories and new methods as thwarting comparison and evaluation) is just as bad as dogmatism. All methods, theories, and their respective knowledge claims can (and must) be subjected to critical scrutiny; nothing is exempt.

The importance of any inquiry's being "critical" can be traced to Plato's method of critical discussion, the very cornerstone of Western philosophy (Popper 1968, p. 16). By necessity, all critical methods must have appraisal standards. It is important and appropriate for rapprochement that advocates of alternative methodologies have been actively developing such standards. As an exemplary example, Wallendorf and Belk (1989, p. 69) rightly point out that any research approach requires standards to assess its "trustworthiness," the importance of which is "postulated to be a scientific universal." They encourage naturalistic consumer researchers to pursue "triangulation of sources, methods, and researchers" (p. 70) to evaluate the credibility, transferability, dependability, and confirmability of their findings. Their efforts and those of Hirschman (1986) toward developing appraisal standards constitute a significant and positive step, but rapprochement could still be thwarted if these standards should render the findings incommensurable with those of contemporary social science. However, as we shall see, "incommensurability" is no longer considered a major problem in the philosophy of science and, therefore, it should pose no problem for rapprochement here.

Kuhn introduced "paradigm incommensurability" into the philosophy of science in 1962, and Feyerabend (1965) continued to develop it. Because paradigm incommensurability seemed to imply relativism, irrationalism, and nihilism, it became one of the most thoroughly investigated topics in the philosophy of science.[18] Those investigations uniformly concluded that no coherent, interesting, nontrivial version of "paradigm incommensurability" could be justified: "The frequent arguments that strive to use the absolute or relative incommensurability of scientific theories as a reason for thinking that they are inaccessible to purely scientific (rational) comparisons are simply fallacious" (Hintikka 1988, p. 38). Only eight years after introducing "paradigm incommensurability," Kuhn retreated from his "Gestalt shift" views on paradigm change and incommensurability because he recognized that such views implied relativism (1970a, pp. 234, 260) and solipsism (1970b, p. 193). Since then, Kuhn's (1978) most prominent scholarly work has focused on exploring the history of the shift in physics toward quantum mechanics. It is most telling that he finds no use for *either* "paradigm" or "incommensurability," let alone, "paradigm incommensurability." Today, even the relativist Feyerabend (1987, p. 81) concedes that incommensurability is a "rare event" and "is a difficulty for philosophers, not scientists."[19] Considering that "paradigm incommensurability" has been so thoroughly discredited in philosophy as to be virtually abandoned by Kuhn, its originator, and considering that even a relativist philosopher such as Feyerabend now concedes it poses no difficulty for science, one must conclude that a priori grounds for believing that "incommensurability" is a problem in consumer research are nonexistent. Examining the actual appraisal criteria currently being developed provides additional proof.

As previously discussed, advocates of alternative methodologies propose triangulation of sources, methods, and researchers to evaluate the credibility, transferability, dependability, and confirmability – in short, the trustworthiness of research. Three conclusions may be drawn from these efforts. First, the use of triangulation should again assuage those who may be concerned that advocates of alternative methods embrace reality relativism. There would be absolutely no reason to triangulate if researchers genuinely believed the relativistic position that rival "multiple realities" were incapable of comparison and evaluation, which is a view necessarily implying all "multiple realities" are equally valid, likely, and trustworthy. Second, the position that all so-called multiple realities are not equally valid, likely, and *trustworthy* appears to converge with that of advocates of contemporary social science who in the past have been (mis)labeled as "positivists," that is, all *perceptions of* reality are not equally valid, equally likely, equally *true*. In other words, "multiple realities" appears to be more a preferred form of discourse, a figure of speech, than a substantive, differentiating position. Third, the specific appraisal criteria being developed by advocates of alternative methodologies, far from being "paradigm encapsulated," or "incommensurable," actually seem very consistent or *commensurate* with contemporary research views, a conclusion readily acknowledged by Hirschman (1986, p. 244). Thus, these factors imply the total absence of objective grounds for the contention that "paradigm incommensurability" prevents rapprochement in consumer research.[20]

What should be our prognosis? Will rapprochement succeed? If the positivists could effect a rapprochement between communities as diverse as science and philosophy at the beginning of this century, cannot those in the single community of consumer research do the same at the century's close? If truth tellers in the 1980s could destroy political walls so tall, so thick, that many believed they would never fall, cannot truth seekers in the 1990s breach puny intradisciplinary walls? Even Holbrook's (1989) instructive call for accepting "poetic insights" gives grounds for optimism. As Robert Frost reminds us in the epigraph, "Something there is that doesn't love a wall."

## Notes

1. The belief that contemporary social science and consumer research are dominated by positivism is a consensus position (Anderson 1986, p. 155; Arndt 1985, p. 11; Belk, Sherry, and Wallendorf 1988, p. 467; Deshpande 1983, p. 101; Firat 1989, p. 93; Hirschman 1986, p. 237; Hirschman 1989, p. 209; Holbrook, Bell, and Grayson 1989. p. 35; Holbrook and O'Shaughnessy 1988, p. 402; Hudson and Ozanne 1988, p. 508; Lavin and Archdeacon 1989, p. 60; Lutz 1989, p. 3; Mick 1986, p. 207; Ozanne and Hudson 1989, p. 1; Peter and Olson 1983, p. 118; Thompson *et al.* 1989, p. 134; Venkatesh 1989, p. 101).

2. To avoid mischaracterization, I make maximum use of direct quotations to the extent that journal space allows. Moreover. when a view is attributed to a particular author by paraphrase, page numbers will be included in the citation. This style, regrettably absent in the marketing and consumer literature, shows readers and original authors where to look for attributed views; they can then determine whether there might possibly be misinterpretations or mischaracterizations.

3. Except where noted, this article's historical material draws from Ayer (1959), Bergmann ( 1967), Joergensen ( 1970), Manicas (1987), and Suppe (1977). Space limitations dictate that only major themes of the logical positivist movement related to the present debate be developed. For a more complete treatment, see Hunt (1991, pp. 266–278).

4. Nihilism is "the theory that nothing is knowable. All knowledge is illusory, worthless, meaningless, relative, and insignificant." Sophistry holds that "victory in argumentation at whatever cost, outwitting opponents, is the sole aim of disputation, no matter how bad the argument." Solipsism is "the theory that no reality exists other than one's self" (Angeles 1981, pp. 188, 265, 266).

5. Indeed, "scientific realism is a majority position whose advocates are so divided as to appear a minority" (Leplin 1984, p. 1). Examples are: transcendental realism (Bhaskar 1979), ontic realism (MacKinnon 1979), methodological realism (Leplin 1986), evolutionary naturalistic realism (Hooker 1985), referential realism (Harre 1986), and constructive realism (Giere 1988).

6. For the positivists, theories could also contain "theoretical terms," but all such terms must be explicitly and completely definable through "correspondence rules" to "observables." Therefore, a "theoretical term" is a shorthand way of talking about a collection of observable terms and *nothing more*. Most especially, a theoretical term does not refer to anything unobservable.

7. I am indebted to Michael E. Levin of the department of philosophy, City College, City University of New York, for pointing out the Marxist view of reification. I hasten to add, however, that Levin does not subscribe to this view.

8. This appears to be Monieson's (1988) argument.

9. For the limited purpose of this article, "antipositivist" seems a more appropriate label than "interpretivist," since many writers (including Belk) believe that "interpretivism" does not properly characterize their views. They rightly point out that all research necessarily involves interpretation. The fundamental issue in the debate may well be whether all research is *just* interpretation. Those (mis)labeled as "positivist" insist that their inquiry touches base with a reality that is outside their paradigm or theory. Antipositivists at times seem to claim that all research, including by implication their own, is linguistically encapsulated and paradigm bounded, i.e., it is *just* interpretation.

10. For an evaluation of using "proof" as a criterion for "acceptable" science, see Hunt (1990), especially the sections on "inductive realism," the "philosophers' fallacy," and Popper.

11. The ontology and structure of quantum mechanics, at least in the positivist "Copenhagen view," are *exclusively* a series of mathematical equations, i.e., they are *just* mathematics: "The fact is that although the underlying quantum mechanical view of the world is extraordinarily confusing – Bohr is said to have remarked that if it doesn't make you dizzy then you don't understand it – quantum mechanics as a computational tool is entirely straightforward... . The problem is that although the formalism of the quantum theory fits nature like a glove, nobody, not even Bohr or Heisenberg, has ever really understood what it means. The only concise picture the formalism offers the world prior to an act of measurement is the formalism itself" (Mermin 1983, pp. 655–656).

12. August Comte (1798–1857) and his colleague Saint-Simon (1760–1825), the nineteenth-century originators of the word "positivism" to describe a philosophical position, actually opposed the use of statistics in sociology. In fact, Comte coined a new word, "sociology" to distance his own work from the statistical emphasis of what was then called "social physics" (Comte 1877, p. 15). (See also Hunt [1989b] for more on the fallaciousness of the quantitative/qualitative and rigor/relevance dichotomies.)

13. Here, Firat is clearly referring to all science, not just social science or, even more narrowly, "positivistic" social science.

14. For the record, I believe that causality and the realist view with respect to unobservables are prominent – but not dominant – in social science and consumer research, but reject the charges of determinism, adoption of the machine metaphor, and reification.

15. The author is indebted to Jerry Goolsby of the University of South Florida for pointing out this alternative perspective.

16. See Hunt (1991, pp. 305–349) for a discussion of why philosophers associate relativism with nihilism, sophistry, and solipsism.

17. "Critical pluralism" should most definitely not be confused with "critical theory." The "critical" in "critical theory" philosophy is a code word for "Marxist" (Hew 1985, p. 30). So-called critical theorists in philosophy use Marxist dogma (or neo-Marxist after the collapse of Marxist regimes in Eastern Europe) to evaluate Western democracies. In contrast, dogma of any kind is antithetical to critical pluralism.

18. For evaluations of incommensurability see Shapere (1964, 1966), Scheffler (1967, chap. 3; 1986, chap. 13), Kordig (1971, chaps. 2, 3), Kitcher (1978), Moberg (1979), Levin (1979), Laudan (1976, 1977), and Putnam (1981). In marketing, see Hunt (1991, pp. 327–330). No one in consumer research has produced a single, valid example of "incommensurable" knowledge claims. Hunt 1989a, p. 195) points out that some consumer researchers have, unfortunately, confused "different" knowledge claims with "incommensurable" ones. For incommensurability to be a problem, at the minimum, knowledge claims must be rivals, and "different" does not imply "rival." For example, Darwinian theory is *different* from Newton's laws, but neither is a *rival* of the other.

19. Philosophers now acknowledge that the reason they mistakenly saw "paradigm incommensurability" in science was, in Bernstein's (1990, p. 85) words, the "Babel in philosophy": "A primary reason why there has been so much concern with problems of incommensurability and relativism is because this is the condition that we find ourselves in as philosophers, where we speak such radically different tongues that we are unable to understand what even our closest neighbors are saying." Consumer research need not mimic philosophy by lapsing into Babel.

20. This optimistic conclusion notwithstanding, there may be those who wish to stop debate rather than encourage it, freeze positions rather than thaw them, encapsulate research programs rather than open them up, or build disciplinary walls rather than tear them down. "Paradigm incommensurability" can continue to be a useful rhetorical tool for such purposes.

## References

Acton, H.B. (1967), "Idealism," in *The Encyclopedia of Philosophy*, Vol. 4, ed. Paul Edwards, New York: Free Press.

Anderson, Paul F. (1983), "Marketing, Scientific Progress and Scientific Method," *Journal of Marketing*, 47 (Fall), 18–31.

– (1986), "On Method in Consumer Research: A Critical Relativist Perspective," *Journal of Consumer Research*, 13 (September), 155–173.

– (1989), "On Relativism and Interpretivism – with a Prolegomenon to the 'Why Question,'" in *Interpretive Consumer Research*, ed. Elizabeth Hirschman, Provo, UT: Association for Consumer Research, 10–23.

Angeles, Peter A. (1981), *Dictionary of Philosophy*, New York: Barnes & Noble.

Arndt, Johan (1985), "On Making Science More Scientific," *Journal of Marketing*, 49 (Summer), 11–23.

Ayer, A.J. (1959), *Logical Positivism*, New York: Free Press.

Belk, Russell W., John F. Sherry, Jr., and Melanie Wallendorf (1988), "A Naturalistic Inquiry into Buyer and Seller Behavior at a Swap Meet," *Journal of Consumer Research*, 14 (March), 449–470.

–, Melanic Wallendorf, and John F. Sherry (1989), "The Sacred and the Profane in Consumer Behavior: Theodicy on the Odyssey," *Journal of Consumer Research*, 16 (June), 1–38.

Berger, Peter and Samuel Pullberg (1966), "Reification and the Sociological Critique of Consciousness," *New Left Review*, 35, 56–71.

Bergmann, Gustav (1967), *Metaphysics of Logical Positivism*, Madison: University of Wisconsin Press.

Bernstein, Richard J. (1990), "Confusion of Tongues," *Chronicle of Higher Education*, January 17, p. B–5.

Bhaskar, Roy (1979), *The Possibility of Naturalism*, Brighton: Harvester.

Braithwaite, R.B. (1968), *Scientific Explanation: A Study of the Function of Theory, Probability, and Law in Science*, Cambridge: Cambridge University Press.

Brodbeck, May (1962), "Explanation, Prediction and 'Imperfect' Knowledge," in *Minnesota Studies in the Philosophy of Science*, Vol. 3, ed. Herbert Feigl and Grover Maxwell, Minneapolis: University of Minnesota Press.

– (1968), "Models and Measurement," in *Readings in the Philosophy of the Social Sciences*, ed. May Brodbeck, New York: Macmillan, 573-578.

Calder, Bobby J. and Alice M. Tybout (1987), "What Consumer Research Is...," *Journal of Consumer Research*, 14 (June), 136–140.

– and Alice M. Tybout (1989), "Interpretive, Qualitative, and Traditional Scientific Empirical Consumer Behavior Research," in *Interpretive Consumer Research*, ed. Elizabeth C. Hirschman, Provo, UT: Association for Consumer Research, 199–208.

Carnap, Rudolph (1936), "Testability and Meaning," *Philosophy of Science*, 3, 419–471.

– (1966), *Philosophical Foundations of Physics*, New York: Basic.

Comte, August (1877), *Cours de philosophie positive*, Vol. 4, 4th ed., Paris: Baillière & Fils.

Deshpande, Rohit (1983), "'Paradigms Lost': On Theory and Method in Research in Marketing," *Journal of Marketing*, 47 (Fall), 101–110.

Dholakia, Nikhilesh (1985), "Opposing Research Camps in Marketing: Rigor vs. Relevance," *Marketing Educator*, 4(3), 3.

– (1988), "Interpreting Monieson: Creative and Destructive Tensions," *Journal of Macromarketing*, 8 (Fall), 11–14.

Feyerabend, Paul K. (1965), "On the Meaning of Scientific Terms," *Journal of Philosophy*, 62, 267–271.

– (1987), *Farewell to Reason*, London: Verso.

Firat, A. Fuat (1989), "Science and Human Understanding," *AMA Winter Educators' Conference*, ed. Terry Childers *et al.*, Chicago: American Marketing Association, 93–98.

Flew, Antony (1985), *Thinking about Social Thinking: The Philosophy of the Social Sciences*, London: Basil Blackwell.

Fullerton, Ronald (1987), "The Poverty of Ahistorical Analysis: Present Weakness and Future Cure in U.S. Marketing Thought," in *Philosophical and Radical Thought in Marketing*, ed. A.F. Firat *et al.*, Lexington, MA: Lexington.

Giere, Ronald N. (1988), *Explaining Science: A Cognitive Approach*, Chicago: University of Chicago Press.

Harre, Rom (1986), *Varieties of Realism*, Oxford: Basil Blackwell.

Hempel, Carl G. (1965), "Aspects of Scientific Explanation," in *Aspects of Scientific Explanation and Other Essays of the Philosophy of Science*, New York: Free Press.

Hintikka, Jaakko (1988), "On the Incommensurability of Theories," *Philosophy of Science*, 55, 25–38.

Hirschman, Elizabeth C. (1986), "Humanistic Inquiry in Marketing Research: Philosophy, Method, and Criteria," *Journal of Marketing Research*, 23 (August), 237–249.

– (1989), "After Word," in *Interpretive Consumer Research*, ed. Elizabeth C. Hirschman, Provo, UT: Association for Consumer Research, 209.

Holbrook. Morris B. (1989), "Farewell Address," *ACR Newsletter* (December), 1–9,

–, Stephen Bell, and Mark W. Grayson (1989), "The Role of Humanities in Consumer Research," in *Interpretive Consumer Research*, ed. Elizabeth C. Hirschman, Provo UT: Association for Consumer Research, 20–47 .

– and Mark W. Grayson (1986), "The Semiology of Cinematic Consumption: Symbolic Consumer Behavior in 'Out of Africa,'" *Journal of Consumer Research*, 13 (December), 374–381.

– and John O'Shaughnessy (1988), "On the Scientific Status of Consumer Research and the Need for an Interpretive Approach to Studying Consumption Behavior," *Journal of Consumer Research*, 15 (December), 398–402.

Hooker, Clifford A. (1985), "Surface Dazzle, Ghostly Depths: An Exposition and Critical Evaluation of van Fraassen's Vindication of Empiricism against Realism," in *Images of Science: Essays on Realism and Empiricism*, ed. Paul M. Churchland and Clifford A. Hooker, Chicago: University of Chicago Press.

Hudson, Laurel Anderson and Julie L. Ozanne (1988), "Alternative Ways of Seeking Knowledge in Consumer Research," *Journal of Consumer Research*, 14 (March), 508–521.

Hunt, Shelby D. (1989a), "Naturalistic, Humanistic, and Interpretive Inquiry: Challenges and Ultimate Potential in *Interpretive Consumer Research*, ed. Elizabeth C. Hirschman, Provo, UT: Association for Consumer Research.

– (1989b), "Reification and Realism in Marketing: in Defense of Reason," *Journal of Macromarketing*, 9 (Fall), 4–10.

– (1990), "Truth in Marketing Theory and Research," *Journal of Marketing*, 54 (July), 1–15.

– (1991), *Modern Marketing Theory,: Critical Issues in the Philosophy of Marketing Science*, Cincinnati: SouthWestern.

Jacoby, Jacob (1978), "Consumer Research: A State of the Art Review," *Journal of Marketing*, 42 (April), 87–96.

Joergensen, Joergen (1970), "The Development of Logical Empiricism," in *Foundations of the Unity of Science*, Vol. 2, ed. Otto Neurath *et al.*, Chicago: University of Chicago Press.

Kassarjian, Harold H. (1989), Review of *Philosophical and Radical Thought in Marketing*, ed. A. Fuat Firat *et al.*, *Journal of Marketing*, 53 (January), 123–126.

Kitcher, P. (1978), "Theories, Theorist, and Theoretical Changes," *Philosophical Review*, 87, 519–547.

Kordig. C.R. (1971), "Feyerabend and Radical Meaning Variance," *Nous*, 9, 399–404.

Kuhn, Thomas S. (1962), *The Structure of Scientific Revolutions*, Chicago: University of Chicago Press.

– (1970a), "Reflections on My Critics," in *Criticism and the Growth of Knowledge*, ed. Imre Lakatos and Alan Musgrave, Cambridge: Cambridge University Press, 231–278.

– (1970b), *The Structure of Scientific Revolutions*, 2d ed., Chicago: University of Chicago Press.

– (1978), *Black-Body Theory and the Quantum Discontinuity 1884–1912*, New York: Oxford University Press.

Kyburg, Henry E., Jr. (1968), *Philosophy of Science: A Formal Approach*, New York: Macmillan.

Laudan, Larry (1976), "Two Dogmas of Methodology," *Philosophy of Science*, 55, 25–38.

- (1977), *Progress and Its Problems*, Berkeley: University of California Press.

Lavin, Marilyn and Thomas J. Archdeacon (1989), "The Relevance of Historical Method for Marketing Research," in *Interpretive Consumer Research*, ed. Elizabeth C. Hirschman, Provo, UT: Association for Consumer Research, 60–68.

Leplin, Jarrett (1984), *Scientific Realism*, Berkeley and Los Angeles: University of California Press.

– (1986), "Methodological Realism and Scientific Rationality," *Philosophy, of Science*, 53, 31–51.

Levin, Michael E. (1979), "On Theory Change and Meaning Change," *Philosophy of Science*, 46, 407–424.

Lukacs, Georg (1971), *History and Class Consciousness. Studies in Marxist Dialectics*, Cambridge, MA: MIT Press.

Lutz, Richard J. (1989), "Presidential Address, 1988 – Positivism, Naturalism and Pluralism in Consumer Research: Paradigms in Paradise," in *Advances in Consumer Research* Vol. 16, ed. Thomas K. Srull, Provo, UT: Association for Consumer Research, 1–8.

MacKinnon, Edward (1979), "Scientific Realism: The New Debates," *Philosophy of Science*, 46, 501–532.

Manicas, Peter T. (1987), *A History of Philosophy of the Social Sciences*, New York: Basil Blackwell.

McMullin, Ernan (1984), "A Case for Scientific Realism," in *Scientific Realism*, ed. Jarrett Leplin, Berkeley and Los Angeles: University of California Press.

Mermin, N.D. (1983), "The Great Quantum Muddle," *Philosophy of Science*, 50 (December), 651–656.

Mick, David Glen (1986), "Consumer Research and Semiotics: Exploring the Morphology of Signs, Symbols, and Significance," *Journal of Consumer Research*. 13 (September), 196-213.

Moberg, D.W. (1979), "Are There Rival, Incommensurable Theories?" *Philosophy of Science*, 46, 244–262.

Monieson, David D. (1988), "Intellectualization in Macromarketing: A World Disenchanted," *Journal of Macromarketing*, 8 (Fall), 4–10.

Nunnally, Jum C. (1978), *Psychometric Theory*, 2d ed., New York: McGraw-Hill.

Ozanne, Julie L. and Laurel Anderson Hudson (1989), "Exploring Diversity in Consumer Research," in *Interpretive Consumer Research*, ed. Elizabeth C. Hirschman, Provo, UT: Association for Consumer Research, 1–9.

Pechmann, Cornelia (1990), "Response to President's Column, September 1989," *ACR Newsletter*, (June), 5–7.

Peter, J. Paul and Jerry C. Olson (1983), "Is Science Marketing?" *Journal of Marketing*, 47 (Fall), 111–125.

– and Jerry C. Olson (1989), "The Relativist/Constructionist Perspective on Scientific Knowledge and Consumer Research," in *Interpretive Consumer Research*, ed. Elizabeth C. Hirschman, Provo, UT: Association for Consumer Research, 24–28.

Phillips, D.C. (1987), *Philosophy, Science, and Social Inquiry*, Oxford: Pergamon.

Popper, Karl R. (1968), *The Logic of Scientific Discovery*, New York: Harper & Row.

Putnam, Hilary (1981), *Reason, Truth, and History*, Cambridge: Cambridge University Press.

Rudner, Richard (1966), *Philosophy of Social Science*, Englewood Cliffs, NJ: Prentice-Hall.

Ryan, Michael J. and Julia M. Bristor (1987), "The Symbiotic Nature of Hermeneutical vs. Classically Generated Knowledge," in *1987 AMA Winter Educators' Conference*, ed. Russell W. Belk *et al.*, Chicago: American Marketing Association, 191–194.

Scheffler, Israel (1967), *Science and Subjectivity*, Indianapolis: Bobbs-Merrill.

– (1986), *Inquiries: Philosophical Studies of Language*, Science, and Learning, Indianapolis: Hackett.

Shapere, D. (1964), "The Structure of Scientific Revolutions," *Philosophical Review*, 73, 383–394.

– (1966), "Meaning and Scientific Change," in *Mind and Cosmos: Explorations in the Philosophy of Science*, ed. R. Colodny, Pittsburgh: University of Pittsburgh Press, 41–85.

Sherry, John F., Jr. (1983), "Gift Giving in Anthropological Perspective," *Journal of Consumer Research*, 10 (September), 157–168.

Siegel, Harvey (1988), "Relativism for Consumer Research? (Comments on Anderson)," *Journal of Consumer Research*, 15 (June), 129–132.

Stern, Barbara B. (1989a), "Literary Explication: A Methodology for Consumer Research," in *Interpretive Consumer Research*, ed. Elizabeth C. Hirschman, Provo, UT: Association for Consumer Research.

– (1989b), "Literary Criticism and Consumer Research: Overview and Illustrative Analysis," *Journal of Consumer Research*, 16 (December), 322–334.

Sternthal, Brian, Alice M. Tybout, and Bobby J. Calder (1987), "Confirmatory versus Comparative Approaches to Judging Theory Tests," *Journal of Consumer Research*, 14 (June), 114–125.

Stove, David (1982), *Popper and After*, Oxford: Pergamon.

Strong, Morgan (1990), 'Playboy Interview: Steven Hawking," *Playboy*, 37 (April), 63–74.

Suppe, Frederick (1977), *The Structure of Scientific Theories*, 2d ed., Chicago: University of Illinois Press.

Thompson, Craig J., William B. Locander, and Howard R. Pollio (1989), "Putting Consumer Experience Back into Consumer Research: The Philosophy and Method of Existential-Phenomenology," *Journal of Consumer Research*, 16 (September), 133–146.
Venkatesh, Alladi (1989), "Modernity and Postmodernity," in *AMA Winter Educators' Conference*, ed. Terry L. Childers *et al.*, 99–104.
Wallendorf, Melanie and Russell W. Belk (1989), "Assessing Trustworthiness in Naturalistic Consumer Research," in *Interpretive Consumer Research*, ed. Elizabeth Hirschman, Provo, UT: Association for Consumer Research, 69–84.

# 9

# Interpreting Consumer Mythology: A Structural Approach to Consumer Behavior

**Sidney J. Levy**

**Source:** *Journal of Marketing* 45 (3) (1981): 49–61.

Qualitative research in current marketing study usually involves focus group interviews, sometimes depth interviews, and projective techniques (Bellenger *et al.* 1976). There is a resurgence of interest in the analysis of expressive verbal materials elicited by such data-gathering methods, but little contemporary marketing literature exists about such analysis. The goal of this paper is to explore and illustrate the idea that verbal materials elicited from people in the marketplace are a form of storytelling that can be analyzed as projective. The responses of a consumer telling about the purchase and use of products may be approached from varied viewpoints. Here, the remarks (the protocol) are taken as a literary production we might interpret in ways comparable to those of clinical psychologists, social anthropologists, and literary critics. A recent view of anthropological concepts (Levy 1978) especially stimulated the attempt to use the Lévi-Strauss structuralist approach by likening consumers' household anecdotes to the myths that he has mined so richly.

In open-ended interviewing about the consumption of products, respondents are often asked to describe the product features the family members prefer, to characterize family consumption patterns, to tell about recent instances of using the product, and to explain how and why given products are used. The results of such interviews are commonly reported in a somewhat literal manner, in tabulations of use frequencies, in lists of features cited, in verbal summaries that most people said this or that, or even in lists of verbatim comments without additional comments by the researchers. Ordinarily, the goals are to learn facts of usage and reasons given for and against the product.

Such handling of the data often seems barren and frustrating because it is not sufficiently penetrating, does not tell enough about the meaning of the product in relation to the lives of the users, and its place among other products. The approach suggested here is to avoid accepting the responses as if they are scientific observations to be tabulated as measures. Rather, the assumption is that the products are used symbolically, and that the telling about their uses is a way of symbolizing the life and nature of the family, thus it requires a theory of interpretation that determines how the data are to be related and understood. Sanche de Gramont (1970. p. 7) illustrates the point:

> I like to imagine these Three Wise Men of the Occident bent in contemplation over a South American Indian myth about a boy who steals a pet pig

> from his father and roasts it in the forest. Freud would conclude that the boy is symbolically killing his father because he desires his mother. Marx would say that this youthful member of the proletariat is seizing control of the methods of production in the class struggle against the landed gentry. Lévi-Strauss would find that in cooking the pig, the primitive Indian boy had achieved the passage from nature to culture and shown that his thought processes are no different from Einstein's.

A conventional marketing approach would probably accept the boy's explanation at face value and conclude that he was hungry, that the pig was convenient, cheap, and tasted good.

The question is raised: If consumer responses are stories (or parts thereof) that tell about the family, how shall the stories be interpreted? Some guidance may come from observing how various kinds of stories are studied, as their analysts search for meanings in such as fairy tales, plays, novels, psychological test responses, and myths, en route to studying consumer research protocols.

In reading fairy tales, as a first example, the reader (consumer) reacts directly with ideas and feelings. Bruno Bettelheim explains in detail the sources of the consumer satisfaction, showing how fairy tales enrich psychological development and assist in solving fundamental human problems. He points out the message the fairy tales get across to the child in manifold form: "... that a struggle against severe difficulties in life is unavoidable, is an intrinsic part of human existence – that if one does not shy away, but steadfastly meets, unexpected and often unjust hardships, one masters all obstacles and at the end emerges victorious" (Bettelheim 1977, p. 8).

As people mature, the literature of plays and novels remains endlessly absorbing, as is the storytelling on radio, in the movies, and on television. The audience is insatiably curious to know what the characters did, what happened next, and how did it come out. Underlying is the belief that the fictions are significantly related to real events, that experiencing the simulated version in this vicarious way is intellectually and emotionally beneficial and/or destructive.

By extension, the lives of authors are of interest to their readers. Even people who have not read the writer's work can enjoy reading about the writer as a person (to have more knowledge, to feel like an insider, to reduce the stature of great figures, to be reassured or titillated by their humanity, their ordinariness, or their bizarre genius). Other analysts want to find clues to illuminate the writings, to understand better the meaning of *Finnegan's Wake* or *Alice in Wonderland.* And others want to explore the nature and processes of creativity as they go on in creators or as they are manifest in their productions.

Thus, the search for meanings expressed in a story goes on at various levels: (1) The experiencing and direct interpretation by the reader is fundamental. (2) That experience is abstracted, generalized, and explained by a scholar for the insight it provides into human nature. (3) The work (product) is interpreted for the means by which it achieves its effects. (4) The teller of the story is studied as a unique source of inspiration or an example of a type. Where the authorship is anonymous, as in folk tales, myths, and many fairy tales, or has its roots recognized in ancient chronicles, the source may be interpreted as part of some national or ethnic character. (5) The author is studied to develop and illuminate the meaning of the work. (6) Relationships between the author and the work are studied and interpreted as examples of general processes of expression, whether the focus is on how the author's personality is visible in the writing or on the means by which self-expression was concealed or transformed. In the same ways, a protocol in which a consumer tells the story of how the product is consumed can be examined for how the consumer interprets the consumption experience, what it tells about people in general, to see how the product features are related to consumption, to learn what the protocol says about the segment it represents, to observe how the individual consumer's character, personality, and life-style help explain the nature of the product, and what the instance explains about the general nature of that kind of consuming.

Having suggested the problem in a general way, this paper will examine the nature of interpretation of self-expression, lay groundwork for application to the study of consumer behavior, and give an example of such application.

## Modes of Analysis

There is intuitive recognition that authors of stories must express their personalities in the story. Projective techniques as research and clinical tools explore the ways people transform and externalize their experience in some narrative form, as a general phenomenon and specifically in response to given materials, in accordance with David Rapaport's formulation of the projective hypothesis, as follows.

> All behavioral manifestations of the human being, including the least and the most significant, are revealing and expressive of his personality, by which we mean that individual principle of which he is the carrier. This formulation of the projective hypothesis implies a specific definition of the term "behavior," which includes all of the following aspects: (a) behavior historically viewed in the life-history; (b) behavior statically viewed as reflected in the environment with which the subject surrounds himself, as the furniture of his house, the clothes he wears, etc.: expressive movements; (d) internal behavior, including percepts, fantasies, thoughts. (Rapaport 1942, p. 213)

Characteristically, interpretation of projective techniques follows two paths. (1) Specific components of the story (test protocol) are tabulated and used systematically to evaluate either an individual's responses or the empirical validity of generalizations about groups. An example of this approach is the case of the Rorschach: Certain perceptions of the inkblots are so common they are designated as popular responses. One element of an individual's adjustment is then derived from the number of popular responses he/she gives, as norms suggest it is too many or too few. However, counting popular responses or the length of stories to establish norms for population groups in a purely empirical manner is relatively superficial, compared, say, to having a theory about conformity, rigidity, deviance, and the meanings of the specific perceptions. (2) Qualitative analysis accepts introspection as data and looks for subjective meanings, thus facing the necessity for interpretation. It is phenomenological and interested in symbolic interactionism, trying to see what lies behind or is meant by the manifest behavior. This viewpoint considers social events to be unlike events in the natural sciences. The social events are selected and attended to because of their significance to the people involved, and thus are psychological events in social contexts.

By the logic of the projective hypothesis and the definition of human events as symbolic, interpretation becomes a process of searching for meaning, that is, finding out how mental phenomena – such inner representations of experiences as ideas, imagery, and consumption fantasies as forms of storytelling to the self – are related to interactions with other people and the physical world.

Leslie Stephen wrote that people's doctrines do not become operative in behavior until they have generated an imaginative symbolism. We make distinctions among these imaginative symbolisms by classifying types of narratives. One kind of tale commonly told within a social group is the myth. Formal interpretation of myths is concerned with classifying and explaining grand myths – those tales of the gods, beasts, and heroes that are about the creation of the world, human birth and death, taking form as accounts of floods, supernatural creatures, matings of gods and mortals, heroic family romances, saviors, and seers, and cataclysmic physical events. The aim is to demonstrate the similarities and differences among cultures of their grand myths, the sources of the myths, and to explicate the realities to which the mythological symbols referred (Frazer 1927).

In recent years, the study of myths was much invigorated by the work of Claude Levi-Strauss. He notes reasons why distinctions are made between tales and myths, but does not regard them as fundamental. He calls tales miniature myths and sees them all as susceptible to the same type of analysis. This analysis involves certain main features at the heart of Lévi-Strauss's contribution.

- The purpose of myth is to provide a logical model capable of overcoming contradictions or paradoxes in natural and social experience.
- Interpretation of myths seeks their essential structural characteristics (in contrast to a functional analysis that links the myth to the social situation that is its local context).
- The structural analysis reveals universal human cognitive processes. These mental operations consist of creating patterns rooted in the perceptions of opposites, manipulating binary relations, and developing mediating terms and triads in various sequences and aggregations.
- A holistic attitude is required, the analysis being addressed to the clustering and interdependency of elements.

The fundamental character of a myth points to its universal mode of thought, the way it transcends local culture. As Lévi-Strauss says, "its substance does not lie in its style, its original music, or its syntax, but in the story which it tells" (Lévi-Strauss, 1963. p. 210). When one takes the many versions of the myth (for example, the stories of Oedipus, including the Homeric, Styphoclean, and Freudian), a structural analysis takes account of all the variants, to arrive at the structural law of the myth. That is, what is it really about? The analysis reaches the conclusion that the myth struggles with the contradiction between the idea that human beings originate autochthonously and the idea that they are born of the union of man and woman – out of one or out of two.

Stories are analyzed by breaking them down into gross constituent units Lévi-Strauss calls mythemes. The mythemes result from a play of binary or ternary oppositions. For example, in a tale a king is not only a king and a shepherdess a shepherdess, but these words and what they signify become tangible means of constructing an intelligible system formed by the oppositions: male/female (with regard to nature) and high/low (with regard to culture), as well as the possible permutations among the six terms. In this way, Lévi-Strauss discerns a universal metalanguage, recognizing, as Miriam Rodin says, the way in which underlying relational principles order cognition across several domains.

Edmund Leach (1974, p. 76) offers broad structural schema in Figure 1 summarizing the relative positions of men, animals, and deities in Greek mythology in a matrix formed by the oppositions above/below, this world/other world, and culture/nature. The analysis will be extended in this paper by amplifying the left side of this structure, elaborating Men in Cities as men, women, and children in high and low social statuses.

If we take the idea that myths are ways of organizing perceptions of realities, of indirectly expressing paradoxical human concerns, they have consumer relevance because these realities and concerns affect people's daily lives. The issues of male/female, nature/culture, and high/low, for example, are not reserved to story-telling occasions about kings and shepherdesses but are also being acted out in everyday behavior. Some marketing study approaches the same generalized, universal level as the grand myths. In his dissertation on *The Social Construction* of *Consumption Patterns*, Firat wrestles with the paradox of poor and disadvantaged consumers establishing irrational consumption patterns in cars and expensive foods. He seeks to show how society induces patterns that express such fundamental structural antinomies in consumption as individual/collective, private/pulic, and passive/active. At this level of analvsis, individual choice behavior is almost irrelevant, being interpreted as a manifestation of conformity to the culture's dominant consumption pattern (Firat 1978). In another universal vein, the work of Daniel B. Williams (1976) examines individual consumer purchasing behavior, interpreting the decision making process to a highly generalized level. In analyzing the problem spaces or mediums for problem solving used by the individual purchase problem solver, Williams identifies such space attributes as within the organism/outside the organism, fast/slow, high/low, and phenomenal/transphenomenal.

The idea of taking the consumer protocol as a kind of story to be interpreted draws from various traditions. Robert P. Abelson, for instance, discusses the concept of cognitive script, defining script as "a coherent sequence of events expected by the individual, involving him either as a participant or as an observer" (Abelson 1976, p. 33). Scripts are formed by the linking of chains of vignettes, the latter being "the raw constituents of remembered episodes in the individual's experience." He insists on this holism and criticizes the "elementaristic, stilted, and static" positions common among cognitive and social psychologists, and stresses the way vignettes are "coherently linked." Vignettes in the consumer's script correspond to the mythemes Lévi-Strauss observes in myths, where he similarly insists on the necessity for analysis of clusters or bundles of mythemes. As with scripts, myths may be dealt with particularistically as factual descriptions of recalled events, as traditional marketing research questionnaires typically do; or as revealing basic universal human structures, as Lévi-Strauss seeks to do. In between, we may seek to interpret sufficiently to get below the surface, and concretely enough to apply the ideas to consumer events.

**Figure 1** Structural Relations in Greek Mythology

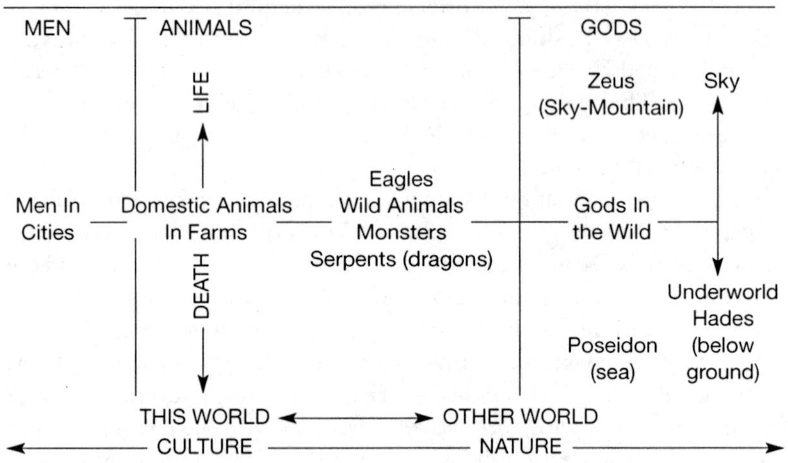


## The Present Study

To gather scripts, vignettes, or mythemes as an illustrative instance for this paper, a sample of six consumers was interviewed at length about the various family members, their individual characteristics, and especially their attitudes and behavior in relation to food. The respondents are married, middle-class housewives with young children living at home. Each was asked to talk about her husband and children and how they like and dislike their foods prepared. The women were particularly asked to relate family stories, those little tales or bits of family lore that are repeated to family and friends as ways of typifying the family members. These interviews were interpreted using a background of hundreds of depth interviews from marketing studies of many food products. It should be understood that numbers are not relevant here. The purpose is to illustrate the use of a qualitative, structuralistic approach, not to sample for representativeness, to measure distributions, nor to compute the significance of differences.

The tales that were gathered are taken as susceptible to interpretation at the various levels and in the various modes noted earlier: as descriptions of consumer experiences, as projections of the housewife storyteller, as revealing the family members, as symbolizing the abstracted functions serving the participants and the social unit, and as mundane, secular little myths that organize consumer reality in accordance with underlying logical structures. Lévi-Strauss points to three levels at which versions of myths may be situated: myths of origin and emergence, myths of migrations, and village tales in which "the great logical or cosmological contrasts have been toned down to the scale of social relations" (Levi-Strauss 1969, p, 333). The little myths of the family are a fourth level of toning down. Little myths are generalizations about the family and its members, told in the form of anecdotes that use selected facts drawn from the fund of past experiences.

The analysis proceeded by close reading of verbatim transcriptions of the interviews. Observing how respondents project their perceptions of themselves and their families, their language, assumptions, emotional tone, logic, and choice of incidents, the following issues were interpreted.

- Purposes served by the telling of little myths.
- Values preference portrayed.
- Theories used in accounting for the behavior of family members.
- Structural relationships of characteristics and categories that are used.

### Purposes

The stories serve an interwoven set of purposes. Like grand myths, they refer to origins of the group and explain how ancestors came together and what life was like in those days. Typically, there is a Paradise Lost aura to the stories – "What fun we used to have going to the lake."

> I remember we used to all get together, and my uncle had a truck with just wooden sides on it and we would go up and picnic, the whole family, aunts, uncles, cousins, and everyone would ride on the back of the truck. There was always somebody there for you. We would go up to lakes and swim; we would have a picnic out at the lake. It was just nice because everybody went: it was something that everybody joined in on.

The stories act as retrospective affirmations of ties and conflicts when relatives reminisce, and to induct new group members by marriage, birth, and friendship into family traditions by transmitting a fund of important values, ideas, and characteristics. They instruct in the life-style of the lineage, the kind of housing, clothing, transportation, recreation, and food it was and is customary to consume.

The stories illustrate specific relationships and personalities. Often, there is a self-justifying quality: The story proves that the people really are (or were) like that.

> I had a car when I was sixteen: I got it as a graduation present, and my sisters and I and my cousins – my one cousin, we're all very close – we were out. I don't know, I think we went to McDonalds, or whatever, and we were

> supposed to be home by nine o'clock, and we didn't get in until nine-thirty, and, sure enough, we came to the door and my mom says. "Where have you been?" and I just said, "oh, ask Jean" who was my cousin, who was behind me. And my mom says something about "this time you're really going to get it," and out shot a hand, and I ducked and Jean ducked, and my baby sister got it. And that – wasn't that it was that hard, but it was harder than a love tap. Sure enough, Jean and I were always the ones that were ducking, and my sister was always the one who was getting it. That's typical.

Abstracted from the flow of childhood events, this little myth becomes paradigmatic and polished. Some of the details are offered as less important. Maybe it was not McDonald's, although saying that it was indicates the innocence of the occasion. The "sure enoughs," the "always," and "that's typical" highlight the mythic character of the story, the way it verifies and generalizes the teller's virtue and cleverness, the sibling rivalry, the mother's role, etc.

### Values and Preferences

In selecting stories to tell, the respondents project their concern with certain values. Middle-class women highlight middle-class values deemed important for transmission through the generations. As telling stories is a method of maintaining family traditions, it is not surprising that the importance of family unity is repeatedly asserted as such a value. One's childhood was part of a close family or regretfully was not, the mother now strives to have a close family, or regrets that maturation and modern life-styles are destroying that closeness. Closeness is evidenced in doing things together, sharing enjoyable experiences such as family picnics, sports outings, travel, hobbies, meals, household projects, in living nearby, in helping one another, showing concern about the children's companions and occasionally in some special intimacy of emotional communication or understanding.

The dimension of conformity to or deviation from manly norms comes up in relation to food. The traditional husband is a "meat and potatoes man."

> His favorite meal is pot roast with potatoes and carrots and onions in a big pot. He likes roast and gravy. That would be his most special meal. Roast and potatoes, and a vegetable, and lots of bread and butter. He's kind of a meat and potatoes man.

This pattern reflects the central American diet; therefore, it seems proper and hardly requires explanation. It often goes on in the context of "he eats everything" except perhaps the conventional hatreds (liver) or less usual foods, such as artichokes.

As a cultural subgroup each family also has its local values. It is easy to gather an array of summaries of family tastes. Women generalize that They all love chicken, They're not crazy about fish, We don't eat any raw vegetables, They all like it rare, They like casseroles. Such remarks are usually not literally true (as fuller discussion reveals): but are imaginative generalizations (not imaginary) that symbolize the kind of family being described as stubborn eaters, narrow eaters, easy to feed, and so on, and show what kind of woman the homemaker is to cope with such a family.

## Consumers' Theories

The above kinds of behavior may seem conventional but are often left unexplained because they are so taken for granted or seem so easily accounted for as a common learning. But husbands who are not meat and potatoes men require explanation; when a family member departs from the norm of eating what the mother regards as an ordinary diet, a problem is posed. The ideas put forth by the women to explain food handling and preferences or aversions take many forms; as shown by examples in Table 1. Some stories are mystery stories; the behavior seems baffling, arbitrary, inexplicable.

> The two kids split an egg, the older one takes the yellow, and the younger one takes the white. I haven't the faintest idea why they feel that way, I really don't.
>
> For instance, he won't eat the potatoes and gravy if it runs into the meat. I don't know why. He has this huge plate, and he separates it all on the edges, nothing in the middle.

A framework that operates in the thinking of the respondents has such elements as these:

- The process of acquiring and inculcating tastes in the service of health beliefs and propriety is a conflict-filled one. Cooks are motivated to get the family to eat what is served by various moral imperatives. such as that's what people like us eat, the food comprises a healthy diet, and providing it and eating it are ways of showing love (and other emotions). Although there is more pleasure and satisfaction involved than in the cleaning part of housekeeping, families do not harmoniously eat everything, but refuse, resist, or disparage, as well as praise.
- There is a natural hierarchy of desirable to offensive attributes of foods. Any extreme may be troublesome, such as in foods that are too fatty, greasy, spicy, rich, etc. The extremes (e.g. salty, slimy) may be enjoyed (caviar, anchovies, oysters), but go on at the periphery of what is ordinarily healthy or suited to usual tastes. Some foods are thought likely to affect anyone with their typical actions of producing burping or wind (radishes, cucumber, beans, onions), looseness (spinach, prunes), or hardness (rice). Sweet foods seem naturally easy to like.
- Individuals vary in being physiologically vulnerable, perhaps prone to weight gain or peculiarly sensitive to certain substances. Illness, skin eruptions, respiratory distress, etc., may be explained as simply idiosyncratic reactions or as allergies rooted in either psychological or social factors, or in just that kind of body.
- Taste preferences are explained at all levels – as due to some sheer physiology of the taste buds, as inherited in the genes, as socialized by ethnic context and by family practices, and as due to novel patterns of individual experiences, beliefs, and habituations.

**Table 1** Consumer Explanations

| Behavior | Explanation |
|---|---|
| Chicken liver, calves liver, I don't even prepare. | I think the whole world hates liver. |
| I used to make tongue quite a bit. | My older son said, "How can you eat tongue with your tongue?" So that was the last time we had tongue. |
| I learned to modify the wine and butter: I cook very simply now. | My husband got terrible chest pains. |
| Polish sauerkraut. He hates it. | He says the whole house stinks for weeks after you make it ... he takes after my father. They both have a queasy stomach and they hate smells. |
| All of a sudden I find myself taking a piece of cake or something, if it's yummy looking. | I don't even like it, but I've got this idea that it's going to help me bowling. It sounds silly, but that's the truth. |
| I'm the only one that likes eggplant. | You kind of have to develop a taste for it. I like all those weird vegetables. |
| They like everything. | Probably because I don't give them a choice. Even when they were little kids, I started getting them into all sorts of different vegetables because I like vegetables. |
| My daughter would not eat meat at all. | A neighbor is a vegetarian, and the woman would tell her they kill that poor little animal, how can you eat their meat? |

## Structural Relations

Food preparation, service, manners, and consumption are all used in symbolic ways. As Lévi-Strauss notes in *The Origin of Table Manners*. "Thus we can hope to discover how, in any particular society, cooking is a language through which that society unconsciously reveals its structure" (Lévi-Strauss 1978, p. 495). The participants communicate through their food behaviors, using the underlying structure both consciously and unconsciously.

The American situation is difficult to interpret in a clearcut way because the available vocabulary is so large. The food products and artifacts come from the whole globe and reflect a mixing of traditions from many societies. The possibilities for different patterns become useful in expressing cultural pride, intergenerational and assimilational conflicts, and individual peculiarities. New little myths about microwave ovens, kiwi fruit, alfalfa sprouts, and pouch cooking need to be gathered to learn the fundamental meanings they will have in the American cuisine. However, the present interviews, interpreted against a background of numerous studies of food products and attitudes, suggest how individual and familial variations draw upon the general vocabulary.

*Sex and age grading.* The roles of sex and age grading are pronounced in distinguishing between the varied suitabilities of foods and methods of preparation. We can distinguish between babies and teenagers, boys and girls, and also observe some of the dimensions at work that affect different food suitabilities.

Babies need milk and soft, mushy, undifferentiated foods. Ideas of nurturance, comfort, and easily digested nutrition go in this direction, so that similar foods are regarded as suited to the elderly and the sick. The organisms are weak and should not have strong stimulation in spiciness nor in being too hot or cold. Boys are stereotypically expected to prefer chunky peanut butter, girls the smooth, and gradually, the preference for homogenous dishes yields to mixtures and combinations. With some maturity the hamburger comes into its own as a youth food, especially appealing to teenagers. A lamb chop or salad is perhaps just right for a woman and a roast or steak for a man. Figure 2 illustrates some typical relationships of age, sex, foods, and their attributes.

**Figure 2** Age and Sex Differentiations in Foods and Their Meanings

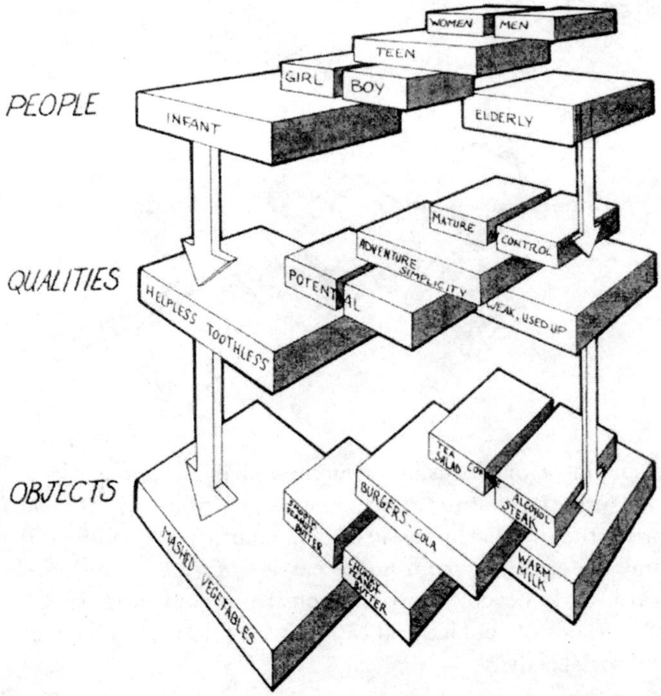


*Social status*. Along with age and sex dimensions with their varying degrees of strength and weakness, social class distinctions are pervasive. These are interwoven, thus, there is a tendency to equate higher social position with strength, maturity, and food professionalism, and lower status preferences with softness, greasiness, and sweetness. Going up the scale, conventionality of preparation fields increasingly to elaboration of methods, greater use of herbs and spices, and usage of unusual foods and ingredients. These qualities are not reserved to the upper classes, of course, but form part of the aspirations of lower status groups as well, and are emulated on special occasions. The ability to cook with appropriate sophistication and skill may be achieved through special study or left in the hands of professional chefs, and enjoyed while eating out. Figure 3 indicates a status hierarchy and some of its attributes.

**Figure 3** The Social Status Structure of Food Symbolism

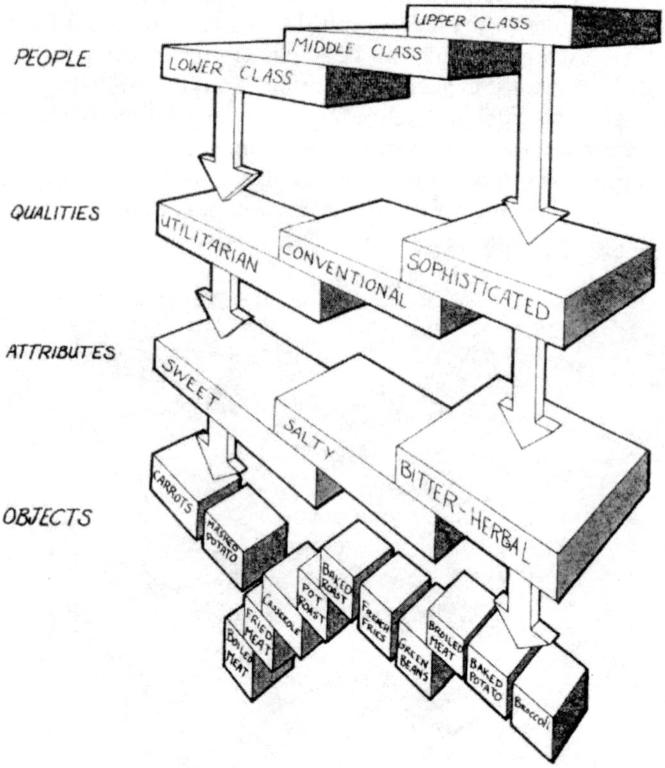


*Eating out(side).* The in-or-out locus is a structural element that speaks of conventionality and festivity, family unity and separation (Figure 4). The conventional core is the meal at home, maternal, comfortable, familiar, dependent, and routine. To eat away from home carries more exciting meanings, Outdoor, backyard, park, beach, imply freedom from conventions, return to nature, primitive methods of cooking and eating (with fingers), no manners, and lively physical and social activity.

**Figure 4** Eating at Home and Eating Out

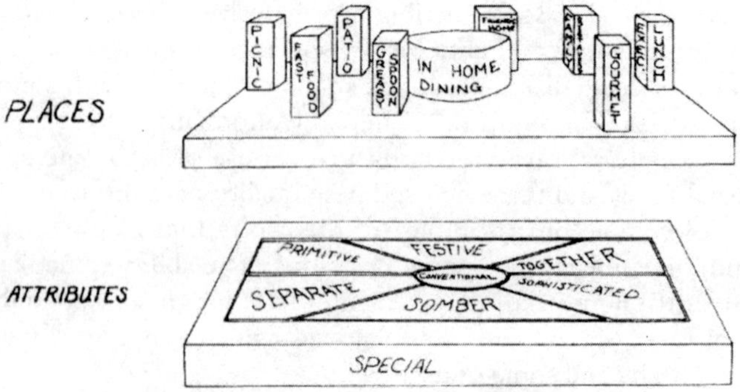

Going out to eat at another home implies some formality, dress-up, a step up in the elaboration of preparation or distinctiveness of the dishes.

The idea of going out to eat at a restaurant interacts with the meanings of the various types of establishments to fit the sex and age grading, and family status dimensions. The choices range from lower class, greasy spoons and forthright EATS cafes, through miscellaneous youthful fast food and family style restaurants, to elegant, cosmopolitan dining rooms. Moving the family unit from the home to the restaurant tends to express a festive attitude and the relaxation of parental responsibility; this attitude becomes even more pronounced for children and adds elements of separation and liberation when they go to fast food restaurants on their own. Lower class cafes and fancy restaurants are adult in meaning, places for adults at work away from home (truck stops, executive business lunches). At the heights, haute cuisine with its subtle sauces and other exotic efforts symbolizes an elite use of leisure, an extreme degree of refinement of the palate, and attendant sybaritic sensibilities. People eat dishes they never have at home and go beyond ordinary meats to expensive cuts and seafoods.

*Beyond the cooked.* Cooking is aimed at numerous objectives – making substances more chewable, more digestible, safer, warm and comforting, and more interesting to the taste. It is a process of culture, as opposed to the natural, and its degrees of status tend to be equated with distancing from the primitive and animal eating of raw food. As indicated above, these degrees of status are expressed in complexity, subtlety, particular foods, methods of preparation, and settings. Basic qualities range from an infantile, homogeneous, mushy, boiled grossness to a highly differentiated awareness of textures, ingredients, seasonings and nuances of preparation.

Little myths are dynamic and change as new experiences become available. Recently added in the raw-to-cooked dimension is a new myth of high status consumption that might be termed transcendental or self-conscious rawness. Like a kind of conspicuous underconsumption or like the French court dressing as Watteau shepherds and shepherdesses, one finds elegantly dressed partygoers eating various raw vegetables with their fingers (*crudités*), and exclaiming over their daring in eating raw hamburger *(steak tartar) or* raw fish (*sushi*). With a heightened physicality (exercising, jogging), the sophisticated return to nature goes with natural rather than processed cheeses, live bacterial processes in yogurt, yeasts, and yerba, peasant grains and dark breads. It is a retreat from over-refinement, a cycling down to rescue the effete body and restore its sexual vigor, mingled with the elite cosmopolitanism, of imported dishes.

In much of this consumer behavior there is no contradiction; rather, the social group prescribes roles and their accompanying symbols; and consumers participate by adopting the roles and symbols suited to their identities. However, animating the process are the deeper contradictions and conflicts that question whether the physical differences attributed to age and sex differences are properly fitted to the culinary and dietary differences. That is, are we preparing and eating the right things? Women should be good cooks by their maternal nature; but the highest art and science of cookery paradoxically tend to be attributed to male chefs (*pace*, Julia Child). Is hierarchy real? Are the foods, dishes, methods, and deferential service sufficient in their symholism to reassure the elite that it is truly elevated? Does eating and thinking make it so?

Perhaps even more fundamental to the little myths, given the insistent refinements of gustatory perception and the aesthetic superiorities with which mothers and elites seek to socialize the young and those of lower status, is the struggle with the basic question: Am I an animal or am I a person? How do we reconcile the animal nature of the eaters with the human culture of the cooks, the intractable fact of the body with the refinements of civilization?

## Marketing Implications

This article has been an exploration and stops with some concluding comments. It has demonstrated a qualitative approach to the study of consumer behavior, as follows:

We can enrich our understanding of consumer behavior by taking consumer protocols as stories that use a sociocultural vocabulary. The analysis blends functional-symbolic-structural logics to observe that a dietary behavior is probably not well understood in isolation or by focusing narrowly on product attributes in the way that much marketing research does. Soler reminds us of this.

> It must be placed into the context of the signs in the same area of life; together they constitute a system, and this system in turn must be seen in relation to the other systems in other areas, for the interaction of all these systems constitute the sociocultural system of a people (Solter 1979. p. 25).

**Figure 5** The Food Mythology Complex

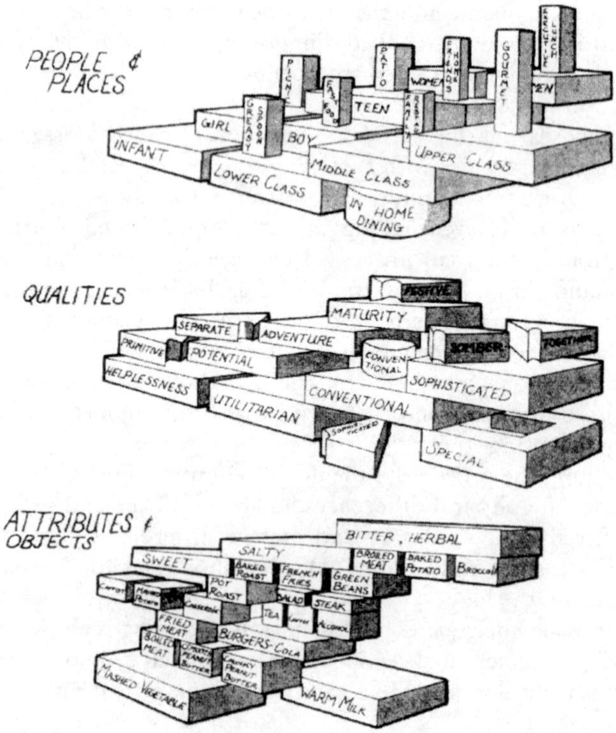

Consumer behavior in the food area uses fundamental generalizations about the meanings of products in a broadly conventional way, within which dynamic processes of individuation and differentiation go on. The little myths show how the basic vocabulary of cooking and eating is used to express identities by males and females, the young and the mature, and people in low, middle, and high status positions. General modeling by age, sex, and social status is a familiar one to marketers; here the analysis observes how specific symbolic distinctions are being made among specific foods, ways of preparing them, and in some of the ideas they represent, such as family unity/dispersion, naivete/sophistication, routine/festivity, sickness/health, grossness/subtlety, conformity/deviation, sacred/profane, etc.

Figure 5 sums up the complex structure of the food mythology. It is drawn to resemble a three-dimensional urban scene, suggesting the cultural sophistication operating to organize biological statuses, sex roles, age gradings, and social positions in terms of both psychological dimensions and food attributes such as taste, texture, appearance, and method of preparation. The marketer works within this complex, using the symbolic vocabulary to define and position the product.

The broad brush strokes indicated above may encourage further study of how families develop their particular little myths: how common cultural little myths change over time; how facts of behavior are modified in the telling; what the facts or the modified tellings are being used to say; how marketers participate in creating the symbolic vocabulary, and how they may use the consumers' mythology on behalf of their specific products and brands in their continuing dialog with consumers.

## References


Abelson. Robert P. (1976), "Script Processing in Attitude Formation and Decision Making," in *Cognition and Social Behavior*, J. Carroll and J. Payne, eds., Hilldale, NJ: Lawrence Erlbaum Associates.

Bellenger, D., Kenneth L. Bernhardt, and Jac L. Goldstucker (1976), *Qualitative Research in Marketing*, Chicago: American Marketing Association.

Bettelheim, Bruno (1977), *The Uses of Enchantment*, New York: Vintage Books.

de Gramont Sanche (1970), "There Are No Superior Societies," in *Claude Lévi-Strauss: The Anthropologist as Hero*, E. Nelson Hayes and Tanya Hayes. eds., Cambridge, MA: MIT Press, p. 3–21

Firat, A. Fuat (1978). "Social Construction of Consumption Patterns," unpublished Ph.D. dissertation, Northwestern University.

Frazer, James G. (1927), *The Golden Bough: A Study in Magic and Religion*, New York: Macmillan.

Leach, Edmund (1974). *Claude Lévi-Strauss*, New York: Viking Press.

Lévi-Strauss, Claude (1963), *Structural Anthropology, Book I*, New York: Basic Books.

– (1969) *The Raw and the Cooked*, Introduction to a Science of Mythology, 1, New York: Harper and Row.

– (1978), *The Origins of Table Manners*, Introduction to a Science of Mythology, 3, New York: Harper and Row.

Levy, Sidney J. (1978), "Hunger and Work in a Civilized Tribe," *American Behavioural Scientist*, 21 (March–April), 557–570.

Rapaport, D. (1942), "Principles Underlying Projective Techniques," *Character and Personality*, Vol. X, No, 3 (March), pp, 213–219.

Soler, Jean (1979). "The Dietary Prohibitions of the Hebrews" *New York Review of Books*, 27 (June 14), 24–25.

Williams, Daniel B. (1976), "An Information Processing Theory of Individual Purchasing Behavior," unpublished Ph.D. dissertation, Northwestern University.

# 10

# Roots of Marketing and Consumer Research at the University of Chicago

**Sidney J. Levy**

**Source:** *Consumption, Markets and Culture* 6 (2) (2003): 99–110.

I have been invited to reflect on the origins of theories of marketing and consumer research at the University of Chicago. This assignment gratifies me considerably; I enjoy remembering my student days at the University, and how I have channeled my social science education into the study of consumption. I appreciate the chance to express gratitude for my fulfilling education. In order to do that, I will engage in some intellectual autobiography and a lot of name-dropping.

## The Role of Education

I attended the University on the G.I. Bill, and after an intensive 21 months earned a Bachelor of Philosophy degree in 1946. The Ph.B. was a liberal arts degree for which I studied the Great Books when Robert Maynard Hutchins headed the University. My social science instructors in the College included Reinhard Bendix, Ernest Burgess, and Edward Shils. I remember Bendix gladly signing G.I. Bill vouchers that enabled me to buy numerous books to build a social science library. In class, we obsessed endlessly on the great issues and complexities of personal freedom and social control, with their reciprocal fears of anarchy and oppression. Shils found me to be a promising student and invited me to work with him at the graduate level. However, in my naiveté, I did not accept his invitation, as I did not appreciate his scholarly stature nor understand what a great opportunity it would have been. But his influence remains; I recently re-read his essays collected under the title of *The Virtue of Civility* (Shils 1997).

Also, fatefully enough, I had become acquainted with three doctoral students whom Carl R. Rogers had brought with him from Ohio State University to establish the Counseling Center at the University of Chicago. These students – Arthur Assum, Natalie Reader, and William Thetford – were enrolled in the Committee on Human Development. We four became close friends. We studied together; I helped them with their teaching assistant duties; and I worked as a typist at the Counseling Center, transcribing recordings of interviewing sessions of non-directive therapy. I did a study with Assum and published a paper comparing the academic ability and achievement of counseled students with non-counseled students (Levy and Assum 1947). Assum drifted away; Natalie married Morris Haimowitz. They went on to specialize in group psychotherapy and we stayed friends in Evanston for many years. Until he died several years ago, Thetford was the closest friend I ever had (other than Bobette Adler, my wife of 47 years). Bill Thetford and I shared an apartment where I learned about his work with Mandel Sherman studying the effects of stress and with Samuel Beck studying the Rorschach Test. Bill went on to become the founding guru of a psycho-religious cult, *A Course in Miracles* (Thetford 1975), that has gained many adherents.

I signed on as a graduate student with the interdisciplinary Committee on Human Development where I gained an M.A. in 1948, writing a master's thesis under Carl Roger's direction that combined the use of his non-directive approach as a research method with Robert Havighurst's concept of developmental tasks (Levy, 1949). The perspectives I derived in the late 1940s came mainly from the topics and methods of the behavioral sciences that were the fashion of the period. More of my teachers were outstanding figures in the behavioral sciences. I studied with or was exposed to the thinking of Robert Redfield, W. Lloyd Warner, Everett Hughes, Herbert Blumer, David Reisman, Allison Davis, William E. Henry, Don Campbell, and others. In a seminar with Lloyd Warner, presciently titled The Web of Life, I became imbued with Warner's views on symbolism and on social stratification; and Erving Goffman presented his dissertation research. Bill Henry (1956) launched me into the study of the Thematic Apperception Technique; and I subsequently became expert in applying it to personality evaluation and did so for numerous organizations (Levy and Moore 1951; Levy 1963). J.L. Moreno, a founder of sociometrics, visited and demonstrated sociodrama; and sociometric analysis formed an important part of my dissertation on the psychodynamics of interpersonal relations (Levy 1956). I also used a multi-method approach, as Don Campbell famously endorsed. Bill Henry was my dissertation chair; Bernice Neugarten and Robert Hess were members of my committee.

The so-called "Second Chicago School" of sociology was flourishing (Fine 1995) and my home base, The Committee on Human Development, provided a multi-disciplinary and eclectic education. I learned about Everett Rogers and Leon Festinger, about diffusion, social influence, and cognitive dissonance. I had a course with the fearsome Bruno Bettelheim. I leamed early about smart women professors, such as Carolyn Tryon, Helen Koch, and Bernice Neugarten; and later Helena Lopata. Among my fellow students and friends were Herbert Gans, Anselm Strauss, Marc Swartz, Ben Wright, Gerald Handel, Lee Rainwater, and Erving Goffman. There was great intellectual stimulation as we argued over philosophies, subject matter, methods, and even attitudes toward how to live. Erving Goffman and Schuyler Choate were friends who lived together not far from my Hyde Park basement apartment. One evening in the Spring of 1953, Bobette and I visited them, and while Schuyler and Bobette were in the kitchen (traditionally enough), I told Erving that Bobette and I had become engaged to be married. Such a bourgeois notion entertained Erving who laughingly exclaimed, "Oh, Sidney, cut the shit!"

## Working at Social Research, Inc.

After completing my master's degree and the required course work for my doctorate, I slowed my academic pace. I had to earn money to pay for my six years in psychoanalysis, so in 1948 I applied for part-time work with Social Research, Inc. (SRI). I had heard that it was a local consulting company (conveniently housed then in the Hyde Park Bank building) that had been created in 1946 by Lloyd Warner and Bill Henry, along with Burleigh B. Gardner of the Industrial Relations group. Gardner, who was known for the pioneering work reported in his *Human Relations in Industry* (1945), managed the company along with Earl Kahn. The company was branching out from organizational consulting to studying consumer behavior. Harriett Bruce Moore and Lee Rainwater, who joined us in 1950, and I were soon immersed in analyzing projective tests of managerial personnel for some companies, and interpreting consumer reactions to products and marketing communications for an array of advertising agencies and their clients. (For more details about Social Research, Inc, see Michael Karesh's recent paper (1995).)

The next ten years were among the most exciting and intensely absorbing in my life. We lived SRI from breakfast until bedtime, brooding over methods of data-gathering and seeking penetrating insights. Despite economic ups and downs, SRI grew and in a short while included Lee Rainwater, Ira O. Glick, Richard P. Coleman, and Gerald Handel in our core intellectual group, and other important individuals who worked with us for various periods and projects, whose names are too many for me to list. Shirley Greene and Albert Robles worked especially closely with me in carrying out research projects, Bobette, my wife, a graduate of the Social Service Administration department, psychiatrically trained, and an astute researcher, was always there to help in a pinch.

Almost all of our research was custom designed, with instruments created to study the qualitative kinds of problems in which we came to specialize. The basic approach was the so called depth interview, a free-style conversational method in which interviewers encouraged respondents to talk fully and to express themselves freely. Within this more or less non-directive approach, we embedded various projective devices (Levy 1985). These were variants on the clinical techniques available at the time, such as the TAT, the Rorschach, Sentence Completion, Word Association, Draw-A-Person, and even the curious Szondi test (Rainwater 1956). We invented devices such as matching people, animals, cars; pictorial symbols, and soliciting dreams (Levy 1995). We took pictures of people's houses and living rooms, we sent interviewers to spend whole days observing and making detailed notes on what the respondents did. Essentially, we engaged in accumulating case studies, personal histories, and ethnographies. We also conducted group interviews before they came to be called focus groups.

Using Warner's Index of Status Characteristics (Warner *et al.* 1949), we classified all our respondents, so we could examine the role of social class in its effects on consumer behavior (Levy 1966). We studied social status positions in detail: for example, *Workingman's Wife* by Lee Rainwater, Richard P. Coleman, and Gerald Handel (1959) was based on studies of readers of true romance publications for Macfadden-Bartell Corporation. We taught our clients about social stratification and the structure of American society, the relations between the Evaluated Participation that identifies an individual's social class position and the Index of Status Characteristics by which we measured it. At times along the way, I sought to apply my interdisciplinary training in a deliberate manner. I wrote one article to show the use of sociological concepts ("Social Class and Consumer Behavior," Levy 1966), another arguing for the psychological perspective ("Mammon and Psyche," Levy 1968), and another to show the relevance of anthropological study ("Hunger and Work in a Civilized Tribe," Levy 1978).

## The Brand Image

With the constant inflow of interviews on a diversity of topics, we learned a lot about American culture, social life, social change, the role of media and advertising, the nature of consumption, kinds of consumers, and perceptions of products and brands. As social scientists we were not content just to write proprietary research reports for our clients. We thought about the larger implications of our specific research projects, published several books and numerous articles, and made presentations at professional conferences. One concept that emerged from our work was that of *the brand image*. In my schoolwork I had learned about body image from Paul Schilder (1950). More significantly, I remembered William James (1892) writing as follows;

> A man's Social Self is the recognition which he gets from his mates ... Properly speaking, a man has as many social selves as there are individuals who recognize him and carry an image of him in their mind. But as the individuals who carry the images fall differently into classes we may practically say that there are as many different social selves as there are distinct groups of persons about whose opinion he cares. (James 1892: 180)

At SRI we saw that this same idea was true for organizations, their products, and their brands, and the notion of imagery is a marketing apperception came to the fore in our interpretation of these phenomena. Consequently, (with Burleigh Gardner) I wrote "The Product and the Brand," for the *Harvard Business Review* (1955) explaining that each product or brand exists in people's minds as a symbolic entity, an integrated resultant of all their experiences with it in the marketplace. This idea also reflected my college study of Plato's idealized forms. One resulting notion, then, of an advertisement being not an isolated communication but "an investment in the long run reputation of the brand," was seized upon by the advertising community and, if I may immodestly – or guiltily – say so, the brand image idea subsequently swept the world, becoming part of the lingua franca of modern times.

## Symbolic Analysis

The brand image was also a vehicle for spreading the notion of symbolic analysis. My own interest in symbolism was inspired from childhood by reading of folk tales, fairy tales, mythology, and James Frazer; and furthered by later encountering the work of Alfred Korzybski, S.I. Hayakawa, George Herbert Mead, Sigmund Freud, Carl Jung, and through my own psychoanalysis. This interest was reinforced by Lloyd Warner's work on symbol systems (1959), the symbolic interactionists at the University of Chicago, and the application of symbolic analysis to the protocols of projective methods. At SRI, we came to regard almost all of our consumer studies as exercises in the interpretation of symbols. This activity is exemplified in the series of studies, carried out in the early1950s on behalf of *The Chicago Tribune*, that Pierre D. Martineau (1957) provided to potential advertisers in several industries, where they were usually the first of their kind:

- *Cigarettes: Their Role and Function* analyzed the physical, psychological, sociological, and cultural significance of cigarettes and smoking. Smoking was described as an activity that symbolized the smoker's virility and potency.
- *Motivations Relating to Soaps and Chemical Detergents* analyzed how these products assisted housewives in coping with and controlling the negative aspects of their social role.
- *Automobiles: What They Mean to Americans* explored the highly ramified significance of the automobile in people's lives as all extension of the self, in terms of its practical use, economic value, social status symbolism, psychological motives, and perceptions of the cars' images,

Ira O. Glick and I wrote *Living with Television* (1962), based on several studies of television shows and their audiences, conducted for the Campbell-Ewald advertising agency of Detroit. In its Foreword, Warner described it as a "contribution to our body of knowledge about the meanings and function of the symbol systems commonly shared by most Americans." This volume built on Warner and Henry's (1948) study, *The Radio Day Time Serial: A Symbolic Analysis*. We did the first qualitative study for the Coca-Cola company on why people drink soft drinks, the first qualitative study for AT&T on the meaning of the telephone. For the Wrigley Company we studied what baseball meant to Cubs fans. A study for FTD, the flower delivery system, analyzed the poignancy of flowers as symbolic of the life cycle, representing and celebrating its beauty, its fragility, and the inevitability of death. With all this kind of work in mind, in 1959 I wrote the article "Symbols for Sale." In May 2000, the American Marketing Association and the University of Illinois named me a recipient of the Converse Award in recognition of that article's original and enduring contribution to the discipline of marketing.

## Broadening the Concept of Marketing

Another idea that grew out of the work of SRI came to be called *the broadening concept*. SRI had many clients that were major organizations. We engaged in executing innovative qualitative marketing rescarch for corporations, hospitals, schools, banks, politicians, and government agencies, From this breadth and variety of work it became evident to me that marketing was a function of all individuals and organizations. Therefore, I later wrote (with Philip Kotler) an article making that point, called "Broadening the Concept of Marketing," that appeared in the *Journal of Marketing* (1969). Awareness of this idea spread among marcologists, a term I suggested (Levy 1976) to distinguish marketing scholars from marketing practitioners. Our article led to the broadening title being given to the 1970 American Marketing Association Summer Educators' Conference, and has since continued to foster the diffusion of the marketing concept into the management of non-business fields of education, health, government, and the arts. One, of my personal favorites is an article I wrote for the volume *Marketing the Arts* (1980), "Arts Consumers and Aesthetic Attributes." The broadening idea created a stir. It was criticized by some people as obvious, wrongheaded, and even as evil. One piece (Laczniak and Michie 1979) in the *Journal of the Academy of Marketing Science* accused us of creating social disorder by distorting the definition of marketing.

## Battles of Intellect, Philosophy, and Morality

This reaction was another manifestation of the perpetual struggle between individual freedom and social control, and of resistance to change. From the beginnings of Social Research, Inc., we ran into a lot of flak. The commercial application of qualitative research came to be called motivation research, a term I suggested to Pierre Martineau (1957) to help him distinguish our work from traditional surveying and its preoccupation with measurement. Opponents at the time flailed around, characterized it as the work of the devil or as a Freudian aberration.

After the 1950s motivation research was said to have died. But of course it continued to grow as qualitative research. The receptivity to qualitative research by business offends people who despise business and those who study consumers on its behalf. Morris Holbrook (1995) regards such consultants as obsequious dogs (p. 303). In one Great Book, *The Theory of the Leisure Class*, that pioneering study of consumption, Thorstein Veblen (1899) commented that "knowledge of latter-day men and things is ... 'lower,' 'base,' 'ignoble,' – one even hears the epithet 'sub-human,' applied to this matter-of-fact knowledge of mankind and of everyday life" (p. 391), To this day, many academic disciplinary purists hold themselves aloof. While some have an awakened interest in studying consumers, they commonly ignore the work reported in the marketing and consumer research journals, sometimes as a result busying themselves with reinventing the wheel.

Of course, reinventing the wheel is a common occurrence. Regardless of the long history I am describing here, it is a sign of the irregular situation of qualitative research that examples of its application still turn up in the press as if it were some remarkable newcomer. Recently, *The Wall Street Journal* (1999) reported Chrysler's "first vehicle designed entirely through an unconventional market-research process known as 'archetype research' (Ah, Carl Jung!) ... overseen by a ... French-born medical anthropologist named G. Clotaire Rapaille..." The research involved poring over focus group protocols in which participants were asked to drift back to their childhoods and jot down the memories invoked by the prototype of the vehicle. A project about Procter and Gamble's Folgers Coffee was also mentioned in which "Rapaille concluded that aroma sells coffee more than taste does because aroma invokes feelings of home." If this was news to P&G, perhaps the "unconventionality" and ever-renewed sense of novelty about qualitative research is due to the persisting naiveté and capacity for astonishment of corporate personnel.

Other fundamental intellectual battles continue. One of them goes on between the partisans of nomothetic approaches and the partisans of idiographic study. Gary Fine (1995) gives an account of this struggle at Chicago, describing the conflict between the advocates of measurement and those committed to the prewar (WWII) emphasis upon qualitative methods and field research methodologies, with the later resisting the incoming proponents of quantitative methods. He notes that Herhert Blumer criticized "those who were attempting to achieve exactitude in social science at the price of direct and naturalistic study" (1995: 145), and cites David Reisman's recollection that

> [T]he enmity was a problem for graduate students who worked with Hughes and with me, as well as for nontenured colleagues, particularly with Nelson Foote and Anselm Strauss ... unrealistically, if understandably, translating acidulous comments by faculty members into actual prescriptions of what would pass muster, some able graduate students feared to write a dissertation without tables in it ... I sometimes had the dismal experience of having as a doctoral candidate someone who had been a spirited undergraduate and watching that person become more timid and less original as time went by. (Reisman, in Berger 1990: 63)

More than 50 years after that statement, when I recently ran a university workshop on qualitative research, one of the doctoral students responded with this fretful statement:

> I suppose what I mean is that there has to be a certain consistency in epistemology, ontological assumptions, and the use of techniques of data collection and presentation. Why do we have to constantly justify the use of certain techniques and why do we willingly or unwillingly participate in perpetuating the dominance of a particular discourse of doing research; in other words, why are we ashamed to be purely qualitative, just as we are not ashamed to be purely quantitative? I find that I am constantly grappling with this in my own

research, and would like to find a way of dealing with this issue, so that we can have other ways of collecting, analyzing, and presenting data.

I marvel at the persistence of this contentiousness, and the lack of scientific objectivity about different methods shown by so many academicians with doctorates to their names. These remarks are true for fields other than marketing: a professor of finance recently raved in my presence that he hated the behavioral people he asserted were ruining his field. Generally, the dominant paradigm people resist, show hostility, and at many schools refuse to hire any faculty who are qualitatively oriented. They behave defensively, foolishly acting as though their livelihoods are jeopardized by the projective techniques and ethnographies that they imagine will replace their surveys, regressions, and multivariate methods. At the 1998 conference of the Association for Consumer Research, such persons complained that qualitative researchers were taking over the conference.

However, the ebb and flow of intellectual conflict is an ordinary thing, in the nature of science, and is a requirement for ideas to demonstrate their viability. It does not afflict only qualitative consumer researchers. Historians who pursue the ancient tradition of qualitative study of the past sputtered and fumed when the cliometricians arrived with their threatening statistical techniques for measuring history and their use of tables as well as tales. In a volume about *Marketing, Society, and Conflict*, written with Gerald Zaltman (Levy and Zaltman 1975), I noted that conflict in and about marketing is pervasive and essential, to its nature.

Social scientists also have diverse preferences for the kinds of explanations they seek. Emile Durkheim, the paradigmatic sociologist, made a strong and explicit case for social causation in his brilliant study of suicide (1951). Although he shows great sensitivity to the psychological sititation of the individuals who take their own lives, his goal is sociological, that is, "to state precisely what the social element of suicide consists of" (p. 52). He meticulously teases out the influence on suicide rates of membership in social groups defined by religion, gender, age, marital and economic status, in attempting to establish laws of general ocurrence, the way individuals are dominated by collective reality to produce non-random results. Other scientists (biologists, psychologists, etc.) seek to explain the way individuals resist or succumb to the force of the collective reality. At Social Research, Inc., we avoided these territorial divisions and tried to blend the social and psychological approaches and the different methodologies they employed.

## Choice Versus Restraint

There is another perpetual conflict that goes on between those who foster the proliferation of choices in the marketplace and those would reduce or more austerely rationalize consumption. Early in the last century, social critics, social workers, moralists, and home economists fussed about the deleterious effects on

American families of having more money, and wasting it on "theaters, amusement parks, nickelodeons, and resorts" (Horowitz 1985: 76), and then hoped that the rigors of World War II might bring back traditional morality and sensible frugality. As it happened, the post-war period saw instead the flowering of the Consumer Revolution. With the industrial capacity and skills that had been created the great accumulation of capital and personal prosperity joined with the pent-up demand for consumer goods and the desires for liberated forms of self-expression. The impact of increasing education, contraception, sexual freedom, feminism, and the assertion of civil rights became more pronounced. The critics remained, offering their negative depictions of contemporary life. David Riesman (1950) regretted the rise of other-directedness in *The Lonely Crowd*, John Galbraith, in *The Affluent Society* (1958), lamented the squirrel-caged character of consumers being motivated by advertising rather than by the public good. And Vance Packard (1957) viewed with alarm *The Hidden Persuaders*, who were corrupting consumers with their insidious analyses and advertising subtleties.

## Value-Laden Social Science

At the same time, scholars of the social scientific disciplines came to study the family in a less visibly moralistic and critical fashion, seeming to seek a more objective understanding of how and why consumers behaved. In 1954 and 1955, New York University Press published two volumes titled *Consumer Behavior*, edited by Lincoln H. Clark. Volume I had the subtitle "The Dynamics of Consumer Reaction," and Volume II, "The Life Cycle and Consumer Behavior." These volumes reported the proceedings of programs sponsored by the Committee for Research on Consumer Attitudes and Behavior, and contain several thoughtful and seminal articles by a diversity of contributors from the professions of economics, sociology, and psychology. Actually, only the editor, Clark, was a professor of marketing. Nelson N. Foote (1954), a University of Chicago sociologist, wrote on "The Autonomy of the Consumer," pointing to the economic background for changes in American culture: "a nationwide multiplication of middle-income farnilies, a correlative shrinking of upper and lower income groups, a substantial rise in real income every year, and, as a result, a mounting ratio of discretionary income" (1954: 15). He saw growing opportunities for consumers to make choices and to show their self-determination. On the other hand, William H. Whyte, Jr (1954), another Chicago sociologist, wrote on "The Consumer in the New Suburbia," with emphasis on the conformity he saw among the residents of the famous suburban development in Park Forest, Illinois.

The thematic and evaluative differences apparent between Foote and Whyte are persistant and general. There are those partisans who see an expansive marketplace that has created a remarkable modern era of prosperity with a wide array of goods, services, experiences, and ideas that enables more consumers than ever to make choices and create the kinds of lifestyles they prefer. Then there are those critics who deplore the effects of an expansive marketplace that creates mass markets of consumers whose choices they see as illusory, whom they perceive being manipulated into conforming modes of consumption by overwhelming capitalistic corporate powers. The critiques of modern urban and suburban life as harried, time-deprived, and obsessed with consuming, in an excess of market choices, radiate in many directions to include the depravity of the entertainment media with their preoccupation with sex and violence, a general decline in morality, and a collapse of family life. For a while it seemed that cocooning might save us, keeping the family cozily ensconced at home, even if self-absorbed and faithfully eating popcorn in front of the television set, the VCR, and the computer. A perceived growing desire for a simpler life is probably exaggerated or is urged upon us by those who claimed to be living it (although one wonders how primitive their homes actually are, how they acquire their clothes, and what cars they drive). The old remedies are again offered lately by *Voluntary Simplicity: Toward a Way of Life That is Outwardly Simple, Inwardly Rich* by Duane Elgin (1993) and Juliet B. Schor's *The Overspent American: Upscaling, Downshifting, and the New Consumer* (1999), while consumer debt increases astronomically.

Modern doomsayers are no more likely to be correct than they were in the Renaissance, the Enlightenment, and the early days of the twentieth century. Intellectual elites appear to resent it or begrudge when large masses of people are able to improve their circumstances by having more to eat, the ability to travel, and the freedom to live as they please. The various positions taken on the virtue or vice of consumption are age-old. David Hume, in his *Essays and Treatises on Several Subjects* (1764) that I studied in the College, describes four philosophical postures that naturally form themselves in the world and entertain different ideas of human life and of happiness. He describes the Epicurean, the man of elegance and pleasure, who justifies living in the present and finding happiness in the pursuit of sensuous enjoyment, and ever new stimulation. The Stoic is the man of action and virtue to whom the most urgent need is to be industrious, to find that we should "but taste the sweets of honest labour" (p. 169) and worthy social actions. He looks with contempt on all the allurements of pleasure, seeing virtue as its own reward as well as the path to fame. The Platonist is the man of contemplation and philosophical devotion. He is surprised at how people differ in their use of the same faculties, ignobly and insatiably, seeking pleasure or public applause, when it is evident that the highest good is the contemplation of the most perfect object. That can be most perfectly done in another state of existence, worshiping our maker through eternity. However, the Sceptic entertains a suspicion that philosophers on all subjects "confine too much their principles, and make no account of that vast variety, which nature has so much affected in all her operation" (p. 181). Hume shows his greatest sympathy with this relativist view, one that post-modern researchers hold at the core of their thinking. These ideal typcs still exist, acting out and recommending the motives of their exemplars.

The dialog among proponents of these philosophies and their attitudes toward consumption by families continues apace in all their contemporary guises. Joanne B. Ciulla (2000) sees the workplace as demanding too much in time, energy, and motivation, and recommends contemplative rather than material values. Brian C. Robertson (2000) also blames the workplace for being too engrossing and feminism as well for resulting in a systematic devaluation of home life, leading to social pathology in children raised without full-time parents. In the March 2000 issue of the *Journal of Consumer Research*, Albert Borgmann ruminates on these matters, casting them in a modern vocabulary, but playing the same old tunes. He seems to believe in a utopian time when there was a higher Platonic general command of science, literature, politics, and economics, which seems all unlikely nostalgia, given that such versions of "our mental lives" have never been common. He is judicious, willing to tolerate a high degree of epicurean pleasure but wishing it balanced with greater stoic exertion, despite those who say we are working too hard.

Modern household politics take advantage of technology, of liberating philosophies and theories, and access to an opulence of goods and services, and show general indifference to the Platonic and Stoic utopias that never were or ever will be. Jeremy Rifkin in *The Age of Access* (2000) sees the dangers of capitalism as so commodifying time and human relationships that the culture will be mined to exhaustion, drained of meaning, and our civilization destroyed. Consumers do exhibit a general desire to be judicious about allocations and decisions in their household policies, and show their goodwill by recycling materials and by supporting efforts to sustain and improve the environment, while they continue avidly to consume and stuff the landfills with refuse. No doubt, as humans and animals, we will continue to be both productive and wasteful, and as scholars, observe ourselves doing it.

## References

Berger, Bennett (ed.) (1990). *Authors of Their Own Lives: Intellectul Autobiographies by Twenty American Sociologists* (University of California Press, Berkeley, CA).

Borgmann, Albert (2000). The moral complexion of consumption, *Journal of Consumer Research*, 26 (March), 418–422.

Ciulla, Joanne B. (2000). *The Working Life* (Times Books, New York).

Clark, L.H. (ed.) (1954). *Consumer Behavior*, Vol. I (New York University Press, New York).

Clark, L.H. (ed.) (1955). *Consumer Behavior*, Vol. II (New York University Press, New York).

Durkheim, Emile (1951). *Suicide* (The Free Press, New York).

Elgin, Duane (1993). *Voluntary Simplicity: Toward a Way of Life that is Outwardly Simple, Inwardly Rich* (Quill, New York).

Fine, G.A. (1995). *A Second Chicago School*? (University of Chicago Press, Chicago, IL).

Foote, Nelson N. (1954). The autonomy of the consumer, In: Clark, Lincoln H., ed., *Consumer Behavior*, Vol. I (New York University Press, New York), pp. 15–24.

Galbraith, John K. (1958). *The Affluent Society* (Houghton Mifflin, Boston, MA).

Gardner, Burleigh B. (1945). *Human Relations in Industry* (Richard R Irwin, Homewood, IL).

Gardner, Burleigh B. and Levy, Sidney J. (1955). The product and the brand, *Harvard Business Review*, 33(March–April), 33–39 and in Levy (1999).

Glick, Ira O. and Levy, Sidney J. (1962). *Living with Television* (Aldine, Chicago, IL).

Henry, William F. (1956). *The Analysis of Fantasy* (John Wiley and Sons, New York).

Holbrook, Morris B. (1995). *Consumer Research* (Sage Publications, Thousand Oaks, CA).

Horowitz, Daniel (1985). *The Morality of Spending* (Ivan R. Dee, Chicago, IL).

Hume, David (1764). *Essays and Treaties on Several Subjects*, Vol. I (Millar, Kincaid and Donaldson, London).

James, William (1892). *Psychology* (Henry Holt, New York).

Karesh, Michael A. (1995). The social scientific origins of symbolic consumer research: Social Research, Inc., Master's Paper, Department of Sociology, University of Chicago.

Laczniak, G.R. and Michie, D.A. (1979). The social disorder of the broadened concept of marketing, *Journal of American Academy Marketing Science*, 7(3) (Summer), 214–232.

Levy, Sidney J. (1949). Non-directive techniques in the study of developmental tasks of adolescence, *School Review* (May–June).

Levy, Sidney J. (1956). A study in psychodynamics of interpersonal relations, Doctoral dissertation, University of Chicago.

Levy, Sidney J. (1959). Symbols for sale, *Harvard Business Review*, 37 (July-August), 117–124, and in Levy (1999).

Levy, Sidney J. (1963). Thematic assessment of executives, *California Management Review*, V(4) (Summer), 3–8.

Levy, Sidney J. (1996). Social class and consumer behavior, In: Newman, J., ed., *On Knowing the Consumer* (John Wiley and Sons, New York), pp. 146–160, and in Levy (1999).

Levy, Sidney J. (1968). Mammon and Psyche, In: Sommers, M.S. and Kernan, J.B., eds, *Explorations in Consumer Behavior* (University of Texas, Austin, TX), pp, 119–134.

Levy, Sidney J. (1976). Marcology 101, or the domain of marketing, In: Bernhardt, K. L., ed., *Marketing: 1776–1976 and Beyond* (American Marketing Association, Chicago, IL), pp. 577–581, and in Levy (1999).

Levy, Sidney J. (1978). Hunger and work in a civilized tribe: Or, the anthropology of market transactions, *American Behavioral Scientist*, 21(4) (March/April), 557–570, and in Levy (1999).

Levy, Sidney J. (1980). Arts consumers and aesthetic attributes, In: Mokwa, Michale P., Dawson, William M. and Prieve, E. Arthur, eds, *Marketing the Arts* (Praeger, New York), pp. 29–46, and in Levy (1999).

Levy, Sidney J. (1985). Dreams, fairy tales, animals, and cars, *Psychology and Marketing*, 2(2), 67–81, and in Levy (1999).

Levy, Sidney J. (1999). *Brands, Consumers, Symbols, and Research*, ed. Dennis W. Rook (Sage Publications, Inc., Thousand Oaks, CA).

Levy, Sidney J. and Assum, Arthur (1947). A comparative study of the academic ability and achievement of two groups of college students, *Journal of Educational Psychology*, 38 (May), 46–50.

Levy, Sidney J. and Kotler, Philip (1969). Broadening the concept of marketing, *Journal of Marketing*, 33 (July), 10–15, and in Levy (1999).

Levy, Sidney J, and Moore, Harriett Bruce (1951). Artful contrivers: a study of engineers, *Personnel, September*, 12–14.

Levy, Sidney J. and Zaltman, Gerald (1975). *Marketing, Society, and Conflict* (Prentice-Hall, Englewood Cliffs, NJ).

Martineau, Pierre (1957). *Motivation in Advertising* (McGraw-Hill, New York).

Packard, Vance (1957). *The Hidden Persuaders* (Pocket Books, New York).

Rainwater, Lee (1956). *A Study of Personality Differences Between Middle and Lower Class Adolescents: The Szondi Test in Culture-Personality Research*, Genetic Psychology Monographs, 54, 3–86.

Rainwater, Lee, Coleman, Richard P, and Handel, Gerald (1959). *Workingman's Wife* (Oceana, New York),

Riesman, David (1950). *The Lonely Crowd* (Yale, University Press, New Haven, CT).

Rifkin, Jeremy (2000). *The Age of Access* (Tarcher/Putnam, New York).

Robertson, Brian C. (2000). *There's No Place Like Work* (Spence Publishing, New York).

Schilder, Paul (1950). *The Image and Appearance of the Human Body* (International Universities Press, New York),

Schor, Juliet B. (1999). *The Overspent American: Upscaling, Downshifting, and the New Consumer* (Harper, New York).

Shils, Edward (1997). *The Virtue of Civility* (Liberty Fund, Indianapolis, IN).
Thetford, William N. (1975). *A Course in Miracles* (Foundation for Inner Peace, New York).
Veblen, Thorstein (1899) *The Theory of the Leisure Class* (The Viking Press, New York).
*Wall Street Journal* (1999). But how does it make you feel? (3 May), BI.
Warner, W. Lloyd (1959). *The Living and the Dead: A Study of the Symbolic Life of Americans* (Yale, University Press, New Haven, CT).
Warner, W.L., and Henry W.E. (1948). *The Radio Day Time Serial: A Symbolic Analysis*, Genetic Psychology Monographs, 37, 3–7
Warner, W.L., Meeker, M., and Bells, K. (1949). *Social Class in America* (Science Research Associates, Chicago, IL).
Whyte, William H,, Jr, (1954). The consumer in the new suburbia, In Clark, Lincoln H., ed., *Consumer Behavior* (New York University Press, New York), pp. 1-14.

## Related readings

Ariés, Phillipe and Duby, Georges (gen. eds) (1989). *A History of Private Life: Passions of the Renaissance*, Vol. III (Harvard University Press, Cambridge, MA),
Brown. S. (1999). Marketing and literature: the anxiety of academic influence, *Journal of Marketing*, 63 (January) 1–15.
Burgess, Ernest and Locke, Harvey J. (1960). *The Family*, 2nd edn (American Book Co., New York).
Chartier, Roger (ed.) (1989). *A History of Private Life: Passions of the Renaissance*, Vol. III (Harvard University Press, Cambridge, MA),
Cohen, J. B. (ed.) (1972). *Behavioral Science Foundations of Consumer Behavior* (The Free Press, New York)
Foote, Nelson N. (ed.) (1961). *Household Decision-Making* (New York University Press, New York).
Handel, Gerald (1967). Psychological study of whole families, In: Handel, Gerald, ed., *The Psychosocial Interior of the Family* (Aldine, Chicago, IL), pp, 517–546.
Hess, Robert D. and Handel, Gerald (1959). *Family Worlds: A Psychosocial Approach to Family Life* (University of Chicago Press, Chicago, IL).
Kassarjian, H.H. (1994). Scholarly traditions and European roots of American consumer research, In: Laurent, G., Lilien, Gary L. and Pras, Bernard, eds, *Research Traditions in Marketing* (Kluwer Academic Publishers, Boston, MA), pp, 265–179.
Klapper, J.T. (1960). *The Effects of Mass Communication* (The Free Press, New York).
Levy, Sidney J. (1957). The cake eaters, Speech to the Association of Canadian Advertisers, Toronto, May, and in Levy (1999).
Levy, Sidney J. (1963) Symbolism and life style, In: Greyser, S., ed., *Proceedings, American Marketing Association* (December), pp, 140–150, and in Levy (1999).
Levy, Sidney J. (1967). Psychosocial reactions to the abundent society. Speech to the Allied Social Sciences Associations, Washington, DC, December, and in Levy (1999).
Levy, Sidney J. (1970). The discretionary society, Speech to the American Marketing Association, Boston, August, and in Levy (1999).
Levy, Sidney J. (1991). President's column: a brief history, *Association for Consumer Research Newsletter* (March), pp. 2–6.
Levy, Sidney J. (1994). Commentary by Sidney J. Levy, In: Laurent, G., Lilien, Gary L. and Pras, Bernard. eds, *Research Traditions in Marketing* (Kluwer Academic Publishers, Boston, MA), pp. 283–287.
Levy, Sidney J. (1996). Stalking the Amphisbaena, *Journal of Consumer Research*, 23(3) (December), 163–176, and in Levy (1999).
Rainwater, Lee. (1974). *What Money Buys: Inequality and the Social Meanings of Income* (Basic Books, New York).

# 11

# Consumer Research and Semiotics: Exploring the Morphology of Signs, Symbols, and Significance

**David Glen Mick**

**Source:** *Journal of Consumer Research* 13 (1986): 196–213.

The consumer world is a web of meanings among consumers and marketers woven from signs and symbols ensconced in their cultural space and time. Authors who have theorized about communication in general, and the formation and use of symbols in particular, have argued that this ability is the central and differentiating characteristic of the human species – "the peculiarity and the glory of man" (Boulding 1956, p. 44).

Today's research on symbolism and consumer behavior has been cultivated from such seminal articles as Gardner and Levy's "The Product and the Brand" (1955), Levy's "Symbols for Sale" (1959), and Levitt's "The Morality (?) of Advertising" (1970), and derives from works by Goffman (1959, 1979), Hall and Trager (1953), Henry (1956), Newman (1957a, 1957b), Veblen (1899), Warner (1953), and Warner and Lunt (1941). Recent research has fostered multiple viewpoints on symbolism and a deepening appreciation for its province in the marketplace and in the lives of consumers. The preeminent scholar and spokesman on the importance of symbolism in consumer behavior has been Sidney Levy (1959, 1971, 1978, 1981, 1982). Lately, Russell Belk has become a major voice as well (1976; Belk, Bahn, and Mayer 1982; Belk, Mayer, and Driscoll 1984).

Despite the increasing attention paid to symbolism in the marketplace and consumer life, the field so far lacks a solid theoretical base and is mired in inherently descriptive research (Hirschman 1981 and Holman 1980a have made similar claims). Levy has lamented (1971, p. 113):

> It is hard to keep thinking about the symbolic meaning of objects and behavior. To do so requires practice in adopting a view of actions that is sufficiently detached to permit analysis and interpretation, and sufficiently empathetic to produce insights. It is usually simpler to deal with the objects and behaviors themselves.

Holman (1981b) has concluded that notwithstanding the volume of research on products as communication vehicles, no theory *per se* has been specified. Belk, Bahn, and Mayer (1982) and Ward (1974), making analogous statements about the evolution of consumption symbolism in children, have called for increased theory building and research in the area. Likewise, Holbrook and Hirschman (1982) have charged that the prevalent information-processing theory has failed to address significant consumption phenomena like leisure activities, fantasies, and emotional responses that are replete with symbolic meaning.

To date, few symbolism researchers in the consumer behavior field have acknowledged and integrated the semiotic doctrine that focuses on the morphology of signs, symbols, and meaning. This article contends that through its distinctive and wide-ranging literature, semiotics can advance theory development and substantiate expanded methodologies for symbolism research from acquisition and consumption to disposition behaviors. This article sketches the history of semiotics, discusses semiotic approaches to symbolism research, and presents the implications of semiotics for consumer behavior theory and research.

## Semiotics: Origins and Evolution

The roots of semiotics trail back at least as far as the pre-Socratic era, where Hippocrates identified bodily manifested symptoms (signs) as conveyors of messages about physical and mental states. Though Plato, Aristotle, Poinsot, Locke, Leibnitz, and Vico all discussed signs, symbols, and communication, it was not until the turn of the 20th century that semiotics achieved its identity through the independently developed works of the Swiss linguist Ferdinand de Saussure and the American philosopher Charles Sanders Peirce.

Broadly speaking, semiotics analyzes the structures of meaning-producing events, both verbal and nonverbal. Sebeok has written that the scope of semiotics and its subject matter includes "the exchange of any messages whatever and of the systems of signs which underlie them," with the *sign* always the fundamental concept (Sebeok 1976, p. 1). Semiotics takes two forms: (1) a general semiotics that seeks to answer, "What is the nature of meaning?"and (2) a specific semiotics that asks, "How does our reality–words, gestures, myths, products/services, theories–acquire meaning?" (Ransdell 1977). To address these questions, semioticians investigate the sign systems or *codes* essential to all types of communication for the latent rules that facilitate sign production and interpretive responses.

Semiotics stands apart from the bulk of the social sciences, and not uncontroversially, with a more intense focus on meaning. Harman (1981) has argued that since meaning is not something physical or directly measurable, it is awkward for contemporary scientifically minded researchers to deal with. For many of them, meaning is beyond the purview of science, and what is non-science is nonsense. Semiotics, in large part, rebukes that view.

### F. de Saussure

Saussure was a respected linguist of his time who challenged the very foundations of his field (1915). He maintained that since language was a system of signs, linguistics should be enveloped by a larger science of signs within society. Saussure called that science *semiology*, i.e., the study of what signs are made of and what laws command them.[1] Saussure defined a linguistic sign as a wholly arbitrary, diadic relationship between a concept that is the signified (e.g., blouse) and a sound image that is the signifier (e.g., the spoken word "blouse").

Saussure sought to overthrow the traditional view of linguistics wherein language was seen as an aggregation of separate units (words), each with a distinct meaning. From Saussure's perspective, the relationships and interactions between words take precedence over individual words when meaning is formed or derived. According to his chessboard metaphor, moving one piece alters all the relationships between pieces on the board. Thus, Saussure's chief contribution to the study of signs resided in shifting a longstanding philosophical emphasis on the nature of things in and of themselves to a relational world view whereby meaning derives from the priorities human beings construct and perceive among signs in a system.

*Synchronic/Diachronic Research.* For Saussure, language was the epitome of a self-contained relational structure. To study the principles of language (or any sign system) Saussure advocated *synchronic* approaches, which measure the adequacy and self-sufficiency of the current system, in addition to customary *diachronic* methods, which place the system in an historical dimension for observing and recording cause-effect laws of change.

*Paradigmatic/Syntagmatic Relations.* Synchronic analyses specify two genres of relations, *paradigmatic* and *syntagmatic*, that determine how signs are organized. A paradigm in the Saussurean sense is a set of signs; a syntagm is the message formed by signs chosen from several paradigms. Paradigmatic relations are those that reveal the oppositions and contrasts between signs in a set. For example, scenes or background settings form an important paradigm from which a key selection is made in the development of advertising messages (e.g., beach, kitchen, office, city street). A paradigmatic choice conveys meaning through the differences between the sign selected and those not selected. Syntagmatic relations are evident in combinations of paradigmatic choices, revealing the rules or conventions that facilitate sign combinations to form messages (in language these rules constitute grammar). In a consumer context, a family picnic is a syntagm of choices from the paradigms of food, drink, entertainment, picnic sites, apparel, participants, and so on.

*Langue/Parole.* Saussure also drew an important distinction between *langue* and *parole*. The former stands for the abstract rules and conventions of language (or any code) that pre-exist any individual's use of it; the latter represents the manipulation of the language system via individual utterances in everyday situations. For Saussure, *parole* is the level at which meaning arises. Meaning ultimately emerges through the existence of differences among words in a language as they are chosen and combined in actual verbalizations. In economic contexts the Saussurean perspective of meaning through difference has been implicated as both the fuel of healthy market competition (brand differentiation; Gardner and Levy 1955) and an institutionalized flaw of Western cultures (social class distinctions promoted by differential product ownership; Sahlins 1976).

*Language and Reality.* Saussure's acute focus on synchronic analyses and on difference as the key to meaning reinforced the self-defining nature of linguistic structures and made them peer inward at their own rules instead of outward at an objective world. According to Hawkes, Saussure further reasoned that (1977, p. 28):

> since this self-regarding, self-regulating form constitutes our characteristic means of encountering and of coping with the world beyond ourselves, then perhaps we can say that it constitutes the characteristic human structure. From there, it is only a small step to the argument that perhaps it also constitutes the characteristic structure of human reality.

Thus, along with Vico and Piaget, Saussure believed that reality is sensible because it is pre-coded for us at birth. "What we learn is not the world," according to Thayer, "but particular codes into which it has been structured so that we may 'share' our experiences of it" (1982, p. 30). And since, in the Saussurean perspective signs are arbitrary and conventional, to learn the codes is to adopt the values and biases that guarantee the indigenous world view.

### Sapir and Whorf

Unaware of Saussure's ideas, the American linguists Edward Sapir and Benjamin Whorf recorded and analyzed North American Indian languages from synchronic and structuralist perspectives. Together they played prominent roles in developing the notion of relativity of culture and in promoting the idea that a culture's life patterns are determined, or at least structured, according to its language. In a provocative classic statement, Sapir wrote (1949, p. 162):

> Human beings do not live in the objective world of social activity as ordinarily understood, but are very much at the mercy of the particular language which has become the medium of expression for their society… . The fact of the matter is that the 'real world' is to a large extent built up on the language habits of the group… . We see and hear and experience very largely as we do because the language habits of our community predispose certain choices of interpretation.

Hence, the so-called Sapir-Whorf hypothesis maintains that communication is not just a mere conduit of information and meaning, but a process that actually establishes reality, including who we are and who we will be. In a unique extension of consumer research, Holman (1981c) has pointed out that cultures incorporate different perceptions of time in the verb structures of their languages and, therein, culture-specific images of the future may affect investment and buying patterns, perceived risks in buyer behavior, and buyer-seller interactions across cultural borders.

**Figure A** Peirce's Triadic Semiosis

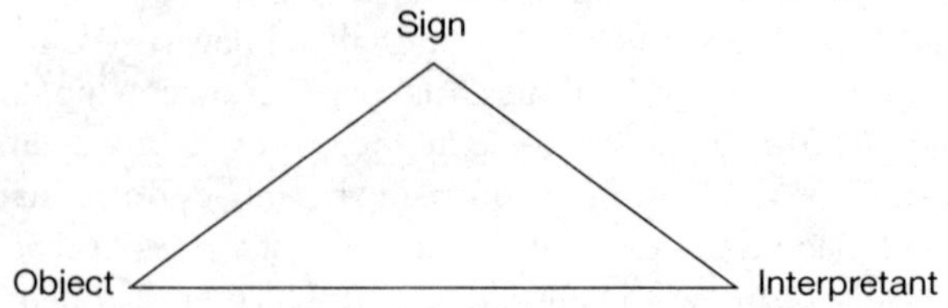

## C.S. Peirce

Peirce's lifelong inquiry into the nature of signs stemmed from his reading of John Locke, who apparently was the first to suggest that semiotics might provide novel insights on human understanding (Peirce 1931–1958). Trained in philosophy and chemistry, Peirce adopted Locke's vision of semiotics and set out from a logic-centered orientation grounded in empirical observation–invariably more pervasive than Saussure's language-centric focus–to examine "the essential nature and fundamental varieties of possible semiosis" (5.488).[2]

*Semiosis, Interpretant, Meaning.* For Peirce, semiosis is the process of communication by any type of sign, a sign being anything that stands for something (its object), to somebody (its interpreter), in some respect (its context). Like Saussure, Peirce explained sign processes in terms of relations. But Peirce spoke of "triadic" instead of "diadic" relations (Peirce 5.484):

> By 'semiosis' I mean, on the contrary [to diadic relations], an action, or influence, which is, or involves, a cooperation of *three* subjects such as a sign, its object, and its interpretant, this tri-relative influence not being in any way resolvable into actions between pairs.

Peirce's model of semiosis is shown in Figure A.

Peirce's semiotics is a philosophy anchored in the real world Saussure de-emphasized, as indicated by the essential role of objects therein. Moreover, it stresses the import of people, social institutions, and culture through the often misunderstood notion of "interpretant." The interpretant is not the interpreter (as Hawkes and others have claimed); nor is it just an interpretation (see Eco 1976, pp. 68–69). According to Sebeok, "By 'interpretant' Peirce appeared to mean the interpreter's reaction to the sign, that is, the sign's transmutation into an inferred neural code" (1976, p. 7). Ultimately, the interpretant is transformed into a language or other symbolic code by which it is shared with and transmitted through the social environment.

Peirce wrote extensively on the interpretant, proposing several subtle gradations of the construct. Nonetheless, Peirce scholars like Buczynska-Garewicz (1981, 1983) and Eco (1976, 1979) have argued that essentially the interpretant is the meaning of the sign; put differently, the interpretant is actually another sign referring to the same "object." Since any initial meaning can be re-interpreted (and often is), each interpretant is thus a sign leading to another interpretant, and so on ad infinitum. This double nature of the interpretant – as both the interpreted sign and the interpreting sign–confers unlimited regress or extrapolation in semiosis and led Peirce to conclude that man "is the thought," in fact, "a sign himself" (5.314, 6.344). This restive tautology apparent in Peirce's interpretant is "at the same time its force and the conditions of its theoretical purity… . Semiosis explains itself by itself" (Eco 1976, p. 7 1). As a more concrete example, consider that a dictionary is a perfect case of similar circularity.

*Icons, Indexes, Symbols.* As his reflections on semiotics evolved, Peirce's taxonomy of signs reached 10 trichotomies, eventually yielding 66 types. The three sign categories he most often utilized (8.368) were based on the relationship between sign and object posed in Figure A. An iconic sign relates to its object in so far as it imitates or resembles the object. An actor portraying Benjamin Franklin in an advertisement and a flow diagram of a consumer choice model are iconic signs. An indexical sign relates to its object by some correspondence of fact, and the relationship is frequently causal. For instance, consumer satisfaction is an indexical sign in marketing theory that some desire has been fulfilled. A symbolic sign relates to its object in an entirely conventional manner and, as such, requires the participative presence of an interpreter to create the signifying connection. Thus, a point-of-purchase display for wine depicting a young couple lounging by a fireplace may represent "the good life" or decadence, love or licentiousness, depending upon the codes of the interpreter's background.

For Peirce, these three important sign categories are not mutually exclusive, since a sign may function in all three capacities. According to Hawkes (1977), the trichotomy is usually hierarchical, with the context of semiosis establishing the priorities of the sign types and the interpretants generated.

*Deduction, Induction, Abduction.* The sign-interpretant relationship in semiosis was also a major focus of Peirce's work. Influenced heavily by Kant, Peirce's epistemology could be termed constructivist; that is, he held that all knowledge and meaning is derived. For Peirce, cognition is a process of knowledge and meaning generation through signs and it takes three forms: deduction, induction, and abduction. To illustrate, suppose a person believes that, as a rule, all women who are good mothers serve their families three nutritionally balanced meals per day. By deduction, the rule and a given case entail a result:

| | |
|---|---|
| rule | 1. All women who... . |
| case | 2. Jane is a good mother. |
| result | 3. Therefore, Jane serves her family three nutritionally balanced meals per day. |

By induction, given a case and a result, the rule is inferred probabilistically:

| | |
|---|---|
| case | 1. Jane is a good mother. |
| result | 2. Jane serves her family three nutritionally balanced meals per day. |
| rule | 3. Therefore, all women who... . |

By abduction, a result and the rule infer the given case probabilistically:

| | |
|---|---|
| result | 1. Jane serves her family three nutritionally balanced meals per day. |
| rule | 2. All women who serve... . |
| case | 3. Therefore, Jane is a good mother. |

The potency of abduction is particularly obvious if we consider Jane a new neighbor or a fictional character in an advertisement about whom little else is known. For the person who wonders why Jane acts as she does, abductively the person need only invent or, more likely, instantiate a rule that has been socio-culturally learned and rehearsed, and the explanation for Jane's actions is derived. Since codes and rules are necessary for an interpretive response, each time a sign is confronted abduction occurs (Eco 1976).

*Peirce's Philosophy of Science.* Peirce's semiotics is a doctrine of experience–indeed, a phenomenological doctrine of consciousness (Zeman 1977). But for Peirce and his man-as-sign conclusion, consciousness is of signs only; it cannot obtain an indubitable science of reality. Though he stressed that his semiotics was an observational normative doctrine, Peirce also emphasized that humanity's primary tools of understanding are symbols: words, diagrams (iconic symbols), mathematical formulas, statistical tests, etc. All are arbitrary and conventional and depend on social agreement for their significance. Peirce also wrote that all of our "knowledge of the internal world is derived by [abductive] reasoning from our knowledge of external facts" through the multiple and potentially endless chain of interpretants (5.317). Taken together, these views exemplify, on the one hand, Peirce's realism, and on the other, his tenet of fallibility, i.e., that exactitude in science can never be attained (1. 135–149).

### Other Contributors and Orientations

*Charles Morris.* Shortly after Saussure and Peirce, Ogden and Richards (1923) spurred the development of semiotics with their classic work, *The Meaning of Meaning.* Though few acknowledge it, the venerable semantic differential has direct origins in Ogden and Richards and in the American semiotician Charles Morris (Osgood, Suci, and Tannenbaum 1957, pp. 310). As the most influential American semiotician up to the present day, Morris's goal was to fuse semiotics with developments in the social sciences to produce a comprehensive science of signs (1938, 1946, 1964, 1971, 1976). Morris defined semiotics as (1946):

> The science of signs. Its main subdivisions are *semantics*, syntactics, and *pragmatics.* Each of these and so semiotics as a whole, can be *pure, descriptive*, or *applied.* Pure semiotics elaborates a language to talk about signs, descriptive semiotics studies actual signs, and applied semiotics utilizes knowledge about signs for the accomplishment of various purposes.

Accordingly, syntactics is the study of sign-sign relations, semantics is the study of sign-object relations, and pragmatics is the study of sign-interpretant relations. Note that in terms of theories of meaning, syntactics is Saussure's focus, semantics is the traditional emphasis, and pragmatics is Peirce's concentration. Contrary to Morris's claims, Singer (1984) and others have since argued that pragmatics presupposes both syntactics and semantics because semiosis occurs only through the irreducible Peircean triad of sign-object-interpretant. Regardless, the trichotomy of syntactics-semantics-pragmatics is probably the most enduring aspect of Morris's semiotic legacy (cf., in sociolinguistics. Greenburg 1964; in marketing, Holbrook 1978). However, the infusion of behavioral psychology into his semiotics and the ongoing controversy over his alleged misapplications of Peircean concepts has tended to diminish Morris's position in contemporary semiotics (Rochberg-Halton and McMurtrey 1983; Steiner 1978).

*A Semiotic Cube.* Nauta (1972) has built from Morris's work a cube that serves as a useful framework for multifaceted semiotic inquiry. We adapt the cube here (Figure B) with minor alterations in terminology to illustrate how Peirce's trichotomy of icon-index-symbol can be united with Morris's trichotomies of syntactics-semantics-pragmatics and pure-descriptive-applied semiotics.[3]

For example, pure semiotics elaborates a metalanguage to talk about signs of any type at any level of semiosis. Historically, theoretical semioticians such as Eco, Morris, Nauta, Peirce, and Saussure dominate this slice of the cube. Componential specifications of consumer semiosis are virtually nonexistent. A fruitful start would be to consider what aspects of acquisition, consumption, and disposition behaviors involve or, perhaps, accentuate certain signs (and combinations thereof) over others. Further, it is likely that icons, indexes, and symbols themselves can be taxonomized to provide more precise theoretical foundations for semiosis in consumer behavior. Consider gift-giving behaviors that are intrinsically semiotic and that have drawn increased attention from consumer researchers (Belk 1976, 1979, 1982; Sherry 1983). Taking a pure semiotics approach, signs can be taxonomized as intrapersonal and interpersonal; gifts as symbols can be similarly classified. Yet, the majority of gift-giving literature in consumer behavior emphasizes the latter over the former despite various consumer indulgences to "reward" the self for past behavior. As a symbolic self-dialogue, intrapersonal gifts are likely to have important, unexplored distinctions from interpersonal gifts along social, personal, and economic dimensions.

**Figure B** A Semotic Cube

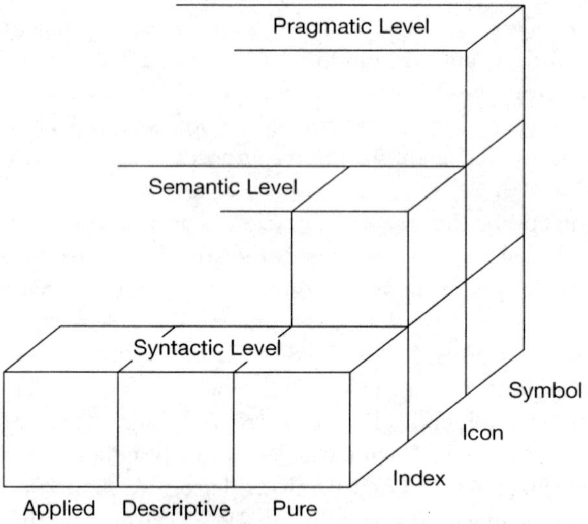


*Source*: Nauta, Doede (1972), *The Meaning of Information*, The Hague: Mouton De Gruyter.

Continuing the pure semiotics slice of the cube, gifts are also iconic and indexical and can be further taxonomized as aesthetic, educational, utilitarian, and so on. A print of a Monet painting and a child's spelling calculator may be thought of, respectively, as aesthetic icons and educational icons (the latter being an iconic sign for a personal computer). Indexically, the print-as-gift may be a sign of a desire to appear "sophisticated" while the calculator-as-gift may reflect a parent's prioritized values on education and on the child's initiation rites for a technological culture.

For descriptive semiotics, inquiry focuses on actual signs. Advertisements in particular have been subjected to descriptive semiotic analyses by Fiske (1982), Leymore (1975), Umiker-Sebeok (1979, 1981), Wernick (1983) and Williamson (1978). In fact, our gift-giving illustration became a partial descriptive semiotic as the actual signs (the print and calculator) were referred to.

By placing actual signs in specific contexts of acquisition, consumption, and disposition, one engages applied semiotics. Instances of applied semiotics include physician-patient relations (Shands 1970; Shands and Meltzer 1977), advertising-information consumption (Fiske 1982), and cultural anthropology research (Geertz 1973, 1983; Singer 1984).

In all three modes of pure, descriptive, and applied inquiry, the signs can be detailed in relation to other signs (syntactics: Does a Monet print fit with art deco furniture?), in relation to their objects (semantics: Do a spelling calculator and a video game refer similarly to the computer culture?), and in relation to their interpretants (pragmatics: What consequences do the Monet print and spelling calculator have for their users today and how do those impacts change with use over time?). The semiotic cube can be employed to analyze consumer semiosis diachronically as well as synchronically as advocated by Saussure.

*Contemporary Semiotics*. Although Morris is probably the most openly recognizable link between Peirce/ Saussure and current semiotics in North America, semiotics has subtly permeated a broad spectrum of disciplines worldwide. Among others, many philosophers (Cassirer, Langer, Whitehead), linguists (Halliday, Hjelmslev, Jakobson), anthropologists (Douglas, Geertz, Levi-Strauss, Singer), and sociologists (Warner) have argued for the primacy of signs in human experience, especially the symbolic dimension. In addition, theoretical and methodological positions espoused by field theorists (Lewin), symbolic interactionists (Blumer), ethnomethodologists (Garfinkel), phenomenologists (Schutz), structuralists (Levi-Strauss), conversational analysts (Sacks), and socialization theorists (Goffman) share numerous indirect affinities with semiotics. As a result, Culler (1981) has commented that a precise tracing of the intellectual tradition of semiotics after Peirce and Saussure is difficult since "one suspects that semiotics could well have defined itself [without Peirce or Saussure] as the logical outcome of an intellectual reorientation that had been under way for some time" (p. 24).

Barthes (1968, 1972, 1983) is perhaps the person most responsible for bringing semiotics to contemporary public light. Currently, Eco (1976, 1979, 1984) and Sebeok (1972, 1974, 1976, 1981) stand as the two predominant semioticians in an enveloping, interdisciplinary doctrine that now includes a vast range of topics in both human and nonhuman communication (see Eco 1976, pp. 9–14, for a panorama of the field).

To be sure, semiotics is not without its critics (Pettit 1975; Sperber 1974). Sperber has claimed that semioticians assume that the human environment overflows with meaning, a premise he maintains is no less ethnocentrically arbitrary than the symbols in which semioticians find so much arbitrary meaning (see Winner 1978 for a rejoinder to Sperber). Despite such criticism and the considerable challenge most readers first encounter with semiotic texts, the field continues to grow and influence.[4]

*Summary*. This concise introduction to semiotics has identified the sign as the fundamental vehicle connecting objects in the broadest sense and human reactions (interpretants). This overall process of semiosis is the basic subject of semiotics and the mechanism by which meaning is created, maintained, and altered. There are different kinds of signs by virtue of their relations with their objects (e.g., icons, indexes, symbols); signs also relate to their interpretants in various ways (e.g., deductively, inductively, abductively). Since signs cannot function independently, the systemic structural level of sign relations is focused upon as codes with underlying rules. Saussure's specification of paradigmatic and syntagmatic relations and Morris's distinctions among syntactics-semantics-pragmatics and pure-descriptive-applied semiotics are exemplars of semiotic approaches to the study of codes, semiosis, and meaning. As Peirce emphasized, signs in the human environment – especially symbols – must be understood by the way they are situated within a wider social context, where both their arbitrariness and meaningfulness are revealed.

So why semiotics and consumer research? Because consumers behave based on the meanings they ascribe to marketplace stimuli. And yet consumer researchers, with few exceptions, have characteristically avoided detailed and systematic inquiry into meaning processes. Perhaps this reflects the shortcomings of current theory and methodologies in consumer research. Or perhaps the role of meaning appears obvious, but also ineffable or intractable. To its advantage, semiotics is a mosaic of terminology and methods that can help us clarify and understand the role of meaning as embodied in the semiosis of consumer behavior as well as researcher behavior. Fortunately, a few in our field have already recognized the value of a semiotic perspective and their work deserves review.

## Explicit Semiotics in Consumer Research

### Advertising Language

The first reference and use of semiotics in consumer behavior literature appeared in Holbrook's 1978 article on the differential impact of varied information characteristics on attitudes. Holbrook evoked Morris's work in discussing the isolation of key content dimensions in persuasive communication (1978, p. 547):

> Especially conspicuous by its absence [from advertising research] is any message variable derived from a systematic consideration of the nature of language – its semantic substance, syntactic structure, and pragmatic uses.

Holbrook focused his study on the semantic properties of verbal advertising messages, making a distinction between factual vs. evaluative content – i.e., "1ogical, objectively verifiable descriptions of tangible product features" vs. "emotional, subjective impressions of intangible aspects of the product" (p. 547). Although Holbrook did not use the term "semiotics" in his article, the influence of his semiotics-derived factual/evaluative dichotomy has been sustained (Hirschman 1980; Shimp and Preston 1981; Yalch and Elmore-Yalch 1984). The Morris trichotomy was later renewed by Hirschman and Holbrook in their introduction to *Symbolic Consumer Behavior* (1981).

### Artifactual Communication

Holman's 1976 dissertation on the communicational properties of women's clothing was the first extensive exposition and application of semiotics by a marketing and consumer behavior researcher. Much of her subsequent work, which is not reviewed here, has built upon semiotic orientations (1980a, 1980b, 1981a, 1981b, 1983). Her 1976 study investigated syntactic and semantic levels of consumer semiosis from pure, descriptive, and applied perspectives (see Figure B) by examining the clothing system as a code and particular clothing ensembles as messages. Looking for the sociocultural rules that endow clothing with meaning, Holman sought first to identify the multiple messages possible within a context-specific clothing system through the description of its structural form. She then examined the strength and consistency of correlations between specific ensembles and attributions made about ensemble wearers.

Among the distinctive features of Holman's study was her insistence on thoroughly specifying the paradigmatic alternatives (among ensemble components) before exploring how they combine to form a coherent message. Thus, only after performing a pure and descriptive analysis at the syntactic level did she embark on semantic analysis.

Holman began by unobtrusively photographing 392 women students and describing their ensembles in terms of a 171-item numerical taxonomic procedure. From cluster analyses of the data, six groups of ensembles emerged, which then guided additional photographing of women students dressed similarly to one of the six groups. Subjects from a student population were then each shown one of the second-phase photographs and asked to make attributions about the woman in the photograph using 31 six-point scale items. Eight variables were found to be statistically significant in attribution differences across ensemble clusters (e.g., sorority membership, femininity, beer drinking habits) though the total variance explained was small.

Outside of introducing semiotics, Holman's work emphasizes the value of unraveling the meaning of a conspicuous product by seeking its interpretation not from the individual user (to whom much of the meaning is likely obscured in subconsciousness), but from the user's audience, which readily detects subtleties of meaning in uninhibited artifactual semiosis. Although she did not acknowledge abductive inferencing as the cognitive mechanism her subjects employed, in fact Holman's study centered on the sociocultural rules that facilitate abduction in consumption symbolism. The abductions were of the form:

1. This coed in the photograph is dressed in a *Z* ensemble.
2. College coeds who are characteristically *X* dress in ensembles like *Z*.
3. Therefore, this coed is characteristically *X* (probably).

As such, Holman's work represents a semiotic perspective on symbolic consumer behavior and advances a sociology of consumption meaning (cf., Nicosia and Mayer 1976).

Sharing Holman's focus on artifactual communication, Kehret-Ward's dissertation invoked Saussurean perspectives to study how children perceive products as conveyors of information about themselves and others.[5] Her subsequent work also reflects Saussure's semiotics (1982; Kehret-Ward, Johnson, and Louie 1985). In particular, she has argued that products-as-symbols are like linguistic units in that meaning emerges fron differences between them, scarcity being the guarantor of difference. These differences in products, in association with their owners, signal social positioning of various modes.

Her study of 7-, 10-, and 13-year-olds confirmed that certain situational and developmental variables mediated the relationship between a product's communication value and its relative scarcity. For example, after manipulating the perception of scarcity, she found that older subjects (aged 13) more often than younger subjects (aged 10 and 7) preferred a scarce brand to a common brand and attributed their preferences directly to the scarcity factor. Kehret-Ward concluded that both younger and older children treat commercial products as linguistic units, but that only the older ones have acquired the ability to choose and display scarce artifacts for purposes of communication. From a semiotic viewpoint, this shows how pragmatic context and the semantic properties of products arise directly from perceived syntactic relations between products.

Kehret-Ward has also extended Saussurean semiotics to consumption symbolism in adults (1982). She has pointed out that as product designs and styles evolve, the meaning of already-owned products and the perceptions of (attributions about) their owners are altered even though the products themselves and their owners have not changed. For instance, the domestic car owner who is perceived as successful in part because she drives a large automobile (Belk, Mayer, and Bahn 1982) may be seen as indulgent or wasteful years later when the new model of the car brand is downsized along with competitors in its class to emulate imported automobiles and improve fuel efficiency. Thus, neither the automobile nor the owner is an autonomous, unarbitrary sign; each is a symbol made meaningful by its distinction from and relationship to competing symbols.

Kehret-Ward (1982) reiterates her argument that products qualify as linguistic signs and goes on to invoke the Peircean icon-index-symbol trichotomy. She argues that a semiotic approach to consumption symbolism leads to two immediate insights (the Peircean terminology in brackets is ours):

1. If a product is purchased for its communication value, then product differentiation [sign alteration by the marketer] for its own sake is meaningless [no interpretant] in the absence of a corresponding consumer trait, need, or desire [objects].

2. The pragmatic meaning of a product [interpretant], especially for its owner [who is both an interpreter and a sign to others], can change when the product's competitors make design or style changes [sign alterations], in effect making a move on the Saussurean chessboard, and in doing so affecting syntactic, semantic, and pragmatic relations throughout.

While the first point is straightforward though crucial, as product failure rates attest to, the second point benefits from further illustration. The emergence of advertising product tags like "all natural ingredients," "lite," and "low fat content" imbue competitors' products with meaning-by-implication like "few or less natural ingredients," "high caloric levels," and "high fat content" – this despite the fact that the competitors' products have not been changed. As the tags proliferate and eventually saturate different product constellations, their communication value paradoxically diminishes (they are no longer scarce) and inflates (in Eco's sense, becomes "overcoded;" 1976). Thus, the "lite" symbol now stands for nothing and many things, including contradictions: low calories, less filling, must continue to use to become or stay thin (no escape), but can eat more portions, can eat more often, can substitute other food for the saved calories (freedom).

### Advertising-Marketing Communication

Sherry has recently adopted a provocative semiotic orientation in arguing that "advertising is a cultural document, a way of presenting and apprehending the world" (1985, p. 1). As Peirce perceived symbols as "man made" and "man making," Sherry sees advertising "as a way of construing the world, in much the same way as religion, science, common sense, art, ideology, or play represent ways of knowing ... advertising [is] a way of understanding" (p. 3). Beyond Williamson's (1978) claim that advertising creates meaning, Sherry rightly contends that advertising also discerns and discovers meaning; i.e., through its verbal and nonverbal rhetoric and its symbolic and iconic conventions, advertising transports its audience via ritualized enactments through the dimensions of experience the culture esteems (Fox 1984). The repetitive ritualizations conserve the culture by reducing the variance in the distribution of cultural behaviors, and thereby move it toward resolving inherent contradictions. At the same time, however, the extensive ritualization leads cultural perceptions to become natural perceptions; in other words, instead of a cultural representation, advertisements come to be seen as representations of the whole world or of definitive reality. Besides the resulting ethnocentrism, Sherry suggests that other aberrant results may manifest themselves in commodity fetishism (Marx 1876), product therapy (Henry 1956), and overconsumption (Bodley 1982). To date, however, these troubling propositions have not been adequately researched (Pollay 1986).

In another article, McCracken and Pollay (1981) argue that advertising seeks regularly to bestow a product with properties beyond its intrinsic features by exploiting two principles that frequently figure into semiotic inquiry: contiguity and similarity (cf., Leach 1976). The former involves bringing together in the ad a select set of objects, persons, and activities with the product. The latter takes over as the audience is invited to acknowledge resemblances and, in effect, transfer properties between the co-present entities. For example, critics of cigarette ads cast on beaches or in locker rooms often claim that the invigorating, healthy qualities of natural settings and athletic exertion are improperly signified in the cigarettes through the resemblances advocated by contiguity.

Finally, Mick (1987) has blended semiotics with schema theory, which specifies the structure, content, and processes involving attitudes, memory, and cognition as well as written and spoken texts (Brewer and Nakamura 1984; Hastie 1981; Thorndyke and Yekovich 1980). Mick proposes incorporating three genres of schema theory into marketing communication research as a first approximation of more wholistic research: goal, knowledge, and text schemata. The goal and knowledge schemata relate to both the marketer and the consumer; the text schemata involve the linguistic messages in marketing communication. Mick argues that as schema theory and schema-specification methodologies are refined, these schemata should be stipulated before and after marketing communication occurs, i.e., moving beyond post-test-only designs and using more within-subjects approaches. Mick also engages Morris's semiotics to foster a metalanguage and a framework within which schema theory can enrich marketing communication research. For example, the structural elements and combinatory forms of schemata can be examined at the syntactic level, the conceptual ramifications of the schema as a research metaphor can be investigated at the semantic level, and developmental issues and context-specific uses of schemata can be approached at the pragmatic level.

## Implicit Semiotics in Consumer Research

There is other consumer research possessing implicit affinities with semiotic orientations. While practically all consumer research on symbolism, and an array of tangential topics, could be explicated within semiotic philosophy, the following studies have actually used similar concepts.

### Consumption Use Systems

Wasson, for example, emphasizes at one point in his consumer behavior text consumption use systems: "consumption of a product involves the use of more items than just the product alone, and requires a step-by-step procedure of some sort" (1975. pp. 9–10). For example, oatmeal as a breakfast food and oatmeal as an ingredient in baking cookies require different companion ingredients and kitchen utensils to make and consume the end product. Thus, "oatmeal is not one product, but several different products, each with its own use system" (p. 10). These use systems are reminiscent of Saussure's structural analysis of language, particularly paradigmatic and syntagmatic relations: oatmeal-as-sign has changeable value and identity, dependent upon its selection and combination with other components of use systems.

### Consumer Mythology

Levy has drawn from the work of the French anthropologist Levi-Strauss to study consumer myths. For Levy, "myths are ways of organizing perceptions of realities, of indirectly expressing paradoxical human concerns [which] affect people's daily lives" (1981, p. 52). Thus, consumer mythology is a type of code. To study consumer myths Levy interviewed housewives about food consumption attitudes and behaviors involving various family members and found an affluence of values and preferences reflected in family traditions and activities. He uncovered symbolic distinctions among certain foods, preparation methods, and consumption behaviors directly related to mythic proportion oppositions, including family togetherness versus separation and celebratory versus everyday cuisine. In all, the study demonstrated the usefulness of anthropological field methodologies and the insightfulness of semiotic and structuralist analyses of consumer mythology: like many other topics in consumer research, dietary behavior has been studied too narrowly in the past when considered only in isolation or with over-emphasis on product attributes.

### Symbolic Interactionism

Several consumer studies have invoked symbolic interactionism, a sociological theory sizably influenced by Peirce (Kernan and Sommers 1968; MacCannell 1976; Schenk and Holman 1980; Solomon 1983). Solomon writes that "symbolic interactionism focuses on the process by which individuals understand their world ... [it assumes] that people interpret the actions of others rather than simply reacting to them." Moreover, the interpretations are a function of the meaning attached to such actions ... which is, in turn, mediated largely by symbols" (Solomon 1983, p. 320). Solomon's overview of the history and tenets of symbolic interactionism suggests many overlaps with semiotics and, as he himself hints, the more refined metalanguage of semiotics holds significant promise for symbolic interaction theory and research (p. 322, footnote 7).

Like most semioticians, symbolic interactionists view human minds as fundamentally social-existentially dependent upon shared symbols. According to both, meaning is negotiated and constructed through intrapersonal and interpersonal discourse; it is not an individual enterprise, but rather "a social procedure for defining objects to achieve a practical effect" (Gallant and Kleinman 1983, p. 5). Thus, the two perspectives share Peirce's pragmatic conception of meaning.

### Experiential Aspects and Abduction

Finally, Holbrook and Hirschman (1982) have called for more concerted attention to the "experiential" aspects of consumer behavior, emphasizing the importance of pre-reflexive reactions to the less objective features of products, nonverbal cues in stimuli, and syntactic versus semantic characteristics of communication. The hedonic responses Holbrook and Hirschman focus on are akin to what Peirce called the emotional interpretant, and their emphasis on syntactics is clearly Saussurean. Furthermore, the authors' appeals to the latent levels of knowledge, emotion, and consumption symbolism as well as their discussions of creativity, play, and artistic endeavors all point to the semiotic concern with the codes and underlying rules of intrapersonal and interpersonal communication, including abductive inferencing.

Peirce also conceived abduction as the method by which the hunches, intuitions, and revelations of human experience take place (Spinks 1983). Eco (1976) argues that this mode of abduction occurs especially in undercoded contexts, i.e., when pre-established rules are deficient or absent. A person who uses a product in an inventive fashion – for instance, adding a previously untried ingredient to a recipe or using aluminum foil in a window to block the summer sun – has taken certain objects not normally associated and, based on some provisional hypothetic rule, has made an abductive inference and impacted the relevant code. A more thorough understanding of this aspect of abductive inferencing can contribute insights into the experiential events of consumer behavior as well as the mechanisms by which hypotheses are generated in consumer research.

## Discussion

### As Old is New

Many who confront semiotics for the first time often remark that, in one manner or another, they have been "doing semiotics" all along. In fact, however, until recently consumer behavior theorists and researchers have tended to treat signs and their functions indiscriminately. Moreover, meaning has been merely ancillary to the inquiry on fundamental human behavior we choose artificially to call consumer behavior. If, as Crosson maintains, "... the problem of meaning is central to our age" (1967, p. 99), and if meaning and consumption are as commingled in the residue of the industrial and consumer revolutions as McCracken (1985) contends, then we must marshall a new orientation for these ancient concerns that will elevate meaning to the same priority in consumer research that it compels in consumer life. First, semiotics satisfies the three epistemic requirements laid out by Hirschman (1981) for the construction of a novel paradigm for the study of symbolic consumption: a sociological level of analysis, because symbols require agreement in meaning for the social construction of reality; a focus on both the production and consumption of symbols; and a concern with the rhetoric of symbols or who controls their meaning over time. Second, semiotics promotes a degree of retrospection and open-mindedness about prevailing theories and methods we are usually unaccustomed to. In so doing it offers the opportunity to improve consumer research by identifying conceptual ruts and by encouraging multiple modes of research. Third, as researchers and consumers of the signs of our time, semiotics can make us better communicators among ourselves, with our subjects, and with our students.

Human experience is mediated by a panorama of signs and codes both linguistic and non-linguistic and it is the meanings of these phenomena that we act upon, not the objects of quasi-existence that we assume supports them. This is a crucial semiotic premise for consumer research in an era of ethnocentric Western materialism where "the belief that the ultimate goals of personal life can be fulfilled by things and sensations ... is losing credibility in the face of facts" (Csikszentmihalyi and Rochberg-Halton 1981, p. ix).[6]

### Acquisition, Consumption, Disposition as Semiosis

In Peirce's semiotics, meaning ultimately issues from the symbolic qualities of signs through the pragmatic implications and realizations of semiosis. Anthropologist and semiotician Mary Douglas (1970; Douglas and Isherwood 1979) has criticized economists – and by implication their marketing progeny – for concocting theories about rational individuals abstracted from their symbol-perfused sociocultural habitat. Olshavsky and Granbois (1979) have reproved consumer researchers for an equivalent myopia.

Although Schenk and Holman (1980) and a handful of other consumer researchers have shared the Douglas and Isherwood opinion, few have gone beyond the perception of goods as subsistence or competitive display tools to the more penetrating semiotic perspective espoused by Douglas and Isherwood – namely, that goods are "needed for making visible and stable the categories of culture" (p. 59). Douglas and Isherwood maintain that "the essential function of consumption is its capacity to make sense" and they exhort researchers to "forget that commodities are good for eating, clothing, and shelter ... treat them as a nonverbal medium for the human creative faculty" (p. 62). Probably no single programmatic study has as thoroughly substantiated this conception of consumption-as-semiosis as Csikszentmihalyi and Rochberg-Halton's (1981). Extending semiotics to the universe of all acquisition, consumption. and disposition behaviors, whether directed at goods and services or at information, can point toward similar new vistas on consumer life.

Considering advertising research especially, we must move beyond conceiving advertising in terms of what it does to people and view it more in terms of what people do with advertising (Lannon and Cooper 1983; Mick 1987). Advertising is both "a model of and a model for reality" (Sherry 1985, p. 9) – in the Geertzian metaphor (1973), a flowchart and a blueprint. Such a perspective enlightens our comprehension of the dynamics of global and national advertising. In the cross-cultural scene, semiotics finds obvious the source of communication gaffes that have been well-documented (Aman 1982; Ricks, Arpan, and Fu 1974). Intracultural codes of language, beauty, proxemics, animals, and colors have been unwittingly and variously violated. For instance, in 1963 Dow Breweries introduced a new beer in Quebec, Canada and liberally borrowed French-Canadian nationalistic emblems in the hopes of enticing patriotic loyalty to its product. Instead, an enormous public outcry erupted and the campaign was scrapped within fifteen days (Elkin 1969).

More generally, Bryant and Jordan (1978), Goffman (1979), and Umiker-Sebeok (1979, 1981) have argued that advertising renders human behavior in predictable, repeatable patterns and depicts an artificial world of anachronistic role models. An illusory "realism" is achieved through the use and abuse of the semiotic concept *metonymy*. Whereas *metaphor* transposes the qualities of one object to a dissimilar object by way of implied comparison, crossing strata of reality through imaginative association, metonymy remains on a single stratum and through the principle of contiguity chooses a part of something to represent the whole. For instance, laundry commercials regularly depict people in the contracted roles of bumbling husband, homebound and antisepsis-expert wife, and careless children. As Fiske points out (1982, p. 97), "The selection of the metonym is clearly crucial, for from it we construct the unknown remainder of reality." Since it is part of what is represents (consumer life), the laundry scene metonym, along with the role behaviors portrayed, is an indexical sign. This accounts for its power. But the part that represents the whole is a paradigmatic and arbitrary choice of the advertiser. Moreover, in its rhetorical usage the arbitrariness of the selection is often glossed over and undetected.

Goffman and Umiker-Sebeok have also shown how widespread sociocultural changes, fueled especially by the women's movement, have been either ignored or trivialized by many advertisers (see also Bartos 1983; Courtney and Whipple 1983; Roberts and Koggan 1975). Continued insensitivity to these pervasive but often recondite changes in the signs of our time are likely contributing to the darker opinions expressed about advertising (Barksdale and Perreault, Jr. 1980; Zanot 1984), particularly by subgroups like single parents, white-collar professional women, and minorities whose beliefs about a common social world are not wholly convergent with traditional American views (cf., Arnould 1983).

### The Primacy of Tacit Knowledge

Semioticians frequently focus on communication coding rules as they account for the interpretability of reality (Culler 1981; Eco 1976; Fiske 1982). In so doing, they probe the realms of both culturally (Hanson and Hanson 1981) and biologically (Gopnik 1981) derived tacit knowledge, identified in various times by Plato, Poinsot, Kant, Freud, Geertz, and Polanyi. By tacit knowledge we mean the store of learned and inherited experiences that serve in the automatic and integrative intuition of the environment and the guidance of behavior. One of Polanyi's examples is the effortless skill of a bicycle rider. For Geertz, tacit knowledge underpins common sense (Geertz 1983). Few consumer researchers have acknowledged the role of tacit knowledge in acquisition, consumption, and disposition behaviors (e.g., Rook 1985) despite the fact that to some degree all forms of knowledge are rooted in tacit knowledge (Polanyi 1958, 1969). According to Hanson and Hanson (1981), tacit knowledge is evidenced in sociocultural principles that act as coding rules in the generation and interpretation of signs. As we grow up and are assimilated socioculturally, these principles are rarely made explicit, though our conventional behavior is grounded in them.

Semiotics can contribute to those emerging areas of consumer theory and research where tacit knowledge is implicated. Consumer values research (Clawson and Vinson 1978; Pitts and Woodside 1984; Pollay 1983), consumer schema and script theory (Crocker 1984; Leigh and Rethans 1983; Mick 1987;

Puto 1985), consumer rituals (Rook 1985), attribution theory (Belk, Mayer, and Bahn 1982; Kehret-Ward and Yalch 1984; Smith and Hunt 1978), and symbolism research in general all focus on the deeper levels of knowledge and consciousness that play vital roles in behavior, though they resist identification.

### Methodological Implications

For Polanyi, Geertz, and semioticians in general, human consciousness and experience is suffused with tacit knowledge. But, enveloped as it is in the signs and meanings of its sociocultural context, and unlike the typical constructs consumer researchers have historically sought to gauge with scales, tacit knowledge eludes specification. To appreciate and approximate the tacit knowledge of consumer behavior, we must realize that it is consumer reality we are studying, not our theory. How do consumers construe the consumer world? How do they formulate and utilize the meanings of acquisition, consumption, and disposition? What is important to them and how do they define those aspects of consumer life (Schneider 1976)?

Consider Figure C, reprinted from Lannon and Cooper (1983). If every consumer study appearing in major publications during the last 20 years was positioned in the figure according to its methodology, the figure would topple over. The upper levels of Figure C reflect the methodological dogma of operationalism which, in its most famous and now debunked form, behaviorism, seeks to explain complex social behavior in terms of select salient variables. For tacit knowledge, consumption symbolism, and consumer life meaning, such approaches are insufficient at best.

**Figure C** An Empirical Research Continuum

| METHOD | LAYER | | | | OUTPUT |
|---|---|---|---|---|---|
| Simple questioning | PUBLIC | COMMUNICABLE | AWARE | Spontaneous | Immediate, spontaneous response |
| Asking/ reminding | | | | Reasoned, conventional | Justifications, explanations |
| Pressing | | | | Preconscious | Detailed elaborations/ introspections |
| Sympathetic probing | PRIVATE | | | Concealed, personal | Personal admissions |
| Play, drama, non-verbal | | NON- | | Intuitive | Symbols, imagination analogy |
| Projective approaches | | | NON- | Unconscious | Repressed attitudes, motives |

*Source*: Lannon, Judie and Peter Cooper (1983), "Humanistic Advertising: A Holistic Cultural Perspective," *International Journal of Advertising* 2: 195–213.

Fortunately, several researchers have mined the lower portions of Figure C. Levy (1978, 1982) has argued for the rich insights to be gained from projective techniques like storytelling, personal consumption-oriented diaries, fantasizing, word associations, Thematic Apperception Tests, and depth interviews. Sherry (1983) and Rook (1985) have called for researchers to immerse themselves in consumer environments as ethnographic, participant observers. Phenomenological ethnography and hermeneutics suggested by Bruyn (1967), Oiler (1982), and O'Shaughnessy (1985) seem useful as well. The much maligned case-study methodology recently revived by Lincoln and Guba (1985) also promotes deeper understanding of tacit knowledge and semiosis. Sherry (1984) and Fine (1985) have advocated closer inspection of consumer anecdotes and oral histories that reveal consumption and mercantile legends containing important symbolic meanings. Ultimately we need a range of methods to obtain a span of data from which a Geertzian "thick description" can be built and interpreted.

Along similar lines, Turner (1967) has suggested that the multilevel nature of symbolic meaning requires varied but funnelled research methods:

1. Exegetical meaning represented by verbal interpretations of symbols by informants
2. Operational meaning represented by actual symbol usage observed by the researcher
3. Positional meaning represented by the researcher's efforts to see a symbol's relationship to others belonging to the same complex or Gestalt

Put another way, as Peirce would surely have supported, we must approach semiotic issues through triangulation – i.e., the convergence of various methodologies and knowledge on the elucidation of consumer semiosis (Deshpande 1983; Hirschman 1985; Webb 1978).

### The Semiotic Challenge

In accentuating naturalistic field research for inquiry into consumer semiosis, the anthropologic-ethnographic vein of semiotics is venerated. However, semiotics is not necessarily contrapuntal to other forms of scientific research like experimentation or survey research (see Anderson *et al.* 1984). What semiotics rebelliously contests is any sort of methodological dogmatism that seeks to govern what is knowable – hence, what can or cannot be true. As Lincoln and Guba (1985) and McCloskey (1983) have argued, the last century has witnessed the rise and domination of a scientific credo grounded in logical positivism, logical empiricism, operationalism, and behaviorism, an amalgam dubbed "modernism" by McCloskey and mockingly called "the Received View" by its critics. One of its precepts holds that only the indubitable can count for knowledge – an article of faith professed loudly in late 19th century physics and mathematics, but today discredited (Capra 1977; Davis and Hersh 1981; Kline 1980). By and large, most social scientists and consumer researchers have honored modernism, or at least its image. Among its axioms, Lincoln and Guba (1985) and McCloskey (1983) list:

- Inquiry is value free
- Knower and known are independent, a dualism
- Time- and context-free generalizations (nomothetic statements) are possible

- Reality is single, tangible, and fragmentable
- Prediction (and control) is the goal of science
- Objectivity is to be treasured; subjective "observation" (introspection) is not scientific knowledge
- Kelvin's Dictum: "When you cannot express it in numbers, your knowledge is of a meagre and unsatisfactory kind"

Thayer describes the pursuit of this *scientism* as "an ideology that permits us to believe that what we are studying is 'out there' rather than 'in here,' and that what we are after is the 'truth,' which is, for those who subscribe to the faith, some function of large masses of data" (1982, p. 35).

There are at least two fallacies at the heart of the Received View. First, objectivity is impossible: theories precede facts and interpretation precedes perception, otherwise how would some signs be singled out and prioritized as more significant or more meaningful? Second, the reality observed is one that pre-exists, precoded to sustain meaning in social spheres, Researchers, like any other group of human beings, admittedly or not, have essential, vested interests in that meaning.

In Peircean semiotics, each person is a sign, in fact principally a symbol – a regenerating spiral of interpretants in a social world of endless semiosis. In consumer research this translates into a higher degree of self-consciousness and self-reflexivity by researchers concerning (1) the pre-existing interpretations they bring to their work, (2) the openendedness of their evolving insights, and (3) the inherited and created symbols they employ in the quest of consumer science. On these exact issues Levy implicitly invoked semiotics while discussing three *ACR* papers on product symbolism (Levy 1982, p. 543):

> The discussion of these three papers highlights to me what we might call a serial regress of perceptions, as in a mirror where an observer sees an observer who sees an observer, to infinity. I am made self-conscious in commenting on and trying to sort out my perceptions of these authors' perceptions of their subjects' perceptions; and you will observe mine, perhaps mention them to others, etc.

Levy's concluding remark injects the semiotic doctrine into consumer research (p. 543):

> We academicians observe and think about the relationships among symbols by studying the ways that selves use them and the interpretation made by others who observe the selves. Although we may dignify our observations and thoughts by calling them data and theories, it may be salutary to recognize that we are just more others observing selves; and that data and theories are symbols of our profession. It is necessary to face up to the subjectivity that is involved on all sides.

Though not explicitly mentioning semiotics, Bristor (1985), Lakoff and Johnson (1980), McCloskey (1983), Palmer (1978), and Ward and Ruekert (1984) have concentrated on exposing researcher/scientist symbol systems. Their insights together with a heightened semiotic competence can contribute to improved scholarship in theory building, testing, and communicating. For instance, popular research metaphors include cognition-as-computerlike and behavior-as-scriptlike. These are symbolic icons whose power derives from agreed-upon similarities. As Ward and Ruekert point out, while such metaphors often facilitate understanding, they also commonly harbor surpluses and deficiencies of meaning that, if unchallenged or unrecognized, can confound more than clarify. As these symbolic icons are promulgated and accepted, they become themselves a code among researchers – an interpretation that precedes the facts. One of Peirce's chief goals was to humanize the sciences by fostering an ethics of scientific terminology and tools, but as Pignatari (1978) notes, though scientists continue to be inveterate metaphor makers, they spend little time examining and re-evaluating their symbolic icons (Palmer 1978).

This may explain why semiotics is intellectually discomforting: it insists on an ongoing reflexivity where the researcher's presuppositions – prior beliefs, theories, models, metaphors, etc. – are regarded as integral to the inquiry's outcome. This active skepticism and resistance to disciplinarity turns semiotics inward to such an extent that Kristeva has suggested that "semiotics cannot develop except as a critique of semiotics" (Kristeva 1969, p. 30). This is a bold prescription, but one that applies equally to consumer research. Semiotics joins with marketing and consumer researchers like Anderson (1983), Bristor (1985), Peter and Olson (1983), and O'Shaughnessy (1985) in fostering a more relativistic, sociological philosophy of science which, as Lincoln and Guba and McCloskey show, is gaining credibility as modernism totters from the weight of its unverifiable epistemological and metaphysical dogmas.

The intense reflexivity expected from its adherents and the provisionality it layers over all explanations conjured by humanity make semiotics as insightful as it is sometimes obtuse. The formidable metalanguage and the virtuosic flair that make some semiotic writings unduly obscure have retarded the diffusion of semiotic thought into areas like consumer research. These problems are, nonetheless, surmountable and worth overcoming, as Eco and Douglas have each argued. On provisionality, Eco has written (1978, p. 83):

> The semiotic approach is ruled by a sort of indeterminacy principle: insofar as signifying and communicating are social functions that determine both social organization and social evolution, to "speak" about "speaking," to signify signification, or to communicate about communication cannot but influence the universe of speaking, signifying, and communicating.

On reflexivity, Douglas has pointed out (1982, p. 199):

> Wherever it has been applied, semiotics has raised controversy. Any academic discipline that has been sleepily taking for granted the conditions of its own communications finds that semiotic analysis can open new depths of awareness and raise new theoretical questions ... Inevitably, exploiting a new

understanding of structures of communication in a given medium brings to the surface thorny epistemological problems that formerly could be ignored by practitioners in that medium.

These remarks provide glimpses of the substantial opportunity semiotics offers to consumer research at a time when one surveyor of our field has opined that our existing methods and tools are obviating our brains (Jacoby 1978; see also Hirschman 1985). No lone perspective, including semiotics, could in itself guide us out of the quagmire thus described. Semiotics, in fact, would suggest that the condition is largely intrinsic to Western thought, if not human nature and the whole symbolic environment; accepting the condition and gaining wisdom through the anxiety is the initial step toward the enlightenment we all seek.

Does this mean that we will wallow in relativism, solipcism, and nihilism? Those who believe the purpose of consumer research is to reach the truth about consumer life will likely answer "yes." What semiotics contends is that the cybernetic matrix of the symbol-human environment will not permit us to arrive at the truth. From this vista, Thayer asks, "Would we go about our business any differently if we sought not to arrive, but to contribute to and enrich the dance of life?" (1982, p. 38). Wood affirms Thayer and implicates semiotics as an essential doctrine in the inquiry into consumer behavior (1982, p. 7):

> Symbolic ability is central to humanity... . Whatever paths we take, we will be acting in ways uniquely human, because we will employ symbols to reach our ends. Humans have such choices only because we can create, use, and abuse symbols to affect our own lives and worlds. This is why symbolic ability defines humanity. It is also why each of us should learn about our symbolic abilities and how we can use these to enhance ourselves and our worlds.

Clearly, semiotics can cultivate our understanding of our symbolic abilities as consumers and as researchers.

## Conclusion

The aim of this article has been to profile the doctrine of semiotics, and to explore and suggest ways in which consumer researchers can achieve added insights in their efforts to comprehend symbolism in the marketplace, in consumer life, and in the research arena itself. Semiotics is not a panacea, or even at this juncture a unified body of thought. In fact, like our own field, semiotics has been criticized for as yet not having produced a core of systematized theorems. In response, some semioticians as well as a few intrepid consumer researchers (Bristor 1985) have taken the position that a general theory for human nature (or consumer behavior) is neither realizable nor germane. Nonetheless, while the absence of unified hypotheses is often considered a weakness, it can also lend flexibility to applications and stimulate expanded research. And while semiotics may seem at first to be best suited as a logic of discovery, to counterbalance an overemphasis on the research of justification (Bouchard 1976; Kassarjian and Sheffet 1981), semiotics suspends if not rejects the discovery/justification distinction along with a host of other reality grids that have taken on the appearance of necessity (MacCannell and MacCannell 1982): self/other, mind/matter, theory/data, form/content, definition/operationalization, independent/dependent variables, and even subject/researcher. Though not a theory in the sense that modernists like Hunt (1983) subscribe to, perhaps the most cogent role semiotics can play is that of an epitheory (Bartels 1970) – that is, as an integrator of previously compartmentalized, incongruent, or unjuxtaposed theories, models, methods, concepts, and so on. In relating semiotics to economic theory, and by implication to marketing and consumer research, Douglas has written (1982, pp. 201–202):

> If semiotics can embed the extremely successful macro-analysis of individual decision-making into a new analysis of cultural interaction, it will be critically important in the history of Western thought. For we suffer from the lack of a methodologically satisfactory way of relating the cognizing individual to his cognized social environment, accounting for the feedbacks and reinforcements each gets from the other. In the growth of a long, slow wave of criticism of the fundamental assumptions of Western thought, semiotics has a unique part to contribute.

Consumer researchers are encouraged to investigate and fulfill the promising contribution semiotics seems poised to make.

## Notes

1. Although synonymous in general reference, Americans tend to use the Greek-derived *semiotics* in deference to Locke and Peirce while Europeans use the Greek-derived *semiology* in the tradition of Saussure (Fisch 1978; Sebeok 1976, Chapters 1 and 2). Specifically however, the Peircean and Saussurean lineages have cardinal contrasts as well as similarities (Fiske 1982; Sherry 1985; Singer 1984).
2. Reference notation for Peirce is volume and paragraph: Volume 5, Paragraph 488.
3. Like most theoretical semiotics, Nauta's original cube extends the doctrine beyond human communication to all possible forms of signification. For example, Nauta incorporates signals into the cube (e.g., hormones, electric signals) that perform teleological control functions in organisms and machines.
4. For the relatively uninitiated, a path of sequential semiotic readings is recommended that moves progressively into more complex semiotic philosophy: Fiske (1982), Innis (1985), Hawkes (1977), Singer (1984), Sebeok (1976), Eco (1976), and Deely (1982).
5. Kehret-Ward's dissertation was completed under the name Murray; for consistency we use Kehret-Ward throughout our discussion. In the reference list, see Murray (1981).
6. For brief but excellent historical inquiries on the acquisition and consumption of worldly goods, see Belk (1983, 1985) and McCracken (1985).

## References


Aman, Reinhold (1982), "Interlingual Taboos in Advertising: How Not to Name Your Product," in *Linguistics and the Professions*, ed. Robert J. DiPietro, Norwood, NJ: Ablex, 215–224.

Anderson, Myrdene, John Deely, Martin Krampen, Joseph Ransdell, Thomas A. Sebeok, and Thure von Uexkull (1984), "A Semiotic Perspective on the Sciences: Steps Toward a New Paradigm," *Semiotica*, 52 (1/2), 7–47.

Anderson, Paul F. (1983), "Marketing, Scientific Progress, and Scientific Method," *Journal of Marketing*, 47 (Fall), 18-31.

Arnould, Eric J. (1983), "Fancies and Glimmers: Culture and Consumer Behavior," in *Advances in Consumer Research*, Vol. 10, eds. Richard P. Bagozzi and Alice M. Tybout, Ann Arbor, MI: Association for Consumer Research, 702–704.

Barksdale, Hiram C. and William D. Perreault, Jr. (1980), "Can Consumers be Satisfied?" *MSU Business Topics*, Spring, 19–30.

Bartels, Robert (1970), *Marketing Theory and Metatheory*, Homewood, IL: Irwin.

Barthes, Roland (1968), *Elements of Semiology*, trans. Annette Lovers and Colin Smith, New York: Hill and Wang.

– (1972), *Mythologies*, trans. Annette Lovers, New York: Hill and Wang.

– (1983), *The Fashion System*, trans. Matthew Ward and Richard Howard, New York: Hill and Wang.

Bartos, Rena (1983), "Wornen and Advertising," *International Journal of Advertising*, 2, 33–45.

Belk, Russell W. (1976), "It's the Thought that Counts: A Signed Digraph Analysis of Gift-Giving," *Journal of Consumer Research*, 3 (December), 155–162.

– (1982), "Effects of Gift-Giving Involvement on Gift-Giving Strategies," in *Advances in Consumer Research*, Volume 9, ed. Andrew A. Mitchell, Ann Arbor, MI: Association for Consumer Research, 531–536.

– (1983), "Worldly Possessions: Issues and Criticisms," in *Advances in Consumer Research*, Vol. 10, eds. Richard P. Bagozzi and Alice M. Tybout, Ann Arbor, MI: Association for Consumer Research, 514–519.

– (1985), "Materialism: Trait Aspects of Living in the Material World," *Journal of Consumer Research*, 12 (December), 265–280.

–, Kenneth Bahn, and Robert Mayer (1982), "Developmental Recognition of Consumption Symbolism," *Journal of Consumer Research*, 9 (June), 4–17.

–, Robert Mayer, and Kenneth Bahn (1982), "The Eye of the Beholder: Individual Differences in Perceptions of Consumption Symbolism," in *Advances in Consumer Research*, Vol. 9, ed. Andrew Mitchell, Ann Arbor, MI: Association for Consumer Research, 523–530.

–, Robert Mayer, and Amy Driscoll (1984), "Children's Recognition of Consumption Symbolism in Children's Products," *Journal of Consumer Research*, 10 (March), 386–397.

Bodley, John (1982), *Victims of Progress*, Palo Alto, CA: Mayfield.

Bouchard, Thomas J. (1976), "Field Research Methods: Interviewing, Questionnaires, Participant Observation, Systematic Observation, Unobtrusive Measures," in *Handbook of Industrial and Organizational Psychology*, ed. Marvin D. Dunnette, Chicago: Rand-McNally, 363–413.

Boulding, Kenneth (1956), *The Image*, Ann Arbor, MI: University of Michigan Press.

Brewer, W. F. and G. V. Nakamura (1984), "The Nature and Functions of Schemas," in *Handbook of Social Cognition*, eds. R. W. Wyer, Jr. and T. K. Srull, Hillsdale, NJ: Lawrence Erlbaum, 119–159.

Bristor, Julia M. (1985), "Consumer Behavior from a Contemporary Philosophy of Science Perspective: An Organizational Framework," in *Advances in Consumer Research*, Vol. 12, eds. Elizabeth C. Hirschman and Morris B. Holbrook, Provo, UT: Association for Consumer Research, 300–304.

Bruyn, Severyn T. (1967), "The New Empiricists: The Participant Observer and Phenomenologist," *Sociology and Social Research*, 51 (3), 317–328.

Bryant, Kathleen and Brigitte Jordan (1978), "The Advertising Couple: The Portrayal of the Couple and Their Relationship in Popular Magazine Advertisements," paper presented at the Sixth Annual Midwest Popular Culture Association Conference, East Lansing, MI: Michigan State University, November.

Buczynska-Garewicz, Hanna (1981), "The Meaning of 'Interpretant'," *Semiosis*, Vol. 21, 10–14.

– (1983), "Sign and Dialogue," *American Journal of Semiotics*, 2 (1–2), 27–43.

Capra, Fritjof (1977), *The Tao of Physics*, New York: Bantam.

Clawson, C. Joseph and Donald E. Vinson (1978), "Human Values: A Historical and Interdisciplinary Analysis," in *Advances in Consumer Research*, ed. H. Keith Hunt, Ann Arbor, MI: Association for Consumer Research, 396–402.

Courtney, Alice E. and Thomas W. Whipple (198 3), *Sex Stereotyping in Advertising*, Lexington, MA: Lexington Books.

Crocker, Jennifer (1984), "A Schematic Approach to Changing Consumers' Beliefs," in *Advances in Consumer Research*, Vol. 11, ed. Thomas Kinnear, Provo, UT: Association for Consumer Research, 472–477.

Crosson, Frederick J. (1967), "Information Theory and Phenomenology," in *Philosophy and Cybernetics*, eds. Frederick J. Crosson and Kenneth M. Sayre, Notre Dame: University of Notre Dame Press.

Csikszentmihalyi, Mihaly and Eugene Rochberg-Halton (1981), *The Meaning of Things: Domestic Symbols in the Self*, Cambridge: Cambridge University Press.

Culler, Jonathan (1981), *The Pursuit of Signs*, Ithaca, N. Cornell University Press.

Davis, Philip J. and Reuben Hersh (1981), *The Mathematical Experience*, Boston: Houghton-Mifflin.

Deely, John (1982), *Introducing Semiotics*, Bloomington, IN: Indiana University Press.

Deshpande, Rohit (1983), "'Paradigms Lost': On Theory a Method in Research in Marketing," *Journal of Marketing*, 47 (Fall), 101–110.

Douglas, Mary (1970), *Natural Symbols*, New York: Panther Books.

– (1982), "The Future of Semiotics," *Semiotica*, (3/4), 197–203.

– and Baron Isherwood (1979), *The World of Goods*, New York: Basic Books.

Eco, Umberto (1976), *A Theory of Semiotics*, Bloomington IN: Indiana University Press.

– (1978), "Semiotics: A Discipline or an Interdiscipliary Method" in *Sight, Sound, and Sense*, ed. Thomas A. Sebeok, Bloomington, IN: Indiana University Press, 73–83.

– (1979), *The Role of the Reader*, Bloomington, IN: Indiana University Press.

– (1984), *Semiotics and the Philosophy of Language*, Bloomington, IN: Indiana University Press.

Elkin, Patrick (1969), "Advertising Themes and Quiet Resolutions: Dilemmas in French Canada," *American Journal of Sociology*, July.

Fine, Gary Alan (1985), "The Goliath Effect: Corporate Dominance and Mercantile Legends," *Journal of American Folklore*, 98 (387), 63–84.

Fisch, Max H. (1978), "Peirce's General Theory of Signs," in *Sight, Sound, and Sense*, ed. Thomas A. Sebeok, Bloomington, IN: Indiana University Press.

Fiske, John (1982), *Introduction to Communication Studies*, London: Methuen.

Fox, Stephen (1984), *The Mirror Makers*, New York: William Morrow.

Gallant, Mary J. and Sherryl Kleinman (1983), "Symbolic Interactionism vs. Ethnomethodology," *Symbolic Interaction*, 6 (1), 1–18.

Gardner, Burleigh B. and Sidney J. Levy (1955), "The Product and the Brand," *Harvard Business Review*, 33 (March April), 33–39.

Geertz, Clifford (1973), *The Interpretation of Cultures*, Nev York: Basic Books.

– (1983), *Local Knowledge*, New York: Basic Books.

Goffman, Erving (1959), *The Presentation of Self in Everyday Life*, Garden City, NY: Doubleday.

– (1979), *Gender Advertisements*, New York: Harper and Row.

Gopnik, Myrna (1981), "Language, Cognition, and the Theory of Signs," *Recherches Semiotiques Semiotic Inquiry*, 1 (4), 310–327.

Greenburg, J. H. (1964), "Linguistics and Ethnology," in *Language in Culture and Society*, ed. Del Hymes, New York: Harper and Row, 27–31.

Hall, Edward T. and George Trager (1953), *The Analysis of Culture*, Washington, D.C.: American Council of Learned Societies.

Hanson, F. Allan and Louise Hanson (1981), "The Cybernetics of Cultural Communication," in *Semiotic Themes*, ed. Richard George, Lawrence, KS: University of Kansas Press, 251–273.

Harman, Willis (1981), "Science and the Clarification of Values: Implications of Recent Findings in Psychological and Psychic Research," *Journal of Humanistic Psychology*, 21 (Summer), 3–16.

Hastie, Reid (1981), "Schematic Principles in Human Memory," in *Social Cognition: The Ontario Symposium*, eds. E.T. Higgins, C.P. Herman, and M.P. Zanna. Hillsdale, NJ: Erlbaum, 39–88.

Hawkes, Terence (1977), *Structuralism and Semiotics*, Berkeley, CA: University of California Press.

Henry, Jules (1956), *Culture Against Man*, New York: Vintage.

Hirschman, Elizabeth C. ( 1980), "Attributes of Attributes and Layers of Meaning," in *Advances in Consumer Research*, Vol. 7, ed. Jerry C. Olson, Ann Arbor, MI: Association for Consumer Research. 7–11.

– (1981), "Comprehending Symbolic Consumption: Three Theoretical Issues," in *Symbolic Consumer Behavior*, eds. Elizabeth C. Hirschman and Morris B. Holbrook, Ann Arbor, MI: Association for Consumer Research, 4–6.

– (1985), "Scientific Style and the Conduct of Consumer Research," *Journal of Consumer Research*, 12 (September), 225– 239.

– and Morris B. Holbrook (1981), "Symbolic Consumer Behavior: An Introduction," in *Symbolic Consumer Behavior*, eds. Elizabeth C. Hirschman and Morris B. Holbrook, Ann Arbor, MI: Association for Consumer Research, 1–2.

Holbrook, Morris B. (1978), "Beyond Attitude Structure: Toward the Informational Determinants of Attitude:" *Journal of Marketing Research*, 25 (November), 545–556.

– and Elizabeth C. Hirschman (1982), "The Experiential Aspects of Consumption: Consumer Fantasies, Feelings, and Fun," *Journal of Consumer Research*, 9 (September), 132–140.

Holman, Rebecca H. (1976), "Communicational Properties of Women's Clothing: Isolation of Discriminable Clothing Ensembles and Identification of Attributions Made to One Person Wearing Each Ensemble," unpublished Ph.D. dissertation, the University of Texas at Austin.

– (1980a), "Clothing as Communication: An Empirical Investigation," in *Advances in Consumer Research*, Vol. 7, ed. Jerry C. Olson, Ann Arbor, MI: Association for Consumer Research, 372–377.

– (1980b), "A Transcription and Analysis System for the Study of Women's Clothing Behavior," *Semiotica*, 32 (1/2), 11–34.

– (1981a), "Apparel as Communication," in *Symbolic Consumer Behavior*, eds. Elizabeth C. Hirschman and Morris B. Holbrook, Ann Arbor, MI: Association for Consumer Research, 7–15.

– (1981b), "Product Use as Communication: A Fresh Look at a Venerable Topic," in *Review of Marketing*, eds. Ben M. Enis and Kenneth J. Roering, Chicago: American Marketing Association, 106–119.

(1981c), "The Imagination of the Future: A Hidden Concept in the Study of Consumer Decision Making," in *Advances in Consumer Research*, Vol. 8, ed. Kent B. Monroe, Ann Arbor, MI: Association for Consumer Research, 187–191.

– (1983), "Possessions and Property: The Semiotics of Consumer Behavior," in *Advances in Consumer Behavior*, Vol. 10, eds. Richard P. Bagozzi and Alice M. Tybout, Ann Arbor, MI: Association for Consumer Research, 565–568.

Hunt, Shelby D. (1983), *Marketing Theory*, Homewood, IL: Irwin.

Innis, Robert E. (1985), *Semiotics: An Introductory Anthology*, Bloomington, IN: Indiana University Press.

Jacoby, Jacob (1978), "Consumer Research: A State of the Art Review," *Journal of Marketing*, 42 (April), 87–96.

Kassarjian, Harold H. and Mary Jane Sheffet (1981), "Personality and Consumer Behavior," in *Perspectives in Consumer Behavior*, 3rd ed., eds. Harold H. Kassarjian and Thomas Robertson, Glenview, IL: Scott Foresman, 160–180.

Kehret-Ward, Trudy (1982), "A Strategy for Understanding the Semiology of Product Choice," paper presented at 1982 Association for Consumer Research Convention, San Francisco, CA.

–, Marcia W. Johnson. Therese A. Louie (1985), "Improving Recall by Manipulating the Syntax of Consumption Rituals," in *Advances in Consumer Research*, Vol. 12, eds. Elizabeth C. Hirschman and Morris B. Holbrook, Provo, UT: Association for Consumer Research, 319–324.

– and Richard Yalch (1984), "To Take or Not to Take the Only One: Effects of Changing the Meaning of a Product Attribute on Choice Behavior," *Journal of Consumer Research*, 10 (March), 410–416.

Kline, Morris (1980), *Mathematics: The Loss of Certainty*, New York: Oxford.

Kristeva, Julia (1969), *Semiotike: Recherches pour une Semanalyse*, Paris: Sevil.

Lakoff, George and Mark Johnson (1980), *Metaphors We Live By*, Chicago: University of Chicago Press.

Lannon, Judie and Peter Cooper (1983), "Humanistic Advertising: A Holistic Cultural Perspective," *International Journal of Advertising*, 195–213.

Leach, Edmund (1976), *Culture and Communication*, Cambridge: Cambridge University Press.

Leigh, Thomas W. and Arno J. Rethans (1983), "Experiences with Script Elicitations within Consumer Decision Making Contexts," in *Advances in Consumer Research*, eds. Richard P. Bagozzi and Alice M. Tybout, Ann Arbor, MI: Association for Consumer Research, 667–672.

Levitt, Theodore (1970), "The Morality (?) of Advertising," *Harvard Business Review*, 48 (July–August), 84–92.

Levy, Sidney J. (1959), "Symbols for Sale," *Harvard Business Review*, 37 (July–August), 117–124.

– (1971), "Symbolism and Life Style," in *Perspectives in Marketing Management*, Glenview, IL: Scott, Foresman, 112–118.

– (1978), *Marketplace Behavior: Its Meaning for Management*, New York: AMACOM.

– (1981), "Interpreting Consumer Mythology: A Structural Approach to Consumer Behavior," *Journal of Marketing*, 45 (Summer), 49–61.

– (1982), "Symbols, Selves, and Others," in *Advances in Consumer Research*, Vol. 9, ed. Andrew Mitchell, Ann Arbor, MI: Association for Consumer Research, 542–543.

Leymore, Varda (1975), *Hidden Myth*, New York: Basic Books.

Lincoln, Yvonna S. and Egon G. Guba (1985), *Naturalistic Inquiry*, Beverly Hills, CA: Sage.

MacCannell, Dean (1976), "The Past and Future of Symbolic Interactionism," *Semiotica*, 16 (2), 99–114.

– and Juliet F. MacCannell (1982), *The Time of the Sign*, Bloomington, IN: Indiana University Press.

Marx, Karl (1876/1976), *Capital*, Vol. 1, trans. Ben Fowkes, Middlesex, England: Penguin Books.

McCloskey, Donald N. (1983), "The Rhetoric of Economics," *Journal of Economic Literature*, 21 (June), 481–517.

McCracken, Grant (1985), "Clio in the Marketplace: Theoretical and Methodological Issues in the History of Consumption," in *Historical Perspective in Consumer Research. National and International Perspectives*, eds. Chin Tiong Tan and Jagdish N. Sheth, Provo, UT: Association for Consumer Research.

– and Richard W. Pollay (1981), "Anthropology and the Study of Advertising," Working Paper #815, History of Advertising Archives, Faculty of Commerce and Business Administration, University of British Columbia.

Mick, David Glen (1987), "Schema-theoretics and Semiotics: Toward More Wholistic, Programmatic Research on Marketing Communication," *Semiotica*, in press.

Morris, Charles W. (1938), *Foundations of the Theory of Signs*, Chicago: University of Chicago Press.

– (1946), *Signs, Language, and Behavior*, New York: Prentice-Hall.

– (1964), *Signification and Significance: A Study of the Relations of Signs and Values*, Cambridge, MA: M.I.T. Press.

– (1971), *Writings on the General Theory of Signs*, The Hague: Mouton.

– (1976), *Image*, New York: Vantage.

Murray, Trudy L. (1981), "Developing the Ability to Relate Scarcity and Communication Value: How Children Come to Use Products as Linguistic Units," unpublished Ph.D. dissertation, the University of Washington.

Nauta, Doede (1972), *The Meaning of Information*, The Hague: Mouton.

Newman, Joseph W. (1957a), "New Insights, New Progress for Marketing," *Harvard Business Review*, 35 (November–December), 95–102.

– (1957b), "Toward Conceptual Schemes of Consumer Behavior," *Motivation Research and Marketing Management*, Boston: Harvard University Graduate School of Business Administration, Division of Research.

Nicosia, Francesco M. and Robert N. Mayer (1976), "Toward a Sociology of Consumption," *Journal of Consumer Research*, 3 (September), 65–74.

Ogden, C.K. and I.A. Richards (1923), *The Meaning of Meaning*, New York: Harcourt Brace.

Oiler, Carolyn (1982), "The Phenomenological Approach in Nursing Research," *Nursing Research*, 31 (3), 178–181.

Olshavsky, Richard W. and Donald H. Granbois (1979), "Consumer Decision Making – Fact or Fiction," *Journal of Consumer Research*, 6 (September), 93–100.

Osgood, Charles E, George J. Suci, and Percy H. Tannenbaum (1957), *The Measurement of Meaning*, Urban IL: The University of Illinois Press.

O'Shaughnessy, John (1985), "A Return to Reason in Consumer Research: An Hermeneutical Approach," in *Advances in Consumer Research*, Vol. 12, eds. Elizabeth Hirschman and Morris B. Holbrook, Provo, UT: Association for Consumer Research, 305–311.

Palmer, Stephen E. (1978), "Fundamental Aspects of Cognitive Representation," in *Cognition and Categorization*, eds. Eleanor Rosch and Barbara B. Lloyd, Hillsdale, NJ: Lawrence Erlbaum, 259–303.

Peirce, Charles Sanders (1931–58), *Collected Papers*, ed Charles Hartshorne, Paul Weiss, and Arthur W. Burke, Cambridge, MA: Harvard University Press.

Peter, J. Paul and Jerry C. Olson (1983), "Is Science Marketing?" *Journal of Marketing*, 47 (4), 111–125.

Pettit, Phillip (1975), *The Concept of Structuralism: A Critical Analysis*, Berkeley, CA: University of California Press.

Pignatari, Decio (1978), "The Contiguity Illusion," in *Sight Sound, and Sense*, ed. Thomas A. Sebeok, Bloomington IN: Indiana University Press, 84–97.

Pitts, Robert E., Jr. and Arch G. Woodside, eds. (1984), *Personal Values and Consumer Psychology*, Lexington, MA Lexington Books.

Polanyi, Michael (1958), *Personal Knowledge*, Chicago, IL: University of Chicago Press.

– (1969), *Knowing and Being*, Chicago, IL: University of Chicago Press.

Pollay, Richard W. (1983), "Measuring the Cultural Value Manifest in Advertising," in *Current Issues and Research in Advertising*, eds. James H. Leigh and Claude R. Martin, Jr., Ann Arbor, MI: University of Michigan Press 71–92.

– (1986), "The Distorted Mirror: Reflections on the Unintended Consequences of Advertising," *Journal of Marketing*, 50 (2), 18–36.

Puto, Christopher P. (1985), "Memory for Scripts in Advertisements," in *Advances in Consumer Research*, Vol. 12, eds. Elizabeth C. Hirschman and Morris B. Holbrook, Provo, UT: Association for Consumer Research, 404–409.

Ransdell, Joseph (1977), "Some Leading Ideas of Peirce's Semiotic," *Semiotica*, 19 (3/4), 157–178.

Ricks, David A., Jeffrey S. Arpan, and Marilyn Y. Fu (1974), "Pitfalls in Advertising Overseas," *Journal of Adverlising Research*, 14 (6), 47–51.

Roberts, Mary Lou and Perri B. Koggan (1975), "How Should Women be Portrayed in Advertisements? – "A Call for Research," in *Advances in Consumer Research*, Vol. 6, ed. William L. Wilkie, Ann Arbor, MI: Association for Consumer Research, 66–72.

Rochberg-Halton, Eugene and Kevin McMurtrey (1983), "The Foundations of Modern Semiotic: Charles Peirce and Charles Morris," *American Journal of Semiotics*, 2 (1–2), 129–156.
Rook, Dennis W. (1985), "The Ritual Dimension of Consumer Behavior," *Journal of Consumer Research*, 12 (December), 251–264.
Sahlins, Marshall (1976), *Culture and Practical Reason*, Chicago: University of Chicago Press.
Sapir, Edward (1949), *Selected Writings in Language, Culture, and Personality*, ed. David G. Mandelbaum, Berkeley, CA: University of California Press.
Saussure, Ferdinand de (1915/1966), *Cour de Linguistic Generale (Course in General Linguistics)*, trans. Wade Baskin, New York: McGraw-Hill.
Schenk, Carolyn Turner and Rebecca H. Holman (1980), "A Sociological Approach to Brand Choice: The Concept of Situational Self Image," in *Advances in Consumer Research*, Vol. 7, ed. Jerry C. Olson, Ann Arbor, MI: Association for Consumer Research, 610–614.
Schneider, David M. (1976), "Notes Toward a Theory of Culture," in *Meaning in Anthropology*, eds. Keith H. Basso and Henry A. Selby, Albuquerque, NM: University of New Mexico Press, 197–220.
Sebeok, Thomas A. (1972), *Perspectives in Zoosemiotics*, The Hague: Mouton.
– (1974), *The Sign and Its Masters*, Austin, TX: University of Texas Press.
– (1976), *Contributions to the Doctrine of Signs*, Bloomington, IN: Indiana University Press.
– (1981), *The Play of Musement*, Bloomington, IN: Indiana University Press.
Shands, Harley C. (1970), *Semiotic Approaches to Psychiatry*, The Hague: Mouton.
– and James D. Meltzer (1977), "Unexpected Semiotic Implications of Medical Inquiry," in *A Perfusion of Signs*, ed. Thomas A. Sebeok, Bloomington, IN: Indiana University Press.
Sherry, John F, Jr. (1983), "Gift Giving in Anthropological Perspective," *Journal of Consumer Research*, 10 (September), 157–168.
– (1984), "Some Implications of Consumer Oral Tradition for Reactive Marketing," in *Advances in Consumer Research*, Vol. 11, ed. Thomas Kinnear, Provo, UT: Association for Consumer Research, 741–747.
- (1985), "Advertising as a Cultural System," unpublished manuscript, Marketing Department, Northwestern University.
Shimp, Terence A. and Ivan L. Preston (1981), "Deceptive and Nondeceptive Consequences of Evaluative Advertising," *Journal of Marketing*, 45 (1), 22–32.
Singer, Milton (1984), *Man's Glassy Essence*, Bloomington, IN: Indiana University Press.
Smith, Robert E. and Shelby D. Hunt (1978), "Attributional Processes and Effects in Promotional Situations," *Journal of Consumer Research*, 5 (December), 149–158.
Solomon, Michael R. (1983), "The Role of Products as Social Stimuli: A Symbolic Interactionism Perspective," *Journal of Consumer Research*, 10 (December), 319–329.
Sperber, Dan (1974), *Rethinking Symbolism*, Cambridge, MA: Cambridge University Press.
Spinks, C.W. (1983), "Peirce's Demon Abduction: Or How to Charm the Truth Out of a Quark," *American Journal of Semiotics*, 2 (1–2), 195–208.
Steiner, Wendy (1978), "Modern American Semiotics," in *The Sign: Semiotics Around the World*, eds. R. W. Bailey, L. Matejka, and P. Steiner, Ann Arbor, MI: University of Michigan Press, 99–118.
Thayer, Lee (1982), "Human Nature: of Communication, of Structuralism, of Semiotics," *Semiotica*, 41 (1/4), 25–40.
Thorndyke, Perry W. and Frank R. Yekovich (1980), "A Critique of Schemata as a Theory of Human Story Memory," *Poetics*, 9, 23–49.
Turner, Victor (1967), *The Forest of Symbols*, Ithaca, NY: Cornell University.
Umiker-Sebeok, D. Jean (1979), "Nature's Way? Visual Representations of American Life Cycles," in *Semiotics of Culture*, eds. Irene Portis Winner and D. Jean Umiker-Sebeok, The Hague: Mouton, 173–220.
– (1981), "The Seven Ages of Woman: A View from American Magazine Advertisements," in *Gender and Nonverbal Behavior*, eds. Clara Mayo and Nancy M. Henley, New York: Springer-Verlag.
Veblen, Thorstein (1899), *The Theory of the Leisure Class*, New York: The New American Library.

Ward, James and Robert W. Ruekert (1984), "The Use of Metaphor in Marketing Theory and Research," in *Proceedings of the Fourteenth Annual Albert Haring Symposium*, Graduate School of Business, Bloomington, IN: Indiana University, 111–129.

Ward, Scott (1974), "Consumer Socialization," *Journal of Consumer Research*, 1 (September), 1–15.

Warner, W. Lloyd (1953), *American Life: Dream and Reality*, Chicago: University of Chicago Press.

– and Paul S. Lunt (1941), *The Social Life of a Modern Community* ("Yankee City Series," Vol. 1), New Haven, CT: Yale University Press.

Wasson, Chester R. (1975), *Consumer Behavior: A Managerial Viewpoint*, Austin, TX: Lone Star.

Webb, Eugene J. (1978), "Unconventionality, Triangulation, and Inference," in *Sociological Methods: A Sourcebook*, ed. Norman K. Denzin, New York: McGraw-Hill, 322–328.

Wernick, Andrew (1983), "Advertising and Ideology: An Interpretive Frarnework," *Theory, Culture, and Society*, 2 (1), 16–33.

Winner, Irene Portis (1978), "Cultural Semiotics and Anthropology," in *The Sign: Semiotics Around the World*, eds. R.W. Bailey, L. Matejka, and P. Steiner, Ann Arbor, MI: University of Michigan Press, 335–363.

Williamson, Judith (1978), *Decoding Advertisements: Idealogy and Meaning in Advertising*, London: Marion Boyars.

Wood, Julia T. (1982), *Human Communication-A Symbolic Interactionist Perspective*, New York: Holt, Rinehart, and Winston.

Yalch, Richard and Rebecca Elmore-Yalch (1984), "The Effect of Numbers on the Route to Persuasion," *Journal of Consumer Research*, 11 (June), 522–527.

Zanot, Eric (1984), "Public Attitudes Towards Advertising: The American Experience," *International Journal of Advertising*, 3, 1–15.

Zernan, J. Jay (1977), "Peirce's Theory of Signs," in *A Perfusion of Signs*, ed. Thomas A. Sebeok, Bloomington, IN: Indiana University Press, 22–39.

# 12

# Philosophical Tensions in Consumer Inquiry

**J. Paul Peter**

**Source:** *Handbook of Consumer Research* (1991): 533–547.

## Introduction

Consumer inquiry has many difficulties that make it a challenging vocation. For example, the field has never set any obtainable objectives by which progress could be measured, nor has it agreed upon the appropriate benefactors of its efforts. Agreement has not been reached on what aspects of the human condition, if any, qualify for exclusion from consideration, leaving the field with an infinite number of phenomena to account for. Other social sciences, which provide the majority of the field's intellectual grist, are commonly considered by their leaders to be in various states of disarray, if not outright crisis, leaving them questionable sources for research ideas and methods. Integrating these diverse and often incommensurable borrowings is a challenge far greater than any faced by Newton. If immutable laws or empirical generalizations are considered to be the standards for judgment, then consumer inquiry must be considered ineffectual.

It is not surprising, then, that consumer inquirers have turned to yet other fields in seeking solutions to their problems or at least solace for their condition. These fields include the philosophy of science, the history of science, and the sociology of science, which collectively are called the "science studies." It is likely that most consumer inquirers look to the science studies literature in hopes of finding better ways of doing science.

Certainly, much has been learned about the nature of science from the excursion into the science studies literature. However, simple answers to the question of how to do science better were not found. Rather, one of the major lessons learned has been that the philosophy of science is in a state of disarray and that there is much disagreement about the nature of science and how it works. In fact, Laudan states the condition quite clearly when he writes:

> Unfortunately, of course, the efforts of philosophers to identify precisely the components of the scientific method have fallen on hard times. So gloomy is the situation these days that few active philosophers of science would still venture to claim that they knew what the scientific method was. But to put it that way is to give too rosy a picture of the present state of disarray in my field, for what I really mean to say is that many philosophers of science, present company included, would go so far as to deny that there was anything corresponding to a unified set of methods which characterized what we customarily call science. (1984, p. 1)

Given this situation, it is not surprising that there are different, conflicting philosophical views concerning the nature of science and that a number of them have been advocated as the appropriate foundation for consumer inquiry.

The purpose of this paper is to review and evaluate the major philosophical positions advanced in consumer inquiry and to suggest implications for practicing researchers. The paper is divided into three sections. In the first section, three positivistic accounts of science are reviewed and evaluated. These include logical empiricism, naive falsification, and sophisticated methodological falsification. It is the premise of this paper that these accounts are fundamentally defective and do not provide a sound philosophical foundation for consumer inquiry. In the second section, a relativistic account of science is described and evaluated. It is the position of this paper that a relativistic view provides the best account of science that is currently available and the most useful philosophical foundation for consumer inquiry. The final section discusses general implications for practicing consumer researchers for adopting various philosophical positions.

## Positivistic Accounts of Science

Logical positivism was created by the mathematicians and philosophers of the Vienna Circle in the 1920s and dominated the philosophical landscape for the next thirty years. This approach was often discussed by its developers as though it provided a description of how scientific theories develop, or as though it detailed an explication of what constitutes a scientific theory. However, these scholars became so enamored with developing stringent criteria for scientific theories that their work lost sight of what was humanly possible. In fact, in spite of exemplary developments in many areas of science, there are likely no theories ever created by earthlings that could satisfy the requirements of the positivistic Received View.

There have been a number of attempts to modify logical positivism while still maintaining a number of its major tenets. These attempts share in common a strong belief in the objectivity of empirical data and its power to sort out truth (or something like it, such as verisimilitude or confirmation) from falsity, or at least to refute false theories. These positivistic accounts of science advocate a single scientific method. Although the particulars of this method have not been detailed, it is this method that is assumed to differentiate science from nonscience. These views focus on the processes involved in attempts to justify knowledge claims, and they do not seriously consider the processes by which theories are created.

### Logical Empiricism

Logical empiricism is usually considered a moderate version of logical positivism that attempts to avoid the "problem of induction." The induction problem refers to the fact that no matter how many empirical observations support a statement, it cannot be concluded that the statement is universally true.

Thus, unlike logical positivists, logical empiricists reject the idea that scientific theories can be conclusively verified. However, they do argue that theories can be increasingly confirmed through empirical research and logical analysis.

In marketing and consumer inquiry, Hunt has written extensively on his interpretations of this perspective (e.g., 1976, 1983a, 1983b, 1984, 1989; Hunt and Speck 1985), and he has been its major advocate. While these accounts are sometimes contradictory, below is an attempt to summarize several of the major points in Hunt's interpretation.

According to Hunt, logical empiricists believe that the world is real, and that there are real phenomena which have an existence independent of the observer. The purpose of science is, therefore, to increase understanding of these real phenomena. While all scientific activity is not completely objective, objectivity as a goal for science is and ought to be a valuable norm (Hunt and Speck, 1985, pp. 30–31). The difference between science and nonscience is the open empirical testing of knowledge claims. This testing is called "intersubjective certification" (Hunt 1983a).

Logical empiricism holds that explanation is central to science and that the occurrence of a phenomenon is explained by showing that the phenomenon was expected to occur as a result of some regularity or "lawlike generalization." Scientific prediction has the same logical structure as scientific explanation, the major difference being the time frame. Theories and lawlike generalizations are used to explain past events and to predict future events (Hunt and Speck, 1985, p. 31).

According to Hunt, "Theories are systematically related sets of statements, including some lawlike generalizations, that are empirically testable … *lawlike* denotes nothing more than the observed regularity in the occurrence of two or more phenomena" (1983b, p. 10). Hunt argues that the deductive-nomological model (with the additional requirement of causal mechanisms or causal laws in the explanans) and the inductive-statistical model (without the requirement that premises suggest a conclusion with "high probability") "remain the most viable models available for explaining phenomena" (Hunt 1983a, p. 99). Hunt also notes that the discovery/justification, the analytic/synthetic, and the observational/theoretical dichotomies play central roles in logical empiricism:

> The discovery/justification dichotomy reminds us that it is useful to distinguish between procedures that scientists use to create or discover hypotheses, lawlike generalizations, and theories from the procedures that are used to evaluate [justify] the truth-content of these same theories, lawlike generalizations, and hypotheses …

The analytic/synthetic dichotomy proposes that the truth content of different kinds of sentences is ascertained in different ways. Some statements (analytical statements) are true or false depending solely on how certain terms in the statements are defined. For example, consider the statement "all department stores that have 81,000 square feet of floor space have 900 square yards of floor space." This statement is true by virtue of our definitions of "square feet, and "square yards." It is *analytically* true. On the other hand, the truth-content of other statements can be determined only by comparing them with certain aspects of the real world. For example, "all department stores that have 81,000 square feet of floor space will have at least ten separate departments" is synthetic and its truth content must be determined by examining actual characteristics of department stores.

The observational/theoretical dichotomy points out that some of the terms in science (observables) have relatively direct empirical referents whereas other terms (theoreticals) seem "far removed" from the empirical world ... (Hunt and Speck, 1985, pp. 31–32).

*Evaluation of Logical Empiricism.* There are many reasons why logical empiricism has long been rejected in the science studies literature. (Only a few of them will be mentioned here. Chalmars 1976, Lincoln and Guba 1985, and Suppe 1977 provide more detailed accounts.) First, it fails to overcome the problem of induction, since it still depends on a finite number of observations to support the assertion that a universal statement is "probably true" (see Anderson 1983). In fact, philosophers have long agreed that there is no defensible method for determining the truth-content of statements.

Second, no defensible criterion has ever been found that differentiates science from nonscience. Hunt's criteria of empirical testability and intersubjective certification are notoriously ambiguous and met by a variety of nonscientific areas (see Laudan 1983).

Third, the supposed symmetry between explanation and prediction has been severely criticized, leading even Hempel (1965) to change his views, and Bromberger (1966) demonstrated the deductive-nomological model to be seriously defective. Suppe (1977, p. 623) concluded that both the deductive-nomological and inductive-statistical models are defective. Hunt's requirement of causal laws in the explanans of the deductive-nomological model makes it impossible to create such explanations. This is because causal laws that meet the requirements of logical empiricism cannot be developed (see, for example, Hunt 1983, pp. 96–97; 125). In terms of Hunt's suggestion for dropping the "highly probable" statement from the inductive-statistical model, it should be clear that this leaves the model with no criterion for judgment. Thus, the value of these models has not been demonstrated.

Further, if "lawlike" denotes nothing more than "observed regularity," as proposed by Hunt, then a correlation of any kind can be considered a lawlike generalization. For example, a correlation between hemline lengths and the stock market prices meets his criterion, yet it seems unlikely that many people would accept this as a lawlike generalization. Similarly, Hunt's definition of theory fails to distinguish scientific theories from other forms of statements. For example, astrology, parapsychology and witchcraft can be shown to meet his requirements, yet few people accept these areas as scientific.

Finally, the analytic/synthetic distinction was shown to be untenable, as was the observational/theoretical dichotomy (see Suppe 1977). Without these distinctions, logical empiricism must be viewed as inadequate.

Although this discussion provides only a brief sketch and evaluation of logical or modern empiricism, it should be clear that the approach has been repudiated in the science studies literature. One positivistic attempt to provide an alternative to logical empiricism is naive falsification. Rather than seeking gradual confirmation of theories through induction as advocated by logical empiricism, naive falsification emphasizes the refutation of deductively derived hypotheses.

### Naive Falsification

Among empirical researchers in consumer inquiry, particularly those who advocate laboratory experimentation, naive falsification is often championed. For example, while there were serious disagreements in a recent debate on external validity (Calder *et al.* 1981, 1982, 1983; Lynch 1982, 1983), apparently the participants agreed that "... Popper's falsification principle is at the heart of the process by which we advance both our scientific knowledge and our confidence in that knowledge" (McGrath and Brinberg 1983, p. 116).

While not providing a detailed account of Popper's views, the Calder-Lynch debate did provide an interpretation of some of its tenets. For example, Calder *et al.* (1981) argue that:

> Theory applications call for falsification test procedures. These procedures are used to test a theory by creating a context and measuring effects within that context that have the potential to disprove or refute the theory ... Theories that repeatedly survive rigorous falsification attempts are accepted as scientific explanations (subject to more stringent testing) and are candidates for application. (p. 198)

They further point out that studies should be done to provide the most rigorous possible tests for a theory. Theories that do not pass these tests are to be ruthlessly rejected. Any disconfirming evidence falsifies a theory, as Lynch (1983) explains:

> In an earlier paper, Calder *et al.* (1981) argued from the standpoint of a falsification philosophy of science (Popper 1959) and quite correctly noted that theories can be rejected if their predictions can be shown to be false for *any* subjects, settings, and events within their domain. (p. 109)

Thus, we have the main elements of naive falsification as interpreted in consumer inquiry. Theories are to be proposed and then rigorous empirical research is done to try to falsify them. Since science seeks universal propositions, any nonsupportive finding leads to immediate rejection of a theory. Supportive findings do not confirm a theory but give it a stature of a theory that "has not yet been falsified."

*Evaluation of Naive Falsification.* It is easy to demonstrate why this form of falsification is naive. According to this view a theory is falsified if predictions are disconfirmed for any subjects, settings, or events within the domain of the theory. Clearly, almost all theories would be immediately falsified if this criterion were applied. For example, consider a theory that states that there is a particular difference between two groups. Even with a reasonably large effect size, a large percentage of individuals in the two groups will be essentially similar or ordered contrary to the direction of the overall group mean. For example, a difference of 0.8 of a standard deviation is considered large for much social research (Cohen 1977). With such a difference, however, 52.6 percent of the two populations overlap (see Sawyer and Peter 1983). Thus, according to naive falsification, since some of the subjects are ordered contrary to the hypothesis, the hypothesis and theory must be rejected. Clearly, few theories would survive even a single empirical study if scientists took naive falsification seriously! Additional problems with this perspective are discussed in a later section of this paper.

### Sophisticated Methodological Falsification

Although many would argue that sophisticated methodological falsification is not a positivistic view, it is commonly interpreted as such in consumer inquiry (e.g., see Calder and Tybout 1987). This approach to falsification was developed by Lakatos (1970) in part to overcome the problem with naive falsification outlined previously. The main difference between it and naive falsification, according to Lakatos, is that

> ... in my conception criticism does not – and must not – kill as fast as Popper imagined. Purely negative, destructive criticism, like "refutation" or demonstration of an inconsistency does not eliminate a research programme. Criticism of a programme is a long and often frustrating process and one must treat budding programmes leniently. One may, of course, show up the degeneration of a research programme, but it is only *constructive criticism* which, with the help of rival research programmes, can achieve real success. (quoted in Suppe 1977, pp. 660–661)

In this view the focus is not on a single theory but on a sequence of ever improving theories, which are the research programs that, according to Lakatos, characterize mature sciences. Research programs have both a "positive heuristic," which directs the path of inquiry, and a "negative heuristic," which indicates which paths not to follow. Research programs also have an irrefutable "hard core" of fundamental assumptions that are determined by methodological decisions and are insulated from refutation by a "protective belt" of auxiliary hypotheses.

Research programs follow the positive heuristic and successively attempt to falsify theories. The theories consist of the negative heuristic and auxiliary hypotheses and, when falsified, are modified by the addition of new hypotheses, making a new theory. Each such cycle is a "problem shift" and is "theoretically progressive" if each successor predicts some novel, unexpected fact. A problem shift is "empirically progressive" if it leads to the discovery of a new fact. A problem shift that is not both theoretically and (at least intermittently) empirically progressive is degenerating and should be stopped (Suppe 1977, pp. 662–663).

*Evaluation of Sophisticated Methodological Falsification.* Both Leong (1985, pp. 36–37) and Suppe (1977, pp. 664–670) provide detailed criticisms of sophisticated methodological falsification. These criticisms generally focus on the idea that Lakatos has failed to explain how scientists could a priori choose a research program that would be progressive. Further, his work ignores the facts that many other factors besides theoretical and empirical progressiveness are involved in scientific theorizing and that what is theoretically reasonable is conditioned by the subject matter of the science. These and other criticisms led Suppe to conclude that this perspective is a "seriously defective account" (p. 669) and that

> In short, we can conclude that Lakatos has exposed *partially* one reasoning pattern in the growth of scientific knowledge which in some circumstances, *is* characteristic of good reasoning in science; but even in the cases he examines, much of the reasoning involved is not reflected in his account. Moreover, it is at best a pattern of good reasoning, and very often science does, and ought to, employ other, incompatible, patterns in proceeding rationally. Other than this limited achievement, Lakatos's work does little to illuminate the role of rationality in the growth of scientific knowledge. (1977, p. 670)

### General Evaluation of Falsification

There are many reasons why falsification in all of its forms has been rejected as an adequate philosophy of science. One of the most telling problems is that while falsificationists recognize that theories cannot be proven to be true, they typically accept the idea that theories can be proven to be false. However, Duhem (1953), Laudan (1977), and others have demonstrated that it is not possible to prove a theory to be false. This is because there is much more involved in any empirical study than the substantive hypothesis of interest. There are a whole set of assumptions about initial conditions, auxiliary hypotheses, and the validity of measuring instruments, of sampling, and of data analysis procedures. No study can completely unravel these and "test" only the substantive hypothesis of interest. Thus, any attempt to conclude that a theory has been falsified can easily be deflected by suggesting that something else in the maze of assumptions and premises caused the "falsifying" result (Laudan 1977, Anderson 1983).

In addition, imaginative researchers can make *ad hoc* modifications to a theory to dispute the inconsistent results or to argue that any unsupportive results demonstrate certain boundary conditions to the theory, but do not falsify it. They may also produce another set of empirical results that again support their favored theory, and they may attempt to persuade the research community that their theory remains valid.

The early history of psychology provides an interesting example of scientists rejecting empirical results that disagreed with their theories. Although Wündt and Tichener disagreed about the content of consciousness, both believed that thinking depended on mental images and their introspective research supported this idea. However, in a series of association experiments performed by Külpe at the University of Würzburg, subjects reported they were able to make associations and decisions without having any images in their consciousness. Kendler explains what happened:

> Neither Wündt nor Tichener was willing to accept the conclusion that the Würzburg studies were damaging to their respective positions. Wündt rejected the results because they were due to a faulty methodology; one cannot observe thought without thinking. In addition, thinking cannot be studied by rigorous experimental methods because an introspector cannot repeatedly observe the mental processes associated with the original presentation of a problem ...
>
> Tichener rejected the results of the Würzburgers, not because thought could not be introspectively served but, instead, because their observations were faulty. When thoughts were analyzed at Cornell, images were always reported. This encouraged Tichener to conclude that the unanalyzable imageless thought experiences reported by the Würzburgers were really unanalyzed. When observed at Cornell, imageless thought was revealed to be complexes of kinesthetic sensations and images. (1987, p. 74)

Thus, theories cannot be falsified by empirical data alone. It would be most unusual for advocates for a theory to simply abandon it because someone produced a set of empirical results that were inconsistent with the theory. In fact, Mitroff (1974) found in his research on the NASA moon scientists that the most respected scientists believed strongly in their theories and ignored data that did not support them.

The history of science provides many other examples of theories that survived and prospered in spite of the availability of empirical data that refuted them. Some common examples include Newtonian theory, relativity theory, Copernican astronomy, the theory of oxidation, natural selection, kinetic theory, and continental drift (see Chalmars 1976, Anderson 1983). Thus, it is clear that falsification does not provide a viable descriptive model of how some of the greatest scientific achievements in history came about. Further, if the greatest scientists in history did not follow falsification tenets, then it is unreasonable to accept falsification as the only model for science.

In consumer inquiry, some researchers have argued that falsification provides the only methodology for scientific knowledge (Calder and Tybout 1987, 1989). However, such a position is untenable (see Laudan 1983), and it should be clear that few social science researchers seriously attempt to falsify theories. Rather, in most cases, they attempt to falsify the null hypothesis in order to claim support for their favored theory (Peter 1983). Greenwald *et al.* (1986) have discussed at length the strong confirmation bias in social science and have pointed out that publication practices overwhelmingly favor supportive results. In fact, Greenwald *et al.* argue that researchers who do not obtain supportive results are unlikely to even try to publish the work. In many cases, then, there is little chance that a "falsifying" result will be widely disseminated in the field and become part of scientific knowledge.

In consumer inquiry, it is clear that theories survive and prosper with either no or only marginal empirical research support. Familiar examples include need theory, a number of personality theories, and theories of the attitude-behavior relationship. In addition, many of the procedures advocated for conducting empirical research are biased against the null hypothesis and are designed to create supportive results (see Peter 1984). Also, statistical criteria used to judge the adequacy of empirical results, such as *p*-values less than 0.05, provide almost no hurdle for empirical results to surmount in order to be judged supportive. This is because obtaining a small *p*-value depends only on factors controlled by the researcher (see Sawyer and Peter 1983). Finally, it is clear that researchers fail to reject theories that have only a modicum of empirical support (see Peterson *et al.* 1985). Thus, it is clear that falsification does not provide an adequate description of consumer inquiry.

As a normative model, falsification also fails for several reasons. First, as noted previously, the history of science demonstrates that falsification cannot account for the activities of many great scientists and the acceptance of many great theories. Thus, to argue that the field should follow falsification tenets is to constrain the field to a single method when the history of science shows that a variety of methods have been productive.

Second, it is not clear operationally how the field could follow falsification tenets. If the "*any* subject, settings, or events" criterion was applied, then almost all theories in the field must be rejected, leaving the field essentially void of content. However, if this criterion is not used, then how much disconfirming evidence is enough to conclude that a theory is falsified? If ten studies support the theory, and two studies refute the theory, is the theory falsified or supported, overall? Falsificationists have no solution to this problem that is consistent with their analysis of science.

Finally, there are serious logical inconsistencies in the recently advocated position of those claiming to be falsificationists in consumer inquiry. For example, these writers argue that

> It is our position that a falsificationist orientation (in the very simple sense of continuing to subject theories to tests in which they *could* fall or have their weaknesses revealed) coupled with a commitment to selecting theories comparatively (i.e., preferring ones that provide the most complete yet parsimonious account of available data) can and should be the general methodology for generating scientific knowledge. Note that these principles do not assume that theories can be demonstrated to be either true or unequivocally false, nor is there any inductive implication that the greater the number of tests a theory has survived the "better" it is... . All we suggest is that a process of ongoing testing, and a preference at any point in time for theories that provide a better explanation than their rivals offers the *possibility* of scientific progress. This is the best we can hope for. (Calder and Tybout 1989, p. 202).

If it is to be argued that theories cannot be shown to be true or false, then it is not clear what role empirical "testing" plays in this account of falsification.

Theories cannot "fail or have their weaknesses revealed" since nonsupportive results cannot lead to the conclusion that the theory is false. Similarly, supportive results cannot lead to the conclusion that the theory is true. Empirical results also cannot be used to conclude that one theory is "better" than another in this account. This is because (1) it is denied in the preceding quotation that "the greater the number of tests a theory [survives] the 'better' it is" and (2) no empirical method is offered for determining the degree to which empirical results must differ to determine that one theory is superior to another. Apparently, then, empirical testing has no valuable role to play in this account, yet "ongoing testing" is encouraged.

This account of falsification differs from previous accounts. Subjective judgments are now seen to play an important role in science. For example, subjective judgments are required for such things as determining how complete a theory is, how parsimonious it is, and whether it is superior to another theory. In fact, this view of "falsification" shares much common ground with relativistic accounts of science.

## Relativistic Accounts of Science

Several factors led a group of scholars interested in consumer inquiry to adopt relativistic views of science. First, having read a good deal of the science studies literature in the late 1970s and early 1980s, it became increasingly clear to these scholars that positivistic accounts of science were repudiated by contemporary philosophies of science. Second, there is no question that books by Kuhn (1970), Feyerabend (1975), and Laudan (1977) had a profound impact on shaping new perspectives advocated for the field. In addition, work in the cognitive sociology of science, such as Bloor (1976), Barnes (1977), Latour and Woolgar (1979), and Zukav (1979), were very influential. Third, the lack of progress in the field and the search for better ways of doing science led to interest in these views.

Perhaps the two best known relativistic accounts of science are critical relativism (Anderson 1983, 1986, 1988b) and the relativistic/constructionist perspective (Olson 1982, Olson and Peter 1984, Peter 1983, 1984, Peter and Olson 1983, 1989). Although there are differences in these perspectives, this paper will focus on the major tenets that underlie both views.

### Fundamental Tenets of Relativism

Relativists in consumer inquiry believe that while there may be (or may not be) a reality independent of the observer, there is no way to know such a reality. In other words, scientists create views of reality and attempt to develop social consensus about these views. What counts as knowledge and the standards by which it is judged are relative to particular times in history, particular research communities, and particular contexts. For example, most of the early studies in our field would be unlikely to meet today's publication standards in terms of theoretical development or methodological sophistication. Similarly, mathematical modelers, behavioral researchers, and interpretive researchers typically use different standards for judging the quality of the work in their domains. Thus, relativists reject the positivistic idea that there are universal standards for judging knowledge claims.

To relativists, science is clearly a social process performed by interacting human beings. Thus, much more is involved in the acceptance or rejection of theories than the logic involved or the empirical evidence collected. As Kuhn (1970) noted, "the superiority of one theory to another is something that cannot be proved in debate. Instead, I have insisted, each party must try, *by persuasion*, to convert the other" (p. 198; emphasis added). Thus, relativists recognize that both psychological and sociological phenomena have strong influences on the acceptance of scientific knowledge.

As a social process, science is clearly subjective. In fact, any statement of objectivity must be based on a subjective belief. Since perceptions are governed by sense impressions and previous learning, humans can only "see" what they have been taught to see. For example, medical students do not see cancer or other diseases in lung X-rays until they are taught to do so. Children do not see "tables" or "chairs" until they are taught to associate these concepts with various pieces of furniture. Similarly, previous knowledge and beliefs determine what researchers perceive when creating and interpreting empirical data (see Arndt 1985).

A major difference between relativistic and positivistic views concerns the nature of empirical data. While positivistic researchers recognize that data have measurement error, they typically view data as being objective and independent of the researcher. As such, data are assumed to be the reality against which theories are tested.

However, relativists recognize that there is no purely observational language, i.e., all data are theory-laden. This means that at least implicit theories are involved in the construction of all empirical data. Any attempt to attach a meaning to a set of numbers also involves theory. Thus, empirical data do not represent a reality independent of the scientist. The scientist selects the theory, the specific hypotheses to be examined, the research setting, the test stimuli, the subjects, the measures, the statistics to be used, and he or she provides the interpretation of the results. In fact, the entire production of research is completely controlled by the scientist (Peter 1984). Further, scientists typically have biases concerning what they want the data to demonstrate, and, in the long-run, perseverance often yields the desired results (Greenwald *et al.* 1986). From this viewpoint, it is small wonder that McGuire (1973) referred to laboratory experimenters as "stage managers."

Relativists recognize that a theory has meaning only within its own context, i.e., theories are not universal. In fact, no universal laws or theories have ever been advanced that meet positivistic requirements (see Feyerabend 1975, Munevar 1981). Thus, relativists view knowledge as context-dependent.

Relativists accept the idea that there is no way to prove the truth or falsity of theories with empirical data. Thus, various types of heuristic power or usefulness are recommended for judging theories (see Peter and Olson 1983, 1989). In addition, it is recognized that the particular beliefs, values, standards, methods, and cognitive aims of the scientists in a research community strongly influence what is accepted as scientific knowledge (see Anderson 1986).

*Evaluations of Relativistic Views.* Since the publication of Anderson (1983) and Peter and Olson (1983), a number of comments have been published critiquing relativistic views. Hunt (1984) argues that intersubjective certification demarcates science from nonscience and that there is a single scientific method; however, he provides no proof of these assertions. He also argues that many philosophers today do not accept relativism, which seems to be an accurate assessment.

Of course, many philosophers do not accept relativism, nor can they, if they wish to maintain the importance of the philosophy of science. Since relativism recognizes that science is subjective, and that perceptions and consensus generation processes are critical to understanding science, the role of philosophers of science is sharply downgraded. Thus, many philosophers of science may have a vested interest in maintaining that science has a particular form of rationality, as well as in advocating realism and in rejecting relativism.

Muncy and Fisk (1985) critique versions of relativism that are, for the most part, far removed from the positions advocated for consumer inquiry, and their work will therefore not be discussed. Cooper (1987) presented his opinion that "the truth of an assertion can be evaluated against the collective evidence in the domain" (p. 127) and suggested that, although there are practical impediments, there is a truth worth seeking. No support is offered for these contentions, however.

As noted previously, Calder and Tybout (1987) champion falsification as the only method of doing science and treat relativism as a philosophy useful only for nonscientific, interpretive work. This position was refuted by Anderson (1988b) and Peter and Olson (1989). Siegel (1988) argues that Anderson's critical relativism is not really relativistic because it implicitly has standards that cut across different research programs. He argues that Anderson's position should be called "critical pluralism." Anderson (1988a) offers a defense of his position noting that his view is relativistic in terms of both objectives and time frames.

Hunt (1989) repeats his opinion that science differs from nonscience in its method of verifying knowledge claims, but again provides no evidence. He also misconstrues relativistic views on the nature of science. Hunt (1989, p. 188) claims that relativists argue that "there are no fundamental differences separating the sciences and the nonsciences," and that this statement logically implies that "the knowledge claims of the nonsciences have as much epistemological warrant as the sciences." Hunt goes on to argue that the second statement implies that "if a palmist should diagnose a person as not having bone cancer (an example of a nonscience knowledge claim), such a diagnosis would have equal warrant as the diagnosis of a medical doctor that the person did have bone cancer (an example of a science knowledge claim)."

Of course, such an argument misstates the relativistic position in consumer inquiry. Surely, relativists in consumer inquiry recognize, as do most philosophers of science, that universal criteria that successfully demarcate sciences from nonsciences have not been created and that neither science nor nonscience can produce objective truth. This logically implies that the acceptance of knowledge claims depends on many factors and that in some cases, some people will and should accept the knowledge claims of science, but in other cases, nonscience claims will and should be accepted. For example, it seems likely that most people in Western cultures would accept the diagnosis of a medical doctor rather than that of a palmist in the situation outlined by Hunt. However, this does not mean that the medical doctor is always right and the palmist is always wrong; certainly there are many cases where medical doctors misdiagnose diseases.

It should be clear that science does not always offer more useful knowledge claims. For example, chiropractic medicine and acupuncture are considered by many to be nonscientific, yet many consumers believe in these therapies and claim to have been healed by them when traditional medical science failed to do so. Thus, the acceptance or rejection of knowledge claims is relative to particular contexts, research communities, and historical periods.

## Implications for Consumer Inquiry

Although the differences in positions discussed previously are of great interest to philosophically minded consumer inquirers, they have had little influence on many empirical researchers in the field. Following their positivistic training, these researchers seem primarily concerned with how to do science "correctly" at the operational level. To them, the primary question seems to be "what difference does it make which philosophy of science I choose when I design my research?"

In that aspects of philosophy undergird all methods and approaches to seeking knowledge, philosophical issues have both direct and indirect influences on workbench level researchers. These issues influence what researchers think they are doing, what they think research is capable of achieving, what topics they choose to study, and what methods they choose to use.

Empirical researchers in social science tend to advocate positivistic views for a number of reasons. First, these views typically champion empirical research as the sole arbitrator of truth and falsity, thus apparently giving empirical researchers a privileged status in the scientific community. Second, these views provide sets of operational rules that, while of questionable epistemological value, do simplify the process of doing and evaluating research. Third, these views have long been taught in doctoral programs as the accepted framework for science and are consistent with the ordinary person's view of science. Fourth, these views underlie traditional research methods that are strongly ingrained in social science. Fifth, these views relegate the insight and creativity necessary to construct theories to a secondary role, making science a comfortable job for even the dullest of minds. Thus, even though it can be demonstrated that positivistic views are untenable and positivistic practices have played a strong role in the current crisis in social science, it is unlikely that many empirical researchers will abandon them or change their views or practices.

Philosophical beliefs can either constrain or free scientists in a research community. Many consumer inquirers have chosen to constrain themselves to following the tenets of various positivistic views. While relativism is still an emerging view, listed subsequently are some tentative suggestions for freeing researchers in consumer inquiry.

### Theory Construction

Perhaps because of a positivistic concern with "testing" theories, consumer researchers have done little in the way of creating useful theories. A clear implication of relativism is that theory construction is a critical activity in science and one worthy of much greater attention in the field. Works by Zaltman *et al.* (1982) and Wicker (1985) should provide useful starting points for developing more creative and more useful theories.

### Type of Research

Positivistic views may well be responsible for establishing basic research as the most prestigious type of science. However, since the truth or falsity of theories cannot be determined in basic research, then other criteria and other types of research deserve greater attention.

One criterion for considering the usefulness of research concerns its contribution to society and society's welfare. At present, it is unlikely that much consumer research would score high marks according to this criterion. There are many important social problems that involve consumption issues that are ignored in the field. For example, issues concerning the problems and responsibilities for delivering a reasonable standard of living to the poor and homeless are ignored in our literature. We should direct our attention to the question of why our society has one of the highest standards of living in the world yet has the largest number of people stealing and killing others in order to obtain various products. Issues concerning the distribution of surplus food to starving Third World countries deserve consideration. Even a partial, tentative solution to one of these problems would far outweigh a complete solution to many of the trivial issues addressed in current consumer inquiry. Positivistic views may discourage such research since it is not of the basic, more "scientific" type. Frankly, positivistic methods are often not well suited for dealing with highly complex social phenomena in natural settings. Relativistic views, however, encourage consumer researchers to expand their research agendas to include meaningful, applied research and to avoid denigrating such research as something less "scientific," and therefore less important, than basic research.

### Research Methods

While positivistic researchers believe there is a single scientific method, relativists recognize that no single method can be universally applied to guarantee scientific knowledge. Relativistic researchers recognize many approaches to creating scientific knowledge, including qualitative, quantitative, and interpretive approaches, and they recognize that no single method is always better than another for constructing scientific knowledge.

One obvious implication of this view is that researchers have complete freedom to select whatever methods are appropriate for achieving their objectives. However, there is more to it. Frankly, positivistic methods in consumer research are commonly used to "justify" theories that are already supported in other fields and already accepted by many consumer researchers. These theories are already accepted by many consumer researchers because they are consistent with the ideology underlying the cognitive paradigm that dominates the field. Relativists would encourage more creative use of these methods, greater use of qualitative and interpretive methods, and the creation of new methods that are not constrained to reaffirming existing beliefs and practices in the field and in society (see Peter 1983, Sampson 1981).

A final issue in research design concerns the status of methodology developed under the guidance of positivism to achieve positivistic goals. This includes the research directives of such areas as sampling theory, measurement theory, experimentation, and inferential statistics. The problem is determining the logical status and value of these methods when the philosophy they are based on has been repudiated. While it is unlikely that these methods will soon be abandoned, serious consideration should be given to determining what "scientific goals" these methods are capable of achieving.

### Research Reporting Practices

The reporting practices and language used in consumer inquiry make the research appear as though it followed a particular sequence and is capable of achieving positivistic goals. Typically, research reports are created to appear as though they were hypothesis-testing, falsification attempts that either support or refute the validity of a theory.

Relativists recognize that empirical data and results are constructed by scientists and constitute only a part of an overall argument for a theory. They have no special, privileged status beyond this. Thus, there should be much more open reporting of what was done to create such results. For example, if the results were created by fishing through a correlation matrix, it should be reported as such without fear of rejection. Similarly, it is common practice in some areas of social science to not report such things as how many "pretests" were done before the desired result was obtained, how many subjects were dropped (called "aberrant data" or "outliers") in order to make the results come out favorably, or how many different manipulations were tried before finding one that worked. Relativists would encourage researchers to report such information and be open concerning how their research was conceptualized and conducted.

From a relativistic viewpoint, the language of research is laden with misleading positivistic terms. For example, theories cannot be "tested" by data, nor can they be "proven" or "confirmed." All studies are case studies that are constrained to particular times and circumstances and the value of inferential statistics is greatly overestimated. Thus, a less pretentious language and a more honest reporting of research practices could free the field from the hypocrisy created when researchers prepare research reports to look like positivistic science.

Research Evaluation

Relativists argue that there is no single criterion or set of criteria that can be universally applied to judge theories, research results, or scientific knowledge. Rather, which criteria are or should be applied depends on the particular context and the relevant goals and values of individual researchers and research communities. For example, mathematical modelers, laboratory experimenters, survey researchers, and interpretive researchers vary in the emphasis they place on criteria such as managerial relevance, mathematical sophistication, theoretical significance, generalizability, and simply whether or not the research is interesting. It is likely that even researchers claiming to be falsificationists recognize that more is involved in assessing scientific knowledge than extant empirical results, and that relativism provides a superior description of research evaluation.

## Summary

This paper investigated a variety of philosophical positions and suggested the implications of accepting them for consumer researchers. Three positivistic accounts of science, including logical empiricism, naive falsification, and sophisticated methodoiogical falsification were reviewed and evaluated. It was argued that these approaches are defective and have been eschewed in the science studies literature. A relativistic account of science was presented, evaluated, and offered as an appropriate philosophy of science for consumer inquiry. Although relativistic views are still emerging and have not answered all of the questions about science, several implications of adopting them were suggested.

## References

Anderson, Paul F. (1983). "Marketing, Scientific Progress, and Scientific Method," *Journal of Marketing*, 47 (Fall), 18–31.

Anderson, Paul F. (1986). "On Method in Consumer Research: A Critical Relativist Perspective," *Journal of Consumer Research*, 13 (September) 155–173.

Anderson, Paul F. (1988a). "Relative to What – That is the Question: A Reply to Siegel," *Journal of Consumer Research*, 15 (June), 133–137.

Anderson, Paul F. (1988b). "Relativism Revidivus: In Defense of Critical Relativism," *Journal of Consumer Research*, 15 (December), 403–406.

Arndt, Johan (1985). "On Making Marketing Science More Scientific: Role of Orientations, Paradigms, Metaphors, and Puzzle Solving," *Journal of Marketing*, 49 (Summer), 11–23.

Barnes, Barry (1977). *Interests and the Growth of Knowledge*. London: Routledge & Kegan Paul.

Bloor, David (1976). *Knowledge and Social Imagery*. London: Routledge & Kegan Paul.

Bromberger, S. (1966). "Why Questions," in R. Colodny (Ed.), *Mind and Cosmos: Explorations in the Philosophy of Science*. Pittsburgh, PA: University of Pittsburgh Press, 86–111.

Calder, Bobby J., Lynn W. Phillips, and Alice M. Tybout (1981). "Designing Research for Application," *Journal of Consumer Research*, 8 (September), 197–207.

Calder, Bobby J., Lynn W. Phillips, and Alice M. Tybout (1982). "The Concept of External Validility," *Journal of Consumer Research*, 9 (December), 240–244.

Calder, Bobby J., Lynn W. Phillips, and Alice M. Tybout (1983). "Beyond External Validity," *Journal of Consumer Research*, 10 (June), 112–114.

Calder, Bobby J., and Alice M. Tybout (1987). "What Consumer Research is ..." *Journal of Consumer Research*, 14 (June), 136–140.

Calder, Bobby J., and Alice M. Tybout (1989). "Interpretive, Qualitative, and Traditional Scientific Empirical Consumer Behavior Research," in Elizabeth C. Hirschman (Ed.), *Interpretive Consumer Research*. Provo, UT: Association for Consumer Research, 199–208.

Chalmars, A. F. (1976). *What Is This Thing Called Science?* St. Lucia, Queensland: University of Queensland Press.

Cohen, Jacob (1977). *Statistical Power Analysis for the Behavioral Sciences*, New York: Academic Press.

Cooper, Lee G. (1987). "Do We Need Critical Relativism? Comments on 'On Method in Consumer Research,'" *Journal of Consumer Research*, 14 (June), pp. 126–127.

Duhem, Pierre (1953). "Physical Theory and Experiment," in Herbert Feigl and May Brodbeck (Eds.), *Readings in Philosophy of Science*. New York: Appleton-Century-Crofts, 235–252.

Feyerabend, Paul (1975). *Against Method*. London: Redwood Burn.

Greenwald, Anthony G., Anthony R. Pratkanis, Michael R. Leippe, and Michael H. Baumgardner (1986). "Under What Conditions Does Theory Obstruct Research Progress?" *Psychological Review*, 93, No. 2, 216–229.

Hempel, Carl G. (1965). *Aspects of Scientific Explanation and Other Essays in the Philosophy of Science*. New York: The Free Press.

Hudson, Laurel Anderson, and Julie L. Ozanne (1988). "Alternative Ways of Seeking Knowledge in Consumer Research," *Journal of Consumer Research*, 14 (March), 508–521.

Hunt, Shelby D. (1976). *Marketing Theory: Conceptual Foundations of Research in Marketing*. Columbus, OH: Grid.

Hunt, Shelby D. (1983a). *Marketing Theory: The Philosophy of Marketing Science*. Homewood, IL: Irwin.

Hunt, Shelby D. (1983b). "General Theories and the Fundamental Explananda of Marketing," *Journal of Marketing*, 47 (Fall), 9–17.

Hunt, Shelby D. (1984). "Should Marketing Adopt Relativism?" in Paul F. Anderson and Michael J. Ryan (Eds.), *Scientific Method in Marketing*. Chicago: American Marketing Association, 30–34.

Hunt, Shelby D. (1989), "Naturalistic, Humanistic, and Interpretive Inquiry: Challenges and Ultimate Potential," in Elizabeth C. Hirschman (Ed.), *Interpretive Consumer Research*. Provo, UT: Association for Consumer Research, 185–198.

Hunt, Shelby D., and Paul S. Speck (1985). "Does Logical Empiricism Imprison Marketing?" in Nikhilesh Dholakia and Johan Arndt (Eds.), *Changing the Course of Marketing: Alternative Paradigms for Widening Marketing Theory, Research in Marketing, Supplement 2*. Greenwich, CT: JAI Press, 27–35.

Kendler, Howard H. (1987). *Historical Foundations of Modern Psychology*. Chicago: Dorsey Press.

Kuhn, Thomas S. (1970). *The Structure of Scientific Theories*, 2nd ed. Chicago: University of Chicago Press.

Lakatos, Imre (1970). "Falsification and the Methodology of Science Research Programs," in Imre Lakatos and Alan Musgrave (Eds.), *Criticisms and the Growth of Knowledge*. London: Cambridge University Press, 91–195.

Latour, Bruno, and Steve Woolgar (1979). *Laboratory Life*. Beverly Hills, CA: Sage.

Laudan, Larry (1977). *Progress and Its Problems*. Berkeley, CA: University of California Press.

Laudan, Larry (1983). "The Demise of the Demarcation Problem," in Rachael Laudan (Ed.), *The Demarcation Between Science and Pseudo-Science*, Vol. 2. Blacksburg, VA: Center for the Study of Science in Society, Virginia Polytechnic Institute.

Laudan, Larry (1984). "Reconstructing Methodology," in Paul F. Anderson and Michael J. Ryan (Eds.), *Scientific Method in Marketing*. Chicago: American Marketing Association, 1–4.

Leong, Siew Ming (1985). "Metatheory and Metamethodology in Marketing: A Lakatosian Reconstruction," *Journal of Marketing*, 49 (Fall), 23–40.

Lincoln, Yvonna S., and Egon G. Guba (1985). *Naturalistic Inquiry*. Beverly Hills, CA: Sage.

Lynch, John G., Jr. (1982). "On the External Validity of Experiments in Consumer Research," *Journal of Consumer Research*, 9 (March), 225–239.

Lynch, John G., Jr. (1983). "The Role of External Validity in Theoretical Research," *Journal of Consumer Research*, 10 (June), 109–111.

McGrath, Joseph E., and David Brinberg (1983). "External Validity and the Research Process: A Comment on the Calder/Lynch Debate," *Journal of Consumer Research*, 10 (June), 115–124.

McGuire, William J. (1973). "The Yin and Yang of Progress in Social Psychology: Seven Koan," *Journal of Personality and Social Psychology*, 26 (June), 446–456.

Mitroff, Ian (1974). "Norms and Counter-Norms in a Select Group of Apollo Moon Scientists: A Case Study of the Ambivalence of Scientists," *American Sociological Review*, 39 (August), 579–595.

Muncy, James A., and Raymond P. Fisk (1985). "Cognitive Relativism and the Practice of Marketing Science," *Journal of Marketing*, 51 (January), 20–33.

Munevar, Gonzalo (1981). *Radical Knowledge: A Philosophical Inquiry into the Nature and Limits of Science*. Indianapolis, IN: Hackett.

Olson, Jerry C. (1982). "Presidential Address – 1981: Toward a Science of Consumer Behavior," in A. Mitchell (Ed.), *Advances in Consumer Research*, Vol. 9. Chicago: Association for Consumer Research, v–x.

Olson, Jerry C. and J. Paul Peter (1984). "External Validity?" in Paul F. Anderson and Michael J. Ryan (Eds.), *Scientific Method in Marketing*. Chicago: American Marketing Association, 81–84.

Peter, J. Paul (1983). "Some Philosophical and Methodological Issues in Consumer Research," in Shelby D. Hunt, *Marketing Theory: The Philosophy of Marketing Science*. Homewood, IL: Irwin, 382–394.

Peter, J. Paul (1984). "On Ignoring a Research Education," in Stephen W. Brown and Raymond P. Fisk (Eds.), *Marketing Theory: Distinguished Contributions*. New York: Wiley, 324–327.

Peter, J. Paul, and Jerry C. Olson (1983). "Is Science Marketing?" *Journal of Marketing*, 47 (Fall), 111–125.

Peter, J. Paul, and Jerry C. Olson (1989). "The Relativistic/Constructionist Perspective on Scientific Knowledge and Consumer Research," in Elizabeth C. Hirschman (Ed.), *Interpretive Consumer Research*. Provo, UT: Association for Consumer Research, 24–29.

Peterson, Robert A., Gerald Albaum, and Richard F. Beltramini (1985). "A Meta-Analysis of Effect Sizes in Consumer Behavior Experiments," *Journal of Consumer Research*, 12 (June), 97–103.

Popper, Karl R. (1959). *The Logic of Scientific Discovery*. New York: Harper Torchbooks.

Sampson, Edward E., (1981). "Cognitive Psychology as Ideology," *American Psychologist*, 36 (July). 730–743.

Sawyer, Alan G., and J. Paul Peter (1983). "The Significance of Statistical Significance Tests in Marketing Research," *Journal of Marketing Research*, 20 (May), 122–133.

Siegel, Harvey (1988). "Relativism for Consumer Research (Comments on Anderson)," *Journal of Consumer Research*, 15 (June), 129–132.

Suppe, Frederick (1977). *The Structure of Scientific Theories*, 2nd ed. Urbana, IL: University of Illinois Press.

Wicker, Allan W. (1985). "Getting Out of Our Conceptual Ruts," *American Psychologist*, 40 (October), 1094–1103.

Zaltman, Gerald, Karen LeMasters, and Michael Heffring (1982). *Theory Construction in Marketing: Some Thoughts on Thinking*. New York: Wiley.

Zukav, Gary (1979). *The Dancing Wu Li Masters: An Overview of the New Physics*. New York: Bantam.

# 13

# Consumer Research: In Search of Identity

**Itamar Simonson, Ziv Carmon, Ravi Dhar, Aimee Drolet, and Stephen M. Nowlis**

**Source:** *Annual Review of Psychology* 52 (2001): 249–275.

## Introduction

The first chapter on "Consumer Analysis" to appear in the *Annual Review of Psychology* (Guest 1962) focused on survey techniques and other methodological aspects of consumer research, with a brief review of the hot topics of the 1950 – motivation research and subliminal advertising. The field of consumer research has made great progress since then, with a significant expansion of the range of topics studied and of the academic community of consumer researchers (for reviews, see e.g. Bettman 1986, Cohen and Chakravarti 1990, Jacoby 1976, Kassarjian 1982, Tybout and Artz 1994). The Association for Consumer Research (ACR) was founded in 1969, and the first consumer behavior textbooks and courses appeared in the late 1960s (e.g. Engel *et al.* 1968, Kassarjian and Robertson 1968). Today, consumer researchers account for close to half of all (business school) marketing faculty, and the study of consumption is also a growing area in other disciplines, such as sociology, communication, and anthropology (e.g. Miller 1995). However, despite the rapid development of the field, there are still significant disagreements about what consumer research is, what its objectives are, and how it should differ from related disciplines. As a result, the field appears to be rather fragmented and even divided on some fundamental issues.

In this chapter, instead of following the format of providing a review of articles published in the previous 4 years, we take a broader perspective and examine the developments, the main influences, and the current state of consumer research. We also explore some of the ongoing debates regarding the identity and objectives of consumer research. Although we try to represent the different subfields and points of view, our own bias undoubtedly affects our interpretation of the developments and the alternative approaches to consumer research.

This review consists of three main sections. In the first we examine the original vision regarding the objectives of consumer research and the subjects of investigation, as well as the limitations of that research agenda. In the second section we explore the consequences of the ambiguity about the domain and identity of consumer research and the multidisciplinary influences on the field. In particular, we review the key trends and "camps" in consumer research, which represent complementary and, in some cases, conflicting views regarding the main topics of investigation and how research is conducted. This review is based, in part, on systematic analyses we conducted of articles that have been published in the leading consumer research journals over the past 30 years. Finally, in the third section we revisit the question of what might differentiate the consumer research field from related fields, as well as the role of theory testing, studies of substantive phenomena, and relevance in consumer research.

## In the Beginning: Domain-Specific Topics and Grand Theories of Consumer Behavior

Ronald Frank, the first editor of the *Journal of Consumer Research* (*JCR*), expected research to be published in the journal to encompass such topics as family planning behavior, occupational choices, mobility, determinants of fertility rates, attitudes towards and use of social services, and determinants of educational attainment (Frank 1974, p. i). Although this is not representative of the types of consumer research conducted at that time (see e.g. Bettman 1971, Jacoby *et al.* 1974, Monroe 1973, Wright 1973), one is struck by the emphasis on topics that are specific to particular consumption categories, such as occupations and social services, and the omission of more general issues, such as persuasion and choice. An apparent assumption underlying this vision for *JCR* was that consumer researchers and researchers from related disciplines would primarily adapt, apply, and possibly extend theories developed in the basic disciplines, such as psychology, sociology, economics, and communication, to specific consumption categories.

It is noteworthy that the most influential frameworks in the early days of the consumer research field were comprehensive models of buyer behavior (e.g. Engel *et al.* 1968, Howard and Sheth 1969, Nicosia 1966). The implicit assumption was that buyer behavior can be captured in one comprehensive model or "grand theory." The emphasis on comprehensive models of buyer behavior declined significantly during the 1980s, which appears to be a natural progression for the field. First, consumer behavior is too complex to be meaningfully captured in a single model. After all, consumer psychology involves most of the elements of human psychology, which cannot be meaningfully represented in any single model or theory. Second, although comprehensive models of buyer behavior served a purpose in integrating various components and, in some ways, defining the field, they could not be effectively tested, and the significance of the actual insights they provided may be debatable.

These models, as well as Frank's (1974) vision for *JCR*, did not resolve the question of what differentiates the consumer research field. In particular, whereas studying topics such as attitudes towards educational services and contraceptives might be relevant and useful for those interested in these subjects, many researchers are likely to perceive as more important and interesting, more general issues, such as how attitudes are formed and choices made. However, focusing on more generic questions raises other "problems" relating to the unique identity and role of consumer research. As described in the next section, owing to this ambiguity and the overlap with more established fields, consumer research has been shaped to a large degree by developments and sometimes conflicting criteria and methods of related disciplines.

## Multidisciplinary Influences on Trends and Camps in Consumer Research

In this section we examine the current state of consumer research, focusing on the multidisciplinary influences on the field with respect to both topics of investigation and research methods. In particular:

1. Because most key aspects of buyer behavior are also central research topics in other disciplines, especially psychology, one would expect developments in consumer research to reflect approaches and developments in the related disciplines. In this review we examine the trends in consumer research with respect to (*a*) the share of "social" versus "cognitive" topics and (*b*) the share of research on "cold" (e.g. attitudes, multi-attribute models, decision rules) versus "hot" (e.g. emotions, arousal, conflict) aspects of consumer behavior.
2. Although psychology has had the greatest impact on consumer research, other fields, such as economics and anthropology, have also had significant influences. Many consumer researchers have tended to be associated with particular other disciplines, representing alternative approaches to research. Consequently, consumer research camps have correspondingly differed in their views regarding important research questions and acceptable research methods. In this review we examine two distinctions within the consumer research field that can be traced to multidisciplinary influences: (*a*) behavioral decision theory (BDT) compared with social cognition consumer research and (*b*) postmodern (or interpretive) compared to positivist consumer research (including both social cognition and BDT research).
3. To further explore the changes in disciplinary impact on consumer research, we analyze the trend in the share of articles representing applications of theories developed in other fields compared with work involving original theory development and/or identification of new phenomena and explanations.

### The Correspondence Between Trends in Psychology and Consumer Research: Social Versus Cognitive and "Hot" Versus "Cold" Topics

***Social Versus Cognitive Consumer Research*** Unlike researchers in psychology, consumer researchers are not identified as social or cognitive, and many researchers in the field have examined issues in both domains. However, following the common distinction in psychology between the social and cognitive domains and the increasing importance and sophistication of research on cognition, it is of interest to study whether there has been a corresponding increase in the share of cognitive relative to social topics studied by consumer researchers. To explore this question, two independent judges (doctoral students working in the area of consumer behavior) classified all consumer behavior articles that have appeared in the leading consumer research journals (*JCR* 1974–1999, *Journal of Marketing Research* 1969–1999, and *Journal of Consumer Psychology* 1990-1999) based on whether they dealt with issues that fall in the domain of social or cognitive psychology.

The exact results of this analysis depend on the manner in which articles in the general area of social cognition (e.g. attitude, persuasion, information processing), which is central to consumer research, are classified. However, regardless of whether social cognition topics are classified as social or cognitive, the qualitative conclusion made from this analysis is that the proportion of social topics has declined significantly, whereas the proportion of cognitive topics has correspondingly increased. Social areas of consumer research that have declined in importance include such topics as family and social influences, reference groups, attribution, and self-perception (e.g. Bearden and Etzel 1982; Folkes 1984, Scott and Yalch 1980). Some of the cognitive topics that have increased in importance include behavioral decision making (see Bettman *et al.* 1998 for a review), memory and knowledge (e.g. Alba and Hutchinson 1987), language (e.g. Schmitt and Zhang 1998), variety seeking (e.g. McAlister 1982, Ratner *et al.* 1999, Simonson 1990), and preconscious processing (e.g. Janiszewski 1988). It is noteworthy that some social topics have become more central, such as cross-cultural and ethnic influences on buyer behavior (e.g. Deshpande and Stayman 1994), the development of children as consumers (e.g. Gregan-Paxton and Roedder-John 1997), and gender differences (e.g. Meyers-Levy and Maheswaran 1991).

A major change has been the decline of attitudes as the central topic of research. In particular, the Fishbein and Ajzen (1975) multi-attribute attitude model and theory of reasoned action received a great deal of attention from consumer researchers in the 1970s and early 1980s, examining such questions as whether intentions mediate the effect of attitudes on behavior and the role of the normative component in the formation of attitudes (e.g. Lutz 1977, Miniard and Cohen 1983, Shimp and Kavas 1984; see also Bagozzi *et al.* 1992).

Since the early 1980s, the elaboration likelihood model of Petty and Cacioppo (e.g. Petty *et al.* 1983) and related dual process models (Chaiken 1980, Fiske and Pavelchek 1986) have been accepted by most consumer researchers as the approach that can best account for the diverse findings on the formation of attitudes, persuasion, and related information processing issues (e.g. Aaker and Maheswaran 1997, Sujan 1985). In addition, consumer researchers have started to examine persuasion processes that relate specifically to marketing and were not derived from existing psychological theories, such as the persuasion knowledge model (Friestad and Wright 1994).

Another important development, which likely contributed to the decrease in the proportion of attitude and persuasion research, has been the growing interest in consumer decision making and the rise of BDT consumer research. In particular, Bettman's (1979) influential book, *An Information Processing Theory of Consumer Choice*, inspired by the work of Newell and Simon (1972), Payne (1976), and other decision-making researchers, presented a framework that describes how information inputs are processed to achieve a decision. It emphasized the role of short- and long-term memory, decision rules and heuristics, and other issues that have subsequently received much attention from consumer researchers.

Finally, memory and cognitive elaboration is another cognitive area that has received growing attention from consumer researchers, including the use of principles of memory operation to explain persuasive communication effects (e.g. Johar and Pham 1999, Keller 1987). For example, according to the resource-matching hypothesis (Norman and Borrow 1975; see Anand and Sternthal 1990 for a review), persuasion is enhanced or hindered depending on the match between the level of cognitive resources available for message processing and the level of cognitive resources that the message requires (e.g. Meyers-Levy and Tybout 1997, Unnava *et al.* 1996).

*Research on "Hot" Versus "Cold" Aspects of Consumer Behavior* A great deal of attitude and decision-making research has examined what might be considered "cold" aspects of consumer behavior. "Cold" aspects include such topics as the role of beliefs in attitude formation, attention, perception, information acquisition, learning, expertise, attribution, and decision rules. Conversely, "hot" aspects include such topics as the role of affect and mood, arousal, regret, low-involvement peripheral persuasion, hedonic aspects of consumption, conflict, and self- expressive motives for brand preference. In psychology there has been growing emphasis on the role of emotions and other "hot" aspects of cognition (see, e.g. Zajonc 1998).

We examined the proportion over time of "cold" and "hot" topics in consumer research based on a classification of articles that have been published in the leading consumer research journals (*JCR* 1974–1999, *Journal of Marketing Research* 1969-1999, and *Journal of Consumer Psychology* 1990–1999). Counting only articles that the judges coded as "cold" or "hot" (excluding the "other" category), there has been a decline in the relative proportion of "cold" topic articles from about 85% in the 1970s, to 75% in the 1980s, and 64% in the 1990s. For example, until recently decision-making research was clearly a "cold" domain, perhaps reflecting the cold economic benchmark often used by decision researchers. However, BDT consumer researchers have recently started to study the role of emotions in decision making (e.g. Bettman 1993). For example, Luce (1998) examined the effect of emotional tradeoff difficulty on the type and amount of information processing (see also Pham 1998, Shiv and Fedorikhin 1999). Other "hot" topics include, for example, affective responses to advertising (e.g. Baumgartner *et al.* 1997, Edell and Chapman-Burke 1987), consumers' fun and fantasies (Holbrook and Hirschman 1982), and measures of consumption emotions (Richins 1997).

In summary, a review of articles published in the leading consumer research journals reveals two trends, both reflecting similar trends in psychology. There has been a decline in the proportion of classic social topics and an increase in the proportion of cognitive topics. Further, the proportion of "hot" topics has increased relative to "cold" topics, though the latter category still accounts for the majority of consumer research articles.

### Disciplinary Influence and Alternative Orientations in Consumer Research: Behavioral Decision Theory Versus Social Cognition and Positivist Versus Postmodern

As indicated, consumer researchers who have been influenced by particular fields have tended to work on different topics and employ different research methods. In this section we explore two contrasts: (*a*) BDT versus social cognition consumer research and (*b*) positivist versus postmodern consumer research.

*The Behavioral Decision Theory and Social-Cognition Approaches to Consumer Research* Whereas the distinction between social and cognitive research does not play nearly as significant a role in consumer research as it does in psychology, the somewhat loose distinction between social cognition-based research and so-called BDT is more prominent in consumer research. In psychology, BDT accounts for a relatively small segment of the literature, although leading BDT researchers such as Daniel Kahneman and Amos Tversky have had great impact on both the cognitive and social psychological literatures. In the consumer behavior literature, research that follows the BDT research paradigm has accounted for a large and growing proportion of all nonpostmodern articles published in the leading journals. Indeed, the central BDT issues of judgment and choice are directly relevant to the most researched area in marketing and consumer behavior, namely, influences on purchase decisions. Furthermore, BDT research serves as a bridge between the "behavioral" and "quantitative" sides of marketing because both BDT and quantitative research share the link to economics and the focus on consumer choice. Conversely, quantitative research in marketing tends to have less in common with social cognition consumer research (and even less with postmodern research).

First, it should be emphasized that social cognition and BDT researchers in marketing share many of the same research values and methods. For example, in the debate between the positivist and postmodern approaches to research, both social cognition and BDT researchers, by and large, are on the same (positivist) side. Furthermore, there are differences in emphasis among researchers within the consumer BDT and social cognition subfields, making it difficult to generalize regarding differences between the two camps. In particular, much BDT consumer research has investigated the processes underlying judgments and decisions (e.g. Coupey 1994, Dhar and Nowlis 1999, Sen and Johnson 1997). Conversely, other BDT research has focused more on judgment and decision-making phenomena, such as the manner in which consumers integrate the opinions of multiple critics (e.g. West and Broniarczyk 1998) or the impact of anticipating regret (e.g. Simonson 1992), where process measures are either not used at all or provide additional insights but are not the focus of the research. Similarly, there are large differences among social cognition consumer researchers with respect to both research methods and topics (see, e.g. Kisielius and Sternthal 1984 and Tybout *et al.* 1983, compared with Alba *et al.* 1999 and Lynch *et al.* 1988).

With the caveat that there are exceptions to each of the following generalizations, there are several key differences between BDT and social cognition consumer research:

1 . One obvious difference relates to the primary influences on each area. Social cognition consumer research has been influenced primarily by social cognition research in psychology (e.g. Chaiken 1980, Fiske and Taylor 1984).

Conversely, the primary influence on BDT consumer research has been the BDT literature, including the work of Kahneman and Tversky (e.g. 1979), Thaler (1985), and other researchers. Furthermore, similar to BDT research published in nonmarketing journals, BDT consumer research has tended to use the normative benchmark of value maximization and time-consistent preferences for evaluating the significance of research findings. Thus, findings that demonstrate violations of the classical economic assumptions regarding buyer behavior have typically been regarded as interesting and important. For example, BDT consumer researchers have demonstrated that, (*a*) the framing of product attributes (e.g. ground beef that is "80% lean" or has "20% fat") influences product evaluation even after actual experience ("80% lean beef" tasted better than "20% fat beef;" Gaeth and Levin 1988); (*b*) when costs significantly precede benefits, the sunk cost effect is greatly diminished (Gourville and Soman 1998); (*c*) the interaction between the pleasure of consumption and the pain of paying has predictable impact on consumer behavior and hedonics (Prelec and Loewenstein 1998); and (*d*) preference elicitation tasks involving comparison of options (e.g. choice), judgments of individual options (e.g. ratings), and matching of two options varying in price and quality, produce systematically different preferences (e.g. Carmon and Simonson 1998, Hsee and Leclerc 1998, Nowlis and Simonson 1997). In recent years, the focus has shifted from demonstrations of value maximization violations to studies that are designed to gain a better understanding of the factors that influence the construction of preferences (e.g. Drolet *et al.* 2000; for a review, see Bettman *et al.* 1998).

2. Social cognition and BDT consumer research have tended to build on different underlying models of buyer behavior and the communication process. One often referenced response hierarchy model (e.g. McGuire 1969), which has its origin in the communications area, includes the following stages: exposure/attention → reception/encoding → cognitive response → attitude → intention → behavior. The other model, which focuses on consumer decision making (or buying process), includes the following stages (e.g. Peter and Olson 1993): problem recognition information search → evaluation of alternatives → purchase decision/choice → postpurchase evaluation. Although these two models highlight somewhat different elements in the consumer response and decision-making process (e.g. attention and intention versus search and evaluation) and employ different terminology, the essential components are quite similar. Thus, for example, most studies that examine influences on attitudes and attitude change also effectively investigate the formation of preferences and alternative evaluation, and vice versa (e.g. Morwitz *et al.* 1993). However, whereas social cognition consumer research has focused on the stages in the communications (or hierarchy-of-effects) model and on how judgments and attitudes are formed, BDT consumer research has tended to examine the decision-making model and particularly the determinants of choice.
3. Related to item 2, whereas BDT consumer researchers have studied primarily stimulus-based phenomena (e.g. Dhar 1997, Kahn and Louie 1990),

social cognition research has focused more on memory-based tasks (e.g. Alba *et al.* 1991; Biehal and Chakravarti 1982, 1983). For example, building on the influential accessibility-diagnosticity model of Feldman and Lynch (1988), Lynch *et al.* (1988) proposed that decisions arise from a process whereby inputs are sequentially retrieved from memory, with the consumer updating the implications of already considered evidence with each new input retrieved. The order of retrieval is a function of the accessibility of each input, but accessible information can be actively disregarded if it is perceived to be nondiagnostic.

4. Although there are certainly exceptions to this generalization, BDT research has tended to focus more on substantive phenomena, which are explained based on existing theories or lead to theoretical extensions. Conversely, a greater share of social cognition consumer research has involved theory testing and extensions that have implications for the consumer environment (e.g. Ratneshwar and Chaiken 1991).
5. There are also differences in the process measures that social cognition and BDT consumer researchers tend to use. Social cognition researchers often employ measures such as cognitive response (e.g. Sternthal *et al.* 1978) and recall to gain insights into cognitive processes. In the BDT area, researchers who have used process measures tended to rely primarily on measures of information acquisition, verbal protocols, and response time (e.g. Bettman and Park 1980, Brucks 1988, Johnson 1984, Sen and Johnson 1997). There is no obvious explanation for the different process measures employed. Finally, the use of mediation and path analysis is more common in social cognition than in BDT consumer research.

Despite the differences between the social cognition and BDT approaches to consumer research, the main topics of investigation are closely related and the research methods, by and large, are similar. Thus, decreasing the division between the two areas and increasing communication and collaboration can advance the consumer research field. Consider, for example, the currently dominant view of consumer persuasion based on the elaboration likelihood model (e.g. Petty *et al.* 1983). Briefly, evaluation of arguments presented in an ad is a frequent example of processing through the central route, whereas the impact of background music represents an example of persuasion through the peripheral route. However, depending on the motivation and ability to process the information, the same cue (e.g. the product endorser) might influence persuasion through either the central or peripheral route (e.g. Petty *et al.* 1991).

In the BDT literature researchers have made a related distinction between compensatory and heuristic-based decision rules (see, e.g. Bettman 1979). This distinction, however, refers typically to the manner in which consumers process attribute information, as opposed to different types of information. Interestingly, BDT researchers have not paid much attention to the manner in which typical peripheral cues, such as source characteristics and background music, impact consumer preferences. On the other hand, BDT consumer researchers have studied extensively the impact of various contextual factors, such as task characteristics (e.g. Fischer *et al.* 1999) and the configuration of the option set under consideration (e.g. Huber *et al.* 1982, Huber and Puto 1983, Wernerfelt 1995), on consumer preferences. These contextual moderators have not received much attention in social cognition research on attitude and persuasion, even though such factors appear quite relevant to our understanding of attitude and persuasion.

Another area that could potentially benefit from increased integration of BDT and social cognition research involves the BDT notion of construction of preferences and the related concepts in social cognition of attitude accessibility and diagnosticity (e.g. Fazio *et al.* 1989, Feldman and Lynch 1988), as well as the notions of attitude strength and ambivalence (e.g. Priester and Petty 1996). For example, Krosnick and Shuman (1988) showed that, contrary to common assumptions, measured attitudes of individuals whose attitudes are intense, important, and held with certainty, are just as susceptible to response order effects as other respondents'. A related finding from BDT consumer research is that expertise and involvement (e.g. owing to accountability) often do not diminish and, in some cases, enhance the susceptibility of consumers to judgment and decision errors such as overconfidence and the attraction effect (e.g. Mahajan 1992, Simonson 1989; but see Coupey *et al.* 1998). Thus, by integrating findings from the social cognition and BDT areas, we are likely to gain a better understanding of the moderators of consumer susceptibility to various biases.

Another example of a finding social cognition research that might have significant BDT implications is the observation that stronger, more accessible attitudes diminish sensitivity to changes in the attitude object (Fazio *et al.* 2000). In particular, it suggests that, although well-formed, stable preferences might represent the ideal sovereign consumer, it might actually reduce consumer welfare and choice effectiveness. Finally, social cognition research on the measurement and construction of attitudes (e.g. Menon *et al.* 1995; for a review, see Schwarz and Bohner 2000) can have significant implications for decision research, and vice versa. In sum, despite the differences in research traditions, issues, and methods, we believe there is a need and opportunity for greater interaction and collaboration between social cognition and BDT consumer researchers.

Postmodern and Positivist Consumer Research So-called postmodern consumer research emerged in the 1980s (see also Levy 1959) and offered an alternative perspective to the purpose of consumer research, the important topics of investigation, and the research methods. An analysis of articles published between 1980 and 1999 in the major journal in the field, *JCR*, reveals that the proportion of postmodern research increased during the 1980s and represented approximately 20% of the published articles since 1990 (with the majority of the remaining articles representing positivist research). Briefly, whereas positivist research attempts to uncover cause-and-effect relationships and focuses on explanations, the postmodern approach focuses more on interpretation than causation and believes in a more subjective view of data interpretation (for a contrast of the two approaches, see Hudson and Ozanne 1988).

Postmodern researchers have also emphasized the need to distinguish consumer research from other fields and to avoid using managerial relevance as a criterion for evaluating research. For example, Belk (1986, p. 423) writes, "My own vision is one of consumer behavior as a discipline unto itself, with a variety of constituent groups, but with no overriding loyalty to any existing discipline or interest group. That is, consumer behavior should not be a subdiscipline of marketing, advertising, psychology, sociology, or anthropology, nor the handmaiden of business, government, or consumers. It should instead be a viable field of study, just as these other disciplines are, with some potential relevance to each of these constituent groups." Holbrook (1987, p. 128) proposes that consumer research refers to the "study of consummation in all its many aspects." Indeed, whereas most positivist research has focused on issues related to purchase decisions, a main emphasis in postmodern consumer research has been on specific consumption experiences and aspects of consumer behavior that had not previously been considered important areas for consumer research. For example, Belk and Costa (1998) recently published a paper regarding the mountain man myth, Thompson (1996) studied the juggling lifestyles of mothers, Arnould and Price (1993) studied the experience of river rafting, and Holbrook and Grayson (1986) provided a semiotic perspective of the movie *Out of Africa*. Also, in his 1998 presidential address to the Association of Consumer Research, John Sherry argued that traditional prose articles might be insufficient vessels for our understanding of consumer behavior and that other vehicles, such as poetry, can more effectively capture the subjective experience of inquiries about consumer behavior.

It should be noted that, in addition to what many positivist researchers regard as unusual topics, some post modern consumer researchers have examined mainstream topics, such as customer satisfaction (Fournier and Mick 1999). However, by and large, postmodern researchers have introduced both new methods and new kinds of topics, inspired by research in anthropology, literature, and other fields that had previously had limited impact on consumer research. Similar to postmodern researchers in other disciplines such as anthropology, postmodern consumer researchers have employed different methodologies, including existential phenomenology (e.g. O'Guinn and Faber 1989, Thompson *et al.* 1989), hermeneutics (Arnould and Fischer 1994), participant observation (Schouten and McAlexander 1995), in-depth interviews (Hirschman 1994), ethnography (Arnould and Wallendorf 1994), critical theory (Murray and Ozanne 1991), literary criticism (Stern 1989), and introspection (Gould 1991; but see Wallendorf and Brucks 1993).

The combination of what was perceived as a different kind of science, which deviates from traditional methods of analyzing and interpreting data, with what was perceived as unusual topics, has evoked strong opposition from many positivist researchers. For example, Cohen (1989) criticizes Belk's research on the role of consumer possessions (1988), arguing that it lacks meaning, empirical identification, and explanatory power. On the other hand, Firat and Venkatesh (1995, p. 260) appeal to positivist researchers to be more receptive to alternative paradigms, stating, "We therefore ask the consumer researchers who are steeped in the methods of cognitive psychology to come out of their protective shells, to set themselves free from unidimensional conceptions. ...It means that we must opt for multiple theories of consumer behavior rather than a single theory that silences all other theories."

At this stage, after the positions of proponents of the two convictions have been expressed in different forums, there is rather limited ongoing communication between them. Looking ahead, it is reasonable to expect that the intensity of the postmodern-positivist debate will diminish. Furthermore, because current marketing doctoral students in some schools are exposed to both positivist and postmodern professors, they are likely to be more receptive to both approaches. Most importantly, despite the current differences in methodology and topics, there are significant opportunities for collaboration. McQuarrie and Mick (1992) provided a fine example of the virtues of combining semiotics analysis and experiments in their research on advertising resonance. Indeed, with more openness and tolerance on both sides, there is significant room for collaboration and combining the advantages of both approaches. Although many positivist researchers are unlikely to change their views regarding data collection and analysis, the limitations of the traditional experimental methodologies and measures may enhance their willingness to combine quantitative data with less structured, more qualitative methods. Also, although positivist and postmodern consumer researchers have so far focused on different kinds of topics, as indicated, the methods employed by postmodern researchers could also be applied to more traditional topics, such as decision making, persuasion, regret, and affect.

### Types of Consumer Research: Theory Development Versus Theory Application

Consumer research can be classified along a continuum from basic research, involving new theories, concepts, and explanations, to applications and minor extensions of existing theories and concepts. One might expect that in the early development of a new applied field such as consumer research there would be greater emphasis on applications of existing theories and borrowing from other, more established fields. However, over time, consumer researchers may seek to go beyond mere applications and minor theoretical extensions and introduce significant theoretical extensions and concepts, and in some cases, new theories relating to buyer behavior.

To examine this question more systematically, two independent judges (doctoral students specializing in consumer behavior) coded consumer research articles (not including postmodern articles) that have appeared in the August issues of the *Journal of Marketing Research* between 1969 and 1999 and articles that appeared in the September issues of the *JCR* between 1974 (the journal's first year) and 1999. Specifically, the judges coded articles dealing with consumer behavior on 1–4 scale, where 1 represents applications or minor extensions of established theories and phenomena (e.g. an investigation of a particular moderator or boundary condition, or ruling out an alternative explanation), and 4 represents articles introducing new constructs, theories, and/or phenomena.

The results show a significant time trend (correlation = 0. 15), with the linear regression model yielding a significant coefficient for year as a predictor ($p < 0.005$). Specifically, looking at 5-year periods from 1969 through 1998, the proportion of articles coded as applications of existing theories and minor extensions (i.e. articles coded 1 or 2 on the 1–4 scale) declined continuously, from 94% in 1969–1973 to 66% in 1994–1998. This trend is consistent with the notion that, as the field has evolved, the appreciation for research that merely applies theories developed elsewhere has declined. Although the consumer environment places some interesting constraints, and demonstrations that certain theories have implications for consumers and marketers can be important, such research is increasingly regarded as making limited (conceptual) contributions and not worthy of publication in the leading journals. Indeed, to the extent that the consumer environment is just another instance of the relevant constructs, there is no conceptual reason to expect the theories not to apply.

We also examined whether there has been a trend with respect to research topics that examine issues that are specific to and relevant primarily to consumer research and marketing as opposed to topics of general interest that might have been published in psychology and other basic discipline journals. For example, whereas the topic of brand equity and extension is central to marketing (e.g. Aaker 1997, Aaker and Keller 1990, Broniarczyk and Alba 1994, Fournier 1998, Keller 1993, Gardner and Levy 1955, Park *et al.* 1991), it has limited significance to other fields. Excluding postmodern articles from the analysis, there has not been a significant change on that dimension; during 1969–1973, 67% of the articles were classified as consumer/marketing specific (1 or 2 on the 1–4 scale), and since 1973 the two topic categories (consumer-specific versus general) have accounted for approximately the same share of consumer research articles.

In summary, our review of the state of consumer research and developments in the field over the past 30 years points to several key trends. First, research topics continue to be influenced by trends in other disciplines, especially psychology. Second, related to the multidisciplinary impact, the consumer research field is characterized by significant divisions between subareas, which not only tend to study different topics, but also differ in terms of their research orientation and methods. Finally, our analysis points to a growing emphasis on original topics and theories compared with applications of existing theories adopted from other fields.

## In Search of Identity: The Role of Relevance, Theory Testing, and Substantive Phenomena

As the preceding review of developments in consumer research and multidisciplinary influence on the field suggests, despite the progress in terms of the quality and quantity of published articles, some of the fundamental debates regarding the objectives and the appropriate topics and methods have not been resolved. The view that consumer research "seeks to produce knowledge about consumer behavior" (Calder and Tybout 1987, p. 136) implies that the important consumer research topics are also main topics in other disciplines, creating ambiguity as to what distinguishes consumer research (other than being a "one-stop shop" for studies of relevance to consumer behavior). Another "constraint" that significantly affects the priorities of many consumer researchers is the fact that most of them are marketing professors in schools of business and might have (explicit and/or implicit) incentives to focus on research topics that are potentially relevant to managers and, to a lesser degree, other constituencies. In this concluding section we examine the different perspectives on the role of relevance and the emphasis on theory-testing versus substantive phenomena-driven research (which leads to theory development), as well as the implications of these approaches for the purpose and identity of the consumer research field.

*The Objectives and (Ir)Relevance of Consumer Research* One would expect any research field or discipline to have a unique identity and purpose that separate it from other fields. Earlier we cited the vision of the first editor of the *JCR*, Ronald Frank (1974), regarding the domain-specific aspects of consumer behavior that he expected researchers from multiple disciplines to examine. At about the same time, the Association for Consumer Research (ACR) was founded with the goal of providing "a forum for exchange of ideas among those interested in consumer behavior research in academic disciplines, in government at all levels from local through national, in private business, and in other sectors such as nonprofit organizations and foundations" (Pratt 1974, p. 4). In 1993, Wells argued that the original vision for the consumer research field has faded and the discipline "faces inward, toward a narrower range of issues, and away from the real world."

Whether or not one shares this assessment of the state of the field, it appears that the original vision regarding the direction and objectives of the ACR and *JCR* has not materialized. With relatively few exceptions, *JCR* and the ACR have not become forums in which researchers from multiple fields exchange ideas about consumer behavior. Also, although some articles published in *JCR* and other journals have examined specific consumer issues, such as food and energy consumption and the provision of nutrition information (e.g. Reilly and Wallendorf 1987, Ritchie *et al.* 1981, Russo *et al.* 1986), most articles published in the leading journals have examined more generic topics such as choice and attitudes. Thus, it is sometimes unclear what differentiates consumer research from other disciplines, except for the experimental stimuli used (e.g. choice between cars versus choice between bets) and the research positioning.

It is also noteworthy that consumer research has not differed significantly from psychology with respect to the proportion of laboratory studies and the use of student subjects. Specifically, our analysis of articles published in the leading consumer research journals[2] indicates that (*a*) the proportion of laboratory studies (defined as studies in which participants were aware that they were participating in a study) climbed from about 80% to around 90% in the mid-1970s and has stayed at that level ever since and (*b*) whereas the proportion of studies using student subjects was only about 30% until the early 1980s, the use of student subjects has increased steadily since then, representing approximately 75% of (positivist) studies published during the 1995–1999 period (see McGrath and Brinberg 1983, Calder *et al.* 1981, and Lynch 1982 for a discussion of the virtues of using homogeneous subject populations such as students).

A related question regarding the role and identity of consumer research is the issue of relevance (see Shimp 1994 for a comprehensive and insightful discussion of this question). Should consumer research be relevant and useful in a concrete way to particular constituencies, or should consumer research produce general knowledge about consumer behavior that could potentially be relevant to various constituencies? Shimp argues that, although consumer research may not be directly relevant to managers and other particular constituencies (other than fellow academics), the knowledge produced by consumer researchers is eventually diffused through teaching, books, consulting, and other channels.

The (ir)relevance of consumer research to managers has received particular attention, and as business schools become more sensitive and responsive to criticism of companies, students, and the popular media, this issue has gained prominence. Although there is continuing disagreement among consumer researchers regarding the virtues of being relevant to managers (e.g. Holbrook 1985), there appears to be general consensus that (academic) consumer research has had rather limited actual impact on managerial practice (e.g. Lutz 1991, Wells 1993; an exception to this generalization is some of the studies dealing with new research methodologies [e.g. Green and Srinivasan 1978]). Interestingly, consumer research articles increasingly emphasize the managerial implications of the findings, and in some journals, having specific managerial implications is one of the conditions for publication. Yet, few managers (or consumers) read consumer research articles that are published in the major journals, and the issues investigated are typically not at a level that is of much use for them.

Also, the proportion of articles published in the major marketing journals that have public policy implications declined in the 1990s compared with the 1970s and 1980s (though this trend might be explained in part by the introduction of the *Journal of Public Policy and Marketing*). Our analysis[3] indicates that, during the second half of the 1970s through the 1980s, approximately 20% of the consumer research articles published in major consumer research journals included public policy implications (e.g. Andreasen 1985, Beales *et al.* 1981), but the proportion of public policy–relevant articles declined to approximately 3% in the 1990s (e.g. Block and Anand-Keller 1995, Pechmann and Ratheshwar 1994).

This situation, whereby a field of research has limited concrete relevance or immediate impact on particular constituencies, is certainly not unique to consumer research. Furthermore, it is easy to identify reasons for the limited relevance of consumer research, including (*a*) the emphasis on theoretical contribution, rigor, and statistical (rather than practical) significance tends to limit the practical relevance; (*b*) the research, review and publication process typically takes several, years; (*c*) unlike researchers in other departments (e.g. medical researchers), who depend on external funding, many consumer researchers require limited funds, and these funds are typically provided by the business schools; (*d*) the gatekeepers of the leading consumer research journals are almost exclusively academics (for example, in 1999, 88 of the 90 members of the *JCR* Editorial Board were university professors); and (*e*) many consumer researchers have limited institutional knowledge and may be removed from the concerns and problems faced by managers, public policy makers, and even consumers (e.g. Armstrong 1991, Hoch 1988).

*Theory-Testing Versus Substantive phenomena-Driven Consumer Research* Calder and Tybout (1999; see also Calder *et al.* 1981) distinguish between (*a*) theory testing, which involves testing of explanations and relations among underlying constructs as well as "intervention testing" (i.e. theory applications) and (*b*) effect applications, in which the research question is whether previously observed effects derived from a particular theory extend to specific other settings. In the former a study is designed to provide the strongest test of the theory, with an emphasis on internal rather than external validity, whereas the latter requires that the experimental design represents most accurately the settings of interest. Importantly, both types of research are driven by existing theories – either theory testing or applications and extensions of theories to particular settings. The argument for emphasizing research that is designed to test and apply theories is that it generates universal principles that "explain any real-world situation within their domain" (Calder *et al.* 1981). From that perspective, theoretical explanations are the most important product of research, whereas generalized empirical phenomena have a lower status and are primarily designed to test and potentially falsify the theory. However, the starting point and motivation for a research project might be either theory testing or a study of a particular substantive (or methodological) domain that yields a set of observations (see discussion of the validity network schema [McGrath and Brinberg 1983, Brinberg and McGrath 1985]). Such empirical observations are typically interpreted based on existing theories, and they often suggest extensions or modifications of existing theories.

Although both theory tests and research that begins with substantive issues and phenomena can contribute to theory building, there are important differences between them. First, with the latter approach, the substantive phenomena investigated are considered interesting in their own right, as opposed to being merely arenas for theory testing. For example, understanding whether and under what conditions consumers discount missing attribute values (e.g. Meyer 1981), draw spontaneous inferences when processing ads (e.g. Kardes 1988), tend to confirm hypotheses generated by ads (e.g. Deighton 1984, Hoch and Ha 1986), prefer pioneering brands (e.g. Carpenter and Nakamoto 1989, Kardes *et al.* 1993), and prefer to co-consume items (e.g. a tasty, unhealthy appetizer and a healthier, less tasty entree) that "balance" each other (e.g. Dhar and Simonson 1999) are research-worthy questions in their own right. The findings of such investigations, in turn, often contribute to theory development.

A second implication of substantive issue-driven research is that identifying generalized empirical phenomena is an important step in the research process. For example, Huber *et al.* (1982) made an interesting observation whereby the addition of an asymmetrically dominated option to a two-option set increases the (absolute) choice share of the dominating option, in violation of the economic assumption of value maximization. Although Huber *et al.* offered several possible explanations, there was no clear theoretical account for this phenomenon when the article was published. However, this finding generated a great deal of interest, leading subsequently to the development of theoretical accounts for such "context effects" (e.g. Ariely and Wallsten 1995, Simonson and Tversky 1992). In that respect, consumer researchers can learn from the "quantitative" researchers in marketing, who often begin with an examination of relevant empirical phenomena, leading to empirical generalizations and theory building (Bass and Wind 1995).[4]

Relatedly, Alba (1999) suggested that less emphasis on theory tests and greater emphasis on obtaining data points would help advance the consumer research field. He writes, "Despite its multidisciplinary positioning, consumer research has been influenced by a narrow set of scientific traditions. A characteristic trait of these traditions is an emphasis on 'theory,' which is loosely conceived but frequently embodied in structural models or process explanations of empirical phenomena. ... The irony for consumer research, however, is that it places premium on theory when in reality it is starved for reliable data points." This point of view is consistent with the approach employed, for example, in medical research, where robust effects are regarded as interesting and important in and of themselves, with the theory often developed at a later time.

This does not mean that theory testing is not an important priority for consumer researchers (e.g. Petty and Cacioppo 1996). Indeed, theories such as the elaboration likelihood model (e.g. Petty *et al.* 1983) and prospect theory (Kahneman and Tversky 1979) have had tremendous impact on the field. However, a question that arises is whether the dominant emphasis on theory-tests as opposed to substantive domain-driven consumer research has indeed enhanced the contribution and the impact of consumer research on its various constituencies. Lutz (1991) argued that the likelihood that theory-tests will yield insights into substantive phenomena of interest is quite remote and that the most likely yield is with respect to the theory being tested. He further proposed that one way to ensure better representation of the substantive domain is to conduct research in naturally occurring consumer purchase, consumption, and communications situations (see also Winer 1999). This argument is related to the debate in the consumer research literature regarding the proper role and significance of external validity in theory tests (e.g. Calder *et al.* 1981, Lynch 1982). Consistent with Lutz's position, if in addition to theory testing, the goal of a research program is to gain a better understanding of particular substantive phenomena and the boundaries of relevant theories, then inclusion of field studies, even if they require some compromise with respect to internal validity, becomes important. As Taylor argued (1998, p. 84), "... to the extent that any program of research must ultimately address both what can happen and what does happen, making use of laboratory experiments to the exclusion of parallel field studies is unwise. Moreover, field studies ... provide valuable insights into the natural contexts in which phenomena occur; they provide information about the strength of the phenomena, given correlated environmental circumstances; they may be helpful in elucidating mediation; and they are extremely important for identifying variables both internal to the person and the environmental nature that moderate the phenomenon."

Similarly, Shimp (1994; see also Lehmann 1996) proposed that consumer research needs to put far greater emphasis on "consumer behavior that occurs within the milieu of actual marketplace phenomena." He suggested that theories taken from other disciplines should be used as instruments rather than as the primary objectives of empirical inquiry. The ultimate goal, he argues, is "the development of theory about actual consumer behavior that may serve the needs of all markets interested in consumer research: academics, students, business-people, public policy officials, and society at large" (p. 5).

## Conclusion

We have examined the current state of consumer research, the multidisciplinary influences on the field and their consquences, as well as the question of what differentiates it from other fields. Multiple influences on an applied area and an identity problem are probably not unique to consumer research (see, e.g. Tetlock's 1998 discussion of the "reductionist syllogism" in his review of research on world politics). However, because consumer behavior is such a broad area in which the central topics are shared with other fields and disciplines, it is particularly susceptible to division and disagreement regarding the key research topics and how research should be conducted. In this review we have explored the differences between three particular subfields – social cognition, BDT, and postmodern consumer research – and highlighted the opportunities for greater collaboration.

Importantly, although multiple and, in some cases, incompatible influences tend to generate disagreements, the exposure to multidisciplinary influences and the different approaches represented in consumer research are also a significant strength that contributes to the quality and diversity of scholarly work. Thus, some studies conducted by consumer researchers represent basic research, dealing with the same fundamental issues that researchers in the related disciplines investigate. In fact, in certain basic research areas that are particularly relevant to businesses and consumers, such as decision making, business schools, including consumer researchers, appear to have taken the lead from the relevant disciplines (e.g. psychology). In addition to basic research, consumer researchers will also continue to apply, test, and extend theories developed in other disciplines. Such research can have significant impact on the field and often contributes to theory development. In particular, the consumer environment imposes relevant constraints and the stimuli used are often richer and more complex than those employed by researchers in psychology. This, in turn, forces the researcher to evaluate the boundaries of the theory, which can lead to theoretical extensions and improve our understanding of the moderating factors and the conditions under which the theory is applicable.

A third type of consumer research, which we believe deserves greater emphasis, focuses on substantive phenomena of interest and often leads to theory development (e.g. Alba 1999, Lutz 1991, Shimp 1994; see also Cialdini 1980). Because such research tends to be motivated by phenomena rather than by theory-testing, it is sometimes viewed as atheoretical and of lower status. However, rigorous studies of substantive phenomena build on the relative advantages and incentives of consumer researchers (and business school faculty more generally), and in many cases make significant contributions to theory development. Furthermore, compared to researchers in the basic disciplines, consumer researchers often have greater exposure to "real world" problems (e.g. of organizations and consumers) and easier access to data relating to substantive phenomena.

The saying that "there is nothing more practical than a good theory" notwithstanding, another advantage of substantive phenomena-driven research is that it is usually more relevant, particularly to the phenomena being investigated. Whether or not researchers believe it is good for consumer research (e.g. Holbrook 1985), the pressure on business school faculty to be relevant and the incentives to conduct research that is relevant in a reasonably concrete way to managers and/or other constituencies continue to play a significant role that many researchers are unlikely to ignore. Although ulterior motives have some negative associations, an emphasis on relevance should not come at the expense of rigor and, ultimately, theoretical contribution. Furthermore, in addition to tightly controlled lab studies that allow unconfounded tests of cause and effect. substantive domain-focused investigations will benefit from the inclusion of studies in more naturalistic settings, even if such tests involve a certain compromise in terms of internal validity. Also, when conducting lab studies, consumer research will benefit from greater attention to using stimuli and tasks that include the essential characteristics of the relevant substantive domains.

Consider, for example, a study of buyer behavior in online auctions, which examines various factors that influence bidding behavior and the willingness to pay for items being auctioned. In addition to improving our understanding of online auctions, such research might have significant theoretical implications regarding escalation, competitive behavior, inference making, perceived value, and other conceptually important issues. A researcher embarking on such a project may begin the investigation by observing actual online auctions, which might offer some tentative hypotheses regarding relevant influences. However, in all likelihood, the presence of confounding factors will limit the researcher's ability to establish unambiguously the generality of the observed phenomena and their causes. Accordingly, the researcher may conduct lab studies using simulated auctions, possibly providing incentives to participants, such as indicating that one or more of the auctions will actually be applied. This lab research, in turn, may lead to additional field experiments that might provide further insights.

In summary, the relative emphasis on theory-testing versus substantive domain-driven research and on external validity is relevant also to the question of the identity of the consumer research field. A greater emphasis on substantive phenomena and the combination of tightly controlled lab studies with investigations in more naturalistic settings, we believe, will differentiate the field and enhance its impact on both theory and practice. Indeed, buyer behavior offers an exceptionally rich domain for studying a wide range of real world phenomena that have potentially important theoretical implications. Furthermore, with the advancement of new technologies and the rise of the Internet, consumer researchers are in a much better position today to conduct investigations that deal with marketplace phenomena while maintaining experimental control. Finally, a greater emphasis on rigorous, systematic, substantive phenomena-driven research has the potential to produce major contributions to theory, precisely because the starting point is not an existing theory. Thus, such research can significantly enhance the impact of the consumer research field on researchers in the consumer and related fields, industry, and public policy makers.

## Acknowledgments

This chapter has benefited greatly from the suggestions of many leading consumer researchers; special thanks to James Bettman, Richard Lutz, and Terry Shimp for their helpful comments.

## Notes

1. Given space limitations, we report only the main findings from these analyses. Additional information regarding the method of analysis and findings can be obtained from the authors.
2. This analysis is based on an examination of consumer behavior articles published in the August issues of the *Journal of Marketing Research* between 1969 and 1999, and articles published in the September issues of the *JCR* from 1974 till 1999.
3. Two independent coders rated each consumer research article published in August issues of the *Journal of Marketing Research* (since 1969), September issues of the *JCR* (since 1974), and Summer issues of the *Journal of Consumer Psychology* (since 1991) in terms of the relevance of its findings and conclusions to public policy makers. The coders used a 0–3 scale where 0 = not at all relevant and 3 = very relevant.
4. A possible limitation of substantive domain-driven research is that there are no clear criteria for determining which questions are interesting and worthy of research, whereas theory tests might offer clearer guidelines. However, the research community, in general, and journal reviewers, in particular, can help educate researchers as to the types of substantive issues considered interesting.

## Literature cited

Aaker D, Keller K. 1990. Consumer evaluations of brand extensions. *J. Mark.* 54:27–41
Aaker JL. 1997. Dimensions of brand personality. *J. Mark. Res.* 34:347–56

Aaker JL, Maheswaran D. 1997. The effect of cultural orientation on persuasion, *J Consum. Res.* 24:315–28

Alba J. 1999. President's column: loose ends. *Assoc. Consum. Res. Newsl.*, Dec., p. 2

Alba J, Hutchinson W. 1987. Dimensions of consumer expertise. *J. Consum. Res.* 13:411–45

Alba J, Hutchinson W, Lynch J. 1991. Memory and decision making. See Robertson and Kassarjian 1991, pp. 1–49

Alba JW, Mela CF, Shimp TA, Urbany JE. 1999. The effect of discount frequency and depth on consumer price judgments. *J Consum. Res.* 26:99–114

Anand P, Sternthal B. 1990. Ease of message processing as a moderator of repetition effects in advertising. *J Mark. Res.* 27:345–53

Andreasen AR. 1985. Consumer responses to dissatisfaction in loose monopolies. *J Consum. Res.* 12:135–41

Ariely D, Wallsten TS. 1995. Seeking subjective dominance in multidimensional space: an explanation of the asymmetric dominance effect. *Organ. Behav. Hum. Decis. Process.* 63(3):223–32

Armstrong JS. 1991. Prediction of consumer behavior by experts and novices. *J Consum. Res.* 18(2):251–56

Arnould E, Wallendorf M. 1994. Market oriented ethnography: interpretation building and marketing strategy formulation. *J Mark. Res.* 31(4):484–504

Amould EJ, Fischer E. 1994. Hermeneutics and consumer research. *J Consum. Res.* 21(l):55–70

Arnould EJ, Price LL. 1993. River magic: extraordinary experience and the extended service encounter. *J Consum. Res.* 20(1)24–45

Bagozzi RP, Baumgartner H, Yi Y. 1992. State versus action orientation and the theory of reasoned action: an application to coupon usage. *J Consum. Res.* 18:505–18

Bass FM, Wind J. 1995. Introduction to the special issue: empirical generalizations in marketing, *Mark. Sci.* 14(3) Part G6–19

Baumgartner H, Sujan M, Padgett D. 1997. Patterns of affective reactions to advertisements: the integration of moment-to-moment responses into overall judgments. *J Mark. Res.* 34:219–32

Beales H, Mazis MB, Salop SC, Staelin R. 198 1. Consumer search and public policy. *J Consum. Res.* 8:11–22

Bearden WO, Etzel MJ. 1982. Reference group influence on product and brand purchase decisions. *J Consum. Res.* 9:183–94

Belk RW. 1986. Generational differences in the meaning of things. *Advert. Consum. Psychol.* 3:199–213

Belk RW. 1988. Possessions and the extended self. *J Consum. Res.* 15(2):139–68

Belk RW, Costa JA. 1998. The mountain man myth: a contemporary consuming fantasy. *J Consum. Res.* 218–40

Bettman J, Luce MF, Payne JW. 1998. Constructive consumer choice processes. *J Consum. Res.* 25:187–217

Bettman JR. 1971. The structure of consumer choice processes. *J Mark. Res.* 8:465–71

Bettman JR. 1979. *An Information Processing Theory of Consumer Choice.* Reading, MA: Addison Wesley

Bettman JR. 1986. Consumer psychology. *Annu. Rev. Psychol.* 37:257–89

Bettman JR. 1993. The decision maker who came in from the cold. In *Advances in Consumer Research*, ed. L McAlister, M Rothschild, 20:7-11. Provo, UT: Assoc. for Consum. Res.

Bettman JR, Park CW. 1980. Effects of prior knowledge and experience and phase of the choice process: a protocol analysis. *J Consum. Res.* 7:234–48.

Biehal G, Chakravarti D. 1982. Information presentation format and learning goals as determinants of consumers' memory retrieval and choice processes. *J Consum. Res.* 8:43–141

Biehal G, Chakravarti D. 1983. Information accessibility as a moderator of consumer choice. *J Consum. Res.* 10: 1–14

Block LG, Anand Keller P. 1995. When to accentuate the negative: the effects of perceived efficacy and message framing on intentions to perform health-related behavior. *J Mark. Res.* 32:192–203

Brinberg D, McGrath J. 1985. *Validity and the Research Process*. Beverly Hills, CA: Sage
Broniarczyk SM, Alba J. 1994. The importance of the brand in brand extension. *J Mark. Res.* 31:214–28
Brucks M. 1988. Search monitor: an approach for computer controlled experiments involving consumer information search. *J Consum. Res.* 15:117–21
Calder BJ, Phillips LW, Tybout AM. 1981. Designing research for applications. *J Consum. Res.* 8:197–207
Calder BJ, Tybout AM. 1987. What consumer research is. *J Consum. Res.* 14(l):136–40
Calder BJ, Tybout AM. 1999. A vision of theory, research, and the future of business schools. *J Acad. Mark. Sci.* 27(3):359–66
Carmon Z, Simonson I. 1998. Price-quality tradeoffs in choice vs. matching: new insights into the prominence effect. *J Consum. Psychol.* 7:323–43
Carpenter GS, Nakamoto K. 1989. Consumer preference formation and pioneering advantage. *J Mark. Res.* 26:285–98
Chaiken S. 1980. Heuristic versus systematic information processing and the use of source versus message cues in persuasion. *J Pers. Soc. Psychol.* 39:752–66
Cialdini RB. 1980. Full cycle social psychology. In *Applied Social Psychology Annual*, ed. L Bickman, 1:21–47. Beverly Hills, CA: Sage
Cohen JB, Chakravarti D. 1990. Consumer psychology. *Annu. Rev. Psychol.* 41:243–88
Cohen JB. 1989. An overextended self? *J Consum. Res.* 16:125–28
Coupey E. 1994. Restructuring: constructive processing of information displays in consumer choice. *J Consum. Res.* 21:83–99
Coupey E, Irwin JR, Payne JW. 1998. Product category familiarity and preference construction. *J Consum. Res.* 24:459–68
Deighton J. 1984. The interaction of advertising and evidence. *J Consum. Res.* 11:763–70
Deshpande R, Stayman DM. 1994. A tale of two cities: distinctiveness theory and advertising effectiveness. *J Mark. Res.* 31:57–64
Dhar R. 1997. Consumer preference for a nochoice option. *J Consum. Res.* 24:215–31
Dhar R, Nowlis SM. 1999. The effect of time pressure on consumer choice deferral. *J Consum. Res.* 25:369–84
Dhar R, Simonson I. 1999. Making complementary choices in consumption episodes: highlighting versus balancing. *J Mark. Res.* 36:29–44
Drolet A, Simonson I, Tversky A. 2000. Indifference curves that travel with the choice set. *Mark. Lett.* 11: 199–209
Edell JA, Chapman Burke M. 1987. The power of feelings in understanding advertising effects. *J Consum. Res.* 14:421–33
Engel J, Kollat D, Blackwell R. 1968. *Consumer Behavior*. New York: Holt, Rinehart & Winston
Fazio RH, Ledbetter JE, Towles-Schwen T. 2000. On the cost of accessible attitudes: detecting that the attitude object has changed. *J Pers. Soc. Psychol.* 78:197–20
Fazio RH, Powell MC, Williams CL 1989. The role of attitude accessibility in the attitude-to-behavior process. *J Consum. Res.* 16:280–88
Feldman JM, Lynch JG Jr. 1988. Self generated validity and other effects of measurement on belief, attitude, intention and behavior. *J Appl. Psychol.* 73:421–35
Firat AF, Venkatesh A. 1995. Liberatory postmodernism and the reenchantment of consumption. *J Consum. Res.* 22:239–67
Fischer G, Carmon Z, Ariely D, Zauberman G. 1999. Goal-based construction of preference: task goals & the prominence effect. *Manage. Sci.* 45:1057–75
Fishbein M, Ajzen I. 1975. *Belief Attitude, Intention and Behavior: An Introduction to Theory and Research*. Reading, MA: Addison-Wesley
Fiske ST, Taylor SE. 1984. *Social Cognition*. New York: McGraw-Hill
Fiske ST, Pavelchek MA. 1986. Category-based versus piecemeal-based affective responses: development in schema-triggered affect. In *Handbook of Motivation and Cognition: Foundations of Social Behavior*, ed. RM Sorrentino, ET Higgins, pp. 167–203. New York: Guilford

Folkes VS. 1984. Consumer reactions to product failure: an attributional approach. *J Consum. Res.* 10:398–409
Fournier S. 1998. Consumers and their brands: developing relationship theory in consumer research. *J Consum. Res.* 24:343–73
Fournier S, Mick DG. 1999. Rediscovering satisfaction. *J Mark.* 615–23
Frank R. 1974. Letter from the editor. *J Consum. Res.* 1:i
Friestad M, Wright P. 1994. The Persuasion Knowledge Model: how people cope with persuasion attempts. *J Consum. Res.* 2 1: 131
Gaeth G, Levin I. 1988. How consumers are affected by the framing of attribute information before and after consuming the product. *J Consum. Res.* 15:374–78
Gardner BB, Levy SL. 1955. The product and the brand. *Harv. Bus. Rev.* Mar-Apr:3338
Gilbert D, Fiske ST, Lindzey G. 1998. *The Handbook of Social Psychology*, Vol. 1, New York: McGraw-Hill. 4th ed.
Gould SJ. 1991. The self manipulation of my pervasive, perceived vital energy through product use: an introspective-Praxis perspective. *J Consum. Res.* 18:194–207
Gourville JT, Soman D. 1998. Payment depreciation: the behavioral effects of temporally separating payments from consumption. *J Consum. Res.* 25:160–74
Green PE, Srinivasan V. 1978. Conjoint analysis in consumer research: issues and outlook. *J Consum. Res.* 5:103–23
Gregan-Paxton J, Roedder-John D. 1997. The emergence of adaptive decision making in children. *J Consum. Res.* 24:43–56
Guest L. 1962. Consumer analysis. *Annu. Rev. Psychol.* 13:315–344
Hirschman EC. 1994. Consumers and their animal companions. *J Consum. Res.* 20:616–32
Hoch SJ. 1988. Who do we know: predicting the interests and opinions of the American consumer. *J Consum. Res.* 15:315–24
Hoch SJ, Ha Y. 1986. Consumer learning: advertising and the ambiguity of product experience. *J Consum. Res*. 13:221–33
Holbrook MB. 1985. Why business is bad for consumer research: the three bears revisited. *Adv. Consum. Res.* 12:145–56
Holbrook MB. 1987. What is consumer research? *J Consum. Res*. 14:128–32
Holbrook MB, Grayson MW. 1986. The semiology of cinematic consumption: symbolic consumer behavior in *Out of Africa*. *J Consum. Res.* 13:374–81
Holbrook MB, Hirschman E. 1982. The experiential aspects of consumption: consumer fantasies, feelings, and fun. *J Consum. Res.* 9:132–40
Howard JA, Sheth JN. 1969. *The Theory of Buyer Behavior*. New York: Wiley
Hsee CK, Leclerc F. 1998. Will products look more attractive when presented separately or together? *J Consum. Res.* 25:175–86
Huber J, Payne J, Puto C. 1982. Adding asymmetrically dominated alternatives: violations of regularity and the similarity hypothesis. *J Consum. Res.* 9:90–98
Huber J, Puto C. 1983. Market boundaries and product choice: illustrating attraction and substitution effects. *J Consum. Res.* 10: 31–44
Hudson LA, Ozanne JL. 1988. Alternative ways of seeking knowledge in consumer research. *J Consum. Res.* 14:508–21
Jacoby J, Speller DE, Berning CK. 1974. Brand choice behavior as a function of information load. *J Consum. Res.* 1:33–42
Jacoby J. 1976. Consumer psychology: an octennium. *Annu. Rev. Psychol.* 27:331–58
Janiszewski C. 1988. Preconscious processing effects: the independence of attitude formation and conscious thought. *J Consum. Res.* 15:199–209
Johar G, Pham MT. 1999. Relatedness, prominence, and constructive sponsor identification, *J Mark. Res.* 26:299–312
Johnson MD. 1984. Consumer choice strategies for comparing noncomparable alternatives. *J Consum. Res.* 11:741–53
Kahn BE, Louie TA. 1990. Effects of retraction of price promotions on brand choice behavior for variety-seeking and last-purchase-loyal consumers. *J Mark. Res.* 27:279–89

Kahneman D, Tversky 1979. Prospect theory: an analysis of decision under risk. *Econometrica* 47:263–91

Kardes FR. 1988. Spontaneous inference processes in advertising: the effects of conclusion omission and involvement on persuasion. *J Consum. Res.* 15:225–33

Kardes FR, Kalyanaram G, Chandrashekaran M, Dornof RJ. 1993. Brand retrieval, consideration set composition, consumer choice, and the pioneering advantage. *J Consum. Res.* 20:62–75

Kassarjian H. 1982. Consumer psychology. *Annu. Rev. Psychol.* 33:619–49

Kassarjian H, Robertson T. 1968. *Perspectives in Consumer Behavior*. Englewood Cliffs, NJ: Prentice Hall

Keller KL. 1987. Memory factors in advertising: the effect of advertising retrieval cues on brand evaluations. *J Consum. Res.* 14:316–33

Keller KL. 1993. Conceptualizing, measuring, and managing customer-based brand equity. *J. Mark.* 57:1–22

Kisielius J, Sternthal B. 1984. Detecting and explaining vividness effects in attitudinal judgments. *J Mark. Res.* 21:54–64

Krosnick JA, Shuman H. 1988. Attitude intensity, importance, and certainty and susceptibility to response effects. *J. Pers. Soc. Psychol*, 54:940–52

Lehmann DR. 1996. Presidential address: knowledge generalization and the conventions of consumer research: a study in inconsistency. In *Advances in Consumer Research*, ed. KP Corfman, JG Lynch Jr, 23:1–5. Provo, UT: Assoc. Consum. Res.

Levy SL. 1959. Symbols for sale. *Harv. Bus. Rev.* Jul–Aug: 117–24

Luce MF 1998. Choosing to avoid: coping with negatively emotion-laden consumer decisions. *J. Consum. Res.* 24:409–22

Lutz RJ. 1977. An experimental investigation of causal relations among cognitions, affect, and behavioral intention. *J. Consum. Res.* 3:197–208

Lutz RJ. 1991. Editorial. *J Consum. Res.* 17: i–v

Lynch JG Jr. 1982. On the external validity of experiments in consumer research. *J Consum. Res.* 9:225–39

Lynch JG Jr, Marmorstein H, Weigold ME 1988. Choices from sets including remembered brands: use of recalled attributes and prior overall evaluations. *J Consum. Res.* 15:169–84

Mahajan J. 1992. The overconfidence effect in marketing management predictions. *J Mark. Res.* 29:329–42

McAlister L. 1982. A dynamic attribute satiation model of variety seeking behavior. *J Consum. Res.* 9:141–50

McGrath JE, Brinberg D. 1983. External validity and the research process: a comment on the Calder/Lynch dialogue. *J Consum. Res.* 10(l):115–24

McGuire WG. 1969. The nature of attitudes and attitude change. In *Handbook of Social Psychology*, ed. G Lindzey, E Aronson, 3:136–3 14. 2nd ed.

McQuarrie EF, Mick DG. 1992, On resonance: a critical pluralistic inquiry into advertising rhetoric. *J Consum. Res.* 17:180–97

Menon G, Raghubir P, Schwarz N. 1995. Behavioral frequency judgments: an accessibility-diagnosticity framework. *J Consum. Res.* 22:212–28

Meyer RJ. 1981. A model of multiattribute judgments under attribute uncertainty and informational constraint. *J Mark. Res.* 18:428–41

Meyers-Levy J, Maheswaran D. 1991. Exploring differences in males' and females' processing strategies. *J Consum. Res.* 18:63–70

Meyers-Levy J, Tybout AM. 1997. Context effects at encoding and judgment in consumption settings: the role of cognitive resources. *J Consum. Res.* 24:1–14

Miller D. 1995. Consumption and commodities. *Annu. Rev. Anthropol.* 24:141–61

Miniard PW, Cohen J. 1983. Modeling personal and normative influences on behavior. *J Consum. Res.* 10: 169–80

Monroe KB. 1973. Buyer's subjective perceptions of price. *J Mark. Res.* 10:70–80

Morwitz VG, Johnson E, Schmittlein D. 1993. Does measuring intent change behavior? *J Consum. Res.* 20:46–61

Murray JB, Ozanne JL. 1991, The critical imagination: emancipatory interests in consumer research. *J Consum. Res.* 18:129–44

Newell A, Simon HA. 1972. *Human Problem Solving*. Englewood Cliffs, NJ: Prentice-Hall

Nicosia F. 1966. *Consumer Decision Processes*. Englewood Cliffs, NJ: Prentice-Hall

Norman DA, Borrow DG. 1975. On data-limited and resource-limited processes. *Cogn. Psychol.* 7:44–64

Nowlis S, Simonson I. 1997. Attribute-task compatibility as a determinant of consumer preference reversals. *J Mark. Res.* 34:205–18

O'Guinn TC, Faber R. 1989. Compulsive buying: a phenomenological exploration. *J Consum. Res.* 16:147–57

Park CW, Milberg S, Lawson R. 1991. Evaluation of brand extensions: the role of product feature similarity and brand concept consistency. *J Consum. Res.* 18:185–93

Payne J. 1976. Task complexity and contingent processing in decision making: an information search and protocol analysis. *Organ. Behav. Hum. Perform.* 16:366–87

Pechmann C, Ratneshwar S. 1994. The effects of antismoking and cigarette advertising on young adolescents' perceptions of peers who smoke. *J. Consum. Res.* 21:236–51

Peter JP, Olson JC. 1993. *Consumer Behavior and Marketing Strategy*. Homewood, IL: Richard D. Irwin, Inc. 3rd ed.

Petty RE, Cacioppo JT. 1996. Addressing disturbing and disturbed consumer behavior: Is it necessary to change the way we conduct behavioral science? *J Mark. Res.* 311–8

Petty RE, Cacioppo JT, Schumann D. 1983. Central and peripheral routes to advertising effectiveness: the moderating role of involvement. *J. Consum. Res.* 10: 134–48

Petty RE, Unnava R, Strathman A.J. 1991. Theories of attitude change. See Robertson & Kassarjian 1991, pp. 241–80

Pham MT. 1998. Representativeness, relevance, and the use of feelings in decision making. *J. Consum. Res.* 25:144–59

Praft RW. 1974. ACR: a perspective. In *Advances in Consumer Research*, ed. S Ward, P Wright, 1: 1–8. Urbana, IL: Assoc. Consum. Res.

Prelec D, Loewenstein GF. 1998. The red and the black: mental accounting of savings and debt. *Mark. Sci.* 17:4–28

Priester JR, Petty RE. 1996. The gradual threshold model of ambivalence: relating the positive and negative bases of attitudes to subjective ambivalence. *J Pers. Soc. Psychol.* 71:431–49

Ratner RK, Kahn BE, Kahneman D. 1999. Choosing less-preferred experiences for the sake of variety. *J Consum. Res.* 26:1–15

Ratneshwar S, Chaiken S. 1991. Comprehension's role in persuasion: the case of its moderating effect on the persuasive impact of source cues. *J Consum. Res.* 18:52–62

Reilly MD, Wallendorf M. 1987. A comparison of group differences in food consumption using household refuse. *J Consum. Res.* 14:289–94

Richins M. 1997. Measuring emotions in the consumption experience. *J Consum. Res.* 24:127–46

Ritchie JRB, McDougall GHG, Claxton JD. 1981. Complexities of household energy consumption and conservation. *J Consum. Res.* 8:233–42

Robertson TS, Kassarjian HH, eds. 1991. *Handbook of Consumer Behavior.* Englewood Cliffs, NJ: Prentice–Hall

Russo JE, Staelin R, Nolan CA, Russell GJ, Metcalf BL. 1986. Nutrition information in the supermarket. *J Consum. Res.* 13:48–70

Schmitt BH, Zhang S. 1998. Language structure and categorization: a study of classifiers in consumer cognition, judgment, and choice. *J Consum. Res.* 25:108–22

Schwarz N, Bohner G. 2000. The construction of attitudes. In *Blackwell Handbook of Social Psychology: Intrapersonal Processes*, ed. A Tesser, N Schwarz. Oxford: Blackwell. In press

Schouten JW, McAlexander JH. 1995. Subcultures of consumption: an ethnography of the new bikers. *J Consum. Res.* 22:43–61

Scott CA, Yalch RF. 1980. Consumer response to initial product trial: Bayesian analysis. *J Consum. Res.* 7:32–41

Sen S, Johnson EJ. 1997. Mere-possession effects without possession in consumer choice. *J Consum. Res.* 24:105–17

Shimp T. 1994. Presidential address: academic Appalachia and the discipline of consumer research. *Adv. Consum. Res.* 21:1–7

Shimp TA, Kavas A. 1984. The theory of reasoned action applied to coupon usage. *J Consum. Res.* 11:795–809

Shiv B, Fedorikhin A. 1999. Heart and mind in conflict: the interplay of affect and cognition in consumer decision making. *J Consum. Res.* 26:278–92

Simonson I. 1989. Choice based on reasons: the case of attraction and compromise effects. *J Consum. Res.* 16:158–74

Simonson I. 1990. The effect of purchase quantity and timing on variety seeking behavior. *J Mark. Res.* 27:150–62

Simonson I. 1992. The influence of anticipating regret and responsibility on purchase decisions. *J Mark. Res.* 19:105–18

Simonson I, Tversky A. 1992. Choice in context: tradeoff contrast and extremeness aversion. *J Mark. Res.* 29:281–95

Stern BB. 1989. Literary criticism and consumer research: overview and illustrative analysis. *J Consum. Res.* 16:322–34

Sternthal B, Dholakia R, Leavitt C. 1978. The persuasive effect of source credibility: tests of cognitive response. *J Consum. Res.* 4:252–60

Sujan M. 1985. Consumer knowledge: effects on evaluation strategies mediating consumer judgments. *J Consum. Res.* 12:31–46

Taylor SE, 1998. The social being in social psychology. See Gilbert *et al.* 1998, pp. 58–95

Tetlock P. 1998. Social psychology and world politics. In *The Handbook of Social Psychology*, ed. D Gilbert, S Fiske, G Lindzey, 2:868–912. New York: McGraw-Hill. 4th ed.

Thaler R. 1985. Mental accounting and consumer choice. *Mark. Sci.* 4:199–214

Thompson CJW. 1996. Caring consumers: gendered consumption meanings and the juggling lifestyle. *J Consum. Res.* 22: 388–407

Thompson CJW, Locander WB, Pollio HR.1989. Putting consumer experience back into consumer research: the philosophy and method of existential-phenomenology. *J Consum. Res.* 16:133–46

Tybout A, Artz N. 1994. Consumer psychology. *Annu. Rev. Psychol.* 45:131–69

Tybout A, Sternthal B, Calder B. 1983. Information availability as a determinant of multiple request effectiveness. *J Mark. Res.* 20:280–90

Unnava R, Agarwal S, Haugtvedt C. 1996. Interactive effects of presentation modality and message-generated imagery on recall of advertising information. *J Consum. Res.* 23:81–93

Wallendorf M, Brucks M. 1993. Introspecting in consumer research: implementation and implications. *J Consum. Res.* 20:339–59

Wells WD. 1993. Discovery-oriented consumer research. *J Consum.* Res. 21:319–31

Wernerfelt B. 1995. A rational reconstruction of the compromise effect: using market data to infer utilities. *J Consum. Res.* 21:627–33

West PM, Broniarczyk SM. 1998. Integrating multiple opinions: the role of aspiration level on consumer response to critic consensus. *J Consum. Res.* 25:38–51

Winer RS. 1999. Experimentation in the 21st century: the importance of external validity. *J Acad. Mark. Sci.* 27:349–58

Wright P. 1973. The cognitive processes mediating acceptance of advertising. *J Mark. Res.* 10:53–62

Zajonc R. 1998. Emotions. See Gilbert *et al.* 1998, pp. 591–632

# 14

# Putting Consumer Experience Back into Consumer Research: The Philosophy and Method of Existential-Phenomenology

**Craig J. Thompson, William B. Locander and Howard R. Pollio**

**Source:** *Journal of Consumer Research* 16 (1989): 133–146.

This article presents existential-phenomenology as a paradigm for studying consumer experience. A paradigm refers to a group of researchers sharing common assumptions about the nature of reality, utilizing common methodologies, and dealing with similar problems (Kuhn 1970). Adherents of a paradigm have both a philosophy of what the world is like and investigative methods deriving from that perspective. Existential-phenomenology is a paradigm that blends the philosophy of existentialism with the methods of phenomenology (Valle and King 1978). The result is a contextually based, holistic psychology that views human beings in non-dualistic terms and seeks to attain a first-person description of experience (Giorgi 1983).

Jacob (1987) notes that much confusion about descriptive methodologies has arisen from treating all such methods as though they were homogeneous. In consumer research, "interpretive" methods (Hudson and Ozanne 1988) primarily have proceeded in the ethnographic (Belk 1987; Belk, Sherry, and Wallendorf 1988; Hirschman 1986; Holbrook 1987; Wallendorf 1987), semiotic (Holbrook and Grayson 1986; Mick 1986; Sherry and Camargo 1987), or structuralist (Levy 1981; O'Shaughnessy 1985) traditions. Although these approaches sometimes take a phenomenological perspective, they are not *per se* existential phenomenology.

Existentialism, the philosophy underlying existential-phenomenology, is associated with the works of Dilthey (1958/orig. 1890), Sartre (1962/orig. 1943), Heidegger (1962/orig. 1927), and Merleau-Ponty (1962/orig. 1945). The research methods of existential-phenomenology derive primarily from Gestalt psychology (Koffka 1935; Kohler 1947; Wertheimer 1945) and clinical practice (May and Yalom 1984; Van den Berg 1970). For example, existential-phenomenological methods have been employed in research concerning the experiences of anxiety (Fischer 1978), learning (Colaizzi 1973; Giorgi 1971), time (Dapkus 1985), and special possessions (Myers 1985).

As Kuhn (1970) noted, understanding a paradigm different from one's own is a difficult task because it requires seeing the world from a new perspective. As a means of making this task easier, an analysis of metaphors describing assumptions of the "traditional" view and those of existential-phenomenology will be employed. A benefit of this approach is that it provides a means of describing a given paradigm's core assumptions, assumptions that are not put to empirical test but are treated as unquestionable givens (Lakatos 1970. Metaphors have been used to highlight assumptions implicit in many different programs of philosophy, cognitive science, and natural science (Gerhart and Russell 1984; Johnson 1987; Kohler 1969; Lakoff 1987; Lakoff and Johnson 1980; Morgan 1980; Pepper 1942). Metaphoric analyses also have been used to examine research issues in marketing science (Arndt 1985; Rosenberg 1984).

In this article, we will focus on basic tenets of existential-phenomenology and will describe a research methodology based on them. The discussion will be organized into four sections. First, the core assumptions of traditional approaches to consumer behavior will be delineated to highlight areas where existential-phenomenology differs from them. Second, core assumptions of existential-phenomenology will be outlined and their implications for consumer research discussed. Third, a specific research method will be described. And, fourth, a discussion of epistemological criteria for this methodology will be given.

## The Cartesian View

The dominant paradigm in marketing and consumer research is logical positivism (or a more current version known as modern empiricism), and the implications of this philosophy for research methodology have been widely discussed (Anderson 1983, 1986; Arndt 1985; Bogdan and Taylor 1975; Hirschman 1986; Holbrook and Hirschman 1982; Hunt 1983; Lincoln and Guba 1985; Peter and Olsen 1983). Logical positivism has an epistemological focus and seeks to determine the "truth value" of statements (Pepper 1942). Some have noted, however, that a broader set of assumptions underlies the use of positivist methods (Giorgi 1971; Van den Berg 1961).

These meta-assumptions have been placed under the more global philosophical rubrics of "Cartesianism" or "rationalism" (Giorgi 1983; Pollio 1982; Valle and King 1978; Zaner 1970). Some of the more well-known tenets of Cartesianism are the distinction between mind and body and the assumption that "reality" must be deduced and then rendered in mathematical terms (Zaner 1970). The legacy of Cartesianism affects the way in which consumer research is done today. The following discussion will focus on the Cartesian metaphors of the machine and the container.

### The Machine Metaphor

One major metaphor of Cartesianism is that of the machine (Pepper 1942; Van den Berg 1961), a theoretical system in which all free dynamics in the system are restricted by constraints taking the form of principles and laws (Kohler 1969). Pepper (1942) notes the certain assumptions that follow from the machine metaphor:

1. Properties of the machine, such as psychological ones, can be calibrated and measured.
2. The machine has primary qualities that are essential to its function and are measurable, such as mass and motion. Any aspects of the machine not quantifiable are viewed as incidental to its function.

3. The machine is composed of independent components. By taking the machine apart and studying components in isolation, the essence of its function can be determined. Analysis does not change machine function, since components in isolation are assumed to operate the same as components in unison.

These assumptions are manifested in many normative methodological prescriptions: (1) science should use formalized language systems (mathematics and operationally specified terms) to express knowledge; (2) science should uncover causal laws that explain the functioning of phenomena; (3) science should employ analytic procedures by which separate parts of the phenomenon can be studied singularly and in detail; and (4) science should reduce a given phenomenon to a set of necessary and sufficient properties.

Mechanism and its accompanying assumptions motivate a variety of research programs that have emerged in psychology, including behaviorism, where behavior is determined by the mechanism of stimulus-response associations (Bower and Hilgard 1981; Howard 1965; Hull 1943); information processing, where cognition is determined by structural mechanisms, such as short-term memory capacity (Bettman 1979; Miller, Galanter, and Pribram 1960; Newell and Simon 1972; Wyer and Srull 1986); and certain natural science approaches to psychoanalysis, where neurotic symptoms are determined by unconscious mechanisms operating within the person (Horowitz 1963; Pumpian-Mindlin 1952).

### The Container Metaphor

Dualism, the proposed separation of the mental and the physical worlds, has been one of the more enduring remnants of the Cartesian legacy (Pollio 1982). The assumptions of dualism are described by another Cartesian metaphor in which the body is viewed as a container for "mind," while the "mind" is viewed as a container for symbolic representations and conceptual structures (Lakoff and Johnson 1980). These aspects have certain implications for studying human cognitive activity.

1. External events, those occurring outside the body container, are objective, while internal events, those occurring inside the body container, are subjective. Experience is a private, internal, and, therefore, subjective event (Churchland 1985).
2. Mind is an entity that manipulates symbols representing the external world (Dreyfuss 1982). These manipulations allow the external world to be brought into internal consciousness. Since the cognitive processes by which the symbol is manipulated are internal, cognitive structures and functions can be isolated and studied in a decontextualized manner.
3. Objects in the world exist as a brute reality independent of human experience and, thus, there is one true description of the world waiting to be discovered (Johnson 1987). This "true" description will be mathematically precise and free of linguistic ambiguity.

## The Existential-Phenomenological View

The purpose of examining the metaphors of Cartesianism is not to argue that they are wrong but to point out that this is one particular world view. It may be limiting for consumer researchers to conclude that this is the only perspective from which to view human phenomena. There are alternative, epistemologically viable world views for exploring human experience. One such world view is that of existential-phenomenology (Giorgi 1983; Merleau-Ponty 1962/orig. 1945; Pollio 1982; Sartre 1962/orig. 1943). The core assumptions of this alternative world view are described by the metaphors of pattern, figure/ground, and seeing.

### The Pattern Metaphor

A pattern is a segregated perceptual whole that emerges from a context (Kohler 1947). While being perceptually distinguishable, a pattern does not exist as a complete and separate entity from its surrounding context (Gibson 1979; Koffka 1935; Kohler 1947). In keeping with the pattern metaphor, existential-phenomenology subscribes to a contextualist world view. Existential-phenomenologists do not seek to study individuals separate from the environments in which they live or the interaction of the two (which implies separation), rather, the study is of the totality of human-being-in-the-world (Heidegger 1962/orig. 1927).

**Figure A** An Illustration of Emergent Phenomena

*Source*: Fraser, James B. (1908), "A New Visual Illusion of Direction," *British Journal of Psychology*, 2 (January) 307–320 (figure appears on p. 318). Reprinted with permission from the *British Journal of Psychology*.

The differences arising from viewing experience dualistically or as being-in-the-world can be presented pictorially. Figure A appears to be a spiral. By decontextualizing the figure, such as by tracing over the spiral with a compass, the diagram is decomposed into a series of embedded circles. Spiralness is an emergent phenomenon of the perceptual context. The dualist would contend that explaining the diagram requires separating the circles from their surrounding context and that spiralness is a pseudo-observation, one that may avoided by employing analytic procedures. The contextualist would counter that spiralness is a phenomenon appropriate for study and that there is no epistemological necessity for holding that only an analytic view can be scientific and valid.

Existential-phenomenology seeks to describe experience as it emerges in some context(s) or, to use phenomenological terms, as it is "lived." The concept of *Lebenswelt*, or life-world, is one manifestation of existential-phenomenology's focus on lived experience (Valle and King 1978). The world of lived experience does not always correspond with the world of objective description because objectivity often implies trying to explain an event as separate from its contextual setting (Pollio 1982). In the field of artificial intelligence, for example, some researchers contend that future breakthroughs in building expert systems will require describing the life-world of the human expert so that background (tacit) and common-sense knowledge can be modeled (Dreyfus 1982; Newell 1982; Searle 1982; Winograd and Flores 1987). The implication is that experts live their knowledge in a way that is not fully representable by a set of decontextualized rules and statements.

**Figure B** An Illustration of Figure/Ground Phenomena

*Source*: Rubin, Edgar (1921), *Visuelle Wahregenommene Figuren*, Copenhagen, Denmark: Glydendalske.

The major point deriving from the pattern metaphor is that existential-phenomenology seeks to be a descriptive science that focuses on the life-world of the individual. Rather than separating and then objectifying aspects of the life-world, the purpose is to describe human experience as it is lived. On this view, the meaning of an experience is always situated in the current experiential context and is coherently related to the ongoing project of the life-world (Sartre 1962). Experiences and their meaning may change but these changes are not arbitrary. This conception of experience as being both dynamic and organized leads to a second metaphor of existential-phenomenology, that of figure/ground.

### The Figure/Ground Metaphor

Figure B offers a well-known example of figure/ground that typically is presented in psychology texts as an interesting perceptual "trick" and little else. The important point to this, and other reversible figures, is that certain aspects of the drawing stand out or become figural while other parts recede into the background (or ground). What is figural from one perspective may be ground from another.

A particular setting can afford different experiences as certain aspects of the context stand out while others recede and become background for the experience (Valle and King 1978). Consider a mother and child shopping in a store. Initially, the mother is focally aware of the store's offerings and the child is in the background of her experiential field. Let the child begin crying and, suddenly, the store recedes into background as the child becomes the focal aspect of the mother's life-world.

Three points may be derived from the figure/ground metaphor. First, experience is conceptualized as a dynamic process in which certain events become figural (stand out) in the individual's life-world while others recede into ground. Second, the figure that stands out is never independent of its ground and vice versa. Neither figure nor ground cause the other; instead, both are co-constituting. Third, all modes of human experience, such as thinking, feeling, knowing, imagining, and remembering, are viewed as intentional phenomena, that is, as having some focus toward which the experience is directed.

The figure/ground metaphor and its attendant concept of intentionality have two major implications for the study of human experience. First, experience emerges in a contextual setting and, therefore, cannot be located "inside" the person as a complete subjectivity nor "outside" the person as a subject-free objectivity. The traditionally defined objective event is but one particular form of experience that seeks to view a phenomenon from the perspective of a detached observer. Second, experience is understood in the context of person-in-the-world. For example, the experience of time changes as a person matures from childhood to adulthood or moves from a boring task to an interesting one (Dapkus 1985; Van den Berg 1961). A parallel can be drawn to the ecological school of psychology, which defines the perceptual unit as person-in-an-environment and holds that the nature of perceiving varies across contexts (Gibson 1979).

## The Seeing Metaphor

Existential-phenomenology describes human experience as both unreflected and reflected (Pollio 1982). In clinical practice, for example, existential-phenomenological therapists view phenomena, traditionally classed as unconscious, in terms of reflected and unreflected experiences (Pollio 1982). The existential-phenomenological therapist locates the person's difficulties in the present life-world and not in an unconscious mechanism determined by historical antecedents (May and Yalom 1984; Merleau-Ponty 1962/ orig. 1945; Van den Berg 1961, 1970). The mechanism of repression is redefined as an existential choice: "the memory that is lost is lost only insofar as it belongs to a region of my life that I refuse" (Merleau-Ponty 1962/orig. 1945). An individual is seen as living in the world in a repressed way and as having to reflect on these experiences to see the pattern of such repression.

Artificial intelligence has recently embraced the distinction between reflected and unreflected experience (Henley 1988). Consider the following quote from Winograd and Flores (1987, p. 97):

> The essence of our being is the pre-reflective (unreflected) experience of being thrown in a situation of acting without the opportunity or need to disengage and function as detached observers. Reflection and abstraction are important phenomena, but are not the basis for our everyday action.

The relationship between reflected and unreflected experience is one of figure/ground. Reflected meanings and symbols emerge from the ground of unreflected experiences. The following excerpt from a phenomenological interview offers an example of a respondent reflecting upon what had previously been an unreflected aspect of her shopping experiences. During the interview, the respondent realizes she is happier with products bought on impulse than those purchased for practical reasons (her term). Prior to the interview, the respondent had not seen the experiential pattern of liking impulse purchases more than planned ones. The respondent's reflecting on a specific lived event allowed this pattern to emerge in the interview.

R: But I am an impulse buyer. Say you go to a wedding or a christening and you are looking for a particular outfit. You could go to 50 stores and never find anything, nothing looks interesting. But you could be absolutely broke, overdrawn with your checking account, and have two kids with you, and you just walk by a store window and you see something that has got your name on it and you just absolutely have to have it. And the nicest things I have gotten are things that I have bought like that. Oftentimes, I have purchased something that is right now the best I have found, and you know, it never fails, after you have worn it, you don't feel that great in it and it turns out to be wasted money.

I: Can you tell me about a time you made a purchase like that?

R: I did that about two months ago. It was a skirt and a top and it was on sale. I got it because it was on sale. When I think back, it wasn't that striking. It fit well and it was a very reasonable price. Honestly, I think it was on sale, it fit me, and I did need another skirt. But the bottom line was, it was not something I could take a look at and say I LOVE this. It was almost like I was being too practical. It's on sale, you need a summer skirt, and it fits you. Those are practical reasons. What I would have enjoyed more is if I had not been looking for something at the time, and something caught my eye and, okay, maybe it wouldn't have been on sale and maybe I didn't need a skirt but I really and truly loved the skirt and I would wear it a lot and I would feel good every time I wear it, that would have been a better purchase.

## Summary and Overview

The Exhibit represents a summary of significant issues that differentiate existential-phenomenological and Cartesian approaches to consumer research. Existential-phenomenology's world view is a *contextualist* view in which experience is seen as a pattern that emerges from a context. The ontology (nature of being) is in-the-world: experience and world are viewed as co-constituting. The research focus is on *experience* as described from a *first-person* view. The research logic is *apodictic*, meaning that researchers seek to apprehend a pattern as it emerges (Husserl 1960/orig. 1925). The research strategy is *holistic* and seeks to relate descriptions of specific experiences to each other and to the overall context of the life-world. The research goal is to give a *thematic description* of experience.

**Exhibit** Two Approaches to Consumer Research

| Tenets of paradigm | Existential phenomenology | Cartesianism |
|---|---|---|
| World view | Contextual | Mechanistic |
| Nature-of-being | In-the-world | Dualistic |
| Research focus | Experience | Theoretical structure |
| Research perspective | First-person | Third-person |
| Research logic | Apodictic | Predictive |
| Research strategy | Holistic | Componential |
| Research goal | Thematic description | Causal reductionism |

Cartesianism's world view is a *mechanistic* view in which reality is perceived as a machine-like event determined by forces and constraints. The ontology is *dualistic:* human beings exist independently of the physical world. The research focus is on determining underlying *theoretical structures* as described from a *third-person* view. The research logic is *predictive;* future manifestations of a phenomenon are deduced from theoretical laws and axioms or induced from historical antecedents. The research strategy is *componential* and seeks to understand phenomena through the analysis of component parts. The research goal is to *reduce* phenomena to an essential set of quantitative dimensions that adhere to determining laws and principles.

Both approaches lead to different research goals and methods for consumer research, but the distinction is not just that one approach is qualitative and the other quantitative. There are widely used qualitative research methods based on Cartesian postulates. For example, a major divergence exists between the phenomenological interview and the more Cartesian method of protocol analysis (Bettman 1979; Ericsson and Simon 1984; O'Shaughnessy 1987). Whereas protocol analysis is interested in uncovering the underlying propositional structure of decision making, existential-phenomenological interviews focus on identifying recurring experiential patterns. Although both techniques are qualitative, different interview outcomes are sought.

## Existential-Phenomenology as Method

To benefit consumer research, existential-phenomenology must provide not just an alternative set of metaphors, but also alternative methods for studying consumer phenomena. The following section details one such research method – the phenomenological interview. Although there are other methods for conducting phenomenological research, such as the analysis of written statements, the interview is perhaps the most powerful means for attaining an in-depth understanding of another person's experiences (Kvale 1983).

Throughout the ensuing discussion, data from actual phenomenological interviews will be used to illustrate methodological considerations. These examples are provided to aid the reader in "seeing" how the method is implemented; they are not meant to offer the results of a complete study.

### The Phenomenological Interview

*Interview Format.* Due to the in-depth nature of the phenomenological interview, ethical concerns arise. Before beginning an interview, informed consent is attained. Respondents are told of the study's purposes and that the interview will be audiotaped, and are assured of anonymity. During all stages of the study, a concerted effort is made to protect respondent confidentiality.

The goal of a phenomenological interview is to attain a first-person description of some specified domain of experience. The course of the dialogue is largely set by the respondent. With the exception of an opening question, the interviewer has no a priori questions concerning the topic. The dialogue tends to be circular rather than linear; the descriptive questions employed by the interviewer flow from the course of the dialogue and not from a predetermined path. The interview is intended to yield a conversation, not a question and answer session.

*The Interview Context.* The role of the interviewer is to provide a context in which respondents freely describe their experiences in detail. The interviewer does not begin an interview feeling that he or she knows more about the topic than the respondent. Since the topic is the respondent's experience, an opposite assumption is probably more useful. An important aspect of the interview is that the interviewer and respondent are in positions of equality (Kvale 1983). The interviewer does not want to be seen as more powerful or knowledgeable because the respondent must be the expert on his or her own experiences.

The questions and probes used by the interviewer follow the course of the dialogue and are aimed at bringing about descriptions of experiences; they are not intended to confirm theoretical hypotheses. A question such as, "What does this product symbolize for you?", is in most instances too theoretical and/or abstract for purposes of a phenomenological interview. A better line of questioning might be, "Can you tell me about a time when you used this product?" Such a question keeps the dialogue focused on a specific experience rather than on an abstraction. Focusing on specific events enables the respondent to provide a fuller, more detailed description of an experience as it was lived.

The interviewer employs descriptive questions, such as "What was X like?", "How did you feel when...?, and relies on the respondent's own words and phrases when asking follow-up questions. For example, if a respondent were to state, "Sometimes I get stressed out by shopping," an appropriate follow-up question might be "Can you describe a time when you were stressed out by shopping?" Using respondent terms is an important means for remaining unencumbered by conceptual predilections.

During the course of the interview, the interviewer should avoid asking "why" questions. Such questions shift the focus of the dialogue away from describing the experience as it was lived to a more distant and abstract discussion.

*Why Not Ask "Why"?* The emphasis on avoiding "why" questions is an area in which phenomenological interviews differ from traditional methods, and this warrants further elaboration. "Why" questions, or an equivalent such as "What caused you to do that?", are often ineffective for generating descriptions of lived experiences. "Why" questions can be perceived as requests for rationalizations and can engender feelings of prejudgment and defensive responses (Argyris 1982). Such questions may also put the respondent in the position of a "naive scientist" seeking to find a plausible explanation for his or her actions. For example, a respondent states, "I generally don't compare prices much when I buy things." A follow-up question such as "Why don't you compare prices?" demands a rationalization for not comparing prices. To answer the question, the respondent singles out one aspect of his or her experience and designates it as a cause. Perhaps the respondent might have answered, "I don't have time." This short, completely plausible response isolates both the interviewer and respondent from the experience as lived.

A more useful follow-up question might be: "Can you tell me about a time you bought something without comparing prices?" The aim of the question is to focus the dialogue on a specific experience of "not comparing prices." What emerged from an actual interview using this question was that the respondent chose not to compare prices on certain items that she described as "have-to-buy products." For such items, she described feeling constrained and lacking an ability to make a choice. The act of not comparing prices was a means for minimizing the time devoted to purchasing these items. For other items that were not seen as "have-to-buys," the respondent felt a choice existed, and comparing prices among these items was "fun and a high." This more extended description revealed the meaning of "not comparing prices" within the respondent's own life-world. From the descriptive detail of how the respondent lived this experience, an experientially based understanding of "not comparing prices" was gained.

*Attaining a Phenomenological Dialogue.* Operationally, the interviewer desires to be a non-directive listener. The interview guidelines of establishing equality among participants, having questions follow from respondent discourse, employing short descriptive questions, and not asking "why" are some methodological procedures for preventing the interviewer from assuming an overly intrusive role. The transcript is a record of the interview dialogue and should reveal whether the interviewer assumed a domineering or directive role. In most cases, such an interview would not be acceptable as data. The ideal interview format occurs when the interviewer's short descriptive questions and/or clarifying statements provide an opening for a respondent's lengthier and detailed descriptions.

*What Can You Do With "What"?* It is often stated that science must go beyond "mere description" – must move from the "what" to the "why" – to provide a real understanding of a phenomenon. Thus, descriptive methods are seen as propaedeutic (preliminary steps) to scientific research (Deshpande 1983; Hunt 1976; MacLeod 1964). Some scholars, however, have asserted that such a view fails to appreciate the power of description (Gibson 1979; Giorgi 1983; Merleau-Ponty 1962/orig. 1945; Wittgenstein 1953). In the usual sense of description, a researcher adopts a detached third-person perspective and views some phenomenon in an objective (object-like) sense. Existential-phenomenology, in contrast, seeks to render a first-person description of the phenomenon as lived.

The differences between first-person and third-person description can readily be shown. For example, a third-person description of a phenomenon, such as a salesperson/customer encounter, might take the form of "the encounter lasted ten minutes," "the customer asked three questions concerning price, quality, and, service," "the salesperson responded by quoting the current retail price," and so on. Such a description does seem propaedeutic since it provides little insight into the nature of the encounter. The emptiness of this description is not necessarily due to a lack of causal inferences; what is missing is experience.

Consider the following description of the experiences of encountering salespersons that emerged from a series of phenomenological interviews. When shoppers felt knowledgeable about a product and enjoyed shopping for it, salespeople were viewed as coercive, intrusive agents, and shoppers did not wish to be "helped" or even approached by them. When shoppers felt ignorant about a product and did not enjoy shopping for it, salespersons were seen as information providers who helped take the "nuisance" out of shopping – to use one respondent's phrase. In this context, shoppers wanted salespeople to come quickly to their assistance rather than having to wait. In the first case, salespeople are seen as manipulative and coercive. In the latter case, they are seen as being helpful and providing information that removes an unenjoyable feeling of ignorance.

Two points may be made in regard to this type of existential-phenomenological description. First, it is an experiential description, not an objective one. With an objective description, one five-minute interaction with a salesperson is equivalent to another five-minute interaction. From an experiential point of view, two five-minute encounters may be radically different. The customer not wanting assistance may view the salesperson as intrusive or manipulative and therefore may experience the encounter as agonizing and interminable. The customer wanting assistance may view the salesperson as a knowledgeable guide, possibly experiencing the encounter as brief and pleasurable. The two encounters may be equivalent on an objective temporal measure, but they differ experientially.

Second, the existential-phenomenological description stays at the level of the respondent's life-world. In the previous example, there is no hypothesis as to "why" shoppers want to be left alone or want to be helped; rather, a description is provided of what shoppers report experiencing when encountering salespeople. For those who would argue this description is in fact a causal analysis, one point needs to be realized. When engaging in a causal analysis, the researcher is abandoning the major tenet of existential phenomenology that understanding must be at the level of lived experience. For example, an explanation that knowledgeable shoppers did not want sales assistance *because* they enjoyed shopping for the product leads to a subsequent question of why enjoyment of shopping *causes* people not to want sales help. After hypothesizing a cause at this level, another question arises. Why does this hypothetical construct *cause* people to enjoy shopping, which *causes* the observable effect of not wanting sale help? At each level, the analysis moves, from lived experience to a theoretical abstraction.

Existential-phenomenological understanding is attained by describing lived experiences and the meanings that emerge from them. Those who ascribe no scientific merit to description perhaps have only considered descriptive research conducted and reported from a third-person perspective. If experiential descriptions are considered, existential-phenomenology may be seen as a descriptive science (Giorgi 1983).

### Interpreting the Interview

After interviews have been transcribed from the audiotapes, the interpretation phase begins. The transcribed interviews become the text from which interpretation ensues (Kvale 1983). The exclusive reliance on verbatim interview transcripts reflects three methodological criteria of phenomenological interpretation – the emic approach, autonomy of the text, and bracketing.

In an emic approach, the interpretation relies on the respondent's own terms and category systems rather than the researcher's (Kvale 1983). The goal of phenomenological investigation is to describe experience in lived rather than conceptually abstract terms. For example, in one interview, a respondent made repeated references to wanting "good service" from salespersons. Whereas a conceptual definition of good service might include attributes such as courtesy, promptness, and knowledge about the product, this respondent had two particular meanings of "good service": not being made to feel "dumb" (her term) by a knowledgeable salesperson, and being told what to buy in a way that did not make her feel manipulated. Using respondent terms is one methodological procedure for staying at the level of lived experience.

The text of the interview is treated as an autonomous body of data comprised of respondent reflections on lived experiences. "Autonomous" has two methodological aspects. First, there is no attempt to corroborate a respondent's descriptions with external verification. If a respondent were to reflect that, "this was an important purchase for me so I went to X for advice," a researcher could seek to verify the reflection by some external criterion of whether the purchase was actually "important" or if indeed X's advice was sought. From the perspective of existential-phenomenology, the relevant issues are that at the time of the interview the purchase is seen as "important" and person X is seen as someone whose advice is sought. The goal is to understand the meaning of "important purchase" and the role of person X in the context of the reflected experience. Respondent descriptions are not to be construed as recalled "copies" of past events, but as reconstructions emerging in the interview.

A second methodological aspect of the autonomy criterion is that the interpretation should not incorporate hypotheses, inferences, and conjectures that exceed the evidence provided by the transcript. For example, if a respondent describes certain frustrations she has in shopping for her spouse, a conjecture that the frustration "really" mirrors underlying marital difficulties is inappropriate unless a discussion of marital problems occurs in the text. Similarly, explaining the respondent's frustrations in theoretical terms, such as psychoanalytic mechanisms, is inappropriate because theoretical explanations are abstractions rather than descriptions of lived experience.

To treat the transcript as an autonomous body of data, preconceived theoretical notions about the phenomena must be bracketed (held in abeyance). Bracketing does not imply a neutral view, as researchers must always see and describe the world from some perspective (Merleau-Ponty 1962/orig. 1945). The interpretation will have as its ground the meta-assumptions of existential-phenomenology, such as those summarized in the Exhibit.

Holding to these meta-assumptions does not preclude bracketing specific preconceptions, such as a theoretical model or hypothesis, about the phenomenon. For example, a respondent might describe the purchase of a sports car. The researcher could entertain a Goffman-like hypothesis that the purchase is intended as a public symbol. Such a presumption must be recognized and bracketed. It may be that the purchase is experienced as symbolizing and projecting certain traits, but, then again, it may not. When bracketing, the researcher relates to respondent reflections in a nondogmatic fashion and attempts to grasp, rather than impose, meanings emerging from the dialogue.

Although bracketing is necessary for attaining an understanding of respondents' lived experiences, the ability of researchers to bracket is sometimes doubted (Hudson and Ozanne 1988). Part of this doubt may stem from a lack of explicit methodological procedures on how to bracket. Without such procedures, bracketing seems vague and mysterious. One methodological procedure for bracketing is to conduct interpretation in a group setting. Aside from facilitating bracketing, the interpretive group affords several other advantages in conducting existential-phenomenological research.

### The Interpretive Group

An interpretive group is composed of the researcher(s) and other individuals familiar with existential-phenomenological research. Members of the group, however, are not required to be experts in phenomenological research or with the phenomenon being studied. The major requirements are that group members are willing to commit the time and effort to interpret a series of interviews and that they seek to apprehend experiences as described in interview dialogues.

The interpretive group facilitates bracketing by conscientiously questioning the assumptions each member employs. If one member is unaware that he or she has failed to bracket a preconception, other members of the group are in a position to see this failure. Members of the group have available to them the interview transcript and whatever interpretation is proposed. Each interpretation is always evaluated by referring back to the transcript. For any interpretation put forth by a member of the group, follow-up questions are asked.

One question from the group should be, "Is the proposed interpretation at the level of the respondent's lived experience?" A theme must emerge from respondent descriptions rather than from abstract or theoretical conjectures. Each group member must be able to show that the proposed interpretation describes the respondent's experience. One means for doing this is by showing in the transcript where the respondent's *own* words support the interpretation. Only interpretations that can be supported in this way are considered.

Another question put forth by the group should be, "Does the proposed interpretation take into account previous passages of the transcript?" No part of an interview is taken out of its overall context. Interpretation is a continuous back and forth process of relating parts to the whole. Earlier sections of a transcript must be re-evaluated constantly in light of what follows later in the interview.

Unlike critical hermeneutics (Ricoeur 1976), which allows the text to yield a multitude of equally adequate interpretations, existential-phenomenological interpretation seeks to describe respondent perspectives. The criteria employed by the group recognize that not all interpretations are equally adequate for this purpose.

The interpretive group affords other benefits as well. The perspective of the group is broader than that of any one individual and, thus, a pattern that might not have been noticed by a single researcher may be "seen" by the group. Also, the perspective of a single researcher may become *sedimented;* that is, the researcher may become focused on certain aspects of the transcript while failing to see others. The group, which is comprised of multiple perspectives, maintains a "fresh" vision and is less likely to approach the transcript in a stereotyped fashion.

The group also offers a means for overcoming difficulties arising from the sheer volume of data involved in dialogical research. For example, 10 interviews easily may generate more than 200 pages of single-spaced text. The lone researcher is likely to become overwhelmed by the interpretive task and may rush the interpretation, thereby overlooking details and interrelations in the transcripts. The lone researcher also may rely on "cognitive heuristics," such as availability and representativeness (Kahneman, Slovic, and Tversky 1982). The interpretive group offers a means of sharing the burden of interpretation because the ability of the group to remember aspects of transcripts is greater than that of any one individual.

The group approach also offers a means of avoiding any sense of monotony and doubt that may plague a lone researcher. Interpretation involves going over each interview transcript a multitude of times. The glamour and excitement of phenomenological research soon gives way to repetition of the task. More problematical, the lone researcher receives no immediate feedback on the adequacy of a proposed interpretation, which is not only discouraging but may have high costs in terms of time. Several months might be spent working on an inadequate interpretation that does not describe lived experience before external raters note some problem. The interpretive group circumvents these difficulties by serving two functions. The dynamic of the group has an energizing effect on the interpretive process and brings the transcript to "life" by its being read and discussed among people who share a common interest, and the group serves a recognition function. If an interpretation describes a pattern in the data, then other individuals will be able to see this pattern (Giorgi 1983). Group members provide the researcher(s) with immediate feedback by noting whether they can also see the interpretation in the transcript.

### Hermeneutical Circles and Global Themes

The hermeneutical circle refers to a part-to-whole mode of interpretation (Bleicher 1980). In existential-phenomenological interpretation, the part-to-whole process occurs in two phases. First, the interpretive group seeks an idiographic (individual) understanding of each interview, which involves viewing each transcript as a whole and relating separate passages of the transcript to its overall content. After each transcript has been interpreted at the idiographic level, a new part-to-whole phase begins in which separate interviews are related to each other and common patterns identified. These patterns of commonalities are referred to as global themes (Kvale 1983; Wertz 1983). This is not to imply that global themes offer exhaustive descriptions of the phenomenon, only that they capture figural aspects emerging from a given set of experiences.

Identifying global themes across interviews is another methodological means for improving interpretive vision, not a means for attaining some type of convergent validation. The interpretation seeks to describe common patterns in experiences. A pattern can present itself in many ways; for example, a song played in two different octaves exhibits the same perceptual pattern even though every note has been changed (Valle and King 1978). In terms of experience, "different" situations (as seen from a third-person perspective) may be experienced in the same way, or the "same" situation (as seen from a third-person perspective) may be experienced differently. One respondent may experience money as a restriction on what they can do as a consumer while another may experience time as a like restriction. Both consumers experience restriction even though the specifics differ. Seeing such a pattern involves a type of "seeing as" (Wittgenstein 1953). That is, researchers are seeing where one situation is experientially similar to another or, in phenomenological terms, where respondent intentionalities are the same.

Although global themes are identified across interviews, support for each theme must be available in individual transcripts. A researcher must continuously refer back to individual transcripts to ensure that global themes are not rendered in abstract terms removed from respondent experience. Even at the level of global themes, the researcher should be able to point to specific passages in the transcripts that afford a clear statement of the theme.

## Epistemological Criteria of Existential-Phenomenology

### A Positive Look at Positivism

Logical positivism provides epistemological criteria for evaluating research. It is sometimes assumed that qualitative research, by definition, cannot meet these positivist criteria and, therefore, must employ alternative standards of "truth" (Lincoln and Guba 1985). A concern of logical positivists is that allowing such a relativistic construal of truth will lead to conclusions that are not empirically based, open the way for dogma and superstition to pass as knowledge, and result in the absence of usable criteria for evaluating knowledge claims (Hunt 1984).

The use of non-positivist research methods, however, does not preclude existential-phenomenology from addressing and/or sharing some of logical positivism's epistemological concerns. If certain philosophical assumptions and methodological constraints that often accompany logical positivist thought are bracketed, it can be seen that positivism's broad evaluative criteria are reasonable standards for existential-phenomenological research. That is, research conclusions should be empirically based; research should strive to be free of personal biases, prejudices, and dogma; other individuals should be able to agree that conclusions are justified by the data; and criteria should be provided for evaluating competing knowledge claims.

Existential-phenomenological research *is* empirical. Its evidence is respondent descriptions of lived experience. In addition, all aspects of the method are aimed at maintaining fidelity to interview transcripts. Any proposed interpretation must be supported by evidence. Existential-phenomeologists do not wish for prejudice, dogma, and superstition to pass for knowledge any more than their positivist counterparts do. Moreover, the group interpretive method does not violate any doctrine of intersubjective certifiability. A major requirement of an interpretation is that it can be "seen" by others. Lastly, criteria exist by which one interpretation can be judged as more viable for existential-phenomenological purposes than another.

In this so-called era of "post-positivism," there is a tendency by interpretive methodologists to treat all aspects of the positivist program as completely antithetical to their own. It is, nonetheless, a categorical mistake to contend that the broad epistemological concerns of one paradigm cannot be relevant to an alternative paradigm. Although the ontological and methodological assumptions of existential-phenomenology and logical positivism differ, both share a common commitment to conducting rigorous, empirical research that is open to careful scrutiny.

## Discovery as Verification

Noting that existential-phenomenology shares some of positivism's broad epistemological concerns does not mean that a methodological eclecticism is being advocated. Pepper (1942) observed that eclecticism often suffers from problematic inconsistencies arising from an uneasy juxtaposition of differing world views. Attempts to synthesize methods (i.e., "hardening" interpretive methods with a dose of positivist procedures) often result in failure to reach the aims of either approach. Although existential-phenomenology and logical positivism may share some broad epistemological concerns, their differing world views necessitate a methodological pluralism.

A major facet of existential-phenomenological philosophy is that experience is not partitioned into the categories of objective and subjective. No methods are seen as purely objective in the sense of being free of human experience nor are any methods seen as purely subjective in the sense of being free of worldly phenomena. It is from this perspective that the positivist distinction between discovery and justification becomes inapplicable to existential-phenomenological research.

For logical positivism, the discovery/justification distinction holds that the means by which knowledge claims are generated must be independent of the methods used to verify them (Hunt 1976). The view seems to be based on the assumption that discovery is a subjective process and verification is an objective one, free of human experience. The distinction's consequence for qualitative research is that the methods used to verify an interpretation are separated from the interpretive process. For example, with a typical verification procedure, such as an inter-rater reliability estimate, verification occurs after the interpretation has been rendered and is external to the interpretive process.

For a descriptive methodology, where no conceptual distinction is made between discovery and justification, the method of interpretation affords its own justification (Giorgi 1986). The descriptive metaphors of existential phenomenology (pattern, figure/ground, and seeing) are all perceptual metaphors, which implies that verification procedures should be internal to the interpretive process. From such a perspective, verification procedures should capitalize on insight and intuition instead of replacing them with external criteria.

Intuition and insight are empirically based: the "seeing" is of things-in-the-world (i.e., empirical phenomena) and not of things-in-the-head of the observer (Gier 1981; Wittgenstein 1953). For example, when a problem is solved by insight, an understanding emerges from grasping the pattern or organization present in the phenomena (Kohler 1947). The problem and the pattern yielding its solution are not subjective entities but are in-the-world. The correctness of an insight is experienced because it allows the problem to be solved and, once informed of the insight, other individuals are able to see the solution as well.

In verifying an insight, first-person experience cannot be removed from the process. When other individuals see a pattern describing some event, they are doing more than providing intersubjective certification; they are experiencing the understanding afforded by the insight. Verification is given in the direct experience of seeing a meaningful pattern.

The group interpretive method was designed to take advantage of the experiential nature of insight described as a Wittgensteinian process of "seeing as." The group does not seek a compromise interpretation, but one that is seen as correct by all members. The fact that different patterns initially may be "seen" is not problematic since group members can discuss each proposed claim in terms of the transcript data and the following evaluative criteria: (1) interpretations must be based on respondents' own terms: (2) passages must be taken in their proper context; (3) theoretical explanations and abstractions must be avoided; and (4) support for proposed themes must be available in all transcripts.

An internal verification procedure, such as the one just outlined, is not an idiosyncratic judgment. In this procedure, there are criteria by which claims should be evaluated and judged by all members of the group. Although this method does not necessarily preclude more conventional verification procedures such as inter-rater reliability, its use of such "internal" verification does frame human insight as a methodological resource rather than as a liability.

Viewing interpretive insight as a "seeing as" process also helps overcome the potential problem of variability in interpretive methods. Unlike quantitative research, where standardized statistical procedures are used, there is no reason to expect that all existential-phenomenological interpretations are produced in the same manner or with the same rigor. The answer to this problem seems to be that, like all research, results of the procedure will become public and other people will judge whether the themes are viable, useful, and meaningful. True to its roots in existential and phenomenological philosophy, the final use and value of any given piece of research is determined by the scientific consumer who will either see and agree or will not see and agree with the themes of a specific existential-phenomenological analysis.

## Final Reflections

The term "consumer behavior" is an anachronism reflecting an era in which psychology was dominated by behaviorism (Howard 1965; Hull 1943). At the height of the behaviorist movement, it was assumed that human beings could be reduced to "nothing but" behavior (Kohler 1938). That is, when a full understanding of behavior was attained, concepts such as "mind," "thinking," and, "imagining," would be unnecessary (Skinner 1974). Indeed, the use of such terms was deemed patently unscientific. The dominance of behaviorism has been overturned by cognitive psychology, and mentalistic terms have been restored to the scientific vocabulary. The majority of contemporary consumer research should be more aptly labeled "consumer cognition."

Although cognitive psychologists now talk freely of "mental structures," "information processing," and "decision making," the term "experience" is still viewed with some of the same metaphysical suspicions behaviorists held for "mind." The "nothing but" hypothesis is again at work. Cognitivists believe that when a full understanding of cognitive structure and process is attained, terms such as experience will be unnecessary. After all, isn't experience really "nothing but" an epi-phenomenon of cognitive structure?

To this question, existential-phenomenology answers no. Studying human experience is different from studying an epi-phenomenon of cognitive structure. Other theorists have also noted that much of consumer research ignores experience (Belk 1984; Fennell 1985; Holbrook and Hirschman 1982; Levy 1981; Mick 1986). Proponents of ethno-methodologies, such as naturalistic inquiry, have similarly noted the inadequacies of conventional methods for studying consumer experience (Belk *et al.* 1988; Hirschman 1986; Hudson and Ozanne 1988; Wallendorf, Belk, and Heisley 1988).

One response to these critiques is the "embryonic defense": consumer research is a young and developing field that will eventually fill in these gaps as it matures. The difficulty is that maturation alone solves nothing. Few would argue that Hullian behaviorism, given sufficient time to mature, would eventually have come to understand cognitive phenomena, because its methods and assumptions did not allow for such phenomena even to *exist*. For consumer researchers to understand experience, they must first employ methods and assumptions that allow for experience to exist.

Existential-phenomenology employs a "something different" hypothesis: experience is something different than response patterns or cognitive structures. As such, existential-phenomenology provides a philosophical base from which to explore consumer experience in non-dualistic terms. It seeks to develop and use methods that allow for a first-person description of lived experience. In both philosophy and method, existential-phenomenology offers a means for putting consumer experience back into consumer research.

## References


Anderson, Paul F. (1983), "Marketing, Scientific Progress, and Scientific Methods," *Journal of Marketing*, 47 (Fall), 44–54.

– (1986), "On Method in Consumer Research: A Critical Relativist Perspective," *Journal of Consumer Research*, 13 (September), 155–173.

Argyris, Chris (1982), *Reasoning, Learning, and Action: Individual and Organizational Dynamics*, San Francisco: Jossey-Bass.

Arndt, Johan (1985), "On Making Marketing More Scientific: The Role of Orientations, Paradigms, Metaphors, and Puzzle Solving," *Journal of Marketing*, 49 (Summer), 11–23.

Belk, Russell (1984), "A Manifesto for a Consumer Behavior of Consumer Behavior," in *1984 AMA Winter Educators' Conference: Scientific Method in Marketing*, eds. Paul F. Anderson and Michael J. Ryan, Chicago: American Marketing Association, 163–167.

– (1987), "The Role of the Odyssey in Consumer Behavior and in Consumer Research," in *Advances in Consumer Research*, Vol. 14, eds. Melanie Wallendorf and Paul Anderson, Provo, UT: Association for Consumer Research, 357–361.

– John F. Sherry, Jr., and Melanie Wallendorf (1988), "A Naturalistic Inquiry into Buyer and Seller Behavior at a Swap Meet," *Journal of Consumer Research*, 14 (March), 449–470.

Bettman, James R. (1979), *An Information Processing Theory of Consumer Choice*, Reading, MA: Addison-Wesley.

Bleicher, Josef (1980), *Contemporary Hermeneutics*, London: Routledge & Kegan Paul.

Bogdan, Steve and Robert Taylor (1975), *Introduction to Qualitative Research Methods*, New York: John Wiley.

Bower, Gordon H. and Ernest R. Hilgard (1981), *Theories of Learning*, Englewood Cliffs, NJ: Prentice-Hall.

Churchland, Paul M. (1985), *Matter and Consciousness*, Cambridge, MA: Bradford Books.
Colaizzi, Paul F. (1973), *Reflection and Research in Psychology: A Phenomenological Study of Learning*, Dubuque, IA: Kendall/Hunt.
Dapkus, Marilyn A. (1985), "A Thematic Analysis of the Experience of Time," *Journal of Personality and Social Psychology*, 49 (August), 408–419.
Deshpande, Rohit (1983), "Paradigms Lost: On Theory and Method in Research in Marketing," *Journal of Marketing*, 47 (Fall), 101–110.
Dilthey, Wilhelm (1958), *Gesammelte Schriften*, Stuttgart, Germany: Teubner.
Dreyfus, Richard, ed. (1982), *Husserl, Intentionality, and Cognitive Science*, Cambridge, MA: MIT Press.
Ericsson, Anders K. and Herbert A. Simon (1984), *Protocol Analysis: Verbal Reports as Data*, Cambridge, MA: MIT Press.
Fennell, Geraldine (1985), "Things of Heaven and Earth: Phenomenology, Marketing and Consumer Research," in *Advances in Consumer Research*, Vol. 12, eds. Elizabeth C. Hirschman and Morris B. Holbrook, Provo, UT: Association for Consumer Research, 544–549.
Fischer, William F. (1978), "An Empirical-Phenomenological Investigation of Being Anxious: An Example of the Meanings of Being Emotional," in *Existential-Phenomenological Alternatives for Psychology*, eds. Ronald Valle and Mark King, New York: Oxford University Press, 166–181.
Gerhart, Mary and Allan Russell (1984), *Metaphoric Processes: The Creation of Scientific and Religious Understanding*, Fort Worth: Texas Christian University Press.
Gibson, James J. (1979), *The Ecological Approach to Visual Perception*, Boston: Houghton Mifflin.
Gier, Nicholas F. (1981), *Wittgenstein and Phenomenology*, Albany: State University of New York Press.
Giorgi, Amedeo (1971), "A Phenomenological Approach to the Problem of Meaning and Serial Learning," in *Dusquesnes Studies in Phenomenology*, Vol. 1, eds. Amedeo Giorgi *et al.*, Pittsburgh, PA: Dusquesne University Press, 88–100.
– (1983), "Concerning the Possibility of Phenomenological Research," *Journal of Phenomenological Psychology*, 14 (Fall), 129–170.
– (1986), "The Context of Discovery-Context of Justification: Distinction and Descriptive Science," *Journal of Phenomenological Psychology*, 17 (Fall), 151–167.
Heidegger, Martin (1962), *Being and Time*, New York: Harper & Row.
Henley, Tracy B. (1988), "Impact of Humanistic Psychology on Cognition and Artificial Intelligence," paper presented at the 1988 American Psychological Association Conference, Atlanta, GA.
Hirschman, Elizabeth C. (1986), "Humanistic Inquiry in Marketing Research: Philosophy, Method, and Criteria," *Journal of Marketing Research*, 13 (August), 237–249.
Holbrook, Morris B. (1987), "From the Log of a Consumer Researcher: Reflections on the Odyssey," in *Advances in Consumer Research*, Vol. 14. eds. Melanie Wallendorf and Paul Anderson, Provo, UT: Association for Consumer Research, 357–36 1.
– and Mark W. Grayson (1986), "The Semiology of Cinematic Consumption: Symbolic Consumer Behavior in *Out of Africa*," *Journal of Consumer Research*, 13 (December), 374–381.
– and Elizabeth C. Hirschman (1982), "The Experiential Aspects of Consumption: Consumer Fantasies, Feelings, and Fun," *Journal of Consumer Research*, 9 (September), 132–140.
Horowitz, Lee (1963), "Theory Construction and Validation in Psychoanalysis," in *Theories in Contemporary Psychology*, New York: Macmillan.
Howard, John A. (1965), *Marketing Theory*, Boston: Allyn & Bacon.
Hudson, Laurel Anderson and Julie L. Ozanne (1988), "Alternative Ways of Seeking Knowledge in Consumer Research," *Journal of Consumer Research*, 14 (March), 508–521.
Hull, Clark L. (1943), *Principles of Behavior*, New York: Appleton-Century-Crofts.
Hunt, Shelby D. (1976), *Marketing Theory: Conceptual Foundations of Research in Marketing*, Columbus, OH: Grid.
– (1983), *Marketing Theory: The Philosophy of Marketing Science*, Homewood, IL: Irwin.
– (1984), "Should Marketing Adopt Relativism?" in *1984 Winter Educators' Conference: Scientific Method in Marketing*, eds. Paul F. Anderson and Michael J. Ryan, Chicago: American Marketing Association, 30–34.

Husserl, Edmund (1960), *Cartesian Meditations: An Introduction to Phenomenology*, Atlantic Highlands, NJ: Humanities Press.

Jacob, Evelyn (1987), "Qualitative Research Traditions," *Review of Educational Research*, 57 (Spring), 1–50.

Johnson, Mark (1987), *The Body in the Mind: the Bodily Basis of Meaning, Imagination, and Reason*, Chicago: University of Chicago Press.

Kahneman, Daniel, Paul Slovic, and Amos Tversky (1982), *Judgment Under Uncertainty: Heuristics and Biases*, Cambridge, England: Cambridge University Press.

Koffka, Kurt (1935), *Gestalt Psychology*, New York: Harcourt Brace & World.

Kohler, Wolfgang (1938), *The Place of Value in a World of Facts*, New York: Liveright Publishing.

– (1947), *Gestalt Psychology*, New York: New American Library Press.

– (1969), *The Task of Gestalt Psychology*, Princeton, NJ: Princeton University Press.

Kuhn, Thomas S. (1970), *The Structure of Scientific Revolutions*, Chicago: University of Chicago Press.

Kvale, Steinar (1983), "The Qualitative Research Interview: A Phenomenological and a Hermeneutical Mode of Understanding," *Journal of Phenomenological Psychology*, 14 (Fall), 171–196.

Lakatos, Imre (1970), "Falsification and the Methodology of Science Research Programs," in *Criticism and the Growth of Knowledge*, eds. Imre Lakatos and Alan Musgrave, London: Cambridge University Press.

Lakoff, George (1987), *Women, Fire, and Dangerous Things*, Chicago: University of Chicago Press.

– and Mark Johnson (1980), *Metaphors We Live By*, Chicago: University of Chicago Press.

Levy, Sidney J. (1981), "Interpreting Consumer Mythology: A Structural Approach to Consumer Behavior," *Journal of Marketing*, 45 (Summer), 49–62.

Lincoln, Yvonna S. and Egon G. Guba (1987), *Naturalistic Inquiry*, Beverly Hills, CA: Sage.

MacLeod, Robert B. (1964), "Phenomenology: A Challenge to Experimental Psychology," in *Behaviorism and Phenomenology: Contrasting Bases for Psychology*, ed. Thomas W. Mann, Chicago: University of Chicago Press, 47–73.

May, Rollo and Irvin Yalom (1984), "Existential Psychotherapy," in *Current Psychotherapies*, ed. Raymond J. Corsini, Itasca, IL: F.E. Peacock, 354–391.

Merleau-Ponty, Maurice (1962), *The Phenomenology of Perception*, London: Routledge & Kegan Paul.

Mick, David Glen (1986), "Consumer Research and Semiotics: Exploring the Morphology of Signs, Symbols, and Significance," *Journal of Consumer Research*, 13 (September), 196–213.

Miller, George A., Eugene Galanter, and Karl H. Pribram (1960), *Plans and the Structure of Behavior*, New York: Holt, Rinehart & Winston.

Morgan, Gareth (1980), "Paradigms, Metaphors, and Puzzle Solving in Organization Theory," *Administrative Science Quarterly*, 25 (December), 605–622.

Myers, Elizabeth (1985), "Phenomenological Analysis of the Importance of Special Possessions," in *Advances in Consumer Research*, Vol. 12, eds. Elizabeth C. Hirschman and Morris B. Holbrook. Provo, UT: Association for Consumer Research. 560–565.

Newell, Allan (1982), "The Knowledge Level," *Artificial Intelligence*, 18 (January), 87–127.

– and Herbert A. Simon (1972), *Human Problem Solving*, Englewood Cliffs, NJ: Prentice-Hall.

O'Shaughnessy, John (1985), "A Return to Reason in Consumer Behavior: An Hermeneutical Approach," in *Advances in Consumer Research*, Vol. 12, eds. Elizabeth C. Hirschman and Morris B. Holbrook, Provo, UT: Association for Consumer Research, 305–311.

– (1987), *Why People Buy*, New York: Oxford University Press.

Pepper, Stephen (1942), *World Hypotheses: A Study in Evidence*, Los Angeles: University of California Press.

Peter, J. Paul and Jerry C. Olson (1983), "Is Science Marketing?" *Journal of Marketing*, 47 (Fall), 111–125.

Pollio, Howard R. (1982), *Behavior and Existence*, Monterey, CA: Brooks/Cole.

Pumpian-Mindlin, Esther (1952), *Psychoanalysis as Science*, Palo Alto, CA: Stanford University Press.

Ricoeur, Paul (1976), *Interpretation Theory*, Fort Worth: Texas Christian University.
Rosenberg, Larry A. (1984), "The Pervasive Role of Metaphors in Marketing Science," in *1984 Winter Educators' Conference: Scientific Method in Marketing*, eds. Paul F. Anderson and Michael J. Ryan, Chicago: American Marketing Association, 74–77.
Sartre, Jean P. (1962), *Being and Nothingness*, New York: Washington Square Press.
Searle, John (1982), "What Is an Intentional State," in *Husserl, Intentionality, and Cognitive Science*, ed. Hubert Dreyfus, Cambridge, MA: MIT Press, 259–276.
Sherry, John F., Jr. and Eduardo G. Camargo (1987), "'May Your Life Be Marvelous': English Language Labelling and the Semiotics of Japanese Promotion," *Journal of Consumer Research*, 14 (September), 174–188.
Skinner, B.F. (1974), *About Behavior*, New York: Knopf.
Valle, Ronald S. and Mark King (1978), "An Introduction to Existential-Phenomenological Thought in Psychology," in *Existential-Phenomenological Alternatives for Psychology*, eds. Ronald S. Valle and Mark King, New York: Oxford University Press, 6–17.
van den Berg, Jan H. (196 1), *The Changing Nature of Man*, New York: W. W. Norton.
– (1970), *A Different Existence: Principles of a Phenomenological Psychopathology*, Pittsburgh, PA: Dusquesne University Press.
Wallendorf, Melanie, Russell Belk, and Deborah Heisley (1988), "Deep Meaning in Possessions: The Paper," in *Advances in Consumer Research*, Vol. 15, ed. Michael J. Houston, Provo, UT: Association for Consumer Research, 528–530.
Wertheimer, Max (1945), *Productive Thinking*, New York: Harper & Row.
Wertz, Frederick J. (1983), "From Everyday to Psychological Description: Analyzing the Moments of a Qualitative Data Analysis," *Journal of Phenomenological Psychology*, 14 (Fall), 197–242.
Winograd, Terry and Fernando Flores (1987), *Understanding Computers and Cognition*, New York: Addison-Wesley.
Wittgenstein, Ludwig (1953), *Philosophical Investigations*, Oxford, England: Basil Blackwell.
Wyer, Robert S. and Thomas K. Srull (1986), "Human Cognition in Its Social Context," *Psychological Review*, 93 (3), 322–359.
Zaner, Richard M. (1970), *The Way of Phenomenology*, New York: Pegasus.

# 15

# Beyond Consumerism: New Historical Perspectives on Consumption

**Frank Trentmann**

**Source:** *Journal of Contemporary History* 39 (3) (2004): 373–401.

If there is one agreement between theorists of modernity and those of post-modernity, it is about the centrality of consumption to modern capitalism and contemporary culture. To thinkers as different as Werner Sombart, Emile Durkheim and Thorstein Veblen at the turn of the twentieth century, consumption was a decisive force behind modern capitalism, its dynamism and social structure. More recently, Anthony Giddens has presented consumerism as simultaneous cause and therapeutic response to the crisis of identities emanating from the pluralization of communities, values and knowledge in "post-traditional society". Post-modernists like Baudrillard have approached consumption as the semiotic code constituting post-modernity itself: ultimately, signs are consumed, not objects. Such has been the recent revival of theoretical interest in consumption that the historian might feel acutely embarrassed by the abundance of choice and the semiotic and, indeed, political implications of any particular approach. Which theory is most appropriate for the historical study of "consumer society"? What is being consumed, by whom, why, and with what consequence differs fundamentally in these writings: should we study objects, signs or experiences, focus on the drive to emulate others or to differentiate oneself, analyse acquisitive mentalities or ironic performances, condemn resulting conformity or celebrate subversion?

It is helpful to note that the theoretical debate about consumption in the last two decades has in the main been driven by a philosophical engagement with "modernity" (or its disappearance), not by an empirical reassessment of the historical dynamics of consumption; in stark contrast with, say, Sombart's earlier empirical work on luxury, or the Frankfurt School's research into mass society. The changing pictures of consumption thus followed on a changing assessment of "modernity", not vice versa, and this theoretical dynamic inevitably had a decisive effect on how consumption and the consumer are portrayed in these texts. We encounter the "modern consumer", the "traditional consumer" and the "post-modern consumer" as ideal-typical constructs. These may be well suited to provide commentary on the condition of "modernity" or "post-modernity". They are less helpful for a historical understanding of consumption, since they present holistic, static and finished end-products rather than problematize how (and whether) these different types have emerged, developed, and stood in relation to each other in different societies at different times.

What, then, should be the unit of enquiry for historical research? Should we write a history of "consumerism' or "consumer society", of "consumption regimes" or "consumer culture"? Historians have largely sidestepped this interpretive problem. The prolonged debate about the merit of "class" and "society" shows that this is not because the profession is theory-challenged. Far from it, it might be argued that "consumer society" or "consumerism" have been adopted just as "class society" became problematic. One reason for this conceptual silence may be found in the formative split between the two principal approaches to consumption in the first wave of historical studies in the late 1970s and 1980s, a split that has effectively limited the contribution of history to the broader debate about consumption in the social sciences and humanities. Two largely self-referential enterprises emerged. One project traced the birth of "modern consumer society" in seventeenth- and eighteenth-century Western Europe and the Atlantic world. The second focused on shopping and mass consumption, particularly the late nineteenth-century department store. These selective enterprises not only ignored many other forms, sites and meanings of consumption, but the temporal gulf between them disguised the incommensurability of their respective notions of modernity. Historians interested in the former project turned to the "modern" acquisitive desire for commodities and "novelties" amongst a broadening middling sort and some artisans. Historians working on the latter, by contrast, argued that a modern consumer society only developed once the large bulk of society, freed from the regime of needs, was able to enter a system of ever-expanding goods and desires. The conceptual and empirical gulf between the two groups was deepened further by different methodological upbringings, the first steeped in anthropology and culture, the latter in social history and gender studies. Whereas historians of seventeenth- and eighteenth-century Holland and Britain worked with a theory of culture inspired, in part, by Durkheim and Mary Douglas, where "need" is as much a cultural construct as "desire", writers privileging the twentieth century often employed an essentialist definition of needs that stood in stark contrast with the "culture" of consumerism. In short, here was a disagreement about the very essence of human existence and culture.

The theoretical divide underlying the chronological gulf in studies of consumption was deepened by competing national traditions of historiography. In Germany, the belated turn to consumption emerged from within the Weberian development of social history as *Gesellschaftsgeschichte.* Rather than being present at the birth of modernity, consumption here was one of its offspring; and even then (like other cultural subjects) it was less a subject in its own right than a source of answers to questions about class and status.[1] Hence the almost iconic status of Bourdieu (rather than, say, Baudrillard) in German history seminars. Bourdieu's treatment of taste and consumption in the formation of habitus can be easily accommodated within *Gesellscbaftsgescbichte;* after all, Bourdieu's idea of "the choice of the necessary", though not economistic in the strict sense, continues to present the "habitus" of the working class as the learned outcome of their material situation.[2] In North America, by contrast, the recent revival of interest in consumption has been driven by a very different historiographical dynamic:

the disillusionment with social history, especially with the "working class", and the shift to gender and poststructuralism. Instead of producing "false" needs, new sites of consumption, such as the department store, offered opportunities for an emancipation of the self and the transgression of dominant gender hierarchies. The late Victorian metropole suddenly exhibited some of the very features of post-modernity *avant la lettre*.

If the strategy of *Gesellschaftsgeschichte* was to use consumption to buttress social history by showing just how subtle and distinctly "modern" class and status were, feminist and post-structuralist approaches turned to consumption to question the very notion of modernity underlying social history. Either way, consumption was instrumentalized. It was not the principal subject or problem. Interest in consumption remained highly selective and fragmented. The department store spoke to questions about the gendering of public spaces, identities and desires. Advertising spoke to questions about semiotics. There were few connections here with the historiography on food, leisure and fashion.[3] There was little dialogue with the fresh and expanding literature in anthropology and geography exploring systems of provision, material culture, life-histories and the processes and spaces connected to consumption before and after purchase.[4] The synergy between the social sciences, history and the arts that had fostered studies of the birth of the consumer society stands in stark contrast to the situation for the nineteenth and twentieth centuries.[5]

There were simply too few historical building blocks for a general debate about the changing physiology of "modern consumer society" in its subsequent adolescence, maturity or old age, let alone for a general historical narrative.

The aim of this article is to outline some of the questions that may help structure such a debate. Should we think in terms of a linear expansion of western consumerism ending in global convergence? What was the underlying dynamic of this expansion and where should we locate its modernity? What was the place of consumption in social and political relations, and what do these connections (and disconnections) tell us about the nature of "consumer society"? More broadly, what are the meanings of consumption and what should historians include or exclude? "Consumerism" and "modern consumer society", it will be argued, are concepts with diminishing analytical and conceptual usefulness that have privileged a particular western version of modern consumption at the expense of the multi-faceted and often contradictory workings of consumption in the past and are increasingly at odds with the current debate about the cultures and politics of consumption.

Despite the explosion of books on subjects related to consumption in the nineteenth and twentieth centuries. many studies address self-sufficient communities rather than engaging in a shared dialogue. In an insightful article five years ago, Peter Stearns observed the lack of connection between discussions of early modern and modern consumer society and turned to a stage theory to link the two.[6] Stage one witnessed the emergence of consumerist desire in early modern Europe and focused on dress and household items. Stage two saw the expansion of consumerism in the mid-late nineteenth century and was marked by a profusion of goods and leisure, the proliferation of retail outlets, and the spread of consumerist values into social spheres as diverse as child-rearing and pornography. As Stearns acknowledged, such a simple two-stage model called for a sharper periodization and more regional diversification. *Consumerism in World History* is the result of his further reflections and extends his question about European stages to the rest of the world. The geographic extension of the subject, however, was not accompanied by a rethinking of the underlying assumptions of western modernity. What is distinctive about modern society, Stearns reiterates, is "consumerism", defined as the lure of material goods. This consumerism first emerged in eighteenth-century Western Europe, and from there was exported to the rest of the globe. The thesis follows directly from two interrelated a priori ways of viewing the subject: the definition of an acquisitive individualist mentality as the defining feature of modern consumer behaviour and, since this originated in the West, a view of expansion that looks from the epi-centre (West) outwards. Both of these views are open to question.

"Consumerism", for Stearns, "describes a society in which many people formulate their goals in life partly through acquiring goods that they clearly do not need for subsistence or for traditional display."[7] Analytically this collapses different units of enquiry. Consumerism appears as mentality, behavioural motivation and individual action, as well as commercial institutions and a defining feature of society at large. It is problematic to read back from increased consumer spending the dominance of consumerist mentalities. For many people, it might be very "necessary" for subsistence to purchase a car in suburban America, because of the lack of public transport and a dispersed socio-economic and cultural infrastructure, not because of a consumerist definition of one's goals in life.[8] Does this make these Americans more consumerist than the privileged citizens of New York or London or Tokyo who can forgo car purchase because they have the spending power to purchase a centrally-located flat? The acquisitive, materialist focus of "consumerism" neglects the significance of forms and modes of consumption which do not centre on the commercial purchase of goods, such as visits to a club or museum, and the consumption of services and experiences more generally. Even shopping, that most basic form of consumption, involves a variety of functions from voyeurism to a search for "authentic sociality"; Daniel Miller's ethnographic studies in London have noted "how shoppers struggle to make specific purchases that will not just reflect but act directly upon the contradictions they constantly face between the normative discourse that tells them who they and their family members should be, and how they find them in their specificity as individuals".[9] Consumption can be about managing familial and social relationships, not merely self-centred acquisitiveness.

The first consequence of the narrow concept of "consumerism" is thus a self-fulfilling prophecy. Stearns finds what he is looking for: materialist consumerism as a key feature of western modernity. A less tautological approach would have been to compare acquisitive consumerist behaviour with the full spectrum of forms of consumption and their motivations; there is little here about alternative radical, social-democratic or nationalist consumer politics, and what there is is viewed only in terms of resistance to consumerism. Yet, alternative visions of consumption have often been integral to the very shape and development of capitalist societies; for example, through the popular Free Trade movement in Victorian and Edwardian Britain which was driven by ideals of the citizen-consumer and dark fears of alien materialism and excess.[10]

To group contemporary mobilization under "anti-consumer protests" misses the attraction of different approaches to consumption and the contribution of consumer movements in the European Union and, with lesser success, more globally to a widening transnational system of trade regulations.[11]

The second consequence is to reinforce a sharp dichotomy between "traditional" and "modern" society, East and West, societies defined by reciprocity and status versus societies driven by individualism and markets.[12] Just as the consumerist fixation obscures the diverse forms and alternative modernities of consumption shaping western societies (which include reciprocity), so it reinforces a picture of less dynamic, "traditional" societies in the East (ignoring their economic dynamism). As for the modern West, so for the traditional East, the cultural dynamics shaping subsistence and what sociologists have termed "ordinary consumption" is simply bracketed.[13] For the early modern period, Stearns thus grants China the display of expensive goods and high quality cloth, but these, he argues, were isolated instances of luxury, limited to the very wealthy, and incorporated into traditional styles and values. Eastern tradition, in other words, killed the dynamic energy of consumerism and the ever-changing tastes and goods this set free in the West.

This equation of tradition with a lack of dynamism side-steps the considerable significance of consumption to social order and change in non-western societies. In the Mughal empire, "a great king was a great consumer", in Chris Bayly's words.[14] Legitimacy of rule depended on a diversity of styles and the encouragement of artisans and traders to produce them. It was not any absence of fashion or diverse and changing tastes that marked the principal difference between this phase of "archaic globalisation" (Bayly) and later global consumption systems, but the push towards uniform, standardized goods in the latter. Even more than India, China in the Ming period exhibits plenty of examples of what Veblen would later term "conspicuous consumption".[15] At the level of popular consumption, more people consumed everyday luxuries like tea and sugar in eighteenth-century China than in eighteenth century Europe outside England. Nor was European consumption at this stage marked by some distinctive, uninterrupted development. As Kenneth Pomeranz has emphasized, a conventional contrast between a "normal" European trend of continued expansion and a defective pattern of interrupted growth in luxury consumption elsewhere is undermined by evidence that European consumption levels remained static during a period of overall economic growth in the first half of the nineteenth century.[16] The advance of Western Europe might have had less to do with some original European revolution of consumerist desire than with other sources, such as access to coal and the exploitation of the New World.

Attention to parallels and contingency in the earlier period might also radically shift our understanding of contemporary global consumption. For Stearns, the question of consumption in Asia and Africa is one of reception and degrees of resistance. In what is perhaps the most ambitious part of the book, Stearns turns to religion to explain where the tidal wave of consumerism swamped societies and where it has been blocked or channelled into different directions. Where a rival value system with strong notions of otherworldliness existed, as with Confucianism in China or Islam in the Middle East, advance was slow. Where no such alternative value system existed, as in sub-Saharan Africa, consumerism advanced more easily. How consumption relates to other value systems and moral institutions is an important question that deserves more comparative analysis. Yet, the reduction of consumerism into an acquisitive mentality might unnecessarily cast consumption and religion as competing self-defining universes. Why presume that an expanding consumer society requires a decline in religious intensity? "In the West", Stearns argues, "consumerism rose amongst powerful strains of Christianity, but in an atmosphere where religious intensity, on the whole, was in decline."[17] This is curious. For in Britain, that paradigm of the first consumer society, religious intensity was steadily increasing in the late eighteenth and nineteenth centuries; evangelicals might have stressed the link between Christianity and commerce but they remained vocal opponents of consumerism. As with Victorian Britain, so with postwar Japan, there is an implicit assumption about the rival forces of "markets" and "culture" at work. Stearns is surely right about the pressure of Americanization in postwar Japan, yet, again, the contrast between traditional values and an alien individualist materialism misses much that is most interesting and distinctive about Japanese consumption. For millions of housewives who made up the Japanese consumer movement, consumption was embedded within a larger universe of civic values that blended ideas of citizenship, national identity and the organic interest of producers and consumers.[18]

How much global convergence is there around consumerism? Stearns points to pockets of resistance, Islamic revival, the indigenization of goods, blending of styles, and uneven distribution of wealth and leisure, but on the whole his evidence, from Disney to Pokemon, suggests the steady global advance of consumerism. Stearns, in a concluding reflection on "Who wins?", is careful to balance an older élitist critique of mass consumption with an emphasis that for many people consumption serves "social and personal interests . . . [and] is not, always, as shallow as it seems".[19] Yet, again, the tendency to reduce consumption to a materialist acquisition of goods by individuals makes it difficult to explore the multi-faceted workings of consumption in society and politics. Consumerism erodes identities and can disorient individuals, it is argued, even though it does not necessarily mean a complete surrender to "western values". Consumerism, measured in a rise in material standards, ceases to add happiness in established consumer societies. Stearns' book might be read most profitably as a final twentieth-century reflection working within an older tradition of historical sociology, reaching back to Weber, turning to materialist consumerism as a way of explaining the rise of the West. Yet consumption in the late twentieth century has become as much about services, experiences, and citizenship as about the acquisition of goods. In Britain, to take a society where this shift in discourse, practice and identity advanced especially rapidly in the 1990s, consumption and consumers entered the workings of such diverse spheres as health care, transport and government. The postwar consumer movement is on the verge of becoming a citizens' movement. The older model of "consumerism", which, after all, originated with an élitist and academic critique of mass consumer society, is ill-equipped to penetrate the different transmutations of consumption in society.[20] Weber's fear of a "*Genussmensch ohne Herz*" (hedonist without heart) and Marcuse's later "one-dimensional man" consumed by a compulsive desire to purchase goods, were important chapters in the history of ideas. They may not be not the best analytical tools to come to grips with contemporary developments, where consumer identities have become suffused with questions of civic participation, cultural identities, and social and global justice, as well as with a drive to acquire goods.

Social differentiation and uneven penetration is the contrasting theme of Heinz-Gerhard Haupt's critical survey of *Konsum und Handel* in nineteenth- and twentieth-century Europe. Haupt puts South-Western and Eastern Europe back into a story normally dominated by their north-western neighbours. Whereas "consumerism" presumes the growing autonomy of a consumerist mentality, Haupt's approach is more concerned with consumption as a process and its role in stabilizing or eroding social solidarities. This has three related analytical advantages. First, it gives as much attention to food and clothing as to more spectacular forms of consumption. Second, it rightly insists on the importance of scarcity as well as abundance in the making of consumer societies, and on the contribution of the state. Finally, it situates consumption in important non-commercial settings, like the household and public spaces, as well as in retailing.

Haupt argues for a categorical distinction between the nineteenth and the twentieth century. Nineteenth-century Europe was a "consumer society", a social context in which a particular set of goods was available to certain groups who used them for self-representation. Twentieth-century "mass consumer society" was qualitatively different, not only because an expanding set of goods became accessible to more people, but because "distinction" through possession was becoming more complex as consumption became connected with many more social, political and cultural formations.[21] Haupt offers a kaleidoscopic picture of "consumer society" giving due space to differences between regions, generations, genders and professions. If there is little doubt about the general upward trend in the consumption of meat and alcohol, the picture remains one of sharp divergence across Europe well into the twentieth century. Skilled workers in France enjoyed lean meat while their unskilled brethren remained dependent on offal. In Spain, many were facing famine after the drought of 1905. In rural Austria, coffee only became part of the diet after the second world war.

Nor was the triumph of "modern", nationally-integrated markets over "traditional" subsistence systems complete in early twentieth-century Europe. In Italy, less than one-third of all farms produced for the market as late as the 1930s. Again, the increase in real wages and disposable income in the late nineteenth century, well established for Britain, France, Germany and Sweden, was a far from general European phenomenon, side-stepping much of the Habsburg empire. Even in the 1950s, 60 per cent of income was spent on food and drink in Southern and Eastern Europe, a figure already left behind in Britain and amongst skilled workers in Germany by the turn of the century.[22] Even for North-Western Europe, this is not a simple narrative of modernization. The arrival of the department store proceeded parallel to a rise in the number of travelling salesmen and hawkers.[23] And the spread of the department store was not an automatic reaction to urbanization and industrialization either – comparatively, France was advanced in the first, but not in the latter. Here, as elsewhere, Haupt's sensibility as a comparativist sheds fresh light on old subjects, urging future research to leave the nation state as the natural unit of enquiry and instead to compare phenomena across societies, such as the distinct conditions that favoured the emergence of particular retail organizations in some cities but not in others.

How consumption relates to collective identities and social solidarities has been a subject more extensively explored by sociologists and anthropologists than by historians. Haupt's short reflections on consumption in relation to gender, ethnicity and nation are thus welcome; generational changes, so crucial to current debates,[24] are a subject historians have yet to explore more fully. Normative discourses of separate gender roles did not necessarily match social realities of consumption – some men did cook – but they set the framework in which consumers oriented themselves. At the same time, the identification of women as consumers also opened up new spaces of action, as in the department store, and, we might add, in civil society more broadly, especially through the expanding network of co-operative women at the turn of the twentieth century, where questions of consumption and citizenship were intimately linked.[25]

The transformation of Europe into a "mass consumer society" in the course of the twentieth century is the theme of the second half of Haupt's study. Here again, the emphasis is as much on limits as on triumphs, and on ruptures as much as linear expansion. Scarcities and rationing during and after the two world wars receive as much attention as the growing consumer spending on furniture, clothing and entertainment. The reader is reminded of the social exclusion that continues to keep the material dreams of consumerism out of reach of large segments of European societies, not least pensioners and single mothers. Throughout, *Konsum und Handel* situates changing trends within the broader social contexts of economic growth and welfare patterns.

Recognition of the multiple and often divergent functions and meanings of consumption raises questions about the very usefulness of working with two large ideal-typical systems of "consumer society" and "mass consumer society". The picture of a nineteenth-century "consumer society" emerges more ambivalent than the concept signals. It suggests boundedness and fractures rather than any unstoppable or defining social system. As a dominant social formation it was limited to particular regions and cities as well as to particular classes. There may have been growing consumption, but very few societies and social solidarities had yet become defined by the practices or mentalities associated with it. Just as it is debatable to speak of a "class society" if its members do not principally define themselves in terms of class, so we might ask when it was that individuals and groups came to define themselves as "consumers". Though the economic use of the term can be traced back to rare instances in the early eighteenth century, the "consumer" as a distinctive identity, as a form of self-description by individuals and groups and as a universal category of ascription and analysis by business, politics and academia only appears to have come fully into its own in mid-, late nineteenth- and early twentieth-century Europe and North America. Even then, the neo-classical view of the rational, utility-maximizing individual that emerged out of the marginalist revolution of the 1870s was not the only (or the principal) representation of "the consumer" competing for social and political attention at the turn of the twentieth century. To many radicals and liberals, "consumers" were informed, ethical users of necessaries, performing important civic roles, as in J.A. Hobson's image of the "citizen-consumer" in Edwardian Britain or in the work of the National Consumers' League (NCL) to improve working conditions and civil rights in early twentieth-century America.[26] A more open, descriptive and less normative definition of "consumer", based on the act of purchase rather than its underlying motivation or set of commodities, appears a rarer, second stage, such as when the NCL in 1925 proclaimed that "every person who buys anything, from a bun to a yacht, is a consumer".[27]

Greater attention to contested meanings of the consumer in societies with different political traditions and socio-economic dynamics might tell us much about the changing salience of "consumer society".[28] In South Korea, for example, where the second half of the 1980s alone saw a 75 per cent real increase in the rate of consumption expenditure, a public debate developed about "excessive consumers". Yet polls asking South Koreans to identify where they thought that excessive consumption lay in their everyday lives, produced children's education at the top of the list, above leisure and travel.[29] The meaning of "consumption" and the identity of the "consumer" and its place in social and political processes here is a radically different one from that in the luxury debates of eighteenth-century imperial Britain, or well-known western debates about mass consumer culture and "conspicuous consumption" in the early twentieth century, premised on a binary of *Bildung*/culture versus consumption/leisure.

How uniform and distinctive is European "mass consumer society", the ideal-type used by Haupt for the twentieth century? Is there sufficient coherence and similarity amongst patterns of consumption in the last half-century to make this term as useful for the 1990s as for the 1950s? Here Haupt follows, on the one hand, Hartmut Kaelble's argument for a general trend of convergence, even though pointing to disruptive moments and qualitative shifts (from class to life-style) and, on the other, Victoria de Grazia's seminal distinction between an American "consumption regime" characterized by individual choice in the marketplace and a European regime where consumer citizenship is sought through social participation and economic redistribution via the state.[30] It is debatable how well these two arguments fit with the analysis of a "mass consumer society". These ideal-typical distinctions might capture particular dimensions of consumption in particular societies at particular times while obscuring alternative developments at others; growing awareness of the limited significance of Fordist "mass" production suggests caution about models of "mass" consumption.[31] European developments in the twentieth century might be even more diverse than Haupt allows. First, it can be argued that the "European model" contained different types of political organization and economic redistribution through which consumer citizenship was exercised – focusing more on civil society at the turn of the twentieth century and to some degree again at the turn of the twenty-first, but on the state in the period in between. Second, the consumption of social and public services (from welfare to culture) should be a more integral part of the analysis of "mass consumer society". Groups suffering from social exclusion and low income, for example, may very well be left out of a consumerist dream world, but they nonetheless are significant consumers of other things – water, social housing, education, television and so forth. Even for more privileged consumers, the place and force of mass consumption (through markets) will remain inadequately explained unless it is connected to a study of the changing provision and understanding of public services; the presence of consumer discourse and practices in health care, to take one example, is pronounced in Britain. Some consumer movements argue that the contrast between "choice" and political organization that underlies the ideal-typical contrast between America and Europe was a false choice in the first place and can be overcome. Transnational trends, not least through European integration and consumer advocacy, make for different regulations and possibilities in the sphere of consumption today from those in the first half of the twentieth century, often eroding the autonomous powers of states.

So far we have discussed the attraction (and limitations) of distinguishing between different large-scale systems (consumerism, consumer society, mass consumer society). Yet how to account for the dynamism generated by consumption in societies in transition from one system to another? For societies in Northern and Western Europe, this question is especially pertinent for the late nineteenth and early twentieth centuries, partly because of growing overall purchasing power, but even more so because of the changing institutions, practices and sensibilities of consumption. The transformation of retailing was the engine of this change. Recognition of its centrality, however, has generally been framed through a narrow definition of modernity. The department store, in particular, has become synonymous with the rise of "modern" consuming practices and sensibilities. The department store, which began to dot the urban landscape of Europe in the last third of the nineteenth century, owes part of its image as a pioneer of modernity to being contrasted with an atavistic, backward-looking and older community of small retailers. This negative assessment, Uwe Spiekermann argues convincingly in *Basis der Konsumgesellschaft*, needs to be historicized as a construct inherited from earlier academic and party-political contestation in imperial Germany. Gustav Schmoller, the doyen of the historical school of political economy, deliberately downplayed the contribution of retailers to German modernization in order to highlight that of the German state.[32]

Between 1867 and 1910 shops expanded by 512 per cent in Germany, a greater rate of increase than that of the population (343 per cent). These numbers, Spiekermann shows, hide a tremendous evolution and diversification of retailing. Instead of the caricature of the *gemütliche*, single shopkeeper, a spectrum of shops and retailing forms emerge, from the *Magazin* and travelling depots *(Wanderlager)*, to itinerant traders and chain stores. The department store was merely one amongst several functional responses to the commercialization of society and one that incorporated evolutionary changes first developed in other settings. As Spiekermann points out, the department store in Germany was not only small in terms of material significance, with less than 2.5 per cent of retail sales on the eve of the first world war, but its fragmented lay-out, such as different cashiers for different parts of each floor, discouraged the emergence of the "*flâneur*", the rambling and browsing shopper.[33]

Diversification and differentiation, not concentration, emerge as the engines of modernity. Spiekermann's principal historiographical aim is to write retailing back into narratives of modern German history. He recovers very different "modern" forms of retailing, many of which fit poorly a Weberian image of modernization – an observation that can be extended to other spheres of consumer culture, such as advertising.[34] Communal experiments with centralizing sales in marketing halls could not compete successfully with the small shops and street traders who worked closer to customers and offered more attractive sales and credit. The *Wanderlager*, often decried by contemporaries as the very essence of shoddiness, here are reassessed for their modernizing potential: they developed efficient business structures, commercialized rural areas and distributed the surplus of industrial society in the form of remainders. The study thus complements the recent rediscovery of "modern" elements of shopping in arcades and shop-windows in the early modern period.[35] Looking ahead, it should also encourage a more ecumenical appreciation of the persistence of rival retailing practices and spaces, including street markets, second-hand consumption, car-boot sales and charity shops.[36] There needs to be more exchange between theorists, sociologists and historians, before any transition to "post-modern" or "post-traditional" consumer culture can be meaningful.

The modernizing force of retailing partly lay in its heterogeneity and its ability to learn from rival challenges. Rather than presenting organizations and movements locked in ideological conflict, Spiekermann focuses on processes of collective learning. The battle between consumer co-operatives and profit-oriented shopkeepers thus becomes a story of successful adaptation, as the latter formed purchase federations on the model of the former to benefit from economies of scale. Far from lagging behind, retail continued to outspend industry on advertisement well into the interwar years, and far from being passive outlets for industry's products, small shops emerge as a vital source of marketing. Shopkeepers not only adjusted their display and (increasingly finished) goods with a view to a particular social clientèle, but this differentiation went hand in hand with a growing routinization of communication and sales techniques within the shop. Professionalization and sales-training self-consciously advanced this process. Customers and retailers alike lost their personal distinction and habits. Shopkeepers and sales personnel were asked to discipline their own chattiness and bad moods, and refrain from self-expression (such as the use of strong perfume), while managing customers with universal sales techniques rather than individual charm. New skills were needed to classify consumers entering the shop, to anticipate a type's desires, but also to demonstrate the meaning of consumer sovereignty by pointing towards a range of higher quality, more expensive goods.[37] Spiekermann's study suggests a new normative trend at the turn of the twentieth century, though, at times, a concern with retrieving the agency of retailers threatens to ignore the agency of consumers. Clearly, the changing relationship between personal and routinized interactions involved both consumers and retailers. Future research will need to explore the different ways in which shops and customers could mix elements of the universal commercial and uniquely personal, even intimate, in different areas of consumption. To what degree modernity resulted in depersonalization, as Spiekermann suggests, needs to be tested against the different forms of self-representation people perform in different arenas of consumption. As the American example of sales personnel introducing themselves by first name and place of origin suggests, there may be no linear trend or normative yardstick. Consumers (and retailers) may want to encourage personal exchange and a sense of community in a particular space – the fancy neighbourhood store which sells personal identity as much as goods – but not in others – the wholesale or outlet centre selling for price. Historians have yet to chart how different societies have developed and managed these different offerings of the consuming self.[38]

Any serious discussion of consumer society must trace the practices and meanings of consumption as they are woven into social structures and actions that lie beyond the shop counter. Instead of oppositional models of analysis (consumption versus production) and of sequential models (consumer society after class society), the challenge of the next generation of work will be one of integration. The study of consumption has the potential to bring together the study of work, politics, family and collective identity in fresh ways. Indeed, it needs to do so if it wants to avoid the fate of historiographical marginalization experienced by earlier "leisure studies".[39] New studies on shopping and factory meals offer new approaches for broadening the social relations of consumption.

How much the ideological valorization of consumption has changed in the last few decades is reflected in Erika Rappaport's significant study of shopping in London's West End in the late nineteenth and early twentieth centuries. Instead of commercial exploitation or oppression, *Shopping for Pleasure* is a story of consumers' agency. Shopping became an emancipatory activity through which middle-class women defined a new sense of bourgeois feminine identity, carved out new public spaces, and became energized as political actors. This approach carries obvious affinities with recent theoretical interest in the "subversive" nature of consumption.[40] Rappaport makes several important revisions to popular theories. Thus, the analysis of credit purchasing and legal cases regarding married women's debts reveals the significance of the legal context for familial consumption. Instead of supporting Veblen's idea of "conspicuous consumption" as a source of social status, Rappaport shows how "legislators, judges, and husbands perceived 'excessive' consumption as potentially undoing that position".[41] There is a keen eye for distinct perceptions of consumer culture within groups as well as tensions between them. The arrival of department stores divided residents and retailers alike, some anxious about its disruption of established gender roles and idyllic neighbourhoods, others greeting it as a vehicle of female improvement.

In the commercial expansion of the West End in the late Victorian and Edwardian period, both the nature of consumption and the identity of the shopper were redefined. The gaze of the *flâneuse*, developed in several magazines, extended the spatial and emotional dimension of consumption beyond the materiality of commodities. One way of reading Rappaport's book is to see here one stage in the contestation of "the consumer" as a new social actor. Middle-class women and organizations as well as journalists, playwrights and businessmen all tried to capture "the consumer", and in the process redefined pre-existing social identities, especially those of women. Musical comedies of the department store, Rappaport argues, "housed socially acceptable yet erotic narratives about the mingling of classes, sexes, and money" that shaped rnodern identities.[42] Other genres distinguished between the educated *flâneuse*, whose window-shopping expanded a sense of humanity, and the irrational shopper, whose addictive pursuit of fashion resulted in a loss of individuality. Who did the women think they were? There is at times a conceptual slippage here that obfuscates the genealogy of "the consumer" as a social identity. "Consumers no doubt came away with many readings of the [department store] plays", Rappaport acknowledges.[43] But did theatre-goers necessarily see themselves as "consumers" when they went to a music hall? How did individuals respond to being bombarded with rival images and expectations of "the consumer"? The utopian and dystopian dimensions are important in themselves, but they also alert us to the need to know more about the spectrum in between.

How the growing interest in consumption can refresh our thinking about industrial society is illustrated by Jacob Tanner in *Fabrikmahlzeit*, a highly original book on food at the industrial workplace in Switzerland in the first half of the twentieth century. The canteen functions as a prism of overlapping discourses and practices that connect work and home, individual productivity and social welfare, profit and health. Tanner encourages us to see workplace and family, production and consumption in the same frame of analysis, rather than as separate universes attracting separate communities of historians. The story begins with the scientific shift at the turn of the twentieth century from labour physiology to nutritional physiology. Whereas the first conceived of the human body in terms of energy and thermodynamics, the latter privileged a biochemical model in which hormones and vitamins provided vital signals and information. Instead of a fuel tank, the body became a communication system. Consequently, "muscular thermodynamics" came to be less influential than previous studies of industrial modernity and Taylorism assumed.[44] At the workplace and beyond the factory gate, a new politics of food emerged that approached questions of productivity, social harmony and national hygiene through a nutritional programme favouring vegetables and juice and discouraging meat and alcohol. The canteen became a social laboratory for creating healthy Swiss bodies.

Tanner approaches this laboratory via two principal avenues, the work of the *Schweizer Verband Volksdienst* (SVV), founded in 1914, and the canteens at the firms of Sandoz, Ciba and Geigy. The SVV became increasingly influential in the creation and management of Swiss canteens, running well over 100 canteens in the metal and chemical industries as well as the public sector. In the 1930s, American ideas of industrial management were displaced by German fascist associations between nutrition and eugenics. Tanner shows how much the SVV's programme was transformed at the workplace by acts of resistance and stubborn cultural trends. The SVV was a pioneering advocate of self-service, which synthesized ideas of rationalization in production and individualization in demand. By 1929, 37 per cent of canteen meals were offered à la carte through self-service. But how successful was this attempt to turn workers into individual consumers with a clear sense of choice? According to Tanner, no sharp break in food culture occurred. Many workers continued to bring their food from home and found increasingly ingenious ways of heating it up at the workplace. Rather than working against familial, domestic settings, the factory canteen came to absorb family traditions, setting itself up as an "alcohol-free substitute home",[45] in which women provided men with food. The SVV"s hopes of transforming Swiss nutrition had only limited success. Canteen budgets reveal a slight but steady increase in expenditure on vegetables and fruit in the late 1920s and 1930s, and only a marginal drop in that for meat. Meal practices, too, proved resilient, as most workers were unwilling to abandon the lengthy two-hour break in the middle of the day.

The overlap of labour and consumption, of factory culture and domestic culture, poses a challenge for the picture of functional and spatial differentiation between mass consumption and mass production in the age of Taylorism. The dominant argument has been that, as capitalism switched to an intensive regime of capital accumulation in the early twentieth century, a functional and spatial separation emerged between the workplace with its task of rationalizing labour and the domestic sphere with its task of keeping workers fit and healthy by managing consumption.[46] Consumer culture, in this account, followed the dictates of capitalist production – the private family used the goods produced by mass production (cars, radios, washing machines, etc.). Expanding the focus of consumption beyond private acts of purchase in the market-place complicates this functionalist argument and cuts across a simple divide of work-place versus private consumption. Even in advanced capitalist societies, or perhaps especially there, collective consumption has played an important role, from public services to energy consumption to canteens. Why some forms of public consumption have proved less viable than others (such as wartime government restaurants) is a challenging question. What is clear from the role of new nutritional ideas is that consumption at the work-place shaped as well as responded to the process of production. Thus, the practice of workers taking several short breaks – a pathological sign of laziness and inefficiency under the thermodynamic model – was promoted from the mid-1930s for its contribution to superior health and productivity.[47]

*Fabrikmahlzeit* opens a successful dialogue between historical study and sociological models of consumption, ranging from Simmel's discussion of the meal to Bourdieu's work on habitus. In contrast to Bourdieu, Tanner shows that eating practices are not only used for "distinction", but also have a cultural force of their own. At the same time, Tanner shows how right Bourdieu was to see food as a retarding element in social transformations, preserving older habits for which there may be little role in a changing society. Historians and pundits hanging onto notions of "basic needs" or economistic interpretations of changing consumption patterns will find a lot to chew on in this study; those proclaiming an automatic correlation between a rise in income and a rise in meat consumption might want to note that Swiss people in 1952 still consumed less meat than they did in 1922.[48] What is debatable is the concluding thesis of a sharp break around 1950, a conviction that unnecessarily prevents Tanner from exploring continuities in Swiss consumer culture. Here the argument relies heavily on shifts in nutritional science rather than the cultural practices of eating in the work-place. As early as 1948 Tanner finds academic commentary on "overfeeding" displacing earlier concerns about how best to manage scarcity. This conceptual shift, it is argued, had dramatic consequences for the influence of nutritional science, which, after all, had acquired its institutional power-base and social legitimation through its position at the centre of the productivist project. But how many workers in how many canteens were troubled by "overfeeding" or "overeating" in the 1950s and 1960s? When did state policies and consumer legislation shift priority from nutrition to obesity? And are there not significant continuities in the expansion of self-service into other areas of consumption in the second half of the twentieth century? Studies of British diet and food cultures suggest it was only in the late 1960s that significant changes took place.[49] Histories of West Germany in the 1950s suggest that memories of pre-war "scarcity" continued to inform working families' understanding and evaluation of growing affluence after the war.[50]

What to do with politics in the study of consumption? This question has been a long-standing headache for students of modern consumer societies. In contrast to the literature on early modern "moral economy" and popular protests, modern and contemporary historians have been slow to debate systematically the changing interface between politics and consumption. This is ironic, given the renewed importance of consumption for recent national and international social movements, as well as for some Western governments and political élites, most notably New Labour in Britain. Methodological assumptions, based on an instinctive bias towards the individual as the core unit of modern consumer society, may account for this historiographical lag. One assumption, which some economic historians continue to fall back upon, is that consumers are a messy agglomerate of utilitarian individuals with different interests and desires: they might briefly be driven to protest because of specific material grievances, but by definition any collective action is difficult to sustain. The other, more culturalist and sometimes explicitly post-structuralist approach has been to explore consumption in the construction of individual identity. What matters here is the relationship between individual lifestyle and the commercial and institutional preparation of a "self" fit for consumer society. The focus is on governmentality, the generation of self and choice – no doubt a process saturated with power, but nonetheless one in which the political imaginary of consumers, their mobilization, and self-understanding as collective actors have featured rarely. Yet this focus on "individual" and "choice" presumes a shift from tradition/community to liberal modernity/individual that is at odds with the many occasions in modern and contemporary history when consumption has been a political site for collective mobilization concerning civil society, democracy and global justice.

The last few years have witnessed a new convergence of interest in modern consumer politics, driven partly by a broader academic and political rediscovery of civil society, partly by historians' turning away from an older male, production and class-oriented vision of social democracy, partly by attention to the politics of everyday life, family and gender.[51] The study by Ina Zweiniger-Bargielowska on *Austerity in Britain* and the collection edited by Hartmut Berghoff on *Konsumpolitik* in twentieth-century Germany now take us two steps forward in thinking about the politicization of consumption, and one step back.[52] The politics in which they are interested here is in the first place the state and organized party politics: how do policies affect consumption, and how do parties use consumer interest and grievances? Consumption here is more or less taken as a given and of instrumental interest. Lizabeth Cohen's *A Consumer's Republic*, by contrast, pursues the larger question of how mass consumption became a dominant mode of political culture and political economy in the USA after the second world war.[53] Here the interest is the changing meanings and functions of consumption and how these transformed the politics of space, community and, eventually, the democratic imagination itself. To a degree, the difference in these approaches reflects the different paths taken by consumer politics in these societies – but only to a degree. They also reflect the persisting force of national historiographical traditions and debates. In spite of an advancing global system of provision and debate about consumption, the primary focus of these studies is not consumer politics as a subject in its own right but as a way of answering questions about power and political culture in particular national settings.

Read next to each other, these books offer fundamentally contradictory conclusions about the state's impact on consumption. The essays in *Konsumpolitik* point to the limitations of state power and to long-term continuities in twentieth-century consumer politics across the divide of the second world war. *Austerity in Britain*, by contrast, presents the decade after 1945 as a sharp break in policy and party allegiance, manifesting itself in a new Conservative drive for markets and choice, away from wartime regulation. *A Consumer's Republic* highlights the centrality of government resources and county and state policies and regulations in sustaining and moulding a more consensual project of mass consumption as an engine of material prosperity and democratic life in postwar America.

A good argument for continuity is Christoph Nonn's discussion of agricultural policies between Weimar and the Federal Republic – here the first world war, rather than 1945, emerges as a decisive break, as the memories of hunger create a new consensus of regulatory politics.[54] Agricultural policies, he emphasizes, cannot simply be understood in terms of élite lobbying but reflect a shift in sentiment within popular parties, including the Social Democrats, who by the 1920s were pressing for a politics of productivity. This fits in well with a significant shift in opinion amongst organized labour and consumer movements in Britain in the same period, away from free trade towards trade regulation to reconcile producer and consumer interests.[55] Speitkamp's discussion of censorship and youth culture in the first half of the twentieth century finds a persistent gulf between the realities of expanding consumer culture and the unwillingness of political and cultural élites to entrust taste and choice to the market. Nineteen forty-five did not amount to a sharp break in popular attitudes to advertising either, as Berghoff's critical evaluation of the profession's role in the nazi and postwar years makes clear. These chapters are forceful reminders of the danger of positing some natural, essential consumer society. Businessmen, politicians and bureaucrats turned to regulation with a specific view of how consumer society worked and could be moulded. Yet they often generated the very opposite consumption patterns from those intended; nazi hopes to limit consumer demand by advertising about scarce resources instead drew attention to these goods and exacerbated bottlenecks. How contradictory consumer policies could be is illustrated in Schröter's discussion of the young Federal Republic in the 1950s. Here clothes and food retailing were deregulated, but energy, housing and transport were not. For Ludwig Erhard, markets and competition offered a substitute for a genuine consumer policy, although even this was compromised by cartel legislation (1952) which allowed some vertical price-fixing favouring producers and traders at the expense of consumers. German competition policy was distinctly shaped by ordo-liberal ideas, equipped with tough laws, and, arguably, more centrally connected to debates about democracy than in postwar Britain where it was more an administrative arm of the state seeking to advance efficiency.[56]

*Austerity in Britain* is more tightly drawn around a specific aspect of consumer politics: the rationing of basic consumption in Britain during and after the second world war, its administration, social consequences and growing politicization. Zweiniger-Bargielowska takes on the myth of the "postwar consensus".[57] As her detailed reconstruction of popular attitudes shows, far from universally accepting continued rationing after the second world war with a stiff upper lip, a growing number of British people turned against it. The groundswell of rising frustration, especially pronounced amongst women, favoured the Conservative revival in the late 1940s and 1950s.[58] Put differently, Labour's fair shares policies, far from symbolizing the popularity of the welfare state and shared sacrifice moulded in wartime, were deeply unfair and, from an electoral point of view, suicidal, as voters turned to Conservative candidates promising choice and free markets.

The question with these points is not whether they are separately true, but what do they mean in a longer and comparative framework? There is little engagement with the multidisciplinary field of consumer studies. Gender is given argumentative privilege, although much of the evidence suggests equally interesting divisions by generation, region, income and skill. Housewives were worse off than their husbands under rationing, but this is hardly surprising. It is well documented that food consumption in working-class families in previous free market situations was also highly gendered and hierarchical.[59] The question is: did rationing exacerbate this gendered inequity and was it experienced as doing so? Labour's fair share policies, likewise, might have been removed in practice from ideals of egalitarianism, and not have been universally popular.

Yet this does not necessarily mean that there was a general loss of public faith in controls. In an ideal world, few people would voluntarily choose rationing, so the question becomes by whose standards was British rationing popular or unpopular?

*Austerity in Britain* is most impressive when using social surveys and opinion polls to chart shifts in popular opinion. Here evidence does not always provide conclusive answers, however. Some polls point to a remarkable degree of continued popularity for controls. As late as 1953 a Gallup poll revealed 43 per cent opposed to the gradual disappearance of rationing, with 47 per cent in favour[60] – many democratic parties form governments with less support. This was far from a dramatic sea-change from wartime opinion. In 1942, for example, 49 per cent wanted a continuation of rationing.[61] Women in the cooperative and labour movements organized mass demonstrations and petitions in support of controls in 1953–54. Observers from societies like Japan, also keen to curb spending and promote saving, found the degree of acceptance of rationing in Britain mind-boggling.[62] How many politicians in other societies have dared to implement austerity measures after a total war and managed to win the next election?

In addition to the popularity of a particular consumer policy, it might be useful, then, to ask about solidarity, compliance and legitimacy – that is, the willingness of people to accept a political framework as legitimate and to live by its rules without challenging the authority and social norms of the community. How do individual feelings translate into individual and collective action? Opinion polls are poor guides for this process, as the frequent gulf between consumer opinions and behaviour makes amply clear; most people indicate a preference for organic food, but very few buy it. Postwar Britain may not have generated a "consensus" about policies but was perhaps nonetheless a society distinguished by a marked degree of cohesion and willingness to accept sacrifices without opting for wide-spread protests, violence or criminalization; even black markets in Britain were distinguished by a high sense of morality and social conscience.[63] This contrasts significantly, for example, with the charged street politics and violent attacks on privileged consumers, shopkeepers and Jews in Germany during and after the first world war. To understand this, however, the study of consumer politics must connect material patterns of everyday life to the ideas and values which provide them with political meaning and direct their collective action.

From this perspective, how much of a break in consumer politics are the immediate postwar years? Arguably, the debate about austerity resumed and sharpened an earlier divide between proponents of regulation and choice, institutional co-ordination and market, that had erupted during the first world war and widened in the interwar years. Tories absorbed the remaining Liberal free traders but made sure to complement their attack on rationing with trade controls and subsidies in other spheres of the economy. Labour consolidated its programme of controls, with sections of the party seeking to design a direct consumer policy and supporting state agencies, like the Council of Industrial Design, in their effort to "rationalize" consumer habits.[64] New arrivals, like the Consumers" Association, developed further the interwar interest in consumer information and protection. In contrast to the late Victorian and Edwardian free trade settlement, the consumer interest was now politically and culturally fragmented, with different meanings and spokespeople, and no longer at the centre of political economy and political culture.

The middle of the twentieth century, arguably, sees a role reversal in the status of the consumer in the political imagination in Britain and America. Whereas consumption (and the representation of consumers) came to play a fragmented and subordinate role in the British political system,[65] in America, as Lizabeth Cohen shows, the opposite dynamic was at work: mass consumption moved to the centre of American politics – and in due course transformed the nature of politics. The creation of "*A Consumer's Republic*", in Cohen's words, became the consensual political project of the postwar years, promising Americans greater prosperity, equality and freedom. This is less a story of sharp breaks than one of a series of organic mutations between different settlements of consumer politics. Citizenship and consumption are omnipresent categories, rather than successive ideal-types, but the respective weight and functional relationship between them change in these three settlements. Cohen's account takes us from the ideal of "citizen consumer" of the New Deal, where consumption was informed by collective interests, to "the purchaser as citizen" of the Consumers' Republic, where the individual pursuit of mass consumption would benefit the public interest, to that of the "consumer/citizen/taxpayer/voter' of the Consumerized Republic, where politics itself is viewed as a market.

It would be too easy (politically and historically) to subsume this account under a narrative of "economic imperialism" in which the ideas and practice of a liberal market increasingly colonize other spheres of politics and society. Inevitably, this book is written within the context of a long-standing and distinctive American debate about whether consumer culture undermines democracy and community.[66] Politicians' appropriation of the language of markets and the invasion of marketing knowledge and market sensibilities into political culture form the end-point of this study. Its main historical contribution, however, is in unravelling the political dynamics behind the confluence of consumption and citizenship at a micro and macro level of power and social relations. The Consumer's Republic created a broad consensual agreement in a vision of society in which American citizens enjoyed greater affluence and freedom by participating in a mass consumption economy. This "consensus", however, never amounted to political stasis. It was neither a natural, self-sustaining economic arrangement, nor did it preclude contestation. Cohen shows masterfully how the ideal of the ever-expanding American pie with growing slices for all changed in shape and distribution as the realities of class, race and gender came to structure mass consumption. Her discussion does for consumer politics what the "systems of provision" approach has done for consumer goods:[67] it follows consumer politics from early ideas to their contestation and implementation as policies, to what we might call the social and political externalities of mass consumption. The spatial dimensions of mass consumer culture are a crucial link in the chain of analysis. At the level of federal policies concerning taxation and mortgage guarantees, she shows how the ideal of greater equality in a dynamic mass consumption economy was compromised from the beginning by inegalitarian, gendered social policies, such as the GI Bill. At the level of local politics, suburbanization and localism made for class and racial segregation. Public spaces became regulated or eliminated altogether. In turn, the spatial reconfiguration of consumption fed back into a revised image of "the consumer" in the 1950s. The previously dominant female representation of the shopper was giving way to "Mr Consumer", whose name is on the mortgage, who drives with his wife to the mall, and who controls access to credit. For Cohen, this regendering was symptomatic of the broader transmutation of the public-minded female citizen-consumer into the male purchaser as citizen.

Cohen's emphasis on the negative social and political externalities of the Consumer's Republic, however, is balanced by her appreciation of how its egalitarian ideals also legitimized grass roots struggles for civic rights and social inclusion. Above all, African-Americans' battle against discrimination made effective use of the new convergence of citizenship and consumption by demanding their share in a mass consumer society; here, too, there was a political commodification of space as civil rights' groups defined housing as one of the most "basic consumer goods".[68] These campaigns' achievements became difficult to maintain, however, once public accommodations were jeopardized by suburbanization.

Politics here stretches beyond a functional connection between material interest and party-political preferences to an inquiry into the consequences of a system of mass consumption for the political deliberation of public questions and for social inclusion and exclusion. For all its emancipatory potential, *A Consumers' Republic* leaves behind a negative balance sheet. It is a social-democratic, historical pendant to communitarian analyses of the erosion of American community and civil society.[69] As a historian, Cohen places little hope in the communitarian vision of disentangling the long-term intertwining of citizenship and consumption. She is at pains to emphasize how mass politics can generate common ideals, a theme of her earlier work.[70] At the same time, there is a good deal of shared diagnostics. The economic recession after 1973 exposed how skin-deep and fragmented the public interest had become under the previous regime of mass consumption. Reaganism reaped the benefits of the historical convergence of consumption and citizenship. The "consumer" had become a dominant identity of self-interest and personal entitlement. Americans have degenerated into a nation of shoppers, shopping for politics just as they shopped for goods.

This approach to consumer politics opens up several vistas, but it also, perhaps, shuts off others. Cohen introduces an important historical dimension to the current debate about neo-liberal hegemony. Rather than presenting neo-liberalism as a paradigmatic shift in political culture in the age of deregulation and Reagan, she traces a long-term fragmentation of public politics to the proliferation of suburban malls and the application of market segmentation by politicians in the 1960s. The book's second achievement is to contribute to present work seeking to place consumer movements within political economy, rather than following a social movement narrative casting consumer advocates as opponents of a dominant regime. Naderism here emerges as much a symptom of the Consumer's Republic as its proffered cure, reinforcing both the consensual ideal of mass consumption that marginalized alternative reform projects and the fragmentation of entrepreneurial interest politics. For all its strengths, this narrative obscures, perhaps unnecessarily, the growing contribution of international developments to consumer politics. The debate about GATT in the 1980s sparked a rediscovery of global issues for American consumer advocates. There has been a vibrant debate about global trade, environmental issues and civil society amongst consumer movements in America as elsewhere. *Consumers' International* has been an influential forum for reintroducing questions of social justice. In Japan in the last two decades, consumption has become an increasingly strong social and political movement as well as a cultural formation.[71] In China, the communist party state's endorsement of "the consumer" as an essential agent in modernization in the 1990s has opened up new (and often unintended oppositional) spaces for political action and association.[72] These developments, and the way in which consumption has become linked to questions of identity, fit poorly the concluding image of the consumer's having descended from being the voice of collective interests to the pursuer of personal entitlement.

*A Consumers' Republic* also raises a question about the causal correlation between mass consumption and public political apathy, which calls for more comparative work along the lines of Almond and Verba's earlier project on civic culture.[73] Concern about selfishness replacing a commitment to collective interests, and a decline in political engagement are as old as history.[74] Yet why necessarily presume a trade-off between a sense of personal entitlement and a sense of social commitment? People might become more involved and assertive consumers because they feel a sense of entitlement *and* because they want to support their community.[75] Finally, the anti-Whiggish account of the fragmentation of the American republic raises questions about the public spirit Americans lost. How collective, how public, how open, how shared was politics before the confluence of citizenship and consumption? There is sometimes an asymmetry in historical method here. The sensitivity attached to the changing meanings of the consumer, the critical questioning who is imagined by whom and who not, who had power in constructing which image and who did not, is rarely extended to the meaning of "citizenship" or "the public," which are left standing as if they possess some essential meaning that does not require equal historicization. There is an implicit, debatable assumption that, prior to the transmutation of consumer politics into consumerized politics, there was a lot more of the shared public space and common stake on which a vibrant democracy depends. Yet is this not somehow at odds with the growing appeal of consumer politics for social movements in the first half of the twentieth century as the very instruments for overcoming barriers to full democracy, social justice and material well-being?

Consumer culture is at the centre of contemporary debates about freedom, identity and social justice. These debates have been most advanced in geography, sociology and cultural studies. Historians' early interest focused on two phenomena: the birth of consumer society in early modern Western Europe and the Atlantic world, and the spread of "modern" consumerism in the late nineteenth and twentieth centuries. This article has argued for expanding the focus of historical enquiry into consumption and for critically re-examining the concepts and periodization underlying it. The task ahead is to write histories of consumption, not consumerism. Consumerism, or the lure of material goods for individuals, is only one point on a broad cultural spectrum in which consumption operates in modern and contemporary societies. The consumption of basic goods (water, grain, meat) continues to be a vital subject of identity and politics in societies which do not lack the disposable income for hedonism. Likewise "mass" consumer society was only one particular social formation, particularly prominent around the mode of production of certain goods and not others. Two related problems have been highlighted: first, the danger of writing a stage narrative of consumption through a supposed transition from need to desire; second, that of framing the analysis in terms of the global expansion of a particular western type of consumption. Instead of working within a self-defined theory of mass consumer society or modern consumer society, historians now need to contextualize the different forms and functions of consumption, and the affiliated social visions and political systems competing with each other at the same time. This requires a more ambitious and ecumenical view of consumption, no longer limited to shopping and the market but looking beyond to what sociologists have called "ordinary consumption", to social services and to systems of public provision.

A new generation of historical work is emerging, seeking to weave consumption back into social and political processes. Yet there remains a notable tension between what has remained a predominantly national frame of analysis and what is after all a subject and process of transnational nature. There is, then, a considerable gulf between the study of commodities through a global system of provisions and historians' preferred study of consumer societies in a national setting. National studies can reveal the significance of particular traditions in moulding consumption and weaving it into the social and political fabric. Sticking too solidly to national frames of analysis, however, risks reinforcing national historiographical subjects and debates, rather than leading to a new dialogue about consumer societies in different settings. What is needed now is greater awareness of transnational and comparative processes, so that historians of different consumer societies can discuss questions of convergence and divergence, consumption and citizenship, and the changing meanings and functions of consumption in the modern and contemporary period.

There can be little doubt that the boundaries of "consumption" and "the consumer", as a subject and identity, expanded enormously in the course of the twentieth century, from goods to services, and from personal wants and social justice to questions of political governance – and did so with different speed and ambition in different societies. This inflation of "consumption" and "consumer" poses a challenge as well as an opportunity for historians. If everything is now consumption – from a museum visit to a hospital stay – the subject risks becoming too broad for any meaningful analysis. What historians can contribute in wrestling with this eternal dilemma of consumer studies is to show how we need to be more sensitive to the ways and contexts in which historical actors have appropriated languages of consumption to make sense of their actions and described themselves and others as "consumers". There is need for a greater and more subtle distinction between the processes that we, as historians, want to describe as purchases, digestion or services (all consumption now) and the activities and subjects which historical subjects themselves thought of as consumption, and the boundaries that distinguished these from other spheres of life.

## Notes

1. E.g. H.-U. Wehler in a paper on "Deutsches Bürgertum nach 1945" at Bielefeld University, June 2001, now in H.-U. Wehler (ed.), *Konflikte zu Beginn des 21. Jahrhunderts* (Munich 2003), chap. 9. For a different kind of social history in Germany, see W. Schivelbusch, *Tastes of Paradise: A Social History of Spices, Stimulants, and Intoxicants* (New York 1992; orig. 1980).

2. As the sociologist Don Slater has observed, this "is a disappointing conclusion, one that recapitulates some now familiar prejudices and wishful thinking – that somehow the working class (or women or others) are unclouded by ideology (or by 'mythology' in Barthes) because they are compelled by real necessity, by a functional relation to things, or because they know things through direct labour, through their hands". *Consumer Culture and Modernity* (Cambridge 1997), 163.

3. For important exceptions, see P. Bailey, *Popular Culture and Performance in the Victorian City* (Cambridge 1998); F. Mort, *Cultures of Consumption: Masculinities and Social Space in Late Twentieth-century Britain* (London 1996) and C. Breward, *The Hidden Consumer: Masculinities, Fashion and City Life 1860–1914* (Manchester 1999).

4. D. Miller (ed.), *Acknowledging Consumption* (London 1995), which remains the best critical entry into debates in the social sciences and humanities. See also now the second edition of Ben Fine, *The World of Consumption* (London 2002).

5. Synergy that is well reflected in J. Brewer and R. Porter (eds), *Consumption and the World of Goods* (London 1993).

6. P. Stearns, "Stages of Consumerism: Recent Work on the Issues of Periodization", *Journal of Modern History*, 69 (1997), 102–17.

7. P. Stearns, *Consumerism in World History: The Global Transformation of Desire* (London 2001), ix.

8. E.g. see J.M. Segal, "Consumer Expenditures and the Growth of Need-required Income" in D. Crocker and T. Linden (eds), *Ethics of Consumption: The Good Life, Justice, and Global Stewardship* (Lanham 1998), 176–97; and the debate in J. Schor (ed.), *Do Americans Shop Too Much? A New Democracy Forum* (Boston 2000).

9. D. Miller, *The Dialectics of Shopping* (Chicago 2001), 55f.

10. See F. Trentmann, "Civil Society, Commerce and the "Citizen Consumer": Popular Meanings of Free Trade in Modern Britain" in F. Trentmann (ed.), *Paradoxes of Civil Society: New Perspectives on Modern German and British History* (New York 2003), 2nd edn, 306-31; F. Trentmann, "National Identity and Consumer Politics: Free Trade and Tariff Reform" in D. Winch and P.K. O'Brien (eds), *The Political Economy of British Historical Experience, 1688–1914* (Oxford 2002), 215–42; E. Furlough and C. Strikwerda (eds.), *Consumerism against Capitalism?* (Oxford 1999).

11. D. Vogel, *Trading Up: Consumer and Environmental Regulation in a Global Economy* (Cambridge, MA 1995).

12. For critiques, see A. Appadurai (ed.), *The Social Life of Things: Commodities in Cultural Perspective* (Cambridge 1986), 3–63; M. Bevir and F. Trentmann (eds), *Markets in Historical Contexts: Ideas and Politics in the Modern World* (Cambridge 2004).

13. J. Gronow and A. Warde (eds), *Ordinary Consumption* (London 2001).

14. C.A. Bayly, "The Origins of Swadeshi (Home Industry): Cloth and Indian Society, 1700–1930" in Appadurai, *Social Life of Things*, op. cit., 300 and C.A. Bayly, "'Archaic' and 'Modern'" Globalization in the Eurasian and African Arena, c. 1750–1850" in A.G. Hopkins (ed.), *Globalization in World History* (London 2002), 47–73.

15. G. Clunas, *Superfluous Things: Material Culture and Social Status in Early Modern China* (Chicago 1991).

16. K. Pomerartz, *The Great Divergence: China, Europe, and the Making of the Modern World Economy* (Princeton, NJ 2000), 117–22. Cf. Prasannan Parthasarthi, "The Great Divergence", *Past and Present*, vol. 176 (2002).

17. Stearns, *Consumerism*, op. cit., 112.

18. P. Maclachlan, *Consumer Politics in Postwar Japan* (New York 2002). See also L.C. Nelson, *Measured Excess: Status, Gender, and Consumer Nationalism in South Korea* (New York 2000).

19. Stearns, *Consumerism*, op. cit., 141.

20. This argument is at odds with U. Wyrwa's idea that "'consumer society' can be a useful analytical concept only if it preserves its original critical impulse and takes consumption's destructive aspects into account". "Consumption and Consumer Society" in S. Strasser, C. McGovern and M. Judt (eds), *Getting and Spending: European and American Consumer Societies in the Twentieth Century* (Cambridge 1998), 447. See also M. Prinz (ed.), *Der lange Weg in den Überfluss: Anfänge und Entwicklung der Konsumgesellschaft seit der Vormoderne* (Paderborn 2003).

21. H.-G. Haupt, *Konsum und Handel: Europa im 19. und 20. Jahrhundert* (Göttingen 2002), 20f.

22. Ibid., 25, 26, 29.

23. See also M. Finn, "Scotch Drapers and the Politics of Modernity: Gender, Class and National Identity in the Victorian Tally Trade" in Daunton and Hilton, *Politics of Consumption*, op. cit., 89–107.

24. B. Gunter, *Understanding the Older Consumer: The Grey Market* (London 1998); P. Thane, *Old Age in English History: Past Experiences, Present Issues* (Oxford 2000); J. Vincent, "Consumers, Identity and Old Age", *Education and Ageing*, 14, 2 (1999), 141–581 M. Nava and A. McRobie (eds), *Gender and Generation* (London 1984); Stephen Kline, *Out of the Garden: Toys, TV, and Children's Culture in the Age of Marketing* (London 1993); B. Gunter and A. Furnham, *Children as Consumers: A Psychological Analysis of the Young People's Market* (London 1998).

25. F. Trentmann, "Bread, Milk and Democracy: Consumption and Citizenship in Twentieth-century Britain" in Daunton and Hilton, *Politics of Consumption*, op. cit., 129–63; G. Scott, *Feminism and the Politics of Working Women: The Women's Co-operative Guild, 1880s to the Second World War* (London 1998).

26. K.K. Sklar, "The Consumer's White Label Campaign of the National Consumers' League" in Strasser *et al.*, *Getting and Spending*, op. cit., 17–35; F. Trentmann, "Civil Society, Commerce and the 'Citizen Consumer'" in Trentmann, *Paradoxes*, op. cit., 306–31; N. Thomson, "Social Opulence, Private Asceticism" in Daunton and Hilton, *Politics of Consumption*, op. cit., 51–68. E. Furlough, *Consumer Cooperation in France. The Politics of Consumption*, 1834–1930 (Ithaca 1991).

27. In the NCL's official history, as quoted in L. Storrs, *Civilizing Capitalism: The National Consumer's League, Women's Activism, and Labor Standards in the New Deal Era* (Chapel Hill, NC 2000), 22.

28. See P. Maclachlan and F. Trentmann, "Civilising Markets: Traditions of Consumer Politics in Twentieth-century Japan, Britain, and America" in M. Bevir and F. Trentmann (eds), *Markets in Historical Contexts*, op. cit., chap. 9.

29. With 23.5 per cent for education, and 19.8 per cent for entertainment, leisure and travel, and well below, durables with a mere 8.7 per cent; from a 1993 national survey cited in S. Kim, "Changing Lifestyles and Consumption Patterns of the South Korean Middle-class and New Generations" in C. Beng-Huat (ed.), *Consumption in Asia: Lifestyles and Identities* (London 2000), 71f.

30. H. Kaelble, "Europäische Besonderheiten des Massenkonsums" in H. Siegrist, H. Kaelble and J. Kocka (eds), *Europäische Konsumgeschichte: Zur Gesellschafts- und Kulturgeschichte des Konsums* (Frankfurt/Main 1998), 169–204; V. de Grazia, "Changing Consumption Regimes in Europe, 1930–1970" in Strasser, *Getting and Spending*, op. cit., 59–83.

31. See J.A. Tooze, "Endless Possibilities? Historical Alternatives to Mass Production Fifteen Years On", *Social History*, 25 (2000), 247–50.

32. U. Spiekermann, *Basis der Konsumgesellschaft: Entstehung und Entwicklung des modernen Kleinhandels in Deutschland*, 1850–1914 (München 1999).

33. Ibid., 381.

34. The infant profession of advertising had to manoeuvre within a cross-fire of competing projects of modernity and tradition, and its successful expansion depended partly on its ability to incorporate some traditional criticism, for example by championing aesthetic communication; see C. Lamberty, *Reklame in Deutschland, 1890–1914: Wahrnehmung, Professionalisierung und Kritik der Wirtschaftswerbung* (Berlin 2000).

35. See C. Walsh, "The Newness of the Department Store: A View from the Eighteenth Century" in G. Crossick and S. Jaumain (eds), *Cathedrals of Consumption: The European Department Store, 1850–1939* (Aldershot 1999), 46–71; and M. Hilton, "Review Article: Class, Consumption and the Public Sphere', *Journal of Contemporary History*, 35, 4 (October 2000), 655–66. J. Benson and L. Ugolini (eds), *A Nation of Shopkeepers* (London 2003).

36. A. Clarke, "'Mother Swapping': The Trafficking of Nearly New Children's Wear" in P. Jackson, M. Lowe, D. Miller and F. Mort (eds), *Commercial Cultures: Economies, Practices, Spaces* (New York 2000), 85–100.

37. Spiekerman, *Konsumgesellschaft*, op. cit., 596ff. N. Gregson and L. Crewe, *Second-Hand Cultures* (forthcoming).

38. For the transition from critiques of mass consumption to its acceptance in mid-twentieth century Germany, see most recently, D. Briesen, *Warenhaus, Massenkonsum und Sozialmoral* (Frankfurt/Main 2001), albeit with a narrow focus on select academic and conservative élites.

39. Recent historical studies of tourism have tried to capitalize on the seminal sociological works by Urry and MacCannell on the centrality of touristic sensibilities for the experiential dimension of modern consumption: S. Baranowski and E. Furlough (eds), *Being Elsewhere: Tourism, Consumer Culture and Identity in Modern Europe and North America* (Ann Arbor, MI 2001).

40. J. Fiske, *Reading the Popular* (Boston 1989) and also M. de Certeau, *The Practice of Everyday Life* (Berkeley, CA 1984).

41. E. Rappaport, *Shopping for Pleasure: Women in the Making of London's West End* (Princeton 2000), 69. See also M. Finn, "Working-class Women and the Contest for Consumer Control in Victorian County Courts", *Past and Present*, 161 (1998), 116–54 and her forthcoming book *The Character of Credit*.

42. Rappaport, *Shopping*, op. cit., 180.

43. Ibid., 187.

44. Cf. A. Rabinbach, *The Human Motor: Energy, Fatigue, and the Rise of Modernity* (Berkeley, CA 1990).

45. J. Tanner, *Fabrikmahlzeit: Ernährungswissenschaft, Industriearbeit und Volksernährung in der Schweiz 1890–1950* (Zürich 1999), 315.

46. M. Aglietta, *A Theory of Capitalist Regulation: The US Experience* (London 1979).

47. Tanner, *Fabrikmahlzeit*, op. cit., 245ff.

48. Ibid., 160f.

49. A. Murcott, "Food and Nutrition in Post-war Britain" in J. Obelkevich and P. Caterall (eds), *Understanding Post-war British Society* (London 1994), 155–64. Cf. D.J. Oddy, *From Plain Fare to Fusion Food. British Diet from the 1890s to the 1990s* (Woodbridge, Suffolk 2003).

50. M. Wildt, *Vom kleinen Wohlstand: Eine Konsumgeschichte der fünfziger Jahre* (Frankfurt/Main 1996).

51. F. Mort, "The Politics of Consumption" in S. Hall and M. Jacques (eds), *New Times: The Changing Face of Politics in the 1990s* (London 1989), 160–72; de Grazia, *Sex of Things*, op. cit.; Daunton and Hilton, *Politics of Consumption*, op. cit.; Strasser *et al.*, *Getting and Spending*, op. cit.; Bevir and Trentmann, *Markets in Historical Contexts*, op. cit.; M. Bevir and F. Trentmann (eds), *Critiques of Capital in Modern Britain and America* (London 2002); M. Jacobs, "'Democracy's Third Estate'. New Deal Politics and the Construction of a 'Consuming Public'", *International Labor and Working-Class History*, 55 (1999), 27–51; see also the forthcoming books by L. Black, *The Political Culture of the Left in Affluent Britain, 1951–64* and M. Hilton, *Consumerism in Twentieth-century Britain*.

52. I. Zweiniger-Bargieloswka, *Austerity in Britain: Rationing, Controls, and Consumption 1939–1955* (Oxford 2000); H. Berghoff (ed.), *Konsumpolitik: die Regulierung des privaten Verbrauchs im 20. Jahrhundert* (Göttingen 1999).

53. L. Cohen, *A Consumer's Republic: The Politics of Mass Consumption in Post-war America* (New York 2003).

54. C. Nonn, "Vom Konsumentenprotest zum Konsens: Lebensmittelverbraucher und Agrarpolitik in Deutschland, 1900–1950" in Berghoff (ed.), *Konsumpolitik*, op. cit., 23–46.

55. Trentmann, "Bread, Milk and Democracy" in Daunton and Hilton, *Politics of Consumption*, op. cit.

56. See D. Gerber, *Law and Competition in Twentieth-century Europe: Protecting Prometheus* (Oxford 2001); S. Wilks, *In the Public Interest: Competition Policy and the Monopolies and Mergers Commission* (Manchester 1999).

57. See also H. Jones and M. Kandiah (eds), *The Myth of Consensus: New Views on British History, 1945–64* (Basingstoke 1996).

58. How much of this is a causal correlation? As Labour's increase of the vote from 47.8 percent in 1945 to 48.8 per cent in 1951 suggests, rationing and controls did not hurt Labour; the Conservatives did increase theirs from 39.8 per cent to 48 per cent, but this gain was made largely by absorbing the Liberal vote. As Zweiniger-Bargielowska points out, the swing in 1951 to the Conservatives was more pronounced amongst women than men. Yet, to what degree was this relative decline in female Labour preference since 1945 due to austerity, and to what degree was it a return to pre-war patterns with 1945 being the aberrant outcome? As she acknowledges, it was only in 1945 that Labour had ever obtained a small lead among female voters.

59. E. Ross, *Love and Toil: Motherhood in Outcast London, 1870–1918* (Oxford 1993).

60. Zweiniger-Bargielowska, *Austerity*, op. cit., 87. The evidence, largely taken from opinion polls and social surveys, is ambivalent and inconclusive, with high instances of "don't know" or "unable to say".

61. Ibid., 115.

62. See S. Garon, "Savings Promotion and the Dissemination of Economic Knowledge: Transnational Insights from the Japanese Experience" in M. Daunton and F. Trentmann (eds), *Worlds of Political Economy* (forthcoming).

63. See M. Roodhouse, "Black Market Activity in Britain, 1939–1955", Cambridge PhD thesis 2003.

64. For this, see C. Beauchamp, "Getting *Your Money's Worth*: American Models for the Remaking of the Consumer Interest in Britain, 1930s–1960s" in Bevir and Trentmann, *Critiques of Capital*, op. cit., 127–50.

65. M. Hilton, "Consumer Politics in Post-war Britain" in Daunton and Hilton, *Politics of Consumption*, op. cit., 241–59; Hilton, *Consumerism*, op. cit.

66. J.K. Galbraith, *The Affluent Society* (London 1969); J. Schor, *The Overspent American: Upscaling, Downshifting and the New Consumer* (New York 1998); R. Frank, *Luxury Fever: Why Money Fails to Satisfy in an Era of Excess* (Princeton, NJ 1999); M. Sandel, *Democracy's Discontent* (Cambridge, MA 1996), A. Schäfer, "German Historicism, Progressive Social Thought, and the Interventionist State in the US Since the 1880s" in Bevir and Trentmann, *Markets in Historical Contexts*, op. cit., chap. 8.

67. Fine, *World of Consumption*, op. cit.

68. Cohen, *A Consumer's Republic*, op. cit., 175. For the civil rights' politics of the NCL in the 1930s, see Storrs, *Civilizing Capitalism*, op. cit.; for the 1960s, see F. Kornbluh, "To Fulfil their 'Rightly Needs': Consumerism and the National Welfare Rights Movement", *Radical History Review*, 69 (1997), 76–113.

69. See here especially, R. Putnam, *Bowling Alone: The Collapse and Revival of American Community* (New York 2000); cf. the debate in R. Kuttner (ed.), *Ticking Time Bombs: The New Conservative Assaults on Democracy* (New York 1996).

70. L. Cohen, *Making a New Deal: Industrial Workers in Chicago, 1919–1939* (Cambridge 1990).

71. J. Clammer, *Contemporary Urban Japan: A Sociology of Consumption* (Oxford 1997); Maclachlan, *Consumer Politics in Post-war Japan*, op. cit.

72. D. Davis (ed.), *The Consumer Revolution in Urban China* (Berkeley, CA 2000).

73. G.A. Almond and S. Verba, *The Civic Culture: Political Attitudes and Democracy in Five Nations* (Princeton, NJ 1963).

74. J. Davidson, *Courtesans and Fishcakes: The Consuming Passions of Classical Athens* (London 1997).

75. Since I wrote this article, a recent Mori survey for the National Consumer Council in Britain found an almost even balance of motivations behind consumer activism: 24 per cent of responses were "to support the community", 23 per cent "to help other people", 22 per cent "got very angry about service provided", and 20 per cent "to help support myself/my family". NCC, *Consumer Activism Omnibus Survey* (London 2002). Note, this research presented the people polled with a ready definition of the consumer "whether this is as a shopper, a patient, a passenger, or someone who uses water and energy services", reflecting trends discussed above. It would be interesting to know to what degree people themselves have incorporated this broadening of consumer identity.

# 16

# Discovery-Oriented Consumer Research

**William D. Wells**

**Source:** *Journal of Consumer Research* 19 (1993): 498–504.

The first years of the *Journal of Consumer Research (JCR)* were heady times indeed. Initiated by 10 professional associations, *JCR* was meant to be "an interdisciplinary communications vehicle for theory, empirical research and methodology of the study of consumer behavior" (Frank 1974).

Ronald Frank, *JCR's* first editor, construed consumer behavior in the broadest of terms:

> What do we mean by consumer behavior? For our purposes, consumer behavior is broadly construed to include media and family planning behavior, occupational choices, mobility, determinants of fertility rates, attitudes toward and use of social services and determinants of educational attainment.
>
> Studies of the purchase, consumption or usage of durables or nondurables including financial assets such as stocks, bonds, and insurance, or services such as medical care and police are welcome in *JCR* as well as studies which focus on brand or package size consumption for a particular product or upon broad aggregates such as total consumer expenditures.
>
> *JCR* will also include material concerned not only with the behavior of households and individuals but also with other parties in their roles as purchasers, if not consumers, of goods and services such as government agencies, hospitals, manufacturers, retailers and wholesalers. [Frank 1974, pp. i, ii]

Within that wide domain, *JCR* was to be "the first journal to which professionals sharing an interest in consumer behavior across disciplines send their material" (Frank 1974): no small task.

At about the same time, the new Association for Consumer Research (ACR) announced equally ambitious goals:

1. To provide a forum for exchange of ideas among those interested in consumer behavior research in academic disciplines, in government at all levels from local through national, in private business, and in other sectors such as nonprofit organizations and foundations.
2. To stimulate research focusing on a better understanding of consumer behavior from a variety of perspectives.
3. To disseminate research findings and other contributions to the understanding of consumer behavior through professional seminars, conferences and publications. [ACR Constitution, as quoted in Pratt 1974, p. 4]

The hubris of that era rings through these words by Sheth: "Within a very short period of time, we seem to have firmly laid the foundation for building a distinct discipline of buyer behavior which will neither be a subsystem of marketing nor that of any of the other older social sciences. [An] even more pleasant observation is that we seem to have achieved better with respect to richness of thinking, comprehensiveness of theorizing, and testing of theories in naturalistic and realistic settings than many of the older behavioral science disciplines in their comparative periods of development" (Sheth 1972, pp. 565–566).

Sheth went on to predict: "Within a decade, it is very likely that other disciplines will be actively interested in buyer behavior and consequently borrow from it a set of concepts and research tools [and] sooner or later, the hard sciences are likely to be exposed to, and interested in, buyer behavior. When that happens, it is equally inevitable that they will extensively borrow both the substantive findings and research methodology [of consumer research]" (Sheth 1972, pp. 571, 573).

A key element of this forecast was Sheth's belief that consumer research would address "critical areas of human behavior" and that consumer researchers would "test their theories in naturalistic and realistic settings." Real solutions to real problems would prevent the "crisis of relevance" that had harmed the social sciences even then (Sheth 1972, p. 572). With an established intellectual base and with a constituency that included business, government, and foundations as both clients and collaborators, the future seemed clear and bright.

It is not that problems were ignored. In a 1972 review, Kollat, Blackwell, and Engel noted that, while 1968–1972 output was "nearly as large as the total body of knowledge that existed at the beginning of the period," consumer research had made "no progress" in standardizing variables or in setting priorities and only "limited progress" in testing theories, establishing a tradition of replication, broadening horizons, or exploiting the advantages of longitudinal designs (Kollat, Blackwell, and Engel 1972, pp. 576, 583).

Four years later, Jacoby decried a litany of sins: misuse of measuring instruments borrowed from other disciplines; lack of attention to reliability and validity; single-shot, nonprogrammatic studies; confusion of correlation with causation; lack of replication; lack of attention to important social issues; over-reliance on verbal (as distinguished from behavioral) data; and preoccupation with the antecedents of brand choice, especially critical of research motivated by "the availability of easy-to-use measuring instruments, the existence of more-or-less willing subject populations, the convenience of the computer, and/or the almost toy-like nature of sophisticated quantitative techniques" (Jacoby 1976, p. 2).

These shortcomings led him to declare that "much too large a proportion of the contemporary consumer research literature is not worth the paper it is printed on or the time it takes to read it" (Jacoby 1976, p. 2).

Despite all that, the mood was upbeat. New courses were attracting new students. New textbooks were describing interesting new work. In government and business, consumer research was gaining credibility. It seemed only a matter of time before Kollat, Blackwell, and Engel's reservations, and Jacoby's dark verdict, would seem dated and quaint.

## This is Now

After nearly two decades, which of the early goals were met, and which are yet to be achieved? As we now know, Sheth's forecast was a little premature. Consumer research has not "achieved better" than the other social sciences with respect to "richness of thinking, comprehensiveness of theorizing, and testing of theories in naturalistic and realistic settings," and it has not yet become the methodological Mecca to which others turn.

Although *JCR* and ACR are now cited by outside authors, the flow is far more in than out (Cote, Leong, and Cote 1991; Leong 1989). Replication is still rare. Validity is still uncertain. And one-shot studies of more or less willing subject populations are still in vogue. The *Journal of Consumer Research* has not become a genuinely interdisciplinary journal. And ACR has not become the central forum for consumer behavior broadly defined.

What could change all that? What could broaden our horizons? What could give the discipline its own creative base? What could make *JCR* the first journal to which professionals sharing an interest in consumer behavior send their material? What could make ACR the catalyst for the next great discovery in consumer research?

A close and critical reading of *JCR* and of ACR's *Proceedings* suggests five guidelines that would advance those worthy goals: Leave home. Forsake mythodology. Reach out. Start small and stay real. Research backward.

### Guideline 1: Leave Home

In an analytical discussion of the consumer research agenda, Johan Arndt (1976) noted that consumer decisions have five parts:

I. Problem recognition
II. Search for information to evaluate alternatives
  A. Internal search
  B. External search
III. Implementation of the purchase
IV. Physical consumption
V. Postconsumption activities

He also noted that decisions differ in importance:

I. Acquisition of strategic items
II. Central budget allocation decisions
III. Generic product or service decisions
IV. Variant selection

By "strategic items," Arndt meant items that have life-altering effects – for instance, a college education, a new home, a new child. By "central budget allocation decisions" he meant allocation among important groups of products and services – new furniture for the living room instead of a vacation trip. By "generic product or service decisions" he meant specific purchases within those groups of products and services. And by "variant selection" he meant brand choice.

**Figure 1** Arndt's Diagram

| | Recognition | Search | Purchase | Consumption | Post-consumption |
|---|---|---|---|---|---|
| Strategic | | | | | |
| Central | | | | | |
| Genetic | | | | | |
| Variant | | | | | |

*Source*: Figure adapted from Arndt 1976, p. 215

Cross classifying stages by levels creates a matrix of consumer choice (Fig. 1). As Arndt and others (e.g., Belk 1987, 1991; Holbrook 1985; Jacoby 1976; Kassarjian 1978; Olson 1982; Pollay 1972) have noted, academic consumer researchers spend most of their time on the early-stage, low-level decisions in the lower-left-hand corner of this chart.

One way to discover more about consumer behavior would be to move upward and to the right. This territory includes life-altering decisions. It also includes the whole consumption sequence, from preconsideration to ultimate result. Fifteen years later, Elizabeth Hirschman (1991, p. 4) urged us to leave home another way:

> As we meet there today, comfortable not only in our attractive surroundings, but in our personal affluence and success, let us not ignore some uncomfortable statistics about other people's realities as consumers. At the present time, 100,000 homeless people dwell in the cities and towns of America, the wealthiest country on earth. . . . What have we done to help their plight?
>
> There are currently 2 to 3 million cocaine and crack addicts in the United States. 375,000 drug-addicted babies were born in 1989, alone. . . . What have *we* done to help them? . . .
>
> Every year over 10 million American consumers suffer financial losses from their addiction to gambling and over 500,000 file for personal bankruptcy as a result of credit card abuse. . . .
>
> There are currently 10 million alcoholics and 80 million cigarette smokers in the United States. . . . Every year 25,000 people die as a result of alcohol-related traffic accidents; and 20,000 consumers die from the disease of alcoholism, itself. . . .
>
> All of these disturbing and disturbed behaviors result from consumption gone wrong. . . . Consumers could likely recover from these damaging behaviors, if adequate research were conducted into their origin and treatment.

> We are a bright, and talented, and productive group. How much we could accomplish if we would turn even a portion of our talents toward understanding and ameliorating the dark side of consumer behavior.

Finally, the discipline would surely benefit from more interaction with the world outside the United States. Of the first 23 format ACR conferences, 21 were in North America, while only two – one in Singapore in 1985 and one in Amsterdam in 1992 – were not. Given the sharp regional differences in consumers' opportunities, resources, and perceptions, it seems obvious that the franchise would be extended and enlightened by more sophisticated appreciation of consumer behavior throughout the world (Fornell 1992; Graham *et al.* 1988; McCracken 1986, 1988; Mehta and Belk 1991; Takada and Jain 1991; Wallendorf and Arnould 1988; Zandpour, Chang, and Catalano 1992).

One does not need to believe that Arndt's categories are comprehensive or mutually exclusive to know that major discoveries lie upward and to the right. One does not need to be a seer to know that effective response to Hirschman's challenge would avert any "crisis of relevance" that might otherwise take place. And one does not need international experience to know that worldwide purviews would increase our range and depth.

Academic research on consumer behavior would be stronger, more creative, more interesting, and more valuable if researchers would pay attention to consumer behavior more broadly defined.

### Guideline 2: Forsake Mythodology

Consumer research has its own myths, inherited from the past. These myths isolate researchers from reality and impede discovery of how real things really work.

*Students Represent Consumers.* As everyone knows, students are not typical consumers. When we ignore this fact we can easily be incorrect. Robert Ferber, *JCR's* second editor, was absolutely clear on this point: "It is not sufficient to say something like, 'the subjects for this study were 83 students at Lower Slobovia State University' and then proceed to formulate and test highly sophisticated behavior models. If the researcher cannot justify the use of that group in terms of [relevance to the problem and representativeness of the sample] there is no reason why the GIGO principle should not be applied immediately, namely, 'garbage in, garbage out'" (Ferber 1977, pp. 57–58).

Nine years later, David Sears hit the same mark:

> Undergraduates usually come from a very narrow age range and are concentrated all the upper levels of educational background.
>
> Their social and political attitudes tend to be considerably less crystallized at this stage than later in life.
>
> They also tend to be substantially more egocentric than older adults.
>
> They have a stronger need for peer approval, manifested in dependency, conformity and overidentification with peers.

> They have been carefully preselected for having unusually adept cognitive skills.
>
> They have also been selected for compliance to authority.
>
> They have greater geographical and social mobility, and later entry into the work force and family life. [Sears 1986, p. 521]

These differences affect research outcomes in many ways. Age and education – and variables correlated with age and education – get inadequate attention, and other less important variables get too much weight. Students' cognitive skills, peer relationships, family relationships, and family responsibilities mediate a wide range of independent variables. These powerful interactions place student-based conclusions at substantial risk. And, possibly most important, overuse of students focuses research content on products that students buy, like CDs, soft drinks, and ballpoint pens. This restriction highlights the lowest portion of Arndt's diagram and obviates the tasks that Hirschman challenged us to undertake.

This is not to say that findings based on students are always wrong. It is only to say that findings based on students are always suspect. Our findings would be substantially more credible if students were not so often the first and only choice.

*The Laboratory Represents the Environment.* The laboratory misrepresents the real world in several important ways. First, it permits control that is impossible outside. When that control produces laboratory-only circumstances, generalizations to the real world can be wrong.

Here is one example: in the laboratory, very interesting television programs interfere with cognitive processing of the commercials they contain (Schumann and Thorson 1990). This finding has led to suggestions that very interesting programs might be very poor carriers of advertising.

Yet field studies show that very interesting television programs are very good carriers of advertising (Clancy and Kweskin 1971; Home Testing Institute 1963; Priemer 1983). The explanation for the contradiction is that laboratory conditions create an artificial, even level of attention, while normal in-home viewing conditions do not. Under normal in-home viewing conditions, very interesting programs attract and hold high levels of attention. Increased attention carries over to the advertising and swamps any decrement that interference might take away (Thorson 1990). Thus, a finding that was valid in the laboratory led to spurious generalization to the world outside.

A second difference between the laboratory and the environment is in the content of "schemer schema": "When someone encounters a sales message or promotional or pricing move . . . the response strategy they select is contingent on . . . their working hypotheses about selling or marketing tactics. To be sure, their schema about [the specific product] *per se* is activated. But the control schema – 'what I believe about likely persuasion and promotion strategies' – is first activated, and that guides the situation-specific process of response" (Wright 1986, p. 2).

Schemer schema also operate in the laboratory; but, in the laboratory, the schemer is the experimenter. When subjects encounter sales messages or pricing or promotional moves in the laboratory, their responses are contingent on their working hypotheses about the intentions of the experimenter. To the degree that these working hypotheses are unique, so also are the "situation-specific processes of response."

In the real world, consumers know that the schemer is a stranger who may do them harm. They also know that their choices may have long-range consequences and that they must be vigilant in their own defense.

In the laboratory, subjects know that the schemer is an experimenter who is seeking "truth." They believe (correctly) that the experimenter will not intentionally harm them and that the experiment is intended to have no permanent effect. To the extent that these "working hypotheses" are laboratory specific, the laboratory misrepresents real-world response. This misrepresentation is not a mere "demand effect" that can be evaded with "manipulation checks." It is a distinction that cannot be erased.

A third difference between the laboratory and the real world is that an experiment has a sudden beginning and a sudden end. As economists continually remind us, most nontrivial consumer behavior is contingent on current or expected changes in life circumstances and mid- to long-range expectations as to how long these changes will last. When experiments focus on instant action, they starkly underestimate these critical effects.

The differences between the laboratory and the environment are so powerful that extrapolations are always problematic. Maybe the laboratory findings will have external validity, and maybe they will not.

We have inherited a myth that says that internal validity is adequate and external validity, if any, is up to someone else. That myth is distinctly inappropriate for consumer research. Consumer research promises to increase our knowledge of consumer behavior. No matter how elegantly fabricated, an experiment does not add to that knowledge until its limits have been tested in the world outside.

Finally, the laboratory is hindered by an inverse correlation between importance and control. Like overuse of student subjects, this inverse correlation directs disproportionate resources to the lowest portion of Arndt's matrix of consumer choice.

The laboratory has one exclusive asset: it is the best way to separate cause from effect. But neither that unquestioned asset nor the trappings of "science" should beguile us into believing that internal validity will suffice. That is why Sheth believed that "realistic and naturalistic settings" would be so vital to the future of our work.

*Statistical Significance Confers Real Significance.* It is easy to see why managers misunderstand "statistical significance." After all, if a finding has passed all that official-looking certification, it ought to be right. It is not easy to see why researchers make the same mistake. Although researchers know better, they often conclude that "significant" relationships are also strong: " 'Everyone' knows that all [statistical significance] means is that the effect is not nil, and nothing more. Yet how often do we see such a result to be taken to mean, at least implicitly, that the effect is significant, that is, important, large. If a result is highly significant, say $p < .001$, the temptation to make this misinterpretation becomes all but irresistible" (Cohen 1990, p. 1307).

This mistake is particularly dangerous in theoretical work. Most theories imply strong relationships among variables. When findings are statistically significant, the theory is said to be "confirmed." But of course, a statistically significant relationship might be a strong relationship, or it might be very weak (Chow 1988; Cohen 1965; Cooper 1981; Rozeboom 1960; Sawyer and Peter 1983); $p < .05$ does not indicate a strong effect.

Furthermore, a great many experiments compare one "experimental" group with one "control" group. If the difference between the groups is significant at $p < .05$, the (unstated) conclusion is that the effect goes on and on forever, in the same direction and at the same rate. But many kinds of consumer behavior follow the law of diminishing returns: a little makes a big difference, and a little more does not. Others follow the Three Bears' law: too little is too little, too much is too much, and just enough is just right. Under those common circumstances, an assumption of infinite linearity makes little sense.

Critics have noted the weak (and sometimes missing) correspondence between theories of consumer behavior and the behavior of real consumers in the real world. How can that correspondence ever increase when we ask no more than whether effects are nil? How can we discover the true nature of consumer behavior if we ignore effect size and shape?

*When Suitably Disguised, Correlation Becomes Causation.* Elementary textbooks warn against assuming that correlation means causation. They explain that *X* may have caused *Y*, *Y* may have caused *X*, or both may have been caused by something else.

More advanced textbooks say exactly the same thing. However, as more variables enter the picture, an insidious change takes place. In multiple regression, for example, a set of *X's* "predict" *Y*, even when all the variables were measured at the same time. And each *X* receives a weight that indicates "importance" or "influence." Suddenly – even though *Y* may have caused all the *X's*, or something else may have caused the whole works – the *X's* have become causes, and the weights have become degrees of effect (Henderson and Denison 1989).

In path analysis, LISREL, and other "causal" models, the illusion becomes more complete. Now the *X's* "influence" each other and jointly "influence" *Y* – and the data are all hidden in the model's inner parts. If the model "fits," it is said to describe "causal" pathways. If it does not quite fit, post hoc explanations keep it safe. Test-retest reliabilities are not usually investigated, nor are alternative explanations of the observed events.

What is needed is a return to the assumption that *X* may have caused *Y*, *Y* may have caused *X*, and both may have been caused by something else. What is also needed is return to the basic requirement that competing explanations be taken seriously and given reasonable amounts of mental space. The more complex the model, the more critical are these cautions to the credibility of our work.

*Mentioning Limitations Makes Them Go Away.* Many journal articles conclude with sections on "limitations." If taken seriously, the limitations would invalidate the findings. It is surprising to outsiders that the authors then go on to state broad, general conclusions – as though the limitations had vanished on being confessed.

This practice leads to "knowledge" that consists of dubious conclusions, and it breeds waste and disappointment in subsequent research. When Jacoby (1976, p. 2) declared that "too large a proportion of the contemporary research literature is not worth the paper it is printed on or the time it takes to read it," this was part of what he meant.

*Five Myths. So* here we have five myths that cultivate the "crisis of relevance" that Sheth had hoped we would avoid: Students represent consumers. The laboratory represents the environment. Statistical significance confers real significance. Correlation means causation. And limitations, once mentioned, simply go away.

We can and should forsake these myths. They do more harm than good. The next three guidelines outline strategies for doing that and for establishing conditions in which discoveries can take place.

### Guideline 3: Reach Out

To judge from Table 1, consumer research is a branch of marketing or a branch of social psychology. Yet both Arndt's diagram and Frank's initial editorial suggest that other academic disciplines have much to add.

Here is one example. In *JCR*'s first issue, Jean Crockett – an economist – noted that expectations affect every choice:

> Even in the pre-Keynsian age economists were aware that expectations are important, not only as to their content but also in terms of the certainty with which they are held. . . .
>
> An observed change in an economic variable may sometimes generate an expectation of return toward the previous level (when the change is believed to result from purely temporary factors) or an expectation that the new level

**Table 1** Cross-disciplinary References in the *Journal of Consumer Research*, 1974–1988

| Discipline | Amount |
|---|---|
| Psychology (%) | 26.8 |
| Marketing (%) | 20.4 |
| Consumer research (%) | 18.0 |
| Economics (%) | 5.6 |
| Mathematics and statistics (%) | 4.2 |
| Sociology (%) | 4.1 |
| Communication and journalism (%) | 3.8 |
| Family and home economics (%) | 1.9 |
| Business (general) (%) | 1.7 |
| Social science (general) (%) | 1.6 |
| Anthropology (%) | 1.5 |
| Medicine (%) | 1.2 |
| Culture, humanities, and the arts (%) | 1.0 |
| Other (%) | 8.2 |
| Total citations (*n*) | 6,867 |

*Source*: Data are from Leong (1989).

will be maintained (when the change is due to a one-shot shift in structure, establishing a new equilibrium which is promptly attained) or an expectation of further change in the same direction (when the causal factors are continuing to shift or when the full effects of a shift are realized only gradually over time). [Crockett 1974, p. 9]

These comments remind us that expected change and expected permanence of change play pivotal roles in consumer behavior. Yet many of our current models omit expectations altogether, and most experiments attempt to rule them out. When we discount expectations – and other economic concepts (Becker 1976; Deaton and Muellbauer 1980; Murphy and Staples 1979) – we ignore causes that have powerful effects.

Sociologists understand many of the forces that influence consumers. Not the least of these forces are the profound effects of cultural and ethnic background, age, and social class (Coleman 1983; Katz and Lazarsfeld 1955; Martineau 1957, 1958). With more acute awareness of sociological models and sociological methods, consumer researchers would see new approaches to old problems. And they would not build universal theories on student-based results.

In the 1980s, ideas from anthropology and ethnography generated healthy controversy, new vitality, and new and important ways of thinking about consumer behavior (Belk 1991; Hirschman 1989; McCracken 1986, 1988). In one sense these imports are radical. In another, they revisit our roots. Realistic and naturalistic settings, attention to important choices, focus on the real behavior of real consumers, and willingness to experiment with unusual methods are squarely in line with the aspirations that brought ACR and *JCR* to life. Still in the offing, and possibly just as evocative, are imports from historical analysis (Nevett 1991) and from humanities and the arts (Deighton, Romer, and McQueen 1989; Harris *et al.* 1986; Stern 1989, 1991; Stern and Gallagher 1991).

The great value of outsiders is of course their outside point of view. Often, when a problem seems intractable, an outside insight shows it can be solved: "For many years physiologists could not understand the purpose of the long loops in the kidney tubules: it was assumed that the loops had no special function and were a relic of the way the kidney had evolved. Then one day an engineer looked at the loops and at once recognized that they could be part of a counter-current multiplier, a well-known engineering device for increasing the concentration of solutions. In this instance, a fresh look from outside provided an answer to something that had been a puzzle for a long time" (De Bono 1968, p. 148).

Neighboring disciplines harbor concepts, data, and problem-solving strategies that expand horizons, heighten creativity, and increase validity in consumer research. By participating in these disciplines – learning their models and their methods and enlisting them as partners – consumer researchers can bring new power to their work.

*The More Distant Neighbors.* The founders of ACR wanted to mix academia, business, government, and foundations because they thought each sector had perspectives that the others lacked.

At first this vision seemed right. Joel Cohen, ACR's first president, was then a member of National Analysts, a commercial research firm. Robert Pratt, ACR's second president, was a General Electric research executive. Researchers from Procter & Gamble and the Leo Burnett Company were on ACR's first program committee. A Federal Trade Commission staff member was on ACR's first board.

The first *Proceedings* of ACR included articles by researchers from AT&T, General Electric, Standard Oil, Procter & Gamble, the Ford Motor Company, Leo Burnett, Bozell and Jacobs, Westat Research, National Analysts, Market Facts, Elrick & Lavidge, the Consumer Research Institute, the Consumer Federation of America, the U.S. Department of Agriculture, the Food and Drug Administration, the U.S. Department of Commerce, the Federal Trade Commission, and the National Science Foundation (Venkatesan 1972). These articles provoked controversy, offered methods and substance, and furnished food for thought.

In the decade that followed, government-based researchers presented articles on surveys as legal evidence, taste-test methods, reactions to advertising, energy conservation, driver behavior, consumption segmentation, economic effects of information, random-coefficient models, and consumer information systems.

Industry-based researchers discussed trade-off analysis, multidimensional scaling, computerized content analysis, trimode factor analysis, survey reliability, group interview methods, life-style and psychographics, the consumer life cycle, brand adoption models, children's influence on adults' purchases, consumers' reactions to sex in advertising, changing tastes in popular music, and estimates of the demand for style. These articles energized discussion and propagated diverse points of view. Much of their substance and many of their methods reappeared in later scholarly research.

But as time went on, industry participation lessened, and government and foundations all but disappeared. As consumer research entered the 1990s, about nine of 10 ACR members, and more than nine of 10 *JCR* authors, were business school faculty. The discipline was turning inward. Academic, government, and industry neighbors were dropping out.

In part, this introversion was a symptom of success. When ACR was newborn, it needed outside support. But as ACR prospered, its academic leaders realized that it could stand by itself.

Some of ACR's academic leaders argued that scholars should be wary of outsiders, especially outsiders wearing business suits. In debating the benefits and hazards of consulting – and being deliberately provocative – Holbrook said: "Business executives tend to approach training programs with a resolute bias against scholarship and science. For them, 'conceptual' is a pejorative term, 'theory' virtually a dirty word" (Holbrook 1985, p. 146). Holbrook and others believed that scholars should be shielded from outside influences that might contaminate their work.

The opposing argument is that industry and government researchers command data, concepts, and methods that have much to contribute to academic consumer research. Consider data first. Government data have supported many influential academic publications: Anderson and Shugan (1991), Fournier, Antes, and Beaumier (1992), Garner and Wagner (1991), and Sinha and Chandrashekaran (1992) are just a few. Industry data have inspired journal articles and books: Aaker and Stayman (1990), Adams and Blair (1992), Biel and Bridgwater (1990), Deighton *et al.* (1989), Greenleaf (1992), Mayhew and Winer (1992), Novak, de Leeuw, and MacEvoy (1992), Pechmann and Stewart (1991), Schlinger (1979), Simonson and Winer (1992), Stewart and Furse (1986), Wells, Leavitt, and McConville (1971), Young and Robinson (1992), and many more.

To make use of such resources, academic consumer researchers must overcome two barriers. The first is a knowledge barrier. They must know that the information exists and perceive its relevance to their own work. The second is an administrative and mechanical barrier. They must gain access to the data base itself. When industry, government, and academic researchers meet in person, opportunities to break both barriers greatly increase.

On the conceptual side, government and industry researchers have broadened the discipline's construct base. "Involvement," a key construct if there ever was one, came from Krugman's (1965) industry-based analysis of advertising effects. Benefit segmentation and means-end analysis began in the research department at Grey Advertising (Haley 1968; Young and Feigin 1975). Occasion-based segmentation (Greenberg 1982) came from National Analysts, and the Lavidge-Steiner model (Lavidge and Steiner 1961) came from Elrick and Lavidge – both commercial research firms. Researchers at Foote, Cone and Belding developed the FCB Grid (Vaughn 1980). This set of constructs has been important in its own right and has inspired influential later work (Rossiter and Percy 1987; Rossiter, Percy, and Donovan 1991). Researchers at corporations, research companies, and advertising agencies made valuable contributions to life-style and psychographic research (Wells 1972).

Multidimensional scaling and trade-off analysis began in industry (Fiedler 1972; Johnson 1972), as did telephone and central location interviewing, and many of the most significant advances in advertising copy testing and focus group research (Goldman and McDonald 1987; Haley and Baldinger, 1991; Schlinger 1979).

While contributions from academia, government, and industry are hard to separate, the record shows that government and industry inputs have expanded, enriched, and enlivened academic consumer research. It seems most reasonable to assume that more interaction among industry, government, and academia would cause more of this desirable effect.

Most fundamentally, the argument against introversion is that introversion threatens intellectual integrity. Introversion insulates myths from logic and offers reassurance that outsiders must be irrelevant, incompetent, or morally perverse.

What is needed is more, not less, outreach – both to scholars in other academic disciplines and to researchers who deal directly with the real world. Outsiders' goals and customs may be different, and they may well denounce what they do not like. On the other hand, they advance the enterprise with new data and new perspectives. And, like the engineer who saw that kidney loops were countercurrent multipliers, they increase the probability that discoveries will take place.

## Guideline 4. Start Small and Stay Real

Here is how things are supposed to work: a theory is at first a rough approximation. Objective scientists "test" it. The tests detect errors. The scientists improve and retest the theory. Eventually, the theory explains and predicts.

About this view of progress, skeptics would ask four questions. First, are theory tests objective? Second, are they reliable enough to detect errors? Third, do errors get corrected? And fourth, do consumer behavior theories reach the point where they explain and predict real world events?

These questions are important because theory and theory testing absorb much of the time and effort devoted to academic consumer research. If the process does not work as advertised, this time and effort could be put to better use.

One meaning of "theory" is a general notion about causes and effects. Without such theories, investigators would be helpless. They would not know what to study, or what questions to ask. This meaning of theory – theory with a small *t* – is not the topic here.

The topic here is Theory with a capital *T*: "universal" principles that "explain any real-world situation within their domain" (Calder, Phillips, and Tybout 1981, p. 198). The fundamental question is, Does the process work as advertised? Does progress actually occur this way?

*Are Theory "Tests" Objective?* First, are Theory "tests" objective? In a review of Theory in the behavioral sciences, Greenwald *et al.* (1986, p. 227) concluded that objectivity is rare: "Theory obstructs research progress when the researcher is an ego-involved advocate of the theory and may be willing to persevere indefinitely in the face of prediction-disconfirming results. Regrettably, because the social systems of many scientific disciplines encourage researchers to be ego-involved theory advocates, the conditions under which theory is likely to obstruct scientific progress are ones that occur commonly."

If anyone believes that consumer researchers are immune to ego involvement, consider Sheth's evaluation of Farley and Ring's (1970, 1974) "test" of Howard and Sheth's (1969) theory of buyer behavior. At the 1992 Converse Symposium, Sheth commented (in passing) on Farley and Ring's work. With a wave of his hand, he dismissed disconfirmation: "The concepts were not operationalized correctly; the correspondence rules were all misapplied." Defense of intellectual offspring is not a rare event.

*Are Theory "Tests" Reliable Enough to Detect Errors?* Second, are Theory "tests" reliable enough to detect errors? The hallmark of reliability is replication. If a finding cannot be replicated, it cannot be a valid test. In commenting on replication, Shimp, Hyatt, and Snyder (1991, p. 276) said: "When an experiment is replicated, chances are that the exact or even similar findings will not be obtained. . . . This can be explained by at least five factors, including improper replication (e.g., nonequivalent manipulations), nonrobust theory, the presence of demand artifacts in the original or replicated data, sampling effects, and laboratory effects." They added: "Laboratory effects involve differences across experiments in such context-specific factors as physical and temporal conditions, experimenters, and procedures. It is hard to control or even assess the magnitude of laboratory effects" (Shimp *et al.* 1991, p. 276).

In a sample of 1,120 empirical papers from the major marketing journals, Hubbard and Armstrong (1991) found no exact replications, and only 20 extensions of earlier work. Of the 20 extensions, 12 contradicted the earlier findings, and only three fully confirmed the original results.

If findings are that capricious, any Theory "test" that fails to support the Theory can be written off as spurious. And given the ego forces that defend Theories, it is far more likely that Theorists will discount disconfirmation than that they will admit their ideas were wrong.

*Do Theories Get Corrected?* Third, do Theories get corrected? The Theory-oriented account of scientific progress holds that even when Theorists remain obdurate, the discipline as a whole corrects mistakes. Through "rigorous falsification," the discipline eliminates invalid propositions and "supports" others, which stay in place (Calder *et al.* 1981). Do theory tests correct mistakes? In a review of Theory tests in psychotherapy, Mahrer concluded:

> I know of no established theory of psychotherapy that declared bankruptcy because of research that failed to confirm, disconfirmed, or falsified its theoretical propositions and network of theoretical assumptions; nor is there a logical necessity for that to occur.
>
> Theories of psychotherapy wax and wane because of considerations that have virtually nothing to do with the testing of hypotheses bearing on their theoretical propositions. "It is simply a sad fact that in soft psychology theories rise and decline, come and go, more as a function of baffled boredom than anything else." [Mahrer 1988, p. 694; internal quote from Meehl (1978), p. 807]

Mahrer explained:

> The space between a theory of psychotherapy and a derived or deduced testable hypothesis is so extensive, loose, and filled with implicit and explicit clauses and conditions that the theory is in no grave danger from whatever findings are obtained. . . .
>
> Not only are firm believers easily able to refute and discount unfriendly findings of hypothesis-testing research, always managing to stay safely out of range, but their research lieutenants can inevitably be counted on to generate counterbalancing friendly studies. . . .
>
> I suggest that hypothesis testing is essentially unable to fulfill its self-assigned mission of confirming or disconfirming psychotherapeutic propositions or theories. Indeed, in the field of psychotherapy, the mission itself is fruitless. [Mahrer 1988, pp. 695–696]

Does consumer research fare better? Consider the Theory of cognitive dissonance. In 1976, Cummings and Venkatesan reviewed 23 studies that had "examined empirically the arousal and reduction of cognitive dissonance in the context of consumer behavior." In agreement with earlier reviews, Cummings and Venkatesan concluded that the theory of cognitive dissonance was "not proven." However, they then went on to conclude that, despite numerous disconfirmations and despite methodological and conceptual flaws in all of the research they had studied, "the evidence in favor of dissonance theory in the consumer behavior literature looks good" (Cummings and Venkatesan 1976, p. 307). What could have made the evidence look bad?

Or consider the Fishbein attitude model. This model has been the object of more "tests" than any other model in all of consumer research. Despite a long and complex list of mutually contradictory findings (Ahtola 1975; Lutz and Bettman 1977; Mazis, Ahtola, and Klippel 1975; Sampson and Harris 1970; Wilkie and Pessemier 1973) the original model stands as stated. Interest in "testing" it has now faded – another victim of "baffled boredom" in consumer research.

*Do Consumer Behavior Theories Predict Real-World Events?* Does the process work as advertised? A fourth element of that basic question is, Do consumer behavior Theories predict real-world events?

In their overview of the research process, McGrath and Brinberg (1983, p. 118) described three stages. Stage 1 is "groundwork" – "development, clarification, and selection of elements and relations" to be used in an investigation. Stage 2 is execution of the investigation itself. Stage 3 is "following up the findings of stage 2, by replication and by a systematic search for both the range and limits of those findings."

Although Theory-oriented consumer researchers have been brilliant in executing stages 1 and 2 of the research process, they have systematically evaded stage 3. As we have already seen, replication almost never happens. And, as McGrath and Brinberg (1983, p. 122) pointed out, "Not only do researchers in our fields seldom deliberately set out to search for the boundaries of their findings, but when they do encounter such disconfirmations . . . they generally regard them as negative findings to be explained away."

But if consumer behavior Theories are to predict behavior in the real world, stage 3 – replication and systematic search for range and limits – is absolutely essential. Replication is essential because findings must be known to be reliable. If findings cannot predict themselves, they cannot possibly predict anything else. Systematic search for range and limits is essential because spurious generalization leads to "inverted expertise." That is, presumed experts who overgeneralize can be less accurate than novices: "Experts overestimate the diagnosticity of their knowledge and intuitions because of the accessibility of abstract representations of the phenomena to be predicted. In contrast, as novices rely on concrete surface features, they perceive the retrieved information to be less diagnostic [and] engage in more detailed processing. . . . Experts, in contrast to novices, rely on a host of irrelevant or weak cues that they perceive as predictive in problem solving. . . . Experts not only overestimate the diagnosticity of the information, but rely on *irrelevant* cues/factors, which leads to a truncation of mental effort and erroneous judgments." (Mahajan 1992, pp. 331–332).

"Inverted expertise" has appeared in banking, engineering, clinical psychology, and marketing (Mahajan 1992). It has also appeared in consumer research. Armstrong (1991) asked *JCR* Editorial Board members to predict how accurately ACR members would "predict" the results of 20 already published *JCR* studies. On the assumption that *JCR* contained a reliable body of knowledge and that ACR members would use that knowledge, the board predicted that accuracy would be about 80 percent. The actual accuracy was 51 percent, significantly worse than chance, and marginally worse than predictions made by high school students and business executives.

This example of "inverted expertise" does not increase confidence that our present body of knowledge can predict real-world events. If the present body of knowledge, employed by presumably knowledgeable members of the discipline, cannot predict consumer behavior within the friendly confines of *JCR*, it cannot possibly predict the real behavior of real consumers in the real world.

The roots of this problem may well lie in systematic evasion of stage 3 of the research process. When findings are not replicated and when their range and limits remain untested, we have no way of knowing which – if any – will explain or predict.

So here we have four counts against Theory-oriented consumer research. Ego-involved Theorists persevere indefinitely in the face of Theory-disconfirming results. Theory "tests" are so imperfect that they can always be written off. When consumer behavior Theories are "tested," they do not get better or even change. And, Theory-oriented consumer researchers neither replicate their findings nor systematically investigate the range and limits of their work. In the absence of this essential segment of the research process, the "body of knowledge" cannot be expected to explain or predict realworld events.

The fault is not with individual researchers, who pursue their craft with skill and dedication. The fault is with the system. Presently accepted practices do not work as advertised. They are not science. They are science fiction.

This fiction is not harmless. When the system fails to work as advertised, it breeds distrust and doubt. Researchers turn to other matters, and knowledge is diminished by the absence of the contributions they could make.

*An Alternative.* An alternative would be to start small and stay real – to forsake pursuit of high-level, abstract representations and seek ground-level generalizations that actually work. These generalizations might be called "theories" with a small *t* (Olson 1982); but they would always refer to real events.

This strategy would ask "so what?" about every outcome of every investigation. Instead of assenting to the notion that any "contribution to Theory" is a contribution to knowledge, it would ask, "all kidding aside, what does this really mean?"

The answer to the "so what?" question need not be "managerial implication." It might be a public policy implication or an implication that individual consumers could put to use. It might be, "Here is a powerful new method," "Here is a confirming replication," "Here is a convincing contradiction of a strongly held opinion," or "Here is a useful insight from reanalysis of earlier work." But, by definition, the answer to "so what?" would have external validity. It would always tell us something about how real consumers really behave.

The "so what?" strategy differs from the Theory-oriented version of scientific progress in four important ways. First, as already noted, it seeks theories with a small *t*: valid, ground-level generalizations about real events. The finding that very interesting television programs are very good carriers of advertising would be one example of a theory with a small *t*.

Second, the "so what?" strategy asserts that the laboratory is neither necessary nor sufficient for scientific research. Instead, it endorses "full-cycle" problem solving, which starts with real-world behavior, tests abstractions from that behavior in the laboratory as appropriate, submits the laboratory results to external validation, returns to the laboratory for further analysis, submits the new analysis to external validation, and continues this cycle until the reliability, range, and limits of the findings are well understood (Cialdini 1980; Lutz 1991; Ray 1975).

The key element of this strategy is that it starts with real-world behavior and returns to the real world every time. It does not devote resources to "falsification" of abstract Theories, and it insists that – in consumer research – findings are not contributions to knowledge until their boundaries have been ascertained and reconfirmed outside.

Third, the "so what?" strategy does not stop at $p < .05$. Instead of quitting with a verdict of "not nil," it demands that investigators find out whether the effect is large enough to be important and whether it is curved or straight. To the $p < .05$ test of statistical significance, the "so what?" strategy adds the more rigorous test of real significance: "What does this finding really mean?"

And fourth, the "so what?" strategy highlights stage 3 of the research process. It does not admit unreplicated findings. And it insists that range and limits be determined before generalizations are made.

When the topic is an abstract, universal Theory, these standards cannot be met (Calder *et al.* 1981). But when the topic is a useful, ground-level generalization, researchers – and their successors and their critics – have every incentive to recheck stability and to find out when and where they can depend on what was found. Granted, this strategy will not generate high-level Theories any time soon. But it will prevent "inverted expertise," and it will generate a reliable body of knowledge about how real consumers really behave.

The next and final guideline depicts a knowledge-generating process that has "so what?" at its base.

### Guideline 5: Research Backward

In a perceptive article on method, Alan Andreasen (1985) proposed that research be conducted backward. "Backward"research proceeds as follows (Andreasen 1985, pp. 176–180):

1. Determine how the research results will be implemented.
2. To ensure the implementation of the results, determine what the final report should contain and how it should look.
3. Specify the analyses necessary to "fill in the blanks" in the research report.
4. Determine the kind of data that must be assembled to carry out these analyses.
5. Scan the available secondary sources and/or syndicated services to see whether the specified data already exist or can be obtained quickly and cheaply from others.
6. If no such easy way out presents itself, design instruments and a sampling plan that will yield the data to fit the analyses you have to undertake.

7. Carry out the field work, continually checking to see whether the data will meet your needs.
8. Do the analysis, write the report, and watch it have its intended effect.

In applied research, these steps have led to findings that decision makers use and trust. In academic settings, they encourage researchers to be proactive about the meaning of their work.

Backward research contrasts sharply with Theory "testing" in all the ways described above. It also contrasts sharply with "looking at," "playing with," or "finding out as much as possible about" a topic – open-ended undertakings that are all too liable to have no definite result.

Backward research starts with an answer to the "so what?" question. Regardless of setting, it follows one clear route.

1. Determine how the research will be implemented. What will anyone do with the findings? Will the findings be useful for solving a specific applied problem? If so, what is the problem and how will the findings be used? Will the findings be useful for settling a theoretical dispute? If so, what is the dispute? Will the findings really settle it? Will the findings set limits on an accepted proposition? If so, who will be interested in the outcome, and how will it add to what we already know?

In commenting from his perspective as *JCR* editor, Richard Lutz (1990, p. ii) observed: "Conducting a piece of research and only later considering the audience for it is a classic example of the sales orientation (i.e., a product in search of a market). Instead, research, like a product, should be designed with a constituency in mind, whether it be managers, public policy officials, or other academic researchers."

The backward strategy seconds that advice. Ironically, some who lecture on the folly of the sales orientation return to their offices and commit that very error in their own research. Instead of asking "so what?" from the beginning, they proceed on the assumption that their customers will value whatever they happen to make.

2. To ensure implementation of the results, determine what the final report should contain and how it should look.

In a continuation of his emphasis on the audience, Lutz (1990, p. ii) recommended that research designs be "test-marketed": "Many futile researcher hours could be saved if authors were to 'test-market' their intended contributions and research designs before executing the research. Many of the more successful authors in our field routinely test-market their manuscripts via a peer review process, but the idea-generation and research-design stages of projects are not generally subjected to the same degree of scrutiny. Taking this simple step . . . would greatly increase the potential yield of our collective research efforts."

To this valuable suggestion, backward research adds three explicit steps: (1) look ahead to a reasonable range of possible outcomes, (2) commit those outcomes to paper, and (3) ask yourself – and colleagues and critics – about each outcome, "all kidding aside, what would this really mean?" If no outcome would mean anything to anyone, the contribution question has been answered, and the answer is "nothing".

3, 4. Specify the analyses necessary to "fill in the blanks" in the research report, and determine the kind of data that must be assembled to carry out these analyses. As obvious as these steps may sound, they are rare in academic consumer research.

Without clear objectives, researchers generate enormous quantities of data only to discover that they cannot locate what they need. When they do get the data organized, they find – too late – that something vital was left out. Had they started with an incomplete report, they would have known which data would, and which would not, fill in the blanks.

By starting with an incomplete report, backward research encourages "triangulation." Many conclusions require more than one kind of evidence. Prespecification shows which combinations of which data and which methods will be needed to make the case.

5. Scan the available secondary sources and/or syndicated services to see whether the specified data already exist or can be obtained quickly and cheaply from others. In consumer research, the "secondary sources and/or syndicated services" extend beyond the local literature. Here is where "reach out" pays off.

6. If no such easy way out presents itself, design instruments and a sampling plan that will yield the data to fit the analysis you have to undertake. As Jacoby (1976), Kollat *et al.* (1972), and many other critics have noted, instruments designed for one task seldom fit another. In backward research, the researcher defines the job, and only then selects or – more usually – designs the tools that will be needed to complete the work.

The same principle applies to all other elements of the investigation, including – most essentially – the sample. In backward research, the researcher thinks first about conclusions and only then about the sample needed to establish credible support. Foresight is the best possible safeguard against Ferber's verdict: "garbage in, garbage out."

7. Carry out the fieldwork, continually checking to see whether the data will meet your needs. In backward research, data are not collected until they "come out right." They are collected until they "settle down." Small samples – samples of the size used in many *JCR* experiments – stop the investigation while chance factors still have too much impact on the findings (Cohen 1990, 1992; Wilcox 1992). On the other hand, excessive samples spend resources well beyond diminishing returns.

When the strength of the relationship and the amount of variability in the data can be estimated, power analysis (Cohen 1990, 1992; Sawyer 1982) can yield a rough forecast as to where the settling-down point might be. But, even then, a close watch on what is happening as data accumulate provides the best view of where more data will not be worth the extra cost.

8. Do the analysis, write the report, and watch it have its intended effect. In the context of Andreasen's original proposal, the "intended effect" was real-world implementation. In the present context, the "intended effect" is a consequential contribution to our understanding of consumer behavior.

In discussing the slow progress of marketing research, an American Marketing Association task force (1988) lamented "burnouts" – promising academic researchers who turn to other pursuits because they believe that no one cares much about their work. Backward research prevents burnout because it is designed from the beginning to produce outcomes that audiences need and want.

*Three Routes to Discovery.* If backward research starts with conclusions, how can it produce discoveries? If it starts with limited objectives, how can it expand the field?

In backward research, step 1 sets the creative goal. Instead of advocating "falsification" of some abstract construct, instead of suggesting that investigators should "look at," "play with," or "find out as much as possible about" some general idea, step 1 initiates a process that directs resources toward a definite result.

This strategy is not without precedent. When Watson and Crick set out to find the structure of DNA, they did not start by "falsifying" a high-level Theory, or by "looking at," "playing with," or "finding out as much as possible about" molecules. Instead, they oriented all their efforts toward one limited, specific, and important end (Weisberg 1986, chap. 6).

In backward research, step 2 promotes discovery via test market. Step 2 asks research planners to specify a range of outcomes and then ask themselves and colleagues, "If this were to be the outcome, who would care?" If the answer to that question is "everyone," the outcome is a discovery by definition. If the answer is "no one," the planner needs a different plan.

And finally, like every other kind of research, backward research benefits from sheer good luck. But, unlike less planful procedures, it establishes cognitive structures that interpret unforeseen results.

These observations are not intended to imply that the backward approach is the only way to make discoveries. As we all know, discovery takes many routes. They are intended to assert, however, that creative solutions to complex problems are most likely to occur when problem solvers start with clear ideas of where they must come out.

## Summary

The *Journal of Consumer Research* and ACR aspired to leadership in a rapidly accelerating academic and applied field. Over the years, that plan has faltered. Now, *JCR* and ACR turn inward, toward a less ambitious set of issues and a less expansive set of goals.

Five guidelines would change all that.

1. Leave home. Consumer behavior starts with the antecedents of decisions and ends with ecological effects. Consumer choices run from life-altering options to brands of gum. In the past, too much effort has been spent on the least important intersections of those two dimensions. Consumer researchers who move upward and to the right will add value to their work.
2. Forsake mythodology. Five myths impede progress: Students represent consumers. The laboratory represents the environment. Statistical significance confers real significance. When suitably disguised, correlation becomes causation. And, once mentioned, limitations simply go away. These myths do more harm than good. They can and should be given up.

3. Reach out. Business, government, and foundations – and adjacent academic disciplines – command data, constructs, methods, and perspectives that can enrich our work. Consumer researchers who participate in these resources gain sophistication, range, and depth.
4. Start small and stay real. Search for abstract, universal theories has not increased our understanding of consumer behavior. Consumer researchers who ask "so what?" about every investigation will fulfill the promise that authenticates the field.
5. Research backward. The surest route to an important discovery is to start with a definite objective and work backward. Researchers who work backward conserve resources, maintain motivation, and produce valuable results.

### Benefits

These guidelines offer different benefits to different groups.

*Early Career Researchers.* To early career researchers, the guidelines offer direct aim at the real behavior of real consumers. This is no trivial concern. Consumer behavior is important in its own right, and it has extensive consequences throughout American society and throughout the world.

The guidelines do not reject science. They reject only blind submission to conventions that have short-circuited contact with reality. The guidelines do not reject theory. They reject only the notion that high-level abstractions are dependable when critical decisions must be made.

The guidelines urge seriousness of purpose. They insist that internal validity is not enough and that external validity is too important to be postponed. They urge directed, focused effort against important problems, and they hold that innovative, valuable solutions to those problems can be found.

In a few years, present early career researchers will be the pacemakers of the field. Now is not too soon to start.

*Current Cadre of Established Researchers.* To the current cadre of established researchers, the guidelines offer renewal. They say, "Open doors. Expand and elevate the discipline. Increase its credibility. Be even more creative than in the past 20 years."

Unquestionably, ACR is a "bright and talented and productive group." And *JCR* is the most prestigious journal in the field. What is needed now is a creative integration that will both preserve those values and import resources from outside. What is also needed is more attention to the dark side of consumer behavior and to Sheth's early insight that credibility is worth the hardships of real-world research.

As role models, gatekeepers, and active contributors, the current cadre can advance the discipline in those directions, or they can defend the status quo. As between innovation and defense, innovation promises broader horizons, more opportunities to source important findings, and greater stature – both within the academic community and throughout the outside world.

*Academic Leaders of ACR.* To ACR's academic leaders, current and future, the guidelines offer growth. The guidelines say, "Turn outward, not inward. Recruit outsiders. Fulfill the vision of the early years."

A larger role in fashioning the conference program would invite outsiders in. External validity would bring outsiders back each year. The result would be better understanding of consumer behavior. It would also be less confidence, more agitation, more controversy, and more ferment – just as ACR's founders had hoped.

*JCR's Editors and Reviewers.* To *JCR's* editors and reviewers, the guidelines offer opportunities to make the journal more important and more widely used. The guidelines seek less willingness to settle for stages 1 and 2 of the research process and more serious attention to the rigors of stage 3. The guidelines do not ask that *JCR* become a managerial journal. They ask only that *JCR* disseminate what intelligent outsiders would regard as knowledge – serious conclusions about how real consumers really behave.

The intention behind the founding of *JCR* was to create a store of insight into consumer behavior, broadly defined. Were it to become that, it would become the journal to which professionals sharing an interest in consumer behavior across disciplines send their material, and it would be of greater value to anyone with any interest in the field.

*Department Heads and Deans.* To administrators, the guidelines offer opportunities to grow a world-class discipline. This objective would require closer contact with other segments of the university and more constructive use of ideas and material resources from outside. It would also require vigorous support of innovative programs and unwavering conviction that horizons can and must exceed their current bounds.

The rewards would be substantial. In this field, credible discoveries have worldwide implications. And intrinsic interest brings first-rate faculty – and first-rate students – into the fold. The discipline's potential is outlined in *JCR*'s first editorial and ACR's constitution. The right incentives would lead to fulfillment of those worthy goals.

## References


Aaker, David A. and Douglas M. Stayman (1990), "Measuring Audience Perceptions of Commercials and Relating Them to Ad Impact," *Journal of Advertising Research*, 30 (August/September), 7–17.

Adams, Anthony J. and Margaret Henderson Blair (1992), "Persuasive Advertising and Sales Accountability," *Journal of Advertising Research*, 32 (March/April), 20–25.

Ahtola, Olli (1975), "The Vector Model of Preferences: An Alternative to the Fishbein Model," *Journal of Marketing Research*, 12 (February), 52–59.

AMA Task Force on the Development of Marketing Thought (1988), "Developing, Disseminating, and Utilizing Marketing Knowledge," *Journal of Marketing*, 52 (October), 1–25.

Anderson, Eugene W. and Steven M. Shugan (1991), "Repositioning for Changing Preferences," *Journal of Consumer Research*, 18 (September), 219–232.

Andreasen, Alan R. (1985), "Backward' Market Research," *Harvard Business Review*, 63 (May–June), 176.

Armstrong, J. Scott (1991), "Prediction of Consumer Behavior by Experts and Novices," *Journal of Consumer Research*, 18 (September), 251–256.

Arndt, Johan (1976), "Reflections on Research in Consumer Behavior," in *Advances in Consumer Research*, Vol. 3, ed. Beverlee B. Anderson, Ann Arbor, MI: Association for Consumer Research, 213–221.

Becker, Gary (1976), *The Economic Approach to Human Behavior*, Chicago: University of Chicago Press.

Belk, Russell W. (1987), "ACR Presidential Address: Happy Thought," in *Advances in Consumer Research*, Vol. 14, ed. Melanie Wallendorf and Paul Anderson, Provo, UT: Association for Consumer Research, 1–4.

– ed. (1991), *Highways and Buyways: Naturalistic Research from the Consumer Behavior Odyssey*, Provo, UT: Association for Consumer Research.

Biel, Alexander and Carol A. Bridgwater (1990), "Attributes of Likable Television Commercials," *Journal of Advertising Research*, 30 (June/July), 38–44.

Calder, Bobby J., Lynn W. Phillips, and Alice M. Tybout (1981), "Designing Research for Application," *Journal of Consumer Research*, 8 (September), 197–207.

Chow, Siu L. (1988), "Significance Test or Effect Size?" *Psychological Bulletin*, 103 (January), 105–110.

Cialdini, Robert B. (1980), "Full-Cycle Social Psychology," in *Applied Social Psychology Annual*, Vol. 1, ed. Leonard Bickman, Beverly Hills, CA: Sage, 21–47.

Clancy, Kevin J. and David M. Kweskin (1971), "TV Commercial Recall Correlates," *Journal of Advertising Research*, 11 (April), 18–20.

Cohen, Jacob (1965), "Some Statistical Issues in Psychological Research," in *Handbook of Clinical Psychology*, ed. Benjamin B. Wolman, New York: McGraw-Hill, 95–121.

– (1990), "Things I Have Learned (So Far)," *American Psychologist*, 45 (December), 1304–1312.

– (1992), "Statistical Power Analysis," *Current Directions in Psychological Science*, 1 (June), 98– 101.

Coleman, Richard P. (1983), "The Continuing Significance of Social Class to Marketing," *Journal of Consumer Research*, 10 (December), 265–280.

Cooper, Harris M. (1981), "On the Significance of Effects and the Effects of Significance," *Journal of Personality and Social Psychology*, 41 (5), 1013–1018.

Cote, Joseph A., Siew Meng Leong, and Jane Cote (1991), "Assessing the Influence of *Journal of Consumer Research:* A Citation Analysis," *Journal of Consumer Research*, 18 (December), 402–410.

Crockett, Jean (1974), "Commentary on Katona, 'Psychology and Consumer Economics,'" *Journal of Consumer Research*, 1 (June), 9–11.

Cummings, William H. and M. Venkatesan (1976), "Cognitive Dissonance and Consumer Behavior: A Review of the Evidence," *Journal of Marketing Research*, 13 (August), 303–308.

Deaton, Angus and John Muellbauer (1980), *Economics and Consumer Behavior*, Cambridge: Cambridge University Press.

De Bono, Edward (1968), *New Think*, New York: Basic.

Deighton, John, Daniel Romer, and Josh McQueen (1989), "Using Drama to Persuade," *Journal of Consumer Research*, 16 (December), 335–343.

Farley, John U. and L. Winston Ring (1970), "An Empirical Test of the Howard-Sheth Model of Buyer Behavior," *Journal of Marketing Research*, 7 (November), 427–438.

– and L. Winston Ring (1974), "Empirical' Specification of a Buyer Behavior Model," *Journal of Marketing Research*, 11 (February), 89–96.

Ferber, Robert (1977), "Research by Convenience," *Journal of Consumer Research*, 4 (June), 57–58.

Fiedler, John A. (1972), "Condominium Design and Pricing: A Case Study in Consumer Trade-off Analysis," in *Proceedings of the Third Annual Conference of the Association for Consumer Research*, ed. M. Venkatesan, College Park, MD: Association for Consumer Research, 279–293.

Fornell, Claes (1992), "A National Customer Satisfaction Barometer: The Swedish Experience," *Journal of Marketing*, 56 (January), 6–21.

Fournier, Susan, David Antes, and Glenn Beaumier (1992), "Nine Consumption Lifestyles," in *Advances in Consumer Research*, Vol. 19, ed. John F. Sherry, Jr., and Brian Sternthal, Provo, UT: Association for Consumer Research, 329–337.

Frank, Ronald E. (1974), "The *Journal of Consumer Research*: An Introduction," *Journal of Consumer Research*, 1 (June), i–ii.

Garner, Thesia I. and Janet Wagner (1991), "Economic Dimensions of Household Gift Giving," *Journal of Consumer Research*, 18 (December), 368–379.

Goldman, Alfred E. and Susan Schwartz McDonald (1987), *The Group Depth Interview*, Englewood Cliffs, NJ: Prentice-Hall.

Graham, John L., Dong Ki Kim, Chi-Yuan Lin, and Michael Robinson (1988), "Buyer-Seller Negotiations around the Pacific Rim: Differences in Fundamental Exchange Processes," *Journal of Consumer Research*, 15 (June), 48–54.

Greenberg, Marshall G. (1982), "Occasion-based Segmentation: Five Years Later," in *Straight Talk about Attitude Research*, ed. Joseph Chasin, Chicago: American Marketing Association, 67–77.

Greenleaf, Eric A. (1992), "Improving Rating Scale Measures by Detecting and Correcting Bias Components in Some Response Styles," *Journal of Marketing Research*, 29 (May), 176–188.

Greenwald, Anthony G., Anthony R. Pratkanis, Michael R. Leippe, and Michael H. Baurmgardner (1986), "Under What Conditions Does Theory Obstruct Research Progress?" *Psychological Review*, 93 (2), 216–229.

Haley, Russell I. (1968), "Benefit Segmentation: A Decision-oriented Research Tool," *Journal of Marketing*, 32 (July), 30–35.

– and Allan L. Baldinger (1991), "The ARF Copy Research Validity Project," *Journal of Advertising Research*, 31 (April/May), 11–32.

Harris, Richard J., Ruth E. Sturm, Michael L. Klassen, and John I. Bechtold (1986), "Language in Advertising: A Psycholinguistic Approach," in *Current Issues and Research in Advertising*, Vol. 9, Ann Arbor: University of Michigan, 1–26.

Henderson, Douglas A. and Daniel R. Denison (1989), "Stepwise Regression in Social and Psychological Research," *Psychological Reports*, 64 (February), 251–257.

Hirschman, Elizabeth C., ed. (1989), *Interpretive Consumer Research*, Provo, UT: Association for Consumer Research.

– (1991), "Secular Mortality and the Dark Side of Consumer Behavior: Or How Semiotics Saved My Life," in *Advances in Consumer Research*, Vol. 18, ed. Rebecca H. Holman and Michael R. Solomon, Provo, UT: Association for Consumer Research, 1–4.

Holbrook, Morris B. (1985), "Why Business Is Bad for Consumer Research: The Three Bears Revisited," in *Advances in Consumer Research*, Vol. 12, ed. Morris B. Holbrook and Elizabeth C. Hirschman, Provo: UT: Association for Consumer Research, 145–156.

Home Testing Institute (1963), "Must Reading about HTI and TVQ," In-House Report no. 22, New York: Home Testing Institute.

Howard, John A. and Jagdish N. Sheth (1969), *The Theory of Buyer Behavior*, New York: Wiley.

Hubbard, Raymond and J. Scott Armstrong (1991), "Replication in Marketing," working paper, Department of Marketing, Wharton School, University of Pennsylvania, Philadelphia, PA 19104.

Jacoby, Jacob (1976), "Consumer Research: Telling It Like It Is," in *Advances in Consumer Research*, Vol. 3, ed. Beverlee B. Anderson, Ann Arbor, MI: Association for Consumer Research, 1–11.

Johnson, Richard M. (1972), *Trade-off Analysis: A Method for Quantifying Consumer Values*, Chicago: Market Facts.

Kassarjian, Harold H. (1978), "Anthropomorphism and Parsimony," in *Advances in Consumer Research*, Vol. 5, ed. H. Keith Hunt, Ann Arbor, MI: Association for Consumer Research, xii–xiv.

Katz, Elihu and Paul F. Lazarsfeld (1955), *Personal Influence*, New York: Free Press.

Kollat, David T., Roger D. Blackwell, and James F. Engel (1972), "The Current Status of Consumer Behavior Research: Developments during the 1968–1972 Period," in *Proceedings of the Third Annual Conference of the Association for Consumer Research*, ed. M. Venkatesan, College Park, MD: Association for Consumer Research, 576–593.

Krugman, Herbert E. (1965), "The Impact of Television Advertising: Learning without Involvement," *Public Opinion Quarterly*, 29 (Fall), 349–356.

Lavidge, Robert J. and Gary A. Steiner (1961), "A Model for Predictive Measurements of Advertising Effectiveness," *Journal of Marketing*, 25 (October), 59–62.

Leong, Siew M. (1989), "A Citation Analysis of the *Journal of Consumer Research*," *Journal of Consumer Research*, 15 (March), 492–497.

Lutz, Richard J. (1990), Editorial, *Journal of Consumer Research*, 17 (December), i–iii.

– (1991), Editorial, *Journal of Consumer Research*, 18 (June), i–vi.

– and James R. Bettman (1977), "Multiattribute Models in Marketing: A Bicentennial Review," in *Consumer and Industrial Buying Behavior*, ed. Arch G. Woodside *et al.*, New York: North-Holland, 137–149.

Mahajan, Jayashree (1992), "The Overconfidence Effect in Marketing Management Predictions," *Journal of Marketing Research*, 29 (August), 329–342.

Mahrer, Alvin R. (1988), "Discovery-oriented Psychotherapy Research," *American Psychologist*, 43 (September), 694–702.

Martineau, Pierre (1957), *Motivation in Advertising*, New York: McGraw-Hill.

– (1958), "Social Classes and Spending Behavior," *Journal of Marketing*, 23 (October), 121–130.

Mayhew, Glenn E. and Russell S. Winer (1992), "An Empirical Analysis of Internal and External Reference Prices Using Scanner Data," *Journal of Consumer Research*, 19 (June), 62–70.

Mazis, Michael B., Olli T. Ahtola, and R. Eugene Klippel (1975), "A Comparison of Four Multi-attribute Models in the Prediction of Consumer Attitudes," *Journal of Consumer Research*, 2 (June), 38–52.

McCracken, Grant D. (1986), "Culture and Consumption: A Theoretical Account of the Structure and Movement of the Cultural Meaning of Consumer Goods," *Journal of Consumer Research*, 13 (June), 71–84.

– (1988), *Culture and Consumption: New Approaches to the Symbolic Character of Consumer Goods and Activities*, Bloomington: Indiana University Press.

McGrath, Joseph E. and David Brinberg (1983), "External Validity and the Research Process: A Comment on the Calder/Lynch Dialogue," *Journal of Consumer Research*, 10 (June), 115–124.

Meehl, Paul E. (1978), "Theoretical Risks and Tabular Asterisks: Sir Karl, Sir Ronald, and the Slow Progress of Soft Psychology," *Journal of Consulting and Clinical Psychology*, 46 (4), 806–834.

Mehta, Raj and Russell W. Belk (1991), "Artifacts, Identity, and Transition: Favorite Possessions of Indians and Indian Immigrants to the United States," *Journal of Consumer Research*, 17 (March), 398–411.

Murphy, Patrick E. and William A. Staples (1979), "A Modernized Family Life Cycle," *Journal of Consumer Research*, 6 (June), 12–22.

Nevett, Terence (1991), "Historical Investigation and the Practice of Marketing," *Journal of Marketing*, 55 (July), 13–23.

Novak, Thomas P., Jan de Leeuw, and Bruce MacEvoy (1992), "Richness Curves for Evaluating Market Segmentation," *Journal of Marketing Research*, 29 (May), 254–267.

Olson, Jerry C. (1982), "Toward a Science of Consumer Behavior," in *Advances in Consumer Research*, Vol. 9, ed. Andrew Mitchell, Ann Arbor, MI: Association for Consumer Research, v–x.

Pechmann, Cornelia and David W. Stewart (1991), "How Direct Comparative Ads and Market Share Affect Brand Choice," *Journal of Advertising Research*, 31 (December), 47–55.

Pollay, Richard W. (1972), "A Model for Research Planning in Consumer Behavior," in *Proceedings of the Third Annual Conference of the Association for Consumer Research*, ed. M. Venkatesan, College Park, MD: Association for Consumer Research, 594–601.

Pratt, Robert W., Jr. (1974), "ACR: A Perspective," in *Advances in Consumer Research*, Vol. 1, ed. Scott Ward and Peter Wright, Urbana, IL: Association for Consumer Research, 1–8.

Priemer, August B. (1983), "The Use of Qualitative Evaluation: Problems, Pitfalls and Potentials," paper presented at the Association of National Advertisers Television Workshop, New York.

Ray, Michael L. (1975), "The Advertising Pretest as Part of a Multimeasure, Multimethod, Multisituation Validation and Application Research System," in *Advances in Consumer Research*, Vol. 2, ed. Mary Jane Schlinger, Ann Arbor, MI: Association for Consumer Research, 577–588.

Rossiter, John R. and Larry Percy (1987), *Advertising and Promotion Management*, New York: McGraw-Hill.

–, Larry Percy, and Robert J. Donovan (1991), "A Better Advertising Planning Grid," *Journal of Advertising Research*, 31 (October/November), 11–21.

Rozeboom, William W. (1960), "The Fallacy of the Null Hypothesis Significance Test," *Psychological Bulletin*, 57 (September), 416–428.

Sampson, Peter and Paul Harris (1970), "A User's Guide to Fishbein," *Journal of the Market Research Society*, (July), 145–166.

Sawyer, Alan G. (1982), "Statistical Power and Effect Size in Consumer Research," in *Advances in Consumer Research*, Vol. 9, ed. Andrew Mitchell, Ann Arbor, MI: Association for Consumer Research, 1–7.

– and J. Paul Peter (1983), "The Significance of Statistical Significance Tests in Marketing Research," *Journal of Marketing Research*, 20 (May), 122–133.

Schlinger, Mary Jane (1979), "A Profile of Responses to Commercials," *Journal of Advertising Research*, 19 (April), 37–46.

Schumann, David W. and Esther Thorson (1990), "The Influence of Viewing Context on Commercial Effectiveness: A Selection-processing Model," in *Current Issues and Research in Advertising*, Vol. 12, Ann Arbor: University of Michigan, 1–24.

Sears, David O. (1986), "College Sophomores in the Laboratory: Influences of a Narrow Data Base on Social Psychology's View of Human Nature," *Journal of Personality and Social Psychology*, 5 1 (3), 515–530.

Sheth, Jagdish N. (1972), "The Future of Buyer Behavior Theory," in *Proceedings of the Third Annual Conference of the Association for Consumer Research*, ed. M. Venkatesan, College Park, MD: Association for Consumer Research, 562–575.

Shimp, Terence A., Eva M. Hyatt, and David J. Snyder (1991), "A Critical Appraisal of Demand Artifacts in Consumer Research," *Journal of Consumer Research*, 18 (December), 273–283.

Simonson, Itamar and Russell S. Winer (1992), "The Influence of Purchase Quantity and Display Format on Consumer Preference for Variety," *Journal of Consumer Research*, 19 (June), 133–138.

Sinha, Rajiv K. and Murali Chandrashekaran (1992), "A Split Hazard Model for Analyzing the Diffusion of Innovations," *Journal of Marketing Research*, 29 (February), 116–127.

Stern, Barbara B. (1989), "Literary Criticism and Consumer Research: Overview and Illustrative Analysis," *Journal of Consumer Research*, 16 (December), 322–334.

– (1991), "Who Talks Advertising? Literary Theory and Narrative 'Point of View,'" *Journal of Advertising*, 20 (September), 9–22.

– and Katherine Gallagher (1991), "Advertising Form, Content, and Values: Lyric, Ballad, and Epic," in *Current Issues and Research in Advertising*, Vol. 13, Ann Arbor: University of Michigan, 79–104.

Stewart, David W. and David Furse (1986), "*Effective Television Advertising – a Study of 1000 Commercials*, Lexington, MA: Lexington.

Takada, Hirokazu and Dipak Jain (1991), "Cross-national Analysis of Diffusion of Consumer Durable Goods in Pacific Rim Countries," *Journal of Marketing*, 55 (April), 48–54.

Thorson, Esther (1990), "Consumer Processing of Advertising," in *Current Issues and Research in Advertising*, Vol. 12, Ann Arbor: University of Michigan, 197–230.

Vankatesan, M., ed. (1972), *Proceedings of the Third Annual Conference of the Association for Consumer Research*, Chicago: Association for Consumer Research.

Vaughn, Richard (1980), "How Advertising Works: A Planning Model," *Journal of Advertising Research*, 20 (October), 27–33.

Wallendorf, Melanie and Eric J. Arnould (1988), "'My Favorite Things': A Cross-cultural Inquiry into Object Attachment, Possessiveness, and Social Linkage," *Journal of Consumer Research*, 14 (March), 531–547.

Weisberg, Robert (1986), *Creativity: Genius and Other Myths*, New York: Freeman.

Wells, William D., ed. (1972), *Lifestyle and Psychographics*, Chicago: American Marketing Association.

–, Clark Leavitt, and Maureen McConville (1971), "A Reaction Profile for TV Commercials," *Journal of Advertising Research*, 11 (6), 11–17.

Wilcox, Rand R. (1992), "Why Can Methods for Comparing Means Have Relatively Low Power, and What Can You Do to Correct the Problem?" *Current Directions in Psychological Science*, 1 (June), 101–105.

Wilkie, William L. and Edgar A. Pessemier (1973), "Issues in Marketing's Use of Multi-attribute Models," *Journal of Marketing Research*, 10 (November), 428–441.

Wright, Peter (1986), "Schemer Schema: Consumers' Intuitive Theories about Marketers' Influence Tactics," in *Advances in Consumer Research*, Vol. 13, ed. Richard J. Lutz, Provo, UT: Association for Consumer Research, 1–3.

Young, Charles E. and Michael Robinson (1992), "Visual Connectedness and Persuasion," *Journal of Advertising Research*, 32 (March/April), 51–59.

Young, Shirley and Barbara Feigin (1975), "Using the Benefit Chain for Improved Strategy Formulation," *Journal of Marketing*, 39 (July), 72–74.

Zandpour, Fred, Cypress Chang, and Joelle Catalano (1992), "Stories, Symbols, and Straight Talk: A Comparative Analysis of French, Taiwanese, and U.S. TV Commercials," *Journal of Advertising Research*, 32 (January/February), 25–38.

# 17

# Consumers and Consumption

**Sharon Zukin and Jennifer Smith Maguire**

**Source:** *Annual Review of Sociology* 30 (2004): 173–197.

## Introduction

Until recently, sociologists in the United States have generally ignored the topic of consumption, but they have done so at their peril. Though consuming basic goods is as ancient as human society, there is reason to believe that consumption of more elaborate goods and services – and the institutions and rituals that make this consumption possible – have assumed an overwhelming significance in modern life. Not only do sales of technologically sophisticated consumer goods like automobiles, DVD players, and personal computers make up a greater portion of the domestic economy around the world, but an increasing part of public culture is shaped by goods and services, advertisements that promote their use, and places – from shopping malls and websites to fitness centers and museum gift shops – where they are displayed, viewed, and bought. Studying consumption is an ideal bridge between research on the economy and the sociology of culture and provides new sites for examining the family, gender, and social class.

Yet aside from widespread use of Bourdieu's (1984) concept of "cultural capital," which includes the differentiated use of consumer goods to establish social status, and Ritzer's (1996) notion of "McDonaldization," which depicts the drive to rationalize contemporary organizations by imposing a self-service format copied from the fast-food chain, most initiatives for studying consumption have come from cultural studies, feminist scholarship, and social history. The works of such social theorists as Walter Benjamin, Zygmunt Bauman, and Jean Baudrillard – which have influenced the study of modernity, culture, and consumption in Europe – are barely read by most sociologists on this side of the Atlantic. Ethnographies of consumer goods in households, and interviews with family members about those goods, are few and far between (Csikszentmihalyi and Rochberg-Halton 1981, Halle 1993, Rochberg-Halton 1986). And the ethnographies of shopping in different London neighborhoods carried out by Miller (1998a, 2001) and other British anthropologists and geographers (Miller *et al.* 1998) are not matched by similarly detailed studies by American sociologists – unless they are employees of marketing firms.

One practical problem is that consumption is a huge topic that overlaps different institutional areas and both the public and private spheres. It is impossible to devise a single analytic framework to grasp its many historical forms and influences or the diverse theoretical perspectives that either praise or condemn it (see Slater 1997). By the same token, the division of intellectual labor among sociological fields makes it difficult to attach consumption to specific areas of the discipline.

Another problem, traceable to classical sociologists of the nineteenth century, is that consumption is broadly taken for granted and often denigrated. Above a minimal level of satisfying physical needs for food, clothing, and shelter, the desire to consume was considered by Marx to be a social need induced by capitalism: a "commodity fetish." Although he acknowledged that men and women like to dress up and eat well, he described these acts as "animal functions" (Marx 1972, p. 60). Weber (1946) viewed consumption instrumentally rather than as a social action carrying meaning in itself. But this does not mean that he thought consumption trivial. The ability to control the use of consumer goods is an important means of marking social status in any society, and in a market society, the ability to buy goods is shared by men and women in the same market position. Significantly, Weber's "Protestant ethic" (1958) has become a key word for referring to consumption as hedonism, pragmatically placed in the service of religious beliefs about salvation. Simmel (1997) was the first of the classical sociologists to discuss both the sensuality and attraction to novelty that supports mass consumption and to suggest that consumers' apparently inconsequential behavior – paying attention to fashion and shopping – is a common expression of modern social life, especially in cities (Simmel 1957). Durkheim, however, put forward a darker theme that underlies much of the contemporary criticism of – and perhaps aversion to studying – consumption. If modern society, and especially the economy, unleashes consumers' boundless desires, it destroys the moral basis of social order (Slater 1997, pp. 74–77).

None of these classical theorists offered empirical demonstrations of their ideas about consumption. They relied on generalized, anthropological observations to support meta-historical ideas. They also placed less emphasis on consumption than on other areas of social life, beginning with production, that were more prominent in their time. By contrast, Thorstein Veblen – a social critic but an economist by profession – was the first theorist to discuss consumption in terms of specific social practices in the United States. But his work on "the leisure class" (Veblen 1959) also uses general, anthropological observations instead of systematic empirical research. Moreover, Veblen's work signals two issues that may also explain why sociologists have held research on consumers in low regard: a moral disapproval of "status consumption" and the preeminent role in consumption that is played by women. From the beginning, then, consumption has been viewed as both amoral and gendered.

A third problem – most vexing for academic sociologists – is that, since the 1930s, applied sociologists and psychologists have dominated consumer research, and there is little crossover between the academic and applied domains. One will look in vain for articles about consumption in the major American sociological journals, and most academic sociologists do not read the journals of consumer research. Market researchers' pragmatic interest in pegging consumption to specific purchases, and in reducing consumers to typological versions of "economic man," is only beginning to be challenged by a more complex understanding of how men and women use consumption to construct social relationships and how consumption is shaped by the "supply side" of economic institutions and culture. But again, it is mainly historians and anthropologists, rather than sociologists, who have addressed these issues. This suggests that the study of consumption has always been multidisciplinary in scope.

Using sociology, then, in a broad rather than a disciplinary sense, we find that most sociological studies of consumption are bracketed, on the one hand, by structural changes in economy, infrastructure, and society that create a system of *mass consumption* and, on the other hand, by individual changes in values, attitudes, and behavior that result in a *consumer culture*. Consumer culture is produced, as well, by agents who work directly in the corporate economy as managers, marketers, and advertising "creatives"; by independent "brokers" who analyze and criticize consumer products; and by dissidents who initiate alternative responses to the mass consumption system. This broad framework allows us to consider consumption as *an institutional field*, i.e., a set of interconnected economic and cultural institutions centered on the production of commodities for individual demand. Even within this framework, there are many different approaches that run along a spectrum from specific, empirical studies to broad, speculative essays. In practice, it is often difficult to separate interpretation from speculation because data on consumers' attitudes are often ambiguous, there is little agreement on analytic frameworks, and the researcher frequently takes on the role of moralist, or at least social critic.

In this review, we begin by examining the basic material setting of the institutional field in studies of the development of specific products, industries, and consumption sites. We move on to consider consumption and the social construction of both the consuming subject and such forms of collective identity as ethnicity, holidays, and national and transnational citizenship. We then turn to the broader question of the transition to consumer society, specifically in the shift from state socialism to a market economy. We end by outlining an emerging sociological approach to studying consumption as an institutional field through multifaceted empirical research on products, texts, and sites that both socialize and serve consumers. Although our approach focuses on only some aspects of consumption – ignoring, for present purposes, such topics as the meaning of things – we think that it holds promise for bridging economic sociology and the sociology of culture (see Zelizer 2004) and for helping us to understand how men, women, and children in modern societies become consumers.

## Consumer Products, Industries, and Sites

Contemporary studies of consumer products and sites date from the 1970s and early 1980s – the very period when the more developed economies of the world were shifting from manufacturing to "postindustrial" production, and consumption was becoming a more visible factor in both the creative destruction of the landscape (Zukin 1991) and the conscious reshaping of the self (Featherstone 1991). At first, the importance of consumption was approached historically, from the rediscovery and English translation of Benjamin's (1999) research on the Paris Arcades of the 1840s, which mainly reached the United States through the filter of British social criticism, to social histories of the late-nineteenth-century department store (Miller 1981, Williams 1982) and early-twentieth-century advertising industry (Ewen 1976). All these studies use archival sources – descriptions of city streets, fashions, and shop windows in Benjamin's work, and memoirs, company records, advertisements, and industry publications in the other cases – to uncover the roots of modem consumer culture. As a whole, this work highlights the innovations of mass consumption: the gradual eclipse of small merchants and pedlars by large, well-capitalized firms; the setting of fixed prices that removed shopping from informal norms of bargaining; the display of piles of goods from distant regions, which transformed abundance into a novelty and made novelty abundant.

Although not theorized in these terms, the research documents the gradual development of an institutional field of mass consumption made up of consumer products, texts, and sites. New retail stores, advertisements, popular magazines, and daily newspapers all brought consumers into contact with goods and tended to make the consumer a powerful role model. To the extent that it is theorized, this work strongly suggests that mass consumption was produced by manipulating consumers' desires to be well dressed, good looking, and beloved; to surround themselves with visions of beauty; and to surrender common sense and sobriety to individual dreams of self-enhancement. Leach's (1993) archival study of the John Wanamaker department store in New York and Philadelphia reaches the height of this form. But, unlike Veblen's critique of the leisure class and contemporary criticism of status consumption, Leach refuses to blame consumers. He analyzes the department store's use of new building materials like plate glass and electric light as "strategies of enticement," and, by examining memoirs, speeches, and private communications, he connects retail entrepreneurs to large banks, universities, and art museums – the urban "circuits of power" that dominated both economy and culture. By making standardized consumer goods visible to all, Leach argues, department stores "democratized desire," while motivating men and women to buy.

Feminist historians emphasize the ambiguity of department stores (and later supermarkets) for women's independence (Bowlby 1985, 2000; Nava 1997). Following Emile Zola's fictional depiction of Parisian department stores as capitalist snares of desire, they describe these consumption sites as manipulating women by providing a wide array of sensory delights. But by providing a reason – shopping – for women to appear unescorted in public, as well as arranging safe spaces like rest rooms and tea rooms where women could gather or sit alone without fear of being molested by men, especially men who had been drinking alcohol, department stores also made it possible for women to leave the domestic space of the home and lay claim to the center of the city (Wolff 1985).

These examinations of the roots of consumer culture are based mainly on a cultural analysis of texts and images. Researchers scrutinize existing photographs and descriptions of visual displays in stores and shop windows for visual signs of manipulating consumers' wills; they read novels for detailed descriptions of such changes in character; and they use early advertisements and strategic statements by industry pioneers as evidence for the intention to create ideal – i.e., avid – consumers. But this perspective can be placed in an even wider framework.

Innovations in production technology around 1900 suggest a broad effort by business leaders to control the flow of goods and information, as well as consumers' minds (Beniger 1986). Though increasing capacity in mass production industries pressed companies to try any means – including advertising – to sell their goods, it is not sufficient to explain the rise of mass consumption by demonstrating the manipulation of consumers' wills (Martin 1999). The quantitative growth of mass consumption also reflects qualitative changes in demographics, new trends of social and geographical mobility, and the growing appeal of standardized goods as badges of both democratization and social status (Schudson 1984). In other words, a sociological analysis of consumer culture requires not just a reading of advertisements and appeals to buy goods; it demands familiarity with the standard tools of social history as well as a careful look at the evolution of specific products.

When applied subtly, and with a broad grasp of historical detail, the study of consumer products is both fascinating in itself and indicative of links between cultural representations, business strategies, and social practices. Schudson's (1984) careful study of the growth of cigarette consumption around 1900 makes a case for a multidimensional social and cultural analysis of consumer products in their social context. In his analysis, Schudson (1984) considers the increasing availability of – and ease of using – cigarettes in contrast to other forms of tobacco; the social effects of World War I, including the return of veterans who had smoked during military duty overseas; emerging pressures on the use of time during the workday; and changes in women's public roles and social status. He concludes that both standardization of the product and democratization of public life led to the cigarette's pre-eminent place for nearly a century in American consumer culture. Taking account of all these changes, Schudson explains the rise of modern consumer culture in one society.

The anthropologist Sidney Mintz (1985) likewise looks at changes in both production and consumption to explain the emergence of sugar as a key consumer good – along with alcohol and tea – in modern Britain. For Mintz, however, these two spheres – production and consumption – form two ends of a single, multinational "commodity chain" (although he does not use the term; see Hughes and Reimer 2003): Sugar links slave, and later free, labor on plantations in the Caribbean with the English working class. Looking at aggregate data on sugar production and consumption in the eighteenth and nineteenth centuries, as well as at changes in labor practices on both sides of the Atlantic, he explains the rise of sugar in the British diet as a means of controlling workers at two ends of a colonial, capitalist economy. But, as with cigarettes, consumers' acceptance of sugar would not have occurred without broad cultural changes in the use of time, women's roles, and the opportunity to use sugar in new social rituals – at teatime, for example, and during a separate course at meals called dessert.

Recent studies of "gourmet" coffees in our time (Roseberry 1996) and of the humble tin can in an earlier era (Naylor 2000) continue to connect the two ends of a commodity chain – mainly, in consuming regions of the northern hemisphere and producing regions of the southern hemisphere – by relating changes in consumers' tastes to the business strategies of producers, exporters, and importers. Although this creates a paradigm for global studies of consumption that fits both everyday experience and structural interdependencies, it also requires attention to initiators outside the realm, strictly speaking, of both production and consumption: product designers, trade groups, marketers, and merchants (du Gay *et al.* 1997, Molotch 2003).

Producers' motivations, moreover, may be multidimensional – and so may their *modus operandi.* When a group of British sociologists studied the development of the Sony Walkman, they used company documents, memoirs, and journalistic accounts to illustrate Sony's desire to innovate, lower costs, and appear as a global company – and also Sony's ability to learn from consumers' behavior (du Gay *et al.* 1997). Their study situates the product not only in a sea change of cultural representations – primarily seen in advertisements for the Walkman – but also in organizational practices of the firm and in young people's social practices of self-expression, individuality, and sociality. According to their model, then, production and consumption are not two poles of a commodity chain, but continually interacting processes in a "cultural circuit," where products both reflect and transform consumers' behavior.

This kind of detailed research highlights the complex interdependence of consumption with its social context, a point that is often downplayed by studies of cultural representations. Yet what gives the study of the Sony Walkman sociological weight – in contrast to Molotch's (2003) multidimensional discussion of twentieth-century product design – is its critical engagement with questions of culture, age, and social class, as well as with the relative power of individuals and multinational corporations. A similar engagement underlies Frank's (1997) study of the rise of "hip" fashion for men in the United States in the late 1960s and Parr's (1999) work on the development of modem household appliances and furniture in Canada after World War II. Unlike economic sociologists, Frank and Parr do not frame their research according to an abstract model of the development of markets; instead, as cultural historians, they are concerned with step-by-step processes of changing consumers' attitudes toward obsolescence. How do consumers begin to desire new consumer goods or fashions? And when do they stop desiring them and replace them with others?

Both Frank and Parr demonstrate manufacturers' strong motivation to persuade consumers to buy new products. Like earlier studies of the U.S. automobile industry, their work uses strategic statements by business executives to show how consumer products companies foster "the organized creation of dissatisfaction" (Steele 1993) with existing styles and models. 'They carry out a close reading of the literature of their respective industries – focusing on the editorial content of the trade press and popular magazines, as well as advertisements – and, in Frank's case, interviews with participants who are still alive.

The correspondence between the appliance and auto industries is not coincidental. Parr (1999) documents how, from the 1930s to the 1950s, companies changed refrigerator models every year and copied automobile styling down to the last detail; they planned both the products' physical obsolescence and their "emotional obsolescence" in consumers' eyes (see also Ewen 1999). Although the auto industry for many years tried to appeal to men, appliance manufacturers appealed to women consumers. Yet the almost entirely male manufacturers ignored women's concerns. According to Parr's interpretation of consumer surveys and magazine articles from the 1950s, women wanted fewer product changes in, and easier physical access to, their refrigerators and stoves, but they were defeated by male executives, designers, and sales clerks and alienated by the dominant machine aesthetic of the time. Certainly there was a large latent demand for consumer products after World War II, but Parr dissects the postwar boom with a critical attention to gender, corporate power, links between art museums and product design, and national (i.e., Canadian) interest in encouraging innovative industrial design. This is what we mean by studying the evolution of consumer products in their social context.

Frank (1997) studies how the men's clothing industry succeeded in socializing consumers to the same idea of emotional obsolescence during the 1960s. Faced with declining sales of men's clothes and an apparent male disdain for fashion, manufacturers and store owners adapted to the growing desire, especially among the young, for creative self-expression. While the trade press urged manufacturers to induce a more rapid turnover of goods by a more rapid creation of styles, advertisements exaggerated fears of conformity and praised creativity. Clothing, as well as soft drinks and cars, were presented as a choice of the young, the wild, and the creative. Frank carries out a shrewd, qualitative content analysis of industry advertisements, but he also compares these ads with strategic statements by company executives in the trade press, as well as with prior organizational changes in the advertising industry – the "creative revolution" of the early 1960s – to document the social construction of the ideal type of the "hip" consumer. The object of Frank's study – the integration of a subculture model of "cool" into the heart of capitalism – is so taken for granted today, it is widely assumed to have spread upward into industry with the force of a grassroots cultural shift. But Frank's archival research shows how creativity was used by the advertising and consumer products industries to convince consumers to buy. A briefer but similar study of change in women's fashions during the 1960s and the resulting eclipse of department stores by designer boutiques indicates that manufacturers and store owners were caught unprepared by a demand for individualistic styles (Zukin 2004), but this does not detract from the explanatory power of Frank's analysis. In the end, the evolution of many consumer products depends on power relations among producers, the quest for self-definition and social status among consumers, and floating cultural representations of "cool."

These product biographies and studies of consumer industries highlight the interconnections between production and consumption. They also demonstrate how consumers' desires for goods are socially constructed – partly through industry-fostered changes in cultural models and strategic practices of marketing ("supply"), and partly through changing demographics, shifting means of self-expression, and new social practices ("demand"). A more speculative view, however, relates this demand for goods to changes in the consuming subject.

## The Consuming Subject

In contrast to specific histories of consumer products and industries, a broad historical view links the rise of consumer culture with the modern creation of a "choosing self" (Slater 1997, p. 59). Accounts of modernity trace the development of this new self to the process of individualization (Bauman 2000, Beck and Beck-Gernsheim 2002), in which identity shifts from a fixed set of characteristics determined by birth and ascription to a reflexive, ongoing, individual project shaped by appearance and performance. The roots of this shift lie in urbanization and industrialization, which open access to an array of new goods and experiences, while at the same time permeating the core of the family and extending interdependencies. With people living more rational, anonymous lives, traditionally stable frameworks for group and individual identity – such as family, religion, class, and nationality – weaken and are modified or abandoned. The individual is then free to choose his or her path toward self-realization, taking on an opportunity and obligation once reserved for the elite. This freedom, however, comes at the cost of security; without fixed rules, the individual is constantly at risk of getting it wrong, and anxiety attends each choice. Simply put, modernity's legacy is a mass crisis of identity: we are each faced with the need to "*become* what one *is*" (Bauman 2000, p. 32).

Complementing this theoretically driven account of the contemporary subject are empirical studies of advertising, magazines, and other advice and self-help manuals, all of which offer means of coping with the dilemma of producing one's identity. Historical content analyses of advertising in the early twentieth century note an increasing emphasis on self-realization (Lears 1983), the importance of first impressions (Marchand 1985), and the viability of improving oneself through consumption. Pendergast's (2000) social-historical study of the content of popular men's magazines from 1900 to 1950 highlights how the efforts of editors, writers, advertisers, and readers intersected in the production of new representations of masculinity, as well as a new medium that combined advice, amusement, and appeals to buy. Against the backdrop of changes in the worlds of work and leisure (and the magazine industry), Pendergast's careful reading of changes in advertising and editorial content in such magazines as *Vanity Fair* and *Ebony* is strengthened by an attention to the role of the producers of such content, as evidenced in memoirs, autobiographies, and business correspondence. Tracing the long-term transition from a Victorian, work-oriented masculinity (and, for black men, a masculinity defined through the demand for access to jobs and rights), to a modern, consumerist masculinity, Pendergast demonstrates how products and texts act together to create a consuming subject.

Issues of identity and consumption converge in the concepts of "taste" and "lifestyle," that is, systems of practices through which individuals classify themselves by their classification of consumer goods as more or less desirable, acceptable, or valuable (Bourdieu 1984, pp. 169–75). Using survey data of French consumers' possessions and preferences (e.g., of artists, styles of dress, and cooking), Bourdieu demonstrates how knowledge of status codes, or rules of legitimacy, allows consumers to display "good" taste and thus establish their distinction. Contrary to arguments that categories such as social class have lost meaning in post-traditional, postmodem societies, Bourdieu's research shows how taste is deeply rooted in class position and relative access to economic, cultural, and social capital. If rich, well-educated consumers prefer one kind of art, bread, or travel to that preferred by workers, farmers, or cultured but less-affluent professors, then lifestyles reconfigure (and disguise) – rather than replace – class positions as patterns of consumption (Grusky and Wheedon 2001, Tomlinson 2003). Impressionistic observations of other consumers' choices in their intimate surroundings – a preference for "shabby chic" deecor (Halnon 2002), for example, and the worn patina of antiques (McCracken 1990, pp. 41–43) – confirm that tastes for specific kinds of consumer goods are implicitly socialized by social class and status or are consciously learned as a means of integration into new social groups (for an opposing view on art in the home, however, see Halle 1993).

Simply mapping Bourdieu's (1984) analysis of class and taste onto today's consumer culture in the United States is problematic, not only because of different relations of class identity to local culture, but also because much has changed in France and elsewhere since the survey data was collected in the 1960s. The commodification of culture has intensified, attention to design has become a normal part of the production process, and design aesthetics have converged such that the same "look" is sold across price categories (see Gartman 1991), making it more difficult to draw a distinct line between a (working class) taste for material function and a (bourgeois) taste for symbolic form. However, Bourdieu's work remains useful for its emphasis on the role of "cultural intermediaries" (Bourdieu 1984, p. 359) – the growing ranks of those involved in media, marketing, advertising, tourism, fashion, and other forms of providing symbolic goods and services.

With its attention to self-improvement, and the time, money, and energy to devote to mastering status codes, this new middle class exemplifies the consuming self (Bourdieu 1984, Featherstone 1991, Wynne 1998). After all, choices in appearance and behavior have significant, practical implications for people who work in services and cultural industries. At the very least, their occupational success requires the cultivation of an appropriate "package" through various "body projects" (Shilling 1993), such as dieting, working out, undergoing plastic surgery, and developing a fashionable, personal style.

In her research on career women and the consumption of fashion, Entwistle (2000) examines "power dressing" as a strategic mode of self-presentation. Through interviews with women, content analysis of dress manuals, and an attention to the retail strategies of fashion designers, Entwistle demonstrates how the skirt or trouser suit provides a solution to the problem of identity for professional women, creating an aura of authority through an appropriate appearance (neither overly masculine nor sexual) that negotiates – and ultimately reproduces – gender codes. At the same time, this work "uniform," and the manuals describing how best to assemble it, are a means to cope with the anxiety of choosing from the number of fashion options available to women: The rules of power dressing offer women the security of knowing that they will "look the part." Interviews with image consultants and their clients (Wellington and Bryson 2001) show how "experts" are used to deal with the pressure of creating an appropriate appearance, particularly for those in frontline service work, where a personal image represents the image of the corporation.

Therapeutic texts and services help to cope with the anxiety of identity production not only by changing but also by affirming the self. Interviews with readers of self-help books, for example, reveal their desire to have their problems and experiences recognized and labeled by an expert, and thus rendered *normal* (Cameron 2000, Simonds 1992; see also Miller 2001, p. 16). By combining interviews with discourse analyses and patterns of consumption, such research reveals how individuals learn to negotiate the institutional field of consumption.

Studies of the social formation of the consuming subject often lead to speculation about the political implications of consumer culture. There is a perceived ideological fit between the self-managing, enterprising, choosing self and the model citizen of neoliberal societies who shoulders the responsibility for maintaining social order through his or her "good" choices (Cronin 2000, Entwistle 2000, Slater 1997). In addition, there is the troubling capacity of consumer industries to commodify – and disarm – dissenting voices, recruiting issues of women's empowerment, environmental sustainability, and racial equality into the service of product promotion, thus reducing social justice to the freedom to choose between products (Cohen 2003, Talbot 2000).

Social theorists have critiqued consumers' much-vaunted "freedom of choice" by pointing out that consumption is presented not as an option but as a duty of the consumer-citizen (Baudrillard 1998, p. 80; Bourdieu 1984, p. 367). There is, moreover, a growing gap between the right to choose one's identity and the ability to control one's life (Bauman 2000, p. 38). The illusory nature of consumer freedom is further supported by academic studies of marketing, public relations, and consumer research (Ewen 1996, 1999; Turow 1998). The archival research by Miller and Rose (1997) on the work of the Tavistock Institute of Human Relations in England in the 1950s and 1960s shows how market researchers, influenced by new psychological conceptions of consumption, attempted to direct or "mobilize" consumers' choices by forging intricate, intimate connections between specific product attributes (such as the texture of new, softer toilet paper) and human passions, fears, and values (such as the desire for middle-class comfort).

These critical views of marketing and the social construction of the consuming subject contradict the "lifestyle" paradigm of consumer research that developed from the 1960s to the 1980s and still dominates marketing today. Market researchers trained in anthropology and psychology began to realize that demographics – socioeconomic characteristics like social class, income, and education – did not adequately indicate differences in consumers' behavior or, more seriously for client firms, predict choices of products. They tried to capture differences in consumers' preferences by creating new typologies based on "psychographic" analysis of consumers' answers to survey questions about their self-concepts and their preferences on a broad array of topics – e.g., spouses, household arrangements, pets, leisure time – that have no direct connection with products. These raw data are often refined by focus groups led by a market researcher. The resulting clusters of attitudes are defined as lifestyle values, and market researchers use them as a proxy for consumers' product choices (Turow 1998, Zukin 2004).

Both researchers and client firms claim that values and lifestyles surveys (VALS) are an effective strategy for increasing sales – and, in the case of political clients, for winning elections. They develop more refined typologies of consumers than standard socioeconomic categories like age, gender, and social class by isolating different clusters of attitudes and behavior within these categories. But they also divide communities and nations into market segments, appealing to a smaller number of common symbols, and – by constant references in the media – reifying these differences (Turow 1998). Moreover, by "disaggregating and reconstituting" consumer types (Applbaum 2003), VALS abstract consumers from both their social context and the integrity of their individual lives.

A more labor-intensive research strategy – also directed at product choices – aims to determine consumers' "relationships" with the brands they buy. Assuming that consumers' loyalty to specific brands is based on emotional and family histories as well as performance, researchers carry out intensive interviews with consumers about all aspects of their childhood and present lives. Like VALS, this research strategy tries to determine what consumers want out of life – and how their "brand portfolios provide meaning to the self" (Fourier 1998). Unlike VALS, however, this research uses interviews, focus groups, card sorts, and other laboratory techniques developed by social psychologists to construct typologies based not on self-declared attitudes but on emotional attachments, behavioral ties, and cognitive beliefs. Although this kind of research does acknowledge the complexity of individual choices and the integrity of individual lives, to many sociologists – especially in the academy – it suffers from the instrumentality of treating the consuming subject as a buying machine.

## Consumption and Collective Identity

The most productive studies situate consumer culture with respect to three levels of analysis: changes in demographic, geographic, and social structure; interventions by marketing media; and developing discourses about the consuming subject or individual identity. This framework applies just as well to the role of consumer culture in forming expressions of collective identity such as ethnicity, holidays, and national or transnational citizenship.

In a study of the social construction of Latino identity in the United States today, the anthropologist Arlene Davila (2001) examines the production and consumption of media images of Hispanics in Spanish-language television, print advertisements, and TV commercials. Based on interviews with Latino marketing professionals in New York, Chicago, and San Antonio, and on focus groups with a cross-section of Latino consumers in New York City, she finds that Latinos are sensitive to traditional bias against dark skin tones both in their home countries and in the United States and that they are ambivalent about being identified as Latino by their ability to speak Spanish – an ability that ignores both the facility in English among the second generation and differences in vocabulary and connotation among Hispanics from different countries. Like studies of English-speaking immigrants from the Caribbean, Davila's research shows how Latino immigrants retain their national identities as if they were ethnic identities; she also shows how media-produced images of Latinos in the United States de-emphasize social class differences by implying that all Latinos are poor. Davila's interviews also indicate that both Latino marketers and consumers are ambivalent about the media's role in reproducing traditional Latin stereotypes – such as the virginal mother and the hot-tempered lover – to sell goods. Moreover, both marketers and consumers are suspicious of Hispanics of different national origins: Cuban-run marketing firms, like Cuban consumers, are often disdainful of Mexican or Dominican competitors, and other groups feel the same. But Latinos' "identity politics" also reflect the attitudes they encounter in the larger American society. According to Davila, Latinos often feel – and are made to feel – under suspicion for being both too ethnic and not ethnic enough.

Although Davila's study is limited to the production and consumption of media images, it suggests several important points about consumer culture. Not least, it demonstrates the importance of consumer culture for producing new ethnic identities. Yet the effects of consumer culture are not uniform. On the one hand, Latino consumers compare media images of Latinos with their own experience, and they reject both the images and the products they represent if they contradict their experience. On the other hand, like all consumers, Latinos absorb and internalize some aspects of the media images and think of themselves as connected to the brands and styles of consumption that they promote. Whether Latinos make these connections consciously or not, they are selecting ethnic markers on the basis of a highly mediated consumer culture. And, as with African Americans (Lamont and Molnar 2001), the difficulties of making these choices in a white-dominated society are echoed in interviews with the Latino marketing professionals who create many of the images.

Although many media images suggest Latinos are poor, African Americans have historically been portrayed as having less money than whites but being more conspicuous consumers. Partly to test this stereotype, the anthropologist Elizabeth Chin (2001) did ethnographic research among a small number of working-class African American families in a northeastern city. She did not specifically investigate the reception of consumer culture among her subjects; rather, she observed how they shopped for gifts and other consumer goods and compiled inventories of their individual and household possessions. The low level of purchases and possessions that she sees in "Newhallville" dramatically contrasts with the media image of African Americans, especially teens, as avid consumers. She relates the lack of consumption, however, to low household incomes, the scarcity of small stores in the mainly segregated neighborhood where her respondents live, and the suspicion black teenagers – like all teens, but more so – arouse when they go shopping in a suburban mall. In an experiment, Chin provides her teenage respondents with a small amount of cash to shop at the mall and finds that they mainly purchase practical items.

This sort of ethnography – including both individual interviews and group discussions – corrects the impression that consumers, especially consumers from ethnic minorities, are duped by the dominant consumer culture. It contradicts the media image of some ethnic minorities as overwhelmingly interested in conspicuous consumption. It negates, as well, the myth that mass consumption levels racial hierarchies because "money knows no color." Chin does not directly confront how these teenagers interpret the media image; neither does she investigate whether they *think* about consumer goods even though they cannot afford to buy them. Nonetheless, watching consumers in action – and examining the purchases they really make – confirms the surprisingly strong rational core of consumption, despite the temptations of stores, the pressure of peers, and the pervasive media image of "luxury fever" (Frank 1999; see also Zukin 2004). Although ethnographic research is always carried out on a small scale, the intensity of detail that it evokes is powerful enough to dislodge common assumptions about consumers.

These findings are confirmed by Zukin's (2004) in-depth interviews with working-class, black, and Hispanic consumers in New York City. As with Chin's ethnography, a single anecdote about discrimination experienced by a dark-skinned, male shopper at Tiffany does not prove any social science theory; however, when it is told with a wealth of personal detail and interpreted against a historical background of discrimination against black consumers, the story provides a critical view of how the experience of consumption – in this case, shopping in an exclusive store – helps to construct ethnic identity both within a group and in the larger society. Zukin's work also includes focus groups with black and Hispanic teenage consumers and their mothers. As in Chin's study, what they say about shopping contradicts media images of their conspicuous consumption. Most approach shopping rationally – one teenage boy makes a list of clothes he needs before he goes to a store and another goes to outlet malls outside the city – and all are tempted by, but do not always succumb to, brand-name logos. Davila's, Chin's, and Zukin's studies show that small-scale ethnographic research and traditional, in-depth interviews yield important insights into the formation of ethnic identity through consumption.

The studies we have discussed so far place consumption against a background of structural changes. Davila's research, for example, refers to increased immigration of Latinos to the United States since 1985. But this is not the only context of their development as consumers. In their home countries, men and women enter the mass consumption system through remittances of goods and money from overseas, free trade agreements, and the growth of multinational retail chains like Wal-Mart. New flows of goods and satellite-based media, and the global expansion of brand-name franchises, create a transnational discourse of consumer culture.

Similar structural changes accompanied the development of consumer culture in the United States. Religious and communal holidays provided sites for new social and cultural practices, which yoked consumerism – mainly gift buying – to older beliefs about, and expressions of, collective identity. Historical studies show how, in a burgeoning consumer culture, mainstream religious holidays and other cultural rituals passed from their origins in carnivals and communal rites, through Christianity (or another major religion), to massive campaigns of marketing.

Nissenbaum (1997) uses reports in the popular press, changes in legislation, seasonal songs and traditions, and other archival sources to trace the contested emergence, in the first quarter of the nineteenth century, of the modem form of Christmas, with its strong domestic focus. Nissenbaum counters jeremiads about the commercial corruption of Christmas in our time by drawing attention to the mutual reinforcement of Christmas rituals and consumer culture in the past. Structural changes – including changing conceptions of, and values associated with, domesticity – intersected with interventions by media and manufacturers in the creation of a holiday shopping season (for an account of Macy's role in shaping the Thanksgiving Day parade, see Leach 1993).

In a different way, anthropologists examine the tension in Christmas between, on the one hand, family and religious values and, on the other, commercialism. Ethnographic and historical research suggests that Christmas gift giving is a complex process of resolving the conflicts between the family and economy. The gift transforms the abstract commodity into an expression of love and a means of producing and maintaining kin relationships, while Christmas shopping – the process of wresting significant gifts from the impersonal world of the mall – affirms the family's collective identity against the backdrop of an anonymous market economy (Carrier 1993; see also Miller 2001). Similarly, receiving gifts "from Santa" and "playing Santa" for oneself allow adults to fulfill their desires for luxurious goods without feeling guilty about being acquisitive (Belk 1993).

Christmas consumerism is also implicated in the production of new forms of collective identity. Research on Christmas in Japan (Moeran and Skov 1993) looks at Christmas advertising, store displays, magazines, and catalogs, coupled with ethnographic observations, to explore the holiday's role not in constructing family-oriented domesticity, but romantic love for young couples. Products (special gifts, fashions) and sites (hotels, restaurants) provide means to produce the identity of a romantic couple through Christmas-themed dates, while Christmas brochures and advertising serve as "manuals for consumerism" (Moeran and Skov 1993, p. 129), educating consumers in *how* to celebrate the event. Such research indicates that the materialism of Christmas consumption is more complex than an outcome of marketing hype because it passes through the formation of collective identities. Moreover, the globalization of consumer culture requires attention to local media, contexts, and identities.

The mediated discourse of consumer culture provides a symbolic language – increasingly, a global language – for men and women, teens and children, to think about their needs. The Latin American anthropologist and cultural critic Nestor Garcia Canclini (2001) believes that this may even be "good for thinking," because consumers are well aware of the various distinctions conferred by the use and possession of different commodities. "To consume," then, "is to participate in an arena of competing claims for what society produces and the ways of using it" (Garcia Canclini 2001, p. 39). Examining electoral campaigns in Argentina, Brazil, and Mexico, Garcia Canclini hears politicians promising voters that their macroeconomic policies will maintain the standard of living and access to consumer goods that voters desire. He sees voters protesting policies that restrict credit to buy cars, televisions, and household appliances. In this dialogue, politics and state policies further "the complicity of consumption and citizenship" – which may integrate a public for social justice as well as divide it for selfish ends.

Garcia Canclini is interested in cultural consumption and the use of media images in Latin American cities. Examining surveys of consumers' use of public spaces and participation in cultural festivals, he finds that the spread of a transnational discourse of consumer culture tends to reduce interest, especially among young people, in traditional forms of culture. Striking – but not unexpected, in view of American practice – is the preference of young people in Bogota and São Paulo for hanging out in shopping centers and metro stations instead of in churches, plazas, cafés, or (in Bogota) bakeries (Garcia Canclini 2001, p. 73). It is not that consumption spaces are unimportant to older people; it is that young people have adapted to – and adopted – more privatized consumption spaces as a common public space. Yet that does not mean that they all uncritically accept the discourse of consumer culture promoted by Starbucks, Wal-Mart, and the mall. Traditional consumer products, texts, and sites may themselves encourage a more romantic, and less critical, view of the world. Certainly in earlier years, traditional consumer culture downplayed social class differences, fostered national unity, and encouraged Latin Americans to buy domestic products. Consequently, Garcia Canclini calls for reinterpretation of both traditional and new consumer cultures, with particular ethnographic attention to consumers' participation in the "globalized networks of symbolic production and circulation [where] trends in art, publishing, advertising, and fashion are set" (2001, p. 90).

Whereas Garcia Canclini studies consumers' participation in these global networks as part of a process of changing political ideologies, another anthropologist – Kalman Applbaum (2003) – studies producers' participation in creating the networks themselves. Applbaum interviewed high-level marketing managers in American-owned, transnational consumer products companies about their business strategies and the way they think about consumers around the world. He then compared their behavior and views with the North American business literature on globalization, tspecially with articles published in the *Harvard Business Review*. Like the VALS paradigm of market research, marketing managers tend to reduce consumers to buying machines and to abstract preferences for specific "lifestyles" as a proxy for choices of consumer goods. Moreover, as our discussion of Garcia Canclini suggests, marketing managers in transnational firms assume that all consumers around the world aspire to an "American" model of consumer society as the basis of their needs and desires. The marketing managers understand this model to represent a universal goal of modernization, democracy, and progress – and their marketing strategies aim to eliminate national, cultural, and ethnic differences in the pursuit of a universal consumer culture. Thus, in interviews with Applbaum, senior managers discussed their goal of providing uniform value to customers across the globe. In practice, however, delivering consistent value and achieving global presence tend to mean corporate ownership of a global brand (such as Coca Cola, Heineken, or Pampers) that is sold in exactly the same way, worldwide. The path to globalization, then, is also the path to corporate profitability, with the discourse of consumer culture providing a means toward realizing the "political project" of globalization.

Clearly, ethnographic research and in-depth interviews provide the most cogent base for generalizing about the role of global consumer culture in forming collective identities. Not just the purchase of goods but also the whole experience of using media, sites, and texts of consumption must be observed, recorded, and analyzed. Yet as Miller's (1998b) important essay comparing Trinidadians' use of Coca Cola and other indigenous soft drinks points out, it is important not to overestimate the power of either a "global brand" or global consumer culture. Careful observations, with attention to specific social contexts, yield a nuanced, and even an ambivalent, view. Consumer culture certainly provides a universal toolkit, a material and symbolic repertoire, for expressing collective identities. But consumer culture provides tools for resistance as well as for integration and adaptation. The "doo rag" worn around the head by young men, both black and white, in the United States in the early 2000s may express a subcultural identity of rebellion or ethnic pride, subverting the cultural pressure for hair straightening that many African Americans encounter. But if the doo rag is a sign of resistance to white-dominated consumer society, it also contradicts a strong aesthetic preference within black consumer culture, and denies the achievements of Mme. C.J. Walker, an early twentieth-century entrepreneur of hair products in the black community (Peiss 1998, Weems 2000). By the same token, using elements of global culture may have more subtle political meanings than at first appear. As Garcia Canclini (2001) suggests, listening to American rock music in Latin America may be politically more progressive than listening to traditional ballads, which foster a populist view favored by earlier, undemocratic governments. And consumers who celebrate holidays by shopping for gifts may go to thrift shops or sales instead of buying heavily advertised brands at full price for conspicuous, status consumption.

## Transitions to a Consumer Society

Most writers interpret consumer society as a distinctive product of modernity, yet the timing of its development and its social, cultural, and economic forms vary across societies, time periods, and regions of the world. Certainly we can identify a "generalized shift" in social practices and mentality (Appadurai 1996, p. 72) that unleashes desires to express individuality, directs these desires to consumer products, and creates new spaces where these products can be sampled, purchased, and enjoyed. Historically, these changes depend not only on the development of markets for the exchange of goods but also on the weakening of state, religious, or other normative controls over material means of expression and the rise of new, independent rationalities. Although historians and sociologists have long debated the timing of the transition to consumer society in the capitalist world – fifteenth- and sixteenth-century England (Mukerji 1983), eighteenth-century England (Campbell 1987, McKendrick *et al.* 1982, Wernick 1991), the United States in the 1890s, 1920s, 1930s, or 1950s (Cohen 2003, Cross 2000, Ewen 1976, Fischer 2003, Martin 1999) – these changes seem to have occurred rapidly in our time with the shift from state socialism to a market economy in Russia, China, and Eastern Europe.

The key structural change that leads to a consumer society in these regions of the world is, of course, the fall of communism in Eastern Europe and the adoption of some forms of a market economy in China. In each country, state (and party) officials decide to modernize the economy by introducing market incentives, allowing individual property ownership, and – as both an incentive to the work force and a means of stimulating aggregate demand – encouraging the production of goods to satisfy consumer desires. Other structural changes facilitating the development of a consumer society include a movement of population, especially to cities (and, in China, to special enterprise zones), an increase in single-child families (related, in China, to state policy), and an explosion of innovation, tied not only to the creation of new products and efficiencies, but also to commercial initiatives and individual self-expression. These changes echo the earlier transitions to consumer society in market economies of the West.

In Western Europe, changes in the dominant forms of Christianity after the Middle Ages and the postmedieval disappearance of sumptuary laws eased the way toward conspicuous consumption by all social classes. In China and Eastern Europe, the introduction of a consumer society likewise depended on ideological and legal changes: encouragement of self-expression through consumption practices, tolerance of visible signs of luxury and comfort, and the shifting of goods and services (such as housing, transportation, medical care, and meals) from collective provision by the work unit to individual provision on the open, and often unregulated, market. These changes expand the means of sociability that are both available and desirable to consumers – at the cost of increasing social inequality (Davis 2000).

As in Latin America, access to new consumer products and consumption sites – from McDonald's in Moscow and Beijing to shopping malls in Budapest and the former East Berlin – brings men, women, and especially young people into a global discourse of consumer culture. Consumer surveys show that, at least in big cities like Shanghai, people have increased their purchases of goods and services, raising both their level of comfort and their level of satisfaction (Lu 2000; for a similar effect in the former Yugoslavia's "market socialism," see the interviews in Zukin 1975). Ethnographies and interviews indicate that Shanghainese families spend more money on their children than ever before, including expensive purchases of nonessential clothes, toys, photographs, and ornaments (Davis and Sensenbrenner 2000). Ethnography also reveals how consumers in Shanghai use new consumption sites like dance halls to look for social partners (Yan 2000) and business people in Shenzhen express social hierarchy by inviting their associates to bowling alleys (Wang 2000). Moreover, like the commercialization of religious holidays in other countries, ethnography in the old Muslim quarter of Xi'an shows young Chinese women using traditional rituals like weddings as occasions to spend lavishly on consumer goods (Gillette 2000).

Although we have not seen any published research based on interviews with marketers in China and Eastern Europe, such a project would likely present fascinating comparative material on how the mediated global discourse of consumer culture has spread to the former socialist societies. But sociologists and market researchers have carried out content analysis of media advertisements and articles in new lifestyle magazines. These printed texts and images are extremely important in socializing people to be consumers even before the goods are widely available.

They colonize the imagination with "visions of lifestyle," creating "a theater of familiarity in which readers may envisage themselves at home" (Fraser 2000, pp. 32–33). Thus, content analysis of ads for new housing in Shanghai shows how marketers target a broad public across most income levels while conveying the sense of a stratified housing market, in which each income level finds its own "oasis" (Fraser 2000). Informal interviews and participant-observation in Cuba and the former German Democratic Republic (Clarke *et al.* 2002) confirm the role of the mediated discourse of consumer culture in shaping people's expectations, as well as in educating them in advance about product quality and variety.

Few studies that have been published in English thus far document conflicts and controversies within these societies over the acceptance of global consumer culture. One such case emerged in Budapest, however, where an offer by the Coca Cola Company to decorate the historic Chain Bridge for Christmas 1996 aroused lengthy public debates and action by the city council (Z. Fejos, unpublished paper). Although the company planned to install no overt advertising – not even a corporate logo – on this landmark, the fact that decorations would be sponsored by one of the best-known and most recognizable producers of a multinational consumer product aroused huge expressions of dissent from local citizens, who disapproved of both the company and its adoption of the bridge. Significantly, surveys showed that younger, less-educated men and women tended to approve of Coca Cola's plan. Older people and intellectuals criticized the arrangement as a capitulation to foreign interests and a sellout to global consumer culture. Yet others pointed out that, because the Hungarian government goes to great lengths to encourage capital investment by multinational corporations, it was counterproductive to condemn Coca Cola's offer.

As the case of the Chain Bridge suggests, consumer society may carry different meanings in different localities and offer different opportunities from those that appear at first view. Advertisements, for example, not only stimulate the desire to buy things in order to live a good life but also mark changing notions of desirability as products become more readily available. Content analysis of advertising in former socialist societies reveals a shift from representations of goods as part of Western individuals' desirable lifestyles to goods as symbols of a country's growth and modernization (Clarke *et al.* 2002). Thus, symbolic consumption of advertising is a form of anticipatory socialization to consumer society, educating people in different ways. Likewise, use of consumer sites is polyvalent. Ethnographies in both Beijing and Singapore document how the social space of McDonald's provides young people with a gathering place, as well as with tables where they can do homework assignments (Yan 2000, Chua 2000; see also Fantasia 1995); both are welcome in a society where apartments are usually small and bedrooms are often shared. This kind of restaurant also offers women a place to sit and be served equally with men, a point made by young women respondents in surveys in Beijing (Yan 2000). Thus, as in the late-nineteenth-century department stores in the United States and Western Europe, consumption sites may be, in some sense, spaces of empowerment.

## Conclusion: Consumption as an Institutional Field

Readers who have followed our discussion so far know that we prefer close, detailed studies of consumer products, texts, and sites, which locate consumption at the junction of changing social structures and cultural practices. Like studies of the production of culture, research on consumption should focus on both the production and reception of products, resulting in the production of *consumers*. The brief but suggestive study of the Sony Walkman (du Gay *et al.* 1997) and Mintz's (1985) monumental study of "sugar and power" are exceptional because they cover all three aspects of consumption. Yet we believe that such an integrated approach is vital.

Ferguson (1998) offers the development of gastronomy in France as a "template" of Bourdieu's (1993) concept of a cultural field; her analysis could also serve as a template for studying new forms of consumption. Ferguson uses the cultural field to isolate five "structural factors" supporting gastronomy as a new form of food consumption in the nineteenth century. First, social and cultural changes tending toward democratization stimulated a broad, middle-class public's interest in elaborate, high-value-added culinary preparations. Second, new consumption sites – restaurants – were dedicated to the production and consumption of gastronomic meals. Third, new rules, published in critical texts of gastronomy – more or less cookbooks for professional chefs and early restaurant reviews – legitimated and standardized both the production and consumption of culinary experiences. Fourth, the development of distinct specialties (or specialty markets) crystallized different positions or schools of thought on gastronomy among chefs on the one hand and critics on the other. Fifth, networks of producers and consumers created social prestige for the new form of consumption as a whole.

Whereas Ferguson applies this analytic framework to the early history of gastronomy as a type of consumption, Zukin (2004) adapts it to the development of shopping in the United States from the 1870s to the present. She identifies the formation of shopping as an institutional field by innovations in the mass consumption system of retail stores (and recently, Web sites) that correspond to shifts in social structure and consumer culture. Dividing the institutional field into social spaces (or consumption sites), languages (or consumer guides), and stories (or narratives of shopping experiences), Zukin uses secondary sources in histories and the business and fashion press to trace changes in business strategies that broaden retail institutions over time and democratize access to consumer goods. She shows how consumption sites maintain and expand a bargain culture, from the five-and-dime to the discount store, and how, from the mail order catalog to the Internet, they embody a regime of looking that focuses attention on products rather than on the social context of their production or use. Reading texts from *Consumer Reports* to *New York* magazine, she shows how the language of consumption changes over time, emphasizing the mediating role of the "honest brokers" who write product reviews and consumer guides. Zukin draws attention to a shift of voice and viewpoint in these texts, which gradually widen from scientific discussion of products' composition and durability to personal writing about lifestyle and self-expression. She finds that, in periods when social mobility becomes more fluid, consumers' anxiety increases, and they respond favorably to a broadening of retail institutions and consumer guides that brings them closer to realizing their sense of value.

Zukin also carries out in-depth interviews with a small number of shoppers of different ages, ethnicities, and social classes. These interviews show a more rational core to people's shopping than the image dramatized in many contemporary accounts of "luxury fever" (Frank 1999) or "the overspent American" (Schor 1998). Yet she finds conflict in shoppers' souls: working class mothers' conflict over buying clothes for themselves or their children, conflict between these mothers and their male partners over buying their children clothes (and sneakers) with brand name logos, and conflict between shopping by necessity, as our parents have taught us, and shopping for status, as encouraged by the media. Zukin's research suggests that shopping is both an enormously controlled and a potentially creative activity, which indicates why many consumers feel strongly about it. It also points the way toward more research that would use history, interviews, and ethnography to flesh out other institutional fields of consumption.

A similar framework underlies Maguire's research on the development of the contemporary fitness field in the United States (Smith 2002). Focusing on developments since the 1970s, Maguire examines interactions between a culturally specific site for production and consumption (the commercial health club), a cadre of professional producers (health club managers and fitness instructors), and an array of media to educate both consumers (fitness magazines and manuals; see Maguire 2002) and producers (occupational and trade journals). Combining observations in health clubs, interviews with fitness producers, and a discourse analysis of fitness texts, she draws connections between the development of a commercial fitness industry and changes in the practice of individualism: the ways that health is promoted as an individual's responsibility, appearance is articulated as an individual's resource, and physical activity is defined as a measure of an individual's capacity for social success. In the nineteenth century, physical ability testified to the strength of national character and to courage in war. This has changed, in our day, to an individual's overall ability to compete for social rewards. Moreover, focusing on personal trainers as cultural intermediaries of fitness, Maguire (2001) shows how they are both ideal producers and consumers. Under the trainers' tutelage, participants in the fitness field learn how to "fit" into the consumer culture of a service economy; both their body and self become "fit for consumption."

Everyday life in the twenty-first century offers many other examples of consumption that can be studied in this way. The point of a sociological study is neither to praise nor to condemn consumers, but to understand how, and why, people learn to consume, over time, in different ways.

## References


Andrews M, Talbot MM, eds. 2000. *All the World and Her Husband: Women in Twentieth-Century Consumer Culture*. London. Cassell

Appadurai A. 1996. *Modernity at Large: Cultural Dimensions of Globalization*. Minneapolis: Univ. Minn. Press

Applbaum K. 2003. *The Marketing Era: From Professional Practice to Global Provisioning*. New York/London: Routledge

Baudrillard J. 1998. *The Consumer Society*. London: Sage

Bauman Z. 2000. *Liquid Modernity*. Cambridge: Polity Press

Beck U, Beck-Gernsheim E. 2002. *Individualization*. London: Sage

Belk R. 1993. Materialism and the making of the modern American Christmas. See Miller 1993, pp.75–104

Beniger JR. 1986. *The Control Revolution: Technological and Economic Origins of the Information Society*. Cambridge, MA: Harvard Univ. Press

Benjamin W. 1999. *The Arcades Project*. Transl. H Eiland, K McLaughlin. Cambridge, MA: Belknap

Bourdieu P. 1984. *Distinction: A Social Critique of the Judgement of Taste*. Transl. R Nice. Cambridge, MA: Harvard Univ. Press

Bourdieu R 1993. *The Field of Cultural Production; Essays on Art and Literature*. New York: Columbia Univ. Press

Bowlby R. 1985. *Just Looking: Consumer Culture in Dreiser, Gissing and Zola*. New York: Methuen

Bowlby R. 2000. *Carried Away: The Invention of Modern Shopping*. London: Faber

Cameron D. 2000. A self off the shelf? Consuming women's empowerment. See Andrews & Talbot 2000, pp. 210–23

Campbell C. 1987. *The Romantic Ethic and the Spirit of Modern Consumerism*. Oxford/New York: Blackwell

Carrier J. 1993. The rituals of Christmas giving. See Miller 1993, pp. 55–74

Chin E. 2001. *Purchasing Power: Black Kids and American Consumer Culture*. Minneapolis: Univ. Minn. Press

Chua BH. 2000. Singaporeans ingesting McDonald's. In *Consumption in Asia: Lifestyles and Identities*, ed. BH Chua, pp. 183-201. London: Routledge

Clarke I, Micken KS, Hart S. 2002. Symbols for sale . . . at least for now: symbolic consumption in transition economics. *Adv. Consum. Res.* 29:25–30

Cohen L. 2003. *A Consumer's Republic. The Politics of Mass Consumption in Postwar America*. New York: Knopf

Cronin AM. 2000. *Advertising and Consumer Citizenship: Gender, Images and Rights*, London: Routledge

Cross G. 2000. *An All-Consuming Century: Why Commercialism Won in Modern America*. New York: Columbia Univ. Press

Csikszentmihalyi M, Rochberg-Halton E. 1981. *The Meaning of Things: Domestic Symbols and the Self*. New York: Cambridge Univ. Press

Davila A. 2001. *Latinos Inc.: The Marketing and Making of a People*. Berkeley/Los Angeles: Univ. Calif. Press

Davis DS, ed. 2000. *The Consumer Revolution in Urban China*. Berkeley/Los Angeles: Univ. Calif. Press

Davis DS, Sensenbrenner JS. 2000. Commercializing childhood: parental purchases for Shanghai's only child. See Davis 2000, pp. 54–79

du Gay P, Hall S, Janes L, Mackay H, Negus K. 1997. *Doing Cultural Studies: The Story of the Sony Walkman*. Thousand Oaks, CA: Sage

Entwistle J. 2000. Fashioning the career woman: power dressing as a strategy of consumption. See Andrews & Talbot 2000, pp. 224–38

Ewen S. 1976. *Captains of Consciousness: Advertising and the Social Roots of Consumer Culture*. New York: McGraw- Hill

Ewen S. 1996. *PR! A Social History of Spin*. New York: Basic Books

Ewen S. 1999. *All Consuming Images: The Politics of Style in Contemporary Culture*. New York: Basic Books. Rev. ed.

Fantasia R. 1995. Fast food in France. *Theory Soc.* 24: 201–43

Featherstone M. 1991. *Consumer Culture and Postmodernism*. London: Sage

Ferguson PP. 1998. A cultural field in the making: gastronomy in 19th century France. *Am. J. Sociol.* 104:597–641

Fischer CS. 2003. *Succumbing to consumerism?: Underlying models in the historical claim*. Presented at Annu. Meet. Am. Sociol. Assoc., 98th, Atlanta, GA

Fourier S. 1998. Consumers and their brands: developing relationship theory in consumer research. *J. Consum. Res.* 24: 343–74

Frank RH. 1999. *Luxury Fever: Why Money Fails to Satisfy in an Era of Excess*. New York: Free Press

Frank T. 1997. *The Conquest of Cool*. Chicago, IL: Univ. Chicago Press

Fraser D. 2000. Inventing oasis: luxury housing advertisements and reconfiguring domestic space in Shanghai. See Davis 2000, pp. 25–53

Garcia Canclini N. 2001. *Consumers and Citizens: Globalization and Multicultural Conflicts*. Transl. G Yudice. Minneapolis: Univ. Minn. Press

Gartman D. 1991. Culture as class symbolization or mass reification? A critique of Bourdieu's distinction. *Am. J. Sociol.* 97: 421–47

Gillette M. 2000. What's in a dress? Brides in the Hui quarter of Xi'an. See Davis 2000, pp. 80–106

Grusky DB, Wheedon KA. 2001. Decomposition without death: a research agenda for a new class analysis. *Acta Social.* 44: 203–18

Halle D. 1993. *Inside Culture: Art and Class in the American Home*. Chicago, IL: Univ. Chicago Press

Halnon KB. 2002. Poor chic: the rational consumption of poverty. *Curr. Sociol.* 50: 510–16

Hughes A, Reimer S. 2004. *Geographies of Commodity Chains*. London: Routledge. In press

Lamont M, Molnar V. 2001. How blacks use consumption to shape their collective identity. *J. Consum.* Cult. 1: 31–46

Leach W. 1993. *Land of Desire: Merchants, Power, and the Rise of a New American Culture*. New York: Pantheon

Lears TJJ. 1983. From salvation to self-realization: advertising and the therapeutic roots of the consumer culture, 1880–930. In *The Culture of Consumption*, ed. RW Fox, TJJ Lears, pp. 3–38. New York: Pantheon

Lu H. 2000. To be relatively comfortable in an egalitarian society. See Davis 2000. pp. 124–41

Maguire JS. 2001. Fit and flexible: the fitness industry, personal trainers and emotional service labour. *Sociol. Sport J.* 18:379–402

Maguire JS. 2002. Body lessons: fitness publishing and the cultural production of the fitness consumer. *Int. Rev. Sociol. Sport* 37:449–64

Marchand R. 1985. *Advertising the American Dream*. Berkeley/Los Angeles: Univ. Calif. Press

Martin JL. 1999. The myth of the consumption oriented economy and the rise of the desiring subject. *Theory Soc.* 28:425–53

Marx K. 1972. Economic and philosophic manuscripts of 1844. In *The Marx-Engels Reader*, ed. RC Tucker, pp. 52- 103. New York: Norton

McCracken G. 1990. *Culture and Consumption*. Bloomington: Indiana Univ. Press

McKendrick N, Brewer J, Plumb JH. 1982. *The Birth of a Consumer Society: The Commercialization of 18th Century England*. Bloomington: Indiana Univ. Press

Miller D, ed. 1993. *Unwrapping Christmas*. Oxford: Clarendon

Miller D. 1998a. *A Theory of Shopping*. Oxford: Polity

Miller D. 1998b. Coca-Cola: a black sweet drink from Trinidad. In *Material Cultures*, ed. D Miller, pp. 169–87. Chicago, IL: Univ. Chicago Press

Miller D. 2001. *The Dialectics of Shopping*. Chicago, IL: Univ. Chicago Press

Miller D, Jackson P, Thrift N, Holbrook B, Rowlands M. 1998. *Shopping, Place and Identity*. London/New York: Routledge

Miller MB. 1981. *The Bon Marché: Bourgeois Culture and the Department Store*, 1869–1920. Princeton, NJ: Princeton Univ. Press

Miller P, Rose N. 1997. Mobilizing the consumer: assembling the subject of consumption. *Theory Cult. Soc.* 14:1–36

Mintz SW. 1985. *Sweetness and Power*. New York: Viking

Moeran B, Skov L. 1993. Cinderella Christmas: kitsch, consumerism, and youth in Japan. See Miller 1993, pp. 105– 33

Molotch H. 2003. *Where Stuff Comes From*. New York: Routledge

Mukerji C. 1983. *From Graven Images: Patterns of Modern Materialism*. New York: Columbia Univ. Press

Nava M. 1997. Women, the city and the department store. In *The Shopping Experience*, ed. P Falk, C Campbell. pp. 56–91. London/Thousand Oaks. CA. Sage

Naylor S. 2000. Spacing the can: empire, modernity, and the globalisation of food. *Environ. Plan.* A 32:1625–39

Nissenbaum S. 1997. *The Battle for Christmas*. New York: Knopf

Parr J. 1999. *Domestic Goods: The Material, the Moral, and the Economic in the Postwar Years*. Toronto: Univ. Toronto Press

Peiss K. 1998. *Hope in a Jar: The Making of America's Beauty Culture*. New York: Holt

Pendergast T. 2000. *Creating the Modern Man: American Magazines and Consumer Culture, 1900–1950*. Columbia: Univ. Missouri Press

Ritzer G. 1996. *The McDonaldization of Society*. Thousand Oaks, CA: Pine Forge Press. Rev. ed.

Rochberg-Halton E. 1986. *Meaning and Modernity*. Chicago. IL: Univ. Chicago Press

Roseberry W. 1996. The rise of yuppie coffees and the reimagination of class in the United States. *Am. Anthropol.* 98: 762–75

Schor JB. 1998. *The Overspent American*. New York: Basic Books

Schudson M. 1984. *Advertising, the Uneasy Persuasion*. New York: Basic Books

Shilling C. 1993. *The Body and Social Theory*. London: Sage

Simmel G. 1957. Fashion. *Am. J. Social.* 62: 541–58

Simmel G. 1997. The philosophy of fashion. In *Simmel on Culture*, ed. D Frisby, M Featherstone, pp. 187–206. London: Sage

Simonds W. 1992. *Women and Self-Help Culture: Reading Between the Lines*. New Brunswick, NJ: Rutgers Univ. Press

Slater D. 1997. *Consumer Culture and Modernity*. Cambridge: Polity Press

Smith J. 2002. *Bodies fit for consumption*. PhD thesis. Graduate Center, City Univ. New York

Steele M. 1993. Attention shoppers: Don't look now but you are being tailed. *Smithsonian* Jan: 70–78

Talbot MM. 2000. Strange bedfellows: feminism in advertising. See Andrews & Talbot 2000, pp. 177–91

Tomlinson M. 2003. Lifestyle and social class. *Eur. Sociol. Rev.* 19: 97–111

Turow J. 1998. *Breaking Up America: Advertisers and the New Media World*. Chicago, IL: Univ. Chicago Press

Veblen T. 1959. *The Theory of the Leisure Class*. New York: Viking

Wang G. 2000. Cultivating friendship through bowling in Shentzen. See Davis 2000, pp. 250–67

Weber M. 1946. Class, status, party. In *Max Weber: Essays in Sociology*. ed. HH Gerth, CW Mills, pp. 180–95. New York: Oxford Univ. Press

Weber M. 1958. *The Protestant Ethic and the Spirit of Capitalism*. Transl. T Parsons. New York: Scribner

Weems RE. 2000. Consumerism and the construction of black female identity in twentieth-century America. In *The Gender and Consumer Culture Reader*, ed. J Scanlon, pp. 166–78. New York: New York Univ. Press

Wellington CA, Bryson JR. 2001. At face value? Image consultancy, emotional labour and professional work. *Sociology* 35: 933–46

Wernick A. 1991. *Promotional Culture: Advertising, Ideology and Symbolic Expression*. London:Sage

Williams R. 1982. *Dream Worlds: Mass Consumption in Late 19th Century France*. Berkeley/Los Angeles: Univ. Calif. Press

Wolff J. 1985. The invisible flaneuse: women and the literature of modernity. *Theory Cult. Soc.* 2: 37–48

Wynne D. 1998. *Leisure, Lifestyle and the New Middle Class: A Case Study*. London: Routledge

Yan Y. 2000. Of hamburger and social space: consuming McDonald's in Beijing. See Davis 2000, pp. 201–25

Zelizer V. 2004. Culture and consumption. In *Handbook of Economic Sociology*, ed. N Smelsner, R Swedberg. Princeton, NJ: Princeton Univ. Press. In press

Zukin S. 1975. *Beyond Marx and Tito: Theory and Practice in Yugoslav Socialism*. Cambridge, UK: Cambridge Univ. Press

Zukin S. 1991. *Landscapes of Power: From Detroit to Disney World*. Berkeley/Los Angeles: Univ. Calif. Press

Zukin S. 2004. *Point of Purchase: How Shopping Changed American Culture*. New York: Routledge